2011
Poet's Market®

includes a 1-year online subscription to
Poet's Market on **WritersMarket.com**

WritersMarket.com
Where & How to Sell What You Write

THE ULTIMATE MARKET RESEARCH TOOL FOR WRITERS

To register your *2011 Poet's Market* book and **start your 1-year online genre only subscription**, scratch off the block below to reveal your activation code, then go to www.WritersMarket.com. Click on "Sign Up Now" and enter your contact information and activation code. It's that easy!

UPDATED MARKET LISTINGS FOR YOUR INTEREST AREA

EASY-TO-USE SEARCHABLE DATABASE

RECORD KEEPING TOOLS

INDUSTRY NEWS

PROFESSIONAL TIPS AND ADVICE

Your purchase of *Poet's Market* gives you access to updated listings related to this genre of writing (valid through 1/31/12). For just $9.99, you can upgrade your subscription and get access to listings from all of our best-selling Market books. Visit **www.WritersMarket.com** for more information.

2011
Poet's Market®

24TH ANNUAL EDITION

ROBERT LEE BREWER, EDITOR

**WRITER'S DIGEST
BOOKS**

WritersDigest.com
Cincinnati, Ohio

Publisher & Community Leader: Phil Sexton
Director, Content & Community Development: Jane Friedman

Writer's Market website: www.writersmarket.com
Writer's Digest website: www.writersdigest.com
Writer's Digest Bookstore: www.writersdigestshop.com

Distributed in Canada by Fraser Direct
100 Armstrong Avenue
Georgetown, ON, Canada L7G 5S4
Tel: (905) 877-4411

Distributed in the U.K. and Europe by David & Charles
Brunel House, Newton Abbot, Devon, TQ12 4PU, England
Tel: (+44) 1626 323200, Fax: (+44) 1626 323319
E-mail: mail@davidandcharles.co.uk

Distributed in Australia by Capricorn Link
Loder House, 126 George Street
Windsor, NSW 2756 Australia
Tel: (02) 4577-3555

ISSN: 0883-5470
ISBN-13: 978-1-58297-950-2
ISBN-10: 1-58297-950-2

Cover design by Claudean Wheeler
Production coordinated by Greg Nock
Illustrations © Frederic Cirou/PhotoAlto

Attention Booksellers: This is an annual directory of F + W Media, Inc. Return deadline for this edition is December 31, 2011.

Contents

From the Editor

Usually, I feel like an editor writing these From the Editor notes, because, well, I am an editor. However, this year has been exciting for me as a poet. BloggingPoet.com named me (and Sina Queyras) Poet Laureate of the Blogosphere for 2010. Poets.org invited me to be the guest poet for the month of January on their discussion forum. Plus, I've completed another successful April Poem-A-Day Challenge over at my Poetic Asides blog while also having a handful of poems published in online and print publications. Of course, I'm also excited about assembling my second edition of *Poet's Market*, too!

In this edition, I tried to build upon the great articles included in the previous edition by focusing on social networking, publishing collections (whether traditionally or DIY), audience development and other nitty-gritty details associated with publishing and distributing poetry. Successful poets (and artists in general) do two things well: create and share. If you're using *Poet's Market*, my assumption is that you feel comfortable with creating poetry; now, you're ready to share your poetry.

In this new century (that is no longer so new), an obvious method for sharing poetry and building an audience for your poems is to use the Internet. If you don't have one yet, create a blog today. It only takes a few minutes, and it's free. Also, make sure you have a profile on Facebook, LinkedIn, and Twitter. These are the basic things you can do immediately to start your journey toward building your audience. More strategies should reveal themselves as you read this 2011 edition of *Poet's Market*.

Until next time, keep poeming!

Robert Lee Brewer
Senior Content Editor, *Poet's Market*
http://blog.writersdigest.com/poeticasides
robert.brewer@fwmedia.com

Follow me on Twitter @robertleebrewer (http://twitter.com/robertleebrewer)
Connect with me on LinkedIn at http://www.linkedin.com/in/robertleebrewer

[Note: The *2010 Poet's Market* contained a mistake in which Larina Warnock's "The Age of the E-Poet?" article actually contained the content from Jessy Randall's "Digital Poetry" piece. Both pieces are included in this edition matched up with the correct writer.]

Getting Started

(and Using This Book)

Delving into the pages of *Poet's Market* indicates a commitment—you've decided to take that big step and begin submitting your poems for publication. How do you *really* begin, though? Here are eight quick tips to help make sense of the marketing/submission process:

1. Be an avid reader. The best way to hone your writing skills (besides writing) is to immerse yourself in poetry of all kinds. It's essential to study the masters; however, from a marketing standpoint, it's equally vital to read what your contemporaries are writing and publishing. Read journals and magazines, chapbooks and collections, anthologies for a variety of voices; scope out the many poetry sites on the Internet. Develop an eye for quality, and then use that eye to assess your own work. Don't rush to publish until you know you're writing the best poetry you're capable of producing.

2. Know what you like to write—and what you write best. Ideally, you should be experimenting with all kinds of poetic forms, from free verse to villanelles. However, there's sure to be a certain style with which you feel most comfortable, that conveys your true "voice." Whether you favor more formal, traditional verse or avant-garde poetry that breaks all the rules, you should identify which markets publish work similar to yours. Those are the magazines and presses you should target to give your submissions the best chance of being read favorably—and accepted. (See the Subject Index beginning on page 540 to observe how some magazines and presses specify their needs.)

3. Learn the "business" of poetry publishing. Poetry may not be a high-paying writing market, but there's still a right way to go about the "business" of submitting and publishing poems. Learn all you can by reading writing-related books and magazines. Read the articles and interviews in this book for plenty of helpful advice. Surf the Internet for a wealth of sites filled with writing advice, market news and informative links. (See Additional Resources on page 461 for some leads.)

4. Research the markets. Study the listings in *Poet's Market* thoroughly; these present submission guidelines, editorial preferences and editors' comments as well as contact information (names, postal and e-mail addresses, website URLs). The Magazines/Journals section begins on page 70, the Book/Chapbook Publishers section on page 351, with the Contests & Awards section following on page 390. In addition, the indexes in the back of this book provide insights into what an editor or publisher may be looking for.

However, studying market listings alone won't cut it. The best way to gauge the kinds of poetry a market publishes is to read several issues of a magazine/journal or several of a press's books to get a feel for the style and content of each. If the market has a website, log on and take a look. Web sites may include poetry samples, reviews, archives of past issues, exclusive content, and especially submission guidelines. (If the market is an online publication, the current issue will be available in its entirety.) If the market has no online presence, send for guidelines and sample copies (include a SASE—self-addressed stamped envelope—for guidelines; include appropriate cost for sample copy).

Submission guidelines are pure gold for the specific information they provide. However you acquire them—by SASE or e-mail, online, or in a magazine itself—make them an integral part of your market research.

5. Start slowly. It may be tempting to send your work directly to *The New Yorker* or *Poetry*, but try to adopt a more modest approach if you're just starting out. Most listings in this book display symbols that reflect the level of writing a magazine or publisher prefers to receive. The (☐) symbol indicates a market that welcomes submissions from beginning or unpublished poets. As you gain confidence and experience (and increased skill in your writing), you can move on to markets coded with the (◑) symbol. Later, when you've built a publication history, submit to the more prestigious magazines and presses (the ◕ markets). Although it may tax your patience, slow and steady progress is a proven route to success.

6. Be professional. Professionalism is not something you should "work up to." Make it show in your first submission, from the way you prepare your manuscript to the attitude you project in your communications with editors.

Follow those guidelines. Submit a polished manuscript. (See "Frequently Asked Questions" on page 7 for details on manuscript formatting and preparation.) Choose poems carefully with the editor's needs in mind. *Always* include a SASE with any submission or inquiry. Such practices show respect for the editor, the publication and the process; and they reflect *your* self-respect and the fact that you take your work seriously. Editors love that; and even if your work is rejected, you've made a good first impression that could help your chances with your next submission.

2011 POET'S MARKET KEY TO SYMBOLS

Ⓝ this market is recently established and appearing for the first time in *Poet's Market*

✦ this market did not appear in the previous edition of *Poet's Market*

♜ this market is located in Canada

🌐 this market is located outside the U.S. and Canada

▣ this market publishes primarily online

$ this market pays a monetary amount

◯ this market welcomes submissions from beginning poets

◑ this market prefers submissions from skilled, experienced poets; will consider work from beginning poets

◕ this market prefers submissions from poets with a high degree of skill and experience

◎ this market has a specialized focus

⊘ this market does not consider unsolicited submissions

⊘ this market is currently closed to *all* submissions

● indicates market information of special note

ms, mss manuscript(s)

b&w black & white (art/photo)

SASE self-addressed, stamped envelope

IRC International Reply Coupon (replaces return postage when mailing to countries other than your own)

(For words and expressions relating specifically to poetry and submissions, see the Glossaries in the back of this book.)

Submission Tracker

Poem Title	Publication/ Contest	Editor/Contact	Date Sent	Date Returned	Date Accepted	Date Published	Pay Received	Comments

7. Keep track of your submissions. First, do *not* send out the only copies of your work. There are no guarantees your submission won't get lost in the mail, misplaced in a busy editorial office, or vanish into a black hole if the publication or press closes down. Create a special file folder for poems you're submitting. Even if you use a word processing program and store your manuscripts on disk, keep a hard copy file as well (and be sure to back up your electronic files).

Second, establish a tracking system so you always know which poems are where. This can be extremely simple: index cards, a chart created with word processing or database software, or even a simple notebook used as a log. (You can enlarge and photocopy the Submission Tracker on page 4 or use it as a model to design your own version.) Note the titles of the poems submitted (or the title of the collection if you're submitting a book/chapbook manuscript); the name of the publication, press, or contest; date sent; estimated response time; and date returned *or* date accepted. Additional information you may want to log: the name of the editor/contact, date the accepted piece is published and/or issue number of the magazine, type/amount of pay received, rights acquired by the publication or press, and any pertinent comments.

Without a tracking system, you risk forgetting where and when manuscripts were submitted. This is even more problematic if you simultaneously send the same manuscripts to different magazines, presses or contests. And if you learn of an acceptance by one magazine or publisher, you *must* notify the others that the poem or collection you sent them is no longer available. You run a bigger chance of overlooking someone without an organized approach. This causes hard feelings among editors you may have inconvenienced, hurting your chances with these markets in the future.

8. Don't fear rejection. Learn from it. No one enjoys rejection, but every writer faces it. The best way to turn a negative into a positive is to learn as much as you can from your rejections. Don't let them get you down. A rejection slip isn't a permission slip to doubt yourself, condemn your poetry or give up.

Look over the rejection. Did the editor provide any comments about your work or reasons why your poems were rejected? Probably he or she didn't. Editors are extremely busy and don't necessarily have time to comment on rejections. If that's the case, move on to the next magazine or publisher you've targeted and send your work out again.

If, however, the editor *has* commented on your work, pay attention. It counts for something that the editor took the time and trouble to say anything, however brief, good or bad. And consider any remark or suggestion with an open mind. You don't have to agree, but you shouldn't automatically disregard the feedback, either. Tell your ego to sit down and be quiet, then use the editor's comments to review your work from a new perspective. You might be surprised by how much you'll learn from a single scribbled word in the margin; or how encouraged you'll feel from a simple "Try again!" written on the rejection slip.

Keep these eight tips in mind as you prepare your poetry submissions, and keep *Poet's Market* at hand to help you along. Believe in yourself and don't give up! As the number of listings in this book shows, there are many opportunities for beginning poets to become published poets.

GUIDE TO LISTING FEATURES

On page 6 is an example of a Magazines/Journal listing (Book/Chapbook Publishers listings follow a similar format). Note the callouts that identify various format features of the listing. A key to the symbols displayed at the beginning of each listing is located on page 3.

EASY-TO-USE
REFERENCE
ICONS

TYPES OF
POETRY
CONSIDERED

DETAILED
SUBMISSION
GUIDELINES

WEB SITES

SPECIFIC
CONTACT
NAMES

EDITOR'S
COMMENTS

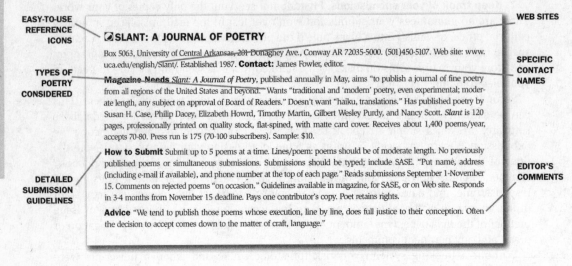

☑ SLANT: A JOURNAL OF POETRY

Box 5063, University of Central Arkansas, 201 Donaghey Ave., Conway AR 72035-5000. (501)450-5107. Web site: www.uca.edu/english/Slant/. Established 1987. **Contact:** James Fowler, editor.

Magazine Needs *Slant: A Journal of Poetry*, published annually in May, aims "to publish a journal of fine poetry from all regions of the United States and beyond." Wants "traditional and 'modern' poetry, even experimental; moderate length, any subject on approval of Board of Readers." Doesn't want "haiku, translations." Has published poetry by Susan H. Case, Philip Dacey, Elizabeth Howrd, Timothy Martin, Gilbert Wesley Purdy, and Nancy Scott. *Slant* is 120 pages, professionally printed on quality stock, flat-spined, with matte card cover. Receives about 1,400 poems/year, accepts 70-80. Press run is 175 (70-100 subscribers). Sample: $10.

How to Submit Submit up to 5 poems at a time. Lines/poem: poems should be of moderate length. No previously published poems or simultaneous submissions. Submissions should be typed; include SASE. "Put name, address (including e-mail if available), and phone number at the top of each page." Reads submissions September 1-November 15. Comments on rejected poems "on occasion." Guidelines available in magazine, for SASE, or on Web site. Responds in 3-4 months from November 15 deadline. Pays one contributor's copy. Poet retains rights.

Advice "We tend to publish those poems whose execution, line by line, does full justice to their conception. Often the decision to accept comes down to the matter of craft, language."

Frequently Asked Questions

The following FAQ (Frequently Asked Questions) section provides the expert knowledge you need to submit your poetry in a professional manner. Answers to most basic questions, such as "How many poems should I send?," "How long should I wait for a reply?" and "Are simultaneous submissions okay?" can be found by simply reading the listings in the Magazines/Journals and Book/Chapbook Publishers sections. See the introduction to each section for an explanation of the information contained in the listings. Also, see the Glossary of Listing terms on page 493.

Is it okay to submit handwritten poems?

Usually, no. Now and then a publisher or editor makes an exception and accepts handwritten manuscripts. However, check the preferences stated in each listing. If no mention is made of handwritten submissions, assume your poetry should be typed or computer-generated.

How should I format my poems for submission to magazines and journals?

If you're submitting poems by regular mail (also referred to as *land mail, postal mail* or *snail mail*), follow this format (also see sample on page 8):

Poems should be typed or computer-printed on white 8½ × 11 paper of at least 20 lb. weight. Left, right and bottom margins should be at least one inch. Starting ½ inch from the top of the page, type your name, address, telephone number, e-mail address (if you have one) and number of lines in the poem in the *upper right* corner, in individual lines, single-spaced. Space down about six lines and type the poem title, either centered or flush left. The title may appear in all caps or in upper and lower case. Space down another two lines (at least) and begin to type your poem. Poems are usually single-spaced, although some magazines may request double-spaced submissions. (Be alert to each market's preferences.) Double-space between stanzas. Type one poem to a page. For poems longer than one page, type your name in the *upper left* corner; on the next line type a key word from the title of your poem, the page number, and indicate whether the stanza begins or is continued on the new page (i.e., MOTHMAN, Page 2, continue stanza *or* begin new stanza).

If you're submitting poems by e-mail (also see sample on page 9):

First, make sure the publication accepts e-mail submissions. This information, when available, is included in all *Poet's Market* listings. In most cases, editors will request that

Mailed Submission Format

DO leave 1/2" margin on top, at least 1" on sides and bottom.

DO list contact information and number of lines in upper right corner.

DO space down about 6 lines.

DO type title in all caps or upper/lower case. Center it or type flush with left margin.

DON'T type a byline but **DO** space down at least 2 lines.

DO double-space between stanzas.

DO type poems single-spaced unless guidelines specify double spacing.

For multi-page poems, **DO** show your name, key word(s) from title, page number, and "continue stanza" or "new stanza."

DO space down at least 3 lines before resuming poem.

S. T. Coleridge
1796 Ancient Way
Mariner Heights, OH 45007
(852)555-5555
albatross@strophe.vv.cy
54 lines

KUBLA KHAN

In Xanadu did Kubla Khan
a stately pleasure dome decree:
where Alph, the sacred river, ran
through caverns measureless to man
down to a sunless sea.
So twice five miles of fertile ground
with walls and towers were girdled round:
and there were gardens bright with sinuous rills,
where blossomed many an incense-bearing tree;
and here were forests ancient as the hills,
enfolding sunny spots of greenery.

But oh! that deep romantic chasm which slanted
down the green hill athwart a cedarn cover!
A savage place! as holy and enchanted
as e'er beneath a waning moon was haunted
by woman wailing for her demon lover!
And from this chasm, with ceaseless turmoil seething,
as if this earth in fast thick pants were breathing,
a mighty fountain momently was forced:
amid whose swift half-intermitted burst
huge fragments vaulted like rebounding hail,
or chaffy grain beneath the thresher's flail:
And 'mid these dancing rocks at once and ever
it flung up momently the sacred river.

S. T. Coleridge
KUBLA KAHN, Page 2, continue stanza

Five miles meandering with a mazy motion
through wood and dale the sacred river ran,
then reached the caverns measureless to man,
and sank in tumult to a lifeless ocean:
and 'mid this tumult Kubla heard from afar
ancestral voices prophesying war!

The shadow of the dome of pleasure
floated midway on the waves;
where was heard the mingled measure
from the fountain and the caves.
It was a miracle of rare device,
a sunny pleasure dome with caves of ice!

A damsel with a dulcimer
in a vision once I saw:
It was an Abyssinian maid,

E-mail Submission Format

DO use a basic typeface and point size.

DO use the appropriate e-mail address.

DO consult guidelines for special instructions about formatting the subject line.

DO follow basic guidelines for a good cover letter.

DO provide contact information, including regular mail address.

DO be aware that formatting can become lost in an electronic submission. Keep it simple.

DO paste all poems within one message, one after the other, unless guidelines specify otherwise.

DON'T send submissions by e-mail unless editor says it's okay (in market listing or guidelines).

Poetry Submission

Arial   12   **B** *I* <u>U</u>

To...   Poetry Editor
Cc...
Bcc...
Subject: Poetry Submission

Pasted below are the following poems I'm submitting for your consideration: "Kubla Khan," "The Nightingale," and "Dejection: An Ode." I've noticed that *Bone-Whittle Review* has published quite a bit of traditional poetry, so I thought my work might be of interest to you.

My poetry has appeared in journals in the U.S. and U.K., including *The Squiggler's Digest* and *Wordsworth's Pal*. I've also won prizes from Stanzaloosa '02 and Lake Country Idol.

Thank you for your time and consideration. I look forward to hearing from you.

S. T. Coleridge
1796 Ancient Way
Mariner Heights OH 45007
(852)555-5555
albatross@strophe.w.cy

KUBLA KHAN

In Xanadu did Kubla Khan
a stately pleasure dome decree:
where Alph, the sacred river, ran
through caverns measureless to man
down to a sunless sea.
So twice five miles of fertile ground
with walls and towers were girdled round:
and there were gardens bright with sinuous rills,
where blossomed many an incense-bearing tree;
and here were forests ancient as the hills,
enfolding sunny spots of greenery.

But oh! that deep romantic chasm which slanted
down the green hill athwart a cedarn cover!
A savage place! as holy and enchanted
as e'er beneath a waning moon was haunted
by woman wailing for her demon lover!
And from this chasm, with ceaseless turmoil seething,
as if this earth in fast thick pants were breathing,
a mighty fountain momently was forced:
amid whose swift half-intermitted burst
huge fragments vaulted like rebounding hail,

Articles & Information

poems be pasted within the body of your e-mail, *not* sent as attachments. Many editors prefer this format because of the danger of viruses, the possibility of software incompatibility, and other concerns associated with e-mail attachments. Editors who consider e-mail attachments taboo may even delete the message without opening the attachment.

Of course, other editors do accept, and even prefer e-mail submissions as attachments. This information should be clearly stated in the market listing. If it's not, you're probably safer submitting your poems in the body of the e-mail. (All the more reason to pay close attention to details given in the listings.)

Note, too, the number of poems the editor recommends including in the e-mail submission. If no quantity is given specifically for e-mails, go with the number of poems an editor recommends submitting in general. Identify your submission with a notation in the subject line. While some editors simply want the words "Poetry Submission," others want poem titles. Check the market listing for preferences. **Note:** Because of spam, filters and other concerns, some editors are strict about what must be printed in the subject line and how. If you're uncertain about any aspect of e-mail submission formats, double-check the website (if available) for information or contact the publication for directions.

If you're submitting poems on disk:

Submit poems on disk *only* when the publication indicates this is acceptable. Even then, if no formatting preferences are given, contact the publisher for specifics before sending the disk. Make sure your disk is virus-free. Always include a hard copy (i.e., printed copy) of your submission with the disk.

What is a chapbook? How is it different from a regular poetry book?

A chapbook is a booklet, averaging 24-50 pages in length (some are shorter), usually digest-sized (5½ × 8½, although chapbooks can come in all sizes, even published within the pages of a magazine). Typically, a chapbook is saddle-stapled with a soft cover (card or special paper); chapbooks can also be produced with a plain paper cover the same weight as the pages, especially if the booklet is photocopied.

A chapbook is a much smaller collection of poetry than a full-length book (which runs anywhere from 50 pages to well over 100 pages, longer for "best of" collections and retrospectives). There are probably more poetry chapbooks being published than full-length books, and that's an important point to consider. Don't think of the chapbook as a poor relation to the full-length collection. While it's true a chapbook won't attract big reviews, qualify for major prizes or find national distribution through chain bookstores, it's a terrific way for a poet to build an audience (and reputation) in increments, while developing the kind of publishing history that may attract the attention of a book publisher one day.

Although some presses consider chapbooks through a regular submission process, many choose manuscripts through competitions. Check each publisher's listing for requirements, send for guidelines or visit the website (absolutely vital if a competition is involved), and check out some sample chapbooks the press has already produced (usually available from the press itself). Most chapbook publishers are as choosy as book publishers about the quality of work they accept. Submit your best poems in a professional manner. (See the Chapbook Publishers Index on page 502 for markets that consider chapbook manuscripts; the Book Publishers Index begins on page 505.)

How do I format a collection of poems to submit to a book/chapbook publisher?

Before you send a manuscript to a book/chapbook publisher, request guidelines (or consult the publisher's website, if available). Requirements vary regarding formatting, query letters and samples, length, and other considerations. Usually you will use 8½ × 11, 20 lb. white paper; set left, right and bottom margins of at least one inch; put your name and title of your collection in the top left corner of every page; limit poems to one per page (although poems certainly may run longer than one page); and number pages consecutively. Individual publisher requirements might include a title page, table of contents, credits page (indicating where previously published poems originally appeared) and biographical note.

If you're submitting your poetry book or chapbook manuscript to a competition, you *must* read and follow the guidelines. Failure to do so could disqualify your manuscript. Guidelines for a competition might call for an official entry form to accompany the submission, a special title page, a minimum and maximum number of pages, and specific formatting instructions (such as paginating the manuscript and not putting the poet's name on any of the manuscript pages).

What is a cover letter? Do I have to send one? What should it say?

A cover letter is your introduction to the editor, telling him a little about yourself and your work. Most editors indicate their cover letter preferences in their listings. If an editor states a cover letter is "required," absolutely send one! It's also better to send one if a cover letter is "preferred." Experts disagree on the necessity and appropriateness of cover letters, so use your own judgment when preferences aren't clear in the listing.

A cover letter should be professional but also allow you to present your work in a personal manner. (See the fictional cover letter on page 12 as an example.) Keep your letter brief, no more than one page. Address your letter to the correct contact person. (Use "Poetry Editor" if no contact name appears in the listing.) Include your name, address, phone number and e-mail address (if available). If a biographical note is requested, include 2-3 lines about your background, interests, why you write poetry, etc. Avoid praising yourself or your poems in your letter (your submission should speak for itself). Include titles (or first lines) of the poems you're submitting. You may list a few of your most recent publishing credits, but no more than five; and keep in mind that some editors find publishing credits tiresome—they're more interested in the quality of the work you're submitting to *them*.

Show your familiarity with the magazine to which you're submitting: comment on a poem the magazine published, tell the editor why you chose to submit to her magazine, mention poets the magazine has published. Use a business-style format for a professional appearance, and proofread carefully; typos, misspellings and other errors make a poor first impression. Remember that editors are people, too. Respect, professionalism and kindness go a long way in poet/editor relationships.

What is a SASE? An IRC (with SAE)?

A SASE is a self-addressed, stamped envelope—and you should never send a submission by regular mail without one. Also include a SASE if you send an inquiry to an editor. If your submission is too large for an envelope (for instance, a bulky book-length collection of poems), use a box and include a self-addressed mailing label with adequate return postage paper-clipped to it.

An IRC is an International Reply Coupon, enclosed with a self-addressed envelope for manuscripts submitted to foreign markets. Each coupon is equivalent in value to the minimum postage rate for an unregistered airmail letter. IRCs may be exchanged for postage stamps at post offices in all foreign countries that are members of the Universal Postal Union (UPU). When you provide the adequate number of IRCs and a self-addressed

Important

Articles & Information

Preparing Your Cover Letter

DO type on one side of 8½ x 11 20 lb. paper.

DO proofread carefully.

DO use a standard 12-point typeface (like Times New Roman).

DO list the poems you're submitting for consideration.

DO mention something about the magazine and about yourself.

DO be brief!

Perry Lineskanner
1954 Eastern Blvd.
Pentameter, OH 45007
(852) 555-5555
soneteer@trochee.vv.cy

April 24, 2009

Spack Saddlestaple, Editor
The Squiggler's Digest
Double-Toe Press
P.O. Box 54X
Submission Junction, AZ 85009

Dear Mr. Saddlestaple:

Enclosed are three poems for your consideration for *The Squiggler's Digest*: "The Diamond Queen," "The Boy Who Was Gromit," and "The Maker of Everything."

Although this is my first submission to your journal, I'm a long-time reader of *The Squiggler's Digest* and enjoy the scope of narrative poetry you feature. I especially enjoyed Sydney Dogwood's poetry cycle in Issue 4.

My own poetry has appeared recently in *The Bone-Whittle Review*, *Bumper-Car Reverie*, and *Stock Still*.

Thank you for considering my manuscript. I look forward to hearing from you.

Sincerely,

Perry Lineskanner

Note: The names used in this letter are intended to be fictional; any resemblance to real people, publications or presses is purely coincidental.

envelope (SAE), you give a foreign editor financial means to return your submission (U.S. postage stamps cannot be used to send mail *to* the United States from outside the country). Purchase price is $2 per coupon. Call your local post office to check for availability (sometimes only larger post offices sell them).

Important note about IRCs: Foreign editors sometimes find the IRCs have been stamped incorrectly by the U.S. post office when purchased. This voids the IRCs and makes it impossible for the foreign editor to exchange the coupons for return postage for your manuscript. When buying IRCs, make sure yours have been stamped correctly before you leave the counter. (The Postal Service clerk must place a postmark in the block with the heading *control stamp of the country of origin*.) More information about International Reply Coupons is available on the USPS website (www.usps.com).

To save time and money, poets sometimes send disposable manuscripts to foreign markets and inform the editor to discard the manuscript after it's been read. Some enclose an IRC and SAE for reply only; others establish a deadline after which they will withdraw the manuscript from consideration and market it elsewhere.

How much postage does my submission need?

As much as it takes—you do *not* want your manuscript to arrive postage due. Purchase a postage scale or take your manuscript to the post office for weighing. Remember, you'll need postage on two envelopes: the one containing your submission and SASE, and the return envelope itself. Submissions without SASEs usually will not be returned (and possibly may not even be read).

Note: New postage rates went into effect on May 12, 2008. There is now a new fee structure for First-Class Postage. For letters and cards (including business-size envelopes), the First-Class rate is 42 cents for the first ounce, and 17 cents per additional ounce up to and including 3.5 ounces. **Letter-sized mail that weighs more than 3.5 ounces is charged the "flats" rate** ("flats" include any envelope large enough to mail an 8½ × 11 manuscript page unfolded) of 83 cents for the first ounce, and 17 cents for each additional ounce up to and including 13 ounces. This means if you send a large envelope that weighs only one ounce, it costs 83 cents at the First-Class flats rate instead of the 42 cents charged for First-Class letters and cards. (See the charts on page 14 for First-Class rates for letters and flats, or go to www.usps.com for complete information on all rates questions.)

The USPS also offers its Click-N-Ship(r) program, which allows a customer to print domestic and international shipping labels with postage, buy insurance and pay for postage by credit card. See the USPS website for a one-time software download, to check system requirements and to register for an account.

The website is also your source for ordering supplies (such as postage scale and labels), reviewing postal regulations, calculating postage and more. Canada Post information and services are available at www.canadapost.com.

What does it mean when an editor says "no previously published" poems? Does this include poems that have appeared in anthologies? What if one of my poems appeared online through a group or forum?

If your poem appears *anywhere* in print for a public audience, it's considered "previously" published. That includes magazines, anthologies, Web sites and online journals, and even printed programs (say for a church service, wedding, etc.). See the explanation for rights below, especially *second serial (reprint) rights* and *all rights* for additional concerns about previously published material.

Postage Information

First-Class Mail Rates: Letters & Cards

1 ounce	$0.44		3 ounces	0.78
2 ounces	$0.61		3.5 ounces	0.95
			Postcard	0.28

First-Class Mail Rates: Flats

Weight not over (ounces)	Rate	Weight not over (ounces)	Rate
1	$0.88	8	2.07
2	1.05	9	2.24
3	1.22	10	2.41
4	1.39	11	2.58
5	1.56	12	2.75
6	1.73	13	2.92
7	1.90		

Source: Web site of the United States Postal Service (www.usps.com)

U.S. and Canadian Postal Codes

AL	Alabama	MN	Minnesota	VA	Virginia
AK	Alaska	MS	Mississippi	WA	Washington
AZ	Arizona	MO	Missouri	WV	West Virginia
AR	Arkansas	MT	Montana	WI	Wisconsin
CA	California	NE	Nebraska	WY	Wyoming
CO	Colorado	NV	Nevada		
CT	Connecticut	NH	New Hampsire	**Canada**	
DE	Delaware	NJ	New Jersey	AB	Alberta
DC	District of	NM	New Mexico	BC	British Columbia
	Columbia	NY	New York	MB	Manitoba
FL	Florida	NC	North Carolina	NB	New Brunswick
GA	Georgia	ND	North Dakota	NL	Newfoundland &
GU	Guam	OH	Ohio		Labrador
HI	Hawaii	OK	Oklahoma	NS	Nova Scotia
ID	Idaho	OR	Oregon	NT	Northwest
IL	Illinois	PA	Pennsylvania		Territories
IN	Indiana	PR	Puerto Rico	NU	Nunavut
IA	Iowa	RI	Rhode Island	ON	Ontario
KS	Kansas	SC	South Carolina	PE	Prince Edward
KY	Kentucky	SD	South Dakota		Island
LA	Louisiana	TN	Tennessee	QC	Quebec
ME	Maine	TX	Texas	SK	Saskatchewan
MD	Maryland	UT	Utah	YT	Yukon
MA	Massachusetts	VT	Vermont		
MI	Michigan	VI	Virgin Islands		

One exception to the above guidelines is if your poem appears online in a *private* poetry forum, critique group, etc. As long as the site is private (i.e., a password is required to view and participate), your poem isn't considered "published." However, if your poem is printed on an online forum or bulletin board that's available for public viewing, even if you must use a password to post the poem or to comment, then your poem is considered "published" as far as rights are concerned.

What rights should I offer for my poems? What do these different rights mean?

Editors usually indicate in their listings what rights they acquire. Most journals and magazines license *first rights* (a.k.a. *first serial rights*), which means the poet offers the right to publish the poem for the first time in any periodical. All other rights to the material remain with the poet. (Note that some editors state that rights to poems "revert to poets upon publication" when first rights are acquired.) When poems are excerpted from a book prior to publication and printed in a magazine/journal, this is also called *first serial rights*. The addition of *North American* indicates the editor is the first to publish a poem in a U.S. or Canadian periodical. The poem may still be submitted to editors outside of North America or to those who acquire reprint rights.

When a magazine/journal licenses *one-time rights* to a poem (also known as *simultaneous rights*), the editor has *nonexclusive* rights to publish the poem once. The poet may submit that same poem to other publications at the same time (usually markets that don't have overlapping audiences).

Editors/publishers open to submission of work already published elsewhere seek *second serial (reprint) rights*. The poet is obliged to inform them where and when the poem previously appeared so they can give proper credit to the original publication. In essence, chapbook or book collections license reprint rights, listing the magazines in which poems previously appeared somewhere in the book (usually on the copyright page or separate credits page).

If a publisher or editor requires you to relinquish *all rights*, be aware that you're giving up ownership of that poem or group of poems. You cannot resubmit the work elsewhere, nor can you include it in a poetry collection without permission or by negotiating for reprint rights to be returned to you. Before you agree to this type of arrangement, ask the editor first if he or she is willing to acquire first rights instead of all rights. If you receive a refusal and you don't want to relinquish all rights, simply write a letter withdrawing your work from consideration. Some editors will reassign rights to a writer after a given amount of time, such as one year.

With the growth in Internet publishing opportunities, *electronic rights* have become very important. These cover a broad range of electronic media, including online magazines, CD recordings of poetry readings and CD-ROM editions of magazines. When submitting to an electronic market of any kind, find out what rights the market acquires upfront (many online magazines also stipulate the right to archive poetry they've published so it's continually available on their websites).

What is a copyright? Should I have my poems copyrighted before I submit them for publication?

Copyright is a proprietary right that gives you the power to control your work's reproduction, distribution and public display or performance, as well as its adaptation to other forms. In other words, you have the legal right to the exclusive publication, sale or distribution of your poetry. What's more, your "original works of authorship" are protected as soon as they are "fixed in a tangible form of expression," i.e., written down or recorded. Since March 1989, copyright notices are no longer required to secure protection, so it's not necessary to include them on your poetry manuscript. Also, in many editors' minds, copyright notices signal the work of amateurs who are distrustful and paranoid about having work stolen.

If you still want to indicate copyright, use the ÞCR symbol or the word *copyright*, your name and the year. If you wish, you can register your copyright with the Copyright Office for a $45 fee, using Form TX (directions and form available for download from www.copyright.gov). Since paying $45 per poem is costly and impractical, you may prefer to copyright a group of unpublished poems for that single fee. Further information is available from the U.S. Copyright Office, Library of Congress, 101 Independence Ave. S.E., Washington DC 20559-6000; by download from www.copyright.gov; or by calling (202)707-3000 between 8:30 a.m. and 5:00 p.m. (EST) weekdays.

Special note regarding Copyright Office mail delivery: The "effective date of registration" for copyright applications is usually the day the Copyright Office actually receives all elements of an application (application form, fee and copies of work being registered). Because of security concerns, all USPS and private-carrier mail is screened off-site prior to arrival at the Copyright Office. This can add 3-5 days to delivery time and could, therefore, impact the effective date of registration. See the website for details about proper packaging, special handling and other related information.

Out of the Slush and Into Print

by Kelly Davio

So you've written some poems. You've shared them with friends you trust for candid feedback, and they genuinely enjoy the poetry. Better still, your writing group, teachers or workshop compatriots think the work is strong enough to send to literary journals. You've done your homework by identifying venues that print poems like yours, and because you're a good literary citizen, you've subscribed to some of your favorite journals. Having identified the strongest three to five poems in your repertoire, you bundle your poems up, stamp the envelopes, rub said envelopes against your dog's head for luck, and say a little prayer as you pop them into the mail.

A few weeks or months pass, a rejection slip or two filtering in as you wait, but you don't worry that "your work does not meet our editorial needs at this time." You keep the faith. Then a few more slips find their way into your mailbox. When the very last journal rejects your work as well, you begin to wonder what's going wrong.

My Writing is Strong, So Why Can't I Seem to Publish?

If you're asking this question, you're in good company with many other poets. Let's be clear: the odds of having work selected for publication are never in your favor. Consider the numbers of poems editors read: for each issue of The Los Angeles Review, for example, we consider more than 1,000 poems, eventually accepting about 40 or so. Many journals have room to showcase only half as many pieces. Not only are your poems pitted against many others, but in some cases, they also have to fight their way past early readers. At many journals, particularly those run by universities, undergraduate students of creative writing make initial calls on poems the "slush pile" (the unsolicited manuscripts considered by journals) and determine whether an editor will even lay eyes on your work.

Depressed yet? Cheer up! There are a number of ways to increase the likelihood that your poetry will make it out of the slush, onto the editor's desk, and into print.

KELLY DAVIO currently serves as the Managing Editor/Poetry Editor at the *Los Angeles Review*, and reads poetry for Fifth Wednesday Journal. Her work can be found in *Women's Review of Books*, *Cincinnati Review*, and *Best New Poets 2009*, among others. Her poetry collection, *Burn This House*, is forthcoming from Red Hen Press, and she is currently working on a novel in verse.

First Impressions

Think of your submission as a blind date with an editor. She doesn't know you, but she's hoping she finds that elusive spark with your work; you want to show her that your poetry is worth her time. When she opens your envelope or e-mail, the first thing she sees is your cover letter. Just as you would dress nicely to meet a possible romantic interest, your cover letter should show that you're competent, classy, and professional.

Start your date well by addressing the editor by name, not as "Sir or Madam," "To Whom it May Concern," or, worst of all, "Friend." Taking a few moments to find an editor's name on a journal's website, rather than dashing off a form letter, shows the editor you care about your submission.

Now that you're off to a good start, keep that cover letter strong by following all guidelines. It baffles editors that many—even most—writers who want to publish don't bother to read or follow guidelines. If an editor asks for three to five poems stapled to a cover letter, don't send six with a paperclip. If the editor asks for the titles of your submitted poems in the cover letter, don't omit them. Taking the time to follow simple instructions will get you places with an editor or reader; when I open that rare submission that is correctly formatted, is addressed to me, and—for the win—spells my name correctly, I automatically want to give more time and attention to that poet's work than to the poems of a writer who sent sloppy slush.

The Right Kind of Attention

Now that you've followed the journal's guidelines, the next step in presenting your work well includes telling a little about yourself. Your cover letter gives an editor a sense of you as a person and as a poet. By including information about where you went to school, what you do for a living, and how you heard about the publication in one, brief paragraph, you'll help the editor warm up to your work. It's also great to remind the editor that you met at a conference or reading, or that you are a loyal subscriber to the magazine (I shouldn't have to tell you it's a bad idea to make these claims if they're untrue). Showing that you're a friendly, engaged person puts an editor in a receptive frame of mind.

There is, however, such a thing as showing too much personality. Sure, using a quirky font, adding glitter to your envelope, or attaching photos of yourself in beachwear will get an editor's attention, but it's the wrong sort of attention. At literary journals, editors develop relationships with writers. If your submission suggests you might not be a person an editor would want to engage—let's say you include a sketch of yourself with your collection of medieval torture devices—she'll be understandably skittish about entering a working relationship with you. Making bold assertions about the importance or innovative nature of the enclosed poetry is a similarly bad idea; however much you may want to explain your work in detail, allow your poetry to speak for itself. As a rule, if you're in doubt as to whether any part of your submission is inappropriate or puts you in a bad light, take it out.

Second Dates

Every poet—fledgling or established—receives rejection. Sometimes rejection slips come as tiny scraps of paper that appear to have been cut by a toddler. Other times, a writer might be lucky enough to receive a whole sheet of paper on actual letterhead. And every now and then, an editor may put ink to paper or cursor to screen to give a writer some constructive feedback or request to see more work.

Let's be clear: being invited to resubmit is like being asked on a second date. There's no commitment at this stage, but there's genuine interest on the editor's part. She likes your poems, and now that you have her attention, you've got a chance to really impress her with the full range of your charms. You may be excited to have a second shot, but follow the rules of playing it cool: don't e-mail a group of poems five minutes after an editor has asked for them, and don't pop a new batch of work into the mail the same day as you receive a rejection. Just as calling your date moments after you've left the restaurant would smack of desperation, don't run the risk of turning your editor off with enthusiasm that resembles stalking. You needn't worry that the editor will forget you; if she's taken the time to ask for a resubmission, it's because she likes the work and finds it memorable. When you do resubmit, after having taken the time to consider what poems might be better suited to the journal's needs, you can jog the editor's memory by mentioning her offer to consider more work.

It's Not Personal Unless You Make It Personal

So let's say your second date doesn't go well, or that you never got to the second date at all. Maybe an editor flatly rejected your best poem, your magnum opus. You feel sure that the editor's taste is sorely lacking. While the editor may, in fact, be missing out, there are a number of reasons a journal might not be able to accept your work. The editor might be looking for variety, and your work may feel too similar to poems already accepted. Perhaps your poems do not fit the theme of the issue. Maybe the editor has already filled her allotted pages, and just can't squeeze another piece in the issue. A rejection of a poem isn't a rejection of a person.

However, some poets, in moments of frustration, have been known to dash off angry missives to editors, questioning levels of taste or qualification for the editorial position. When personal attacks are leveled, it discourages those editors who spend great swaths of their free time working to promote the craft and appreciation of poetry. In an industry that runs less on money than it does on good will, hostility will only breed a bad reputation. Spare yourself from becoming the pariah in the inbox by taking setbacks graciously.

Persistence Pays...In Contributor's Copies

The longer you write and continue to send out work, the more you will find success in publishing. Given the vast number of publications in the Western world, there is undoubtedly a journal for every writer. And as you begin to see your poems come out in print, it will likely be a point of pride for you to see your collection of contributor's copies—copies given in payment for the use of the poet's work—grow to overfill your bookshelf.

But if you have visions of your bank account growing to such seam-bursting proportions, skim back up to the line about the literary world running on good vibes, not on hard cash. Placing poems in journals doesn't pay much, if anything. From time to time, a journal may be able to offer a poet a small honorarium, but publications can generally afford only to give complimentary or discounted copies.

So why put yourself through the rigmarole of writing, submitting, finding rejection and, somewhere down the line, getting some copies of magazines? Hopefully it's because you're genuinely in love with language and with poetry, and it brings you joy to share that love with others. As you go forward in your writing career, remember: be friendly, be courteous, be kind and, by all means, keep going.

Social Networking and Poetry Publishing

by Amy MacLennan

Social networking is transforming the terrain of poetry publishing. Facebook, Twitter and LinkedIn are changing the ways poets interact with their publishers, readers and peers. These tools produce new opportunities and methods of communicating, and all have their limitations. Formerly relegated to postal correspondence or in-person interactions at workshops, MFA programs, conventions, poetry festivals and the like, poets are now able to immediately and regularly connect with publishers and readers of poetry in the virtual realm.

LinkedIn is the least immediate of the current social networking sites. Intended more as an employment network, LinkedIn permits users to find jobs/business opportunities, do research on potential employers, as well as display résumés and references. In the poetry arena, it is probably used best as a way to maintain a teaching, publishing and/or freelancing résumé for the prospect of paid employment. A tool like Twitter is an "intravenous drip" of social interface. It allows for short, 140-character bursts of in-the-moment posts called tweets. Facebook is probably the most robust and flexible of the current social networking services. It provides the opportunity to create and join groups or fan pages, the ability to post photos, videos and notes as well as links to outside web pages, and lets users organize friend lists. Both individuals and literary magazine entities can maintain a presence and interact with other poetry enthusiasts.

The most obvious advantage to social networking is that it does not require in-person contact and can be accessed from computers, laptops and most mobile phones. For almost all poets and publishers, time is a precious commodity. Immediacy and convenience are vital when they try to balance the demands of a paying job (sometimes two or even three) with writing, publishing and a necessary personal life. It is also an excellent alternative for those that do not have the means to travel or attend workshops and Master's programs. Poet Josh Robbins noted, "I've met people on Facebook that I'd never have met otherwise because of geographic distance, etc. Facebook takes the awkwardness and anxiety out of networking. People automatically have something in common, and communication is on a more level field of play."

AMY MACLENNAN has been published in Hayden's Ferry Review, River Styx, Linebreak, Cimarron Review, Folio, and Rattle. Her poems have appeared in the anthologies Not a Muse: The Inner Lives of Women from Haven Books and Eating Her Wedding Dress: A Collection of Clothing Poems from Ragged Sky Press.

Literary magazine publishing opportunities are still available in places like Poet's Market and Allison Joseph's Creative Writers Opportunities List that she delivers through Yahoo! groups. However, there are many ways that social networks place a different spin on the publishing process. Calls for submissions and reminders of closing dates can be sent easily by editors via status updates, wall comments and fan page updates. Collin Kelley, a poet from Atlanta, has been asked "by editors and publishers I've met at Facebook and Twitter to submit work, give interviews or participate in chats and radio programs. There's more instant access and gratification using social networking. It's easier to reach out to literary magazines and presses, too, since so many now have Facebook pages. You get a real sense of who is reading and what the press is working on," he said.

Poet Molly Fisk said that social networking has provided opportunities outside of publishing, "I've been invited to blurb/endorse an on-line litmag, to submit work - both by a guest editor whom I know for a special issue and by a regular editor whom I didn't know, to be part of four or five readings at various venues (bookstore, radio, cafe), and to be part of a big festival in a major nearby city that benefits the library."

From a publisher's point of view, discovering a poet's work from interactions on Facebook occurs, but it depends on the editor. As Chris Hamilton-Emery of Salt Publishing said, "I've contacted several people through Facebook, though mainly as I can reach the people I'm interested in through it, as opposed to find them and their work actually on Facebook."

Nonetheless, Mary Biddinger of Barn Owl Review stated, "I have used Facebook to solicit poets for BOR, and have found that I get replies much more readily than if I'm using e-mail. I also click on a lot of links that folks post, and have read the work of poets who interest me (and who I might not have found otherwise)."

Steven Schroeder, editor of Anti-, said, "I did publish at least one piece of visual 'cover' art that I was initially queried about through Facebook when the artist (also a poet and editor) joined the Anti- Facebook group and saw my call for art."

Another plus for both publishers and poets is the immediate delivery of news to friends, followers and connections. Whether it is publicizing a recent literary magazine issue, offering a discount subscription or announcing a new blog post, social networking can drive a large number people to websites and blogs. Poet and editor Arlene Ang uses "the status update mostly for poems that get published and the 'note' when it comes to letting contributors and (hopefully) interested friends know that the new issue of a 'zine I'm editing is up. We're about to use Facebook to help market the Press 1 anthology," she said.

As with any form of communication, there are some drawbacks to social networking. Over-publicizing is a common complaint. While one of the main points of social networking is to meet new people and broadcast your own successes, "bombardment" with copious self-promotion announcements and invitations to join fan pages is a major irritant to most poets and publishers. The same goes for literary magazines. If someone joins a fan page or group, they clearly want to receive notice of new issues and readings. However, too many tweets or updates will prompt many to disconnect themselves from the overeager editors. There is also the issue of "cozying up" to publishers in a way that makes it difficult for them to preserve boundaries. Editors want to sustain fairness, and many keep some distance in their social networking interactions in order to keep the submission review process as impartial as possible.

Molly Fisk has a very even approach to social networking and stated, "I work hard at it - posting two or three times almost every day, referring people to good poets, poems, teachers, classes, and places to send their work, giving away all kinds of good ideas in the spirit of sharing our art, as well as putting up wacky things I find interesting that are not writing related but give people a sense of the range of my interests and scope."

Know Your Audience

by Joannie Kervran Stangeland

A s a poet, you write the work that needs writing—what wakes you at three in the morning, clamoring to be said. But after you write it, who hears it?

Ellen Bass has said, "I see the poem as real—there's a real person on the other end of the poem, the reader. I'm a real person talking to that reader. When I write the poem, I'm first talking to myself...When I think about the reader then reading it, I want the reader to actually understand what I'm communicating."

If you're writing an occasional poem for a wedding, a birthday, or a special event, you probably have a pretty good idea of who will hear the poem and where they will hear it. You think about what you want to say to that particular audience.

When you don't have an audience you know, your poems still speak. They connect with those who are in the chairs, reading the page, or an audience you don't have or know about yet. Your poems are words and words are communication—a conversation, a confession, a call to action. Even the most intensely private passages become a dialog when you send them into the world.

Who Is Reading Your Poems?

When you're submitting poems, journal editors are your audience—and Poet's Market gives you an opportunity to learn more about that audience. In the listings, the editors of each publication tell you what kinds of work they're looking for.

Get to know their guidelines. The listings in Poet's Market include basic guidelines, such as the publication's reading period, whether e-mail submissions are permitted, and other preferences.

Your audience changes from journal to journal. Some publications focus on specific forms, such as haiku, cinquains, or prose poems. Others want work only from a specific community—for example, people of color, Canadian writers, women, or teens. Find the

JOANNIE KERVRAN STANGELAND's poetry has most recently appeared in CHEST, Horticulture, and Journal of the American Medical Association. She is the author of two poetry chapbooks, A Steady Longing for Flight (winner of the Floating Bridge Press Chapbook Award) and Weathered Steps (Rose Alley Press). Joannie has been writing poetry for nearly 20 years. She has been a Jack Straw Writer, and her poems have appeared on Seattle-area buses. Joannie also blogs at http://poe-query.blogspot.com, and she hosts a video series, "A Writer's Guide to Microsoft Office" (www.youtube.com/officeonlinevideos).

journals that make the best fit with your poems. They are your best and likely most appreciative audience.

Be aware of the themes that are wanted. Some journals are centered on specific subjects, such as nature, science fiction, humor, travel, or medicine and healing. Other publications switch themes from one issue to the next. If your poem fits their theme, they are part of your audience—at least for that issue.

Most entries include a web address, so you can visit the publication's website to confirm that the guidelines are still the same. A publication may have switched over to e-mail submissions or an online submission manager, or the reading period might have closed early. You can also order a sample copy or read any poems posted on the site. Seeing what editors have chosen in the past can give you a better idea of what they're looking for now.

Check for the most recent information you can find. The editors you're sending your poems to read through many submissions, and one that hasn't followed their guidelines is going to get the wrong kind of attention.

Who Is Hearing Your Poems?

You can find an armload of articles that bemoan the decreasing audience for poetry. But let's forget about the masses and focus on the folks who show up.

Your audience needs to hear you. Be sure your audience can hear you. Check the environment: How big is the space? Are you in a coffee shop—with a loud espresso grinder—or in a bar or in a bookstore that uses crinkly plastic bags? If you aren't sure how well your voice is carrying, go ahead and ask. If a microphone is available, use it. You might not be as loud as you think you are, without it.

Your audience is here to hear you. You're here to share your poems. Take charge and be generous with your poems and your voice. I think of it as "owning the room," but it's also like being the hostess of a fabulous party for all your friends. You want to connect with the passion that fired your poem when you were writing it, and you want to connect with your guests in the room.

Your audience wants to know you—a little. Long introductions to each poem might be too much information. After all, it's about sharing the poems. But some background information can help your audience connect with you and the poem. And it's a different kind of listening, giving them a chance to rest a bit before the next poem.

In a 1985 interview, Carolyn Kizer said, "Dylan Thomas was a success not because he was a great poet, but because he read magnificently...I'm modest about my poetry, but I'm not modest about my reading. I've worked hard to be good at it, and I'm proud of it."

Reading well is a gift to your audience and to your poems.

If you have books with you, let people know, quickly. It isn't the best time for a lengthy sales pitch, but someone might want to take your poems home.

At the end of the reading, if at all possible, stay and talk with people. This is another chance to get to know your audience, even after you've read. You'll learn more for the next time.

Are there any content or language restrictions? If children are part of the audience, or if you are being recorded for broadcast on the radio or on television, you might need to adjust your choice of poems or change some of your wording on the fly.

On the about.com website, Bob Holman recounts an all-ages poetry event and describes the readers as poets "who temper when necessary ("France"? for the "F" word? Genius!) but are never anything less than the poets they are."

You are a member of your audience. When you're at an open mic reading, remember to be a good audience to all the participants. They will be part of your audience when it's your turn, so you want to treat the other readers with attention and respect.

Why & How I Self-Published My Collection

by Sage Cohen & Tracy Koretsky

SAGE COHEN

"Anyone who says it can't be done should get out of the way of the person who's doing it."—Chinese proverb

I am a DIY kind of woman. In my late 20's, I founded my own marketing communications firm, which over the years has enabled me to purchase my own house, fund my own writing retreats and hobble together my own, unique expression of a writing life.

What does this have to do with self-publishing, you may ask? Everything! Having sidestepped a prescribed career path for one that makes space for the passion and practice of poetry, the process of authoring my own livelihood primed me well for launching my own books into the world. But that's not where I started.

In 2004, I understood that I had a complete collection of poems on my hands and that it was time to start ushering them into the world in toto. I spent the next two years polishing, ordering, and conceptualizing the trajectory and shape of my manuscript: plucking poems out, shuffling them in, making mazes over my floors, reading and rereading, deciding and second-guessing until the whole body of work coalesced into the organizing principle of three sections: New York, San Francisco, and Portland—the three cities that had framed my life and shaped my poetry consecutively for nearly 15 years.

Come 2006, I had a final poetry manuscript in hand composed of poems spanning more than a decade. A third of the poems had been workshopped and refined in a graduate creative writing program. Nineteen of the poems were previously published in literary journals and magazines. Some had taken ten-to-fifteen years to mature and ripen. And nearly every poem had been field-tested through live readings, where I learned what resonated with listeners, started to get a feel for my own voice, and gained a big-picture understanding and appreciation of my own craft.

SAGE COHEN is the author of the poetry collection Like The Heart, The World and the nonfiction books Writing the Life Poetic: An Invitation to Read and Write Poetry (Writer's Digest Books, 2009) and The Productive Writer: Tips & Tools to Help You Write More, Stress Less, and Create Success (Writer's Digest Books, 2010). She has won first prize in the Ghost Road Press poetry contest and been nominated for a Pushcart Prize. Sage received her BA from Brown University and her MA in poetry from New York University. Learn more at www.writingthelifepoetic.typepad.com, www.writingthelifepoetic.com and www.sagesaidso.com. **TRACY KORETSKY** is the author of the poetry collection Even Before My Own Name.

I chose a title for the collection—*Like the Heart, the World*—proofed the whole shebang three times, printed a final, hard copy of the beautiful beast, made ten photocopies and was ready to go. Then I researched first-book publication contests through Poets & Writers, targeting the opportunities that seemed best suited to me. Out went those heavy, padded packages of hope into the blind future of judgment.

Back came the letters. They were far more personal and detailed than I expected, offering specific appreciation for standout poems and suggestions for improvement for others. Of the eight publishers to which I sent my work in the course of a year, four awarded my manuscript either finalist or semi-finalist status in their competitions. This was a gratifying endorsement of my work's viability in the subjective world of poetry publishing.

As the encouraging rejections were rolling in, I learned that a previous MFA classmate had just published a poetry collection, and I wrote to congratulate her. She sent me a miserable reply about having struggled for more than a decade to get the book published and how it had embittered her to the final result. At the time, I was doing approximately a dozen readings, plus a handful of teaching and lecturing gigs per year. Participants at these events repeatedly approached me about purchasing my poetry; and I didn't have anything to offer them.

When I received the note from my old classmate, something clicked. It occurred to me that I didn't need a publisher to create a book. In fact, having been solely responsible for creating so many client communications over the years, it seemed more natural—preferable, even—to have complete responsibility for the look, feel, and results of my own, most precious communication project.

I thought through the consequences of exiting the creeping crawl of the standard publishing path:

- Was I willing to forgo the validation and status of publication by a traditional press for the freedom of designing, producing and marketing my own book? Yes.
- Was I secure enough in the value of my work to put it into the world without anyone else's official stamp of approval: Yes. (After all, I had a well-seasoned collection of poetry that had been endorsed by poets I trust, published in journals I admire, and—most importantly—that I believed in.)
- Was I planning to teach at a university in the next year or two? No.
- Would I be seeking highly competitive funding or awards such as NEA grants or Guggenheim Fellowships any time soon? No.
- Was I sure the manuscript was ready for publication? Not only was it as good as I thought it was going to get, it was starting to feel in the way of the next collection trying to come through—its time had come to leave the nest.
- Was I prepared to be the one-woman sales and marketing force behind this book? Of course! (See day job above.)
- Would I regret experimenting with this alternative path to publication? Possibly—I wouldn't know without trying. I was ready to find out.

In short, I was very clear about why I was self-publishing and how it would benefit my writing life; I felt confident in the quality of my work; and maybe most importantly, I felt excited and proud about creating a book of my own making. I was both enthusiastic about promoting the book and clear about how much work that involved, from many years of professional experience. I decided to do it.

Just by chance, at the blogher conference that summer, I stumbled upon the fine folks from lulu.com and had the opportunity to handle some of their print-on-demand books.

The production quality was stunning. These books that writers had produced themselves were far more beautiful, quirky and original than anything I had seen from any mainstream publishing house. I started to get really excited about the opportunity to make my own decisions about how my poetry collection would look and feel.

Upon doing a little research, it became clear that the fast and inexpensive print-on-demand option was far preferable to me than the standard print-and-shelve-and-wait process. Instead of printing, let's say, 500 books, storing them in my office, and then mailing each one off as folks ordered them, print-on-demand books get printed digitally the moment someone orders one—and the vendor (in my case, Lulu.com) gets paid a flat fee each time someone purchases a book. The whole order-purchase-fulfillment process (including my own, virtual storefront) is handled online by the vendor. So there's no inventory sitting around, gathering dust. And more importantly, there is not a large, up-front printing (or warehousing) investment required by the author. My only costs were in getting the book ready for production—and a minimal fee for registering myself as publisher and acquiring an ISBN.

I hired a friend who is an editor to proof the manuscript for grammatical and punctuation errors. (I'd seen the poems far too many times over the years to have an eye for such fine detail.) I hired my friend Gregoire Vion, a designer and illustrator I'd been collaborating with for 13 years—the one who illustrated my subsequent book, *Writing the Life Poetic: An Invitation to Read and Write Poetry*—to lay out the book. For the front cover, we simply modified an illustration that we'd created for my holiday card a few years earlier. For the back cover, we chose an illustration previously created for one of my web sites.

Then, through the lulu.com online customer interface, Gregoire submitted the cover and content, I chose a distribution package, proofed a copy of the printed book, decided how much of a cut I was going to take per purchase, and then PRESTO: it was available for sale. Within about a month, *Like the Heart, the World* was available for order through major book retailers everywhere, including amazon.com. I purchased a stash of books to bring with me to events and sell directly to participants; since then, I've never had to send anyone wanting my poetry home empty-handed.

Which leaves me with just one, unanswered question: Would I regret experimenting with this alternative path to publication?

It's been three years since I published *Like the Heart, the World*, and the answer is wholeheartedly: no regrets. Birthing my book how and when I wanted made me giddy—and it still does. Through the process, I have gained confidence in my own authority: to decide when my poetry is ready for publication, and to do what needs to be done to put my book in the hands of people who want to read it.

TRACY KORETSKY

Let me make this clear: I have not just self-published my collection of poetry—I am giving it away. I've posted a free e-book version at www.TracyKoretsky.com, and offer the perfect-bound paperback for $5, the cost of printing and mailing. Every artist should have a gift of their art to give away to the world. This memoir in poems is mine.

Sure, I gave up the rite of adjudication, the incomparable thrill of an editor or guest judge selecting, from amongst its peers, my manuscript. This is what one sacrifices when deciding to self-publish and is the true crux of the choice: which is more important to you, getting expert recognition though it might take years or getting the work out when and how you choose, but without imprimatur.

There is no right answer; I can only speak for myself. In my collection, more than two-thirds of the poems were previously published. They'd received eighteen awards. At one point I fretted that some of the older pieces seemed out of style, so I submitted to anthologies. Their acceptance was reassurance enough—this book felt pre-adjudicated!

Furthermore, I am not paid to teach poetry nor do I seek to be. If I did, self-publishing might not be the best garnish for my resume. I wasn't convinced the contest route was the best choice either. You know the drill: send your manuscript to multiple competitions (at around $25 a submission before postage) and wait for judgment. Wait years sometimes. Then one day, perhaps, you discover you've won; your book will be published, and within the foreseeable future. Drop everything. It's time to get your promotion together because, no matter how accommodating the publisher, for poetry, this work always falls to the author.

So too, with the exception of the manufacturing, do all the sundry expenses: the website, postcards, review copies, etc. Also the legwork of booking readings and getting copies into stores, if that's how you want to go. Moreover, a publisher only produces a limited run, usually 250 copies or fewer, with which to recoup your costs. On the other hand, you can sell your print-on-demand (POD) publication at your own pace for as long as you care to. The fact is that with free software, photo stock houses, downloadable fonts, and surprisingly affordable POD fees, a poetry collection with a beautiful cover and elegantly set text can be produced for less than the cost of entering six competitions.

I also considered the many stories I'd heard of authors getting what should be very happy news at the worst possible time—or sometimes a poet just wants to move on—to put a project behind and not veer from exciting new work to promote something old. I asked myself, what if I get to decide when's a good time. What if, after I feel I satisfied with the book's content and design and have firmly grounded my publicity, I launch my book with greater energy and care than any publisher would? What if I feel that time should be sooner than later? What if I put my work into the world in the way I think will have the most impact? What would that game look like?

Well, for one thing, it would mean removing money from the equation. Instead, I would define success as readers—lots and lots of readers, hundreds more than if I were selling the book.

I'll admit I was daunted. Publishing costs money; it involves technology. Yet, as it turns out, it's the simplest part. Certainly it's the most instant. There's a way to handle every aspect ranging from do-it-yourself to pay-for-service depending on your skill and budget. To sort it out, I went to the Writer's Digest 101 Best Websites and dug in. One final thought before I get more technical: I am a poet, not a rocket scientist, and I if could do this, so can you.

Because it requires almost superhuman forbearance not to press send once the book is designed, focus first on preparing its promotion. After all, this is the major advantage of self-publishing and the difference between a gratifying experience and a hectic frenzy.

If you have no clue where to begin, take a class. Better yet, take two. Then take a breath. There is an infinite amount of work one can do. Get a sense of your options, then lob from the list the one or two you like least. Do what you feel most affective within a time limit. Attack them in batches in rotation, for example, e-mails for one month, booking readings the next, then sending review copies. Remember, if you promote your book for one year, that will be forty-eight weeks more than the best publisher would.

It's never too early to begin. Every time you attend a writer's conference, take a class, or join a forum, capture the e-mail list. Every time you look at a poetry magazine, scour the authors' bios for addresses. Also take note of what publications feature poetry reviews. Any database program can help you keep track of where you know the person from so you can personalize the messages.

If you've never done any of this preparation, seek out colleagues in similar situations. Pool your lists and share the research required to place reviews.

Test run everything, from your announcements to your thank-you notes. If you type "spam filter words" into your browser, you will find lists of words and practices to avoid, such as multiple fonts or embedded images. A mass-mailing program like Turbo Mailer will send to each address discreetly, another way to avoid spam filters.

Some items you will need: your book's description and personal bio in a couple of lengths to suit everything from postcards to your Amazon page, a press release, and a half-sheet review slip with all of the above. It can be helpful to have several guest blogs prepared. You guessed it; you can get examples of all of these online. I even found tips on how to improve my handwriting.

To prepare your book, several steps are required. Its interior must be proofread and typeset, and its cover, designed. (Though, as a self-publisher one can reload the contents of a book for about $40. So if you find mistakes after the fact, or want to update your cover, unlike standard publishing, you have that choice.)

Take your time; proofreading requires patience. If it's not your strength, hire someone. One post on Craigslist will garner more than enough applicants. To weed them, create a short test by embedding errors into a poem. Of course, grammar within poetry is often non-standard; no one says you have to take every suggestion, but input can help.

Typesetting requires desktop publishing software—word processing is not acceptable. First, study published collections to determine your tastes (a separate font for titles, or maybe all caps?) Then search the Internet for free downloadable packages. Most have online tutorials, even videos, to instruct you. If you still find yourself stymied, In-Design—the industry standard—is supported by more than ample classes and tutorials. Before purchasing, try taking a class, then returning to one of the free alternatives.

You will also use your desktop publishing software to produce your cover. Warning: this is so much fun it can become addictive. Create several rough drafts then ask people whose taste you admire for feedback before screwing down the details. The variety of exquisite images and typefaces available from free Internet stock photo and font sites will astonish you. Furthermore, unless explicitly specified, you do not have to take these images as they are. You are permitted to crop or manipulate using Photoshop or similar free software. It is polite to notify the photographer and credit his or her work on the cover and website. While you're at it, provide publicity material for the photographer to share with his or her list.

In addition, you require an ISBN, the unique code assigned to each book. Unfortunately, Bowker is the only vendor for this, and only offer packages of ten.

On the other hand, you can choose to skip all this stuff. Co-publishing may be the most expensive option, but can be very complete. They can set your text, design your cover, even incorporate images you supply. If your co-publisher provides the ISBN, you'll save that expense. Some also offer author webpages or inclusion in their catalogs—a definite asset.

Above all, if you want to be a successful self-publisher, you require the ability to convince yourself that you are having fun when you are learning new software or taking a class on promotion. Here's a test: let's say you locate a journal that asks for a review copy even while warning that they may not review it. Do you think: "What a waste of money" or, "Yay, someone who loves poetry is going to read me?" If you chose the second, you're going to love this game.

Alternative Outlets

Ways to Sell Your Poetry Collection

by H. Palmer Hall

A poet friend of mine in Montreal wrote to let me know that artists there had found a new use for those old, banned cigarette machines. Instead of selling cigarettes from them, artists (including poets) are selling small editions of their work so that interested people can stick two dollars in the machine and have a two-inch by three-inch book of poems plunk down into the area where packs of cigarettes once appeared. Other poets I know routinely send postcards with one of their poems on the verso of the written message and a hand-written "for sale" message.

A few months ago, I was wandering around Jackson Square in New Orleans when a man approached me, pulled open his trench coat, and said, in a rough whisper, "Wanta buy some poems?" Surprised at his approach to selling poetry, I handed him ten bucks and walked off with a book of his poems. Other poets, with more musical talent than I have, frequently busk in the streets, playing fiddles or guitars, and selling books of their poems alongside their CDs.

Granted, not all poets are willing to become "buskers for poetry" or approach strangers in the street and offer to sell them poems. And most of us would have to go through the bureaucratic regulations of our home cities to set up former cigarette machines as poetry dispensers. The point here is that we do not have to go through distributors or bookstores with their heavy discounts to sell our poems. We can sell them in other, more effective and more innovative ways.

One of our poets at Pecan Grove Press, Linda Kittell, wrote a wonderful collection of poems based upon Andrew Wyeth's "Helga Pictures." She contacted the Farnsworth Art Museum in Rockland, Maine, about selling the chapbook in their museum shop since they had an excellent collection of Wyeth paintings. The museum purchased ten copies to sell to patrons who loved Wyeth's work. Curious about whether they had sold or not, I contacted the manager of the shop a year later. He told me all ten had sold within a month

H. PALMER HALL is the author of nine chapbooks and books, most recently Foreign and Domestic (Turning Point, 2009) and Coming to Terms (Plain View, 2007). His work has appeared in various reviews and anthologies including North American Review, The Texas Observer, The Texas Review, Briar Cliff Review, Ascent, American Diaspora, A Fine Frenzy and many others. His press, Pecan Grove Press, celebrated its twentieth anniversary in 2008 by publishing its 100th book. He is a member of the Texas Institute of Letters and recipient of "The Art of Peace Award" from St. Mary's University.

of his stocking them. Until I called, it had not occurred to him to reorder. He did and also suggested some other museums that might be interested.

Not too long ago, I put together a small collection of my own poems to give as Christmas presents to an international group of friends who had met each other by watching a pond in Africa on a 24/7 live webcast from Botswana, Africa. I sent a copy of Reflections from Pete's Pond to the manager of the game preserve. Much to my surprise, he ordered 100 copies to sell in the "Curio Shop" at the Mashatu Game Preserve. Later, another game preserve in the same area ordered an additional 50 copies. Amazing to me: 150 copies of a small, 34-page chapbook being sold in far away Botswana, Africa. Those books sold without my doing a reading and without my giving a steep discount to a book distributor.

I started seriously thinking about the allure of Amazon.com and Ingram and other traditional distribution sources for books and wondered why it seemed that every poet we published wanted to be listed on Amazon and wanted their books sold in bookstores. Part of that, I realize, is vanity. It just feels so good to e-mail friends and relatives and say, "You can buy my new book on Amazon or at Big Box Bookstore." We all do, of course, want our books in bookstores, but the most important thing is to actually sell the books. Very few bookstores really try to sell poetry; most are fairly happy to return them to the publisher after a short shelf life.

Poets need to think of creative ways to sell their poems. Here are just a few examples of some things a few of our poets have done to sell their books:

If the book has a subject/topic level of interest beyond being a collection of poems, look for a tie-in to some other field. Linda Kittell did that with her collection of poems based on Wyeth paintings and I lucked into doing it with my Africa poems. We also published a small miscellany of flower poems called The Rites of Spring. Flower poems? Yes, stapled inside a greeting card by a local artist. Three different florists' shops stocked them and sold them.

We published a book, Humidity Moon, by Michael Rodriguez, a Marine veteran, about his experiences in Vietnam. He got permission from several veterans' organizations to attend their meetings, set up a table, and sell copies of the book. More than 1,000 copies later, we are thinking about doing a new printing.

Other poets have contacted their old high school English teachers and suggested that their current students might benefit from hearing from an alumnus who is a real life poet and has recently published a book. The poets sign the books for the students who are notified in advance about the visiting poet and bring money to buy the books.

One poet had her partner throw a "baby shower" for her and her book. She sent invitations to all the friends who had, over the years, invited her and her partner to showers, expecting correctly that she would buy a present for the newborn, and since she preferred not having a baby thought birthing a book was the closest thing. The invitation she sent announced the birth of a 6 × 9 inch bouncing baby book. Instead of gifts, the guests bought copies of the book and the poet signed them.

The only thing limiting the way poets can sell their books is an unwillingness to think of ways other than bookstores and on-line sales. That's mostly because we have blinders on. Because we have always bought books at bookstores and at poetry readings, we only think of those very traditional ways to sell our books. That does us and our books a disservice.

Poetic Asides From Seven Poets

By Robert Lee Brewer

The best source of information about poetry often comes from actual poets, which is why I interview poets regularly at my Poetic Asides blog (http://blog.writersdigest. com/poeticasides). Here are seven poets sharing their knowledge on poetic forms, revision, what makes a great poem, and more.

MARIE-ELIZABETH MALI

Marie-Elizabeth Mali lives in New York City. She is a co-curator of louderArts: the Reading Series at Bar 13 Lounge and Page Meets Stage at the Bowery Poetry Club and is a poetry editor for *TIFERET: A Journal of Spiritual Literature*. Before receiving her MFA in poetry from Sarah Lawrence College, she practiced Traditional Chinese Medicine. Her work has appeared in *Calyx, MiPOesias*, and *RATTLE*, among others.

Your Facebook profile says you are currently co-editing *The Book of the Villanelle* with Annie Finch. Can you elaborate on this project?

The book begins with an essay by Julie Kane on the history of the villanelle followed by the villanelle by Passerat widely considered to be the first "codified" example of the form, in French and English. It was first published in 1606. The first section contains classic villanelles and it moves chronologically from Emily Pfeiffer through Dylan Thomas, including the famous ones you'd imagine would be in there. The second contains contemporary villanelles and it moves alphabetically. That's the largest section, containing over 150 poems. The third section contains variations, ways that people have played with the form, like free verse and unrhymed villanelles, extra or fewer stanzas, going backwards (the quatrain first), a "Haikunelle," in which each stanza follows the 5-7-5 rule of the Haiku, and a double villanelle, in which there are two voices in dialogue throughout the stanzas, among other variations. The anthology is being looked at by publishers now, and we hope that once it comes out it will be adopted as a textbook, in addition to having popular appeal. Unlike the Penguin Book of the Sonnet, it will most likely be the definitive

ROBERT LEE BREWER is a Senior Content Editor in the Writer's Digest Writing Community. He edits Writer's Market, Poet's Market, and WritersMarket.com, in addition to many other responsibilities, including contributing to the Poetic Asides blog. Brewer is also a poet who has been published in several print and online publications. You can contact him via his My Name Is Not Bob blog (http://robertleebrewer.blogspot.com) or via e-mail (robertleebrewer@gmail.com).

collection of all things villanelle for a long time to come, since there have not been as many poems written in this form as the sonnet.

As a follow-up question, what do you think makes for a good villanelle?

One thing I've learned in reading almost 600 villanelles for this project is that meter plays a larger role in its success than I previously realized. Working with Annie Finch has really trained my ear. It's not simply a matter of coming up with two good refrain lines that work well together in the last quatrain, it's got to sing, too. Most often, they're in iambic pentameter, but we've got some great ones in triple meters in the anthology. Obviously, the free verse ones don't follow this rule, but if you want to write a traditional villanelle, you've got to be taking meter into account. It arose out of folk songs and the original ones were lyrics, often sung by women, in contrast to the more "courtly" madrigals. It's a form that lends itself to our times, given that it arose from humble origins out of improvisation and collaboration among multiple singers and included various registers of speech (dialect, proverbs, puns, etc.).

You received your MFA in poetry from Sarah Lawrence College. How important do you feel an MFA is to the development of a poet? Also, what do you feel are the main benefits of seeking an MFA?

The MFA program was a crucial part of my development as a poet. I didn't start out as a trained writer, having been a bodyworker and then a Licensed Acupuncturist for 14 years after college. So, when I decided to stop seeing patients and dedicate myself to writing poetry, I needed that kind of intensive focus on craft and a supportive community in which to work on my skills. There were people in my program who have studied creative writing since high school. I don't know how necessary the MFA is for someone like that, though it's become pretty much a pre-requisite if one wants to teach.

The main benefit of seeking an MFA (for someone like me) is to have two years to focus intensively on the craft of writing in a community of writers, developing friendships and readers of one's work that will hopefully endure throughout one's writing life. Writing poetry is an otherwise solitary endeavor and it's helpful to have trusted readers who can help you catch habits you tend to lean on too heavily, who can push you to go deeper and farther than you might otherwise push yourself. Like music, in which you practice scales for years before you start improvising, you become a better poet by learning the craft, even if you never end up writing in form or meter. The more you know, the more you can toss out the rules and be yourself on the page. But if you've never learned the rules in the first place, then you have no basis for knowing what works and what doesn't in a poem. And that's a lot of what being a good poet is about: learning to be a good (dispassionate) editor of your own work. Inspiration is one thing, but editing is what really makes a poem a poem, and that's something best learned in a classroom.

That said, we at louderARTS aim to create a space for poets who otherwise might not have access to the kind of learning that goes on in MFA programs by providing free workshops taught by members of our community, paid workshops by some of our big-name features, like Kim Addonizio and Denise Duhamel, and the opportunity to have work critiqued by more senior members of the community. Organizations like this are important because not everyone can get an MFA but everyone has the right to learn the bones and scaffolding of poetic craft, and I'm deeply committed to folks who are interested in growing as writers having access to knowledge, regardless of whether it happens in an academic context or not.

Luckily, many poets are committed to the same thing, so the Acentos Foundation, an organization of Latino/a writers that's an outgrowth of louderARTS, with which I'm also loosely involved, holds a fantastic, free series of weekly writing workshops in the Bronx that have been faciliated by poets like Martín Espada, Lorna Dee Cervantes, Cornelius Eady, Jeffrey McDaniel, Ada Limon, and many more, in return for being taken out to lunch. Their generosity as teachers is astounding and to hear people's writing grow as a result (because many of the attendees then come read their new work on the louderARTS open mic) is amazing and gratifying.

PRIS CAMPBELL

Pris Campbell is the author of *Sea Trails: Poems and 1977 Passage Notes* (Lummox Press). Her poetry has been published in several print and online journals, and she has a website at www.poeticinspire.com.

I first discovered your poetry on MySpace and in poetry forums. Since then, I have kept up with you on Facebook and other sites. How do you think poets can get the most out of online communities and social networks?

I think that meeting good poets is a strong plus for sites such as these. Had it not been for MySpace, for example (where I no longer post), I wouldn't have met S.A. Griffin or A.D. Winans, for example, both of whom have become good friends. That's only to name two people. On Facebook, I find the fan pages or groups for journals extremely helpful since they announce to members when submissions are open. It saves a lot of searching all over the internet.

A caution I would like to express is to not let your work suffer because of the effusive praise that often comes to posted poems. I've seen it given to well crafted poems I love and I've seen it given to poems that needed to be run through poetry 101. Everyone likes praise. I know I do. I've learned to accept it, then ignore it, and remind myself that this still isn't the best I can do. The main advantage I see to posting poems on a place such as Facebook is that people get to know your poetry, recognize your name and will hopefully want to read more of your work.

Your well-crafted poems often feel very personal. For these narrative poems, how personal do you allow yourself to get?

Sometimes, I get very personal. Other times, I change enough of the details of the poem or write in third person for a layer of privacy. I also write a lot about people on the edge of society. Those poems can be inspired by one person I've known or a combination of several people. I don't want to write a tell-all diary but I do want to be authentic in my writing. In my chap, *Hesitant Commitments*, also published as part of the Little Red Book series by Lummox, I wanted to write about some important issues I had with men as a young adult that were affected by things my grandfather did to me when I was younger. That was a really difficult range of time in my life and I needed to remove myself by a level to write it effectively. I did this by setting the poems in Europe, where I've never been, and taking myself back to a younger age, writing in the present tense. A lot of people have read this book as strictly sensual and missed the point of the crucial core poem near the end, "Why I Am Sad."

As a follow-up question, what sort of process do you go through with revision typically for each poem?

I'm very visual with my poems. I see them happening in my head, so I begin writing by scribbling down the scene or scenes unfolding without trying to write well, create line breaks, etc. Next, I scribble over that initial draft, changing words, lines, phrases to better reflect what I saw. At about this point, I type this almost indecipherable mess into the computer and start thinking of such poetic devices as inner rhyme, alliteration, enjambment, the beat of a line and if those things could be used in the service of the poem to improve it. I never add them just to add them. Ninety percent of the time I overwrite initially and much of my revision consists of cutting, then cutting more each time until I've whittled out a decent poem.

HELEN LOSSE

Helen Losse is the author of *Better With Friends* (Rank Stranger Press). Losse has also published two chapbooks and is the editor of *The Dead Mule School of Southern Literature*.

How important do you feel community is for a poet?

I think community is important to life in general not just for poets, but it is essential to promoting (read; publishing and selling) one's work. Writing is a solo experience, but, once written, poems are usually made to be shared. Writing and marketing are two entirely separate aspects of the writing life. It is fine to write poems and put them in a drawer, but it is better to share them with others. My goal—or, at least, one of my goals—is to write so that others see themselves in my poems. I want to be the kind of poet whose images make a reader feel and think. I want to find truth and point other people toward it.

I know it probably changes from poem to poem, but are there certain things you check for when you revise your poems?

I try to make sure I don't have unnecessary words in a poem. That's what makes revision challenging. Poetry differs from prose in its exaggeration of image and the musical element of language, so words that would be unnecessary in prose may be needed in poetry. This is especially true of repeated words or phrases. The very nature of poetry sometimes makes it necessary to say something in a roundabout rather than a straightforward manner, but if I do use repetition, I want to make sure it adds to the overall effect not just the length of the poem. I want to get the pacing and emphasis right and be sure the stanzas occur in the right order not just the order in which they were written.

In serious revision, I often break the poem into sentences—a big "Thank You" to poet Dennis Sampson for telling me to write clear sentences—then rearrange the order of sentences, experiment with line breaks and stanza breaks, using couplets, triplets, quatrains, and stanzas of varying lengths on most poems before I'm finished. And finished is—at least, for me—a relative term. I will revise any poem I have written, published or not, if I see a way to improve it. After all, it's my poem, so I have the right—no, the responsibility—to make it the best I can. I love revising poems.

Do you feel poets should have an online presence?

I do. The world is a technical place now, and poets are expected to have a certain degree of technical competency, actually the more skills the better. No longer can a poet write poems out longhand and expect to be taken seriously. All poets—not just self-published poets or those on a small press—must be, to some degree, their own promoters.

This pertains only to poets who seek publication. I have no interest in telling people how to live their lives. Hand-written one-of-a-kind birthday-poems are lovely. And I am sure that somewhere there is a successful poet with no online presence at all. I just think the Internet is a tool that writers in this day and age ought to learn to use.

NATE PRITTS

Nate Pritts is the author of *Honorary Astronaut* (Ghost Road Press) and *Sensational Spectacular* (BlazeVOX [Books]). Pritts is also the editor of *H_NGM_N*, an online journal of poetry and prose.

In *Honorary Astronaut*, there are times when I feel the poems almost go over the top in their enthusiasm, but there's this sense of sincerity that seems to make them work anyway. Or maybe it's the sincerity and confessional nature that make the poems feel so enthusiastic, but it's the tightness of your poems that makes them work. How much time and work do you typically put into the revision process? And are there things you typically try finding?

There's no one answer here. Sometimes, I work my poems hard, running them through several stress tests and changing lots of little things or some big things. Sometimes, I junk the whole thing and start again, but with a few lines still echoing in the far corners of my heart. Since you ask specifically about Honorary Astronaut, I'll say that with these poems I was trying to find a balance between an ecstatic utterance that seemed improvisational and a crafted sentence. The thing is, I can talk about the "craft" of these poems—the form—or I can talk about what the poems are about - the ostensible subject, the content - but the primary consideration for me has always been to make the poem a responsive index of my thought. I write what I hope is a fluent, discursive line that is grammatically correct (mostly) and that proceeds by way of association. I'm trying to get the poem to the bone of that.

Practically, though, some of the poems in Honorary Astronaut had first been in my MFA thesis (1999?); some popped up in my PhD dissertation (2003). Some, however, were written while the book was in the proof stage! It was my, truly, "first book," though Sensational Spectacular was completed, accepted and published a year before it. Those poems were the ones I had lived with and tinkered with obsessively for almost seven years.

You've published a few collections of poetry now. How do you go about assembling your collections?

I don't know if I have one tried and true method yet. *Sensational Spectacular* was a series, really, and so I knew what went in; in short, I knew it was a book and knew what belonged where. Honorary Astronaut went through so many different forms (at one point, it was broken into 4 numbered sections) that I truly don't remember how I put it together. I know I followed themes from one poem to the next. My new book, *The Wonderfull Yeare*, is a shepherd's calendar—so I just put the seasons in order!

I did just put together a new manuscript and I realize I did the same thing that I did at one point with *Honorary Astronaut* and with my chapbook *Shrug*: I printed off all the poems, found a room with big tables and spread them all out. Then I just walked around the room reading them out loud, thinking about the echoes, the correspondences. And at one point, I started picking up a poem, then grabbing another one that belonged before or after the first one. I kept doing this until I was holding all these poems in my hand, and there were others scattered on the floor that hadn't made the cut, and I had a scrap of paper with notes for a few poems that I might need to write to emphasize or add to the manuscript.

As the editor of *H_NGM_N*, an online journal of poetry and prose, what do you look for in poetry submissions?

Gosh, I guess that's hard to define but I know it when I see it. I'm looking for poems that are looking for me. I mean, first, I expect a certain level of competency and professionalism in the submission; *H_NGM_N* has guidelines for a reason. And if anyone wants to know what kinds of poems we publish, the best thing they could do is read the poems in our nine issues, our various chapbooks and side projects.

We get some poems that have no chance; they show no knowledge of the kinds of work we champion, no attention to language or craft, have nothing to really say. Most of what we get is pretty solid, though, and so we have to make some tough calls. I'm looking for something that knocks my head off with its energy and this could come from the compelling nature of the linguistic utterance, it could come from a sparkly and brilliant image, it could come from anywhere. Though we've been labeled as a home for experimental poetry, I'm not happy with that. My models are Renaissance sonneteers, or Coleridge saying "O!" every time he got to see the sunrise. I think a poem is what one beating heart can say to another beating heart in words.

SYDNEY LEA

Sydney Lea is the author of *Ghost Pain* (Sarabande Books). Lea is the founder and former editor of *New England Review*, and currently teaches at Dartmouth College.

Ghost Pain was your eighth volume of poems. How do you go about assembling a collection?

I was lucky enough to have Robert Penn Warren as a mentor when I was a younger man, and his description of how he knew he was done with a book still strikes home for me. He says that you write and you write and you write, and in due course you realize that a certain curve of energy has completed itself, that the stuff you are writing now is differently motivated from what you've been doing for some time. I know that's vague, but I can't seem to do better, in that I don't conceive of collections in an aprioristic, programmatic way.

You teach at Dartmouth College. Does teaching inform or influence your writing?

I may have answered that question above, at least in part. The plain truth is that I haven't been entirely innocent of stealing "ideas" from students, ones that they may have been too new at the game to have pulled off successfully. But that's a rarity. Teaching is important to me as a hedge against adopting a mood like Hemingway's at his worst: Long time ago good, now no good. For forty years, in every course I have found at least one young woman or man who bolsters my faith not only in poetry but also in human nature. Also, by my own choice I live a long way from alleged centers of sophistication, which is helpful to me in that it keeps me from the occasional belief of writers in this era of Creeping MFAism that EVERYONE is concerned with literature. Few of my neighbors are concerned with it, at least in the way that the MFAer may be. And yet I do need the "fix" of talking passionately about poetry, fiction, creative writing" in general, and I get it via my students; I get it a lot more from them than from academic colleagues at any rate.

Ghost Pain includes the long poem "A Man Walked Out." What's the most challenging aspect of writing a long poem?

Here's the weird thing. I have written a number of long poems, starting perhaps with "The Feud" in my second collection, moving through "To the Bone" from my 1996 new and selected, into "A Man Walked Out" and most lately into something called "Birds: A Farrago" from my forthcoming book, *Young of the Year*. And each of these poems seems somehow to have been given to me. Each seems to have followed on a fairly long period of disinclination from writing. Not writer's block but disinclination (whose causes remain unknown to me). Then these poems come in a rush, and I rarely do much in the way of revising them. Is that "inspiration?" I don't know, don't even know if I believe in such a thing, really; rather, I believe these gimmes are the payoff for all those hours of revision that I have put into shorter poems.

So in a sense I am a poor candidate to answer your question. I don't conceive of long poems; they present themselves to me helter skelter. Weird, as I say.

CATI PORTER

Cati Porter is the author of *Seven Floors Up* (Mayapple Press). Porter is also the founder and editor-in-chief of *Poemeleon: A Journal of Poetry*, as well as the associate editor (poetry) for *Babel Fruit*.

As the Editor-in-Chief of *Poemeleon* and poetry editor of *Babel Fruit*, what do you feel makes a good poem?

There are lots of good poems. So so many competently and compellingly good poems. For me, though, they all have certain things in common. And that's the drawback. What's really rare, though, is the great poem, which is so much harder to define: It's the one that hits me in the gut; It's the one that makes everything become suddenly clear, or makes what was previously clear so utterly muddled that I'm dumbstruck. Good poems make me want to sit down and write until my fingers ache. Great poems leave me wondering if I'll ever be able to write again.

But great poems are difficult. In order to write great poems, we must first write good poems. (And of course, before that and in-between, the essential bad poems.)

Both good poems as well as great poems employ craft, image, music, voice, and use them to forward the ideas embedded in the poem. The devices inform, rather than dictate, the shape of the poem, become integral to the movement of a piece — both on the page and in the head. To take a step back, what separates a good poem from a bad poem? The usage of those same devices: A bad poem uses them to ill effect — sets out to write a sonnet and writes one, no matter whether the end rhymes are forced, syntax needlessly inverted, the phrases stilted and awkward. A good poem never does that, not without good cause.

But the difference between a good poem and a great poem? That's a little more subtle, but I think it's that gut punch. If it's not there, I might be willing to hang around with it for a while, but it's not the one I'm going to remember down the road.

small fruit songs is a collection of prose poems about fruit. What do you like about the prose poem as a poetic form?

At the time I was writing *small fruit songs*, I had previously been in love with received forms and was trying them all out. Often my results fell under the "bad poem" heading. But one day, after deciding that I wanted to write a series that used fruit-related terminology as its impetus, I sat down and just allowed my subconscious to take over, and what came out was very associative, unstructured, and organic, which felt like the right choice for the material.

What I like most about the prose poem is its versatility. I've read prose poems that read like stories, prose poems that read like excerpts from a training manual, lyric prose poems, prose poems as dramatic monologue, prose poems as pseudo-journalism, surrealist prose poems.... That said, as versatile as it is, I don't think the prose poem is the end-all, beat-all. It's not functional if the form is forced.

Do you have a writing routine?

I wish! I prefer writing in the very early morning when the house is quiet, but with kids and with a household to run, I have to be more fluid. I used to get up in the middle of the night, but I can only take so much sleep deprivation. I do get up at about five or five-thirty, sometimes earlier, but most days I need a couple cups of coffee — and an empty house — to be productive. If I can't finish what I'm working on while they're at school, it's catch-as-catch-can. And I can't use anything but a computer. My handwriting is awful so even if I manage to scribble a few lines while out running around, usually I can't read it later!

JIM SCHLEY

Jim Schley is the author of *As When, In Season* (Marick Press). Schley is the former executive director of The Frost Place and is currently a managing editor at Tupelo Press.

In your collection *As When, In Season*, you have a section of nine odes. What do you feel makes an effective ode?

An ode is an ancient verbal-song of praise. Pindar's seminal odes were composed for choral voices, with cresting lines and surging acclaim for athletes and other heroes, and they combine rhythms and images in daring ways, reaching for ecstasy through reasoning and metaphor. I've loved reading and hearing the Greek myths since childhood, and that feeling was refreshed and transmuted as I rediscovered those stories, reading to our daughter when she was tiny (which I still do today, when she's sixteen). In graduate school I wrote a seventy-page essay examining every aspect of Keats's marvelously varied, fluid yet precise "Ode to a Nightingale." I wondered if a poet today could write a compelling ode in a natural contemporary idiom. There's a certain grandeur, in tone and amplitude, I was reaching toward . . .

Years ago I had the idea of writing a series of portraits of crucial female teachers; I intended to make a set of nine, each named for one of the mythological muses, and each representing a certain domain of knowledge and action. In my view, these muses wouldn't be the inspirers of a male artist, but would be virtuosos in their own right. I couldn't find a suitable structure for this "suite" of poems, in which I knew the musical component needed to be particularly strong. In the mid-1990s I began experimenting with an invented form, which I called a chanoine after the French word for chain, and this time (probably my third or fourth attempt) the series came together steadily. Each poem has thirteen rhymes on the same sound, and there are many, many images and allusions; for some readers, my odes may seem too full, as I've tried to see how far I can push the momentum of the sentences in relation to the "staves" or measures of the lines, using syntax for flex and spring. While the form is the tightest I've ever used, the writing process was euphoric, as I learned firsthand how much artists gain (including the most absorbing pleasure) by addressing a resilient, resistive vessel of form.

The muse poems are each a portrait of a specific person (or in one instance two people, entwined), writers and artists, also my wife and our daughter. Only one of them is named outright (the poem for Grace Paley uses "grace" as the rhyme-sound). Whether these poems succeed as odes with respect to the whole tradition, I can't know, but I love reading them to audiences. I have the sense that they reach a listener through the ears more directly than they reach a reader through the eyes, and I'm making plans to do a recording of my delivery, where I can attend closely to pacing and clarity.

This is your first full-length collection, yet you're very experienced in the poetry world. How long did it take you to get this collection together?

From an early age, I knew I wanted to make a living through reading and writing, and soon after college I started work as a literary editor, apprenticing to the boundlessly dedicated and knowledgeable Sydney Lea, founder of the journal *New England Review*. This led to other editorial jobs, which were entwined with my theater work.

Like most young writers, I made efforts to get my work published, with only sporadic success. Meanwhile, I edited more than a hundred books in a variety of fields, including poetry, fiction, and essays. Gradually I came to an understanding of what the book I'd want to publish would be like, in texture and shape. With a state arts council grant, I published a chapbook in 1999, featuring the muse sequence and four lullabies, which was a 150% good experience, and in 2006 after I'd entered a round of book contests to no avail, I decided instead to publish another chapbook, with a new linked series. At that point the poet Ilya Kaminsky asked to see my manuscript for Marick Press. He and publisher Mariela Griffor said "Yes," and all of a sudden the book was being produced, to my surprise (and relief).

You're a managing editor at Tupelo Press, so I imagine you get to see several very fine collections that get published, as well as good and bad collections that don't quite make the grade. As an editor, what do you think makes a great poetry collection?

I'm presently most involved in the step-by-step production of Tupelo's forthcoming books, working closely with authors on editorial adjustments and working very closely with book designers and printers, a part of the process with which I have a lot of experience. It's extremely exciting to navigate the transformation of a book from word-processing to designed pages, comparable to the translation of a dance or theater work from rehearsal studio to stage.

Even after working as a professional editor since 1980, my answer to your question of what makes a powerful, moving, satisfying book isn't so different from the answer I'd have given as a child or teenaged reader (though my frame of reference is wider, as I've read hundreds and hundreds of books in a number of languages and from many eras). I remain an "innocent" reader: longing to be transported, by imagery and story; willing to be challenged, by language and ideas; most drawn to a dynamic, unfolding relationship between the details of a collection, part by part and passage by passage, and the shape of the whole.

The Age of the E-Poet?

by Larina Warnock

From first word on the page to publication, the Internet has changed the way poets approach the business of poetry. Free reference websites help poets find the right metaphor or accurate information. Specialized market listing sites assist with market identification. An increasing number of traditional magazines place some portion of magazine content online so poets can deduce which might be a good fit for their work (and which won't). Beyond all this, Internet writing communities, online submission processes, and the ever-expanding field of Internet publishing have produced significant opportunities—and challenges—for poets today.

Revision

Online workshop forums offer numerous benefits to poets—from discussion of famous poems and poets to critical thinking about your own work to learning about publication opportunities. Christine Klocek-Lim, poet and former site administrator for The Academy of American Poets discussion forum, thinks that a sense of community is one of the primary ways that online workshops help poets. "Because poetry is such a small piece of our larger culture, it's often very difficult to find people to discuss writing in face-to-face situations," she says, "The forum opens up the world and gives us somewhere to meet."

Diverse communities of any kind have challenges, and Klocek-Lim explains one of the most common ones this way: "I think some of the risk is inherent to online interaction: that lack of personal interaction can lead to a great deal of misunderstanding. The person you're talking to doesn't have a face and one is unable to tell if he or she is being sarcastic or serious at times. Of course," she continues, "this also leads those who participate online to become better writers in general, not just in poetry. If you want to make a point clearly, you've got to know how to write persuasive prose that doesn't mislead the reader onto paths you never considered."

If a particular community doesn't suit a poet's needs, there are always other options. Jim Corner founded *Desert Moon Review* in 2001. "The sites where I was posting my work for critique were cruel," he says of the experiences that led him to found a new workshop

LARINA WARNOCK is the site administrator for The Academy of American Poets online discussion forum and editor of The Externalist: A Journal of Perspectives. Her poetry has appeared both online and in print, including placing in the IBPC and being shortlisted with The Guardian Poetry Workshop three times.

board, "Also not willing to work with new poets and help them in improvement of their craft. I decided I was far enough along to provide this kind of mentoring, so I looked for others who felt the same." *Desert Moon Review* continues to increase membership through application and includes "prize-winning poets and poets struggling to become the former."

Feedback can help poets improve significantly. "I believe the forum gives poets perspective. So often we write in the silence of our reality," says Klocek-Lim, "when posting a poem for workshopping, we begin to understand how our poetry interacts with the reader and a larger audience. I can't stress enough the importance of this, especially for beginners." Paradoxically, therein lays the risk of overreliance on criticism to revise. Klocek-Lim puts it this way, "I think we get hooked on the feedback."

While it's unlikely that a poet will find an agent or mainstream publisher through an Internet forum, there are opportunities for publication. For example, many boards participate in the Interboard Poetry Competition (commonly called the IBPC). Winners are announced at each participating board and published on the IBPC website. Selection for the IBPC is sometimes the first publication or award a poet receives and this can be a great boost to their confidence.

Some editors of online journals (myself included) solicit work they've seen on Internet forums, but just as valuable is access to a variety of readers. Over time, poets participating in an Internet workshop develop an audience. Membership often includes poets of all ages, backgrounds, and geography—and they read. It isn't uncommon for members to recommend potential markets to other members when they see a poem that might fit in their favorite literary journal or an anthology they've heard about.

If the eventual goal of a poet is publication in more traditional venues, one cannot consider Internet workshops without considering how participation will affect publishing opportunities. Some workshop boards are private (or even invite-only), but most require registration only for those wanting to post there—that is, the general public can read posted poems and their comments. Fred Sasaki of *POETRY Magazine* explains why this can be troublesome: "*POETRY* publishes new work, and we require first serial rights and first web rights. If the work has appeared elsewhere, then those rights cannot be granted to us. Online writing workshops pose an interesting problem, as the forum itself is not a 'publication,' per se, even though the contents on the site have been 'published.'" *POETRY*'s solution is to only consider work that has not been viewable by the general public.

Most traditional journals, and some online journals, have similar requirements. Poets should always check guidelines before submitting a poem that has appeared on a publically viewable forum. While it can be difficult to understand how it could be bad for a poem to have been reviewed by others before submission, editors need to consider their readers (who are often paying to read new work), as well as their own mission. "It's a special thing to encounter a poem in a lit mag and know that it's the first time that that work has appeared in print or online. There's a magic in that discover," says Sasaki.

If a poet carefully considers their own needs and goals, there are many benefits to participation in online workshops. It can take time, however, to find the workshop that best suits you. Jim Corner says, "Most of the not for profit sites, and there are many, only ask for basic info, so my advice to wandering poets is try *DMR* [*Desert Moon Review*] or any of the others for a while to find which one or ones fit their needs."

Featured Websites

- Writer's Market—www.writersmarket.com
- Duotrope Digest—www.duotrope.com
- The Academy of American Poets Discussion Forum—www.poets.org/forum
- Desert Moon Review—www.thedesertmoonreview.com
- Stirring—www.sundress.net/stirring/
- Wheelhouse Magazine—www.wheelhousemagazine.com
- The Externalist—www.theexternalist.com
- Best of the Net Anthology—www.sundress.net/bestof
- Dzanc Books—www.dzancbooks.org
- Interboard Poetry Competition—ibpc.webdelsol.com

Submission

Gone are the days of sending a SASE with a letter requesting guidelines—most magazines have an online presence where their guidelines are posted. It's rarely necessary now to maintain ten or fifteen subscriptions to journals you may or may not like—most of those websites also have excerpts or web content that you can view to decide whether you would like to become a reader or if your work might fit with the publication. Poet's Market includes website addresses, and online databases like *Writer's Market* and Duotrope Digest maintain listings with links.

The trend that has really simplified things is the availability of Internet-based submission processes by both traditional and Internet journals. At The Externalist, we accept submissions in the body of an e-mail. This is the most common preference for e-submission, though a few journals prefer attachments. Just as you would when submitting by mail, it is very important to read a magazine's guidelines and follow their directions when submitting electronically. If you send an attachment and they don't accept attachments, it's not only possible but probable that the editor will not read your submission. E-mail subject headers should follow the guidelines as well or your submission may find the junk mail filter (the electronic equivalent to "lost in the mail"). Many traditional publications like *AGNI* and *POETRY* are using online submission managers that allow you to upload your submission. Again, it's very important to follow the directions as online submission managers only accept certain file types. Electronic submission not only saves paper and postage, but usually speeds up response time as well.

Publication

The field of online publishing has burgeoned in the last few years, but it can be challenging to determine where to submit. Erin Elizabeth Smith, editor of *Stirring*, says, "Because of the stigma of online publishing—'They just publish anyone!' 'Anyone can start a journal, thus it can't be good!'—I believe that online journals have to work harder to make themselves seem legitimate." Unfortunately, such a stigma exists largely because there are some websites that claim to be "journals" or "magazines," but really do publish everyone that submits. By and large, though, such websites are easy to recognize once a poet looks at the work the site has published, and most online journals practice the same high standards of print journals.

"I think that anyone, poet or editor, who looks upon online publication as being less of a validation of the poem doesn't know the business," says poet Simon Perchik, "Poetry journals have a mortality rate that is scary. My experience is that a fair percentage of the print journals listed in the directories are already defunct by the time the directory is available, or if they accept a poem they will fold before the poem is printed."

Poet Dorianne Laux notes, "There are a handful of excellent print journals and a handful of excellent online journals and that's all you're going to get at any given time in history. I think writers should be less interested in being taken seriously, which is quite subjective, and more interested in the value of a serious readership." Readership is a common theme among poets and editors of online publications.

Smith contends that readership is the primary benefit of publishing online. "*Stirring* has a monthly 'subscription base' of approximately 2,500, which means new issues of the site receive 30,000 readers a year," she says, "Not to mention that archives of the poems are always available, so your work isn't just being read in the newest issue of the journal, but is searchable from then on. I think many writers forget about this when they publish their early or 'secondary' work in online journals—more people will read your work online than in print."

Perchik prefers online publications for this reason. "Consider the readership the poet gets when the poem appears online. There's a whole world out there," he says. Expanding on that point, Laux says, "I've also found new readers, both young and old, who come to my work for the first time online, and then seek out my print publications so I've gained readers I otherwise wouldn't have found, and those readers help to keep my books in print. More and more I hear that a new reader or editor has been found online. These discoveries have led to other publications."

Online journals can also open the door to new styles of poetry. David Michael Wolach, editor of award-winning *Wheelhouse Magazine*, says, "On the flip side, the realities editors and writers face has opened up opportunities, not only formally—e.g., hypertext, concrete and conceptual poetry, etc.—but in terms of building unexpected and diverse writing collectives. Online journals should, ideally, help all of us find the new, the exciting, the unexpected, more easily."

As the field of online publishing has grown, so too have opportunities for award nominations and anthologizing. Best of the Net was the first formalized anthology of online work. Smith, cofounder of Best of the Net, says, "Our list of winners has included famous names like Bob Hicok, Dorianne Laux, and Ron Carlson, but also young writers new into the game, housewives that frequent the online poetry forums, and any other number of non-professional writers. In a lot of ways, I see the Best of the Net Anthology is a preview of the poets that we'll probably be reading in the print anthologies in another decade." That may be true even sooner. Dzanc Books now prints an anthology of work found in online journals, and online journals can (and often do) nominate for Pushcart Prizes.

The same advice applies to both online and print journals. As Laux says, "I think young poets should do what poets have always done: research the journals, find the few that suit you for whatever personal reasons, support that journal by getting a subscription, and send your poems there with the hope of breaking in someday." Wolach agrees, "Seek out journals that you read, that consistently offer you that shock of alterity. If you feel that you want to be part of that conversation, so to speak, then send them your work. If not, then take your lack of interest as a sign to move on."

Digital Poetry

by Jessy Randall

Digital poetry is electronic literature that cannot exist on paper. It can move (an early online journal specializing in digital poetry was called Poems That Go) or include multimedia components, and it is often interactive and/or collaborative.

In 1992 William Gibson (author of the science fiction novel *Neuromancer*) released a precursor to today's net-based digital poetry: "Agrippa (A Book of the Dead)," a self-destructing poem on a floppy disk. As readers used the disk, it erased itself. (You can experience the poem now in the form of a screen-capture at www.boingboing. net/2008/12/09/gibsons-selfdetructi.html.)

Digital poetry is about as old as the internet—which means, of course, that it's still quite young. One of the earliest examples of digital poetry is Peter Howard's 1997 work "Midwinter Fair," (www.hphoward.demon.co.uk/midwin/midwintr.htm), which operates on the same principle as the Choose Your Own Adventure books popular in the 1980s. "Midwinter Fair" contains hyperlinked words, and the reader chooses which of these to follow and in what order. Each reader therefore experiences the poem differently. Like much of the digital poetry that would follow, "Midwinter Fair" is interactive and nonlinear. It is also community-oriented: it has multiple authors, and is not static; even now it changes. Howard invites readers of the poem to participate by linking up their own work. He continues to make digital poems, and says that what appeals to him is that "digital poetry is still very much a new medium, so there aren't any rules, and pretty much everything is up for grabs."

Jason Nelson is currently one of the top artists in digital poetry; his works "game, game, game and again game" and "i made this. you play this. we are enemies" are available at www.secrettechnology.com. These are games, texts, and works of art. You don't just read them, play them, or view them; you experience them. They combine screen shots of the mundane web (Yahoo, Google, etc.), doodle-like artwork, and arcade game tropes, and they reveal poetry at odd moments. For Nelson, as for Howard, the appeal of digital poetry is its lack of history or tradition: "Digital poetry is conventionless. It's a lovely messy space,

JESSY RANDALL'S poems have been hung from trees, recited on closed-circuit television, sold in gumball machines, and made into rock songs. Her first book of poems, A Day in Boyland (Ghost Road Press, 2007) was a finalist for the Colorado Book Award. Randall has a collection of collaborative poems with Daniel M. Shapiro, Interruptions, forthcoming from Pecan Grove Press, another solo collection forthcoming from Red Hen Press.

where poets can create whatever-the-hell they want, truly exploratory/adventurous, with all the fear and unease unknown directions bring."

There's an inherent irony in writing an article on digital poetry for a paper publication. It's such a fast-changing medium that by the time this article appears it will be out of date. But most, perhaps all, of these examples will still be available on the internet. You should be able to go to the archives of Poems That Go, watch poetry videos at Shape of a Box or HERE EXPLODES MY GIANT FACE, and visit academic sites like the Electronic Literature Organization (eliterature.org) or the Electronic Poetry Center (epc.buffalo.edu/e-poetry). Turbulence is also a site to watch: founded in 1996, its mission is to commission and support net art. Among its projects is Tumbaramba, a conceptual artwork in the form of a Firefox extension. It's a sort of stealth literary magazine—you download the extension and, over time, twelve stories appear embedded your browser. Projects like show the unusual and surprising possibilities of digital poetry.

The Art of Failure

by Okla Elliott

The historical importance of translation for English language poetry is undeniable. Henry Howard, the Earl of Surrey, invented blank verse in order to translate Virgil's Æneid in 1554, because the Latin original was unrhymed yet metered, and no equivalent existed in English. Blank verse, brought to us by a translator's ingenuity, allowed for Shakespeare's plays to be written as we know them. The sonnet (sonetto or "little song" in Italian) was created by Giacomo da Lentini and enjoyed a boom among Italian poets such as Calvalcanti, Dante, and Petrarch in the mid-13th and early 14th centuries. It was not until the 16th century that sonnets began appearing in English, in translations from Italian and from French. And the list of gifts translators have brought English poetry goes on—couplets, villanelles, sestinas, and, some have argued, even free verse via attempts to translate Chinese poetry. The question now is: What is the cultural and artistic place of translation in the age of globalization?

According to a Center for Book Culture study on the number of books translated into English between 2000-2006, it's a pretty dismal place. Most countries had fewer than one book per year translated into English, and literary heavyweights such as France, Italy, and Germany had fewer than ten books per year translated into English—and this includes novels and nonfiction as well as poetry. The percentage of books in translation tends to be estimated, by such organizations as the NEA and PEN, at about three percent of the total published in America. (Incidentally, there is an excellent blog about translation, out of the University of Rochester, called Three Percent.) Does this mean the effort of translation is hopeless or unimportant? Not necessarily.

Translation is very complex; the process, the need, and the market for it are not so easily summed up. To understand the landscape, we have to look at the differences between publishing translation as books or in journals, translating contemporary or older work, working alone or collaboratively. Likewise, the politics and ethics of translation play a role. And perhaps most importantly, the process and joys of translation need to be understood.

OKLA ELLIOTT is an Assistant Professor at Ohio Wesleyan University. His nonfiction, poetry, short fiction, and translations have appeared in A Public Space, Cold Mountain Review, Indiana Review, New Letters, The Pedestal Magazine, and other publications. He is the author of The Mutable Wheel and Lucid Bodies and Other Poems. He is also co-editor, with Kyle Minor, of The Other Chekhov.

The process of translation

The primary goal of translation is to recreate the effect of the original poem in the target language (the language into which you are translating). The problem, of course, is that if the poet did her work properly in the original (or source) language, then she made use of every available trick and tactic, thus making the job of recreating the poem almost impossible. This is why Umberto Eco calls translation "the art of failure." But while perfection is perhaps not possible, there are thousands of excellent translations in existence. So, how were they done?

You have to determine whether you want to transport the source text into the target language or transport the reader of your translation to the source culture. If you are translating, for example, a contemporary Mexican poet, and the word buñuelo appears, you have to decide whether to replace this very specific Mexican sweet bun made with orange juice with some American equivalent (a honeybun perhaps) or to simply leave the Spanish word in the English translation and hope the reader knows what a buñuelo is. A third option is to retain the Spanish word and footnote it, though footnotes can ruin the effect of a poem if there are too many of them. The general rule is to avoid them when possible. Of course, the problem with replacing a Mexican pastry with a traditional American pastry is that—forgive the pun—you damage the original flavor of the poem, though you do not run the risk of losing or confusing your reader. But both tactics lead to problems, as nearly everything in translation does. I don't mean to suggest that a translation can't do both. In fact, most good translations do, but each successful translation, in order to have its singular effect as the original had its singular effect, ought to privilege one effort over the other.

Depending on the source text, your level of mastery of the source language, and whether there are pre-existing translations, the first stages of working on a new translation of a poem will differ wildly. When translating Latin and Greek literature, David Slavitt uses pre-existing literal prose translations of the poems as well as his personal knowledge of Latin and Greek "to turn the prose translations back into poems." Slavitt says, "When you translate prose, you are the original author's clerk, but when you translate poetry, you are his partner."

Frequently, translation is also done collaboratively. Likely the most famous contemporary duo is Richard Pevear and Larissa Volokhonsky, who have redone many of the Russian prose masterpieces. A notable team in poetry translation is Peter Burian and Alan Shapiro, who collaborate on translations of ancient literature. The make-up of the team is frequently a scholar of the source language/text and a poet who knows the tricks of English verse and who might have some knowledge of the source language.

But no matter your tactics or whether you work alone or with a collaborator, tough choices will have to be made. My translation of Jürgen Becker's poem "Oderbruch," which appeared in the Indiana Review, offers a simple example of the issues a translator runs into in nearly every line. I had translated "[g]elb graue Dämmerung" as "[g]old gray twilight" which caused the faculty member consulted about the accuracy of my translation to suggest that I change it to the more literal "[y]ellow gray twilight." In one sense, he was right—"gelb" means "yellow." But I felt that "gold" was close enough to the literal meaning, but it had the added poetic benefit of retaining the consonance and the number of syllables in the original. Ultimately, the poetry editors at Indiana Review agreed with me, but not because I was unquestionably right. We were both right about how to translate the line. It was simply that I was willing to make a small sacrifice in literalness to retain the music, whereas he was willing to make a small sacrifice of the music to retain a more exact meaning. Every poem will present a dozen or more moments where the translator must sacrifice one thing for another. Only rarely does a poem submit easily to transfer into a new language/culture. That, however, is also part of the joy. Nearly every translator speaks of the joy of finding an elegant solution to a seemingly insoluble problem. ·

Slavitt says, "I didn't take a Hippocratic Oath when I signed on to be a writer. I feel no obligation to the literal meaning of the text whatsoever." It's the pleasure of the original he is after. Does that mean Twinkies show up in Ovid? Well, fine, let it be so. Or so Slavitt says. But the business of translation is a highly contentious one, and one where opinions are unusually strong and criticisms often bitter.

One of the joys of translation is what you can learn by doing it. Slavitt went to the Eclogues and Georgics of Virgil in order to learn how to make a paragraph work in verse. Matthew Zapruder, author of The Pajamaist and translator of the Romanian poet Eugen Jebeleanu, reports, "I also had a sense right away that it would be a good thing for me, a poet just starting to find his way, to be inside the seriousness of the voice and the directness and implacable structure of the poems."

Publishing translations

The report on the market for poetry in translation is mixed. A recent New York Review of Books article points out that Iran publishes more literature in translation than the United States does—as do all European countries and most Latin American ones. That said, however, it has been my experience that original poetry and fiction are comparably hard to place in journals, whereas translation and nonfiction are much easier to place. This has, predictably, to do with the volume and quality of submissions in each genre, as well as current demand. Brett Fletcher Lauer, a poetry editor at A Public Space and an advisor editor at Columbia University's Circumference, a journal dedicated entirely to poetry in translation, offers the following theory on why translations tend to be better and therefore more likely to be accepted: "A Public Space receives a relatively small number of submissions of poetry in translation compared with the thousands of submissions of English-language poetry. That being said, the overall quality of translations submitted is very high. I'm not sure how to account for this fact." He goes on to speculate, "The process of translating and the dedication it requires makes it so that it cannot be casual work, but, instead, a sort of over-time, and what we receive reflects this."

"Generally journals were happy to publish the poems," says Zapruder of his translations of Jebeleanu. "I had more difficulty publishing the book; in fact, I finished the translations in 1998, and it took almost ten years for the book to eventually come out with Coffee House Press."

Slavitt says, "If you translate a standard classic and are lucky enough to get it adopted as a text in enough courses, it will do much better than original poetry." But he adds, "If you translate someone who needs translating—Ausonius for instance—it's about even [with sales of original collections of poetry]." Given the generally poor sales of poetry collections, this might not be very heartening, but it ought to be. Either a book of translation will sell about the same as an original collection or considerably better, especially if you can recast a classic poet in a new translation.

Some of the journals most supportive of poetry in translation are Absinthe, The Bitter Oleander, Circumference, Indiana Review, International Poetry Review, The Literary Review, Natural Bridge, New Letters, Poetry International, and A Public Space. There are others, of course, but these are journals that are dedicated to translation solely or that publish some translation in nearly every issue. And presses that publish translation regularly include Northwestern University Press, Red Hen Press, Sheep Meadow Press, and Ugly Duckling Presse. If a new translator wants to discover what is happening in translation today, s/he would do well to peruse these publications.

Advice for getting started

If you're a first-time translator, it is unlikely that you'll get the rights to translate and publish the work of a major author whose work is still under copyright—e.g., Günter Grass or Pablo Neruda. Mark Smith-Soto, the editor of International Poetry Review and a poet/translator in his own right, advises that a new translator find an author who enjoys a good reputation in his/her home country but who hasn't yet been translated into English. "If you ask a poet whether he'd like to be translated, the answer is generally going to be yes," Smith-Soto says. And here is where the unfortunate state of literature in translation can actually be a plus. Since there is so much excellent literature that has yet to be translated, you'll have plenty to choose from. But since you'll be spending many hours living in the poet's work, it's important to find work you admire. Otherwise, what should be a joy will become a chore. Once you've established yourself, then the larger gigs will come.

It's also worthwhile to have a working knowledge of translation theory, which sounds daunting but which in fact can be attained by reading two excellent books out from University of Chicago Press, The Craft of Translation and Theories of Translation, both edited by John Biguenet and Rainer Schulte. These two reasonably sized volumes will bring you from Dryden's thinking on translation through Goethe's and up to Gregory Rabassa's with excellent stops at Nietzsche's, Benjamin's, and others'.

So, read these books, read the journals that publish translations, read these two seminal texts on the theory and craft of translation, find poetry you admire, and get to work. It's rewarding for both the translator and for the literary culture as a whole.

Why Publishing a Chapbook Makes Sense

by Jeannine Hall Gailey

Maybe you've published some poems in good literary journals, you've started giving readings around town, and you're ready for the next step. You have a lot of poems in your repertoire, but aren't sure exactly how to get your work into the hands of the public. Now is the time to consider putting together a chapbook. This article describes the benefits of publishing chapbooks and how to go about it, including advice from chapbook publishers and writers with successful chapbooks.

What is a poetry chapbook?

Definitions abound (one is even included in the FAQ section at the beginning of Poet's Market,) but today's chapbooks are primarily defined by length (usually less than thirty pages) and production (usually limited edition, sometimes handmade.) While some are beautiful book-arts products, perfect bound with high-quality covers, like those published by Washington State Chapbook Press Floating Bridge or Tupelo Press, a chapbook can also be a stapled-together affair produced at the local copy shop.

As for the means of production, there are many chapbook presses out there (New Michigan Press, Concrete Wolf, Floating Bridge, Finishing Line Press, Pudding House Press...). But you can also self-publish a chapbook to sell at readings.

Chapbooks used to be mainly an emerging poet's way of getting their work out to the public, but these days, presses like Sarabande Press have created in-demand chapbooks for well-known authors such as Louise Glück and James Tate as well. Dorianne Laux, for instance, recently published a chapbook, "Superman," with Red Dragonfly Press.

Why a poetry chapbook?

The benefits are multiple. First, the task of putting together a chapbook collection of poems—thinking about organization, which poems to include or exclude, polishing up poems you meant to revise but never got around to—is great training for putting together a full-length book. Second, learning to market and sell your own work—getting over the embarrassment of asking bookstores to carry your chapbook, or telling friends about your

JEANNINE HALL GAILEY is a San Diego writer whose first book of poetry, Becoming the Villainess, was published by Steel Toe Books. She was awarded a 2007 Dorothy Sargent Rosenberg Prize for Poetry and a 2007 Washington State Artist Trust GAP grant. Her poems have appeared in several publications, including The Iowa Review, The Columbia Poetry Review, and Smartish Pace. She currently teaches at the MFA program at National University.

chapbook publication—is essential for any poet, because the usual marketing machinery of publishing (talk shows, end-caps at Barnes & Nobles, advertising campaigns) doesn't really exist in the poetry publishing world, which is run on slim margins by a very few overworked but dedicated people.

Kelli Russell Agodon, whose sold-out chapbook, "Geography," was one of Floating Bridge Press' best sellers, talked about how the experience of having a chapbook had benefited her. "Having a chapbook has helped me by opening new doors. It has allowed me to have opportunities such as teaching or reading at poetry festivals and conferences that may not have been open to me if I didn't have a book. It also helped me understand the publishing process a little better before my full length collection. Also, crafting the chapbook really allowed me to focus on one particular subject."

Lana Ayers, editor and publisher at Concrete Wolf, a chapbook publisher, details further benefits. "Chapbooks provide an opportunity for authors to produce tightly woven or themed collections. And since most chapbooks, are less expensive than full-length collections, it is easier to convince a reader to take the plunge. Also, the shorter length of the collection can be less intimidating for readers new to poetry. So chapbooks are an all-around great opportunity for both poets and readers to get acquainted."

Kristy Bowen, editor and publisher at Dancing Girl Press, talks about why she started publishing chapbooks. "I also have a love for the chapbook itself as form, a small morsel of poetry that can be devoured in one sitting. Also, they are an affordable way to get new work into the hands of readers with very little fuss. I'm interested as well in how to expand the traditional notion of chapbooks further into the realm of book arts."

Writers have different motivations for publishing chapbooks—fascination with the form, building a relationship with an audience, or finding a home for a particular set of poems. Dorianne Laux described her decision to publish a chapbook after several highly successful full-length collections.

"I met Scott King, of Red Dragonfly Press while I was at the Anderson Center for the Arts for a writing residency and he was producing letterpress broadsides. He later asked if I'd like to do a chapbook. At the time, I wasn't sure if I had enough poems on a theme to make a book, but said yes anyway, not wanting to miss a chance to work with Scott. It took me about a year to come up with the poems in "Superman" which are all loosely based around pop culture figures, icons and objects of the 20th century. I wasn't yet ready for a fifth book of poems and so a chapbook seemed a great way to have something in the interim. But more important was my desire to have a beautiful book, hand set on gorgeous paper and sewn together, something that would be a small, elegant gift I could give to friends. It was also a way to bring attention to this small press and its poet/editor, Scott King, who had taught me so much about the quality of labor that went into reproducing a page of words before the invention of carbon paper, mimeo and xerox machines, computers and desktop printers. It was exacting, dangerous and dirty work, performed amidst smoke, sparks and fire by some anonymous typesetter bent over in a greasy smock, delicately choosing the next stately letter with the deafening clatter of the molten lead foundry pounding against the drums in his ears. It's also wonderfully ironic to have a book about 20th century characters like Cher and The Beatles produced using a 16th century technology!"

So now you're intrigued. But how, exactly, do you put together a chapbook?

What does putting together a chapbook entail?

The good news is that it's a lot like putting together a book, but a more compact, and perhaps, more tightly-themed collection. Usually, writers have obsessions, and those obsessions manifest themselves over time. You'll find twenty poems on superheroes, for instance, or on abandoned gas stations in the Midwest. Or you'll find twenty poems that tell their own story.

Kelli Russell Agodon's advice for someone putting together a chapbook for the first time? "My advice would be to focus your chapbook on one subject, theme, or story. The best chapbooks look deeply at a topic, but also make new discoveries in their poems throughout the book. I suggest choosing only your strongest poems for your chapbook, then determine if there are certain poems you need to write to make the chapbook stronger and more complete."

Kristy Bowen adds that "sometimes, especially poets at the beginning of their career see a chapbook as a stepping stone to the first book, which it usually is, but I suspect they sometimes see the chapbook merely as a shorter volume sort of tossed together without any real feel of cohesion in the chapbook itself. So what you get is an odd mismatch of the poems they consider best, but without any sort of thematic or formal binding." So what is Dancing Girl Press' editor looking for? "We particularly look for work that has a strong sense of image and music, cohesiveness as a manuscript, interesting and surprising, sometimes unusual, use of language. We love humor when done well, strangeness, wackiness. Hybridity, collage, intertextuality. Manuscripts that create their own worlds."

This brings us to the next subject—how to get your chapbook published.

How are chapbooks published?

You've got your manuscript of 15-30 pages of thematically-engaged, tightly edited poetry together, so now what? Well, many chapbook publishers, just like poetry book publishers, decide what they are going to publish through a contest system. Presses like this include Tupelo Press, Concrete Wolf, Pudding House, and New Michigan Press. If you go this route, you should research the publisher by obtaining at least one of their previous publications, checking out the production and writing quality, and decide if it's a good fit for you. If it is, then you send off your manuscript with a cover letter, a check (usually $10-15), and a SASE, and hope for the best. Some presses publish runners-up and finalists as well as winners. Be sure to read the guidelines thoroughly, and follow them to the letter.

Some chapbook publishers, like Sarabande Press, only publish through solicitation—that is, they contact the person they want to publish directly - so unless you get a call, you won't be getting your chapbook published through them. Some chapbook publishers will read "open submissions," for a few months a year, like Dancing Girl Press, but these are few and far between.

Of course, there's always self-publishing, and this is an easier (and more affordable) feat if you're attempting a saddle-stitched chapbook than a perfect bound book. You could even put it all up—your poems, the cover art, your table of contents and acknowledgements - on your own computer, using basic publishing software, print it out on your own laser printer, and staple it at your kitchen table. If you google "make your own saddle-stitched chapbook" you can find a couple of sets of instructions, or if you're lucky enough to have a book arts center near you, sign up for a class.

Marketing a poetry chapbook

Marketing a chapbook is, admittedly, more difficult to market than a poetry book. Many bookstores won't carry them because they are difficult to store and display. Your best bet is to talk an independent bookstore into carrying a copy or two on consignment. Most review outlets don't take chapbook reviews, and chapbooks are not usually eligible for major book awards.

But chapbooks are by nature ephemeral, and that can be an advantage. A limited run means an especially beautiful or well-written chapbook might later become a collector's item, and no writer keeps too many chapbooks on hand—and, unlike books, they don't take up too much space to store. Many people see chapbooks as a more intimate way to get to know a poet's work, and value the fact that the chapbooks may only be around for a short amount of time. Chapbooks are easy to sell at poetry readings, where the buyer is more likely to want a souvenir of that experience, and on poet's web sites, where the buyers are already familiar with the poet and their work. If you have friends with blogs, send them a review copy of your chapbook and ask them to say a few words.

So, remember this—give readings. Be an interesting, enthusiastic reader who has actually organized their work and practiced it a few times. This will increase the odds that audience members might want to buy your chapbook! And, make sure you have a personal web site or blog that your fans can come to and find out how to buy your chapbook—whether it's directly from you or from a link to your publisher or even Amazon. Don't make them hunt for it!

Why should you consider publishing a chapbook?

A chapbook gives you a way to connect with your reader. It gives your reader a physical reminder of your work, and sometimes it's a beautiful artifact, sometimes a humble set of copies, folded over and stapled. Creating a chapbook helps you practice organizing your work into a coherent collection. Selling your chapbook orients you in the world of marketing poetry, and, if you do it yourself or watch it being produced, a way to understand the physical work of book publishing.

Because of these benefits, it's more than just a step towards a full-length poetry collection—it's a way for you to build an audience, to put your work out into the world in a considered, deliberate way. Take a look at the chapbook publishers listed in Poet's Market, and order some samples to get an idea of the diversity of the production and content of chapbooks available as well as figure out which publisher might be right for you. Before you know it, you'll have something in hand to share at readings and with friends and family.

Finding Readers

How to Get Your Poetry Into Their Hands

by Diane Lockward

Poets who are fortunate enough to have a full-length collection from a large publishing house receive the services of a marketing department with a budget that covers advertising and a book tour. But if you, like most of us, get your book from a small press, you will find that your publisher has little or no budget for promotion. There are a number of benefits to working with a small press publisher, for example, more involvement in the design of the book and a personal relationship with your publisher. However, if you want your book to find its way into the hands of readers, you are going to have to work to make that happen.

Spreading the word

The work of promoting your book begins before the book is even out. Most small press publishers have found that ads are not cost effective, but they will design a press release and do a snail mailing for you. While you wait for your book to get published, compile an up-to-date snail mail list. Since mailings are expensive, include only your best prospects, not everyone you've ever met. Many publishers also do an e-mail blitz, so prepare a list of e-mail addresses. Your publisher will most likely send the press release and a review copy to journals that have published your work. Assemble a list of the names and addresses of those journals, but only the ones that run reviews.

After your book is published, supplement your publisher's mailings with your own. Many publishers provide postcards for this purpose, but if yours doesn't, you can design your own inexpensively at an online service such as vistaprint.com. Upload your cover image onto one side and add ordering information on the other, leaving space for name and address of the recipient. In your e-mail notes include your cover image, but do not add an attachment as many people will not open it. It doesn't matter if people receive more than one notice about your book. Janet Holmes, publisher of Ahsahta Books, says, "Sometimes a reader needs to see the title of a book multiple times before it sinks in as something to acquire." Many recipients will appreciate—and act upon—the reminder.

DIANE LOCKWARD'S second collection, What Feeds Us (Wind Publications), received the 2006 Quentin R. Howard Poetry Prize. Her poems appear in Garrison Keillor's Good Poems for Hard Times and in such journals as Harvard Review, Spoon River Poetry Review, and Prairie Schooner. (www.dianelockward.com)

Ask your publisher to provide you with the press release via attachment. Save it on your computer and include it with any additional review copies you mail out. Send the press release to your college alumni newsletter. Put one up on the bulletin board where you work. Fire off some to local libraries and bookstores. Send another with a fact sheet to your local newspaper. Request an article and offer to go in for an interview. My local paper interviewed me and ran an article for each of my books. That would not have happened if I hadn't asked.

Lining up readings

Tom Hunley, director of Steel Toe Books, says, "Readings are far and away the #1 way for poets to sell books." Let your first reading be a book launch party. Invite your relatives, friends, and poet pals. Have food. This reading may well be your best sales event. If you have a friend with a book coming out around the same time, consider joining forces. Publisher Joan Cusack Handler celebrates each new CavanKerry Press book with a literary salon held in someone's home. Poet Claire Keyes (The Question of Rapture, Mayapple Press, 2008) had house readings held by friends. She and her hosts collaborated on the guest list and shared expenses.

After the initial round of readings, you need to get proactive. Poet Kate Greenstreet (case sensitive, Ahsahta Books, 2006) warns that "if you won't ask—and people aren't already inviting you—obviously, you won't be reading." To get readings, you need to compose a query letter. Keep it informative and succinct. I send most of mine by e-mail with links to my website and online sites where my work is available. Make a list of venues in your area. Try bookstores, libraries, art galleries, coffeehouses—all the usual places. Then get creative. I have friends who've read in chocolate stores, wine bars, and hip jewelry stores. Contact local book clubs and suggest that your book be a selection. Offer to present a reading and discussion for the group. Senior citizens' residences and nursing homes are often looking for social programs. Offer your services for a reading. If you have friends who teach, offer to do a reading, a Q & A, and a workshop. Apply to conferences, festivals, and book fairs.

Target audiences that might likely have an interest in your work and in poetry. For example, I'm a former high school English teacher. One of my most successful readings was for a district-wide English department meeting. I read ten poems and offered ten teaching tips. The supervisor purchased a copy of my book for each department member—all forty of them. That presentation led to an offer to teach a six-hour workshop for a small group of teachers.

Also target groups that don't ordinarily attend readings but are somehow connected to your subject matter. Are your poems about flowers? Query nearby garden clubs and suggest a reading at one of their upcoming meetings. Do your poems deal with woman-related topics? Contact area women's clubs. Marion Haddad (Somewhere Between Mexico and a River Called Home, Pecan Grove Press, 2004) is the American-born daughter of Syrian immigrants and for thirty-five years lived a few minutes from the Mexican border, so she often seeks readings at Arab-American gatherings and border studies events. Richard Jeffrey Newman, whose The Silence of Men (CavanKerry, 2006) deals with gender, sexuality, and recovery from child sexual abuse, solicited and received an invitation to read at the 2008 Wellness and Writing Connections Conference. One of my favorite readings was at New York Life Investment Management, certainly an unlikely place for poetry, but the woman who heads Human Resources runs special programs for women employees. I proposed a reading entitled "Poetry and the Lives of Women." My host pre-ordered six of my books and had a drawing for them, a great alternative when reading at an event where selling books might not be appropriate.

Eventually you will need to seek readings outside of your own area. Remember that the farther you cast your net, the fewer responses you're likely to get. Cast it anyhow because you will get some responses. To find out where readings are held, map out the distance you're willing to travel. Then do a Google search, for example, "poetry venues in New Jersey" or "poetry readings in Boston." That should bring up some listings. If there's contact information, send off your query letter. Check out reading schedules on other poets' websites. Visit online calendars, for example, those at The Academy of American Poets' and Poets & Writers' websites. Use these to suggest possible venues to query. When you get readings, publicize them as widely as possible. List them in online calendars and send out e-mail notices to people you know in the area of the reading. Do not rely solely on the venue host to drum up an audience for you.

Regardless of where you're reading, remember that you're promoting your book, so be prepared to read poems from the book. Greg Kosmicki, of The Backwaters Press, advises poets that while they may get tired of reading the same poems, the audience will be hearing them for the first time. Your listeners will be more inclined to buy your book if you hold it and read from it. Remember, too, that not everyone who attends your reading will buy your book. My own publisher, Charlie Hughes of Wind Publications, suggests that often the "value in a reading or personal appearance is not in the number of books sold at the event, but in getting the writer's name in the newspaper announcing the event—building name recognition." I usually bring along oversized postcards with my cover image on one side and a poem and ordering information on the other. I give these away and like to think that some of the recipients might make a later purchase. I also always carry some business cards with me, cover image on one side, contact information on the other.

Using the internet

The internet is one of your best resources for promoting your book. If you don't already have a website, get one. Even if your publisher has a page for your book at the press' website, you should have your own website. You can get a domain name very inexpensively. Since this is your website's address, use your own name so people can easily locate your website. If you design your own website, you will pay only for the hosting. If you use a free hosting site, be sure it's ad-free. A website with ads looks awful and unprofessional. If you use a web designer's services, you will, of course, pay more, but don't go wild. Your site should include a bio, an image of your book cover, purchase information, sample poems, links to other poems, links to online reviews and interviews, a calendar of your readings, and contact information. Be sure your website is attractive and up to date. A website that is not maintained does not make a good impression.

Consider keeping a blog. There's a big community now of poet bloggers. A blog takes some time, but it's a great place to establish contacts with other poets and another place to display your book cover and list readings. You can add podcasts and videos, thus creating long-distance readings for potential fans who might not otherwise be able to get to a reading. Kate Greenstreet kept a blog for two years. She used it to do a series of more than 100 first-book interviews and undoubtedly earned many friends. As much as she gave to the poetry community, she got back in support when her own book came out.

Join an internet social network such as Facebook, My Space, or Red Room. These are hot gathering places for poets, and all are free. I'm on Facebook where I create event listings for my readings and send out invitations to "friends" who live in the area of an upcoming reading. Without this resource, I would not know these people's names or how to contact them. I've learned about venues and booked readings through Facebook contacts, gotten an online interview, and participated in a college student's poetry course project. Richard Jeffrey Newman received an invitation from a Facebook contact to go to Chile as part of Chile Poesia, an international poetry festival. A poetry listserv will also put you among poets and offer opportunities for sales and readings.

A final suggestion for your internet use, this one fast and easy. Use your e-mail signature to good advantage. Set your e-mail program to automatically add a link to your website at the bottom of each new message you write. If you like, you can add a link to your blog or anything special you have online such as a poem feature. Think of the signature area as free billboard space. You'll be amazed how many people will click on those links and go visiting.

Keeping expectations realistic

Promoting your book is the business of poetry, but don't expect to make money. As Kate Greenstreet says, "When we're talking about selling poetry books, we're talking about doing business, but it isn't conventional business even if you work really hard at it." Richard Jeffrey Newman reminds us that books of poetry "find their audience one reader at a time, slowly, over time." If you want your book to find those readers, you need to be industrious, adventurous, persistent and patient.

10 Tips for the Perfect Reading

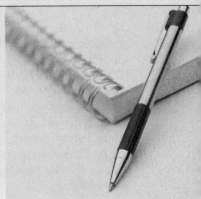

by Taylor Mali

The extent of the advice given to poets for how to present their work aloud at poetry readings usually boils down to reading slower, louder, and clearer. And while those are important improvements to almost anyone's style of recitation (albeit extremely difficult to make yourself do, especially at the same time), there are several other factors to keep in mind if you want your audience to appreciate your skills as a writer and perhaps even buy your book after the reading.

1. **Try to make the first thing out of your mouth poetry.** What else could be more important than immediately giving the audience an example of what they came to the reading to hear? Insipid chatter between poems is bad enough, but introductory insipid chatter is even worse and tends to go on and on. Sometimes it will be five minutes before a poet even gets to the first poem! Everything you think you need to say—thank yous, shout outs, announcements about journals in which your poetry will be forthcoming, or plugs for your books and next appearances—all of this can be mentioned after the first poem. Or maybe not at all (except for the thank yous).

2. **Know what poems you will read and have them close at hand.** Don't burden the audience with having to watch you flip through your own book or resort to looking at the table of contents while you make a self-deprecating joke only to realize finally that the poem you wanted to read is actually in your other book. Have your poems picked out in advance as well as the order in which you will read them. All of your fussing between poems counts toward the time you have been given to read.

3. **Don't be the poet who reads forever!** Time limits do not only apply to bad poets; they apply to brilliant poets like you as well. Unfortunately, it's usually the bad poets who have no concept of time. Before the reading, rehearse your set (with a stopwatch if possible) and do not go over the time you've been allotted. Losing track of how long you've been reading is no excuse for going over. Don't ask the organizer to give you a signal when you have five minutes left or periodically look up and ask, "How am I doing on time?" It's your responsibility to know how you are "doing on time." If anything, be a little under time and leave your audience wanting more.

4. **Keep your chatter between poems to a minimum.** Most of what poets say between

TAYLOR MALI is a teacher and voiceover artist. A classically trained Shakespearean actor, Mali was one of the original poets to appear on the HBO series Russell Simmons Presents Def Poetry. He is a veteran of the poetry slam and the author of What Learning Leaves and several spoken word CDs and DVDs. He lives and writes in New York City. For more information, visit www.taylormali.com.

poems comes from nervousness and not any real need to explicate the poem.

5. **Perform one poem by someone else.** Depending on how much time you have been given, it's a nice idea to celebrate the work of someone else beside yourself. Introduce your audience to one of your favorite poems by one of your favorite poets. Tell them where they can find this particular poem and two things you love about it. Then, at the end of your reading of the poem, say the author's name one last time.

6. **Perform at least one of your poems from memory.** Once you experience the freedom of being able to make constant eye contact while having your hands completely free to gesture or hang naturally at your sides (which doesn't feel natural at all but looks perfectly normal), you will want to memorize more of your work. And you should! The roots of poetry are bardic, not literary, so it is entirely fitting to work on making the recitation of your poem a better performance. Work at memorizing more and more poetry every day. The mind is a muscle; the more you use it, the stronger it gets.

7. **Let the audience clap if they want to clap.** If one definition of a "performance" poem is that after it's over, the audience not only wants to applaud but knows that applause is appropriate, then you could say that one definition of an "academic" poem is that after it's over—assuming you know when that is—the audience doesn't even know if they are supposed to clap. Poets with limited performance skills will often request that audiences not applaud between poems because they are uncomfortable with the awkward silence that fills the room when they finish each poem. In fact, sometimes the only clue that such poets have finished a poem is when they say, "The next poem I'd like to read." Certainly don't telegraph the end of your poem by speeding up or trailing off or both. Rather build toward it, perhaps nodding your head ever so slightly at the end.

8. **Make eye contact.** Real eye contact. Look at different parts of the room as you glance up from your text every now and then. Poets who look at the exact same spot as they methodically lift their heads every seven seconds to pretend they are looking at the same person (whose chair is apparently attached to one of the lighting fixtures) aren't fooling anyone. It is better never to look up at all than to do so perfunctorily to mask your nervousness.

9. **If there is a microphone, use it.** Granted, when the microphone is attached to a podium, you won't have much choice but to use it. But faced with a solitary mic stand and the possibly awkward task of having to adjust it for your height while somehow also managing a bottle of water and the text from which you are about to read, you might decide you don't need a microphone at all. Not a good decision, even if you have a big, boomy voice. Without a microphone, you cannot get quiet when the poem invites it, or else no one will hear you when you do. Unless the system sounds like crap and has for the whole night, use the microphone, even if it takes a few extra seconds at the outset to adjust it.

10. **Enjoy yourself.** This seems obvious, but audiences love to see people who love what they do, especially when they do it well. Smile a lot. Try reciting an entire poem while smiling. Let people suspect you are having the time of your life. And whatever you do, don't ever suggest that your reading is a kind of torture you are inflicting on the audience ("Don't worry. You only have to listen to three more!"). You are a genius, and your words are the proof. Knock 'em dead!

Mistakes Poets Make

In putting together listings for *Poet's Market*, we ask editors for any words of advice they want to share with our readers. Often the editors' responses include comments about what poets should and shouldn't do when submitting work—the same comments, over and over. That means a lot of poets are repeating similar mistakes when they send out their poems for consideration.

The following list includes the most common of those mistakes—the ones poets should work hardest to avoid.

Not reading a publication before submitting work

Researching a publication is essential before submitting your poetry. Try to buy a sample copy of a magazine (by mail, if necessary) or at least see if an issue is available at the library. It may not be economically feasible for poets to purchase a copy of every magazine they target, especially if they send out a lot of poems. However, there are additional ways to familiarize yourself with a publication.

Read the market listing thoroughly. If guidelines are available, send for them by e-mail or regular mail, or check for them online. A publication's website often presents valuable information, including sample poems, magazine covers—and guidelines.

Submitting inappropriate work

Make good use of your research so you're sure you understand what a magazine publishes. Don't rationalize that a journal favoring free verse might jump at the chance to consider your long epic poem in heroic couplets. Don't convince yourself your experimental style will be a good fit for the traditional journal filled with rhyming poetry. Don't go into denial about whether a certain journal and your poetry are made for each other. It's counterproductive and ultimately wastes postage (not to mention time—yours and the editor's).

Submitting an unreasonable number of poems

If an editor recommends sending three to five poems (a typical range), don't send six. Don't send a dozen poems and tell the editor to pick the five she wants to consider. If the editor doesn't specify a number (or the listing says "no limit"), don't take that as an invitation to mail off 20 poems. The editors and staff of literary magazines are busy enough as it is, and they may decide they don't have time to cope with you. (When submitting book or chapbook manuscripts to publishers, make sure your page count falls within the range they state.)

Don't go to the other extreme and send only one poem, unless an editor says it's okay (which is rare). One poem doesn't give an editor much of a perspective on your work, and it doesn't give you very good odds on getting the piece accepted.

Ignoring the editor's preferences regarding formats

If an editor makes a point of describing a preferred manuscript format, follow it, even if that format seems to contradict the standard. (Standard format includes using 8½ × 11 white paper and conventional typeface and point size; avoid special graphics, colors or type flourishes; put your name and address on every page.) Don't devise your own format to make your submission stand out. Keep everything clean, crisp and easy to read (and professional).

Be alert to e-mail submission formats. Follow directions regarding what the editor wants printed in the subject line, how many poems to include in a single e-mail, whether to use attachments or paste work in the body of the message, and other elements. Editors have good reasons for outlining their preferences; ignoring them could mean having your e-mail deleted before your poems are even read.

Omitting a self-addressed stamped envelope (SASE)

Why do editors continuously say "include a SASE with your submission?" Because so many poets don't do it. Here's a simple rule: Unless the editor gives alternate instructions, include a #10 SASE, whether submitting poems or sending an inquiry.

Writing bad cover letters (or omitting them completely)

Cover letters have become an established part of the submission process. There are editors who remain indifferent about the necessity of a cover letter, but many consider it rude to be sent a submission without any other communication from the poet.

Unless the editor says otherwise, send a cover letter. Keep it short and direct, a polite introduction of you and your work. (See "Frequently Asked Questions" on page 7 for more tips on cover letters, and an example.) Here are a few important Don'ts:

- **Don't** list all the magazines where your work has appeared; limit yourself to five magazine titles. The work you're submitting has to stand on its own.
- **Don't** tell the editor what a good poet you are—or how good someone else thinks you are.
- **Don't** tell the editor how to edit, lay out or print your poem. Some of those decisions are up to the editor, assuming she decides to accept your poem in the first place.
- **Don't** point out the poem is copyrighted in your name or include the copyright symbol. All poems are automatically copyrighted in the poet's name as soon as they're "fixed" (i.e., written down), and editors know this.

Not maintaining good editor/poet relations

Most editors are hard-working poetry lovers dedicated to finding and promoting good work. They aspire to turn submissions around as quickly as possible and to treat all poets with respect. They don't want to steal your work. Often they aren't paid for their labor and may even have to dip into their own pockets just to keep their magazines going.

Poets should finesse their communications with editors regarding problems, especially in initial letters and e-mail. Editors (and their magazines and presses) aren't service-oriented businesses, like the phone company. Getting huffy with an editor as if arguing with your cable provider about an overcharge is inappropriate. Attitude isn't going to get you anywhere; in fact, it could create additional obstacles.

That's not to say poets shouldn't feel exasperated when they're inconvenienced or ill treated. None of us likes to see our creations vanish, or to pay good money for something we're never going to receive (like a subscription or sample copy). However, exasperated is one thing; outraged is another. Too often poets go on the offensive with editors and make matters worse. Experts on how to complain effectively recommend you keep your cool and stay professional, no matter what kind of problem you're trying to work out.

Dealing With Problem Editors

There *are* problem editors out there, and we've all encountered them at one time or another. Some rip people off, prey on poets' desires to be published, or treat poets and their work with flagrant disregard. Fortunately, such editors are very much in the minority.

Now and then you may discover the disorganized editor or the overwhelmed editor; these two cause heartache (and heartburn) by closing up shop without returning manuscripts, or failing to honor paid requests for subscriptions and sample copies. More often than not, their transgressions are rooted in chaos and irresponsibility, not malicious intent. Frustrating as such editors are, they're not out to get you.

There are many instances, too, where larger circumstances are beyond an editor's control. For example, a college-oriented journal may be student-staffed, with editors changing each academic year. Funds for the journal may be cut unexpectedly by administration belt-tightening, or a grant could be cancelled. The editorial office may be moved to another part of the university. An exam schedule could impact a publishing schedule. All of these things cause problems and delays.

Then again, a literary journal may be a one-person, home-based operation. The editor may get sick or have an illness in the family. Her regular job may suddenly demand lots of overtime. There may be divorce or death with which the editor has to cope. A computer could crash. Or the editor may need to scramble for money before the magazine can go to the printer. Emergencies happen, and they take their toll on deadlines. The last thing the editor wants is to inconvenience poets and readers, but sometimes life gets in the way.

Usually, difficulties with these kinds of "problem" editors can be resolved satisfactorily through communication and patience. There are always exceptions, though. Here are a few typical situations with problem editors and how to handle them:

An editor is rude. If it's a matter of bad attitude, take it with a grain of salt. Maybe he's having a rotten day. If there's abusive language and excessive profanity involved, let us know about it. (See the complaint procedure on page 64.)

An editor harshly criticizes your poem. If an editor takes time to comment on your poetry, even if the feedback seems overly critical, consider the suggestions with an open mind and try to find something valid and useful in them. If, after you've given the matter fair consideration, you think the editor was out of line, don't rush to defend your poetry or wave your bruised ego in the editor's face. Allow that the editor has a right to her opinion (which you're not obligated to take as the final word on the quality of your work), forget about it and move on.

Complaint Procedure

Important

If you feel you have not been treated fairly by a market listed in Poet's Market, we advise you to take the following steps:

- First, try to contact the market. Sometimes one phone call, letter, or e-mail can quickly clear up the matter. Document all your communications with the market.

- When you contact us with a complaint, provide the details of your submission, the date of your first contact with the market and the nature of your subsequent communication.

- We will file a record of your complaint and further investigate the market.

- The number and severity of complaints will be considered when deciding whether or not to delete a market from the next edition of Poet's Market.

An editor is slow to respond to a submission. As explained above, there may be many reasons why an editor's response takes longer than the time stated in the market listing or guidelines. Allow a few more weeks to pass beyond the deadline, then write a polite inquiry to the editor about the status of your manuscript. (Include a SASE if sending by regular mail.) Understand an editor may not be able to read your letter right away if deadlines are pressing or if he's embroiled in a personal crisis. Try to be patient. If you haven't received a reply to your inquiry after a month or so, however, it's time for further action.

An editor won't return your manuscript. Decide whether you want to invest any more time in this journal or publisher. If you conclude you've been patient long enough, write a firm but professional letter to the editor withdrawing your manuscript from consideration. Request that the manuscript be returned; but know, too, a truly indifferent editor probably won't bother to send it back or reply in any way. Keep a copy of your withdrawal letter for your files, make a new copy of your manuscript and look for a better market.

Also, contact Poet's Market by letter or e-mail with details of your experience. We always look into problems with editors, although we don't withdraw a listing on the basis of a single complaint unless we discover further evidence of consistent misbehavior. We do, however, keep complaints on file and watch for patterns of unacceptable behavior from any specific market.

An editor takes your money. If you sent a check for a subscription or sample copy and you haven't received anything, review your bank statement to see if the check has been cashed. If it has, send the editor a query. Politely point out the editor has cashed your check, but you haven't yet received the material you were expecting. Give the editor the benefit of the doubt: An upcoming issue of a magazine could be running late, your subscription could have been overlooked by mistake, or your copy could have been lost in transit or sent in error to the wrong address.

If your check has *not* been cashed, query the editor to see if your order was ever received. It may have been lost (in the mail or on the editor's desk), the editor may be holding several checks to cash at one time, or the editor may be waiting to cash checks until a tardy issue is finally published.

If you get an unsatisfactory response from the editor (or no response at all), wait a few weeks and try again. If the matter still isn't resolved, let us know about it. We're especially interested in publishers who take money from poets but don't deliver the goods. Be sure to send us all the details of the transaction, plus copies of any correspondence (yours and the editor's). We can't pursue your situation in any legal way or act as mediator, but we can ban an unscrupulous publisher from *Poet's Market* and keep the information as a resource in case we get later complaints.

Should you continue trying to get your money back from such editors? That's your decision. If your loss is under $10 (say, for a subscription or sample copy), it might cost you less in the long run to let the matter go. And the fee for a "stop payment" order on a check can be hefty—possibly more than the amount you sent the editor in the first place. Yes, it's infuriating to be cheated, but sometimes fighting on principle costs more than it's worth.

If your monetary loss is significant (for instance, you shelled out a couple hundred dollars in a subsidy publishing agreement), consider contacting your state attorney general's office for advice about small claims court, filing a complaint and other actions you can take.

Is It a 'Con'?

Think Before You Trust

What is a "con?" Con is short for "confidence," an adjective defined by Webster's as "of, relating to, or adept at swindling by false promise," as in "confidence man" or "confidence game." While the publishing world is full of legitimate opportunities for poets to gain honor and exposure for their work, there are also plenty of "cons." How can you tell the difference? The following are some of the most common situations that cost poets disappointment, frustration—and cash. Learn to spot them before submitting your work, and don't let your vanity be your guide.

ANTHOLOGIES

Has this happened to you? You see an ad in a perfectly respectable publication announcing a poetry contest with big cash prizes. You enter, and later you receive a glowing letter congratulating you on your exceptional poem, which the contest sponsor wants to include in his deluxe hardbound anthology of the best poetry submitted to the contest. The anthology costs only, say, $65. You don't have to buy it—they'll still publish your poem— but wouldn't you be proud to own one? And wouldn't it be nice to buy additional copies to give to family and friends? And for an extra charge you can include a biographical note. And so on . . .

Of course, when the anthology arrives, the quality of the poetry may not be what you were expecting, with several poems crammed unattractively onto a page. Apparently everyone who entered the contest was invited to be published; you basically paid cash to see your poem appear in a phone book-like volume with no literary merit whatsoever.

Were you conned? Depends on how you look at it. If you bought into the flattery and believed you were being published in an exclusive, high-quality publication, no doubt you feel duped. On the other hand, if all you were after was seeing your poem in print, even knowing you'd have to pay for the privilege, then you got what you wanted. (Unless you've deceived yourself into believing you've truly won an honor and now have a worthy publishing credit; you don't.)

If you don't want to add insult to injury, resist additional spiels, like having your poem printed on coffee mugs and t-shirts (you can do this yourself through print shops or online services like www.cafepress.com) or spending large sums on awards banquets and conferences. And, before you submit a single line of poetry, find out what rights the contest sponsor acquires. You may be relinquishing all rights to your poem simply by mailing it in or submitting it through a website. If the poem no longer belongs to you,

Helpful Websites

Important

The following websites include specific information about questionable poetry publishers and awards. For more websites of value to poets, see Additional Resources on page 461.

- An Incomplete Guide to Print On Demand Publishers offers articles on POD publishing, comparisons of POD publishers (contracts, distribution, fees, etc.) and an online forum: http://booksandtales.com/pod/index.php

- Answers to frequently asked questions about poetry awards from the Academy of American Poets: www.poets.org/page.php/prmID/116

- Poets will find warnings and other valuable publishing information on the Preditors & Editors website: www.anotherealm.com/prededitors/

- Writer Beware tracks contests, publishers and literary agents: www.sfwa.org/beware

- "Literary Contest Caution" at http://windpub.com/literary.scams

the publisher can do whatever he wishes with it. Don't let your vanity propel you into a situation you'll always regret.

READING AND CONTEST FEES

Suppose you notice a promising market for your poetry, but the editor requires a set fee just to consider your work. Or you see a contest that interests you, but you have to pay the sponsor a fee just to enter. Are you being conned?

In the case of reading fees, keep these points in mind: Is the market so exceptional that you feel it's worth risking the cost of the reading fee to have your work considered? What makes it so much better than markets that do not charge fees? Has the market been around awhile, with an established publishing schedule? What are you paid if your work is accepted? Are reasonably priced samples available so you can judge the production values and quality of the writing?

Reading fees don't necessarily signal a suspicious market. In fact, they're increasingly popular as editors struggle with the costs of publishing books and magazines, including the man-hours required to read loads of (often bad) submissions. However, fees represent an additional financial burden on poets, who often don't receive any monetary reward for their poems to begin with. It's really up to individual poets to decide whether paying a fee is beneficial to their publishing efforts. Think long and hard about fee-charging markets that are new and untried, don't pay poets for their work (at the very least a print publication should offer a contributor's copy), charge high prices for sample copies or set fees that seem unreasonable.

Entry fees for contests often fund prizes, judges' fees, honorariums and expenses of running and promoting the contest (including publishing a "prize" collection or issue of a magazine). Other kinds of contests charge entry fees, from Irish dancing competitions to bake-offs at a county fair. Why not poetry contests?

That's not to say you shouldn't be cautious. Watch out for contests that charge higher-than-average fees, especially if the fees are out of proportion to the amount of prize money being given. (Look through the Contests & Awards section beginning on page 390 to get a sense of what most competitions charge; you'll also find contests in other sections of this book by consulting the Additional Contests & Awards index on page 453.) Find out how long the contest has been around, and verify whether prizes have been awarded each year and to whom. In the case of book and chapbook contests, send for one of the winning publications to confirm that the publisher puts out a quality product. Regard with skepticism any contest that tells you you've won something, then demands payment for an anthology, trophy or other item. (It's okay if a group offers an anthology for a modest price without providing winners with free copies. Most state poetry societies have to do this; but they also present cash awards in each category of the contest, and their entry fees are low.)

SUBSIDY PUBLISHERS, PRINT-ON-DEMAND

Poetry books are a hard sell to the book-buying public. Few of the big publishers handle these books, and those that do feature the "name" poets (i.e., the major prize winners and contemporary masters with breathtaking reputations). Even the small presses publish only so many books per year—far less than the number of poets writing.

No wonder so many poets decide to pay to have their poetry collections published. While some may self-publish (i.e., take full control of their book, working directly with a printer), others turn to subsidy publishers (also called "vanity publishers") and print-on-demand (POD) publishers.

There are many differences between subsidy publishing and POD publishing, as well as similarities (having to pay to get published is a big one). Whether or not you get conned is entirely up to you. You have to take responsibility for asking questions, doing research on presses, and reading the fine print on the contract to make sure you know exactly what you're paying for. There are landmines in dealing with subsidy and POD publishers, and you have to investigate thoroughly and intelligently to avoid damage.

Some questions to keep in mind: Are fees inflated compared to the product and services you'll be receiving? Will you still own the rights to your book? Does the publisher put out a quality product that's attractive and cleanly printed? (Get a sample copy and find out.) How many copies of the book will you receive? How much will you have to pay for additional copies? How will your book be sold and distributed? (Don't count on seeing your volume in bookstores.)

Will you receive royalties? How much? Does the publisher offer any kind of promotional assistance or is it all up to you? Will those promotion efforts be realistic and results-oriented? (Sometimes "promotion" means sending out review copies, which is a waste—such volumes are rarely reviewed.) Don't wait until *after* you've signed a contract (and a check) to raise these issues. Do your homework first.

Obviously, poets who don't stay on their toes may find themselves preyed upon. And a questionable publishing opportunity doesn't have to be an out-and-out rip-off for you to feel cheated. In every situation, you have a choice *not* to participate. Exercise that choice, or at least develop a healthy sense of skepticism before you fling yourself and your poetry at the first smooth talker who compliments your work. Poets get burned because they're much too impatient to see their work in print. Calm your ego, slow down and devote that time, energy and money toward reading other poets and improving your own writing. You'll find that getting published will eventually take care of itself.

Magazines/ Journals

Literary magazines and journals usually provide a poet's first publishing success. In fact, you shouldn't be thinking about book/chapbook publication until your poems have appeared in a variety of magazines, journals and zines (both print and online). This is the preferred way to develop an audience, build publishing credits and learn the ins and outs of the publishing process.

In this section you'll find hundreds of magazines and journals that publish poetry. They range from small black-and-white booklets produced on home computers to major periodicals with high production values and important reputations. To help you sort through these markets and direct your submissions most effectively, we've organized information in each listing according to a basic format.

HOW LISTINGS ARE FORMATTED

Content of each market listing was provided or verified by a representative of the publication (editor, poetry editor, managing editor, etc.). Here is how that content is arranged within the listing:

Symbols. Icons at the beginning of each listing offer visual signposts to specific information about the publication: (**N**) this market is recently established and new to *Poet's Market*; (✖) this market did not appear in the 2010 edition; (■) this market publishes primarily online (although it may also produce an annual print version or a "best of" anthology); (✪) this market is located in Canada or (⊕) outside the U.S. and Canada; (**S**) this market pays a monetary amount (as opposed to contributor's copies); (□) this market welcomes submissions from beginning poets; (◪) this market prefers submissions from skilled, experienced poets, will consider work from beginning poets; (◖) this market prefers submissions from poets with a high degree of skill and experience; (◎) this market has a specialized focus (listed in parentheses after magazine/journal title); (◪) this market does not consider unsolicited submissions; and (◪) this market is closed to *all* submissions. (Keys to these symbols are listed on the inside covers of this book and on page 3.)

Contact information. Depending on what was provided by each editor, contact information includes: magazine/journal title (in bold) with areas of specialization noted in parentheses where appropriate; regular mail address; telephone number; fax number; e-mail address; website address; year the publication was established; the name of the person to contact (or an editorial title); and membership in small press/publishing organizations. (**Note:** If a magazine/journal publishes only online and/or wants submissions by e-mail exclusively, no street address may be given.)

Magazine Needs. It's important to study this section as you research potential markets. Here you'll find such helpful information as the editor's overview of the publication, with individual poetry needs and preferences; a list of recently published poets; production information (number of pages, printing/binding details, type of cover); the number of poetry submissions the publication receives vs. the number accepted; and press run, distribution and price information.

How to Contact. This section focuses on the specific details of submitting work: how many poems to send; minimum/maximum number of lines per poem; whether previously published poems or simultaneous submissions are considered; submission format preferences (including whether to submit by e-mail, and how); response times; payment; rights acquired and more.

Additional Information. Editors may use this section to explain other publishing activities, elaborate on some aspect of the magazine/journal, suggest future plans—anything beyond the basic details that readers may find of interest.

Contest/Award Offerings. This section discusses prizes and competitions associated with the publication, with either brief guidelines or a cross-reference to a separate listing in the Contests & Awards section.

Also Offers. Describes additional offerings associated with this publication (i.e., sponsored readings, website activities such as blogs and forums, related poetry groups, etc.).

Tips. Provides direct quotes from editors about everything from pet peeves to tips on writing to perspectives on the state of poetry today.

GETTING STARTED, FINDING MARKETS

If you don't have a certain magazine or journal in mind, read randomly through the listings, making notes as you go. (Don't hesitate to write in the margins, underline, use highlighters; it also helps to flag markets that interest you with Post-It Notes). Browsing the listings is an effective way to familiarize yourself with the kind of information presented and the publishing opportunities that are available at various skill levels.

If you have a specific market in mind, however, begin with the General Index. Here all the book's listings are alphabetized along with additional references that may be buried within a listing (such as a press name or competition title).

REFINE YOUR SEARCH

To supplement the General Index, we provide the following indexes to help you refine your marketing plan for submitting your poems to publications. Not every listing appears in one of these indexes, so use them only to reinforce your other research efforts:

Openness to Submissions Index categorizes markets according to the icons (▢ ◨ ◪ ◉) that appear at the beginning of each listing—signposts that indicate the level of writing an editor prefers to see. (For an explanation of these symbols, see page 3, the inside covers of this book or the handy tear-out bookmark just inside the front cover.)

Geographical Index sorts magazines and journals by state or by countries outside the U.S. Some markets are more open to poets from their respective regions, so this index is helpful when pinpointing local opportunities.

Subject Index groups markets according to areas of special focus. These include all specialized markets (appearing with the ◉ symbol) as well as broader categories such as online markets, poetry for children, markets that consider translations and others. When you want to submit a poem that features a certain topic or theme, is written in a specific form or style or addresses a unique audience, check this index first.

THE NEXT STEP

Once you know how to interpret the listings in this section and identify markets for your work, the next step is to start submitting your poems. See "Getting Started (and Using This Book)" on page 2 and "Frequently Asked Questions" on page 7 for advice, guidelines for preparing your manuscript and proper submissions procedures.

▣ ◪ 2RIVER VIEW

7474 Drexel Dr., University City MO 63130. E-mail: long@2River.org. Website: www.2River. org. **Contact:** Richard Long.

Magazines Needs *2River View*, published quarterly online, restricts each issue to ten poets. "We prefer poems with these qualities: image, subtlety, and point of view; a surface of worldly exactitude, as well as a depth of semantic ambiguity; and a voice that negotiates with its body of predecessors." Robert Creeley, R. Virgil Davis, Tony Colella, David Appelbaum, Michelle Askin, Rebecca Givens. Accepts 1-5% of unsolicited submissions.

How to Contact Submit up to 5 poems once per reading period. No previously published poems or simultaneous submissions. Accepts e-mail submissions pasted into the body of the e-mail; no fax or disk submissions. Reads submissions year round (see website for reading period for each issue). Time between acceptance and publication is 3 months. Guidelines on website.

⊕ ◪ 10TH MUSE

33 Hartington Rd., Southampton, Hants SO14 0EW, England. E-mail: a.jordan@surfree. co.uk. **Contact:** Andrew Jordan, editor.

Magazines Needs *10th Muse* "includes poetry and reviews, as well as short prose and graphics." Has published poetry by Richard Caddel, Stephen M. Dickey, Andrew Duncan, Carrie Etter, Becky Gould Gibson, and Bill Griffiths. *10th Muse* is 48-72 pages, A5, photocopied, saddle-stapled, with card cover. Press run is 200. Single copy: £3.50 (UK); subscription: £9 for 3 issues (UK). Make checks payable to *10th Muse*. "U.S. subscribers: Send $10 in bills for single copy (including postage)."

How to Contact Submit up to 6 poems at a time. No e-mail submissions. Include SASE (or SAE with IRCs). Responds in 3 months. Pays one contributor's copy. Staff reviews books of poetry. Send materials for review consideration.

Tips "Poets should read a copy of the magazine first."

▣ ◪ THE 13TH WARRIOR REVIEW

P.O. Box 5122, Seabrook NJ 08302-3511. E-mail: theeditor@asteriusonline.com. Website: www.asteriuspress.com. **Contact:** John C. Erianne, Editor.

Magazines Needs *The 13th Warrior Review*, published 2-2 times annually online, seeks "excellent literary-quality poetry as well as fiction, essays, and reviews. All excellent poetry will be given serious consideration." Has published poetry by P.Q. Perron, Cindy Rosmus, B.Z Niditch, Genine Hanns, John Sweet, and Corey Ginsberg.

How to Contact Submit no more than 5 poems at a time. Considers simultaneous submissions, but "not encouraged"; no previously published poems. Accepts e-mail submissions only, pasted as text into body of message—no attachments. "Use 'submission' as the subject header. Any submission that comes as a file attachment will be deleted without reply." Cover letter is preferred; "should be brief and to the point." Include SASE for postal submissions. Time between acceptance and publication is up to 6 months. Seldom comments on rejected poems. Guidelines available on website. No payment. Acquires first rights, first electronic rights, and non-exclusive anthology rights.

Tips "Write from love; don't expect love in return, don't take rejection personally, and don't let anyone stop you."

☑ ABBEY

5360 Fallriver Row Court, Columbia MD 21044. E-mail: greisman@aol.com. **Contact:** David Greisman, editor.

Magazines Needs *Abbey* is "a more-or-less informal zine looking for poetry that does for the mind what the first sip of Molson Ale does for the palate." Does not want "pornography or politics." Has published poetry by Richard Peabody, Ruth Moon Kempher, Carol Hamilton, Harry Calhoun, Kyle Laws, Joel Poudrier, Wayne Hogan, and Edmund Conti. *Abbey* is usually 20-26 pages, magazine-sized, photocopied, and held together with 1 low-alloy metal staple in the top left corner. Receives about 1,000 poems/year, accepts about 150. Press run is 200. Subscription: $2. Sample: 50¢.

How to Contact Responds in 1 month "except during baseball season." Pays 1-2 contributor's copies.

Additional Information Abbey Cheapochapbooks come out once or twice every 5 years, averaging 10-15 pages. For chapbook consideration, query with 4-6 sample poems, bio, and list of publications. Responds in 2 months "including baseball season." Pays 25-50 author's copies.

Tips "I'm definitely seeing poetry from 2 schools—the nit'n'grit school and the textured/reflective school. I much prefer the latter."

☑ ABLE MUSE

467 Saratoga Ave., #602, San Jose CA 95129-1326. (267)224-7478. Fax: (267)224-7478. Website: www.ablemuse.com. **Contact:** Alex Pepple, editor.

Magazines Needs *Able Muse: a review of metrical poetry,* published 2 times/year, "spotlights formal poetry via an online presentation, in the supportive environment of art, photography, essays, interviews, book reviews, fiction, and a literary forum. Also includes electronic books of poetry. *Able Muse* exclusively publishes formal poetry. We are looking for well-crafted poems of any length or subject that employ skillful and imaginative use of meter, or meter and rhyme, executed in contemporary idiom, that reads as naturally as your free-verse poems." Does not want "free-verse, greeting card verse, or poems in forms with no regard to meter (such as a free verse pantoum, sestina, etc.)." Considers poetry by teens. "High levels of craft still required even for teen writers." Has published poetry by Mark Jarman, A.E. Stallings, Annie Finch, Rhina P. Espaillat, Rachel Hadas, and R.S. Gwynn. Receives about 1,500 poems/year, accepts about 5%.

How to Contact Submit 1-5 poems at a time. No previously published poems or simultaneous submissions. Accepts fax, e-mail, and disk submissions. "E-mail is the preferred medium of submission, but we also welcome snail mail, or submit directly from the website with the automated online submission form." Cover letter preferred. Time between acceptance and publication is 6-12 weeks. Sometimes comments on rejected poems. Sometimes publishes theme issues. Guidelines available for SASE, by e-mail, or on website. Responds in 4 months. Sometimes sends prepublication galleys. Acquires first rights. Reviews books of poetry. Send materials for review consideration.

Also Offers "Able Muse will provide a print version, currently in the works, in the near future. We are also planning a CD anthology of the best poems, stories, articles from previous issues, along with an accompanying audio CD of the poets and writers reading their works." Contest/Award Offerings Sponsors the semiannual Tipsy Muse Poetry Contest "is a light verse competition" with prize offerings of $200. Check website at http://eratosphere.ablemuse.com for contest dates. Entry

Fee: $5/poem. Guidelines available for SASE, by e-mail, and on website.

Tips "Despite the rush to publish everything online, most of web-published poetry has been free verse. This is surprising given formal poetry's recent rise in popularity in the number of print journals that exclusively publish formal poetry. *Able Muse* attempts to fill this void bringing the best contemporary formalists online. Remember, content is just as important as form."

☒ ◪ ABRAMELIN, THE JOURNAL OF POETRY AND MAGICK

E-mail: nessaralindaran@aol.com. Website: www.abramelin.net. **Contact:** Vanessa Kittle, editor.

Magazines Needs *Abramelin, the Journal of Poetry and Magick*, published biannually online and a yearly best of edition each December, offers "literary poetry and essays concerning the western esoteric traditions." Wants "poetry that shows rather than tells. Poems that make me jealous of the writer. Poems that are inspired with wonderful language and imagery. In short—literature. Poetry submissions needn't be about magick at all. I feel that real poetry is magick. In fact, poetry that is literally magickal in theme has to be twice as good." Does not want "rhyming poems. Very short fiction. But beware, I learned from the best." Considers poetry by teens. Has published poetry by Simon Perchik, Rich Kostelanetz, and Lyn Lifshin. *Abramelin* receives about 1,000 poems/year, accepts about 5%. Distributed free online. Number of unique visitors: 3,000/issue.

How to Contact Submit 1-5 poems at a time. Lines/poem: no minimum/maximum. Considers previously published poems and simultaneous submissions (with notification). Accepts e-mail (pasted into body of message) and disk submissions. Cover letter is preferred. Reads submissions year round. Submit seasonal poems 2 months in advance. Time between acceptance and publication is 1-3 months. Often comments on rejected poems. Sometimes publishes theme issues. Upcoming themes available in magazine or on website. Guidelines available by e-mail or on website. Responds in 1 month. Pays 1 contributor's copy. Acquires one-time rights, with option to include in a yearly print anthology. Rights revert to poets upon publication.

Additional Information Publishes an annual print anthology—40 pages, digest-sized, professionally printed, perfect-bound, with glossy full color cover. Single copy: $9.50. Make checks payable to Vanessa Kittle.

Tips "Bring the reader into the moment. Be as specific as possible."

ABZ

P.O. Box 2746, Huntington WV 25727. E-mail: editorial@abzpress.com. Website: www. abzpress.com.

Magazines Needs *ABZ*, published annually, wants poetry using interesting and exciting language. Sample copies and subscriptions: $8.

How to Contact Submit 1 to 6 poems at a time. Reading period is September 1-December 1. Guidelines on website. "Contributors receive a small stipend and two copies of the magazine."

Additional Information Offers the ABZ First Book Poetry Prize for original poetry manuscripts between 48-80 pages.

A CAPPELLA ZOO

A cappella Zoo, 105 Harvard Ave. E. #A1, Seattle WA 98102. (208)705-5070. E-mail: editor@acappellazoo.com. Website: www.acappellazoo.com. **Contact:** Colin Meldrum, editor/publisher. "*A cappella Zoo* invites submissions of memorable prose, poetry, drama, and genre-bending works. We are especially excited about magical realism and works that experiment with technique, form, language, and thought."

Magazines Needs "*A cappella Zoo* invites submissions of memorable prose, poetry, drama, and genre-bending works. We are especially excited about magical realism and works that experiment with technique, form, language, and thought." Wants "avant-garde poetry."

How to Contact Submit up to 3 poems by e-mail. Time between acceptance and publication is 4 months. Accepts simultaneous submissions. Responds in 2 weeks on queries; 3 months on mss. Buys First North American serial rights.

◻ ACM (ANOTHER CHICAGO MAGAZINE)

Another Chicago Magazine, P.O. Box 408439, Chicago IL 60640. Website: www. anotherchicagomagazine.net. **Contact:** Michael Meinhardt, Poetry Editor. *ACM (Another Chicago Magazine)*, published semiannually in May and November, prints work "with emphasis on quality, experimental, politically aware prose, fiction, poetry, reviews, cross-genre work, and essays." Wants "traditional to experimental verse with an emphasis on message, especially poems with strong voices articulating social or political concerns." Does not want "religious verse." Has published poetry by Albert Goldbarth, Maureen Seaton, Sharon Darrow, Simon Perchik, Alice George, and R.T. Castleberry. *ACM* is 220 pages, digest-sized, offset-printed, includes ads. Press run is 2,000. Single copy: $12. $19.95/year.

How to Contact Submit 3-4 typed poems at a time, usually no more than 4 pages. Considers simultaneous submissions with notification; no previously published poems. Reads submissions year-round. Guidelines available on website; however, "The best way to know what we publish is to read what we publish. If you haven't read *ACM* before, order a sample copy to know if your work is appropriate." Responds in 3 months. Sends prepublication galleys. Pays monetary amount "if funds permit," and/or one contributor's copy and one-year subscription. Acquires first serial rights. Reviews books of poetry in 250-800 words. Send materials for review consideration.

Tips Sponsors the annual Chicago Literary Awards. Prize: $1,000 and publication in *ACM*. Entry fee: $12 for 3 poems (300 total lines), $5 for each additional poem (up to 100 lines). Deadline: December 15th. Guidelines available on website.

◻ ◎ THE ACORN

1530 Seventh St., Rock Island IL 61201. (309)788-3980. *The Acorn*, published quarterly, is a "publication for young authors, as well as teachers or anyone else interested in our young authors." Considers poetry and fiction from children and teens in grades K-12. "Young authors submitting to *The Acorn* should put either age or grade on manuscripts." Accepts well over half of submitted mss. Press run is 100. Subscription: $10. Sample: $3. Make all checks payable to *The Oak*.

How to Contact Submit up to 5 poems at a time. Lines/poem: 35 maximum. Considers previously published poems and simultaneous submissions. Include SASE with all submissions. Responds in 1 week. "*The Acorn* does not pay in dollars or copies, but you need not purchase to be published." Acquires first or second rights. All rights revert to poet upon publication. Sponsors numerous poetry contests. Guidelines available for SASE.

⊕ ☑ ACUMEN MAGAZINE

Ember Press, 6 The Mount, Higher Furzeham, Brixham, South Devon TQ5 8QY, England. E-mail: patricia@acumen-poetry.co.uk. **Contact:** Patricia Oxley, Poetry Editor. *Acumen*, published 3 times/year in January, May, and September, is "a general literary magazine with emphasis on good poetry." Wants "well-crafted, high-quality, imaginative poems showing a sense of form." Does not want "experimental verse of an obscene type." Has published poetry by Ruth Padel, William Oxley, Hugo Williams, Peter Porter, Danielle Hope, and Leah Fritz. *Acumen* is 120 pages, A5, perfect-bound. Receives about 12,000 poems, accepts about 120. Press run is 650. Subscription: $45 surface/$50 air. Sample: $15.

How to Contact Submit 5-6 poems at a time. Considers simultaneous submissions (if not submitted to UK magazines); no previously published poems. "If a reply is required, please send IRCs. One IRC for a decision, 3 IRCs if work is to be returned." Willing to reply by e-mail to save IRCs. Responds in 3 months. Pays "by negotiation" and 1 contributor's copy. Staff reviews books of poetry in up to 300 words (single-book format) or 600 words (multi-book format). Send materials for review consideration to Glyn Pursglove, 25 St. Albans Rd., Brynmill, Swansea, West Glamorgan SA2 0BP Wales.

Tips "Read *Acumen* carefully to see what kind of poetry we publish. Also, read widely in many poetry magazines, and don't forget the poets of the past—they can still teach us a great deal."

☐ ADVOCATE, PKA'S PUBLICATION

1881 Little West Kill Rd., Prattsville NY 12468. (518)299-3103.

Magazines Needs *Advocate, PKA's Publication*, published bimonthly, is an advertiser-supported tabloid using "original, previously unpublished works, such as feature stories, essays, 'think' pieces, letters to the editor, profiles, humor, fiction, poetry, puzzles, cartoons, or line drawings." Wants "nearly any kind of poetry, any length. Poetry ought to speak to people and not be so oblique as to have meaning only to the poet. If I had to be there to understand the poem, don't send it. Also looking for horse-related poems, stories, drawings, and photos." Does not want "religious or pornographic poetry." Considers poetry by children and teens (when included with release form signed by adult). Accepts about 25% of poems received. Circulation is 10,000; all distributed free. Subscription: $16.50 (6 issues). Sample: $5 (includes guidelines).

How to Contact Submit any number of poems at a time. Lines/poem: open. No previously published poems or simultaneous submissions. "Please, no work that has appeared on the Internet." Submissions may be typed or legibly handwritten. "Send a SASE with your submission; no postcards, please." Time between acceptance and publication is up to 6 months. Occasionally comments on rejected poems. Responds in 2 months. Guidelines available with sample copy ($5). Pays 2 contributor's copies. Acquires first rights only.

Tips "Always looking for horse/equine-oriented works."

☑ ◎ AFRICAN VOICES

270 W. 96th St., New York NY 10025. **Contact:** Layding Kaliba, poetry editor. *African Voices*, published quarterly, is an "art and literary magazine that highlights the work of people of color. We publish ethnic literature and poetry on any subject. We also consider all themes and styles: avant-garde, free verse, haiku, light verse, and traditional. We do not wish to limit the reader or author." Considers poetry written by children. Has published poetry by Reg E. Gaines, Maya Angelou, Jessica Care Moore, Asha Bandele, Tony Medina, and Louis Reyes Rivera. *African Voices* is about 48 pages, magazine-sized, professionally printed, saddle-stapled, with paper cover. Receives about 100 submissions/year, accepts about 30%. Press run is 20,000. Single copy: $4; subscription: $12. Sample: $5.

How to Contact Submit no more than 2 poems at any one time. Accepts previously published poems and simultaneous submissions. Accepts submissions by e-mail (in text box), by fax, and by postal mail. Cover letter and SASE required. Seldom comments on rejected poems. Guidelines available for SASE or on website. Responds in 3 months. Pays 2 copies. Acquires first or one-time rights. Reviews books of poetry in 500-1,000 words. Send materials for review consideration, attn. Layding Kaliba. Sponsors periodic poetry contests and readings. Send SASE for details.

Tips "We strongly encourage new writers/poets to send in their work. Accepted contributors are encouraged to subscribe."

AGNI

(617)353-7135. Fax: (617)353-7134. E-mail: agni@bu.edu. Website: www.agnimagazine. org. **Contact:** Sven Birkerts, editor. "Eclectic literary magazine publishing first-rate poems, essays, translations, and stories."

• Work published in AGNI has been included regularly in The Best American Poetry and The Pushcart Prize.

How to Contact Submit no more than 5 poems at a time. Considers simultaneous submissions; no previously published poems. No e-mail submissions. Cover letter is required ("brief, sincere")."No fancy fonts, gimmicks. Include SASE or e-mail address; no preformatted reply cards." Reads submissions September 1-May 31. Pays $20/page ($150 maximum), a1 year subscription, and for print publication: 2 contributor's copies and 4 gift copies. Acquires first serial rights.

▣ ☑ AGNIESZKA'S DOWRY (AGD)

A Small Garlic Press (ASGP), 5445 N. Sheridan Rd., #3003, Chicago IL 60640. E-mail: marek@enteract.com; ketzle@ketzle.net. Website: http://asgp.org. **Contact:** Marek Lugowski and Katrina Grace Craig, Co-Editors.

• Send submissions to both e-mail addresses simultaneously.

Magazines Needs *Agnieszka's Dowry (AgD)* is "a magazine published both in print and as a permanent Internet installation of poems and graphics, letters to Agnieszka. The print version consists of professionally crafted chapbooks. The online version comprises fast-loading pages employing an intuitive, if uncanny, navigation in an interesting space, all conducive to fast and comfortable reading. No restrictions on form or type. We use contextual and juxtapositional tie-ins with other material in making choices, so visiting the online AgD or reading a chapbook of an AgD issue is required of anyone making a submission." Single copy: $3 plus $5 shipping, if ordered from website by an individual. Make checks payable to A Small Garlic Press.

How to Contact Submit 5-10 poems at a time. Accepts e-mail submissions only (NOTE: pasted into body of message in plain text, sent to both editors simultaneously; no attachments). "Prisoners may make submissions by regular mail, and we will waive the requirement that they read a print issue." Sometimes comments on rejected poems. Guidelines and annotated catalog available on website only. Responds by e-mail or SASE, usually within 2 months. Pays 1 contributor's copy. Acquires one-time rights where applicable.

Additional Information A Small Garlic Press (ASGP) publishes up to 3 chapbooks of poetry/year. Query with a full online ms, ASCII (plain text) only.

◯ THE AGUILAR EXPRESSION

1329 Gilmore Ave., Donora PA 15033. (724)379-8019. E-mail: xyz0@access995.com. Website: www.wordrunner.com/xfaguilar. **Contact:** Xavier F. Aguilar, editor/publisher.

Magazines Needs *The Aguilar Expression*, published annually in October, encourages "poetics that deal with now, which our readers can relate to. In publishing poetry, I try to exhibit the unique reality that we too often take for granted and acquaint as mediocre." Has published poetry by Martin Kich and Gail Ghai. *The Aguilar Expression* is 4-20 pages, 5x7, typeset, printed on 20 lb. paper. Receives about 10-15 poems/month, accepts about 10-15/year. Circulation is 200. Sample: $8. Make checks payable to Xavier Aguilar.

How to Contact Submit up to 3 poems at a time. Lines/poem: 30 maximum. No e-mail submissions. Cover letter is required (include writing background). SASE (for contact purposes) is required. Manuscripts should be submitted in clear, camera-ready copy. Submit copies, not originals; mss will not be returned. "We encourage all writers to send a SASE for writer's guidelines before submitting." Responds in 2 months. Pays 2 contributor's copies.

◙ ALASKA QUARTERLY REVIEW

University of Alaska Anchorage, 3211 Providence Dr., Anchorage AK 99508. (907)786-6916. Fax: (907)786-6916. E-mail: ayaqr@uaa.alaska.edu. Website: www.uaa.alaska.edu/aqr. **Contact:** Ronald Spatz, Executive Editor.

• Poetry published in *Alaska Quarterly Review* has been selected for inclusion in *The Best American Poetry*, *The Pushcart Prize*, and *Beacon's Best* anthologies.

Magazines Needs *Alaska Quarterly Review*, published in 2 double issues/year, is "devoted to contemporary literary art. We publish both traditional and experimental fiction, poetry, literary nonfiction, and short plays." Wants all styles and forms of poetry, "with the most emphasis perhaps on voice and content that displays 'risk,' or intriguing ideas or situations." Has published poetry by Maxine Kumin, Jane Hirshfield, David Lehman, Pattiann Rogers, Albert Goldbarth, and Billy Collins. *Alaska Quarterly Review* is 224-300 pages, digest-sized, professionally printed, perfect-bound, with card cover with color or b&w photo. Receives up to 5,000 submissions/year, accepts 40-90. Press run is 2,800. Subscription: $18. Sample: $6.

How to Contact No fax or e-mail submissions. Reads submissions mid-August to mid-May; manuscripts are *not* read May 15-August 15. Responds in up to 5 months, "sometimes longer during peak periods in late winter." Pay depends on funding. Acquires first North American serial rights.

Additional Information Guest poetry editors have included Stuart Dybek, Jane Hirshfield, Stuart Dischell, Maxine Kumin, Pattiann Rogers, Dorianne Laux, Peggy Shumaker, Olena Kalytiak Davis, Nancy Eimers, Michael Ryan, and Billy Collins.

☑ ◎ ALBATROSS

The Anabiosis Press, 2 South New St., Bradford MA 01835. (978)469-7085. E-mail: rsmyth@anabiosispress.org. Website: www.anabiosispress.org. **Contact:** Richard Smyth, editor.

Magazines Needs *Albatross*, published "as soon as we have accepted enough quality poems to publish an issue—about 1 per year," considers the albatross "to be a metaphor for the environment. The journal's title is drawn from Coleridge's *The Rime of the Ancient Mariner* and is intended to invoke the allegorical implications of that poem. This is not to say that we publish only environmental or nature poetry, but that we are biased toward such subject matter. We publish mostly free verse, and we prefer a narrative style." Wants "poetry written in a strong, mature voice that conveys a deeply felt experience or makes a powerful statement." Does not want "rhyming poetry, prose poetry, or haiku." Has published poetry by Paul Brooke, Joan Colby, Tom Sexton, Linda King, and Fredrick Zydek. *Albatross* is 28 pages, digest-sized, laser-typeset, with linen cover. Subscription: $8 for 2 issues. Sample: $5.

How to Contact Submit 3-5 poems at a time. Lines/poem: 200 maximum. No simultaneous submissions. Accepts e-mail submissions if included in body of message (but is "often quicker at returning mailed submissions"). Name and address must accompany e-mail submissions. Cover letter is not required. "We do, however, need bio notes and SASE for return or response. Poems should be typed single-spaced, with name, address, and phone number in upper left corner." Time between acceptance and publication is up to 6 months to a year. Guidelines available for SASE or on website. Responds in 1-2 months. Pays 1 contributor's copy. Acquires all rights. Returns rights provided that "previous publication in *Albatross* is mentioned in all subsequent reprintings."

Contest/Award Offerings The Anabiosis Press Chapbook Contest.

Tips "We expect a poet to read as much contemporary poetry as possible. We want to be moved. When you read our poetry, we hope that it moves you in the same way that it moves us. We try to publish the kind of poetry that you would want to read again and again."

☑ ◎ ALIMENTUM, THE LITERATURE OF FOOD

P.O. Box 210028, Nashville TN 37221, Nashville TN 37221. E-mail: info@alimentumjournal. com; submissions@alimentumjournal.com. Website: www.alimentumjournal.com. **Contact:** Cortney Davis, Poetry Editor. (Specialized: poems about/referencing food; menupoems; recipe poems)

Magazines Needs *Alimentum, The Literature of Food*, published semiannually in winter and summer, is "the only literary journal all about food." Wants "fiction, creative nonfiction, and poetry all around the subject of food." Has published poetry by Dick Allen, Stephen Gibson, Carly Sachs, Jen Karetnik, Virginia Chase Sutton. *Alimentum* is 128 pages, 6x7½, perfect-bound, with matte coated cover with 4-color art, interior b&w illustration includes ads. Receives about 2,000 poems/year, accepts about 30-40. Press run is 2,000. Single copy:

$10 ($18 Canada/foreign); subscription: $18 for 1 year ($30 Canada/foreign). Make checks payable to *Alimentum* (payment available online through credit card or PayPal).

How to Contact Submit no more than 5 poems at a time. Lines/poem: no minimum or maximum. Considers simultaneous submissions; no previously published poems. No e-mail submissions; postal submissions only. Include SASE. Check website for reading periods which vary from year to year. Guidelines available on website. Responds 1-3 months. Pays contributor's copy. Acquires First North American Serial rights. Rights revert to poets upon publication.

Also Offers Publishes an annual broadside of "menupoems" for restaurants during National Poetry Month in April.

Tips "While food is our subject, we like poems to be about more than just the food. As in the stories we publish, the poems should also carry a personal element, even a story, not just a list of ingredients. Some special poem categories that we look for are menupoems and recipe poems."

$ ☑ ◎ ALIVE NOW

1908 Grand Ave., P.O. Box 340004, Nashville TN 37203-0004. E-mail: alivenow@ upperroom.org. **Contact:** Melissa Tidwell, editor.

Magazines Needs *Alive Now*, published bimonthly, is a devotional magazine that invites readers to enter an ever-deepening relationship with God. "*Alive Now* seeks to nourish people who are hungry for a sacred way of living. Submissions should invite readers to see God in the midst of daily life by exploring how contemporary issues impact their faith lives. Each word must be vivid and dynamic and contribute to the whole. We make selections based on a list of upcoming themes. Manuscripts which do not fit a theme will be returned." Considers avant-garde and free verse. *Alive Now* is 64 pages. Accepts 20 poems/ year. Circulation is 70,000. Subscription: $17.95/year (6 issues); $26.95 for 2 years (12 issues). Additional subscription information, including foreign rates, available on website.

How to Contact Submit up to 5 poems/theme at a time. Lines/poem: 10 minimum, 45 maximum. Accepts e-mail submissions (pasted into body of message). "Send up to 5 poems per theme in single e-mail, single-spaced, plain text. Put theme in subject line." Postal submissions should be typed, double-spaced, on 8½ × 11 paper; include SASE. "If you're submitting material for more than one theme, send a SASE for each theme represented. On each page you submit, include your name, address, and the theme for which the piece is being sent." Always publishes theme issues; all poems must relate to themes. Upcoming themes and guidelines available for SASE or on website. "We will notify contributors of manuscript status when we make final decisions for a theme, 3 months before the issue date. We place manuscripts on hold for specific issues; authors are free to request their manuscripts be returned to them at any time." Pays $40 or more on acceptance. Purchases newspaper, periodical, and electronic rights; may purchase one-time use.

Tips "*Alive Now* is ecumenical, including both lay persons and church professionals. Our readers are primarily adults, from young adults to older adults, and include persons of many cultures and ethnic backgrounds."

⊕ $ ☑ AMBIT

17 Priory Gardens, Highgate, London N6 5QY, England. E-mail: info@ambitmagazine. co.uk. Website: www.ambitmagazine.co.uk. **Contact:** Martin Bax, Carol Ann Duffy, and Henry Graham, Poetry Editors. *Ambit*, published quarterly, is a 96-page quarterly of

avant-garde, contemporary, and experimental work. *Ambit* is perfect-bound, with 2-color cover with artwork. Accepts about 3% of submissions received. Subscription: £28 UK, £30/ 44 rest of Europe, £32/$64 everywhere else. Sample: £7 UK, £9/ 15 rest of Europe, £10/$20 overseas.

How to Contact Submit up to 6 poems at a time. No previously published poems or simultaneous submissions. No e-mail submissions. "SAE vital for reply;" include IRCs when submitting from outside of UK. Poems should be typed, double-spaced. Never comments on rejected poems. Guidelines available in magazine or on website. Responds in 3-4 months. Pays small token plus 2 contributor's copies. Staff reviews books of poetry. Send materials for review consideration to review editor.

Tips "Read a copy of the magazine before submitting!"

☑ THE AMERICAN DISSIDENT: A JOURNAL OF LITERATURE, DEMOCRACY & DISSIDENCE

1837 Main St., Concord MA 01742. E-mail: todslone@yahoo.com. Website: www. TheAmericanDissident.org. **Contact:** G. Tod Slone, editor.

Magazines Needs *The American Dissident*, published 2 times/year, provides "a forum for, amongst other things, criticism of the academic/literary established order, which clearly discourages vigorous debate, cornerstone of democracy, to the evident detriment of American Literature. The Journal seeks rare poets daring to risk going against that established-order grain." Wants "poetry, reviews, artwork, and short (1,000 words) essays in English, French, or Spanish, written on the edge with a dash of personal risk and stemming from personal experience, conflict with power, and/or involvement." Submissions should be "iconoclastic and parrhesiastic in nature." *The American Dissident* is 56-64 pages, digest-sized, offset-printed, perfect-bound, with card cover. Press run is 200. Single copy: $9; subscriptions: individuals, $18; institutions $20.

How to Contact Submit 3 poems at a time. Considers simultaneous submissions; no previously published poems. E-mail submissions from subscribers only. "Far too many poets submit without even reading the guidelines. Include SASE and cover letter containing not credits, but rather personal dissident information, as well as incidents that provoked you to 'go upright and vital, and speak the rude truth in all ways' (Emerson)." Time between acceptance and publication is up to 2 months. Almost always comments on rejected poems. Guidelines available for SASE. Responds in 1 month. Pays 1 contributor's copy. Acquires first North American serial rights. Reviews books/chapbooks of poetry and other magazines in 250 words, single-book format. Send materials for review consideration.

Tips "For the sake of democracy, poetry needs to be much more than safe, comfortable, diversionary intellectual entertainment, and poets much more than public court jesters. If only poets endeavored to be more than mass-producing versifyers and established-order professors of creative writing. If only they questioned and challenged as individuals, rather than always trying to fit in and exude collegiality. If only they heeded Villon ('Estoit-il lors temps de moy taire'), Wole Soyinka ('Criticism, like charity, starts at home'), Sinclair Lewis ('Every Compulsion is put upon writers to become safe, polite, obedient, and sterile'), and Orwell ('I write because there is some lie I want to expose')."

☑ AMERICAN LITERARY REVIEW

Dept. of English, University of North Texas, 1155 Union Circle #311307, Denton TX 76203-1307. (940)565-2755. E-mail: bond@unt.edu. Website: www.engl.unt.edu/alr. **Contact:** Bruce Bond and Corey Marks, poetry editors.

Magazines Needs *American Literary Review*, published semiannually, considers all forms and modes of poetry, nonfiction, and fiction. "We are especially interested in originality, substance, imaginative power, and lyric intensity." Has published poetry by Kathleen Pierce, Mark Irwin, Stephen Dunn, William Olsen, David St. John, and Cate Marvin. *American Literary Review* is about 120 pages, digest-sized, attractively printed, perfect-bound, with color card cover with photo. Subscription: $14/year, $22 for 2 years. Sample: $7.

How to Contact Submit up to 5 typewritten poems at a time. Considers simultaneous submissions. No fax or e-mail submissions. Cover letter is required. Include author's name, address, phone number, and poem titles. Reads mss October 1-May 1. Guidelines available on website. Responds in up to 3 months. Pays 2 contributor's copies.

Contest/Award Offerings Check website for details.

☑ THE AMERICAN POETRY JOURNAL

P.O. Box 2080, Aptos CA 95001-2080. E-mail: apjsubmissions@yahoo.com. Website: www.americanpoetryjournal.com. *The American Poetry Journal*, published annually (July), seeks "to publish work using poetic device, favoring image, metaphor, and good sound. We like alliteration, extended metaphors, image, movement, and poems that can pass the 'so what' test. *The American Poetry Journal* has in mind the reader who delights in discovering what a poem can do to the tongue and what the poem paints on the cave of the mind." Wants poems "that exhibit strong, fresh imagery, metaphor, and good sound." Does not want "narratives about family, simplistic verse, annoying word hodge-podges." Has published poetry by C.J. Sage, Natasha Sage, Lola Haskins, Dorianne Laux, and Jennifer Juneau. *The American Poetry Journal* is 100 pages, 6X9, perfect-bound. Accepts about 1% of poems submitted. Single copy: $12; subscription: $12. Make checks payable to J.P. Dancing Bear.

How to Contact Submit 3-5 poems at a time. Considers simultaneous submissions; no previously published poems. E-mail submissions only. Cover letter is preferred. Considers unsolicited submissions October 1- April 30 (poets may submit no more than twice during the reading period). "We consider submissions from subscribers year round." Time between acceptance and publication is 8 months. "Poems are read first for clarity and technique, then read aloud for sound quality." Seldom comments on rejected poems. Guidelines available on website. Responds in 3 months. Pays one contributor's copy. Acquires first rights.Offers The American Poet Prize and *The American Poetry Journal* Book Prize (see separate listings in Contests & Awards).

Tips "Know the magazine you are submitting to, before you commit your work and yourself. It's not that difficult, but it helps your odds when the editor can tell that you get what the magazine is about. Reading an issue is the easiest way to do this."

$ ☑ ◎ ANCIENT PATHS

P.O. Box 7505, Fairfax Station VA 22039. **Contact:** Skylar H. Burris, Editor. *Ancient Paths*, published biennially in odd-numbered years, provides "a forum for quality Christian poetry." Wants "traditional rhymed/metrical forms and free verse; subtle Christian themes. I seek poetry that makes the reader both think and feel." Does not want 'preachy' poetry, inconsistent meter, or forced rhyme; no stream of conscious or avant-garde work; no esoteric academic poetry. Has published poetry by Giovanni Malito, Ida Fasel, Diane Glancy, Walt McDonald, and Donna Farley. *Ancient Paths* is 80 + pages, digest-sized, photocopied, perfect-bound, with cardstock cover. Issue 17 will feature the work of two poets. Receives about 600 queries/year, accepts two poets. Press run to be determined. Single copy: $12. Make checks payable to Skylar Burris.

☑ ◎ ANGEL FACE

(Specialized: poems arranged according to Mysteries of the Rosary) c/o MaryAnka Press, P.O. Box 102, Huffman TX 77336. Website: www.maryanka.com. Established 2004. **Contact:** Mary Agnes Dalrymple, editor.

Magazines Needs *Angel Face*, published annually in the spring, prints poems "arranged according to the pattern of the Rosary (according to the Rosary Mysteries), but submitting poets need not be Catholic or Christian. I am open to many different viewpoints and have published poetry by Jewish and other non-Christian poets, as well as Catholic and Protestant poets. My goal is to bring the Rosary 'into life.'" Wants "poetry written from the life of the poet, but I am also open to poems written from the Biblical and traditional source material of the Rosary Mysteries. Some themes of the Rosary are birth, rebirth, joy, light, sorrow, abandonment, death, epiphany, redemption, resurrection, hope, transformation, forgiveness, the seasons of nature, the cycle of life, and the search for God in everyday life. Additional Rosary information can be found through the links page of my website." Does not want "rhyming or didactic poems. Also nothing negative or derogatory." *Angel Face* is 50 pages, digest-sized, desktop-published, hand-bound by the editor with waxed Irish linen thread, with cardstock cover with color artwork. Receives about 300 submissions/year, accepts about 40 poems. Press run is 100. Single copy: $7; subscription: $14 for 2 copies. Make checks payable to Mary Agnes Dalrymple.

How to Contact Submit up to 5 poems at a time. Lines/poem: about 60 maximum. Considers previously published poems and simultaneous submissions. Accepts submissions by postal mail only. "For information on why I do not accept e-mailed submissions, go to guidelines page of website and click on the Editor's Notes." Cover letter is preferred. Reads submissions year round. Time between acceptance and publication is 4 months to one year. Sometimes comments on rejected poems. "If I see something I like but think it still needs work, I will comment." Guidelines available for SASE or on website. Responds in about 3 months ("longer when I am putting an issue together"). Pays one contributor's copy. Acquires one-time rights. Rights revert to poet upon publication. **Currently not accepting admissions. On Hiatus**.

Tips "Write it, and then rewrite it. Consider each poem to be a child. No responsible person would send a child out half-naked on an empty stomach with no way to get back home. Poetry shouldn't be sent out that way, either. Provide the right size SASE with proper postage. Most of the poems published in *Angel Face* were not written with the Rosary in mind. Send your best poems, even if you are not sure they will fit the Rosary prayer pattern."

✿ ☑ THE ANTIGONISH REVIEW

P.O. Box 5000, Antigonish NS B2G 2W5, Canada. (902)867-3962. Fax: (902)867-5563. E-mail: TAR@stfx.ca. Website: www.antigonishreview.com. **Contact:** Jeanette Lynes, co-editor.

Magazines Needs *The Antigonish Review*, published quarterly, tries "to produce the kind of literary and visual mosaic that the modern sensibility requires or would respond to. Subject matter can be anything; the style is traditional, modern, or post-modern limited by typographic resources. Purpose is not an issue." Does not want "erotica, scatalogical verse, excessive propaganda toward a certain subject." Has published poetry by Andy Wainwright, W.J. Keith, Michael Hulse, Jean McNeil, M. Travis Lane, and Douglas Lochhead. *The Antigonish Review* is 144 pages, digest-sized, offset-printed, flat-spined, with glossy card cover with art. Receives 2,500 submissions/year, accepts about 10%. Press run is 1,000. Subscription: $24 CAD, $30 US, International $40. Sample: $7 CAD.

How to Contact Submit 5-10 poems at a time. Lines/poem: "not over 80, i.e., 2 pages." No previously published poems or simultaneous submissions. Accepts fax submissions; e-mail submissions accepted from overseas only. Include SASE (SAE and IRCs if outside Canada; "we cannot use U.S. postage") or we can respond by e-mail. Time between acceptance and publication is up to 8 months. Sometimes comments on rejected poems. Guidelines available for SASE, by e-mail, or on website. Responds in up to 6 months. Pays $30 CAD per page and 2 contributor's copies. Acquires first North American serial rights.

$ ☑ THE ANTIOCH REVIEW

P.O. Box 148, Yellow Springs OH 45387. (937)769-1365. E-mail: mkeyes@antioch.edu. Website: www.antiochreview.org. **Contact:** Judith Hall, Poetry Editor.

• Work published in *The Antioch Review* has been included frequently in *The Best American Poetry, The Best New Poets,* and *The Pushcart Prize.*

Magazines Needs *The Antioch Review* "is an independent quarterly of critical and creative thought. For well over 50 years, creative authors, poets, and thinkers have found a friendly reception—regardless of formal reputation. We get far more poetry than we can possibly accept, and the competition is keen. Here, where form and content are so inseparable and reaction is so personal, it is difficult to state requirements or limitations. Studying recent issues of *The Antioch Review* should be helpful." Does not want "'light' or inspirational verse." Has published poetry by Peter Marcus, Jacqueline Osherow, Joanna Rawson, David Yezzi, and others. Receives about 3,000 submissions/year. Circulation is 3,000; 70% distributed through bookstores and newsstands. Subscription: $40. Sample: $7.

How to Contact Submit 3-6 poems at a time. No previously published poems or simultaneous submissions. Include SASE with all submissions. Reads submissions September 1-May 1 only. Guidelines available on website. Responds in 8-10 weeks. Pays $15/published page plus 2 contributor's copies; additional copies available at 40% discount.

▣ $ ▢ ◎ AOIFE'S KISS

P.O. Box 782, Cedar Rapids IA 52406-0782. E-mail: aoifeskiss@yahoo.com. Website: www.samsdotpublishing.com. **Contact:** Tyree Campbell, managing editor. (Specialized: fantasy; science fiction) Member: The Speculative Literature Foundation (http://SpeculativeLiterature.org).

Magazines Needs *Aoife's Kiss*, published quarterly, prints "fantasy, science fiction, sword and sorcery, alternate history, horror short stories, poems, illustrations, and movie and book reviews." Wants "fantasy, science fiction, spooky horror, and speculative poetry with minimal angst." Does not want "horror with excessive blood and gore." Considers poetry by children and teens. Has published poetry by Bruce Boston, Karen A. Romanko, Mike Allen, Corrine De Winter, Julie Shiel, and Marge B. Simon. *Aoife's Kiss* (print version) is 54 pages, magazine-sized, offset-printed, saddle-stapled, perfect-bound, with color paper cover, includes ads. Receives about 300 poems/year, accepts about 50 (17%). Press run is 150; 5 distributed free to reviewers. Single copy: $7; subscription: $22/year, $40 for 2 years. Make checks payable to Tyree Campbell/Sam's Dot Publishing.

How to Contact Submit up to 5 poems at a time. Lines/poem: prefers less than 100. Considers previously published poems; no simultaneous submissions. Accepts e-mail submissions (pasted into body of message); no disk submissions. "Submission should include snail mail address and a short (1-2 lines) bio." Reads submissions year round. Submit seasonal poems 6 months in advance. Time between acceptance and publication is 2-5 months. Often comments on rejected poems. Guidelines available on website. Responds in 4-6 weeks. Pays $5/poem, $3/reprint, $1 for scifaiku and related forms, and 1 contributor's copy. Acquires first North American serial rights. Reviews books/chapbooks of poetry. Send materials for review consideration to Tyree Campbell.

Tips "It's up to the writer to take the first step and submit work. Some of our best poems have come from poets who weren't sure if they were good enough. Horror poetry is a difficult sell with us."

☑ APALACHEE REVIEW

Apalachee Press, P.O. Box 10469, Tallahassee FL 32302. E-mail: ARsubmissions@hotmail.com. Website: www.apalacheereview.org. **Contact:** Dominika Wrozynski, poetry editor. Member: CLMP, AAP.

Magazines Needs *Apalachee Review*, published about twice/year, appears "as soon as we have enough good material." Has published poetry by Rita Mae Reese and Charles Harper Webb. *Apalachee Review* is 120 pages, digest-sized, professionally printed, perfect-bound, with card cover. Press run is 700. Subscription: $15 for 2 issues ($30 foreign). Sample: $5.

How to Contact Submit 3-5 poems at a time. Considers simulaneous submissions. Accepts submissions by postal mail only. "Submit clear copies, with name and address on each." SASE required. Reads submissions year round. Sometimes comments on rejected poems. Guidelines available for SASE or on website. Responds in 4 months, "but sometimes we get bogged down." Pays 2 contributor's copies. Poet retains rights. Staff reviews books of poetry. Send materials for review consideration.

Ⓝ ☑ APPARATUS MAGAZINE

E-mail: submissions@apparatusmagazine.com. Website: www.apparatusmagazine.com. **Contact:** Adam W. Hart, publisher/editor. "*Apparatus Magazine* strives to bring readers poetry and fiction from around the world that explores the mythos of 'man (or woman) vs. machine,' that conjures up words from the inner machine, and more. Each issue features work from around the world, bringing the reader literary updates from the *internal machine.*"

- "*apparatus magazine*, published monthly, strives to bring readers poetry and fiction from around the world that explores the mythos of "man (or woman) vs. machine," that conjures up words from the inner machine, and more. Each issue of *apparatus magazine* features work from around the world, bringing the reader literary updates from the internal machine."

Magazines Needs Wants "shorter poetry, free verse. Attention given to poems with a strong, natural voice. apparatus magazine accepts poetry on general themes, but does feature monthly thematic issues." Does not want overtly inspirational poetry, poetry aimed at children, or confessional poetry. Avoid "work that is overtly racist, sexist, violent, homophobic, discriminatory, pornographic, or otherwise in questionable taste. Has published poetry by Rayne Arroyo, Anne Brooke, Lesley Dame, Gregg Shapiro, Inara Cedrins, and Chanming Yuan."

How to Contact Submit 3-5 poems at a time, 2 pages maximum/poem. Accepts submissions by e-mail pasted into body of e-mail message. Cover letter is required. "Please include list of submitted poems, as well as a (maximum) 3-line bio listing other publications/journals in which poet has published his/her work." Reads submissions year round. Submit seasonal poems 2-3 months in advance. Time between acceptance and publication is 1-3 months. Often comments on rejected poems. Regularly publishes theme issues. Upcoming themes available in magazine, by e-mail, and on website. Guidelines available in magazine, by e-mail, and on website. Acquires first North American serial rights, electronic rights, option with poet's permission to reprint accepted work in yearly anthology. Rights revert to poet upon publication.

Contest/Award Offerings The apparatus award is offered annually for best poem published in *apparatus magazine* during the publication year (June to May). Award: $100. Guidelines available in magazine, on website, by e-mail.

Tips "Be sure to read the guidelines as posted for *apparatus magazine*. Themes for each issue are typically posted three months (or more) in advance. Include cover letter and bio with e-mail submissions. Submit more than just one poem, so I can get a feel for your work. Also, be sure to read back issues of the magazine. The journal tends to select work that focuses on specific themes, and usually tries to pick work that will complement/ contrast with other pieces selected for the issue. Send your best work, and don't be afraid of trying again. I often suggest other publications/markets if a piece is not a good match for the journal."

⊠ ▣ ◨ APPLE VALLEY REVIEW: A JOURNAL OF CONTEMPORARY LITERATURE

E-mail: editor@leahbrowning.net. Website: www.applevalleyreview.com. **Contact:** Leah Browning, editor. Member: Council of Literary Magazines and Presses (CLMP).

Magazines Needs *Apple Valley Review: A Journal of Contemporary Literature*, published semiannually online, features "beautifully crafted poetry, short fiction, and essays." Wants "work that has both mainstream and literary appeal. All work must be original, previously unpublished, and in English. Translations are welcome if permission has been granted. Preference is given to short (under 2 pages), non-rhyming poetry." Does not want "erotica, work containing explicit language or violence, or work that is scholarly, critical, inspirational, or intended for children." Considers poetry by children and teens; "all work is considered regardless of the author's age." Has published poetry by Vince Corvaia, Michael Lauchlan, Jin Cordaro, Gregory Lawless, Anna Evans, and Keetje Kuipers. Receives about 5,000 + poems/year, accepts less than 1%.

How to Contact Submit 2-6 poems at a time. Lines/poem: "no limit, though we prefer short poems (under 2 pages). No previously published poems or simultaneous submissions. Accepts e-mail submissions (pasted into body of message, with "poetry" in subject line); no disk submissions. Cover letter is preferred. "Include name, address, phone number, e-mail address, and a short biography." Reads submissions year round. Submit seasonal poems 6 months in advance, "though our interest in seasonal poems is very limited." Time between acceptance and publication is 1-2 months. Sometimes comments on rejected poems. Guidelines available by e-mail or on website. Responds in 1 week to 3 months. Sometimes sends prepublication galleys. "This is not a paying market. However, all work published in the *Apple Valley Review* during a given calendar year will be considered for the annual *Apple Valley Review* Editor's Prize." Acquires first rights and first serial rights and retains the right to archive the work online for an indefinite period of time. "As appropriate, we may also choose to nominate published work for awards or recognition. Author retains all other rights."

Contest/Award Offerings Offers the annual *Apple Valley Review* Editor's Prize. Award varies. "From 2006-2009, the prize was $100 and a book of poetry or fiction." Submit 2-6 poems. **Entry fee:** none. **Deadline:** rolling; all submissions to the *Apple Valley Review*, and all work published during a given calendar year will be considered for the prize.

Tips "Try to read as much as possible, and submit to markets that are publishing work that you enjoy. They are more likely to be a good fit."

⧈ A PUBLIC SPACE

323 Dean St., Brooklyn NY 11217. (718)858-8067. Fax: (718)858-8069. E-mail: general@ apublicspace.org. Website: www.apublicspace.org. **Contact:** Brigid Hughes, editor.

Magazines Needs *A Public Space*, published quarterly, "is an independent magazine of literature and culture. In an era that has relegated literature to the margins, we plan to make fiction and poetry the stars of a new conversation. We believe that stories are how we make sense of our lives and how we learn about other lives. We believe that stories matter." Single copy: $15; subscription: $36/year or $60/2 years.

How to Contact Submit up to 4 poems at a time. Considers simultaneous submissions; no previously published poems. Prefers submissions through online process; accepts mail. Include SASE. See website for submission dates and guidelines.

⧉ $ ⧇ ARC POETRY MAGAZINE

P.O. Box 81060, Ottawa ON K1P 1B1, Canada. E-mail: editor@arcpoetry.ca. Website: www.arcpoetry.ca. **Contact:** Pauline Conley, managing editor.

Magazines Needs *Arc Poetry Magazine*, published semiannually, prints poetry, poetry-related articles, interviews, and book reviews. "Tastes are eclectic. International submissions are welcome and encouraged." Has published poetry by Don Coles, Karen Solie, Carmine Starnino, David O'Meara, Elizabeth Bachinsky, George Elliott Clarke, Daryl Hine, Michael Ondaatje, Stephanie Bolster, and Don Domanski. *Arc Poetry Magazine* is 130-160 pages, perfect-bound, printed on matte white stock "with a crisp, engaging design and a striking

Magazines/Journals

visual art portfolio in each issue." Receives about 1,000 submissions/year, accepts about 40-50 poems. Press run is 1,500. Single copy: $12.50 CAD, $18 CAD (U.S.), $20 CAD (overseas); subscription: 2 issues/1 year—$17.95 CAD (in Canada); 4 issues/2 years—$34.95 CAD (in Canada), $42.95 USD, $45.95 USD (overseas). Online ordering available for subscriptions and single copies (with occasional promotions).

How to Contact Submit 4-8 poems at a time. No previously published poems or simultaneous submissions. No e-mail submissions. Cover letter is required. Submissions should be single-spaced, with name and address on each page. Guidelines available for SAE and IRC or on website. Responds in 4-6 months. Pays $40 CAD/page plus 2 contributor's copies. Acquires first Canadian serial rights.

Contest/Award Offerings The Confederation Poets Prize is an annual award of $250 for the best poem published in *Arc* that year. *Arc* also sponsors an international Poem of the Year Contest: 1st Prize: $1,500 CAD; 2nd Prize: $1,000 CAD; 3rd Prize: $750 CAD. Guidelines available on website. **Entry fee:** $23 CAD for 4 poems. **Deadline:** February 1. Other awards include the Lampman-Scott Award for Poetry, Critic's Desk Award, and the Diana Brebner Prize for Poetry.

ARDENT!

Poetry in the Arts, Inc., 1909 Hollow Ridge Dr, Cedar Park TX 78613. E-mail: rimer777@gmail.com. Website: www.ardent.poetryinarts.org. **Contact:** Dillon McKinsey, editor.

Magazines Needs *Ardent!*, published semiannually, is a journal of poetry and art. All forms and styles are considered. *Ardent!* is perfect-bound.

How to Contact Accepts e-mail submissions, "but must adhere to the guidelines. See the *Ardent!* website for details." Submission by postal mail should be sent c/o *Ardent!* editors to the address listed above. Pays contributor's copies.

◪ ARIES: A JOURNAL OF CREATIVE EXPRESSION

1201 Wesleyan St., Fort Worth TX 76105-1536. (817)531-4907. Fax: (817)531-6503. E-mail: sneeley@txwes.edu. **Contact:** Stacia Dunn Neeley, General Editor.

Magazines Needs *Aries: A Journal of Creative Expression*, published annually in fall, prints quality poetry, b&w photography/art, fiction, creative nonfiction, essays, and short plays. Poetry 3 to 50 lines. Original poetry in languages other than English welcome if submitted with English translation as companion. Has published poetry by Virgil Suárez, Richard Robbins, Susan Smith Nash, Gerald Zipper, and Lynn Veach Sadler. *Aries* is 70-100 pages, digest-sized, offset-printed, perfect-bound, with slick cover. Receives about 800 poems/year, accepts about 10%. Press run is 300. Single copy: $7; subscription: $7. Make checks payable to Aries @ Texas Wesleyan University.

How to Contact Send 5 submissions maximum per year. Lines/poem: 3 minimum, 50 maximum. Considers simultaneous submissions with notification; no previously published poems. Cover letter required. Include titles of submissions and 100-word bio required; no names allowed on submissions themselves. Accepts submissions August 1-December 15 only. Submit electronically to aries@txwes.edu or to Aries, c/o Neeley, at the mailing address above. Notification April/May; publication in fall. "At least 3 reviewers read every submission via blind review. Personal response to every submission accompanied by a SASE or functioning e-mail address." Always comments on rejected poems. Guidelines available in magazine, for SASE or by e-mail. Responds in up to 6 months (notification of acceptance in April). Offers 50% off 2 contributor's copies. Acquires first rights.

Tips "Write in the voice that speaks from your unique position in the world. Our editors tend to choose works that show 'there's something at stake.'"

◻ ◎ ARKANSAS REVIEW: A JOURNAL OF DELTA STUDIES

P.O. Box 1890, State University AR 72467-1890. (870)972-3043. Fax: (870)972-3045. E-mail: jcollins@astate.edu. Website: www.clt.astate.edu/arkreview. **Contact:** Janelle Collins, General Editor. **Contact:** Janelle Collins, general editor.

Magazines Needs *Arkansas Review: A Journal of Delta Studies*, published 3 times/year, is "a regional studies journal devoted to the 7-state Mississippi River Delta. Interdisciplinary in scope, we publish academic articles, relevant creative material, interviews, and reviews. Material must respond to or evoke the experiences and landscapes of the 7-state Mississippi River Delta (St. Louis to New Orleans)." Has published poetry by Greg Fraser, Jo McDougall, and Catherine Savage Brosman. *Arkansas Review* is 92 pages, magazine-sized, photo offset-printed, saddle-stapled, with 4-color cover. Receives about 500 poems/year, accepts about 5%. Press run is 600; 50 distributed free to contributors. Subscription: $20. Sample: $7.50. Make checks payable to ASU Foundation.

How to Contact Submit any number of poems at a time. No previously published poems or simultaneous submissions. Accepts e-mail and disk submissions. Cover letter is preferred. Include SASE. Time between acceptance and publication is about 6 months. Occasionally publishes theme issues. Guidelines available for SASE or by e-mail. Responds in 4 months. Pays 3 contributor's copies. Acquires first rights. Staff reviews books/chapbooks of poetry "that are relevant to the Delta" in 500 words, single- and multi-book format. Send materials for review consideration to Janelle Collins ("inquire in advance").

◪ THE ARMCHAIR AESTHETE

Pickle Gas Press, 19 Abbotswood Crescent, Penfield NY 14526. (585)248-8617. E-mail: bypaul@frontiernet.net; thearmchairaesthete@yahoo.com. **Contact:** Paul Agosto, editor.

Magazines Needs *The Armchair Aesthete*, published 1-2 times/year, is a zine of "thoughtful, well-crafted, concise fiction and poetry. Interested in both fiction and poetry." *The Armchair Aesthete* is 140-170 pages, digest-sized, desktop-published, photocopied, with card cover and plastic spiral bound. Receives about 300 poems/year, accepts about 25-30%. Submission must be accompanied by a SASE (#10 envelope). Recently published work by CFrank Andreotti, Andrew Oerke, Randall Brown, Alan Reynolds. Subscription: $14/2 issues. Sample: $7 postpaid and 5 First-Class stamps. Make checks payable to Paul Agosto.

How to Contact Lines/poem: 60 maximum. Fiction: 4,500 words maximum. Considers previously published poems and simultaneous submissions, if indicated. Accepts e-mail submissions (pasted into body of message or attached MS Word file). Cover letter is preferred. Time between acceptance and publication is up to 12 months. Seldom comments on rejected poems. Guidelines available for SASE. Responds in 4-7 months. Pays 1 contributor's copy. Acquires one-time rights.

✥ ▣ ☑ ASCENT ASPIRATIONS MAGAZINE

1560 Arbutus Dr., Nanoose Bay BC V9P 9C8, Canada. E-mail: ascentaspirations@shaw. com. **Contact:** David Fraser, Editor.

Magazines Needs *Ascent Aspirations Magazine*, publishes monthly on-line and publishes one anthology in print as a separate themed title in spring, specializes in poetry, short fiction, essays, and visual art. "A quality electronic and print publication, *Ascent* is dedicated to encouraging aspiring poets and fiction writers. We accept all forms of poetry on any theme. Poetry needs to be unique and touch the reader emotionally with relevant human, social, and philosophical imagery." Does not want poetry "that focuses on mainstream overtly religious verse." Considers poetry by children and teens. Has published poetry by Janet Buck and Taylor Graham. Work is considered for the print *The Yearly Anthology* through contests (see below). Receives about 1,500 poems/year, accepts about 15%.

How to Contact Submit 1-5 poems at a time. Considers previously published poems and simultaneous submissions. Prefers e-mail submissions (pasted into body of message or as attachment in Word); no disk submissions. "If you must submit by postal mail because it is your only avenue, provide a SASE with IRCs or Canadian stamps." Reads submissions on a regular basis year round. Time between acceptance and publication is 3 months or sooner. Editor makes decisions on all poems. Seldom comments on rejected poems. Occasionally publishes theme issues. Upcoming themes available on website. Responds in 3 months. Acquires one-time rights.

Contest/Award Offerings To fund the printing of the1 annual anthology, *Ascent* offers a contest for poetry and fiction. 1st Prize: $100 CAD; 2nd Prize: $75 CAD; 3rd Prize: $50 CAD; 4th Prize: $25 CAD; 5 Honorable Mentions: $10 CAD each. All winners and honorable mentions receive 1-2 copies of anthology; all other entrants published in anthology receive 1 free copy. Guidelines available for SASE, by e-mail, or on website. **Entry fee:** $5 CAD/poem or $10 CAD/3 poems. **Deadlines:** "these vary for each contest." **NOTE: "Fee, awards, and the number of copies for winners of contests can change. Refer always to the website for the most up-to-date information."**

Tips "Write with passion for your material. In terms of editing, always proofread to the point where what you submit is the best it can possibly be. Never be discouraged if your work is not accepted; it may be just not the right fit for the current publication."

☑ ASHEVILLE POETRY REVIEW

P.O. Box 7086, Asheville NC 28802. (828)649-0217. Website: www.ashevillereview.com. **Contact:** Keith Flynn, founder/managing editor.

Magazines Needs *Asheville Poetry Review*, published annually, prints "the best regional, national, and international poems we can find. We publish translations, interviews, essays, historical perspectives, and book reviews as well." Wants "quality work with well-crafted ideas married to a dynamic style. Any subject matter is fit to be considered so long as the language is vivid with a clear sense of rhythm. We subscribe to the Borges dictum that great poetry is a combination of 'algebra and fire.'" Has published poetry by Sherman Alexie, Eavan Boland, Gary Snyder, Colette Inez, Robert Bly, and Fred Chappell. *Asheville Poetry Review* is 160-300 pages, digest-sized, perfect-bound, laminated, with full-color cover. Receives about 8,000 submissions/year, accepts about 5%. Press run is 3,000. Subscription: $22.50 for 2 years, $43.50 for 4 years. Sample: $13. **"We prefer poets purchase a sample copy prior to submitting."**

How to Contact Submit 3-5 poems at a time. No previously published poems or simultaneous submissions. No e-mail submissions. Cover letter is required. Include comprehensive bio, recent publishing credits, and SASE. Reads submissions January 15-July 15. Time between acceptance and publication is up to one year. Poems are circulated to an editorial board. Seldom comments on rejected poems. Occasionally publishes theme issues. Guidelines available for SASE or on website. Responds in up to 7 months. Pays 1 contributor's copy. Rights revert back to author upon publication. Reviews books/chapbooks of poetry. Send materials for review consideration.

▣ ◪ ◎ ASININE POETRY

E-mail: editor@asininepoetry.com. Website: www.asininepoetry.com. **Contact:** R. Narvaez, editor.

Magazines Needs *asinine poetry and prose*, published monthly online, "features 10-12 new works each month. We specialize in poetry that does not take itself too seriously." Wants "any form of poetry, but for us the poetry must be in a humorous, parodic, or satirical style. We prefer well-crafted poems that may contain serious elements or cover serious subjects— but which are also amusing, absurd, or hilarious." Does not want serious, straightforward poems. Has published poetry by Hal Sirowitz, William Trowbridge, Elizabeth Swados, Daniel Thomas Moran, and Colonel Drunky Bob. Receives about 1,000 poems/year, accepts about 10%.

How to Contact Submit 3-4 poems at a time. Lines/poem: 50 maximum. Considers previously published poems and simultaneous submissions. Accepts e-mail (pasted into body of message).

Contest/Award Offerings Sponsors 1 contest/year. Guidelines available on website.

▦ ◪ ASSENT

11 Orkney Close, Stenson Fields, Derbyshire DE24 3LW, England. E-mail: nottposoc@ btinternet.com. Website: nottinghampoetrysociety.co.uk. **Contact:** Adrian Buckner, editor.

Magazines Needs *Assent*, formerly *Poetry Nottingham*, published 3 times/year, features articles and reviews in addition to poetry. Open to submissions from UK and overseas. Has published poetry from Europe, Australasia, the U.S., and Japan. *Assent* is 6x8, perfect-bound, professionally printed. Receives about 2,000 submissions/year, accepts about 120. Press run is 250. Single copy: £4; subscription: £12 UK, £20 overseas. Checks payable to Poetry Nottingham Publications. Subscribers who wish to pay in U.S. dollars please send check for $25, payable to Karen Crosbie, to 1036 Menlo Avenue, Apt 103, Los Angeles, CA, 90006. Single copy $7.

How to Contact Submit up to 6 poems at a time. No previously published poems. Cover letter is required. "Send SAE and 3 IRCs for stamps. No need to query." Responds in 2 months. Pays 1 contributor's copy. Staff reviews books of poetry, usually confined to UK publications.

Contest/Award Offerings The Nottingham Open Poetry Competition offers cash prizes, annual subscriptions, and publication in *Assent*. Open to all. Guidelines available on website.

Tips "We seek to provide an uncluttered environment for poems of wit, poems of concise lyrical intensity, and poems that are bold enough to expand on a theme."

☻ ATLANTA REVIEW

P.O. Box 8248, Atlanta GA 31106. E-mail: atlrev@yahoo.com. Website: www.atlantareview.com. **Contact:** Dan Veach, Editor/Publisher.

- Work published in *Atlanta Review* has been included in *The Best American Poetry* and *The Pushcart Prize*.

Magazines Needs *Atlanta Review*, published semiannually, is devoted primarily to poetry, but occasionally features interviews and b&w artwork. Wants "quality poetry of genuine human appeal." Has published poetry by Seamus Heaney, Billy Collins, Derek Walcott, Maxine Kumin, Alicia Stallings, Gunter Grass, and Thomas Lux. *Atlanta Review* is 128 pages, digest-sized, professionally printed on acid-free paper, flat-spined, with glossy color cover. Receives about 10,000 poems/year, accepts about 1%. Press run is 2,500. Single copy: $6; subscription: $10. Sample: $5.

How to Contact Submit no more than 5 poems at a time. No previously published poems. No e-mail submissions from within the U.S.; postal submissions only. Include SASE for reply. "Authors living outside the United States and Canada may submit work via e-mail." Cover letter is preferred. Include brief bio. Put name and address on each poem. Reads submissions according to the following deadlines: June 1 for Fall; December 1 for Spring. "While we do read year round, response time may be slower during summer and the winter holidays." Time between acceptance and publication is 6 months. Seldom comments on rejected poems. Guidelines available for SASE, by e-mail, or on website. Responds in 1 month. Pays 2 contributor's copies, author's discounts on additional copies. Acquires first North American serial rights.

Contest/Award Offerings *Atlanta Review* sponsors the Poetry 2011 International Poetry Competition.

$ ☑ THE ATLANTIC MONTHLY

The Watergate, 600 New Hampshire Ave, NW, Washington DC 20037. Website: www.theatlantic.com. **Contact:** David Barber, poetry editor.

Magazines Needs *The Atlantic Monthly* publishes some of the most distinguished poetry in American literature. "We read with interest and attention every poem submitted to the magazine and, quite simply, we publish those that seem to us to be the best." Wants "the broadest possible range of work: traditional forms and free verse, the meditative lyric and the 'light' or comic poem, the work of the famous and the work of the unknown." Has published poetry by Maxine Kumin, Stanley Plumly, Linda Gregerson, Philip Levine, Ellen Bryant Voigt, and W.S. Merwin. Has a circulation of 500,000. Receives about 60,000 poems/year, accepts about 30-35. Subscription: $24.50 for 10 issues. Sample: $7.50 (back issue).

How to Contact Submit 2-6 poems at a time. No previously published poems or simultaneous submissions. No e-mail or disk submissions; postal submissions only. SASE required. Responds in 4-6 weeks. Always sends prepublication galleys. Pays about $4/line. Acquires first North American serial rights only.

Tips "We have long been committed to the discovery of new poets. Our one limitation is length; we are unable to publish very long poems, and authors should consult back issues of the magazine for precedents."

☐ ATLANTIC PACIFIC PRESS

279 Gulf Rd., South Dartmouth MA 02748. (508)994-7869. E-mail: abcworks@att.net. Website: atlanticpacificpress.com. **Contact:** Christine Walen, editor.

Magazines Needs *Atlantic Pacific Press*, published quarterly, "is a journal of fiction, drama, poetry, prose poetry, flash fiction, lyrics, cartoons, sci-fi, fantasy, veterans/military, romance, mystery, horror, westerns, family life, children's stories, nonfiction, art, and photography." Does not want porn. Has published poetry by D. Davis Phillips Michael Foster, Lynn Veach Sadler, James Hoggard, Mediha F. Saliba, Sheryl L. Nelms, Marjorie Bixler, Sheila Golburgh Johnson, James Fowler, Claudia Barnett. *Atlantic Pacific Press* is 90 pages, digest-sized, saddle-stapled, with cover art and photography welcome; includes ads. Accepts about 80% of poems/year. Single copy: $10; subscription: $30/year (4 copies). Make checks payable to *Atlantic Pacific Press*.

How to Contact Guidelines available for SASE. Reading periods: Spring, February 20; Summer, May 20; Fall, August 20; Winter, November 20. Acquires first North American serial rights, first rights. All rights revert to poet upon publication. Reviews books, chapbooks of poetry, and other magazines and journals in 200 words.

Tips "Read your work to others. You may find it helpful to attend a writer's conference or take a workshop."

◰ ◎ THE AUROREAN

Encircle Publications, P.O. Box 187, Farmington ME 04938. (207)778-0467. E-mail: Aurorean@encirclepub.com (inquiries only). Website: www.encirclepub.com. **Contact:** Devin McGuire, Assistant Editor.

Magazines Needs *The Aurorean*, published semiannually (spring/summer, fall/winter), uses "well crafted upbeat poetry. Seasonal/New England focus, but open to other subjects." Wants "short poems (4-6 lines). Publishes haiku section each issue. "Mostly free verse and occasional rhyme. We publish newer poets alongside the biggest names in the small press." Does not want "anything hateful, overly religious." Has published poetry by Steve Ausherman, Kevin Marshall Chopson, Ruth Webber Evans, and Carol Hamilton. *The Aurorean* is digest-sized, professionally printed, perfect-bound. Press run is 550. Single copy: $11 U.S., $12 international; subscription: $21 U.S. (2 issues), $25 international. Sample: back issues from previous quarterly format, $3 each; back issues of current semiannual format, $7 each. Make checks payable to Encircle Publications, LLC.

How to Contact Submit 1-5 poems at a time in a #10 envelope (larger envelopes discouraged due to space). Lines/poem: 40 maximum. Considers previously published poems. "Discourages simultaneous submissions "as we always reply in 3 months maximum. If you must submit simultaneously, be aware that none can be withdrawn once we have typeset/mailed a proof." Cover letter with brief introduction is preferred. "Fold cover letter separately and fold poems together. Poems folded individually cannot be reviewed." Include SASE with sufficient postage for return/reply; International submissions, include SAE and IRC. Manuscripts are acknowledged with a postcard or by e-mail upon receipt (e-mail address appreciated). Reads submissions August 16 - February 15 for spring/summer; February 15 - August 15 for fall/winter. Sends proofs with instructions for poets accepted each issue on how to submit bios. Pays 2 contributor's copies per poem published (maximum 4 copies/issue). Acquires one-time rights. Please credit if later published elsewhere. Two featured poets each issue (superb execution of poetic craft; in some way seasonally/New England reflective) receive publication of up to 3 poems with 100-word bio; 10 copies of magazine and 1-year subscription.

Also Offers *The Unrorean* broadsheet, appears twice/year mid-January and mid-July for poems too long, experimental, or dark for magazine. "Still, nothing hateful." 2-4 11x17 pages, laser-printed. Sample: $2 postpaid. Include SASE for return/reply. No proofs, bios; open submission dates. Pays 1 contributor's copy/poem, 1 "editor's pick" receives 2. "Poets may submit for the magazine or broadsheet individually (work submitted individually for broadsheet is not acknowledged by postcard or e-mail). Work sent to the magazine will also be considered for the broadsheet, unless otherwise requested in cover letter."

Tips "Be familiar with your markets; don't ever submit blindly. Keep writing. Support the markets that support poets. *Poet's Market* is your best friend. See our quotes and tips on the writing life for further submission tips from editor."

◪ AUTUMN SKY POETRY

5263 Arctic Circle, Emmaus PA 18049. E-mail: autumnskypoetryeditor@gmail.com. Website: www.autumnskypoetry.com. **Contact:** Christine Klocek-Lim, editor.

• "Reading poetry is a pleasure for which too few of us have the time to spare. Autumn Sky Poetry, published quarterly online, aims to make poetry "as accessible as possible: simple pages, simple formatting, exquisite poetry. To that end, we publish ten poems each issue, one poem per poet."

Magazines Needs Wants formal verse, free verse, prose poetry. "I'm open to everything, but each poem must intrigue me within the first 4-6 lines. I want to be surprised, moved, interested, impressed." Does not want badly rhymed poems, overemphasis on -ing words, too many adjectives, poems that are all emotion, no craft or all craft and no emotion. Technical skill and voice should balance within the poem. Has published poetry by Antonia Clark, Brent Fisk, Gail White, Kelley White, Guy Kettelhack.

How to Contact Submit up to 4 poems at a time, 70 lines maximum. Considers previously published and simultaneous submissions. Accepts e-mail submissions, pasted into body of message. No cover letter necessary. Include a bio with poems, use standard 12 pt font in e-mail. Accepts poems year round, read the last two weeks before issue is released. Submit seasonal poems 3 months in advance. Time between acceptance and publication is 1 week. Sometimes comments on rejected poems. Sometimes publishes theme issues. Themes and guidelines available on website. Responds in 1 week to 3 months. Always sends e-mail receipt of submission. Always sends prepublication galleys. Acquires First Electronic Rights upon acceptance of poems. Rights return to author upon publication. Reserves right to archive poem indefinitely online, but will remove at request of author.

Tips "Don't give up. Submit as much as possible. Work on improving your technical skills; voice will follow. Read contemporary poetry as well as classics."

◪ ◎ AVOCET, A JOURNAL OF NATURE POEMS

P.O. Box 1717, Southold NY 11971. Website: www.avocetreview.com. **Contact:** Peter C. Leverich, Editor.

Magazines Needs *Avocet, A Journal of Nature Poems*, published quarterly, is "devoted to poets who find meaning in their lives from the natural world." Wants "imagist/transcendental poetry that explores the beauty and divinity in nature." Does not want "poems that have rhyme, cliché, or abstraction." Has published poetry by Louis Daniel Brodsky, Gary Every, Ruth Goring, Gayle Elen Harvey, Lyn Lifshin, Holly Rose Diane Shaw, and Kristin Camitta Zimet. *Avocet* is 60 pages, 5 1/2x8 1/2, professionally printed, saddle-stapled, with card cover. Single copy: $6; subscription: $24. Make checks payable to Peter C. Leverich.

How to Contact Submit 3-5 poems at a time. Considers previously published poems, if acknowledged. Cover letter with e-mail address is helpful. Include SASE for reply only; mss will not be returned. Time between acceptance and publication is up to 3 months. Responds in up to 2 months. Pays 1 contributor's copy.

BABEL: THE MULTILINGUAL, MULTICULTURAL ONLINE JOURNAL AND COMMUNITY OF ARTS AND IDEAS

E-mail: submissions@towerofbabel.com. Website: http://towerofbabel.com. **Contact:** Malcolm Lawrence, editor-in-chief.

Magazines Needs "*Babel* is an electronic zine recognized by the UN as one of the most important social and human sciences online periodicals. Publishes regional reports from international stringers all over the planet, as well as features, round table discussions, fiction, columns, poetry, erotica, travelogues, and reviews of all the arts and editorials. We want to see poetry from all over the world, including multicultural or multilingual work, as well as poetry that has been translated from or into another language, as long as it is also in English. We also appreciate gay/lesbian and bisexual poetry. Writers whose work discriminates against the opposite sex, different cultures, or belief systems will not be considered."

How to Contact Submit no more than 10 poems at a time. Considers previously published poems and simultaneous submissions. Accepts e-mail submissions only. Cover letter is required. "Please send submissions with a résumé or bio as a Microsoft Word or RTF document attached to e-mail." Time between acceptance and publication varies; "usually no more than a month or 2 depending on how busy we are." Seldom comments on rejected poems. Guidelines available on website. Responds in 2-4 weeks. Reviews books/chapbooks of poetry and other magazines, single- and multi-book format. Open to unsolicited reviews. Send materials for review consideration.

Tips "We would like to see more poetry with first person male characters written by female authors as well as more poetry with first person female characters written by male authors. We would also like to see that dynamic in action when it comes to other languages, cultures, races, classes, sexual orientations, and ages. The best advice we could give to writers wanting to be published in our publication is simply to know what you're writing about and to write passionately about it."

BABEL FRUIT

E-mail: editors@babelfruit.org. Website: www.babelfruit.com. "We publish literature of exile, expatriation, repatriation, integration and exploration. We want to read poetry under the influence of 'the other.' Travel, look around or reach within. Wherever you see the other."

◻ **BABYSUE®**

P.O. Box 15749, Chattanooga TN 373415. E-mail: LMNOP@babysue.com. Website: www.babysue.com; www.LMNOP.com. **Contact:** Don W. Seven, Editor/Publisher.

Magazines Needs *babysue*, published twice/year, offers obtuse humor for the extremely open-minded. "We are open to all styles, but prefer short poems." No restrictions. Has published poetry by Edward Mycue, Susan Andrews, and Barry Bishop. *babysue* is 32 pages, offset-printed. "We print prose, poems, and cartoons. We usually accept about 5% of what we receive." Sample: $5. Payment may be made in either cash, check, or money order payable to M. Fievet.

How to Contact Considers previously published poems and simultaneous submissions. Deadlines are March 30 and September 30 of each year. Seldom comments on rejected poems. Responds "immediately, if we are interested." Pays 1 contributor's copy. "We do occasionally review other magazines."

◒ **BACKSTREET**

P.O. Box 1377, Berthoud CO 80513. E-mail: clarkreview@earthlink.net. **Contact:** Ray Foreman, Editor.

Magazines Needs *Backstreet*, published 6 times/year, wants "strong, clear narrative poems relevant to the times and the human condition, and appropriate for a readership of experienced poets. We are a 'poet's magazine for poets' whose purpose is keeping them writing by providing an easy and regular publishing outlet. We are privately subsidized, never run contests, and offer subscriptions at minimal cost to poets who read other poets' work." Does not want "poems that are obscure in any way or poems that have meaning only to the writer." Has published poetry by Anselm Brocki, Charles Ries, Laurel Speer, Arthur Gotlieb, and Steven Levi. *Backstreet* "has a special layout that has the equivalent content of a 36-page magazine," laser-printed, stapled, with paper cover. Receives about 600 poems/year, accepts about 200. Press run is 150. Single copy: $2; subscription: $10 for 10 issues. Make checks payable to R. Foreman.

How to Contact Submit 3 poems at a time. Lines/poem: 15 minimum, 50 maximum. "Maximum width is 65 characters per line." Considers previously published poems and simultaneous submissions. No e-mail or disk submissions. "SASE for first submission only. No cover letter, bio, or credits list. No graphic layout. Flush left, preferably in Times Roman or Garamond. No long skinnys. Disposable sharp hard copies. Your work speaks for you." Reads submissions year round. Time between acceptance and publication is 3 months. Sometimes comments on rejected poems. Responds in one week to one month. Acquires one-time rights. Rights revert to poet upon publication.

Tips "To write better poems, read poems in current anthologies to get a feel for what is good. It almost never happens at most poetry readings. Poetry is essentially an abbreviated short story literary art on the page."

▣ ◪ ◉ **THE BAREFOOT MUSE**

P.O. Box 115, Hainesport NJ 08036. (609)702-7407. E-mail: evnsanna@comcast.net. Website: www.barefootmuse.com. **Contact:** Anna Evans, Editor, and Nicholas Friedman, Assistant Editor.

Magazines Needs *The Barefoot Muse*, published semiannually online, prints "only formal/ metrical poetry (rhyme is optional). Poems in formal structures are most welcome. These include (but are not limited to) sonnets, villanelles, sestinas, triolets, pantoums, and rondeaus." Does not want "free verse; also, please do not send me rhyming poetry without first finding out what meter is." Has published poetry by Denise Duhamel, Jared Carter, Gail White, X.J. Kennedy, and Annie Finch. Receives about 1600 poems/year, accepts about 3%.

How to Contact Submit up to 5 poems at a time. Lines/poem: less than 40 preferred. Considers previously published poems ("by invitation only") and simultaneous submissions ("with notification"). Accepts e-mail submissions (pasted into body of message). Reads submissions year round. Time between acceptance and publication is up to 6 months. Sometimes comments on rejected poems. Guidelines available on website. Responds in 2 months. Always sends prepublications galleys. Acquires one-time rights. Rights revert to poet upon publication.

☑ BARROW STREET

P.O. Box 1831, New York NY 10156. E-mail: infobarrow@gmail.com. Website: www. barrowstreet.org. Established 1998. **Contact:** Lorna Blake, Patricia Carlin, Peter Covino, and Melissa Hotchkiss, editors.

• Poetry published in *Barrow Street* is often selected for *The Best American Poetry*.

Magazines Needs *Barrow Street*, published annually, "is dedicated to publishing new and established poets." Wants "poetry of the highest quality; open to all styles and forms." Has published poetry by Molly Peacock, Lyn Hejinian, Carl Phillips, Marie Ponsot, Charles Bernstein, and Stephen Burt. *Barrow Street* is 96-120 pages, digest-sized, professionally printed, perfect-bound, with glossy cardstock cover with color or b&w photography. Receives about 3,000 poems/year, accepts about 3%. Press run is 1,000. Subscription: $18 for 2years, $25 for 3 years. Sample: $10.

How to Contact Submit up to 5 poems at a time. Considers simultaneous submissions (when notified); no previously published poems. Cover letter is preferred. Include brief bio. Must have name, address, e-mail, and phone on each page submitted or submission will not be considered. Reads submissions October 1 - March 31. Poems circulated to an editorial board. Guidelines available on website. Responds 2-9 months. Does not return or respond to submissions made outside the reading period. Always sends prepublication galleys. Pays 2 contributor's copies. Acquires first rights.

Contest/Award Offerings The Barrow Street Press Book Contest.

Tips "Submit your strongest work."

Ⓝ ☑ BATEAU

P.O. Box 1584, Northampton MA 01061. (413)586-2494. E-mail: info@bateaupress.org; ashley@bateaupress.org. Website: www.bateaupress.org. **Contact:** Ashley Schaffer, managing editor. "*Bateau* subscribes to no trend but serves to represent as wide a cross-section of contemporary writing as possible. For this reason, readers will most likely love and hate at least something in each issue. We consider this a good thing. To us, it means Bateau is eclectic, open-ended, and not mired in a particular strain."

Magazines Needs "*Bateau*, published semiannually, subscribes to no trend but serves to represent as wide a cross-section of contemporary writing as possible. For this reason, readers will most likely love and hate at least something in each issue. We consider this a good thing. To us, it means Bateau is eclectic, open-ended, and not mired in a particular strain." Has published poetry by Tomaz Salamun, John Olsen, Michael Burkhardt, Joshua Marie Wilkinson, Allison Titus, Allan Peterson. *Bateau* is around 80 pages, digest-sized, offset print, perfect-bound, with a 100% recycled letterpress cover. Receives about 5,000 poems/year, accepts about 50. Press run is 250. Single copy: $10; subscription $18. Make checks payable to Bateau Press.

How to Contact Submit 5 poems at a time, up to 2 pages. Considers simultaneous submissions, no previously published poems or work concurrently available online. Prefers electronic submissions via online submission manager on website. Reads submissions year round. Time between acceptance and publication is 3-8 months. Poems are circulated to an editorial board. Often comments on rejected poems. Sometimes publishes theme issues. Upcoming themes available on website; guidelines availalbe for SASE or on website. Responds in 3-6 months. Sometimes sends prepublication galleries. Pays 2 contributor's copies. Acquires first North American serial rights, electronic rights. "We reserve the right to display work on internet for promotional, advertising, and to store, transmit, and distribute electronic copies of the work as required to facilitate the printing and distribution process of *Bateau*." Rights revert to poet upon publication.

☐ BATHTUB GIN

Pathwise Press, 4712 Perrier St., New Orleans LA 70115. E-mail: pathwisepress@hotmail.com. Website: www.pathwisepress.com. Established 1997. **Contact:** Christopher Harter, editor.

- **PLEASE NOTE:** "*Bathtub Gin*/Pathwise Press are on hiatus through 2010; interested parties should contact the magazine to check on status."

Magazines Needs *Bathtub Gin*, published semiannually in April and October, has "an eclectic aesthetic—we want to keep you guessing what is on the next page." Wants poetry that "takes a chance with language or paints a vivid picture with its imagery, has the kick of bathtub gin, which can be experimental or a sonnet." Does not want "trite rhymes, Bukowski wannabes (let the man rest), or confessionals." Has published poetry by Kell Robertson, Tom Kryss, Mike James, and Richard Krech. *Bathtub Gin* is about 60 pages, digest-sized, laser-printed, saddle-stapled, with 80 lb. coverstock cover. Receives about 1,200 poems/year, accepts about 5%. Press run is 300-350; 10 distributed free to reviewers, other editors, and libraries. Single copy: $5; subscription: $8. Sample: $3.50 (back issue). Foreign orders add $2. Make checks payable to Christopher Harter.

How to Contact Submit 4-6 poems at a time. Considers previously published poems and simultaneous submissions. Accepts e-mail submissions (pasted into body of message). Cover letter is required. "Three- to five-line bio required if you are accepted for publication; if none provided, we make one up." Include SASE. Reads submissions June 1-September 15 only, but accepts contributions for 2 issues. Time between acceptance and publication is up to 8 months. Sometimes comments on rejected poems. Guidelines available in magazine, for SASE, by e-mail, or on website. Responds in up to 2 months. Pays 2 contributor's copies.

"We also sell extra copies to contributors at a discount, which they can give away or sell at full price."

Additional Information Pathwise Press's goal is to publish chapbooks, broadsides, and "whatever else tickles us." Has published *The Levelling Wind* by Kell Robertson, *Nothing But Love* by Mike James, *The United Colors of Death* by Mark Terrill, and *Living Room, Earth* by Carmen Germain. Guidelines available for SASE or on website.

Also Offers "We feature a 'News' section where people can list their books, presses, events, etc."

☑ BAYOU

English Dept., University of New Orleans, 2000 Lakeshore Dr., New Orleans LA 70148. E-mail: bayou@uno.edu. Website: http://cola.uno.edu/cww/bayou.htm. **Contact:** Poetry Editor. Established 1975 as The Panhandler (University of West Florida); 2002 as Bayou (co-published by University of West Florida and University of New Orleans). Bayou is now solely published by the University of New Orleans. Member: CLMP (Council of Literary Magazines and Presses).

Magazines Needs *Bayou Magazine*, published biannually, is "a young publication with an old soul. Each issue contains stunningly beautiful fiction, nonfiction, and poetry. One issue a year contains an award-winning play from the annual Tennessee Williams/New Orleans Literary Festival One-Act Play competition. From quirky shorts to more traditional stories, we are committed to publishing solid work. Regardless of style, at *Bayou* we are always interested first in a well-told tale. Our poetry and prose are filled with memorable characters observing their world, acknowledging both the mundane and the sublime, often at once, and always with an eye toward beauty. Contains a range of material from established, award-winning authors as well as new voices on the rise." Has published poetry by Eric Trethewey, Virgil Suárez, Marilyn Hacker, Sean Beaudoin, Tom Whalen, and Mark Doty. *Bayou* is 130 pages, digest-sized, professionally printed, perfect-bound, with matte cardstock cover (artwork varies). Receives "hundreds of submissions," accepts "very few." Press run is 500; distributed free to students and faculty of University of West Florida and University of New Orleans. Single copy: $8; subscription: $15. Make checks payable to the UNO Foundation.

How to Contact Submit no more than 5 poems at a time. Lines/poem: "We have no strict length restrictions, though obviously it is harder to fit in very long poems." Considers simultaneous submissions; no previously published poems. No e-mail or disk submissions. "A brief cover letter is necessary, but don't tell us your life story, explain your poems, or tell us how wonderful your poems are. Do give us your contact information." Reads submissions year round, "but we tend to slow down in the summer months." Time between acceptance and publication varies "but we give the author a general idea when the work is accepted." Poems are circulated to an editorial board. Never comments on rejected poems. Guidelines available in magazine, for SASE, or by e-mail. Responds in 4 months. Pays 2 contributor's copies. Acquires first North American serial rights.

☑ ◎ BEAR CREEK HAIKU

P.O. Box 3787, Boulder CO 80307.

Magazines Needs *bear creek haiku* prints haiku/senryu and any form/style less than 15 lines.

How to Contact Submit 5-20 poems at a time. Considers previously published or unpublished poems, translations, and simultaneous submissions. "Include name, address, and several poems on each page. Keep your postage expenses at two first-class stamps, one of which is on the SASE." Pays 2 contributor's copies.

Tips "We appreciate receiving your own personal favorites, be they simultaneously submitted or published elsewhere or never seen before. Write, create your poems—the heart, spirit, shadow, ancestors, readers, other poets, an occasional editor, etc., will benefit deeply."

$ ◎ THE BEAR DELUXE

Orlo, a nonprofit organization exploring environmental issues through the creative arts, P.O. Box 10342, Portland OR 97296-0342. E-mail: bear@orlo.org. Website: www.orlo.org. **Contact:** Tom Webb, Editor. *The Bear Deluxe*, published twice a year, provides "a fresh voice amid often strident and polarized environmental discourse. Street-level, non-dogmatic, and solution-oriented, *The Bear Deluxe* presents lively creative discussion to a diverse readership." Wants poetry "with innovative environmental perspectives." Has published poetry by Judith Barrington, Robert Michael Pyle, Mary Winters, Stephen Babcock, Carl Hanni, and Derek Sheffield. *The Bear Deluxe* is 48 pages, 9x12, newsprint, saddle-stapled, with brown Kraft paper cover. Receives about 1,200 poems/year, accepts about 20-30. Press run is 20,000; 18,000 distributed free on the streets of the western U.S. and beyond. Subscription: $20. Sample: $5. Make checks payable to Orlo.

How to Contact Submit 3-5 poems at a time. Lines/poem: 50 maximum. Considers previously published poems and simultaneous submissions "so long as noted." Accepts e-mail submissions (pasted into body of message) but it is not as preferable as sending hard copy by mail. "We can't respond to e-mail submissions but do look at them." Poems are reviewed by a committee of 3-5 people. Publishes 1 theme issue/year. Guidelines available for SASE. Responds in 6 months. Pays $20/poem, 1 contributor's copy (more if willing to distribute), and subscription. Acquires first or one-time rights.

Tips "The magazine is moving away from using the term environmental writing. Quality writing which furthers the magazine's goal of engaging new and divergent readers will garner the most attention."

◻ ◎ BELLEVUE LITERARY REVIEW

New York University School of Medicine, OBV-A612, 550 First Ave., New York NY 10016. (212)263-3973. E-mail: info@BLReview.org. Website: www.BLReview.org. **Contact:** Stacy Bodziak, managing editor. (Specialized: humanity, health, and healing) Member: CLMP.

• Work published in *Bellevue Literary Review* has appeared in *The Pushcart Prize*.

Magazines Needs *Bellevue Literary Review*, published semiannually, prints "works of fiction, nonfiction, and poetry that touch upon relationships to the human body, illness, health, and healing." Has published poetry by Rafael Campo, Sharon Olds, James Tate, David Wagoner, John Stone, and Floyd Skloot. *Bellevue Literary Review* is 160 pages, digest-sized, perfect-bound, includes ads. Receives about 1,800 poems/year, accepts about 3%. Press run is 5,000; distributed free to lit mag conferences, promotions, and other contacts. Single copy: $9; subscription: $15/year, $35 for 3 years (plus $5/year postage to Canada, $8/year postage foreign). Make checks payable to *Bellevue Literary Review*.

How to Contact Submit up to 3 poems at a time. Lines/poem: prefers poems of one page or less. Considers simultaneous submissions. No previously published poems; work published on personal blogs or Websites will be considered on a case-by-case basis. No e-mail or disk submissions. "We accept poems via regular mail and through our website; when submitting via regular mail, please include SASE." Cover letter is preferred. Reads submissions year round. Time between acceptance and publication is about 6-7 months. "Poems are reviewed by two independent readers, then sent to an editor." Sometimes comments on rejected poems. Sometimes publishes theme issues. Upcoming themes available on website. Guidelines available for SASE or on website. Responds in 3-5 months. Always sends prepublication galleys. Pays 2 contributor's copies and one-year subscription for author, plus one-year gift subscription for friend. Acquires first North American serial rights. Rights revert to poet upon publication.

Contest/Award Offerings The annual Bellevue Literary Review Prize for Poetry.

◙ BELLINGHAM REVIEW

Western Washington University, Mail Stop 9053, Bellingham WA 98225. (360)650-4863. E-mail: bellingham.review@wwu.edu. Website: www.wwu.edu/~bhreview. **Contact:** Brenda Miller, Editor-in-Chief.

Magazines Needs *Bellingham Review*, published twice/year, has no specific preferences as to form. Wants "well-crafted poetry, but are open to all styles." Has published poetry by David Shields, Tess Gallagher, Gary Soto, Jane Hirshfield, Albert Goldbarth, and Rebecca McClanahan. *Bellingham Review* is digest-sized, perfect-bound, with matte cover. Circulation is 1,600. Subscription: $12/year, $20 for 2 years, $20/year for libraries and institutions. Sample: $12. Make checks payable to *Bellingham Review*.

How to Contact Submit 3-5 poems at a time. Considers simultaneous submissions with notification. No e-mail submissions; accepts submissions by postal mail only. Include SASE. Reads submissions September 15-February 1 only (submissions must be postmarked within this reading period). Guidelines available for SASE or on website. Responds in 2 months. Pays 2 contributor's copies, a year's subscription, plus monetary payment (if funding allows). Acquires first North American serial rights.

Contest/Award Offerings The 49th Parallel Poetry Award.

◙ BELLOWING ARK

Bellowing Ark Press, P.O. Box 55564, Shoreline WA 98155. (206)440-0791. E-mail: bellowingark@bellowingark.org. Website: www.bellowingark.org. **Contact:** Robert R. Ward, editor.

Magazines Needs *Bellowing Ark*, published bimonthly, is a literary tabloid that prints "only poetry which demonstrates in some way the proposition that existence has meaning or, to put it another way, that life is worth living. We have no strictures as to length, form, or style; only that the work we publish is, to our judgment, life-affirming." Does not want "academic poetry, in any of its manifold forms." Has published poetry by Jerry Austin, Miriam Schorr, Tobi Cogswell, Esther Cameron, Mary Jo Balistrieri, Dolores Stewart, and Colleen Harris. Beginning in 2008 three cash awards, The Lois and Marine Robert Warden (poetry), The Lucas Doolin (fiction), and The Michael L. Newell (black and white line art), are given. *Bellowing Ark* is 32 pages, tabloid-sized, printed on electrobright stock. Press run is 1,000. Subscription: $20/year. Sample: $4.

How to Contact Submit 3-6 poems at a time. "Absolutely no simultaneous submissions." No e-mail submissions; accepts postal submissions only. Guidelines available for SASE or on website. Responds in up to 3 months; publishes accepted work within the next 2 issues. Occasionally comments on rejected poems if they "seem to display potential to become the kind of work we want." Sometimes sends prepublication galleys. Pays 2 contributor's copies. Reviews books of poetry. Send materials for review consideration.

Additional Information Bellowing Ark Press publishes collections of poetry by invitation only.

☑ ◎ BELL'S LETTERS POET

P.O. Box 2187, Gulfport MS 39505-2187. **Contact:** Jim Bell, editor/publisher. *Bell's Letters Poet*, published quarterly, **must be purchased by contributors before they can be published.** Wants "clean writing in good taste; no vulgarity, no artsy vulgarity." Has published poetry by Betty Wallace, Paul Pascal, C. David Hay & Helen Rilling. *Bell's Letters Poet* is about 60 pages, digest-sized, photocopied on plain bond paper (including cover), saddle-stapled. Single copy: $7; subscription: $28. Sample: $5. "Send a poem (20 lines or under, in good taste) with your sample order, and we will publish it in our next issue."

How to Contact Submit 4 poems at a time. Lines/poem: 4-20. Considers previously published poems "if cleared by author with prior publisher"; no simultaneous submissions. No e-mail submissions; accepts submissions by postal mail only. Submission deadline is 2 months prior to publication. Accepted poems by subscribers are published immediately in the next issue. Guidelines available online or for SASE. No payment for accepted poetry, but "many patrons send cash awards to the poets whose work they especially like." Reviews chapbooks of poetry by subscribers.

Tips "The Ratings" is a competition in each issue. Readers are asked to vote on their favorite poems, and the "Top 40" are announced in the next issue, along with awards sent to the poets by patrons. News releases are then sent to subscriber's hometown newspaper. *Bell's Letters Poet* also features a telephone and e-mail exchange among poets, a birth-date listing, and a profile of its poets. "Tired of seeing no bylines this year? Subscription guarantees a byline in each issue."

☑ BELOIT POETRY JOURNAL

P.O. Box 151, Farmington ME 04938. (207)778-0020. **Contact:** John Rosenwald and Lee Sharkey, editors.

- Poetry published in the *Beloit Poetry Journal* has been included in *The Best American Poetry, Best New Poets, The Pushcart Prize,* and appears regularly on the Poetry Daily and Verse Daily websites.

Magazines Needs *Beloit Poetry Journal*, published quarterly, prints "the most outstanding poems we receive, without bias as to length, school, subject, or form. For 60 years of continuous publication, we have been distinguished for the extraordinary range of our poetry and our discovery of strong new poets." Wants "visions broader than the merely personal; language that makes us laugh and weep, recoil, resist—and pay attention. We're drawn to poetry that grabs hold of the whole body, not just the head." Has published poetry by Sherman Alexie, Mark Doty, Albert Goldbarth, Patricia Goedicke, Karl Elder, Ben Lerner, Sonia Sanchez, and Susan Tichy. *Beloit Poetry Journal* is about 48 pages, digest-sized, saddle-stapled, attractively printed, with "beautiful" 4-color covers. Circulation is 1,250. Subscription: $18/year, $48 for 3 years (individuals); $23/year, $65 for 3 years (institutions). Check website for international subscription rates. Sample: $5.

How to Contact No previously published poems or simultaneous submissions. No e-mail submissions. "Submit any time, without query, in any legible form; no bio necessary. Unless it's a long poem, send what will go in a business envelope for 1 stamp. Don't send your life's work. We respond to most submissions within 2 weeks. Manuscripts under active consideration we keep for up to 4 months, circulating them among our readers, and continuing to winnow. At the quarterly meetings of the Editorial Board, we read aloud all the surviving poems and put together an issue of the best we have." Complete guidelines available on website. Pays 3 contributor's copies. Acquires first serial rights. Reviews books by and about poets. Send books for review consideration.

Additional Information "To diversify our offerings, we occasionally publish chapbooks (for example, our 60th Anniversary Chapbook of Chad Walsh prize-winning poets). These are never the work of a single poet."

Contest/Award Offerings Awards the Chad Walsh Poetry Prize ($3,500 in 2009) to a poem or group of poems published in the calendar year. "Every poem we publish will be considered for the 2011 prize."

Tips "We are always watching for inventive forms and quickened language."

▣ $ ◎ BELTWAY POETRY QUARTERLY

E-mail: beltway.poetry@juno.com. Website: www.beltwaypoetry.com. **Contact:** Kim Roberts, editor. Established 2000.

Magazines Needs *Beltway Poetry Quarterly*, published online, "features poets who live or work in the greater Washington, D.C., metro region. *Beltway* showcases the richness and diversity of Washington, D.C., authors, with poets from different backgrounds, races, ethnicities, ages, and sexual orientations represented. We have included Pulitzer Prize-winners and those who have never previously published. We publish academic, spoken word, and experimental authors—and those whose work defies categorization." Takes unsolicited submissions only for special themed issues. Themes change annually; check website for details. Has published poetry by Cornelius Eady, Anthony Hecht, E. Ethelbert Miller, Jane Shore, Sharan Strange, and Hilary Tham.

How to Contact *"Other than annual themed issue, we consider poems by invitation only.* Theme issues have included poetic responses to Walt Whitman, the war in Iraq, and D.C. Places. 2 issues per year feature 5 poets from the greater-D.C. region, and these issues are open only by invitation. 1 issue per year is guest-edited." Never comments on rejected poems. Guidelines available on website.

Also Offers "Monthly Poetry News section has information on new publications, calls for entries, workshops, readings, and performances. Extensive links also include the most complete listing anywhere of artist residency programs in the U.S."

$ ◩ ◎ BIBLE ADVOCATE

P.O. Box 33677, Denver CO 80233. E-mail: bibleadvocate@cog7.org. Website: www.cog7.org/BA. **Contact:** Sherri Langton, Associate Editor.

Magazines Needs *Bible Advocate*, published 6 times/year, features "Christian content—to be a voice for the Bible and for the church." Wants "free verse, some traditional, with Christian/Bible themes." Does not want "avant-garde poetry." *Bible Advocate* is 32 pages, magazine-sized. Receives about 30-50 poems/year, accepts about 10-20. Press run varies; all distributed free.

How to Contact Submit no more than 5 poems at a time. Lines/poem: 5 minimum, 20 maximum. Considers previously published poems (with notification) and simultaneous submissions. Prefers e-mail submissions. Cover letter is preferred. "No handwritten submissions, please." Time between acceptance and publication is up to 1 year. "I read them first and reject those that won't work for us. I send good ones to editor for approval." Seldom comments on rejected poems. Publishes theme issues. Guidelines available for SASE or on website. Responds in 2 months. Pays $20 and 2 contributor's copies. Acquires first, reprint, electronic, and one-time rights.

Tips "Avoid trite or forced rhyming. Be aware of the magazine's doctrinal views (send for doctrinal beliefs booklet)."

▣ ◪ ◎ THE BIG UGLY REVIEW

490 Second St., Suite 200, San Fransisco CA 94107. E-mail: info@biguglyreview.com. Website: www.biguglyreview.com. **Contact:** Miriam Pirone, Poetry editor.

Magazines Needs *The Big Ugly Review*, published 2 times/year online, showcases "emerging and established writers, photographers, filmmakers, and musicians. Each issue includes fiction (short stories and flash fiction), creative nonfiction, poetry, photo-essays, short films of 5 minutes or less, and downloadable songs, all related to that issue's theme." Wants "vivid and accurate poetry of any style, form, or length." Has published poetry by Edward Smallfield, Jennifer C. Chapis, Valerie Coulton, Stephen Hemenway, Diana Der-Hovanessian, and James Cihlar. Receives about 750-1,000 poems/year, accepts about 20.

How to Contact Submit no more than 6 poems at a time. Considers previously published poems and simultaneous submissions. Accepts e-mail submissions (pasted into body of message and as attachment); no disk submissions. "Send documents in Word or Word-readable attachments. Also paste the poems into the body of the e-mail text. Include your name, address, phone number, and e-mail on the first page." Cover letter is preferred. Reads submissions year round. Time between acceptance and publication is 1-2 months. Sometimes comments on rejected poems. Regularly publishes theme issues. Guidelines available on website. Responds "approximately 1 month after close of the issue's submission deadline." No payment. Author retains all rights.

◪ THE BITTER OLEANDER

4983 Tall Oaks Dr., Fayetteville NY 13066-9776. (315)637-3047. Fax: (315)637-5056. E-mail: info@bitteroleander.com. Website: www.bitteroleander.com. **Contact:** Paul B. Roth, Editor/Publisher.

• Poetry published in *The Bitter Oleander* has been included in *The Best American Poetry*; recognized by Public Radio's *Excellence In Print* award for best literary journal of 2005.

Magazines Needs *The Bitter Oleander*, published semiannually in April and October, seeks "highly imaginative poetry whose language is serious. Particularly interested in translations."

Has published poetry by Alan Britt, George Kalamaras, Duane Locke, Silvia Scheibli, Shawn Fawson, Anthony Seidman, and Christine Boyka Kluge. *The Bitter Oleander* is 128 pages, digest-sized, offset-printed, perfect-bound, with glossy 4-color cover with art, includes ads. Receives about 12,000 poems/year, accepts less than 1%. Press run is 1,200. Single copy: $10; subscription: $18. Make checks payable to Bitter Oleander Press.

How to Contact Submit up to 8 poems at a time. Lines/poem: 30 maximum. No previously published poems. Allows simultaneous submissions. No e-mail submissions unless outside U.S. Cover letter is preferred. Include name and address on each page of ms. Does not read mss during July. Time between acceptance and publication is 6 months. "All poems are read by the editor only, and all decisions are made by this editor." Often comments on rejected poems. Guidelines available for SASE or on website. Responds within 1 month. Pays 1 contributor's copy.

Contest/Award Offerings Sponsors the Frances Locke Memorial Poetry Award.

Tips "We simply want poetry that is imaginative and serious in its delivery of language. So much flat-line poetry is written today that anyone reading one magazine after another cannot tell the difference."

Ⓝ ☑ BLACKBIRD

An online journal of literature and the arts, Virginia Commonwealth University Department of Fic, Richmond VA 23284. (804)225-4729. E-mail: blackbird@vcu.edu. Website: www.blackbird.vcu.edu. **Contact:** Mary Flinn, Gregory Donovan, editors.

How to Contact Send complete ms. In clude cover letter, name, address, telephone number, brief biographical comment. Responds in 6 months to mss. Accepts simultaneous submissions. Sample copy online. Writer's guidelines online. Pays $200 for fiction, $40 for poetry. Pays on publication for first North American serial rights. Does not read from April 15-November 1. Publishes ms 3-6 months after acceptance. **Publishes 1-2 new writers/ year.**

$ ☑ BLACK WARRIOR REVIEW

P.O. Box 862936, Tuscaloosa AL 35486-0027. (205)348-4518. E-mail: bwr@ua.edu. Website: www.bwr.ua.edu. **Contact:** Daniela Olszewska, poetry editor.

• Poetry published in *Black Warrior Review* has been included in *The Best American Poetry* and *The Pushcart Prize*.

Magazines Needs *Black Warrior Review*, published semiannually in February and October, prints poetry, fiction, nonfiction, art and comics by up-and-coming as well as accomplished writers. Has published poetry by Joanna Klink, Claire Donato, Terrance Hayes, Sabrina Orah Mark, K.A. Hays, Andrew Zawacki, Catie Rosemurgy, Jaswinder Bolina, Oliver de la Paz, and JOshua Marie Wilkinson. *Black Warrior Review* is 180 pages, digest-sized. Press run is 2,000. Subscription: $16/year, $28 for 2 years, $40 for 3 years. Sample: $10. Make checks payable to the University of Alabama.

How to Contact Submit up to 7 poems at a time. Considers simultaneous submissions if noted. No e-mail or disk submissions. Responds in up to 5 months. Pays up to $75 and one-year subscription. Acquires first rights. Reviews books of poetry in single- or multi-book format. Send materials for review consideration.

Tips "Subscribe or purchase a sample copy to see what we're after. For 33 years, we've published new voices alongside Pulitzer Prize winners. Freshness and attention to craft, rather than credits, impress us most."

▣ ☑ BLOOD LOTUS

E-mail: bloodlotusjournal@gmail.com. Website: www.bloodlotus.org. **Contact:** Stacia Fleegal, managing editor.

Magazines Needs *Blood Lotus*, published quarterly online, publishes "poetry, fiction, and anything in between!" Wants "fresh language, memorable characters, and beautiful artwork."

How to Contact Submit 3-5 poems of free or formal verse to bloodlotuspoetry@gmail. com. Considers simultaneous submissions; no previously published poems. Will not open attachments. Reads submissions year round. Guidelines on website. Acquires first North American rights, electronic archival rights.

ⓝ ☑ BLOOD ORANGE REVIEW

E-mail: admin@bloodorangereview.com. Website: www.bloodorangereview.com. **Contact:** H.K. Hummel, Stephanie Lenox, Bryan Fry. *Blood Orange Review* publishes fiction, poetry, and nonfiction in an online quarterly. The Review is committed to cultivating an audience for exciting literary voices and promoting its writers.

Magazines Needs *Blood Orange Review*, published online quarterly, is "looking for more than an interesting story or a descriptive image. The pieces we publish are the ones that we remember days or even weeks afterward for their compelling characters, believable voices, or sharp revelations. We're not afraid of anything, but if we bristle or stop having fun, we figure there is a good chance our readers will too. In a word, write deftly. Leave us desiring more."

How to Contact Submit 3-5 poems through online submission manager in one document. Accepts simultaneous submissions; no previously published poems. Responds in 8 weeks. Reads submissions year round. Additional guidelines can be found on website.

☑ ◎ BLUE COLLAR REVIEW

Partisan Press, P.O. Box 11417, Norfolk VA 23517. E-mail: red-ink@earthlink.net. Website: www.partisanpress.org. **Contact:** A. Markowitz, editor, and mary Franke, co-editor.

Magazines Needs *Blue Collar Review (Journal of Progressive Working Class Literature)*, published quarterly, contains poetry, short stories, and illustrations "reflecting the working class experience—a broad range from the personal to the societal. Our purpose is to promote and expand working class literature and an awareness of the connections between workers of all occupations and the social context in which we live. Also to inspire the creativity and latent talent in 'common' working people." Wants "writing of high quality that reflects the working class experience from delicate internal awareness to the militant. We accept a broad range of style and focus—but are generally progressive, political/social." Does not want anything "racist, sexist-misogynist, right wing, or overly religious. No 'bubba' poetry, nothing overly introspective or confessional, no academic/abstract or 'Vogon' poetry. No simple beginners rhyme or verse." Has published poetry by Simon Perchik, Jim Daniels, Mary McAnally, Marge Piercy, Alan Catlin, and Rob Whitbeck. *Blue Collar Review* is 60 pages, digest-sized, offset-printed, saddle-stapled, with colored card cover, includes ads. Receives hundreds of poems/year, accepts about 15%. Press run is 500. Subscription: $15/year, $25 for 2 years. Sample: $5. Make checks payable to Partisan Press.

How to Contact Submit up to 4 poems at a time; "no complete manuscripts, please." Considers previously published poems; no simultaneous submissions. No e-mail submissions; postal submissions only. Cover letter is preferred. Include full-size SASE for response. "Poems should be typed as they are to appear upon publication. Author's name and address should appear on every page. Overly long lines reduce chances of acceptance as line may have to be broken to fit the page size and format of the journal." Time between acceptance and publication is 3 months to a year. Poems are reviewed by editor and co-editor. Seldom comments on rejected poems. Guidelines available on website. Responds in 3 months. Sends prepublication galleys only upon request. Pays 1-3 contributor's copies. Considers reviews of chapbooks and journals.

Additional Information Partisan Press looks for "poetry of power that reflects a working class consciousness and moves us forward as a society. Must be good writing reflecting social realism including but not limited to political issues." Publishes about 3 chapbooks/year; not presently open to unsolicited submissions. "Submissions are requested from among the poets published in the *Blue Collar Review*." Has published *A Possible Explanation* by Peggy Safire and *American Sounds* by Robert Edwards. Chapbooks are usually 20-60 pages, digest-sized, offset-printed, saddle-stapled or flat-spined, with card or glossy covers. Sample chapbooks are $7 and listed on website.

Contest/Award Offerings Sponsors the annual Working People's Poetry Competition.

Tips "Don't be afraid to try. Read a variety of poetry and find your own voice. Write about reality, your own experience, and what moves you."

◎ BLUELINE

125 Morey Hall, Dept. of English and Communication, SUNY Potsdam, Potsdam NY 13676. *Blueline*, published annually in May, is "dedicated to prose and poetry about the Adirondacks and other regions similar in geography and spirit." Wants "clear, concrete poetry that goes beyond mere description. We prefer a realistic to a romantic view." Does not want "sentimental or extremely experimental poetry." Uses poems on "nature in general, Adirondack Mountains in particular. Form may vary, can be traditional or contemporary." Has published poetry by L.M. Rosenberg, John Unterecker, Lloyd Van Brunt, Laurence Josephs, Maurice Kenny, and Nancy L. Nielsen. *Blueline* is 200 pages, digest-sized. Press run is 600. Sample: $3 (back issue).

☑ BOGG: A JOURNAL OF CONTEMPORARY WRITING

Bogg Publications, 422 N. Cleveland St., Arlington VA 22201-1424. **Contact:** John Elsberg, Poetry Editor. *Bogg: A Journal of Contemporary Writing*, published twice/year, combines "innovative American work with a range of writing from England and the Commonwealth. It features poetry (including haiku and tanka, prose poems, and experimental/visual poems), very short experimental or satirical/wry fiction, interviews, essays on the small press scene, reviews, review essays, and line art. We also publish occasional free-for-postage pamphlets." Uses a great deal of poetry in each issue (with featured poets). Wants "poetry in all styles, with a healthy leavening of shorts (under 10 lines). *Bogg* seeks original voices."

Considers all subject matter. "Some have even found the magazine's sense of play offensive. Overt religious and political poems have to have strong poetical merits—statement alone is not sufficient." *Bogg* started in England and in 1975 began including a supplement of American work; it is now published in the U.S. and mixes U.S., Canadian, Australian, and UK work with reviews of small press publications from all of those areas. Has published poetry by Richard Peabody, Ann Menebroker, LeRoy Gorman, Marcia Arrieta, Kathy Ernst, and Steve Sneyd. *Bogg* is 56 pages, digest-sized, typeset, saddle-stapled, in a format "that leaves enough white space to let each poem stand and breathe alone." Receives more than 10,000 American poems/year, accepts about 100-150. Press run is 850. Single copy: $6; subscription: $15 for 3 issues. Sample: $4.

How to Contact Submit 6 poems at a time. Considers previously published poems "occasionally, but with a credit line to the previous publisher"; no simultaneous submissions. Cover letter is preferred ("it can help us get a 'feel' for the writer's intentions/slant"). SASE required or material will be discarded ("no exceptions"). Prefers hard copy mss, with author's name and address on each sheet. Guidelines available for SASE. Responds in 1 week. Pays 2 contributor's copies. Acquires one-time rights. Reviews books/chapbooks of poetry and other magazines/journals in 250 words. Send materials to relevant editor (by region) for review consideration. Bogg Publications occasionally publishes pamphlets and chapbooks by invitation only, with the author receiving 25% of the print run. Recent chapbooks include *Cleft Brow Totem* by Dave Wright, *South Jersey Shore* by David Check and John Elsberg, and *78 RPM* by John Yamrus. Obtain free chapbook samples by sending digest-sized SASE with 2 ounces worth of postage.

Tips "Become familiar with a magazine before submitting to it. Long lists of previous credits irritate us. Short notes about how the writer has heard about *Bogg* or what he or she finds interesting or annoying in the magazine are welcome."

☑ BOMB MAGAZINE

80 Hanson Place, Suite 703, Brooklyn NY 11217. (718)636-9100. E-mail: firstproof@ bombsite.com; generalinquiries@bombsite.com. Website: www.bombsite.com. **Contact:** Monica de la Torre. Magazine: 9 × 11.5; 104 pages; 70 lb. glossy cover; illustrations; photos. Written, edited and produced by industry professionals and funded by those interested in the arts. Publishes writing which is unconventional and contains an edge, whether it be in style or subject matter. Quarterly. Estab. 1981. Circ. 36,000.Experimental, novel excerpts, contemporary. No genre: romance, science fiction, horror, western. Receives 200 unsolicited mss/month. Accepts 6 mss/issue; 24 mss/year. Publishes ms 3-6 months after acceptance. Agented fiction 70%. **Publishes 2-3 new writers/year.** Recently published work by Lynne Tillman, Dennis Cooper, Susan Wheeler, and Laurie Sheck.

How to Contact "*BOMB Magazine* accepts unsolicited poetry and prose submissions for our literary pull-out *First Proof* by mail from January 1- August 31. Submissions sent outside these dates will be returned unread. Manuscripts should be typed, double-spaced (prose only), proofread, and should be final drafts, not exceeding 20 pages in length." Accepts simultaneous submissions. Include SASE. Responds in 4-6 months. Send ms with SASE. Responds in 3-5 months to mss. Accepts multiple submissions. Sample copy for $7.95. Writer's guidelines on website: http://bombsite.com/issues/0/articles/3406 or by email. Accepts submissions from January 1 to August 31; mss sent "outside those dates will be returned unread. "Pays $100, and contributor's copies. Pays on publication for Exclusive first-time serial rights and license in electronic, audio and print form in English language. Sends galleys to author.

☑ ◎ BORDERLANDS: TEXAS POETRY REVIEW

P.O. Box 33096, Austin TX 78764. **Contact:** Editor. *Borderlands: Texas Poetry Review*, published semiannually, prints "high-quality, outward-looking poetry by new and established poets, as well as brief reviews of poetry books and critical essays. Cosmopolitan in content, but particularly welcomes Texas and Southwest writers." Wants "outward-looking poems that exhibit social, political, geographical, historical, feminist, or spiritual awareness coupled with concise artistry. We also seek poems in 2 languages (one of which must be English), where the poet has written both versions." Does not want "introspective work about the speaker's psyche, childhood, or intimate relationships." Has published poetry by Walter McDonald, Naomi Shihab Nye, Mario Susko, Wendy Barker, Larry D. Thomas, and Reza Shirazi, and Scott Hightower. *Borderlands* is 100-150 pages, digest-sized, offset-printed, perfect-bound, with 4-color cover. Receives about 2,000 poems/year, accepts about 120. Press run is 1,000. Sample: $12.

How to Contact Submit 4 typed poems at a time. No previously published poems or simultaneous submissions. No e-mail submissions. Include SASE with sufficient return postage. Seldom comments on rejected poems. Guidelines available for SASE or on website. Responds in 6-8 months. Pays 1 contributor's copy. Acquires first rights. Reviews books of poetry in 1 page. Send materials for review consideration to Editors, *Borderlands*.

▣ ☑ BORN MAGAZINE

P.O. Box 1313, Portland OR 97207-1313. E-mail: editors@bornmagazine.org. Website: www.bornmagazine.org. **Contact:** Anmarie Trimble, Editor. *Born Magazine*, published online, is "an experimental venue that marries literary arts and interactive media. We publish multimedia 'interpretations' of poetry and prose, created by interactive artists in collaboration with poets and writers." Wants poems suited to "interpretation into a visual or interactive form. Due to the unusual, collaborative nature of our publication, we represent a variety of styles and forms of poetry." Has published poetry by Victorian Chang, Bob Hicok, Timothy Liu, Edward Hirsch, Marvin Bell, Michele Glazer, Major Jackson, Ander Monson, and Joyelle McSweeney.

How to Contact Submit 2-5 poems at a time. Considers previously published poems; no simultaneous submissions. Accepts e-mail submissions only (as Word documents or .txt files). Reads submissions year round. Submit seasonal poems 6 months in advance. Time between acceptance and publication is 3-6 months. "Poems must be accepted by the editor and 1 contributing editor. Selected works are forwarded to our art department, which chooses an artist partner to work with the writer. Artist and writer collaborate on a concept, to be realized by the artist. We also accept proposals for collaborating with an artist to create a piece from scratch." Never comments on rejected poems. Guidelines available on website. Responds in "a few months" to e-mail queries. Always sends prepublication galleys. No payment. "We can offer only the experience of participating in a collaborative community, as well as a broad audience (we average 40,000 readers to our site per month)." Acquires one-time rights.

Tips "We accept new and previously published work. *Born*'s mission is to nurture creativity and co-development of new literary art forms on the Web."

$ ☑ BOSTON REVIEW

35 Medford St., Suite 302, Somerville MA 02143. (617)591-0505. Fax: (617)591-0440. E-mail: review@bostonreview.net. Website: www.bostonreview.net.

- Poetry submitted to *Boston Review* has been included in The Best American Poetry Anthology.

Magazines Needs *Boston Review*, published bimonthly, is a tabloid-format magazine of arts, culture, and politics. "We are open to both traditional and experimental forms. What we value most is originality and a strong sense of voice." Has published poetry by Frank Bidart, Lucie Brock-Broido, Peter Gizzi, Jorie Graham, Allen Grossman, John Koethe, and Karen Volkman. Receives about 5,000 submissions/year, accepts about 30 poems/year. Circulation is 15,000 nationally. Single copy: $5; subscription: $25. Sample: $5.

How to Contact Submit 5-6 poems at a time through online submissions system. Does not accept faxed or e-mailed submissions. Include brief bio. Time between acceptance and publication is 6 months to one year. Reads submissions September 15-May 15. Responds in 2-4 months. Payment varies. Acquires first serial rights. Reviews books of poetry, solicited reviews only. Send materials for review consideration.

Contest/Award Offerings The *Boston Review* Annual Poetry Contest.

☑ ◎ THE BRIAR CLIFF REVIEW

Briar Cliff University, 3303 Rebecca St., Sioux City IA 51104-2340. E-mail: jeanne.emmons@briarcliff.edu. Website: www.briarcliff.edu/bcreview/. **Contact:** Jeanne Emmons, Poetry Editor; Managing Editor: Tricia Currans-Sheehan. Member: CLMP; American Humanities Index; EBSCO/Humanities International Complete.

Magazines Needs *The Briar Cliff Review*, published annually in April, is "an attractive, eclectic literary and cultural magazine." Wants "quality poetry with strong imagery and tight, well-wrought language; especially interested in, but not limited to, regional, Midwestern content." Has published poetry by Jeanne Wagner, Gaylord Brewer, and Joe Wilkins. *The Briar Cliff Review* is 100 pages, magazine-sized, professionally printed on 100 lb. Altima Satin text paper, perfect-bound, with 4-color cover on dull stock. Receives about 1,000 poems/year, accepts about 30. Press run is 1,000. Sample: $15.

How to Contact Considers simultaneous submissions, but expects prompt notification of acceptance elsewhere; no previously published poems. No e-mail submissions; postal submissions only. Cover letter is required. "Include short bio. Submissions should be typewritten or letter quality, with author's name and address on each page. No manuscripts returned without SASE." Reads submissions August 1-November 1 only. Time between acceptance and publication is up to 6 months. Seldom comments on rejected poems. Guidelines available on website. Responds in 6-8 months. Pays 2 contributor's copies. Acquires first serial rights.

Contest/Award Offerings The *Briar Cliff Review* Annual Fiction, Poetry and Creative Nonfiction Contest.

⬛ ◎ BRILLIANT CORNERS: A JOURNAL OF JAZZ & LITERATURE

P.O. Box 1206, Ann Arbor MI 48106. (888)359-9188. E-mail: clare@bridgesjournal.org. Website: www.bridgesjournal.org. Established 1990. **Contact:** Clare Kinberg, managing editor.

Magazines Needs *Brilliant Corners*, published semiannually, features jazz-related poetry, fiction, and nonfiction. "We are open as to length and form." Wants "work that is both passionate and well crafted—work worthy of our recent contributors." Does not want "sloppy hipster jargon or improvisatory nonsense." Has published poetry by Amiri Baraka, Jayne Cortez, Yusef Komunyakaa, Philip Levine, Sonia Sanchez, and Al Young. *Brilliant Corners* is 90 pages, digest-sized, commercially printed, perfect-bound, with color card cover with original artwork, includes ads. Accepts about 5% of work received. Press run is 350. Subscription: $12. Sample: $7.

How to Contact Submit 3-5 poems at a time. No previously published poems or simultaneous submissions. No e-mail or fax submissions. Cover letter is preferred. Reads submissions September 1-May 15 only. Seldom comments on rejected poems. Responds in 2 months. Pays 2 contributor's copies. Acquires first North American serial rights. Staff reviews books of poetry. Send materials for review consideration.

⬛ BROKEN SOUL'S INTERNATIONAL LITERARY ARTS JOURNAL

158 Spencer Avenue, Suite 100, Pittsburgh PA 15227. E-mail: brokensoulsinternational@ comcast.net. Website: http://brokensoulsinternationalliteraryartsjournal.webs.com. **Contact:** John Thompson. *Broken Soul's International Literary Arts Journal*, published quarterly, is open to beginners as well as professionals. "We are 'dedicated to the emotional intellectual' with a creative perception of life." Wants strong imagery and accepts free verse, avant-garde poetry, haiku, and senryu. Open to length and subject matter. Does not want porn or violence. Has published poetry by Lyn Lifshin, Rose Marie Hunold, Peter Vetrano, Carol Frances Brown, and Richard King Perkins II. 30-50 pages, magazine-sized, laser-printed, with stock cover with sleeve. Receives about 1,000 poems/year, accepts about 10-15%. Press run is about 100 (more than 60 subscribers, 10 libraries). Single copy: $6; subscription: $20. Sample (when available): $4.Considers previously published poems and simultaneous submissions. Cover letter is preferred. "Give brief bio, state where you heard of us, state if material has been previously published and where. Always enclose SASE if you seek reply and return of your material." Time between acceptance and publication is within one year. Always comments on rejected poems. Guidelines available for SASE. Responds in one month.

Tips "Don't be afraid to submit your material. Take rejection as advice—study your market. Create your own style and voice, then be heard. 'I am a creator, a name beneath words' (from my poem, 'unidentified-Identified')."

⬛ BRYANT LITERARY REVIEW

Faculty Suite F, Bryant University, Smithfield RI 02917. E-mail: blr@bryant.edu. Website: http://web.bryant.edu/~blr. **Contact:** Tom Chandler, Editor. *Bryant Literary Review* is an international magazine of poetry and fiction published annually in May. Features poetry, fiction, photography, and art. "Our only standard is quality." Has published poetry by Michael S. Harper, Mary Crow, Denise Duhamel, and Baron Wormser. Bryant Literary

Review is 125 pages, digest-sized, offset-printed, perfect-bound, with 4-color cover with art or photo. Receives about 3,000 poems/year, accepts about 1%. Press run is 2,500. Single copy: $8; subscription: $8. For more information, contact blr@bryant.edu. To submit work, please review the submission guidelines on our website.

How to Contact Submit 3-5 poems at a time. Cover letter is required. "Include SASE; please submit only once each reading period." Reads submissions September 1-December 31. Time between acceptance and publication is 5 months. Seldom comments on rejected poems. Guidelines available in magazine or on website. Responds in 3 months. Pays 2 contributor's copies. Acquires one-time rights.

Tips "No abstract expressionist poems, please. We prefer accessible work of depth and quality."

☑ BURNSIDE REVIEW

P.O. Box 1782, Portland OR 97207. **Contact:** Sid Miller, Editor. *Burnside Review*, published every 9 months, prints "the best poetry we can get our hands on." Each issue includes one featured poet with an interview and new poems. "We tend to publish poetry that finds beauty in truly unexpected places; that combines urban and natural imagery; that breaks the heart." Open to all forms. Translations are encouraged. "Would like to see more lyric poetry." Has published poetry by Linda Bierds, Dorianne Laux, Ed Skoog, Campbell McGrath, Paul Guest, and Larissa Szporluk. *Burnside Review* is 80 pages, 6x6, professionally printed, perfect-bound. Receives about 2,500 poems/year, accepts about 50. Press run is 500. Single copy: $8; subscription: $13. Make checks payable to *Burnside Review* or order online.

How to Contact Submit 3-5 poems at a time. Considers simultaneous submissions; no previously published poems. Accepts e-mail only. "E-mailed submissions should include all poems and cover letter in one Word or RTF file sent as an attachment. The subject line should read 'Poetry Submission.' Send to submissions@burnsidereview.org. "Please check our website for complete guidelines and possible themed issues. Submissions sent by post will not be read and will be recycled. Please put name and address on each poem." Reads submissions year-round. Submit seasonal poems 3-6 months in advance. Time between acceptance and publication is up to 9 months. "Editors read all poems." Seldom comments on rejected poems. Responds in 2-4 months. Pays one contributor's copy. Acquires first rights.

Contest/Award Offerings The *Burnside Review* offers a Chapbook Competition.

$ ☑ BUTTON MAGAZINE

P.O. Box 77, Westminster MA 01473. E-mail: sally@moonsigns.net. Website: http://moonsigns.net. Established 1993. **Contact:** Maude Piper, poetry editor.

Magazines Needs *Button*, published annually, is "New England's tiniest magazine of fiction, poetry, and gracious living." Wants "poetry that incises a perfect figure eight on the ice, but also cuts beneath that mirrored surface. Minimal use of vertical pronoun." Does not want "sentiment; no 'musing' on who or what done ya wrong." Has published poetry by Amanda Powell, Brendan Galvin, Jean Monahan, Mary Campbell, Kevin McGrath, and Ed Conti. *Button* is 30 pages, 4¼ × 5½, saddle-stapled, with cardstock offset cover with illustrations that incorporate 1 or more buttons. Press run is 1,200. Subscription: $10/6 issues. "Sorry, no overseas subscriptions." Sample: $2, plus $2 S/H and 1 First-Class stamp.

How to Contact Submit no more than 2 poems at a time. "Do not submit more than twice in one year." No previously published poems. Cover letter is required. Time between acceptance and publication is up to 6 months. "Our reading period is April 1-September 30. Work sent at other times will be discarded." Poems are circulated to an editorial board. Often comments on rejected poems. Guidelines available by e-mail. Responds within 4 months. Pays honorarium and at least 2 contributor's copies. Acquires first North American serial rights.

Tips "Writing as therapy is fine. Publishing as therapy is not. Take the vertical pronoun (I) and write your poem without it. Still got something to say? Also, *Button* tries to reflect a world one would want to live in—this does not mean we make the space for various uncatalogued human vices (self-pity, navel gazing). If you can be really amusing about those, that's another story. Finally, writers who need to say they've published 1,200 poems in various magazines and then name all of the magazines—well, we don't really need to know. Aim high, write often, but refine, refine, refine. If you feel your work is ready to stand alongside poems by people who have also published in prominent national journals, please send, but bear in mind we are very exacting about what we publish. Occasionally we respond personally on ms."

N CAKETRAIN

P.O. Box 82588, Pittsburgh PA 15218. E-mail: caketrainjournal@hotmail.com. Website: www.caketrain.org. Established 2003. **Contact:** Amanda Raczkowski and Joseph Reed, editors.

Magazines Needs "*Caketrain* is a literary journal and press based in Pittsburgh, Pennsylvania. Our interest is in bringing you, reader, the very best in contemporary creative writing, full stop. *Caketrain* journals and chapbooks are digest-sized, printed on 60 lb. acid-free, off-white stock, perfect-bound by a ten-point high-gloss cover stock. Price: $8.

How to Contact Submit up to 7 poems, works of fiction or creative nonfiction (no book reviews), works of visual art, or any combination. Considers simultaneous submissions; no previously published poems. Notify immediately if a piece is chosen for publication elsewhere. Accepts submissions by mail or e-mail (attached DOC, RTF or PDF preferred over pasted-in-the-body for text). Cover letter is required. Include SASE. "All unused print submissions will be recycled upon rejection. Please include a brief, press-ready biographical statement and any relevant contact information. Print name and title on the top of each poetry page." Guidelines available on website. Response time up to 6 months. Pays 1 contributor's copy. Rights revert to poet upon publication.

Contest/Award Offerings See Contests and Awards section for Caketrain Chapbook competition.

☑ CALIFORNIA QUARTERLY

P.O. Box 7126, Orange CA 92863-7126. **Contact:** The Editors.

Magazines Needs *California Quarterly*, the official publication of the California State Poetry Society (an affiliate of the National Federation of State Poetry Societies), is designed "to encourage the writing and dissemination of poetry." Wants poetry on any subject. "No geographical limitations. Quality is all that matters." Has published poetry by Michael L. Johnson, Lyn Lifshin, and Joanna C. Scott. *California Quarterly* is 64 pages, digest-sized, offset-printed, perfect-bound with cover art. Receives 3,000-4,000 poems/year, accepts about 5%. Press run is 500. Membership in CSPS is $30/year and includes a subscription to *California Quarterly*. Sample: $7 (includes guidelines).

How to Contact Submit up to 6 poems at a time. Lines/poem: 60 maximum. No previously published poems. Accepts submissions by postal mail only; no e-mail submissions. Put name and address on each sheet, include SASE. Seldom comments on rejected poems. Guidelines available for SASE. Responds in up to 8 months. Pays 1 contributor's copy. Acquires first rights. Rights revert to poet after publication.

Tips "Since our editor changes with each issue, we encourage poets to resubmit."

☐ ◎ CALYX, A JOURNAL OF ART AND LITERATURE BY WOMEN

Calyx Books, P.O. Box B, Corvallis OR 97339-0539. (541)753-9384. Fax: (541)753-0515. E-mail: editor@calyxpress.org. Website: www.calyxpress.org.

Magazines Needs *CALYX, A Journal of Art and Literature by Women*, published 3 times every 18 months, contains poetry, prose, art, book reviews, essays, and interviews by and about women. Wants "excellently crafted poetry that also has excellent content." Has published poetry by Maurya Simon, Diane Averill, Carole Boston Weatherford, and Eleanor Wilner. *CALYX* is 6x8, handsomely printed on heavy paper, flat-spined, with glossy color cover. Single copy: $10 plus $4 shipping; subscription: $23/volume (3 issues), $41 for 2 volumes (6 issues). Sample: $14. See website for foreign and institutional rates.

How to Contact Send up to 6 poems at a time. Considers previously published poems "occasionally" and simultaneous submissions "if kept up-to-date on publication." No fax or e-mail submissions except from overseas. Include SASE and short bio. "We accept copies in good condition and clearly readable. *CALYX* is edited by a collective editorial board." Reads submissions postmarked October 1-December 31 only. **Manuscripts received outside of reading period will be returned unread.** Guidelines available for SASE, by e-mail, or on website. Responds in 4-9 months. Pays one contributor's copy/poem, plus subscription. Send materials for review consideration.

Additional Information CALYX Books publishes one book of poetry/year. All work published is by women. Has published *Storytelling in Cambodia* by Willa Schneberg and *Black Candle: Poems about Women from India, Pakistan, and Bangladesh* by Chitra Banerjee Divakaruni. **Closed to submissions until further notice.**

Contest/Award Offerings The annual Lois Cranston Memorial Poetry Prize and the new Sarah Lantz Memorial Poetry Book Prize.

Tips "Read the publication and be familiar with what we have published."

✿ ☐ ◎ CANADIAN ZEN HAIKU

297 Blake Blvd. #4, Ottawa ON K1L 6L6, Canada. (613)744-1048. E-mail: laissezmoienpaix@gmail.com. Website: http://canadianzenhaikuhome.homestead.com/index.html. *Canadian Zen Haiku*, published quarterly, features Asian poetry forms. Does not want "any poetry genre other than haiku, senryu, tanka, renga, or Japanese form poetry." Considers poetry by children and teens. Has published poetry by Sondra Ball, Richard Doiron, Shigeki Matsumura, Lanie Shanzyra Rebanos, and Deborah P. Kolodji. *Canadian Zen Haiku* is 36 pages, laser-printed, stapled, with 67 bond high-quality acid-free cover. Receives about 5,000 poems/year, accepts about 600 (or 12%). Press run is 100 estimated for first issue;

25 distributed free to contributors. Single copy: $4 CAD; subscription: $16/year CAD for Canadian subscribers only, or $20/year USD for international subscribers (all other countries). Sample: $5 CAD. Make checks payable to Richard Vallance Janke.

How to Contact Submit 12 poems at a time (maximum). Lines/poem: 3; no more than 20 syllables if haiku. Considers previously published poems; no simultaneous submissions. Accepts e-mail submissions (as attachment—2 copies: one in RTF format, one in TXT format—all poems in one digest file); no disk submissions. "Never paste poems into body of e-mail message. Do not submit your haiku separately, one at a time." Cover letter is required. "Include three- to five-sentence bio and link to your poetry home page, if any." Reads submissions year round. Submit seasonal poems 2 months in advance. Time between acceptance and publication is 3 months. Poems are circulated to an editorial board. Never comments on rejected poems. "It is considered courteous form for contributors who are regularly accepted for publication in *Canadian Zen Haiku* to subscribe to the journal." Regularly publishes theme issues. Upcoming themes available in magazine. Guidelines available in magazine or on website. Responds in 3 weeks. Always sends prepublication galleys. Pays one contributor's copy. Acquires first rights and electronic rights. "A small digest of approximately 20% of the haiku published in *Canadian Zen Haiku* will also be published in an online version of the same journal at its home page URL. The digest online version is free, but it is just that, a digest only." Rights revert to poet upon publication. Reviews books/chapbooks of poetry and other magazines/journals in 500 words "or more in each issue, where applicable."

Tips "Professional poetry journal editors such as myself are invariably on the lookout for poetry genres specifically meeting our market's targeted needs. In the case of *Canadian Zen Haiku*, this means we are looking for highly competent Japanese haiku, senryu, renga, tanka, or other Japanese-only verse forms. We accept Japanese poetry form verse in virtually any language, provided there is a parallel English or French translation submitted. Spelling and grammar must be impeccable, regardless of language of submission. The editors read several languages, including English, French, Spanish, Italian, German, Greek, Latin, and Japanese. We encourage competent submissions in as many languages as possible."

⊕ ◑ ◎ CANDELABRUM POETRY MAGAZINE

The Red Candle Press, 1 Chatsworth Court, Outram Rd., Southsea PO5 1RA, England. Website: www.members.tripod.com/redcandlepress. *Candelabrum*, published twice/year in April and October, prints "good-quality metrical verse." Wants "rhymed verse especially. Elegantly cadenced free verse is acceptable. Accepts 5-7-5 haiku. Any subject, including eroticism (but not porn)—satire, love poems, nature lyrics, philosophical." Does not want "weak stuff (moons and Junes, loves and doves, etc.). No chopped-up prose pretending to be free verse. Nothing racist, ageist, or sexist." Has published poetry by Pam Russell, Ryan Underwood, David Britton, Alice Evans, Jack Harvey, and Nick Spargo. Receives about 2,000 submissions/year, accepts about 10% (usually holds poems for the next year). Press run is 900. Sample: $6 (in U.S. bills only; non-sterling checks not accepted).

How to Contact Lines/poem: 40 maximum. No simultaneous submissions. No e-mail submissions. "Submit anytime. Enclose one IRC for reply only; 3 IRCs if you wish manuscript returned. If you'd prefer a reply by e-mail, without return of unwanted manuscript, please enclose one British first-class stamp, IRC, or U.S. dollar bill to pay for the call. Each poem on a separate sheet, please; neat typescripts or neat legible manuscripts. Please, no dark, oily photostats, no colored ink (only black or blue). Author's name and address on each sheet, please." Guidelines available on website. Responds in about 2 months. Pays one contributor's copy.Red Candle Press is "a formalist press, specially interested in metrical and rhymed poetry, though free verse is not excluded. We're more interested in poems than poets; that is, we're interested in what sort of poems an author produces, not in his or her personality."

Tips "Formalist poetry is much more popular here in Britain, and we think also in the United States, now than it was in 1970, when we established *Candelabrum*. We always welcome new poets, especially formalists, and we like to hear from the U.S. as well as from here at home. General tip: Study the various outlets at the library, or buy a copy of *Candelabrum*, or borrow a copy from a subscriber, before you go to the expense of submitting your work. The Red Candle Press regrets that, because of bank charges, it is unable to accept dollar cheques. However, it is always happy to accept U.S. dollar bills."

⊠ $ ☑ THE CAPILANO REVIEW

2055 Purcell Way, North Vancouver BC V7J 3H5, Canada. (604)984-1712. E-mail: tcr@ capcollege.bc.ca; contact@thecapilanoreview.ca. Website: www.thecapilanoreview.ca. **Contact:** Submissions.

Magazines Needs *The Capilano Review*, published 3 times/year, is a literary and visual arts review. Wants "avant-garde, experimental, previously unpublished poetry. *The Capilano Review* is 100-120 pages, digest-sized, finely printed, perfect-bound, with glossy full-color card cover. Circulation is 800. Sample: $14.70 CAD prepaid.

How to Contact Submit 5-6 poems. No simultaneous submissions. No e-mail or disk submissions. Cover letter is required. Include SAE with IRCs; "submissions with U.S. postage will not be considered." Responds in up to 4 months. Pays $50-200 CAD, subscription, and 2 contributor's copies. Acquires first North American serial rights.

Tips "Read the magazine and website before you submit. *The Capilano Review* receives dozens of manuscripts each week; unfortunately, the majority of them are simply inappropriate for the magazine."

⃣ ◎ THE CARIBBEAN WRITER

University of the Virgin Islands, RR 1, P.O. Box 10,000, Kingshill, St. Croix US 00850. (340)692-4152. Fax: (340)692-4026. E-mail: info@thecaribbeanwriter.org. Website: www. TheCaribbeanWriter.com. **Contact:** Opal Palmer Adisa, PhD.

• Poetry published in *The Caribbean Writer* has appeared in The Pushcart Prize.

Magazines Needs *The Caribbean Writer*, published annually, is a literary anthology with a Caribbean focus (Caribbean must be central to the literary work, or the work must reflect a Caribbean heritage, experience, or perspective). Has published poetry by Edwidge Danticat, Geoffrey Philp, and Thomas Reiter. *The Caribbean Writer* is 300+ pages, digest-sized, handsomely printed on heavy stock, perfect-bound, with glossy card cover. Press run is 1,200. Single copy: $15 plus $5 postage; subscription: $25. Sample: $7 plus $5 postage. (Note: postage to and from the Virgin Islands is the same as within the US.)

How to Contact Submit up to 5 poems at a time. Considers simultaneous submissions; no previously published poems. Accepts e-mail as attachment; no fax submissions. Blind submissions only: name, address, phone number, e-mail address, and title of ms should appear in cover letter along with brief bio. Title only on ms. Reads submissions by November 30 annual deadline. Guidelines available in magazine, for SASE, by e-mail, or on website. Pays 2 contributor's copies. Acquires first North American serial rights. Reviews books of poetry and fiction in 1,000 words. Send materials for review consideration.

Contest/Award Offerings All submissions are eligible for the Daily News Prize ($300) for poetry, The Marguerite Cobb McKay Prize to a Virgin Island author ($200), the David Hough Literary Prize to a Caribbean author ($500), the Canute A. Brodhurst Prize for Fiction ($400), and the Charlotte and Isidor Paiewonsky Prize ($200) for first-time publication.

☑ CAVEAT LECTOR

400 Hyde St., Apt. 606, San Francisco CA 94109-7445. (415)928-7431. Fax: (415)928-7431. E-mail: editors@caveat-lector.org. Website: www.caveat-lector.org. **Contact:** Christopher Bernard, Co-Editor.

Magazines Needs *Caveat Lector*, published 2 times/year, "is devoted to the arts and cultural and philosophical commentary. As well as literary work, we publish art, photography, music, streaming audio of selected literary pieces, and short films. Our website includes an art gallery and a multimedia section, including links to websites we think might be of interest to our readers." Wants poems "on any subject, in any style, as long as the work is authentic in feeling and appropriately crafted. We are looking for accomplished poems, something that resonates in the mind long after the reader has laid the poem aside. We want work that has authenticity of emotion and high craft; poems that, whether raw or polished, ring true—and if humorous, are actually funny, or at least witty. Classical to experimental. Note: We sometimes request authors for audio of work we publish to post on our website." Has published poetry by Joanne Lowery, Simon Perchik, Les Murray, Alfred Robinson, and Ernest Hilbert. *Caveat Lector* is 32-48 pages, 11 × 4¼, photocopied, saddle-stapled, with b&w cover. Receives 200-600 poems/year, accepts about 2%. Press run is 250. Single copy: $3.50; subscription: $15 for 4 issues. Sample: $3.

How to Contact Submit up to 6 short poems, 3 medium-length poems, or 1 long poem at a time. Lines/poem:short, up to 50 each; medium, 51-100; long, up to 500. Considers simultaneous submissions, "but please inform us." Cover letter is not required, but appreciated. "Place name, address, and (optional) telephone number on each page. Include SASE and brief bio (100 words or less)." Reads submissions March-June. Time between acceptance and publication is 1 year. Sometimes comments on rejected poems. Guidelines available for SASE. Responds in 1 month. Pays 2 contributor's copies. Acquires first publication rights.

Tips "The 2 rules of writing are: 1) Revise it again. 2) Revise it again. The writing level of most of our submissions is pleasingly high. Being a small publication, Caveat Lector cannot publish all the work liked by its editors, thus a rejection is not necessarily a criticism of the work. We try to provide comments to our more promising submitters."

☐ CC&D/CHILDREN, CHURCHES AND DADDIES

Scars Publications, 829 Brian Court, Gurnee IL 60031. E-mail: ccandd96@scars.tv. Website: http://scars.tv. **Contact:** Janet Kuypers, editor/publisher.

Magazines Needs *CC&D/Children, Churches and Daddies (The Unreligious, Non-Family-Oriented Literary Magazine)*, published monthly, contains poetry, prose, art, and essays. "Also run electronic issues and collection books. We accept poetry of almost any genre, but no rhyme or religious poems (look at our current issue for a better idea of what we're like). We are okay with gay/lesbian/bisexual, nature/rural/ecology, political/social issues, women/feminism." Does not want "racist, sexist (therefore we're not into pornography, either), or homophobic stuff." Has published poetry by Mel Waldman, Pat Dixon, Angeline Hawkes-Craig, Cheryl Townsend, Kenneth DiMaggio. *CC&D/Children, Churches and Daddies* is 84 pages, perfect-bound. Receives hundreds of poems/year, accepts about 40%. Sample: $6 (print for pre-2010 issues); free electronic sample online. 2010 copies can be ordered from our printer. See website for more information. Make checks payable to Janet Kuypers.

How to Contact Submit via e-mail. Lines/poem: accepts longer works, "within 2 pages for an individual poem is appreciated." Considers previously published poems and simultaneous submissions. Accepts e-mail submissions (preferred, pasted into body of message or as attachment in Microsoft Word .doc file) or disk submissions. "When submitting via e-mail in body of message, explain in preceding paragraph that it is a submission; for disk submissions, mail floppy disk with ASCII text, or Macintosh disk." Comments on rejected poems "if asked." Guidelines available for SASE, by e-mail, or on website. Responds in 2 weeks.

Contest/Award Offerings Scars Publications sometimes sponsors a contest "where writing appears in an annual book." Write or e-mail (editor@scars.tv) for information.

Also Offers Also able to publish electronic chapbooks. Additional information available by e-mail or on website.

Tips "The website is a more comprehensive view of what *CC&D/Children, Churches and Daddies* does. All the information is there."

☑ CENTER: A JOURNAL OF THE LITERARY ARTS

202 Tate Hall, University of Missouri-Columbia, Columbia MO 65211-1500. E-mail: cla@missouri.edu. Website: center.missouri.edu. **Contact:** Managing Editor.

Magazines Needs *Center: A Journal of the Literary Arts*, publishes "poetry, fiction, creative nonfiction, and, on occasion, translations. Center publishes from a broad range of aesthetic categories and privileges work that is deliberately crafted, engaging, and accessible." Has published poetry by Kim Chinquee, Mark Conway, Debra Anne Davis, William Eisner, Kathy Fagan, Kathleen Flenniken, and more. *Center: A Journal* is 100+ pages, digest-sized, perfect-bound, with 4-color card cover, includes ads for literary journals. Receives about 1,000 poems/year, accepts about 30. Press run is 500. Single copy: $7 (current issue). Sample: $3.50 (back issue). Make checks payable to *Center: A Journal*.

How to Contact Submit 3-6 poems at a time. Considers simultaneous submissions with notification; no previously published poems. Accepts e-mail submissions from international poets only. Cover letter is preferred. Reads submissions July 1-December 1. "Submissions received outside of the reading period will be returned unread." Guidelines available on website. Responds in up to 4 months. Acquires first North American serial rights. Rights revert to poets upon publication.

⋈ ▣ ☑ CERISE PRESS

C/O Sally Molini, P.O. Box 241187, 10510 Parker St., Omaha NE 68124. E-mail: editors@ cerisepress.com; submissions@cerisepress.com. Website: www.cerisepress.com. **Contact:** Karen Rigby, Fiona Sze-Lorrain, Sally Molini, editors.

Magazines Needs *Cerise Press*, published 3 times/year, is an "international, online journal of literature, arts, and culture (with a forthcoming print anthology) based in the US and France, offering poetry, nonfiction, translations, fiction, artwork, and photography." Has published Mahmoud Darwish, Auxeméry, Tess Gallagher, Yusef Komunyakaa, Eleanor Wilner, Pierre-Albert Jourdan, Abdelwahab Meddeb, Pura López-Colomé, Dorianne Laux, Ray Gonzalez, Victoria Chang.

How to Contact Submit 3-5 poems at a time. Considers simultaneous submissions. Accepts e-mail submissions. Cover letter is required. "Please let us know if work is accepted elsewhere. Do not query until three months from the date of submission." Reads submissions year round. Never comments on rejected poems. Guidelines on website. Responds in 2-3 months. Acquires first North American serial rights. Rights revert to poet upon publication. Reviews books and chapbooks of poetry, fiction, critical essays, biographies, photography, and more.

☑ THE CHAFFIN JOURNAL

Dept. of English, Case Annex 467, Eastern Kentucky University, Richmond KY 40475-3102. (859)622-3080. Website: www.english.eku.edu/chaffin_journal.

Magazines Needs *The Chaffin Journal*, published annually in December, prints quality short fiction and poetry by new and established writers/poets. Wants any form, subject matter, or style. Does not want "poor quality." Has published poetry by Taylor Graham, Diane Glancy, Judith Montgomery, Simon Perchik, Philip St. Clair, and Virgil Suárez. *The Chaffin Journal* is 120 pages, digest-sized, offset-printed, perfect-bound, with plain cover with title only. Receives about 500 poems/year, accepts about 10%. Press run is 300; 40-50 distributed free to contributors. Single copy: $6; subscription: $6/year. Sample (back issue): $5. Make checks payable to *The Chaffin Journal*.

How to Contact Submit 5 poems per submission period. Considers simultaneous submissions (although not preferred); no previously published poems. No e-mail or disk submissions. Cover letter is preferred. "Submit typed pages with only one poem per page. Enclose SASE." Reads submissions June 1-October 1. Time between acceptance and publication is 6 months. Poems are reviewed by the general editor and 2 poetry editors. Never comments on rejected poems. Guidelines available in magazine or on website. Responds in 3 months. Pays 1 contributor's copy. Acquires one-time rights.

Tips "Submit quality work during our reading period; include cover letter and SASE."

⊠ ◯ CHALLENGER INTERNATIONAL

(250)991-5567. E-mail: danlukiv@sd28.bc.ca. Website: http://challengerinternational.20m .com/index.html.

Magazines Needs *Challenger international*, published annually, contains "poetry and (on occasion) short fiction." Wants "any type of work, especially by teenagers (our mandate: to encourage young writers, and to publish their work alongside established writers), providing it is not pornographic, profane, or overly abstract." Has published poetry from Canada, the continental U.S., Hawaii, Switzerland, Russia, Malta, Italy, Slovenia, Ireland, England, Korea, Pakistan, Australia, Zimbabwe, Argentina, and Columbia. *Challenger international* is generally 20-50 pages, magazine-sized, laser-printed, side-stapled. Press run is 50. *Challenger international* is distributed free to McNaughton Centre Secondary Alternate School sudents.

How to Contact Considers previously published poems and simultaneous submissions. Cover letter is required. Include list of credits, if any. Accepts e-mail submissions only; no postal submissions. "Sometimes we edit to save the poet rejection." Responds in 6 months. Payment is 1 e-copy (sent as an e-mail attachment) of the issue in which the author's work appears. Poet retains rights.

Additional Information Island Scholastic Press publishes chapbooks by authors featured in *Challenger international*. Pays 3 author's copies. Copyright remains with author. Distribution of free copies through McNaughton Centre.

Tips "We like imagistic poetry that makes sense."

$ ☑ ◎ CHAMPAGNE SHIVERS

E-mail: ChampagneShivers@hotmail.com. Website: samsdotpublishing.com/vineyard/ Champagne%20Shivers.htm. **Contact:** Cathy Buburuz, Editor. *Champagne Shivers* is "a classy horror magazine. This is not the place to submit offensive language. We prefer poetic, well-written horror." Wants "horror poetry only. We prefer poems that do not rhyme, but all verse will be considered. Poems 20-30 lines stand the best chance for acceptance, especially if they're scary and entertaining." Does not want "anything that isn't horror related, and always proof and edit before you send your submission. If your work does not have high entertainment or high impact, do not send it here." Has published poetry by Lee Clark Zumpe, Nancy Bennett, Steve Vernon, Kurt Newton, W.B. Vogel III, and Keith W. Sikora. *Champagne Shivers* is more than 60 pages, 8 1/2x11, professionally printed and perfect-bound, with full color cover art depicting a chilling, yet beautiful female. Receives about 1,000 poems/year, accepts 15 poems/issue. Press run and subscriber base vary; the only free copies go to reviewers and contributors. Single copy: $12 U.S. and Canada. Sample: $10 U.S. and Canada. ("Foreign countries, please inquire about costs.") Make checks payable to Tyree Campbell, Sam's Dot Publishing, P.O. Box 782, Cedar Rapids IA 52406-0782 (for subscriptions and sample copies only; DO NOT SEND SUBMISSIONS TO THIS ADDRESS).

How to Contact Needs *Not accepting submissions.*. Submit 1 poem at a time. Lines/poem: 20-30. No simultaneous submissions. Accepts e-mail submissions only (pasted into body of message; DO NOT SEND ATTACHMENTS) to ChampagneShivers@hotmail.com. Does not accept snail mail submissions. Cover letter is preferred. "Submit 1 poem with a bio written in the third person, your mailing address, and your e-mail address." Reads submissions year-round. Submit seasonal poems 4 months in advance. Time between acceptance and publication is less than 6 months. Always comments on rejected poems. Guidelines available by e-mail or on website. Pays 10¢/line for unpublished poems, plus 1 contributor's copy.

Acquires first North American serial rights to unpublished poems. All rights revert back to the writer upon publication.

Tips "Submit horror poems only. I love psychological horror poetry, horror poetry about the Old West, horror poems about asylums, or anything that's just plain scary. I do not want poems about werewolves, vampires, ghosts, or traditional monsters. I want to read poetry that's fresh and exciting. Most of all, send me something that's high in entertainment, that's never been done before. Send poems that will give me and my audience the shivers." Sam's Dot Publishing offers The James Award (Trophy) annually. The editor selects one poem per year from the pages of Champagne Shivers to nominate for the award. Entry fee: "None—it's free." Deadline: August. Guidelines available on website. "Never send snail mail submissions; always submit in the body of an e-mail after reading the information under How to Submit."

▣ ◖ CHANTARELLE'S NOTEBOOK

E-mail: chantarellesnotebook@yahoo.com. Website: www.chantarellesnotebook.com. **Contact:** Kendall A. Bell, co-editor.

Magazines Needs *Chantarelle's Notebook*, published quarterly online, seeks "quality work from undiscovered poets. We enjoy poems that speak to us—poems with great sonics and visuals." Wants "all styles of poetry, as long as it's quality work." Does not want "infantile rants, juvenile confessionals, greeting card-styled verse, political posturing, or religious outpourings." Considers poetry by children and teens. "There are no age restrictions, but submissions from younger people will be held to the same guidelines and standards as those from adults." Has published poetry by Donna Vorreyer, Patricia Carragon, Corrine DeWinter, Taylor Graham, Corey Mesler, and Simon Perchik. Receives about 500 poems/year, accepts about 20%. Sample: see website for latest issue.

How to Contact Submit 3-5 poems at a time. Lines/poem: "shorter poems have a better chance, but long poems are fine." Considers previously published poems; no simultaneous submissions. Accepts e-mail submissions (pasted into body of message; "we will not open any attachments—they will be deleted"). Cover letter is required. "Please include a short bio of no more than 75 words, should we decide to accept your work." Reads submissions year round. Submit seasonal poems 2-3 months in advance. "The editors will review all submissions and make a decision within a week's time." Never comments on rejected poems. Guidelines available on website. "Please follow the guidelines—all the information is there!" Responds in 2-3 weeks. Acquires one-time rights. Rights revert to poets upon publication. "*Chantarelle's Notebook* is also accepting photo submissions. Please visit the website for guidelines on how to submit your photos to us."

Also Offers "*Chantarelle's Notebook* will publish a 'best of' print journal that will cull poems from each of the previous 4 quarterly issues in the past year. The authors of the poems chosen will receive 1 contributor's copy and can buy additional copies at half price."

Tips "Read as much poetry as you can. Immerse yourself in work other than your own. Turn off your television. Write from the pit of your stomach. Revise. Edit. Rewrite. Do not let rejections keep you off your path. The only way to become a great poet is to learn from all experiences, good and bad."

⊕ ☑ ◎ CHAPMAN

Chapman Publishing, 4 Broughton Place, Edinburgh EH1 3RX, Scotland. (44)(131)557-2207. E-mail: chapman-pub@blueyonder.co.uk. Website: www.chapman-pub.co.uk. **Contact:** Dr. Joy Hendry, editor. (Specialized: Scottish culture)

Magazines Needs *Chapman*, published 3 times/year, "is controversial, influential, outspoken, and intelligent. Established in 1970, it has become a dynamic force in Scottish culture covering theatre, politics, language, and the arts. Our highly respected forum for poetry, fiction, criticism, review, and debate makes it essential reading for anyone interested in contemporary Scotland. *Chapman* publishes the best in Scottish writing—new work by well-known Scottish writers in the context of lucid critical discussion. It also, increasingly, publishes international writing. With our strong commitment to the future, we energetically promote new writers, new ideas, and new approaches." Also interested in receiving poetry dealing with women's issues and feminism. Has published poetry by Stewart Cpmm. Angus Calder, Alan Riach, George Mackay Brown, Norman MacCaig, Janet Paisley, Gerda Stevenson, Marina Tsvetaeva. *Chapman* is 176 pages, digest-sized, professionally printed in small type on gloss stock, perfect-bound, with glossy card cover. Press run is 2,000. Receives "thousands" of poetry submissions/year, accepts about 200. Single copy: £8.50 including post, £10 overseas ($15); subscription: £24 ($60). Sample: £8.50, $15 (overseas). Payment also via PayPal.

How to Contact Submit 4-10 poems at a time. No simultaneous submissions. Cover letter is required. "Submissions must be accompanied by a SASE/IRC or provide e-mail address for reply. Please send sufficient postage to cover the return of your manuscript. Do not send foreign stamps. Limit 1 poem/page. We do not usually publish single poems." Responds "as soon as possible." Always sends prepublication galleys. Pays a small fee and/or contributor's copies at discount. Staff reviews books of poetry. Send materials for review consideration.

Additional Information *Chapman Publishing is currently not accepting submissions of books or chapbooks.*

Tips "Poets should not try to court approval by writing poems especially to suit what they perceive as the nature of the magazine. They usually get it wrong and write badly."

$ ☑ THE CHARITON REVIEW

The Chariton Review, Truman State University, 100 East Normal Ave., Kirksville MO 63501. E-mail: chariton@truman.edu. Website: http://tsup.truman.edu/item.asp?itemId = 383. **Contact:** Jim Barnes, Editor. Publishes two issues each year. This international literary journal was founded in 1975 by Andrew Grossbardt and edited by Jim Barnes from 1976 to 2010. James D'Agostino is editor effective July 2010. He is the author of *Nude with Anything*, and his work has appeared in numerous poetry magazines and journals. He teaches at Truman State University, which supported *The Chariton Review* for many years. Truman State University Press began managing production and distribution of the journal in 2008. Managing Editor: Barbara Smith-Mandell. See also The Chariton Review Short Fiction Prize. The Chariton Review invites submissions of previously unpublished short fiction, essays, and poetry. Send inquiries to our e-mail. Please send a printout of the submission.

☑ CHAUTAUQUA LITERARY JOURNAL

601 S. College Rd., Wilmington NC 28403. **Contact:** Jill Gerard, editor.

• Poetry published in *Chautauqua Literary Journal* has been included in *The Pushcart Prize* anthology.

Magazines Needs *Chautauqua Literary Journal*, published annually in June, prints poetry, short fiction, creative nonfiction, and book reviews. "The editors actively solicit writing that expresses the values of Chautauqua Institution broadly construed: A sense of inquiry into questions of personal, social, political, spiritual, and aesthetic importance, reglardless of genre. We consider the work of any writer, whether or not affiliated with Chautauqua institution. The qualities we seek include a mastery of craft, attention to vivid and accurate language, a true lyric 'ear,' an original and compelling vision, and strong narrative instinct. Above all, we value work that is intensely personal, yet somehow implicitly comments on larger public concerns—work that answers every reader's most urgent question: Why are you telling me this?" Has published poetry by Robert Cording, Lucille Clifton, Carl Dennis, George Looney, Michael McFee, and many more. *Chautauqua Literary Journal* is 200 pages, digest-sized, offset-printed, with notch adhesive binding and matte cover with original artwork, includes ads. Receives about 4,000 poems/year, accepts about 40. Press run is 2,000; 300 distributed free to contributors and others. Single copy: $14.95. Make checks payable to *Chautauqua Literary Journal*.

How to Contact Submit 3 poems maximum at a time. Considers simultaneous submissions (if notified); no previously published poems. Prefers writers submit via www.manuscripthub. com. Cover letter is preferred. "We prefer single-spaced manuscripts in 12 pt. font. Cover letters should be brief and mention recent publications (if any). SASE is mandatory." Reads submissions February 15-April 15 and August 15-November 15. Time between acceptance and publication is up to 1 year. "The editor is the sole arbiter, but we do have advisory editors who periodically make recommendations." Sometimes comments on rejected poems. Guidelines available on website. Responds in 3 months or less. Always sends prepublication galleys. Pays 2 contributor's copies. Acquires first rights "plus one-time non-exclusive rights to reprint accepted work in an anniversary issue." Reviews books/chapbooks of poetry in 750-1,000 words, single- and multi-book format. Send materials for review consideration to *Chautauqua Literary Journal*/Reviews, P.O. Box 2039, York Beach ME 03910.

Tips "Poets who are not avid readers of contemporary poetry will most likely not be writing anything of interest to us."

☑ ◎ CHEST

3300 Dundee Rd, Northbrook IL 60062. 800-343-2222. E-mail: poetrychest@aol.com. Website: www.chestjournal.org. **Contact:** Michael Zack, M.D., poetry editor.

Magazines Needs *Chest*, published monthly, "is the official medical journal of the American College of Chest Physicians, the world's largest medical journal for pulmonologists, sleep, and critical care specialists, with over 22,000 subscribers." Wants "poetry with themes of medical relevance." *Chest* is approximately 300 pages, magazine-sized, perfect-bound, with a glossy cover, and includes ads. Press run is 22,000. Number of unique visitors: 900,000 to website. Subscription: $192. Make checks payable to American College Chest Physicians.

How to Contact Submit up to 1 poem at a time, between 10 and 80 lines. Only accepts e-mail submissions (as attachment or in body of e-mail); no fax or disk submissions. Brief cover letter preferred. Reads submissions year round. Poems are circulated to an editorial board. Sometimes comments on rejected poems. Never publishes theme issues. Guidelines available in magazine and on website. Responds in 2 months; always sends prepublication galleys. Retains all rights.

☑ CHIRON REVIEW

522 E. South Ave., St. John KS 67576-2212. (620)786-4955. E-mail: editor@chironreview. com. Website: http://chironreview.com. **Contact:** Gerald and Zachary Locklin, poetry editors.

Magazines Needs *Chiron Review*, published quarterly, is a tabloid using photographs of featured writers. No taboos. Has published poetry by Quentin Crisp, Felice Picano, Edward Field, Wanda Coleman, and Marge Piercy. Press run is about 1,000. Subscription: $17/year (4 issues).

How to Contact Please check website before submitting. Submit up to 5 poems at a time. No longer accepts e-mail submissions. Guidelines available for SASE or on website. Responds in 2-6 weeks. Pays 1 contributor's copy, discount on additional copies. Acquires first-time rights. Reviews books of poetry in 500-700 words.

Additional Information Will also publish occasional chapbooks; see website for details.

$ ☑ ◎ THE CHRISTIAN CENTURY

(Specialized: Christian; social issues) 104 S. Michigan Ave., Suite 700, Chicago IL 60603. (312)263-7510. Fax: (312)263-7540. Website: www.ChristianCentury.org. Established 1884; named The Christian Century 1900, established again 1908, joined by New Christian 1970. **Contact:** Jill Peláez Baumgaertner, poetry editor.

Magazines Needs *The Christian Century*, an "ecumenical biweekly," is a liberal, sophisticated journal of news, articles of opinion, and reviews. Uses approximately 1 poem/issue, not necessarily on religious themes but in keeping with the literate tone of the magazine. Wants "poems that are not statements but experiences, that do not talk about the world but show it. We want to publish poems that are grounded in images and that reveal an awareness of the sounds of language and the forms of poetry even when the poems are written in free verse." Does not want "pietistic or sentimental doggerel." Has published poetry by Jeanne Murray Walker, Ida Fasel, Kathleen Norris, Luci Shaw, J. Barrie Shepherd, and Wendell Berry. The *Christian Century* is about 48 pages, magazine-sized, printed on quality newsprint, saddle-stapled, includes ads. Sample: $3.50.

How to Contact Lines/poem: 20 maximum. "Prefer shorter poems." No simultaneous submissions. Submissions without SASE (or SAE and IRCs) will not be returned. Submit poems typed, double-spaced, one poem/page. Include name, address, and phone number on each page. Pays usually $20/poem plus 1 contributor's copy and discount on additional copies. Acquires all rights. Inquire about reprint permission. Reviews books of poetry in 300-400 words, single-book format; 400-500 words, multi-book format.

☑ ◎ CHRISTIANITY AND LITERATURE

Humanities Division, Pepperdine University, 24255 Pacific Coast Highway, Malibu CA 90263. **Contact:** Julia S. Kasdorf, poetry editor (Pennsylvania State University, English Dept., 114 Burrows Bldg, University Park, PA 16802). *Christianity and Literature*, a quarterly scholarly journal, publishes about 4-6 poems/issue. Press run is 1,100. Single copy: $10; subscription: $25/year, $45 for 2 years. Make checks payable to CCL.

How to Contact Submit 1-6 poems at a time. No previously published poems or simultaneous submissions. Accepts submissions by surface mail only. Cover letter is required. Submissions must be accompanied by SASE. Time between acceptance and publication is 6-12 months. "Poems are chosen by our poetry editor." Guidelines available on website. Responds within 4 months. Rights to republish revert to poets upon written request. Reviews collections of literary, Christian poetry occasionally in some issues (no chapbooks). Pays one Contributor's Copy and five offprints of poem.

Tips "We look for poems that are clear and surprising. They should have a compelling sense of voice, formal sophistication (though not necessarily rhyme and meter), and the ability to reveal the spiritual through concrete images. We cannot return submissions that are not accompanied by SASE."

$ ☑ THE CHRISTIAN SCIENCE MONITOR

The Home Forum Page, 210 Massachussetts Ave., P02-30, Boston MA 02115. E-mail: homeforum@csmonitor.com. Website: www.csmonitor.com. http://www.csmonitor.com/About/Contributor-guidelines#homeforum. **Contact:** Editors: Susan Leach, Marjorie Kehe. *The Christian Science Monitor*, an international daily newspaper, regularly features poetry in The Home Forum section. Wants "finely crafted poems that explore and celebrate daily life; that provide a respite from daily news and from the bleakness that appears in so much contemporary verse." Does not want "work that presents people in helpless or hopeless states; poetry about death, aging, or illness; or dark, violent, sensual poems. No poems that are overtly religious or falsely sweet." Considers free verse and fixed forms. Has published poetry by Diana Der-Hovanessian, Marilyn Krysl, and Michael Glaser. Publishes 1-4 poems/week.

How to Contact Submit up to 5 poems at a time. Lines/poem: Prefers short poems under 20 lines. No previously published poems or simultaneous submissions. Accepts e-mail submissions only (by attachment in MS Word, 1 poem/e-mail). Pays $20/haiku; $40/poem.

$ ☑ ◎ CHRYSALIS READER

1745 Gravel Hill Rd., Dillwyn VA 23936. Fax: (434)983-1074. E-mail: rlawson@sover. net. Website: www.swedenborg.com/chrysallis. **Contact:** Robert F. Lawson and Carol S. Lawson.

Magazines Needs *Chrysalis Reader*, published annually in September by the Swedenborg Foundation, is a "contribution to the search for spiritual wisdom, a book series that challenges inquiring minds through the use of literate and scholarly fiction, essays, and poetry." Wants "poetry that surprises, that pushes the language, gets our attention." Does not want anything "overly religious or sophomoric." Has published work by Robert Bly, Linda Pastan, Wesley McNair, Wyn Cooper, William Kloefkorn, and Virgil Suárez. *Chrysalis Reader* is 208 pages, 7x10, professionally printed on archival paper, perfect-bound, with coated coverstock. Receives about 1,000 submissions/year, accepts about 16 poems. Press run is 3,500. Sample: $10. (Sample poems available on website.)

How to Contact Submit no more than 5-6 poems at a time. Considers simultaneous submissions "if notified immediately when work is accepted elsewhere"; no previously published poems.

Include SASE. Reads submissions year round. Time between acceptance and publication is typically 18 months. Regularly publishes theme issues (the 2010 issue theme is "The Marketplace"). Themes and guidelines available with SASE or on website. Responds in 3 months. Always sends prepublication galleys. Pays $25 and 3 contributor's copies. Acquires first-time rights. "We expect to be credited for reprints after permission is given."

Contest/Award Offerings The Bailey Prize.

Tips "Purchase a back issue, go online, or request your bookstore to order a reading copy so that you can better gauge what to submit."

$ ☐ ◎ CICADA MAGAZINE

Carus Publishing, 70 E. Lake St., Suite 300, Chicago IL 60601. Website: www.cricketmag. com. **Contact:** Deborah Vetter, Executive Editor.

Magazines Needs *CICADA Magazine*, published semimonthly, is "the groundbreaking teen literary magazine that raises the issues that today's young adults find most important; a high-quality literary magazine for ages 14 and up." Wants "serious or humorous poetry; rhymed or free verse." Considers poetry by teens. *CICADA* is 128 pages, digest-sized, perfect-bound, with full-color cover. Receives more than 1,200 submissions/month, accept 25-30. Circulation is 17,000. Subscription: $35.97/year (6 issues). Sample: $8.50; sample pages available online.

How to Submit Submit no more than 5 poems at a time. Lines/poem: up to 25. Considers previously published poems. Show line count on each poem submitted. Include SASE. Guidelines available for SASE or on website. Responds in 6 months. Pays up to $3/line on publication. Acquires North American publication rights for previously published poems; rights vary for unpublished poems.

Also Offers "The Slam," an online writing forum "for young writers who want the world to see what they can do with words."

Tips "Our standards are very high, and we will accept only top-quality material. Please familiarize yourself with *CICADA* before submitting."

◪ CIDER PRESS REVIEW

777 Braddock Lane, Halifax PA 17032. E-mail: editor@ciderpressreview.com. Website: http://ciderpressreview.com. **Contact:** Caron Andregg, editor-in-chief, and Ruth Foley, associate poetry editor.

Magazines Needs *Cider Press Review*, published annually, features "the best new work from contemporary poets." Wants "thoughtful, well-crafted poems with vivid language and strong images. We prefer poems that have something to say. We would like to see more well-written humor. We also encourage translations." Does not want "didactic, inspirational, greeting card verse, empty word play, therapy, or religious doggerel." Also welcomes reviews in not more than 500 words of current full-length books of poetry. Has published poetry by Robert Arroyo, Jr., Virgil Suaárez, Linda Pastan, Kathleen Flenniken, Tim Seibles, Joanne Lowery, Thomas Lux, and Mark Cox. *Cider Press Review* is 128 pages, digest-sized, offset-printed, perfect-bound, with 4-color coated card cover. Receives about 2,500 poems/year, accepts about 3%. Press run is 500. Single copy: $13.95; subscription: $24 for 2 issues (1 journal, 1 book from the *Cider Press Review* Book Award). Sample: $12 (journal).

How to Contact Submit up to 5 poems at a time. No previously published poems or simultaneous submissions. Submit by postal mail or through online submission form at website. "International authors or special needs, please query via e-mail. Do not send unsolicited disk or e-mail submissions." Cover letter is preferred. Include short bio (25 words maximum). SASE required for reply. Reads submissions April 1-August 31 only. Time between acceptance and publication is 6-9 months. Poems are circulated to an editorial board. Guidelines available for SASE or on website. Responds in 1-4 months. Always sends prepublication galleys. Pays 1 contributor's copy. Acquires first North American serial rights.

Contest/Award Offerings *The Cider Press Review* Book Award.

◙ CIMARRON REVIEW

205 Morrill Hall, Oklahoma State University, Stillwater OK 74078-0135. E-mail: cimarronreview@okstate.edu. Website: http://cimarronreview.okstate.edu. **Contact:** Lisa Lewis and Alfred Corn, poetry editors.

Magazines Needs *Cimarron Review*, published quarterly, is a literary journal "that takes pride in our eclecticism. We like evocative poetry (lyric or narrative) controlled by a strong voice. No restrictions as to subject matter." Wants "poems whose surfaces and structures risk uncertainty and which display energy, texture, intelligence, and intense investment." Has published poetry by William Stafford, John Ashbery, Grace Schulman, Barbara Hamby, Patricia Fargnoli, Phillip Dacey, Holly Prado, and Kim Addonizio. *Cimarron Review* is 100-150 pages, digest-sized, perfect-bound, with color cover. Press run is 600. Single copy: $7; subscription: $24/year ($28 Canada), $42 for 2 years ($48 Canada), $65 for 3 years ($72 Canada).

How to Contact Submit 3-5 poems at a time. Considers simultaneous submissions. No e-mail submissions; accepts postal submissions only. "Writers outside North America may query by e-mail." No response without SASE. Guidelines available on website. Responds in up to 6 months. Pays 2 contributor's copies. Acquires first North American serial rights only. Reviews books of poetry in 500-900 words, single-book format, occasionally multi-book.

$ ◙ THE CINCINNATI REVIEW

P.O. Box 210069, Cincinnati OH 45221-0069. (513) 556-3954. E-mail: editors@cincinnatireview. com. Website: www.cincinnatireview.com. Established 2003. **Contact:** Don Bogen, poetry editor.

Magazines Needs *The Cincinnati Review*, published semiannually, is devoted "to publishing the best new poetry and literary fiction, as well as book reviews, essays, and interviews. Open to any schools, styles, forms—as long as the poem is well made and sophisticated in its language use and subject matter." Each issue includes a translation feature. For more information on translations please see our website. *The Cincinnati Review* is 180-200 pages, digest-sized, perfect-bound, with matte paperback cover with full-color art, includes ads. Press run is 1,000. Single copy: $9 (current issue); subscription: $15. Sample: $7 (back issue).

How to Contact Submit up to 10 pages of poetry at a time. Considers simultaneous submissions with notification; no multiple submissions or previously published poems.

No e-mail or disk submissions. E-mail submissions accepted beginning fall 2010. Cover letter is preferred. SASE required for hardcopy submissions. Reads submissions September 1-May 31. Time between acceptance and publication is 6 months. "First-round reading by small, trained staff. Final decisions made by genre editors." Seldom comments on rejected poems. Guidelines available for SASE or on website. Responds in 6 to 8 weeks. Always sends prepublication galleys. Pays $30/page and 2 contributor's copies. Acquires first North American serial rights. Reviews books of poetry in 1,500 words, single-book format.

✿ ☑ ◎ THE CLAREMONT REVIEW

4980 Wesley Rd., Victoria BC V8Y 1Y9, Canada. E-mail: bashford@islandnet.com. Website: www.theClaremontReview.ca. **Contact:** Lucy Bashford, managing editor. *The Claremont Review*, published semiannually, prints poetry and fiction by writers ages 13-19. Each Fall issue also includes an interview with a prominent Canadian writer. Wants "vital, modern poetry and fiction with a strong voice and living language. We prefer works that reveal something of the human condition. No clichéd language or copies of 18th- and 19th-century work." Has published poetry by Andrew Battershill, Danielle Hubbard, and Kristina Lucas. *The Claremont Review* is 110 pages, digest-sized, professionally printed, perfect-bound, with an attractive color cover. Receives 600-800 poems/year, accepts about 120. Press run is 700. Subscription: $18/year, $35 for 2 years. Sample: $10.

How to Contact Considers simultaneous submissions; no previously published poems. Cover letter is required. Include brief bio. We do not want rhyming poetry. Type poems one to a page with author's name at the top of each. Reads submissions September-June only. Always comments on rejected poems. Guidelines available in magazine or on website. Responds in up to 6 weeks (excluding July and August). Pays one bound contributor's copy, and funds when grants allow it. Acquires first North American serial rights.

Tips "Read excerpts on the website, and content of back issues."

☑ ◎ CLARK STREET REVIEW

P.O. Box 1377, Berthoud CO 80513. E-mail: clarkreview@earthlink.net. **Contact:** Ray Foreman, Editor.

Magazines Needs *Clark Street Review*, published 6 times/year, uses narrative poetry and short shorts. Tries "to give writers and poets cause to keep writing by publishing their best work." Wants "narrative poetry under 100 lines that reaches readers who are mostly published poets and writers. Subjects are open." Does not want "obscure or formalist work." Has published poetry by Charles Ries, Anselm Brocki, Ed Galling, Ellaraine Lockie, and J. Glenn Evans. *Clark Street Review* is 20 pages, digest-sized, photocopied, saddle-stapled, with paper cover. Receives about 1,000 poems/year, accepts about 10%. Press run is 200. Single copy: $2; subscription: $10 for 10 issues postpaid for writers only. Make checks payable to R. Foreman.

How to Contact Submit 1-5 poems at a time. Lines/poem: 20 minimum, 75 maximum. Considers previously published poems and simultaneous submissions. Send "disposable sharp copies. Maximum width—65 characters. Include SASE for reply. No cover letter." Time between acceptance and publication is 4 months. "Editor reads everything with a critical eye of 30 years of experience in writing and publishing small press work." Often comments on rejected poems. Guidelines available for SASE or by e-mail. Responds in 3 weeks. Acquires one-time rights.

Tips "*Clark Street Review* is geared to the more experienced poet and writer deeply involved in the writer's life. There are tips and quotes throughout each issue that writers appreciate. As always, the work we print speaks for the writer and the magazine. Publishing excellence and giving writers a reason to write is our only aim. Well-crafted, interesting, and accessible human narrative poems will see ink in *CSR*."

$ ☑ COLORADO REVIEW

Center for Literary Publishing, Dept. of English, Colorado State University, Ft. Collins CO 80523. (970)491-5449. E-mail: Stephanie.GSchwind@colostate.edu. Website: http://coloradoreview.colostate.edu. General Editor: Stephanie G'Schwind, and Dan Beachy-Quick, Book Review Editor. **Contact:** Donald Revell, Sasha Steensen, and Matthew Cooperman, Poetry Editors.

- Poetry published in *Colorado Review* has been included in *The Best American Poetry* and *Pushcart Prize Anthology*.

Magazines Needs *Colorado Review*, published 3 times/year, prints short fiction, poetry, and personal essays. Has published poetry by Alice Notley, Rae Armantrout, Tomaz Salamun, Kazim Ali, Rusty Morrison, Joseph Campana, Paul Hoover, and Fanny Howe. *Colorado Review* is about 224 pages, digest-sized, professionally printed, notch-bound, with glossy card cover. Press run is 1,300. Receives about 10,000 submissions/year, accepts about 2%. Subscription: $24/year. Sample: $10.

How to Contact Submit no more than 5 poems at a time. Considers simultaneous submissions, "but you must notify *Colorado Review* immediately if accepted elsewhere"; no previously published poems. No e-mail submissions. SASE required for response. Reads submissions September 1-May 1 only. Responds in 2 months, "often sooner." Pays $5/printed page. Acquires first North American serial rights. Reviews books of poetry, fiction, and nonfiction. "Most book reviews are solicited, but feel free to query." Send materials for review consideration.

Contest/Award Offerings Colorado Prize for Poetry.

☑ COMMON GROUND REVIEW

40 Prospect St. Unit C1, Westfield, MA 01085. Website: www.cgreview.org. Established 1999. **Contact:** Larry O'Brien, editor.

Magazines Needs *Common Ground Review*, published semiannually, prints poetry and original artwork by the art editor Alice Ahrens Williams. Wants poetry with strong imagery; well-written free or traditional forms. Does not want greeting card verse, overly sentimental or political poetry. Has published poetry by James Doyle, Martin Galvin, CB Follett, Kathryn Howd Machan, and Sheryl L. Nelms. *Common Ground Review* is 60+ pages, digest-sized, perfect-bound, with 4-color cover. Receives about 1,000 poems/year, accepts less than 10%. Press run is 125-150. Single copy: $12.50 (includes S&H). Orders: Make checks payable to *Common Ground Review* and send to 43 Winton Rd., East Windsor CT 06088.

How to Contact Submit 1-3 poems at a time. Lines/poem: 60 maximum. No previously published poems. Simultaneous submissions are allowed; see website for details. E-mail submissions are allowed. Cover letter is required, as is biography. "Poems should be single-spaced; include name, address, phone number, e-mail address, brief biography, and SASE (submissions without SASE will not be notified)." Reads submissions year round, but deadline for non-contest submissions is August 31. Submit seasonal poems 6 months in advance. Time between acceptance and publication is 4-6 months. "Editor reads and culls submissions. Final decisions made by editorial board." Seldom comments on rejected poems. Guidelines available in magazine or on website. Responds in 2 months. Pays 1 contributor's copy. Acquires one-time rights.

Contest/Award Offerings Sponsors an annual poetry contest. Offers 1st Prize: $500; 2nd Prize: $200; 3rd Prize: $100; Honorable Mentions. **Entry fee:** $15 for 1-3 unpublished poems. **Deadline:** February 28 for contest submissions only. All contest submissions are considered for publication in *Common Ground Review*.

Tips "Read journal before submitting. Beginning poets need to read what's out there, get into workshops, and work on revising. Attend writers' conferences. Listen and learn."

Ⓝ ▣ ☑ ◎ COMMON SENSE 2

E-mail: slatsboss@gmail.com. Website: www.commonsense2.com. **Contact:** Jack Romig, poetry editor.

Magazines Needs *CommonSense 2*, published monthly online, is "a magazine of progressive political thought with a broad interest in the arts." Wants"any form and style." Jack Lindeman, Richard O'Connell, Jack Conway, Eliza Kelley, and Belle Randall. Receives approximately 100 poems/year, accepts about 50%. Number of unique visitors: 3,500-5,000.

How to Contact Submit 3-5 poems at a time. Considers previously published poetry and simultaneous submissions. Accepts e-mail submissions; no fax or dis. Cover letter is unnecessary. "We require bio information (a paragraph) and request a head shot photo file." Reads submissions year round. Submit seasonal poems 2 months in advance. Time between acceptance and publication is 2-8 weeks. Never comments on rejected poems. Guidelines available by e-mail. Responds in 6 months. Acquires first rights. Rights revert to poet upon publication.

Tips "We're open to excellent poetry on any subject though we're politically oriented."

☐ ◎ COMMON THREADS

3510 North High Street, Columbus OH 43214. (614)268-5094. E-mail: Team@ohiopoetryassn. org. Website: ohiopoetryassn.com.

Magazines Needs *Common Threads*, published semiannually in April and October, is the Ohio Poetry Association's member poetry magazine. **Only members of OPA may submit poems.** "We use beginners' poetry, but would like it to be good, tight, revised. In short, not first drafts. We'd like poems to make us think as well as feel something. I really treasure short poems for spacing's sake." Does not want to see poetry that is highly sentimental, overly morbid, religiously coercive, or pornograpic. Considers poetry by teens "if members or high school contest winners." Has published poetry by Bill Reyer, Michael Bugeja, Timothy Russell, Yvonne Hardenbrook, and Dalene Stull. *Common Threads* is 52 pages, digest-sized, computer-typeset, with matte card cover. "*Common Threads* is a forum for our members, and we do use reprints so new members can get a look at what is going well in more general magazines." Subscription: annual OPA dues, including 2 issues of *Common*

Threads are $18; $15 for seniors (over age 65). Single copy: $2; $8 for students (through college).

How to Contact Lines/poem: "nothing over 40 (unless exceptional)." Considers previously published poems, if "author is upfront about them." Accepts submissions by postal mail only. Reads submissions year round. Frequently publishes seasonal poems. Guidelines available for SASE. All rights revert to poet after publication.

Tips "Read a lot to see what is being done by good poets nationally. Write what you know and love. Revise!!"

$ ☻ ◎ COMMONWEAL

475 Riverside Dr., Room 405, New York NY 10115. E-mail: editors@commonwealmagazine. org. Website: www.commonwealmagazine.org. **Contact:** Rosemary Deen, poetry editor.

Magazines Needs *Commonweal*, published every 2 weeks, is a Catholic general interest magazine for college-educated readers. Wants serious, witty, well-written poems. Does not publish inspirational poems. Circulation is 20,000. Subscription: $55.

How to Contact Lines/poem: 75 maximum. No simultaneous submissions. Only accepts hardcopy submissions with an SASE. Reads submissions September 1-June 30 only. Pays 50¢/line plus 2 contributor's copies. Acquires all rights. Returns rights when requested by the author. Reviews books of poetry in 750-1,000 words, single- or multi-book format.

☻ THE COMSTOCK REVIEW

4956 St. John Dr., Syracuse NY 13215. E-mail: poetry@comstockreview.org. Website: www. comstockreview.org.

Magazines Needs "Soon entering its 25th year of publication, *The Comstock Review* is proud of its long-established reputation of publishing the finest known and unknown poets throughout North America. We choose our poems solely on the basis of what we consider to be their artistic merits. We are not swayed by long publishing histories. We are not afraid of the avant-garde, but shy from the overly obscure, the patently religious and the needlessly graphic." *The Comstock Review* is approximately 100 pages, digest-sized, professionally printed, perfect-bound. Press run is 500. Subscription: $20/year, $36/2 years. Samples issues available for $12.

How to Contact Submit 3-6 poems, one submission per reading period. No previously published poems; simultaneous submissions accepted. "Average poem published is one page in length. Please also consider our 65 character line width when submitting." Postal submissions only; no e-mail. Cover letter is optional, three line bio preferred. Include three line bio. Put name, address, phone number, and e-mail address on each page. Reads submissions January 1-March 15th only. Acceptances mailed out 8-12 weeks after close of reading period. Editorial comments and suggestions sometimes given. Guidelines available in magazine, for SASE, or on website. Pays 1 contributor's copy. Acquires first North American serial rights.

Contest/Award Offerings The annual Muriel Craft Bailey Memorial Award and the biennial Jesse Bryce Niles Memorial Chapbook Award.

☑ CONCHO RIVER REVIEW

P.O. Box 10894, Angelo State University, San Angelo TX 76909. (915)942-2273. Fax: (915)942-2155. E-mail: jerry.bradley@lamar.edu. Website: www.angelo.edu/dept/english/publications/concho_river_review.htm. **Contact:** Jerry Bradley, Poetry Editor; Mary Ellen Hartje.

Magazines Needs *Concho River Review*, published twice/year, is a literary journal "particularly looking for poems with distinctive imagery and imaginative forms and rhythms. The first test of a poem will be its imagery. We prefer shorter poems; few long poems accepted." Has published poetry by David Vancil, Nathan Brown, Robert Cooperman, Mary Winters, Red Shuttleworth, and William Jolliff. *Concho River Review* is 120-138 pages, digest-sized, professionally printed, flat-spined, with matte card cover. Receives 1,000 poems/year, accepts 60. Press run is 300 (200 subscribers, 10 libraries). Subscription: $14. Sample: $5.

How to Contact Submit 3-5 poems at a time. No simultaneous submissions. Accepts e-mail submissions (as attachment in Word). "No reply without SASE or e-mail address. No handwritten manuscripts accepted." Responds in 2-3 months. Pays 1 contributor's copy. Acquires first rights.

Tips "We're always looking for good, strong work—from well-known poets and those who have never been published before."

$ ☑ CONFRONTATION MAGAZINE

English Dept., C.W. Post Campus, Long Island Univ., 720 Northern Blvd., Brookville NY 11548-1300. (516)299-2720. Fax: (516)299-2735. E-mail: confrontationmag@gmail.com. Website: www.liu.edu/confrontation. **Contact:** Belinda Kremer, poetry editor.

Magazines Needs *Confrontation Magazine,* published semiannually, is interested "in all forms. Our only criterion is high literary merit. We think of our audience as an educated, lay group of intelligent readers. We prefer lyric poems." Does not want "sentimental verse." Considers poetry by children and teens. Has published poetry by David Ray, T. Alan Broughton, David Ignatow, Philip Appleman, Jane Mayhall, and Joseph Brodsky. *Confrontation* is about 300 pages, digest-sized, professionally printed, flat-spined. Receives about 1,200 submissions/year, accepts about 150. Circulation is 2,000. Subscription: $15/year. Sample: $3.

How to Contact Submit no more than 10 pages of poetry at a time. Lines/poem: "length generally should be kept to 2 pages." No previously published poems. "Prefer single submissions. Clear copy." No e-mail submissions; postal submissions only. Reads submissions September-May. "Do not submit mss June through August." Publishes theme issues. Upcoming themes available for SASE. Guidelines available on website. Responds in 2 months. Sometimes sends prepublication galleys. Pays $5-50 and 1 contributor's copy with discount available on additional copies. Staff reviews books of poetry. Send materials for review consideration.

Additional Information Occasionally publishes "book" issues or "anthologies." Most recent book is *Plenty of Exits: New and Selected Poems* by Martin Tucker, a collection of narrative, lyrical, and humorous poems.

Tips "We want serious poetry, which may be humorous and light-hearted on the surface."

☑ CONNECTICUT REVIEW

Southern Connecticut State University, 501 Crescent St., New Haven CT 06515. (203)392-6737. Fax: (203)392-5748. E-mail: ctreview@southernct.edu. Website: www.southernct.edu/projects/ctreview. **Contact:** Vivian Shipley, Editor.

- Poetry published in *Connecticut Review* has been included in *The Best American Poetry* and *The Pushcart Prize* anthologies; has received special recognition for Literary Excellence from Public Radio's series *The Poet and the Poem*; and has won the Phoenix Award for Significant Editorial Achievement from the Council of Editors of Learned Journals (CELJ).

Magazines Needs *Connecticut Review*, published semiannually, contains essays, poetry, articles, fiction, b&w photographs, and color artwork. Has published poetry by Jack Bedell, Colette Inez, Maxine Kumin, Tony Fusco, Dana Gioia, and Marilyn Nelson. *Connecticut Review* is 208 pages, digest-sized, offset-printed, perfect-bound, with glossy 4-color cover. Receives about 2,500 poems/year, accepts about 5%. Press run is 3,000; 1,000 distributed free to Connecticut State libraries and high schools. Sample: $8. Make checks payable to Connecticut State University.

How to Contact Submit 3-5 typed poems at a time. Accepts submissions by postal mail only. Name, address, and phone number in the upper left corner of each page. Include SASE for reply only. Guidelines available for SASE. Pays 2 contributor's copies. Acquires first or one-time rights.

☑ THE CONNECTICUT RIVER REVIEW

53 Pearl St, New Haven CT 06511. E-mail: connpoetry@comcast.net. Website: ct-poetry-society.org/publications. **Contact:** Lisa Siedlarz, editor.

Magazines Needs *Connecticut River Review*, published annually in July or August by the Connecticut Poetry Society, prints "original, honest, diverse, vital, well-crafted poetry." Wants "any form, any subject. Translations and long poems welcome." Has published poetry by Marilyn Nelson, Jack Bedell, Maria Mazziotti Gillan, and Vivian Shipley. *Connecticut River Review* is digest-sized, attractively printed, perfect-bound. Receives about 2,000 submissions/year, accepts about 100. Press run is about 300. Membership in the CT poetry society is $25 per year and includes *Connecticut River Review* and *Long River Run*, a members-only magazine.

How to Contact Submit no more than 3-5 poems at a time. Considers simultaneous submissions if notified of acceptance elsewhere; no previously published poems. Cover letter is preferred. Include bio. "Complete contact information typed in upper right corner; SASE required." Reads submissions October 1-April 15. Guidelines available for SASE or on website. Responds in up to 8 weeks. Pays 1 contributor's copy. "Poet retains copyright."

Tips "Read as much good poetry as you can before you write."

▣ ☑ CONTE, AN ONLINE JOURNAL OF NARRATIVE WRITING

23260 Nanticoke Road, Quantico MD 21856. E-mail: poetry@conteonline.net. Website: http://www.conteonline.net. **Contact:** Adam Tavel, poetry editor. *Conte, an Online Journal of Narrative Writing*, published biannually online, prints "narrative writing of the highest quality. Writing that displays some degree of familiarity with our journal is likely to attract our attention, so make sure your work has a narrative bent." Has published poetry by

William Hathaway, Jim Daniels, E. Ethelbert Miller, Erika Meitner, and Roger Weingarten, among others. Receives about 2,000 poems/year, accepts about 24. Number of unique visitors: approximately 1,000/month. Submit up to 3 poems at a time. Query before sending poems over 100 lines in length. Considers simultaneous submissions; "please state clearly in your cover letter that your work is under consideration elsewhere and notify us immediately if it is accepted by another publication"; does not accept previously published poems (considers poetry posted on a public website/blog/forum and poetry posted on a private, password-protected forum as published). Accepts e-mail submissions (pasted into body of message); no fax or disk submissions. Cover letter is preferred.

Magazines Needs Cover letters are optional for some magazines, but we like to know a little about our submitters. "The type of things you should probably include are: 1) how you learned about our journal; 2) a few places you have been published previously, if at all; and 3) whether or not you are sending a simultaneous submission." Reads submissions year-round. Time between acceptance and publication is typically 2-4 months. Since *Conte* is a small journal, it is truly a labor of love for our 3 editors. While we occasionally share work with one another during the screening process, primarily we rely on our respective expertise in poetry and prose when making editorial selections. "Ultimately, a good poem is fresh and engaging from its very first line, so the chief responsibility for any poetry editor is to sift through clichés and mediocrity to share the best submitted work with the world." Sometimes comments on rejected poems. Sometimes publishes theme issues. Upcoming themes and guidelines available on website. Responds in 3-5 months. Sometimes sends prepublication galleys. Acquires one-time rights. Rights revert to poets upon publication.

Tips Here at *Conte*, it is obvious when a writer is unfamiliar with our narrative mission, because he/she will rave about our "avant-garde style" or "embrace of the experimental." Be aware of your own aesthetic leanings and send work to publications that are a snug fit.

$ ☙ ◎ CONTEMPORARY HAIBUN

P.O. Box 2461, Winchester VA 22604-1661. (540)722-2156. E-mail: jim.kacian@redmoonpress.com. Website: www.redmoonpress.com. **Contact:** Jim Kacian, Editor/Publisher.

Magazines Needs *contemporary haibun*, published annually in April, is the first Western journal dedicated to haibun and haiga. Considers poetry by children and teens. Has published poetry by Fran Masat, Carol Pearce-Worthington, Ray Rasmussen, and Jeff Winke. *contemporary haibun* is 128 pages, digest-sized, offset-printed on quality paper, with 4-color heavy-stock cover. Receives several hundred submissions/year, accepts about 5%. Print run is 1,000. Subscription: $17 plus $5 p&h. Sample available for SASE or by e-mail.

How to Contact Submit up to 3 haibun or haiga at a time. Considers previously published poems. Accepts submissions online at www.poetrylives.com/cho/ as well as disk and postal submissions. Include SASE for postal submissions. Time between acceptance and publication varies according to time of submission. Poems are circulated to an editorial board. "Only haibun and haiga will be considered. If you are unfamiliar with the form, consult *Journey to the Interior*, edited by Bruce Ross, *contemporary haibun online* (at www. redmoonpress.com), or previous issues of *contemporary haibun*, for samples and some discussion." Guidelines available in magazine, for SASE, by e-mail, or on website. Pays $1/page. Acquires first North American serial rights.

Also Offers Publishes *The Red Moon Anthology*, "an annual volume of the finest English-language haiku and related work published anywhere in the world." (See separate listing in this section.)

Tips "It is best if you familiarize yourself with what is happening in the genre (and its close relatives) today before submitting. We strive to give all the work we publish plenty of space in which to resonate, and to provide a forum where the best of today's practitioners can be published with dignity and prestige."

▣ $ ☑ CONTRARY

3133 S. Emerald Ave., Chicago IL 60616-3299. E-mail: chicago@contrarymagazine.com. Website: www.contrarymagazine.com. **Contact:** Jeff McMahon, editor. Member: CLMP.

Magazines Needs *Contrary*, published quarterly online, contains "fiction, poetry, literary commentary, and prefers work that combines the virtues of all those categories. Founded at the University of Chicago, it now operates independently and not-for-profit on the South Side of Chicago. We like work that is not only contrary in content, but contrary in its evasion of the expectations established by its genre. Our fiction defies traditional story form. For example, a story may bring us to closure without ever delivering an ending. And we value fiction as poetic as any poem. We look especially for plurality or meaning, for dual reverberation or beauty and concern. *Contrary's* poetry in particular often mimics the effects of fiction or commentary. We find ourselves enamored of prose poems because they are naturally ambiguous about form — they tug overtly on the forces of narrative — but prose poems remain the minority of all the poetic forms we publish."

How to Contact Submit no more than 3 poems per issue. No mail or e-mail submissions; submit work via the website. Considers simultaneous submissions; no previously published poems. Accepts submissions through online form only. Reads submissions year round. See website for submission deadlines per issue. Often comments on rejected poems. Guidelines on website. $20 per byline, $60 for featured work. "Upon acceptance, *Contrary* acquires the following rights: 1) exclusive rights for the three-month period that the accepted work appears in the current issue of *Contrary* magazine, 2) the right to permanent inclusion of the work in *Contrary's* electronic archive, and 3) the right to reproduce the work in print and electronic collections of our content. After the current issue expires, the author is free to seek republication elsewhere, but *Contrary* must be credited upon republication."

☑ CONVERGENCE

E-mail: clinville@csus.edu. Website: www.convergence-journal.com. **Contact:** Cynthia Linville, Managing Editor.

Magazines Needs *Convergence*, published quarterly online, seeks "to unify the literary and visual arts and draw new interpretations of the written word by pairing poems and flash fiction with complementary art. We are open to many different styles, but we do not often publish formal verse. Read a couple of issues to get a sense of what we like; namely, well-crafted work with fresh images and a strong voice." Does not want "poetry with trite, unoriginal language or unfinished work." Has published poetry by Lola Haskins, Grace Cavalieri, Molly Fisk, and Renato Rosaldo. Receives about 800 poems/year, accepts about 10 per issue plus monthly selections for "Editor's Choice." Has about 200 online subscribers.

How to Contact Submit up to 5 poems at a time. Lines/poem: 60 maximum. No simultaneous submissions. Accepts e-mail submissions only. Reads submissions year round. Time between acceptance and publication is 1-2 months. Poems are circulated to an editorial board. Sometimes comments on rejected poems. Guidelines available on website. Responds in 6 months. No payment. Acquires first rights.

◙ COPIOUS MAGAZINE

225 E. 72nd St., #527, New York NY 10021. E-mail: underground@copiousmagazine.com. **Contact:** Andrea Grant, Editor. *Copious Magazine*, published 3-4 times/year online, features poetry, artwork, photographs, pulp fiction novel covers, interviews, music, and fashion. Wants "poems that have that aching knife twist in them; themes of nocturne, mythology, and fairy tales; poems about people. We produce *Copious* so that artists/writers will have an attractive venue in which to showcase. We produce from a place of truth, so that other creatives might be inspired by accounts of overcoming obstacles. When stepping into the *Copious* world, the content is interwoven to create a deliberate environment, sometimes with allegorical humor. We feature thematic imagery of the vixen of film noir and hardboiled pulp novels. She defies social expectations as seduction melds with her tragic side, a strong female force." Does not want "rhyming; horror; crass, overly sentimental poetry." Considers poetry by children and teens. Has published poetry by Ace Boggess, B.M. Bradley, Andrea MacPherson, and Laurel Ann Bogen. Publishes about 20 poems/issue. Readership is 10,000 and growing.

How to Contact Submit 3-5 poems at a time. Considers previously published poems and simultaneous submissions. Accepts e-mail submissions (pasted into body of message only; no attachments) or submit from our website. Cover letter is required. "Please provide a short bio with credits." Reads submissions year round. Submit seasonal poems 6 months in advance. Time between acceptance and publication is up to one year. Occasionally publishes theme issues. Guidelines available by e-mail. Responds in up to one year. Acquires one-time rights; reserves right to republish in future anthologies. Send materials for review consideration to Andrea Grant.

Tips "The best poetry comes from the heart and has that haunting little twist. Don't be afraid to take risks."

▣ ◙ THE CORTLAND REVIEW

P.O. Box 1234, New York NY 10276. (678)428-1323. Fax: (770)956-0850. E-mail: tcr@cortlandreview.com. Website: www.cortlandreview.com. **Contact:** Ginger Murchison, editor.

• Poem published in the *Best American Poetry* in 2007 and Best of the web 2007 and 2008.

Magazines Needs *The Cortland Review*, published 6 times/year, is "an online magazine publishing both established and up-and-coming writers from the print and online worlds. Using audio paired with text to complete the link between reader and poet, TCR provides regular and feature issues with poems and short fiction selected by staff as well as illustrious guest editors." Wants "free verse, formal, avant-garde." Does not want "inspirational, religious, political." Has published poetry by Billy Collins, Stephen Dunn, Seamus Heaney,

Tony Hoagland, Sharon Olds, Philip Levine and Gerald Stern. Receives about 500 poems/year, accepts about 80-100. Receives about 82,000 unique visitors per month.

How to Contact Submit 3-5 poems at a time, up to 100 lines. No previously published poems or simultaneous submissions ("Previously published" work includes poetry posted on public Websites/blogs/forums, and on private, password-protected forums). Poems should be submitted via online form accessible by menu on home page. Cover letter is required. "All work should be single-spaced. Do not use all caps, even for titles. Make sure entire submission is submitted in one online submission form." Poems are circulated to an editorial board or guest editor. Sometimes comments on rejected poems. Sometimes publishes theme issues by solicited contributors only. Guidelines available on website. Responds in about 6 months. Prepublication galleys are available online. "TCR acquires the rights to publish the author's material (text and audio)." Rights revert to author upon publication. Reviews books of poetry. Book reviews should be queried.

☑ COTTONWOOD

Cottonwood Press, 1301 Jayhawk Blvd., Room 400, Kansas Union, University of Kansas, Lawrence KS 66045. (785)864-3777. E-mail: pwedge@ku.edu. **Contact:** Philip Wedge, Poetry Editor.

Magazines Needs *Cottonwood*, published semiannually, emphasizes the Midwest "but publishes the best poetry received regardless of region." Wants poems "on daily experience, perception; strong narrative or sensory impact, non-derivative." Does not want "'literary,' not 'academic.'" Has published poetry by Rita Dove, Virgil Suárez, Walt McDonald, Oliver Rice, and Luci Tapahonso. *Cottonwood* is 112 pages, digest-sized, printed from computer offset, flat-spined. Receives about 3,000 submissions/year, accepts about 20. Press run is 500-600. Single copy: $8.00. Sample: $5.

How to Contact Submit up to 5 pages of poetry at a time with SASE. Lines/poem: 60 maximum. No simultaneous or e-mailed submissions. Sometimes comments on rejected poems. Responds in up to 5 months. Pays 1 contributor's copy.

Additional Information Cottonwood Press "is auxiliary to *Cottonwood Magazine* and publishes material by authors in the region. **Material is usually solicited.**" Has published *Violence and Grace* by Michael L. Johnson and *Midwestern Buildings* by Victor Contoski.

Tips "Read the little magazines and send to ones you like."

☑ THE COUNTRY DOG REVIEW

E-mail: countrydogreview@gmail.com. Website: www.countrydogreview.org. **Contact:** Danielle Sellers, editor.

Magazines Needs *The Country Dog Review*, published quarterly online, publishes "poetry, book reviews, and interviews with poets." Wants "poetry of the highest quality, not limited to style or region. Also accepts book reviews and interviews. Query first." Does not want "translations, fiction, nonfiction." Receives about 400 poems/year, accepts about 10%.

How to Contact Submit 3-5 poems at a time. No previously published poems or simultaneous submissions. Accepts e-mail submissions with attachment; no fax or disk submissions. Cover letter is required. Reads submissions year round. Submit seasonal poems 6 months in advance. Time between acceptance and publication is 1-4 months. Never comments on rejected poems. Sometimes publishes theme issues. Upcoming themes and guidelines available by e-mail and on website. Responds in 1-2 months. Sometimes sends prepublication galleys. Acquires first North American serial rights. Reviews books of poetry in 500 words, single-book format.

☑ CRAB CREEK REVIEW

7315 34th Ave NW, Seattle WA 98117. E-mail: editors@crabcreekreview.org. Website: www.crabcreekreview.org. **Contact:** Lana Hechtman Ayers , poetry editor. Established 2009.

Magazines Needs *Crab Creek Review*, published biannually, is seeking "poetry, short fiction, and creative nonfiction that takes us somewhere unexpected, keeps us engaged, and stays with us beyond the initial reading. We appreciate lyrical and narrative forms of poetry, with a slight bias toward free verse. Translations are welcome—please submit with a copy of the poem in its original language, if possible." Has published poetry by Oliver de la Paz, Dorianne Laux, Greg Nicholl, and translations by Ilya Kaminsky and Matthew Zapruder. Fiction by karen Heuler and Daniel Homan. *Crab Creek Review* is an 80- to 120-page, perfect-bound paperback. Subscription: $15/year, $28/2 year. Sample: $6.

How to Contact Send up to 5 poems between September 1 and April 30, to "Poetry Editor." No e-mail submissions. Cover letter is preferred. Include cover letter and SASE for reply only. "Without one we will not consider your work." Responds in up to 6 months. Pays 1 contributor copy.

Contest/Award Offerings Offers annual poetry contest with deadline of May 31st. Entry fee: $10. Submit up to 5 poems. All entries will be considered for publication. See website for more information.

$ ☑ CRAB ORCHARD REVIEW

Dept. of English, Mail Code 4503, Faner Hall 2380, Southern Illinois Univ Carbondale, 1000 Faner Dr., Carbondale IL 62901. Website: www.craborchardreview.siuc.edu. **Contact:** Allison Joseph, editor.

- *Crab Orchard Review* received a 2009 Literary Award and a 2009 Operating Grant from the Illinois Arts Council; poetry published in *Crab Orchard Review* has appeared in *The Best American Poetry* and *Beacon's Best of 1999* and *2000*.

Magazines Needs *Crab Orchard Review*, published semiannually in March and September, prints poetry, fiction, creative nonfiction, interviews, book reviews, and novel excerpts. Wants all styles and forms from traditional to experimental. Does not want greeting card verse; literary poetry only. Has published poetry by Luisa A. Igloria, Erinn Batykefer, Jim Daniels, Bryan Tso Jones. *Crab Orchard Review* is 256-280 pages, digest-sized, professionally printed, perfect-bound, with (usually) glossy card cover with color photos. Receives about 12,000 poems/year, accepts about 1%. Press run is 3,500; 100 exchanged with other journals; remainder in shelf sales. Subscription: $20. Sample: $12.

How to Contact Submit up to 5 poems at a time. Considers simultaneous submissions with notification; no previously published poems. Postal submissions only. Cover letter is preferred. "Indicate stanza breaks on poems of more than 1 page." Reads submissions April-November for Summer/Fall special theme issue, February-April for regular, non-thematic Winter/Spring issue. Time between acceptance and publication is 6 months to a year. "Poems that are under serious consideration are discussed and decided on by the managing editor and poetry editor." Seldom comments on rejected poems. Publishes theme issues.

Upcoming themes available in magazine, for SASE, or on website. Guidelines available for SASE or on website. Responds in up to 9 months. Pays $20/page ($50 minimum), 2 contributor's copies, and 1 year's subscription. Acquires first North American serial rights. Staff reviews books of poetry in 500-700 words, single-book format. Send materials for review consideration to Jon C. Tribble, Managing Editor.

Contest/Award Offerings The Crab Orchard Series in Poetry Open Competition Awards, The Crab Orchard Series in Poetry First Book Award, and The Richard Peterson Poetry Prize.

Tips "Do not send any submissions via e-mail! Include SASE (#10 or larger) with all submissions and all queries—no postcards or small envelopes. Before you send work, check the website to see what issue we are currently reading submissions for. Being familiar with our reading schedule will help you submit appropriate work at the right time."

$ ☑ CRAZYHORSE

Dept. of English, College of Charleston, 66 George St., Charleston SC 29424. (843)953-7740. E-mail: crazyhorse@cofc.edu. Website: www.crazyhorsejournal.org. **Contact:** Garrett Doherty, Poetry Editor.

- Poetry published in *Crazyhorse* has appeared in *The Best American Poetry 2008*, 2007, 2006 and *The Pushcart Prize*.

Magazines Needs *Crazyhorse*, published semiannually, prints fine fiction, poetry, and essays. "Send your best words our way. We like to print a mix of writing regardless of its form, genre, school, or politics. We're especially on the lookout for writing that doesn't fit the categories. Before sending, ask 'What's reckoned with that's important for other people to read?'" Has published poetry by David Wojahn, Mary Ruefle, Nance Van Winkle, Dean Young, Marvin Bell, and A.V. Christie. *Crazyhorse* is 160 pages, 834x812, perfect-bound, with 4-color glossy cover. Receives about 15,000 poems/year. Circulation is 2,000. Single copy: $9; subscription: $16/year, $27 for 2 years, $36 for 3 years. Sample: $6. Make checks payable to *Crazyhorse*.

How to Contact Submit 3-5 poems at a time. Considers simultaneous submissions; no previously published poems. No fax, e-mail, or disk submissions. Cover letter is preferred. Reads submissions year round. "We read slower in summer." Time between acceptance and publication is 6 months. Seldom comments on rejected poems. Guidelines available in magazine, for SASE, by e-mail, or on website. Responds in 3 months. Sometimes sends prepublication galleys. Pays $20/page, 2 contributor's copies, and one-year subscription (2 issues). Acquires first North American serial rights.

Contest/Award Offerings The annual Lynda Hull Memorial Poetry Prize.

Tips "Feel strongly; then write."

☑ THE CREAM CITY REVIEW

Dept. of English, Univ of Wisconsin—Milwaukee, P.O. Box 413, Milwaukee WI 53201. Website: creamcityreview.org. **Contact:** Emilie Lindemann and Derrick Harriel.

- Poetry published in *The Cream City Review* has been included in *The Best American Poetry*.

Magazines Needs *The Cream City Review*, published twice/year, seeks "all forms of writing, from traditional to experimental. We strive to produce issues that are challenging, diverse,

Magazines/Journals

and of lasting quality." Does not want "sexist, homophobic, racist, or formulaic writings." Has published poetry by Elizabeth Bradfield, Annie Finch, Timothy Liu, Thylias Moss, Lee Ann Roripaugh, and Larissa Szporluk. *The Cream City Review* is about 200 pages, digest-sized, perfect-bound, with full-color cover on 70 lb. paper. Press run is 1,000. Single copy: $12; subscription: $22/year, $41 for 2 years ($35/year for institutions). Sample: $7.

How to Contact Submit no more than 5 poems at a time via electronic submission form. Considers simultaneous submissions when notified. "General submissions are accepted from August 1 to November 1 and from December 1 to April 1. Our online submission management system will not allow submissions to be made at times outside of our reading periods." Sometimes comments on rejected poems. Publishes theme issues." Guidelines available on website. Responds in 2-8 months. Payment includes one-year subscription. Acquires first rights.

Contest/Award Offerings Sponsors an annual poetry contest, The Beau Boudreaux Prize. Awards $1000 plus publication. **Entry fee:** $15 for 3-5 poems. For now, because of the entry fee, all competition submissions must be made by regular mail. All entries are considered for publication. Guidelines available on website.

✿ ◔ ◎ CREATIVE CONNECTIONS

Kwil Kids Publishing, Box 98037, Vancouver BC V6Z 2Y0, Canada. E-mail: creative-connections@hotmail.com. Website: creative-connections.spaces.live.com. **Contact:** Kalen Marquis, editor.

Magazines Needs *Creative Connections*, published quarterly, is a newsletter that prints "essays, articles, short stories, poems, book reviews, dialogues, letters, sidebar lists, and black and white ink sketches." Wants "woven words of wisdom, wonder, and wellness. We promote 'creativity' and 'connection' as well as human growth and development through joy, compassion, and cheerleading—not criticism." Interested in psychology, sociology, philosophy, and spirituality "in the broadest sense" as well as "long-standing universal human themes." *Creative Connections* is 10 pages. Receives about 400 submissions/year, accepts about 80%. Press run is 200. Subscription: $20 CAD (4 issues). Make checks payable to Kalen Marquis.

How to Contact Submit 5 poems at a time. Accepts e-mail submissions (pasted into body of message; no attachments). Cover letter is preferred. Include SASE (or SAE with IRC for those submitting outside of Canada). Reads submissions year round. Time between acceptance and publication is up to 3 months. Always comments on rejected poems. "Kwil always provides encouragement and personalized response with SASE (or SAE and IRC)." Guidelines available for SASE (Canadian-stamped envelope, or IRC, or $1 USD for Canadian postage) or by e-mail. Responds in April, August, and December. Pays 1 contributor's copy. Acquires one-time rights.

Tips "Submit best and submit often; provide Canadian-stamped envelope; sign permission card; have fun writing."

◔ CRUCIBLE

Barton College, College Station, Wilson NC 27893. (252)399-6343. E-mail: crucible@barton. edu. **Contact:** Terrence L. Grimes, editor.

Magazines Needs *Crucible*, published annually in November, uses "poetry that demonstrates originality and integrity of craftsmanship as well as thought. Traditional metrical and rhyming poems are difficult to bring off in modern poetry. The best poetry is written out of deeply felt experience which has been crafted into pleasing form." Wants "free verse with attention paid particularly to image, line, stanza, and voice." Does not want "very long narratives, poetry that is forced." Has published poetry by Robert Grey, R.T. Smith, and Anthony S. Abbott. *Crucible* is under 100 pages, digest-sized, professionally printed on high-quality paper, with matte card cover. Press run is 500. Sample: $8.

How to Contact Submit no more than 5 poems at a time. No previously published poems or simultaneous submissions. "We require electronic submission of work and a short biography including a list of publications." Receives submissions between Christmas and mid-April only. Responds in late summer. Pays in contributor's copies.

Contest/Award Offerings The Sam Ragan Prize ($150), in honor of the former Poet Laureate of North Carolina, and other contests (prizes of $150 and $100). Guidelines available on website.

▦ ☑ CURRENT ACCOUNTS

Journal of the Bank Street Writers, Regency House, Longworth Rd., Horwich, Bolton BL6 7BA, England. (44)(1204)669858. E-mail: bswscribe@aol.com. *Current Accounts*, published semiannually, prints poetry, fiction, and nonfiction by members of Bank Street Writers, and other contributors. Open to all types of poetry. "No requirements, although some space is reserved for members." Considers poetry by children and teens. Has published poetry by Pat Winslow, M.R. Peacocke, and Gerald England. *Current Accounts* is 52 pages, A5, photocopied, saddle-stapled, with card cover with b&w or color photo or artwork. Receives about 300 poems/year, accepts about 5%. Press run is 80; 8 distributed free to competition winners. Subscription: £6. Sample: £3. Make checks payable to Bank Street Writers (sterling checks only).

How to Contact Submit up to 6 poems at a time. Lines/poem: 100 maximum. No previously published poems (unpublished poems preferred) or simultaneous submissions. Prefers e-mail submissions (pasted into body of message). Cover letter is required. SAE or IRC essential for postal submissions. Time between acceptance and publication is 6 months. Seldom comments on rejected poems. Guidelines available for SASE, by fax, e-mail, or on website. Responds in 3 months. Pays 1 contributor's copy. Acquires first rights.

Tips Bank Street Writers meets once/month and offers workshops, guest speakers, and other activities. Write for details."We like originality of ideas, images, and use of language. No inspirational or religious verse unless it's also good in poetic terms."

◪ ☑ DALHOUSIE REVIEW

Dalhouise University, Halifax NS B3H 4R2 Canada. (902)494-2541. Fax: (902)494-3561. E-mail: dalhousie.review@dal.ca. Website: http://dalhousiereview.dal.ca. Editor: Anthony Stewart. **Contact:** Poetry editor. *Dalhousie Review*, published 3 times/year, is a journal of criticism publishing poetry and fiction. Considers poetry from both new and established writers. *Dalhousie Review* is 144 pages, digest-sized. Accepts about 5% of poems received. Press run is 500. Single copy: $15 CAD; subscription: $22.50 CAD, $28 USD. Make checks payable to *Dalhousie Review*.

How to Contact Lines/poem: 40. No previously published poems. No e-mail submissions except from outside North American (all other initial submissions are by means of hard copy only). "Submissions should be typed on plain white paper, double-spaced throughout. Spelling preferences are those of *The Canadian Oxford Dictionary*: catalogue, colour, program, travelling, theatre, and so on. Beyond this, writers of fiction and poetry are encouraged to follow whatever canons of usage might govern the particular story or poem in question, and to be inventive with language, ideas, and form. Please enclose a SASE (or SAE and IRC) for response." Reads submissions year round. Seldom comments on rejected poems. Occasionally publishes theme issues. Guidelines available for SAE and IRC or on website. Pays 2 contributor's copies and 10 off-prints.

◎ DARKLING MAGAZINE

Darkling Publications, 28780 318th Avenue, Colome SD 57528. (605)455-2892. E-mail: darkling@mitchelltelecom.net. **Contact:** James C. Van Oort, editor in chief.

Magazines Needs *Darkling Magazine*, published annually in August, is "primarily interested in poetry. All submissions should be dark in nature and should help expose the darker side of man. Dark nature does not mean whiny or overly murderous, and being depressed does not make an artist's work dark. Pornography will not be considered and will merit no response. Profanity that is meritless or does not support the subject of any piece is unacceptable. Has published poems by Robert Cooperman, Kenneth DiMaggio, Arthur Gottlieb, Simon Perchik, Cathy Porter and Susanna Rich, among others. Subscription: $15 with s&h. Sample copies are $10.00. Make checks payable to Darkling Publications.

How to Contact Submit up to 8 poems at a time. Lines/poem: any length is acceptable, but "epic poems must be of exceptional quality. Considers previously published poems and simultaneous submissions. Will accept e-mail submissions; no disk submissions. Cover letter is required. Reads submissions October to April. Time between acceptance and publication is varies. Poems are circulated to an editorial board. Sometimes comments on rejected poems. Guidelines available in magazine. Announces rejections and acceptance in May or June. Pays 1 contributor's copy. All rights revert to author upon publication.

Contest/Award Offerings Submit approximately 30 pages of poetry for the Darkling Magazine Annual Chapbook Contest. No theme is necessary. Dark poetry is preferred but excellent poetry of any type will be considered. Again no pornography or excessive profanity will be printed. The editors reserve the right to determine which poems and in which order the poems shall be printed and thus the final publication may deviate from the original manuscript sent in by the contestant. A reading fee of $20.00 is required. Checks should be made out to Darkling Publications. Open for chapbook submissions from January 1– April 1. Winner will be notified in July and expected publication will be in October. Each entrant will receive 1 copy of the winning chapbook. The winner will receive 10 copies of the chapbook and a 20% discount on any additional copies they may wish to purchase. Editors may offer comments on chapbooks submitted.

Tips "We are always looking for new poets who have a voice we feel needs to be heard. Do not be afraid to ask questions. Our editorial staff will be very happy to communicate with you."

N ▣ ◷ DEAD MULE SCHOOL OF SOUTHERN LITERATURE

E-mail: deadmule.poetry@gmail.com. Website: www.deadmule.com/. **Contact:** Helen Losse, poetry editor.

Magazines Needs "*The Dead Mule School of Southern Literature* wants stories. Good ones. Your writing? Hmmmmm. Write about sweat-dripping, Bible-thumping, pick-up driving, beer drinking rednecks. Chauvinistic, Mama-loving, hounddog-owning porch sitters - stereotypes we love to hate or hate to love. Heroes who drink sweet tea, eat Moon Pies, grits, and collards, frying in lard… lard pie, lard eggs, lard sandwiches. Lard. Mule skinners and mud runners. The esoteric, the strange, the truly captivating story will make it onto our pages. Be it about folks who are uncouth, semi-literate, tobacco chewing adolescents, or PhDs, Scholars, Scientists, Artists, Inventors, and Entrepreneurs. Write about brilliant, kind, thoughtful folks who will help you in your time of need or spit on your grandma. The South contains them all. There's no New South, there is only The South."

How to Contact Submit 1-4 Poems at a time. No previously published poems or simultaneous submissions. Submit by e-mail, "along with Southern Legitimacy Statement with your submission. *The Dead Mule* does not publish standard bios." Reads submissions year round. Guidelines found on website. "Submission to and acceptance by *Dead Mule* grants us first electronic and indefinite archive rights. All other rights revert to the author upon publication. Please credit *Dead Mule* as the first publisher if you reprint elsewhere; we like seeing our name in print, too."

◖ DENVER QUARTERLY

University of Denver, 2000 E. Asbury, Denver CO 80208. (303)871-2892. Website: www. denverquarterly.com. **Contact:** Bill Ramke. "We publish fiction, articles and poetry for a generally well-educated audience, primarily interested in literature and the literary experience. They read DQ to find something a little different from a stictly academic quarterly or a creative writing outlet." Quarterly. Pays $5/page for fiction and poetry and 2 contributor's copies. Acquires first North American serial rights.

How to Contact "Poetry submissions should be comprised of 3-5 poems. Submit ms by mail, include SASE; 3 months to mss. Accepts simultaneous submissions. Sample copy for $10.

◿ THE DERONDA REVIEW

P.O. Box 55164, Madison WI 53705. E-mail: derondareview@att.net. Website: www. pointandcircumference.com. Mindy Aber Barad, co-editor for Israel. **Contact:** Esther Cameron, editor. Co-Editor for Israel: Mindy Aber Barad, P.O.B. 1299, Efrat 90435.

Magazines Needs *The Deronda Review*, published semiannually, seeks to "promote a literature of introspection, dialogue, and social concern." Wants "poetry of beauty and integrity with emotional and intellectual depth, commitment to subject matter as well as language, and the courage to ignore fashion. Welcome: well-crafted formal verse, social comment (including satire), love poems, philosophical/religious poems. The website will also publish essays and fiction. *The Deronda Review* has a standing interest in work that sees Judaism as a source of values and/or reflects on the current situation of Israel and of Western civilization. Open, in principle, to writers of all ages." Has published poetry by Yakov Azriel, Ruth Blumert, Ida Fasel, Constance Rowell Mastores, Richard Moore, and

Yaacov Dovid Shulman. *The Deronda Review* is 28-36 pages, magazine-sized, photocopied, saddle-stapled, with cardstock cover. Press run is 375. Single copy: $6; subscription: $12.

How to Contact Submit 3-5 poems at a time or, for the website, prose of any length. Longer works will be considered for installment publication. Considers simultaneous submissions. "The paper magazine rarely accepts repritns; the website invites submission of poems already published in paper format. All poems published for the first time on the website will be printed in the magazine." Cover letter is unnecessary. "Do include SASE with sufficient postage to return all manuscripts or with 'Reply Only" clearly indicated. First-time contributors in the U.S. are requested to submit by surface mail. Poets whose work is accepted will be asked for titles of books available, to be published in the magazine." Time between acceptance and publication is up to 1 year. Often comments on rejected poems. Does not offer guidelines because "the tradition is the only 'guideline.' We do encourage contributors to write for a sample." Responds in up to 4 months; "if longer, please query by e-mail." Pays 2 contributor's copies for magazine publication. Acquires first rights.

Additional Information *The Deronda Review* publishes the addresses of poets who would welcome correspondence. "Poets can also submit longer selections of work for publication on the 'Point and Circumference' website." Current projects include a blog that will post longer works, poems as they are accepted by the magazine, correspondence, etc. This should be launched by August 2009; check the website for updates.

Tips "The poem should speak to the ear and to the understanding, and it should be understood that understanding has social consequences. Like all our social functioning, poetry today suffers from a loss of community, which translates into a lack of real intimacy with the reader. Poets can work against this trend by remaining in touch with the poetry of past generations, by forming relationships in which poetry can be employed as the language of friendship, and by at least contemplating the concept of covenant. Publication should be an afterthought."

☑ DESCANT: FORT WORTH'S JOURNAL OF POETRY AND FICTION

English Dept., Texas Christian University, Box 297270, Fort Worth TX 76129. Fax: (817)257-6239. E-mail: descant@tcu.edu. Website: www.descant.tcu.edu. **Contact:** Dave Kuhne, Editor.

Magazines Needs *descant: Fort Worth's Journal of Poetry and Fiction*, published annually during the summer, seeks "well-crafted poems of interest. No restrictions as to subject matter or form." *descant* is 100+ pages, digest-sized, professionally printed and bound, with matte card cover. Receives about 3,000 poems/year. Press run is 500. Single copy: $12 ($18 outside U.S.). Sample: $10.

How to Contact Lines/poem: 60 or fewer, "but sometimes longer." Accepts simultaneous submissions. No fax or e-mail submissions. Reads submissions September-March only. Responds in 6 weeks. Pays 2 contributor's copies.

Contest/Award Offerings Sponsors the annual Betsy Colquitt Award for Poetry, offering $500 to the best poem or series of poems by a single author in a volume. *descant* also offers a $250 award for an outstanding poem in an issue. No application process or reading fee; all published submissions are eligible for consideration.

◙ DEVIL BLOSSOMS

Asterius Press, P.O. Box 5122, Seabrook NJ 08302-3511. Website: www.asteriuspress.com. **Contact:** John C. Erianne, Editor. *Devil Blossoms*, published irregularly 1-2 times/year, seeks "poetry in which the words show the scars of real life. Sensual poetry that's occasionally ugly. I'd rather read a poem that makes me sick than a poem without meaning." Wants poetry that is "darkly comical, ironic, visceral, horrific; or any tidbit of human experience that moves me." Does not want "religious greetings, 'I'm-so-happy-to-be-alive' tree poetry." Has published poetry by Marie Kazalia, Stephanie Savage, Mitchell Metz, Normal, John Sweet, and Alison Daniel. *Devil Blossoms* is 32 pages, 7½ × 10, saddle-stapled, with matte card cover with ink drawings. Receives about 10,000 poems/year, accepts about 1%. Press run is 750. Single copy: $5; subscription: $14. Make checks payable to John C. Erianne.

How to Contact Submit 3-5 poems at a time. Considers simultaneous submissions "if so informed." Accepts e-mail submissions (pasted into body of message; no attachments). Must have "submission" in the subject header. Cover letter is preferred. Time between acceptance and publication is up to one year. "I promptly read submissions, divide them into a 'no' and a 'maybe' pile. Then I read the 'maybes' again." Seldom comments on rejected poems. Guidelines available on website. Responds in up to 2 months. Pays one contributor's copy. Acquires first rights.

Tips "Write from love; don't expect love in return, don't take rejection personally, and don't let anyone stop you."

▣ ◪ DIAGRAM

Dept of English, P.O. Box 210067, University of Arizona, Tucson AZ 85721. E-mail: editor@ thediagram.com. Website: www.thediagram.com. **Contact:** Ander Monson, Editor. Member: CLMP.

- Work appearing in *DIAGRAM* has been reprinted on the Poetry Daily and Verse Daily Websites.

Magazines Needs *DIAGRAM*, published semimonthly online, prints "poetry, prose, and schematic (found or created), plus nonfiction, art, and sound. We're especially interested in unusual forms and structures, and work that blurs genre boundaries." Does not want light verse. Has published poetry by Arielle Greenberg, Jason Bredle, Lia Purpura, GC Waldrep. Receives about 1,000 poems/year, accepts about 5%. Number of unique visitors:1,500/ day.

How to Contact Submit 3-6 poems at a time. Lines/poem: no limit. Considers simultaneous submissions; no previously published poems. Electronic submissions accepted through submissions manager; no e-mail, disk, or fax submissions. Electronic submissions MUCH preferred; print submissions must include SASE if response is expected." Cover letter is preferred. Reads submissions year round. Time between acceptance and publication is 1-10 months. Poems are circulated to an editorial board. Sometimes comments on rejected poems. Sometimes publishes theme issues. Guidelines available on website. Responds in 1-3 months. Always sends prepublication galleys. Acquires first rights and first North American serial rights. Rights revert to poet upon publication. Reviews books/chapbooks of poetry in 500-1,500 words, single- or multi-book format. Send materials for review consideration to Pablo Peschiera, reviews editor. Info on website

Additional Information *DIAGRAM* also publishes periodic perfect-bound print anthologies.

Contest/Award Offerings Sponsors the annual *DIAGRAM*/Michigan Press Chapbook Contest.

▣ ▢ ◎ DIAMOND DUST E-ZINE

725 Third Ave., Pinole CA 94564. E-mail: DiamondEditor@yahoo.com. **Contact:** Laura Rutlind. *Diamond Dust E-zine*, published quarterly online, is "a magazine for teens and adults. Our goal is to inspire our readers in their Christian walk." Wants "poetry, short fiction, articles, book and music reviews, and fillers. Poetry of all types and all topics is considered. Submissions are not required to be religious, but we ask that they include good morals and clean content. 'Inspirational' is key." Does not want "to see anything that does not have clean content or high morals, or anything that is not inspirational." Considers poetry by teens. "Teens are encouraged to submit their work, but they must include their age and name or pen name." Accepts 20 poems/year. Available for free online. "NOTE: due to a backlog of submissions caused by unforeseen circumstances, we will only be considering the manuscripts submitted to us since November 2009. If you submitted a manuscript earlier than that and would like it to be re-considered, please re-submit it."

How to Contact Submit 3 poems at a time. Lines/poem: less than 30. Considers previously published poems. Requires e-mail submissions (pasted into body of e-mail). Cover letter is required. "Tell us who you are and what you write. Include bio. If you're a teen, please include your age." Reads submissions year-round. Submit seasonal poems 4 months in advance. Usually publishes theme issues. Guidelines and themes available by e-mail or on website. Responds within 2 months. No payment, but will include an author bio and contact links on website. "We acquire one-time electronic rights. All rights are given back to the author after publication. All pieces remain on our website for 2 issues and then they are deleted."

Tips "We love to work with beginning writers, so take a look at our current issue online. If you follow our guidelines and themes list, your submission has a good chance of achieving publication."

▣ ▢ THE DIRTY NAPKIN

E-mail: thedirtynapkin@thedirtynapkin.com. Website: thedirtynapkin.com. **Contact:** J. Argyl Plath, Managing Director.

Magazines Needs "Have you ever felt the urgency to write while you were out, at a restaurant, say, and scribbled a thought down on a napkin or the closest thing you could find? Have you ever told your friends to 'hang on a sec' until you finished that thought? As writers, we do not know when the muse will slap us silly. Luckily, there are many napkins filling the world waiting for us to dirty them. Luckily, there are many napkins filling the world waiting for us to dirty them. We believe writing cannot be separated from the voice, breath, and personality of the author. Further, we feel that if a piece of writing is separated from this literal voice, much power is lost. Therefore, we seek to include this voice by providing recordings of each author reading their work." Has published poetry by Alicia Ostriker, Jane Mead, F.D. Reeve, Sarah J. Sloat, Jacqueline Garlitos, and Doug Ramspeck. Single copy: $20-50 for POD (varies based on page count), subscription $16 (includes access to all author recordings and discounts on merchandise).

How to Contact Submit 3 poems at a time. Accepts e-mail submissions (through online form); no fax or disk submissions. Cover letter is preferred. Reads submissions year round. Time between acceptance and publication is 2-3 months. Poems are circulated to an editorial board. Sometimes comments on rejected poems. Guidelines on website. Responds in 1-2 months. Acquires first North American serial and electronic rights. Rights revert to poets upon publication.

Also Offers "Each issue will feature on writer on its cover. The cover will be determined by the staff from the pool of accepted submissions. If you are selected to win the cover prize, we will ask that you hand write your work on a napkin of your choosing. Your work will appear inside the magazine as well."

🔲 ☑ DMQ REVIEW

E-mail: editors@dmqreview.com. Website: www.dmqreview.com. **Contact:** Sally Ashton, editor in chief.

Magazines Needs *DMQ Review*, published quarterly online, is "a quality magazine of poetry presented with visual art." Wants "finely crafted poetry that represents the diversity of contemporary poetry." Has published poetry by David Lehman, Ellen Bass, Amy Gerstler, Bob Hicok, Ilya Kaminsky, and Jane Hirshfield. Receives about 3,000-5,000 poems/year, accepts about 1%.

How to Contact Submit up to 3 poems at a time ("no more than once per quarter"). Considers simultaneous submissions (with notifications only); no previously published poems. Accepts e-mail submissions (pasted into body of message; no attachments will be read) only. "Please read and follow complete submission guidelines on our website." Reads submissions year round. Time between acceptance and publication is 1-3 months. Poems are circulated to an editorial board. Never comments on rejected poems. Responds within 3 months. Acquires first rights.

Additional Information Nominates for the Pushcart Prize. "We also consider submissions of visual art, which we publish with the poems in the magazine, with links to the artists' Websites."

Tips "Read recent issues of *DMQ Review* before submitting, follow our guidelines, and send your best work."

🔲 ⬭ DOWN IN THE DIRT

Scars Publications, 829 Brian Court, Gurnee IL 60031. E-mail: alexrand@scars.tv. Website: http://scars.tv. **Contact:** Alexandria Rand, editor.

Magazines Needs *Down in the Dirt*, published monthly online, prints "good work that makes you think, that makes you feel like you've lived through a scene instead of merely read it." Also can consider poems. Does not want smut, rhyming poetry, or religious writing. Has published work by I.B. Rad, Pat Dixon,Mel Waldman, and Ken Dean. *Down in the Dirt* is published "electronically as well as in print, either on the Web or in e-book form (PDF file)." Sample: available on website.

How to Contact Lines/poem: any length is appreciated. Considers previously published poems and simultaneous submissions. Accepts e-mail submissions (vastly preferred to snail mail; pasted into body of message or as Microsoft Word .doc file attachment) and disk submissions (formatted for Macintosh). Guidelines available for SASE, by e-mail, or on website. No payment. "Currently, accepted writings get their own web page in the "writings" section at http://scars.tv, and samples of accepted writings are placed into an annual collection book Scars Publications produces."

Additional Information Also able to publish electronic chapbooks. Write for more information.

Contest/Award Offerings Scars Publications sponsors a contest "where accepted writing appears in a collection book. Write or e-mail (editor@scars.tv) for information."

Tips "The website is a more comprehensive view of what *Down in the Dirt* does. All the information is there."

▣ ☑ DROWN IN MY OWN FEARS

E-mail: drowninmyownfears@yahoo.com. Website: http://drowninmyownfears.angelfire. com. **Contact:** Chantal Hejduk and Karina Bowman, editors.

Magazines Needs *Drown In My Own Fears*, published quarterly online, "is a poetry journal about the human condition, therefore, we want poems reflecting that. Poems submitted should be about love, hate, pain, sorrow, etc. We don't want maudlin sentimentality, we want the depths of your very being. We want well-written, deeply conceived pieces of work. Anything that isn't about the human condition really isn't for us." Wants "all styles of poetry, as long as it's your best work." Does not want "syrupy sweet, gooey nonsense, religious rants, political grandstandings." Considers poetry by teens. Has published poetry by Kendall A. Bell, April Michelle Bratten, Natalie Carpentieri, MK Chavez, James H. Duncan and Taylor Graham. Receives about 300 poems/year, accepts about 10%.

How to Contact Submit 3-5 poems at a time. "We prefer short poems, but long ones are ok." Considers previously published poems; no simultaneous submissions. Accepts e-mail submissions (pasted into body of e-mail message); no fax or disk submissions. Cover letter is rquired. Include a brief bio with your submission. Reads submissions year round. Submit seasonal poems 3 months in advance. Time between acceptance and publication is 1-2 months. Never comments on rejected poems. Sometimes publishes theme issues. Upcoming themes and guidelines available on website. Responds in 2-4 weeks. Acquires first rights. Rights revert to poets upon publication.

Tips "Try different writing styles and don't limit your poetic view to one way of thinking. Read lots of different poets. Write on little pieces of paper when an idea or a line comes. If you can't finish a poem in one sitting, come back to it later. You might find more inspiration in a day or two. Always rewrite and find avenues to workshop your poems. Several sets of eyes can certainly give you invaluable advice. True poets write because they must."

▣ ▣ ☑ DRUNKEN BOAT

119 Main Street, Chester CT 06412. (860)526-3318. E-mail: editor@drunkenboat.com. Website: www.drunkenboat.com. **Contact:** Ravi Shankar, founding editor; Leslie McGrath, managing editor. Member: CLMP.

Magazines Needs *Drunken Boat*, published twice yearly online, is a multimedia publication reaching an international audience with an extremely broad aesthetic. Considers poetry by teens. "We judge by quality, not age. However, most poetry we publish is written by published poets with training in creative writing. "Has published more than 500 poets, including Heather McHugh, Jane Hirshfield, Alfred Corn, Alice Fulton, Ron Silliman, and Roseanna Warren. Received about 3,000 poems/year, accepts about 5%.

How to Contact Submit up to 3 poems at a time. Considers simultaneous submissions. Accepts submissions through online submissions system on website only. Cover letter is preferred. "Due to the high number of poetry submissions, we limit submissions to 3 poems, in .doc or .rtf format. "Reads submissions year round. Time between acceptance and publication is 2-4 months. "Readers have MFAs in poetry, pass work to assistant poetry editor, who passes to poetry editor. "Sometimes comments on rejected poems. Sometimes publishes theme issues. Guidelines on website. Responds in 4-12 weeks. Always sends prepublication galleys. Acquires one-time rights. "Unless reprinted something already published, *Drunken Boat* has exclusive electronic rights of the work in question. Work that appears in print needs to acknowledge prior publication in *Drunken Boat*. Also, *Drunken Boat* reserves the right to republish work in print or DVD format with the permission of author/artist. "Reviews books, chapbooks of poetry. Will consider reviews of any length. Send materials for review consideration to editor@drunkenboat.com.

Tips "*Drunken Boat* publishes the best of more traditional publication alongside works of art endemic to the medium of the web. We recommend you read the past issues of the magazine to get a sense of what we publish. We are open to a range of styles, from experimental to formal, and are open to collaborations and other non-traditional works."

N ☑ DUCTS

P.O. Box 3203, Grand Central Station, New York NY 10163. E-mail: department: fiction@ducts.org, essays@ducts.org. Website: http://ducts.org. **Contact:** Jonathan Kravetz. DUCTS is a Webzine of personal stories, fiction, essays, memoirs, poetry, humor, profiles, reviews and art. "DUCTS was founded in 1999 with the intent of giving emerging writers a venue to regularly publish their compelling, personal stories. The site has been expanded to include art and creative works of all genres. We believe that these genres must and do overlap. DUCTS publishes the best, most compelling stories and we hope to attract readers who are drawn to work that rises above." Semiannual. CLMP.

How to Contact Reading period is January 1 through August 31. Send complete ms to poetry@ducts.org. Accepts submissions by e-mail to appropriate departments. Responds in 1-4 weeks to queries; 1-6 months to mss. Accepts simultaneous and reprints submissions. Writer's guidelines on ducts.org.

☐ ☑ EARTHSHINE

P.O. Box 245, Hummelstown PA 17036. E-mail: poetry@ruminations.us. Website: www.ruminations.us. **Contact:** Sally Zaino and Julie Moffitt, poetry editors.

Magazines Needs *Earthshine*, published irregularly in print, and online, features poetry and 1-2 pieces of cover art per volume. "When the online journal is full, a printed volume is produced and offered for sale. Subscriptions will be available as the publication becomes regular. The voice of *Earthshine* is one of illumination, compassion, humanity, and reason. Please see submission guidelines Web page for updated information. Poems are the ultimate rumination, and if the world is to be saved, the poets will be needed; they are who see the connections between all things, and the patterns shared. We seek poetry of high literary quality which will generate its own light for our readers." Has published poetry by Rachel Barroso, Fredrik Zydek, Steven Klepetar, Mario Susko.

How to Contact Submit no more than 6 poems at a time. Considers previously published poems; no simultaneous submissions. (Considers poetry posted on a public website/blog/forum and poetry posted on a private, password-protected forum as published.) "We prefer poems that have not been published elsewhere, but occasionally make exceptions. If a work has been published elsewhere, including on a personal website, please include the publication history." Accepts e-mail submissions (pasted into body of message); no fax or disk submissions. Cover letter is preferred. "Please let us know where you heard about *Earthshine*. If submitting by mail, please include a SASE for reply only. Please do not send the only copy of your work." Reads submissions year round. Submit seasonal poems 1 month in advance. Time between acceptance and publication is: "online publication is almost immediate, printed publication TBD." Sometimes comments on rejected poems. Never publishes theme issues. Guidelines available in magazine, for SASE, and on website. Responds in 1-2 months. Pays 1 contributor copy. Acquires first rights, one-time rights, electronic rights (publication rights include online publication and publication in 1 printed volume. Request first rights if poem is previously unpublished; one-time rights if poem has appeared elsewhere. Archive rights negotiated separately. Rights revert to poets upon publication.

Also Offers "The parent of *Earthshine* is also at Ruminations.us, and offers full editing and review services for a fee."

N ⊕ ▣ ◿ ECLECTICA

E-mail: editors@eclectica.org. Website: www.eclectica.org. Online magazine. "Eclectica is a quarterly World Wide Web journal devoted to showcasing the best writing on the Web, regardless of genre or subject matter. 'Literary' and 'genre' work appear side-by-side in each issue, along with pieces that blur the distinctions between such categories. Pushcart Prize, National Poetry Series, and Pulitzer Prize winners, as well as Nebula Award nominees, have shared issues with previously unpublished authors."

Magazines Needs Magazine seeks outstanding poetry, fiction, nonfiction, opinion, and reviews.

How to Contact Accepts submissions by e-mail. "While we will consider simultaneous submissions, please be sure to let us know that they are simultaneous and keep us updated on their publication status." Guidelines available on website. Acquires first North American serial rights, electronic rights.

▨ ◿ THE ECLECTIC MUSE

Suite 307, 6311 Gilbert Rd., Richmond BC V7C 3V7, Canada. (604)277-3864. E-mail: jrmbooks@hotmail.com. Website: mbooksofbc.com. thehypertexts.com. **Contact:** Joe M. Ruggier, publisher.

Magazines Needs *The Eclectic Muse*, published annually at Christmas, is devoted "to publishing all kinds of poetry (eclectic in style and taste) but specializing in rhyme- and neo-classicist revival." Does not want "bad work (stylistically bad or thematically offensive)." Has published poetry by Mary Keelan Meisel, John Laycock, Philip Higson, Roy Harrison, Michael Burch, and Ralph O. Cunningham. *The Eclectic Muse* is magazine-sized, digitally copied, saddle-stapled, with paper cover. The number of pages varies from year to year (32 minimum to 56 maximum). Receives about 300 poems/year, accepts about 15%. Press run is 200; distributed free to all contributing authors plus selected gift subscription recipients. Single copy: $8; subscription: $25. Make checks payable to Joe M. Ruggier.

How to Contact Submit no more than 5 poems at a time. Lines/poem: 60 maximum; "please consult if longer." Considers previously published poems and simultaneous submissions. Accepts e-mail submissions (preferred, as a single .doc or .rtf attachment containing all 5 poems) and disk submissions. "Send your submission by regular mail only if you have no access to a computer or you are computer illiterate. Typeset everything in Times New Roman 12 point. If your poetry features indents and special line spacing, please make sure you reproduce these features yourself in your data entry since it will not be possible for the editor to determine your intentions." Cover letter is preferred. "Include brief bio (100 words maximum) with your name, credentials (degrees, etc.), occupation and marital status, your most major publication credits only, and any hobbies or interests." Provide SASE plus clear e-mail and postal addresses for communication and for sending contributor's copy. Reads submissions year round. Time between acceptance and publication is 1 year. Poems are circulated to an editorial board. Sometimes comments on rejected poems. **"If authors wish to have a manuscript carefully assessed and edited, the fee is $250 USD; will respond within 8 weeks."** Guidelines available in magazine or on website. Responds in 2 months. Pays 2 contributor's copies. Reviews books/chapbooks of poetry and other magazines/journals in 900 words. Send materials for review consideration to Joe M. Ruggier, managing editor.

Also Offers "Look us up on www.thehypertexts.com, where myself and my services are listed (featured) permanently. The host of this splendid poetry website is my U.S. associate, Mr. Michael Burch. He features, on this site, most of the leading names in contemporary North America."

Tips "An author's style is really the only thing which belongs to him as an artist to manipulate for his own purposes as he pleases. Truths and feelings do not belong to him exclusively and may not be bent or manipulated for his own purposes as he pleases. We do not want bad work where the poet feels that the message matters but the style is bad (not good workmanship), nor do we wish to publish work which seems to us to distort and bend truths and human feelings far too much."

☑ ◎ EKPHRASIS

Frith Press, P.O. Box 161236, Sacramento CA 95816-1236. E-mail: frithpress@aol.com. Website: ekphrasisjournal.com. **Contact:** Laverne Frith and Carol Frith, editors.

• Poems from *Ekphrasis* have been featured on *Poetry Daily*.

Magazines Needs *Ekphrasis*, published semiannually in March and September, is an "outlet for the growing body of poetry focusing on individual works from any artistic genre." Wants "poetry the main content of which is based on individual works from any artistic genre. Poetry should transcend mere description. Open to all forms." Does not want "poetry without ekphrastic focus. No poorly crafted work. No archaic language." Has published poetry by Jeffrey Levine, Peter Meinke, David Hamilton, Barbara Lefcowitz, Molly McQuade, and Annie Boutelle. *Ekphrasis* is 35-50 pages, digest-sized, photocopied, saddle-stapled. Subscription: $12/year. Sample: $6. Make checks payable, in U.S. funds, to Laverne Frith.

How to Contact Submit 3-5 poems at a time. Considers previously published poems "infrequently, must be credited"; no simultaneous submissions. Accepts submissions by postal mail only. Cover letter is required, including short bio with representative credits and phone number. Include SASE. Time between acceptance and publication is up to 1 year. Seldom comments on rejected poems. Guidelines available for SASE or on website. Responds in 4 months. Pays 1 contributor's copy. Nominates for Pushcart Prize. Acquires first North American serial or one-time rights.

Additional Information Until further notice, Frith Press will publish **occasional chapbooks by invitation only**.

Contest/Award Offerings The Ekphrasis Prize, a $500 award, "is now being presented to the best poem published in Ekphrasis in each calendar year, as determined by the editors of the journal. There will be no contest. No reading fees will be required. The 2009 contest prize was awarded to Jeanine Stevens for "Frida in a White Dress."

Tips "With the focus on ekphrastic verse, we are bringing attention to the interconnections between various artistic genres and dramatizing the importance and universality of language. Study in the humanities is essential background preparation for the understanding of these interrelations."

$ ☑ ELLIPSIS

Westminster College of Salt Lake City, 1840 South 1300 East, Salt Lake City UT 84105. E-mail: ellipsis@westminstercollege.edu. Website: www.westminstercollege.edu/ellipsis. **Contact:** Poetry Editor. *Ellipsis*, published annually in April, needs "good literary poetry, fiction, essays, plays, and visual art." Has published poetry by Allison Joseph, Molly McQuade, Virgil Suaárez, Maurice Kilwein-Guevara, Richard Cecil, and Ron Carlson. *Ellipsis* is 120 pages, digest-sized, perfect-bound, with color cover. Accepts about 5% of submissions received. Press run is 2,000; most distributed free through college. Sample: $7.

How to Contact Submit 3-5 poems at a time. Accepts e-mail submissions. Considers simultaneous submissions if notified of acceptance elsewhere; no previously published poems. No fax or e-mail submissions; postal submissions only. One poem per page, with name and contact information on every page. Include SASE and brief bio. Reads submissions August 1 - November 1. Responds in up to 8 months. Pays $10/poem, plus two contributor's copies.

Tips "All accepted poems are eligible for the Ellipsis Award, which includes a $100 prize. Past judges have included Jorie Graham, Sandra Cisneros, Phillip Levine, and Stanley Plumly."

☑ ENGLISH JOURNAL

Interdisciplinary Studies in Curriculum & Instruction,, National-Louis University, Tampa FL 33609. (941)629-0541. E-mail: EJPoetry@nl.edu (submissions); asullivan@nl.edu (inquiries). Website: www.ncte.org/journals/EJ. **Contact:** Anne McCrary Sullivan, poetry editor.

Magazines Needs *English Journal*, established 1912, published 6 times annually by The National Council of Teachers of English, is a professional education journal, circulation over 20,000. "Poetry submissions that respond to announced themes, either implicitly or explicitly, are encouraged. Themes are announced in every issue and at the NCTE http://

www.englishjournal.colostate.edu/issuetopics.htm. Poems may be in any form or style, serious or humorous, and do not have to specifically address teaching or classrooms." English Journal accepts fewer than 10% of submissions.

How to Contact Submissions are accepted electronically only via website. "Send by e-mail attachment, for blind review, up to 5 poems with only phone number and initials on the page. In your accompanying message, include 50-60 word biographical statement. In subject line, indicate theme for which you are submitting." No previously published poems or simultaneous submissions. Seldom comments on rejected poems. Responds in 2-4 months after deadline. Pays 2 contributor's copies.

☑ EPICENTER: A LITERARY MAGAZINE

P.O. Box 367, Riverside CA 92502. E-mail: submissions@epicentermagazine.org. **Contact:** Rowena Silver, Editor. *Epicenter: A Literary Magazine*, published semiannually, is open to all styles. "*Epicenter* is looking for poetry, essays, short stories, creative nonfiction, and artwork. We publish new and established writers." Considers translations. Does not want "angst-ridden, sentimental, or earthquake poetry. We are not adverse to graphic images as long as the work contains literary merit." Has published poetry by Virgil Suarez, Alba Cruz-Hacher, B.Z. Niditch, Egon Lass, and Zdravka Evtimova. *Epicenter* is 100 pages, perfect-bound. Receives about 2,000 submissions/year, accepts about 5%. Press run is 800. Single copy: $7. Make checks payable to *Epicenter: A Literary Magazine*.

How to Contact Submit up to 5 poems at a time. Considers previously published poems and simultaneous submissions. Accepts e-mail submissions. Include SASE with sufficient postage for return of materials. Seldom comments on rejected poems. Guidelines available in magazine, for SASE, by e-mail, or on website. Pays 1 contributor's copy. Acquires one-time and electronic rights..

$ ☑ EPOCH

251 Goldwin Smith Hall, Cornell University, Ithaca NY 14853. (607)255-3385. Website: www.arts.cornell.edu/english/epoch.html. **Contact:** Nancy Vieira Couto, Poetry Editor.

Magazines Needs *Epoch*, published 3 times/year, has a distinguished and long record of publishing exceptionally fine poetry and fiction. Has published poetry by Kevin Prufer, Peter Dale Scott, Martin Walls, Maxine Kumin, Heather McHugh, and D. James Smith. *Epoch* is 128 pages, digest-sized, professionally printed, perfect-bound, with glossy color cover. Accepts less than 1% of the many submissions received each year. Has 1,000 subscribers. Subscription: $11/year domestic, $15/year foreign. Sample: $5.

How to Contact No simultaneous submissions. Manuscripts not accompanied by SASE will be discarded unread. Reads submissions September 15-April 15. Responds in up to 10 weeks. Occasionally provides criticism on mss. Pays 3 contributor's copies and at least $10/page. "We pay more when we have more!" Acquires first serial rights.

Tips "Read the magazine."

⊕ ☑ ◎ EUROPEAN JUDAISM

A Journal for the New Europe, LBC, The Sternberg Centre, 80 East End Rd., London N3 2SY, England. E-mail: european.judaism@lbc.ac.uk. Website: www.berghahnbooks. com/journals/ej. **Contact:** Managing Editor. *European Judaism*, published twice/year, is a "glossy, elegant magazine with emphasis on European Jewish theology/philosophy/ literature/history, with some poetry in every issue. Poems should (preferably) be short and have some relevance to matters of Jewish interest." Has published poetry by Linda Pastan, Elaine Feinstein, Daniel Weissbort, and Dannie Abse. *European Judaism* is 110 pages, digest-sized, flat-spined. Press run is 950 (about 500 subscribers, over 100 libraries). Subscription: $45 individual, $20 student, $162 institution.

How to Contact Submit 3-4 poems at a time. Lines/poem: short poems preferred. "I prefer unpublished poems, but poems from published books are acceptable." Cover letter is required. "No material is read or returned if not accompanied by SASE (or SAE with IRCs). We cannot use American stamps." Pays 1 contributor's copy.

$ ☑ ◎ EVANGEL

Light and Life Communications, P.O. Box 535002, Indianapolis IN 46253-5002. **Contact:** J. Innes, Editor.

Magazines Needs *Evangel*, published quarterly, is an adult Sunday school paper. "Devotional in nature, it lifts up Christ as the source of salvation and hope. The mission of *Evangel* is to increase the reader's understanding of the nature and character of God and the nature of a life lived for Christ. Material that fits this mission and isn't longer than one page will be considered." Does not want rhyming work. *Evangel* is 8 pages, 512×812, printed in 4-color, unbound. Accepts about 5% of poetry received. Press run is about 10,000. Subscription: $2.59/quarter (13 weeks). Sample: free for #10 SASE.

How to Contact Submit no more than 5 poems at a time. Considers simultaneous submissions. Cover letter is preferred. "Poetry must be typed on $8\frac{1}{2} \times 11$ white paper. In the upper left-hand corner of each page, include your name, address, phone number, and social security number. In the upper right-hand corner of cover page, specify what rights you are offering. One-eighth of the way down the page, give the title. All subsequent material must be double-spaced, with one-inch margins." Submit seasonal poems 1 year in advance. Seldom comments on rejected poems. Guidelines available for #10 SASE. "Write 'guidelines request' on your envelope so we can sort it from the submissions." Responds in up to 2 months. Pays $10 plus 2 contributor's copies. Acquires one-time rights.

Tips "Poetry is used primarily as filler. Send for sample and guidelines to better understand what and who the audience is."

☑ THE EVANSVILLE REVIEW

1800 Lincoln Ave., Evansville IN 47722. (812)488-1042. E-mail: evansvillereview@ evansville.edu. Website: english.evansville.edu/EvansvilleReview.htm. **Contact:** Kasey Brunner, editor.

• Poetry published in *The Evansville Review* has been included in *The Best American Poetry* and *The Pushcart Prize*.

Magazines Needs *The Evansville Review*, published annually in April, prints "prose, poems, and drama of literary merit." Wants "anything of quality." No excessively experimental work; no erotica. Has published poetry by Joseph Brodsky, J.L. Borges, John Updike, Willis Barnstone, Rita Dove, and Vivian Shipley. *The Evansville Review* is 140-200 pages, digest-sized, perfect-bound, with art on cover. Receives about 2,000 poems/year, accepts about 2%. Press run is 1,500. Sample: $5.

How to Contact Submit 3-5 poems at a time. Considers previously published poems and simultaneous submissions. No fax or e-mail submissions; postal submissions only. Cover letter is required. Include brief bio. Manuscripts not returned without SASE. Reads submissions September 1-December 1 only. Time between acceptance and publication is 3 months. Poems are circulated to an editorial board. Seldom comments on rejected poems. Guidelines available for SASE or on website. Responds within 3 months of the deadline. Pays 2 contributor's copies. Rights remain with poet.

Contest/Award Offerings The Willis Barnstone Translation Prize.

◎ EXIT 13

P.O. Box 423, Fanwood NJ 07023-1162. (908)889-5298. E-mail: exit13magazine@yahoo. com. **Contact:** Tom Plante Editor.

Magazines Needs *Exit 13*, published annually, uses poetry that is "short, to the point, with a sense of geography." Has published poetry by Paul Brooke, Ruth Moon Kempher, Sandy McCord, Sander Zulauf, Paul Sohar, and Charles Rammelkamp. *Exit 13* is about 76 pages. Press run is 300. Sample: $8.

How to Contact Considers simultaneous submissions and previously published poems. Accepts e-mail submissions (no attachments). Guidelines available in magazine or for SASE. Responds in 4 months. Pays 1 contributor's copy. Acquires one-time and possible anthology rights.

Tips "*Exit 13* looks for adventure, a living record of places we've experienced. Every state, region, country, and ecosystem is welcome. Write about what you know and have seen. Send a snapshot of an 'Exit 13' road sign and receive a free copy of the issue in which it appears."

THE EXQUISITE CORPSE

E-mail: submissions@corpse.org. "We will read anything—stories, broken language of the heart and loins (poetry, letters, travel reports, news and gossip, mixed genre media with collage, music, sound and web-wide effects."

Magazines Needs "We will be looking at stories, broken language of the heart and loins (i.e, poetry), letters, reports from obscure places where you traveled for unclear reasons, news, and gossip, mixed genre media with collage, music, sound, and web-wide effects. We prefer works of malignant brilliance to well-practiced euphonies, practical utopianism, sexual delirium, and resolute enmity against mediocrity, which is preaching to the choir. We repeat: mediocrity is preaching to the choir."

How to Contact For your submission to be considered, it must be sent digitally either in the body of your e-mail or as an attachment with extension .rtf (Rich Text Format). Almost all word processing programs on Mac and PC include the option to "save as" Rich Text Format. See website for guidelines.

🅽 ◨ EYE ON LIFE

E-mail: eyeonlife.ezine@gmail.com. Website: http://eyeonlife.squarespace.com. **Contact:** Tom Rubenoff, senior poetry editor.

Magazines Needs *Eye on Life*, published weekly online, wants poems with striking and original imagery. "We like to see poems in which meaning exceeds form." Does not want "forced rhyming, poems stuffed into forms into which they do not fit." Accepts poetry by teens, but "please let us know if you are under 21 years old. Has published poetry by Donal Mahoney and Christopher Shawn Barker. Receives about 500 poems/year, accepts about 150.

How to Contact Submit 5 poems at a time by e-mail, no more than one page in length. Considers simultaneous submissions. Reads submissions year round. Submit seasonal poems one month in advance. Time between acceptance and publication is 2 weeks. Poems are circulated to an editorial board. Never comments on rejected poems. Sometimes publishes theme issues. Guidelines and upcoming themes available on website. Responds in 2 weeks. Acquires one-time rights. Rights revert to poets upon publication.

Contest/Award Offerings Eyes on Life Poetry Prize is awarded annually with a prize of $100 of the entry fees collected. Submit up to 3 poems. Entry fee: $5/poem; deadline: January 31st. Guidelines available on website after November 1.

Tips "Please see the Poetry Unlocked section of our magazine and acquaint yourself with the kinds of poetry we publish before entering."

▣ ◑ ◎ FAILBETTER.COM

2022 Grove Ave., Richmond VA 23220. Andrew Day, Publisher. Member: CLMP. **Contact:** Poetry Editors: Mary Donnelly, Christina Kallery. *failbetter.com*, published online, seeks "that which is at once original and personal. When choosing work to submit, be certain that what you have created could only have come from you." Publishes translations and interviews with such poets as Paul Muldoon, Marie Ponsot, Mary Jo Salter, and Billy Collins. Has published poetry by J. Allyn Rosser, Terrance Hayes, Mary Donnely, and Thaddeus Rutkowski. Receives about 2,000 poetry submissions/year, accepts about 9-12. Publishes 3-4 poets/issue.

How to Contact Submit 4-6 poems at a time. Lines/poem: "we're not concerned with length—one good sentence may find a home here, as the bulk of mediocrity will not." Considers simultaneous submissions; no previously published poems. Encourages e-mail submissions (pasted into body of message). "Send to submissions@failbetter.com only! Please read and follow submission guidelines posted on website. All e-mail submissions should include title in header. All poetry submissions must be included in the body of your e-mail. Please do not send attached files." Also accepts postal submissions; "please note, however, any materials accepted for publication must ultimately be submitted in electronic format in order to appear on our site." Cover letter is preferred. Reads submissions year round. Time between acceptance and publication is 4 months minimum and upward. Poems are circulated to an editorial board. Often comments on rejected poems. "It's not unusual to ask poets to re-submit, and their subsequent submissions have been accepted." Guidelines available on website. Responds in up to 4 months to e-mail submissions; up to 6 months by regular mail. "We will not respond to any e-mail inquiry regarding receipt confirmation or status of any work under consideration." No payment. Acquires exclusive first-time Internet rights; works will also be archived online. All other rights, including opportunity to publish in traditional print form, revert to the poet.

Tips "With a readership of more than 60,000 per issue, *failbetter* is one of the Web's widely read literary magazines, offering exposure of poets' works to a much broader, worldwide audience than the typical print journal. For both established and emerging poets our advice remains the same: We strongly recommend that you not only read the previous issue, but also sign up on our e-mail list (subscribe@failbetter.com) to be notified of future publications."

✒ FAT TUESDAY

560 Manada Gap Rd., Grantville PA 17028. E-mail: lionelstevroid@yahoo.com. Website: http://groups.yahoo.com/group/FatTuesday. **Contact:** FM Cotolo. "For two decades, "Fat Tuesday" has pushed the boundaries of small-press literati. Bring your poetry, prose, lyrics and scribblings to this special group of readers and writers through the internet. Co-founder, editor-in-chief and publisher FM Cotolo moderates this free e-mail "magazine" in the spirit of the publication known the world over. Post your words or forever hold your piece."

How to Contact *Fat Tuesday*, published irregularly, is "a Mardi Gras of literary, visual, and audio treats featuring voices, singing, shouting, sighing, and shining, expressing the relevant to irreverent." Wants "prose poems, poems of irreverence, gems from the gut. Particularly interested in hard-hitting 'autofiction.'" Considers poetry by children and teens. Has published poetry by Chuck Taylor, Charles Bukowski, Mark Cramer, and Cotolo Patrick Kelly. *Fat Tuesday* is up to 60 pages, typeset (large type, heavy paper), saddle-stapled, usually chapbook-style (sometimes magazine-sized, unbound), with card cover, includes ads. Receives hundreds of submissions/year, accepts about 3-5%. Sample: $5, postage paid (all editions). Submit maximum Accepts e-mail submissions (pasted into body of message). Cover letter is "fine, the more amusing the better." Publishes theme issues. Responds in up to 3 months. Pays 2 contributor's copies if audio. Rights revert to author after publication. "Please join our web group (see website above) and submit all the material you want. Get read by other writers, non-writers, and wannabes." poems.

Tips "In 1998, *Fat Tuesday* was presented in a different format with the production of a stereo audio cassette edition. *Fat Tuesday*'s Cool Noise features readings, music, collage, and songs, all in the spirit of *Fat*'s printed versions. *Fat Tuesday* has released other audio projects. In-print magazines will still be produced as planned when funds are available. Support the magazine that publishes your work!"

✒ FAULTLINE

Dept. of English & Comparative Literature, University of California, Irvine, Irvine CA 92697-2650. (949)824-1573. E-mail: faultline@uci.edu. Website: www.humanities.uci.edu/faultline. **Contact:** Elizabeth Wyatt, poetry editor.

• Poetry published by *Faultline* has been included in *The Pushcart Prize*.

Magazines Needs *Faultline*, published annually each spring, features new poetry, fiction, and translation. Has published poetry by C.K. Williams, Larissa Szporluk, Yusef Komunyakaa, Amy Gerstler, and Killarney Clary. *Faultline* is about 200 pages, digest-sized, professionally printed on 60 lb. paper, perfect-bound, with 80 lb. coverstock. Receives about 5,000 poems/year, accepts less than 1%. Press run is 1,000. Single copy: $10. Sample: $5.

How to Contact Submit up to 5 poems at a time. Considers simultaneous submissions, "but please note in cover letter that the manuscript is being considered elsewhere." No fax or e-mail submissions. Cover letter is required. Include name, postal and e-mail addresses, and titles of work submitted; do not put name and address on ms pages themselves. SASE required. Reads submissions September 15-February 15 only. Poems are selected by a board of up to 6 readers. Seldom comments on rejected poems. Guidelines available for SASE or on website. Responds in 3 months. Pays 2 contributor's copies. Acquires first or one-time serial rights.

☑ ◎ FEMINIST STUDIES

0103 Taliaferro Hall, University of Maryland, College Park MD 20742-7726. E-mail: info@ feministstudies.org; creative@feministstudies.org. Website: www.feministstudies.org.

Magazines Needs *Feminist Studies*, published 3 times/year, welcomes "all forms of written creative expression, which may include but is not limited to poetry and short fiction." Has published poetry by Dawn McDuffie, Liz Robbins, Maria Mazziotti Gillan, Mary Ann Wehler, Barbara Wiedemann, and Paola Corso. *Feminist Studies* is 250 pages, elegantly printed, flat-spined, paperback. Press run is 8,000. Sample: $17.

How to Contact No previously published poems ("we only consider original work that is not under review elsewhere") or simultaneous submissions. No fax submissions. Send 1 hard copy of submission as well as an electronic version (disk, CD, or e-mail). "We will not process creative submissions until we receive both a hard copy and electronic version." Retain a copy; work will not be returned. Reads submissions twice/year according to May 1 and December 1 deadlines. Responds by July 15 and February 15 with notice of board's decision. Regularly publishes theme issues. Guidelines available on website. Always sends prepublication galleys. Pays 2 contributor's copies.

▣ ☑ ◎ FICKLE MUSES

315 Terrace St. SE, Albuquerque NM 87106. E-mail: editor@ficklemuses.com. Website: www.ficklemuses.com. **Contact:** Sari Krosinsky, editor.

Magazines Needs *Fickle Muses*, published weekly online, is a journal of myth and legend printing poetry, fiction and art. Open to all styles and forms. Has published poetry by J.V. Foerster, Ray Hinman, Maureen Seaton, Kenneth P. Gurney, Doug Ramspeck. Accepts about 10% of poems received. Number of unique visitors: 160/week.

How to Contact Submit up to 5 poems at a time. Lines/poem: no limits on length. Considers previously published poems and simultaneous submissions. Accepts e-mail submissions (pasted into body of message preferred, unless special formatting requires an attachment); no disk submissions. Cover letter is preferred. Reads submissions year round. Time between acceptance and publication is up to 3 months. Never comments on rejected poems. Guidelines available on website. Responds in up to 3 months. Acquires one-time and archival rights. Rights revert to poets upon publication. Reviews books/chapbooks of poetry and other magazines/journals in 500 words, single-book format. For review consideration, query by e-mail.

$ ☑ FIELD: CONTEMPORARY POETRY AND POETICS

Oberlin College, 50 N. Professor St., Oberlin OH 44074. (440)775-8408. E-mail: oc.press@ oberlin.edu. Website: www.oberlin.edu/ocpress. **Contact:** David Young.

• Work published in *FIELD* has been included frequently in *The Best American Poetry*.

Magazines Needs *FIELD: Contemporary Poetry and Poetics*, published semiannually in April and October, is a literary journal with "emphasis on poetry, translations, and essays by poets." Has published poetry by Michelle Glazer, Tom Lux, Carl Phillips, Betsy Sholl, Charles Simic, Jean Valentine and translations by Marilyn Hacker and Stuart Friebert. *FIELD* is 100 pages, digest-sized, printed on rag stock, flat-spined, with glossy color card cover. Subscription: $16/year, $28 for 2 years. Sample: $8 postpaid.

How to Contact Submit up to 5 poems at a time. No previously published poems or simultaneous submissions. No e-mail submissions. Include cover letter and SASE. Reads submissions year round. Seldom comments on rejected poems. Guidelines available for SASE, by e-mail, or on website. Responds in 6-8 weeks. Always sends prepublication galleys. Pays $15/page and 2 contributor's copies. Staff reviews books of poetry. Send materials for review consideration.

Additional Information Oberlin College Press publishes books of translations in the FIELD Translation Series. Books are usually flat-spined paperbacks averaging 150 pages. Query regarding translations. Also publishes books of poetry in the FIELD Poetry Series, by invitation only. Has published *Tryst,* by Angie Estes; *Kurosawa's Dog,* by Dennis Hinrichsen; *He and I,* by Emmanuel Moses, translated by Marilyn Hacker; *The Sleep Hotel,* by Amy Newlove Schroeder. Write for catalog or visit website to buy sample books.

Contest/Award Offerings Sponsors the annual FIELD Poetry Prize for a book-length collection of poems.

Tips "A sampling of 3-5 poems is desirable. Be sure to include enough postage on SASE if you want poems returned. We try to read promptly; please wait to submit poems elsewhere."

▣ $ ▢ ◎ THE FIFTH DI...

Tyree Campbell, attn: Sam's Dot Publishing, PO Box 782, Cedar Rapids IA 52406-0782. *The Fifth Di...,* published quarterly online, features fiction and poetry from the science fiction and fantasy genres. Open to most forms, but all poems must be science fiction or fantasy. Does not want horror, or anything that is not science fiction or fantasy. Considers poetry by children and teens. Has published poetry by Bruce Boston, Cathy Buburuz, Marge Simon, Aurelio Rico Lopez III, Terrie Relf, and John Bushore. Receives about 200 poems/year, accepts about 20.

How to Contact Submit 1 poem at a time. Lines/poem: no limit. No previously published poems or simultaneous submissions. Accepts e-mail submissions only (as attachment); no disk submissions. Cover letter is preferred. Reads submissions year round. Time between acceptance and publication is 1 month. Sometimes comments on rejected poems. Guidelines available on website. Responds in 1-3 months. Pays $5. Acquires first rights.

▨ ◪ FILLING STATION

P.O. Box 22135, Bankers Hall, Calgary AB T2P 4J5 Canada. (403)234-0336. E-mail: meditor.fs@gmail.com. Website: www.fillingstation.ca. **Contact:** Laurie Fuhr, general editor. Established 1993. *filling Station,* published 3 times/year, prints contemporary poetry, fiction, visual art, interviews, reviews, and articles. "We are looking for all forms of contemporary writing. but especially that which is original and/or experimental." Has published poetry by Fred Wah, Larissa Lai, Margaret Christakos, Robert Kroetsch, Ron Silliman, Susan Holbrook, and many more. *filling Station* is 80-100 pages, 8½ × 11, perfect-bound, with card cover, includes photos and artwork. Receives about 100 submissions for each issue, accepts approximately 10%. Press run is 700. Subscription: $22/year, $38 for 2 years. Sample: $8.

How to Contact E-mailed submissions for text is strongly encouraged. Submissions should include author's name, address, e-mail, and a short biography. Unaccepted submissions will not be returned unless suitable SASE is included. Considers simultaneous submissions, provided this is noted on submissions and they are withdrawn elsewhere if accepted by *filling Station*. No previously published material. Accepts submissions year round; deadlines vary. E-mail managing editor for next deadline. Guidelines available in magazine, for SASE, by e-mail, or on website. Responds in 4 months. Pays one-year subscription. Acquires first North American serial rights and non-exclusive rights to reprint and/or electronically publish material published in *filling Station*. All copyrights remain with that author or artist. "*filling Station* does not accept submissions that are racist, misogynist, and/or homophobic."

Tips "We favour work on the innovative cutting-edge. Please read our magazine before submitting."

☑ FIRST CLASS

Four-Sep Publications, P.O. Box 86, Friendship IN 47021. E-mail: christopherm@four-sep.com. Website: www.four-sep.com. Established 1994. **Contact:** Christopher M., editor.

Magazines Needs *First Class*, published in May and November, prints "excellent/odd writing for intelligent/creative readers." Does not want "traditional work." Has published poetry by Bennett, Locklin, Every, Ui-Neill, Catlin, and Huffstickler. *First Class* is 48-56 pages, 4¼x11, printed, saddle-stapled, with colored cover. Receives about 1,500 poems/year, accepts about 30. Press run is 300-400. Sample: $6 (includes guidelines). Make checks payable to Christopher M.

How to Contact Submit 5 poems at a time. Considers previously published poems and simultaneous submissions. No fax or e-mail submissions. Cover letter is preferred. "Manuscripts will not be returned." Time between acceptance and publication is 2-4 months. Often comments on rejected poems. Guidelines available in magazine, or on website. Responds in 4-8 weeks. Pays 1 contributor's copy. Acquires one-time rights. Reviews books of poetry and fiction. Send materials for review consideration.

Additional Information Chapbook production available.

Tips "Belt out a good, short, thought-provoking, graphic, uncommon piece."

☑ FLINT HILLS REVIEW

Box 4019, Emporia State University, Emporia KS 66801. Fax: (620)341-5547. E-mail: krabas@emporia.edu. Website: www.emporia.edu/fhr/index.htm. **Contact:** The Editors.

Magazines Needs *Flint Hills Review*, published annually in late summer, is "a regionally focused journal presenting writers of national distinction alongside new authors." Wants all forms of poetry except rhyming. Does not want sentimental or gratuitous verse. Has published poetry by E. Ethelbert Miller, Elizabeth Dodd, Walt McDonald, and Gwendolyn Brooks. *Flint Hills Review* is about 100 pages, digest-sized, offset-printed, perfect-bound, with glossy card cover with b&w photo. Receives about 2,000 poems/year, accepts about 5%. Single copy: $7.

How to Contact Submit 3-5 poems at a time. Considers simultaneous submissions; no previously published poems. Accepts submissions by fax or e-mail (pasted into body of message). Cover letter is required. Include SASE. Reads submissions January-March only. Time between acceptance and publication is about one year. Seldom comments on rejected poems. Occasionally publishes theme issues. Guidelines available for SASE or on website. Pays 1 contributor's copy. Acquires first rights.

Contest/Award Offerings FHR hosts an annual nonfiction contest. **Entry Fee**: $10. **Deadline:** March 15.

Tips "Send writing with evidence of a strong sense of place."

☒ FLOYD COUNTY MOONSHINE

720 Christiansburg Pike, Floyd VA 24091. (540)745-5150. E-mail: floydshine@gmail.com. Website: www.floydcountymoonshine.com. **Contact:** Aaron Moore, editor-in-chief.

Magazines Needs *Floyd County Moonshine*, published quarterly, is a "literary and arts magazine in Floyd, Virginia and the New River Valley. We accept poetry, short stories, and essays addressing all manner of themes; however, preference is given to those works of a rural or Southern/Appalachian nature. We welcome cutting-edge and innovative fiction and poetry in particular." Wants "rustic innovation." Has published poetry by Steve Kistulentz, Louis Gallo, Ernie Wormwood, Rodney Smith, Chelsea Adams, and Justin Askins. *Floyd County Moonshine* is 70-100 pages, digest-sized, saddle-stitched, with a heavy glossy cover; includes ads. Receives 200 poems/year, accepts 25%. Press run is 200-500; subscribers 50-100, libraries, 5-10, 50-75 distributed free. Single copy: $8; subscription: $15/1 year, $25/2 years.

How to Contact Submit 3 poems at a time. No previously published poems or simultaneous submissions. Accepts e-mail submissions; no fax or disk. Cover letter is unnecessary. Reads submissions year round.

◪ FLYWAY, A JOURNAL OF WRITING AND ENVIRONMENT

206 Ross Hall, Iowa State University, Ames IA 50011-1201. Fax: (515)294-6814. E-mail: flyway@iastate.edu. Website: www.flyway.org. **Contact:** Stephen Pett, editor-in-chief.

Magazines Needs *Flyway, A Journal of Writing and Environment*, published 3 times/year, "is one of the best literary magazines for the money. It's packed with some of the most readable poems being published today—all styles, forms, lengths, and subjects." Does not want "elite-sounding free verse with obscure meanings, and pretty-sounding formal verse with obvious meanings." *Flyway* is 120 pages, digest-sized, professionally printed, perfect-bound, with matte card cover with color. Press run is 600. Subscription: $24. Sample: $8.

How to Contact Submit 4-6 poems at a time. Cover letter is preferred. "We do not read manuscripts between the first of May and the end of August." Responds in 6 weeks (often sooner). Pays 2 contributor's copies. Acquires first rights.

Contest/Award Offerings Sponsors an annual award for poetry, fiction, and nonfiction. Details available for SASE or on website.

▣ ☑ THE FOLIATE OAK ONLINE

University of Arkansas, Arts and Humanities, Monticello AK 71656. (870)460-1247. E-mail: foliateoak@uamont.edu. Website: www.foliateoak.uamont.edu. **Contact:** Diane Payne.

• Association Collegiate Media Awards

Magazines Needs *The Foliate Oak Online*, published monthly online, prints prose, poetry, and artwork reviewed by college students, edited and added to the website. Wants all genres and forms of poetry are accepted. Does not want: "We're not interested in homophobic, religious rants, or pornographic, violent stories. Please avoid using offensive language." Considers poetry by teens. Has published poetry by Tony Hoagland, Richard Fein, and FJ Bergmann. Receives about 300 poems/year, accepts about 100. Number of unique visitors: 500 monthly.

How to Contact Submit no more than 5 poems at a time, maximum 30 lines. Does not accept previously published poems (considers poetry posted on a public website/blog/forum and poetry posted on a private, password-protected forum as published). Only accepts e-mail submissions as attachment; no fax or disk submissions. Cover letter is unnecessary. See website for guidelines; Word documents are preferred, submit a third person bio. Reads submissions during school year. Submit seasonal poems 1 months in advance. Time between acceptance and publication is 2-3 weeks. Poems are circulated to an editorial board. Guidelines available on website. Responds in 1 month. Acquires one-time rights. Reviews other magazines/journals.

Additional Information "We are accepting submissions at this time! If accepted, the work will be posted in our monthly magazine for a minimum of 4 weeks. Send us what you have via e-mail."

Tips "Be original, have fun with it; if you are rejected, just keep sending us your work - we enjoy reading them!"

☑ FOLIO, A LITERARY JOURNAL AT AMERICAN UNIVERSITY

Dept. of Literature, American University, Washington DC 20016. (202)885-2990. Fax: (202)885-2938. E-mail: folio.editors@gmail.com. Website: www.american.edu/cas/literature/folio. Established 1984. **Contact:** Greta Schuler, editor-in-chief.

Magazines Needs *Folio*, published 2 times/year, Since 1984, we have published original creative work by both new and established authors. Past issues have included work by Michael Reid Busk, Billy Collins, William Stafford, and Bruce Weigl, and interviews with Michael Cunningham, Charles Baxter, Amy Bloom, Ann Beattie, and Walter Kirn. We look for well-crafted poetry and prose that is bold and memorable. *Folio* is 80 pages, digest-sized, with matte cover with graphic art. Receives about 1,000 poems/year, accepts about 25. Press run is 400; 50-60 distributed free to the American University community and contributors. Single copy: $6; subscription: $12/year. Make checks payable to "*Folio* at American University."

How to Contact Submit 3-6 poems or one prose piece at a time. Considers simultaneous submissions "with notice." No fax, e-mail, or disk submissions. Cover letter is preferred. "SASE required for notification only; manuscripts are not returned." Reads submissions August 1 -March 5. Time between acceptance and publication is 2 months. "Poems and prose are reviewed by editorial staff and senior editors." Seldom comments on rejected poems. Occasionally publishes theme issues. Guidelines available on website. Pays 2 contributor's copies. Acquires first North American serial rights.

▣ ☑ FORPOETRY.COM

E-mail: poems@forpoetry.com. Website: www.forpoetry.com. **Contact:** Jackie Marcus, editor.

Magazines Needs *ForPoetry.Com*, published online with daily updates, seeks "to promote new and emerging poets, with or without MFAs. We will be publishing established poets, but our primary interest is in publishing excellent poetry, prose, and reviews." Wants "lyric poetry, vivid imagery, open form, natural landscape, philosophical themes—but not at the expense of honesty and passion." Does not want "city punk, corny sentimental fluff, or academic workshop imitations." Has published poetry by Sherod Santos, John Koethe, Robert Hass, Kim Addonizio, and Brenda Hillman.

How to Contact Submit no more than 2 poems at a time. Considers simultaneous submissions; no previously published poems. Accepts e-mail submissions only (pasted into body of message; no attachments). Cover letter is preferred. Reads submissions September-May only. Time between acceptance and publication is 2-3 weeks. "We'll read all submissions and then decide together on the poems we'll publish." Comments on rejected poems "as often as possible. We receive lots of submissions and are very selective about acceptances, but we will always try to send a note back on rejections." Guidelines available on website. Responds in 2 weeks. Reviews books/chapbooks of poetry and other magazines in 800 words.

Tips "As my friend Kevin Hull said, 'Get used to solitude and rejection.' Sit on your poems for several months or more. Time is your best critic."

☑ FOURTEEN HILLS: THE SFSU REVIEW

Creative Writing Dept., San Francisco State Univ., 1600 Holloway Ave., San Francisco CA 94132. (415)338-3083. Fax: (415)338-7030. E-mail: hills@sfsu.edu. Website: www.14hills. net. **Contact:** Poetry Editor. *Fourteen Hills: The SFSU Review*, published semiannually, is a journal of contemporary literary art. Wants "high-quality, innovative work." Has published poetry by Lawrence Ferlinghetti, Kim Addonizio, Marilyn Hacker, Robert Creeley, Naomi Shihab Nye, and Fanny Howe. *Fourteen Hills* is 170 pages, digest-sized, professionally printed, perfect-bound, with glossy card cover. Receives about 900 poems/year, accepts about 5-10%. Press run is 600. Single copy: $9; subscription: $17/year, $32 for 2 years. Sample: $5 or $7 for back issue, depending on publication date.

How to Contact Always sends prepublication galleys. Pays 2 contributor's copies. Submit 3-5 unpublished, unsolicited poems. Writers may submit once per submission period. The submission periods are: September 1 to January 1 for inclusion in the spring issue (released in May) February 1 to July 1 for inclusion in the winter issue (released in December). Response times vary from four to nine months, depending on where your submission falls in the reading period, but we will usually respond within five months. Manuscripts and artwork should be mailed and addressed to the proper genre editor, and MUST be accompanied by a self-addressed, stamped envelope for notification, in addition to an e-mail and telephone contact. Due to the volume of submissions, manuscripts CANNOT BE RETURNED so please, do not send any originals. We accept simultaneous submissions;

however, please be sure to notify us immediately by email should you need to withdraw submissions due to publication elsewhere. Please note that we do not accept electronic submissions at this time in the form of an email or otherwise.

Tips "Please read an issue of *Fourteen Hills* before submitting."

✷ THE FOURTH RIVER

Chatham University, Woodland Rd., Pittsburgh PA 15232. E-mail: fourthriver@chatham.edu. Website: http://fourthriver.chatham.edu. **Contact:** Peter Oresick, Editor.

Magazines Needs *The Fourth River*, an annual publication of the MFA program at Chatham University, features "literature that engages and explores the relationship between humans and their environments." Wants "writings that are richly situated at the confluence of place, space, and identity, or that reflect upon or make use of landscape and place in new ways." *The Fourth River* is digest-sized, perfect-bound, with full-color cover by various artists. Accepts about 30-40 poems/year. Press run is 500. Single copy: $10; subscription: $16 for 2 years; $22 for 3 years. Make checks payable to Chatham University.

How to Contact Submit 7 poems at a time. Lines/poem: submit 25 pages maximum. No previously published poems. No e-mail or disk submissions. Cover letter is preferred. "SASE is required for response." Reads submissions August 1-February 15. Time between acceptance and publication is 5-8 months. Poems are circulated to an editorial board. Sometimes comments on rejected poems. Sometimes publishes theme issues. Guidelines available on website. Responds in 3-5 months. Acquires first North American serial rights.

✷ FREEFALL

Undead Poets Press, 15735 Kerstyn St., Taylor MI 48180. E-mail: mauruspoet@yahoo.com. Website: www.springfed.org/MDWpublish.html. **Contact:** Marc Maurus, publisher. *freefall*, published 3 times/year in April, July, and October, prints the quality work of beginners as well as established poets. "Free verse or formal poetry is okay, and our acceptance policy is broad." Does not want "concrete, shape, or greeting card verse; no gratuitous language or sex; no fuzzy animals or syrupy nature poems." Has published poetry by B.Z. Niditch, Lyn Lifshin, David Lawrence, Michael Estabrook, and Joe Speer. *freefall* is 40 pages, digest-sized, laser-printed, saddle-stapled, with cardstock cover with photographs. Receives about 200 poems/year, accepts about 50%. Press run is 250; 25 distributed free to small press reviewers. Single copy: $7.50; subscription: $15. Make checks payable to Marc Maurus.

How to Contact Submit 5-10 poems at a time. Lines/poem: 3 minimum, 80 maximum. Considers previously published poems with notification; no simultaneous submissions. Accepts e-mail submissions (pasted into body of message, no attachments); no fax or disk submissions. "Snail mail preferred; please send SASE." Cover letter is preferred. Reads submissions all year. Submit seasonal poems 6 months in advance. Time between acceptance and publication is 6 months. "If a poem is high quality, I accept it right away; poor work is rejected immediately; those on the fence are circulated to as many as three other guest editors." Often comments on rejected poems. Poems may be sent for critique only for $2 each plus SASE. Guidelines available for SASE. Responds in 2 weeks. Pays one contributor's copy. Acquires first rights. Rights revert to author on publication. Reviews chapbooks of poetry and other magazines/journals in 500 words, single-book format. Send materials for review consideration to Marc Maurus.

Tips "We prefer to see crafted work, not unedited one-offs. We welcome as much formal verse as we can because we feel there is a place for it."

✂ $ ⊘ FREEFALL MAGAZINE

Alexandra Writers' Centre Society, 922 Ninth Ave. SE, Calgary AB T2G 0S4 Canada. (403)264-4730. Website: www.freefallmagazine.ca. Established 1990. **Contact:** Member: AMPA and Magazines Canada.

Magazines Needs *FreeFall Magazine*, published in April and October, contains fiction, nonfiction, poetry, and interviews related to writers/writing, and artwork and photographs suitable for b&w reproduction. "*FreeFall*'s mandate is to encourage the voices of new, emerging, and experienced writers and provide an outlet for their work." Wants "poems in a variety of forms with a strong voice, effective language, and fresh images." Has published poetry by Christopher Wiseman, Sharon Drummond, Edna Alford, Joan Clarke, and Barry Butson. *FreeFall* is 100-120 pages, digest-sized, perfect-bound, glossy, with 60 lb. paper cover. Receives about 100 poems/year, accepts about 15%. Press run is 500; 30 distributed free to contributors, promotion. Single copy: $12.50 USD, $10 CAD; subscription: $25 USD, $20 CAD. Sample: $10 USD, $10 CAD.

How to Contact Submit up to 5 poems at a time. No previously published poems or simultaneous submissions. Accepts postal and disk submissions (ASCII, text format, must include hard copy); no e-mail submissions. Cover letter is required. Include 2-line bio and SASE. Reads submissions in January and July only. Time between acceptance and publication is 3 months. "All submissions are read by 8 editors." Seldom comments on rejected poems. Occasionally publishes theme issues. Guidelines available by mail request, for SAE and IRC, by e-mail, or on website. Responds in 3 months. Pays 1 contributor's copy and a nominal amount per page. Acquires first North American serial rights.

Additional Information See website for information about the Alexandra Writers' Centre Society activities and services, and for additional information about *FreeFall Magazine*.

Contest/Award Offerings Hosts an annual fiction and poetry contest. **Deadline:** December 31. Guidelines available by e-mail or on website.

🌐 ⊘ FREEXPRESSION

P.O. Box 4, West Hoxton NSW 2171, Australia. (61)(2)9607-5559. E-mail: frexprsn@tpg. com.au. Website: www.freexpression.net. **Contact:** Peter F. Pike, Managing Editor.

Magazines Needs *FreeXpresSion*, published monthly, contains "creative writing, how-to articles, short stories, and poetry including cinquain, haiku, etc., and bush verse." Open to all forms. "Christian themes OK. Humorous material welcome. No gratuitous sex; bad language OK. We don't want to see anything degrading." Has published poetry by Ron Stevens, Ellis Campbell, John Ryan, and Ken Dean. *FreeXpresSion* is 28 pages, magazine-sized, offset-printed, saddle-stapled, with paper cover. Receives about 2,500 poems/year, accepts about 30%. Press run is 500. Single copy: $3.50 AUS; subscription: $42 AUS ($66 AUS overseas airmail). Sample: A4 SAE with $1 stamp (Australia) or 2 IRCs (overseas).

How to Contact Submit 3-4 poems at a time. Lines/poem: "very long poems are not desired but would be considered." Considers previously published poems and simultaneous submissions. Accepts e-mail (pasted into body of message) and disk submissions. Cover letter is preferred. Time between acceptance and publication is 2 months. Seldom comments on rejected poems. Publishes theme issues. Upcoming themes available in magazine, by e-mail, or on website. Guidelines available in magazine, for SAE and IRC, or by fax or e-mail. Responds in 2 months. Sometimes sends prepublication galleys. Pays 1 contributor's copy; additional copies available at half price. Acquires first Australian rights only. Reviews books of poetry in 500 words. Send materials for review consideration.

Additional Information *FreeXpresSion* also publishes books up to 200 pages **through subsidy arrangements with authors**. "Some poems published throughout the year are used in *Yearbooks* (annual anthologies)."

Contest/Award Offerings Sponsors an annual contest with 3 categories for poetry: blank verse (up to 60 lines); traditional verse (up to 80 lines), and haiku. 1st Prize in blank verse: $200 AUS; 2nd Prize: $100 AUS; 1st Prize in traditional rhyming poetry: $250 AUS; 2nd Prize: $150 AUS; 3rd Prize: $100 AUS. Haiku, one prize $100 AUS. Guidelines and entry form available by e-mail.

Tips "Keep it short and simple."

◎ FROGPOND: JOURNAL OF THE HAIKU SOCIETY OF AMERICA

Haiku Society of America, P.O. Box 122, Nassau NY 12123. E-mail: gswede@ryerson.ca. Website: www.hsa-haiku.org. **Contact:** George Swede, Editor.

Magazines Needs *Frogpond*, published triannually (February, June, October), is the international journal of the Haiku Society of America, an affiliate of the American Literature Association. Wants "contemporary English-language haiku, ranging from 1-4 lines or in a visual arrangement, focusing on a moment keenly perceived and crisply conveyed, using clear images and non-poetic language." Also considers "related forms: senryu, sequences, linked poems, and haibun. Has published poetry by all of the foremost haiku poets around the world. *Frogpond* is 116-128 pages, digest-sized, perfect-bound. Receives about 10,000 submissions/year, accepts about 500. *Frogpond* goes to 800 subscribers as well as to over 14 foreign countries. Sample or back issue: $10; $14 foreign. Make checks payable to Haiku Society of America.

How to Contact Submissions by e-mail preferred. No simultaneous submissions. Include SASE with postal submissions. Guidelines available for SASE or on website. Detailed instructions on website. Responds at the end of each submission period (June 1-August 1; September 15-November 15; February 15-April 15). Reviews books of poetry, usually in 1,000 words or less.

Additional Information Also accepts articles, 1,000-4,000 words, that are properly referenced according to 1 of the 3 style guides: MLA, APA, Chicago Manual.

Contest/Award Offerings The "best of issue" prize of 4100 is awarded to a poem from each issue of *Frogpond* through a gift from the Museum of Haiku Literature, located in Tokyo. The Haiku Society of America also sponsors a number of other contests, most of which have cash prizes: The Harold G. Henderson Haiku Award Contest, the Gerald Brady Senryu Award Contest, the Bernard Lionel Einbond Memorial Renku Contest, the Nicholas A. Virgilio Memorial Haiku Competition for High School Students, the Mildred Kanterman Merit Book Awards for outstanding books in the haiku field. Guidelines available on website.

Tips "Submissions to *Frogpond* are accepted from both members and nonmembers, although familiarity with the journal will aid writers in discovering what it publishes."

$ ☑ FUGUE

200 Brink Hall, University of Idaho, Moscow ID 83844-1102. E-mail: poetrysubmit@uidaho.edu. Website: www.uidaho.edu/fugue. **Contact:** Jennifer Yeatts, Poetry Editor.

Magazines Needs *Fugue*, published semiannually in summer and winter, is a literary magazine of the University of Idaho. "There are no restrictions on type of poetry; however, we are not interested in trite or quaint verse." Has published poetry by Sonia Sanchez, Simon Perchik, Denise Duhamel, Dean Young, and W.S. Merwin. *Fugue* is up to 200 pages, perfect-bound. Receives about 400 poems/semester, accepts only 15-20 poems/issue. Press run is 250. There is also an online version. Sample: $8.

How to Contact Submit 3-5 poems at a time (10 pages maximum). No previously published poems. Considers simultaneous submissions "with the explicit provision that the writer inform us immediately if the work is accepted for publication elsewhere." E-mail submissions only. Include brief cover letter in body of e-mail with name, address, e-mail, phone number, poem titles, and a brief bio citing any awards/publications. Paste poems in body of e-mail and include one attached file which includes all poems in .pdf, .rtf, or .doc format. Reads submissions September 1-May 1 only. Time between acceptance and publication is up to 1 year. "Submissions are reviewed by staff members and chosen with consensus by the editorial board. No major changes are made to a manuscript without authorial approval." Publishes theme issues. Guidelines available for SASE or on website. Responds in up to 5 months. Pays at least 1 contributor's copy plus an honorarium (up to $25 as funds allow). Acquires first North American serial rights.

Contest/Award Offerings "For information regarding our annual spring poetry contest, please visit our website."

Tips "We are looking for poetry that takes risks while demonstrating powerful voice and careful attention to language and craft. Proper manuscript format and submission etiquette are expected; submissions that do not follow guidelines as listed on website will not be read or held on file."

▣ ☐ THE FURNACE REVIEW

E-mail: submissions@thefurnacereview.com. Website: www.thefurnacereview.com. **Contact:** Ciara LaVelle, editor.

Magazines Needs *The Furnace Review*, published quarterly online, is "dedicated to new writers and unique or groundbreaking work." Wants "all forms, from haiku to sonnets to free verse to totally experimental. Just make it interesting." Has published poetry by Carolynn Kingyens, Charles Geoghegan-Clements, Curtis Evans, and Richard Matthes. Receives about 1,500 pieces/year, accepts about 30.

How to Contact Submit up to 5 poems at a time. Lines/poem: 75 maximum. Considers simultaneous submissions; no previously published poems. Accepts e-mail submissions; no disk submissions. Cover letter is preferred. "Include a short biography with all submissions." Reads submissions year round. Time between acceptance and publication is 3 months. Poems are circulated to an editorial board. Sometimes comments on rejected poems. Guidelines available on website. Responds in 6 months. Acquires first North American serial rights.

◙ GARGOYLE MAGAZINE

Paycock Press, 3819 N. 13th St., Arlington VA 22201. E-mail: gargoyle@gargoylemagazine. com. Website: www.gargoylemagazine.com. **Contact:** Richard Peabody, co-editor.

Magazines Needs *Gargoyle Magazine*, published annually, has always been a scallywag magazine, a maverick magazine, a bit too academic for the underground and way too underground for the academics. We generally run short, one-page poems. We like wit, imagery, killer lines." Has published poetry by Naomi Ayala, Nicole Blackman, Kate Braverman, Laura Chester, Thaisa Frank, Thylias Moss, Elizabeth Swados, and Paul West. *Gargoyle* is about 500 pages, digest-sized, offset-printed, perfectbound, with color cover, includes ads. Accepts about 10% of the poems received each year. Press run is 2,000. Subscription: $30 for 2 issues (individuals); $40 (institutions). Sample: $10.

How to Contact Submit 5 poems at a time. Considers simultaneous submissions. Accepts e-mail submissions (preferred; pasted into body of message). Reads submissions "all summer—June, July, and August." Time between acceptance and publication is 12 months. "The 2 editors make some concessions but generally concur." Often comments on rejected poems. Responds in 3 months. Always sends prepublication galleys. Pays 1 contributor's copy and offers 50% discount on additional copies. Acquires first rights.

Additional Information Paycock Press has published 22 additional titles since 1976 and is not currently seeking mss.

◙ GEORGETOWN REVIEW

Box 227, 400 E. College St., Georgetown KY 40324. (502)863-8308. Fax: (502)868-8888. E-mail: gtownreview@georgetowncollege.edu. Website: http://georgetownreview. georgetowncollege.edu. **Contact:** Steven Carter, editor. Member: CLMP.

Magazines Needs *Georgetown Review*, published annually in May, is a literary journal of poetry, fiction, and creative nonfiction. "We have no specific guidelines concerning form or content of poetry, but are always eager to see poetry that is insightful, rooted in reality, and human." Does not want "work that is merely sentimental, political, or inspirational." Considers poetry by children and teens. Has published poetry by Denise Duhamel, X.J. Kennedy, Fred Chappell, Frederick Smock, Mark Halperin, David Citino, William Greenway, James Harms, and Margarita Engle. *Georgetown Review* is 192 pages, digest-sized, offset-printed, perfect-bound, with 60 lb. glossy 4-color cover with art/graphics, includes ads. Receives about 1,000 poems/year, accepts about 50-60. Press run is 1,000. Single copy: $5; subscription: $5. Make checks payable to *Georgetown Review*.

How to Contact Submit 1-10 poems at a time. Lines/poem: open. Considers simultaneous submissions; no previously published poems. No fax, e-mail, or disk submissions. Cover letter is preferred. "In cover letter, please include short bio and a list of publications. Also, must include SASE for reply." Reads submissions September 1-March 15. Submit seasonal poems 1 year in advance. Time between acceptance and publication is 6-12 months. Poems are circulated to an editorial board. "The first reader passes the poem along to the poetry editor, and then a final decision is made by the poetry editor and the head editor." Seldom comments on rejected poems. Guidelines available for SASE, by e-mail, or on website. Responds in 1-3 months. Pays 2 contributor's copies. Acquires first North American serial rights. Reviews books/chapbooks of poetry in 1,000 words, multi-book format.

Contest/Award Offerings Sponsors annual contest, offering $1,000 prize and publication; runners-up also receive publication. Guidelines available for SASE, by e-mail, or on website. **Entry fee:** $10/poem, $5 for each additional poem.

$ ☑ THE GEORGIA REVIEW

The University of Georgia, 285 S. Jackson St., Athens GA 30602-9009. E-mail: garev@uga.edu. Mindy Wilson, Managing Editor. **Contact:** Stephen Corey, Editor. *The Georgia Review*, published quarterly, seeks "the very best work we can find, whether by Nobel laureates and Pulitzer Prize-winners or by little-known (or even previously unpublished) writers. All manuscripts receive serious, careful attention. We have featured first-ever publications by many new voices over the years, but encourage all potential contributors to become familiar with past offerings before submitting." Has published poetry by Rita Dove, Stephen Dunn, Margaret Gibson, Albert Goldbarth, and Lola Haskins. *The Georgia Review* is 200-232 pages, 7x10, professionally printed, flat-spined, with glossy card cover. Publishes 60-70 poems/year, less than .5% of those received. Press run is 4,500. Subscription: $35/year. Single: $15.

How to Contact Submit 3-5 poems at a time. We do not accept submissions via fax or e-mail. If a submission is known to be included in a book already accepted by a publisher, please notify us of this fact (and of the anticipated date of book publication) in a cover letter. Reads year-round, but submissions postmarked May 15-August 15 will be returned unread. Guidelines available for SASE or on website. Responds in 2-3 months. Always sends prepublication galleys. Pays $4/line, one-year subscription, and 1 contributor's copy. Acquires first North American serial rights. Reviews books of poetry. "Our poetry reviews range from 500-word 'Book Briefs' on single volumes to 5,000-word essay reviews on multiple volumes."

Tips "Needless to say, competition is extremely tough. All styles and forms are welcome, but response times can be slower during peak periods in the fall and late spring."

☐ GERONIMO REVIEW

E-mail: geronimoreview@att.net. Website: www.sanjeronimofnd.org. **Contact:** S. Bass, Editor.

Magazines Needs *geronimo review*, published online, will "publish on its website virtually everything submitted. Submit whatever strikes your fancy. Literally. Anything. Overt pornography, hate speech, etc., taken under editorial advisement." Has 2 submission categories: Open (these submissions are graded "mercilessly" by both editors and readers) and Amateur ("graded on an appropriate scale"). Wants "politics and political satire. Anything of unusual excellence, especially the short lyric." Has published poetry by Mark C. Peery, dada rambass, zeninubasho, geronimo bassetti, Élan B. Yergmoul, "and innumerable others."

How to Contact Submit 3 poems at a time. Lines/poem: 100 maximum (or the length demanded by the poem). Considers simultaneous submissions; no previously published poems. Accepts submissions by e-mail only (as Word attachment or pasted into body of message). Submissions in html will appear with poet's formatting. Reads submissions all year. Time between acceptance and publication is 2 weeks. Guidelines available on website. Responds in 3 weeks ("maybe"). Acquires all rights; returns to poet "on request." Send materials for review consideration.

Additional Information MaoMao Press will publish essays on and reviews of poetry in the future. "Not presently accepting book submissions—watch our website. *GR* will soon allow poets to post their work directly online, and will allow readers to comment on and vote, allowing superior material to float to the top." Artists will also be encouraged to post their art. Poets who have published a book may, on request, get their own page on the site.

Also Offers Plans anthology of *geronimo review* material.

Tips "Don't be Susan Wheeler. Be in the tradition of Yeats, Frost, Carroll, Stevens, and be really original and inspire strong reactions."

☑ ◎ GERTRUDE

P.O. Box 83948, Portland OR 97283. E-mail: editor@gertrudepress.org. Website: www. gertrudepress.org. **Contact:** Eric Delehoy, founding editor.

Magazines Needs *Gertrude*, published semiannually, is the literary publication of Gertrude Press (see separate listing in Books/Chapbooks), "a nonprofit 501(c)(3) organization showcasing and developing the creative talents of lesbian, gay, bisexual, trans, queer-identified, and allied individuals." Has published poetry by Judith Barrington, Deanna Kern Ludwin, Casey Charles, Michael Montlack, Megan Kruse, and Noah Tysick. *Gertrude* is 64-112 pages, digest-sized, offset-printed, perfect-bound, with glossy 4-color cardstock cover with art. Receives about 500 poems/year, accepts about 6-8%. Press run is 300; 50 distributed free. Single copy: $8.25; subscription: $15/year, $27 for 2 years. Sample: $6.25. Make checks payable to Gertrude Press.

How to Contact Submit 6 poems at a time. Lines/poem: open. Considers simultaneous submissions; no previously published poems. Accepts e-mail submissions via the website only; no disk submissions. Cover letter is preferred. Include short bio and SASE. Reads submissions year round. Time between acceptance and publication is 3-6 months. Poems are circulated to an editorial board. Sometimes comments on rejected poems. Guidelines available in magazine, by e-mail, or on website. Responds in 3 months. Sometimes sends prepublication galleys. Pays 1 contributor's copy plus discount on additional copies/subscriptions. Acquires one-time rights. Rights revert to poets upon publication.

Contest/Award Offerings The Gertrude Press Poetry Chapbook Contest.

Tips "*Gertrude* publishes the best poetry that is received. While we are a queer publication, poetry need not be lesbigay-specific, and publication is open to all poets regardless of background."

$ ☑ THE GETTYSBURG REVIEW

Gettysburg College, Gettysburg PA 17325. (717)337-6770. Fax: (717)337-6775. E-mail: mdrew@gettysburg.edu. Website: www.gettysburgreview.com. **Contact:** Peter Stitt, Editor. *The Gettysburg Review*, published quarterly, considers "well-written poems of all kinds." Has published poetry by Rita Dove, Alice Friman, Philip Schultz, Michelle, Boisseau, Bob Hicok, Linda Pastan, and G.C. Waldrep. Accepts 1-2% of submissions received. Press run is 4,500. Subscription: $28/year. Sample: $10.

⬒ $ ☑ GRAIN

P.O. Box 67, Saskatoon SK S7K 3K1, Canada. (306)244-2828. Fax: (306)244-0255. E-mail: grainmag@sasktel.net. Website: www.grainmagazine.ca. **Contact:** Gerry Hill, poetry editor.

Magazines Needs *Grain*, published quarterly, is "an internationally acclaimed literary journal that publishes engaging, surprising, eclectic, and challenging writing and images by Canadian and international writers and artists." Has published poetry by Lorna Crozier, Don Domanski, Cornelia Haeussler, Patrick Lane, Karen Solie, and Monty Reid. *Grain* is 128-144 pages, digest-sized, professionally printed. Press run is 1,100. Receives about 2,400 submissions/year. Subscription: $30 CAD/year, $46 CAD for 2 years. Sample: $13 CAD. (See website for U.S. and foreign postage fees.)

How to Contact Submit up to 12 pages of poetry, typed in readable font on one side only. No previously published poems or simultaneous submissions. No fax or e-mail submissions; postal submissions only. Cover letter with all contact information, title(s), and genre of work is required. "No staples. Your name and address must be on every page. Pieces of more than one page must be numbered. Please only submit work in one genre at one time." Reads submissions September-May only. "Manuscripts postmarked between June 1 and August 31 will be returned unread." Guidelines available in magazine, for SASE (or SAE and IRC), by fax, e-mail, or on website. Responds in 2-4 months. Pays $50-225 CAD (depending on number of pages) and 2 contributor's copies. Acquires first Canadian serial rights only. Copyright remains with the author.

Tips "Only work of the highest literary quality is accepted. Read several back issues."

◖ GRASSLANDS REVIEW

E-mail: kedwards18@isugw.indstate.edu; brendan.corcoran@indstate.edu. Website: http://www.indstate.edu/english/team.asp. **Contact:** Dr. Brendan Corcoran, Managing Editor. Established 1989.

Magazines Needs *Grasslands Review*, published semiannually, aims to "to encourage beginning writers and to give adult creative writing students experience in editing fiction and poetry; using any type of poetry; shorter poems stand best chance." Has published poetry by Carol Graser, Marlene Tilton, Don Shockey, Barry Brummett, J.E. McCarthy, and Jennifer Comoll. *Grasslands Review* is 30-50 pages, digest-sized, professionally printed, photocopied, saddle-stapled, with card cover. Receives about 600 submissions/year, accepts about 30-50. Press run is 200. Subscription: $10 for 2 issues (individuals), $20 for 2 issues (institutions). Sample: $5 for older issues, $6 for more recent.

How to Contact Submit no more than 5 poems at a time. No previously published poems or simultaneous submissions. No e-mail submissions. Cover letter is preferred (brief). Include #10 SASE for response. Reads submissions postmarked October and March only. Sometimes comments on submissions. Responds in 4 months. Sometimes sends prepublication galleys. Pays one contributor's copy.

☑ THE GREAT AMERICAN POETRY SHOW

The Muse Media, P.O. Box 69506, West Hollywood CA 90069. E-mail: info@tgaps.net. Website: www.tgaps.net. **Contact:** Larry Ziman, editor/publisher.

Magazines Needs *The Great American Poetry Show*, published about every 3 years, is an 8½ × 11 hardcover serial poetry anthology. Wants poems on any subject, in any style, of any length. Has published poetry by Sara Berkeley, Alan Britt, Hector E. Estrada, Heidi Nye, Tom Smith, and Sarah Brown Weitzman. *The Great American Poetry Show* is 150 pages, sheet-fed offset-printed, perfect-bound, with cloth cover with art/graphics. "For our first volume, we read about 8,000 poems from about 1,400 poets and accepted only 113 poems from 83 poets." Press run is 1,000. Single copy: $35 (print), $7.50 (e-book, download only).

How to Contact Submit any number of poems at a time. Considers previously published poems and simultaneous submissions. Accepts e-mail submissions (as attachment). Cover letter is optional. Include SASE. "If we reject a submission of your work, please send us another group to go through. We have 3 editors who can handle a lot of submissions." Responds in 1-3 months ("depends on how busy we are"). Pays 1 contributor's copy.

Also Offers "Please visit our message boards where anyone can have us post poetry news, reviews, essays, articles, and recommended books."

Tips "We are very hard to please. But we are very easy to submit to. Do not get discouraged by rejections from us. Just keep sending us more poems to consider. Hopefully, we will find something we want to publish in your submissions. If we reject everything you send us, still do not get discouraged. Send your poems to other publishers until you find one who wants to publish your poetry."

🖳 ⃠ GREEN HILLS LITERARY LANTERN

McClain Hall, Truman State University, Kirksville MO 63501. (660)785-4513. E-mail: jbeneven@truman.edu. Website: http://ll.truman.edu/ghllweb/. **Contact:** Joe Benevento, Poetry Editor.

Magazines Needs *Green Hills Literary Lantern*, published annually online in June, is "an open-access journal of short fiction and poetry of exceptional quality." Wants "the best poetry, in any style, preferably understandable. There are no restrictions on subject matter. Both free and formal verse forms are fine, though we publish more free verse overall." Does not want "haiku, limericks, or anything over 2 pages. Pornography and gratuitous violence will not be accepted. Obscurity for its own sake is also frowned upon." Has published poetry by Jim Thomas, David Lawrence, Mark Belair, Louis Philips, Francine Tolf, and Julie Lechevsky. Sample: $7 (back issue).

How to Contact Submit 3-7 poems at a time. Considers simultaneous submissions, "but not preferred"; no previously published poems. No e-mail submissions. Cover letter is preferred. Include list of publication credits. Type poems one/page. Often comments on rejected poems. Guidelines available for SASE, by e-mail, or on website. Responds within 4 months. Always sends prepublication galleys. Acquires one-time rights.

Tips "Read the best poetry and be willing to learn from what you encounter. A genuine attempt is made to publish the best poems available, no matter who the writer. First-time poets, well-established poets, and those in between, all can and have found a place in the *Green Hills Literary Lantern*. We try to supply feedback, particularly to those we seek to encourage."

☑ GREEN MOUNTAINS REVIEW

Johnson State College, Johnson VT 05656. (802)635-1350. Fax: (802)635-1210. E-mail: gmr@jsc.vsc.edu. Website: http://greenmountainsreview.jsc.vsc.edu. **Contact:** Neil Shepard, senior editor, or Elizabeth Powell, poetry editor.

- Poetry published in *Green Mountains Review* has been included in *The Best American Poetry* and *The Pushcart Prize* anthologies.

Magazines Needs *Green Mountains Review*, published twice/year, includes poetry (and other writing) by well-known authors and promising newcomers. Has published poetry by Carol Frost, Sharon Olds, Carl Phillips, David St. John, and David Wojahn. *Green Mountains Review* is 150-200 pages, digest-sized, flat-spined. Receives about 5,000 submissions/year, publishes 60 authors. Press run is 1,550. Single copy: $9.50 including postage; subscription: $15/year. Sample: $7 (back issue).

How to Contact Submit no more than 5 poems at a time. Considers simultaneous submissions. No e-mail submissions. Reads submissions September 1-March 1 only. Sometimes comments rejected poems. Publishes theme issues. Guidelines available for SASE. Responds in up to 6 months. Pays 2 contributor's copies plus one-year subscription. Acquires first North American serial rights. Send materials for review consideration.

☑ THE GREENSBORO REVIEW

MFA Writing Program, 3302 Hall for Humanities and, Research Administration, University of NC at Green, Greensboro NC 27402. (336)334-5459. E-mail: jlclark@uncg.edu. Website: www.greensbororeview.org. **Contact:** Jim Clark, editor.

- Work published in *The Greensboro Review* has been consistently anthologized or cited in *Best American Short Stories*, *New Stories from the South*, *The Pushcart Prize*, and *Prize Stories: The O. Henry Awards*.

Magazines Needs *The Greensboro Review*, published twice/year, showcases well-made verse in all styles and forms, though shorter poems (under 50 lines) are preferred. Has published poetry by Carl Dennis, Jack Gilbert, Linda Gregg, Tung-Hui Hu, A. Van Jordan, and Natasha Tretheway. *The Greensboro Review* is 144 pages, digest-sized, professionally printed, flat-spined, with colored matte cover. Subscription: $14/year, $24 for 2 years, and $30 for 3 years. Sample: $8.

How to Contact Submit no more than 5 poems at a time. Lines/poem: under 50 lines preferred. No previously published poems. Simultaneous submissions accepted. No fax or e-mail submissions. Cover letter is preferred. Include number of poems submitted. Provide SASE for reply; manuscripts arriving after those dates will be held for consideration for the next issue. Reads submissions according to the following deadlines: mss must arrive by September 15 to be considered for the Spring issue (acceptances in December), or February 15 to be considered for the Fall issue (acceptances in May). "Manuscripts arriving after those dates will be held for consideration for the next issue." Guidelines available in magazine, for SASE, or on website. Responds in 4 months. Always sends prepublication galleys. Pays 3 contributor's copies. Acquires first North American serial rights.

Tips "We want to see the best being written regardless of theme, subject, or style."

ⓝ ☑ GUERNICA

A Magazine of Art and Politics, Attn: Michael Archer,, 165 Bennett Ave., 4C, New York NY 10040. E-mail: editors@guernicamag.com. Website: www.guernicamag.com. **Contact:** Meakin Armstrong, Fiction Editor. "*Guernica*, published biweekly, is one of the web's most acclaimed new magazines. 2009: Guernica is called a "great online literary magazine" by *Esquire*. *Guernica* contributors come from dozens of countries and write in nearly as many languages."

Magazines Needs In subject line (please follow this format exactly): "poetry submission." Submit up to five poems, any length-to poetry@guernicamag.com.

☑ GULF STREAM MAGAZINE

English Dept., Florida International University, 3000 NE 151 St., Biscayne Bay Campus, North Miami FL 33181. (305)919-5599. E-mail: gulfstreamfiu@yahoo.com. Website: www.gulfstreamlitmag.com. **Contact:** Peter Borrebach, editor.

Magazines Needs *Gulf Stream*, published semiannually, is associated with the creative writing program at Florida International University. Wants "poetry of any style and subject matter as long as it's of high literary quality." Has published poetry by Robert Wrigley, Jan Beatty, Jill Bialosky, and Catherine Bowman. *Gulf Stream* is 124 pages, digest-sized, flat-spined, printed on quality stock, with matte card cover. Accepts less than 10% of poetry received. Print back-issue sample: $5.

How to Contact Submit no more than 5 poems at a time. Considers simultaneous submissions with notification. Accepts electronic online submissions only; no snail mail/hard copy or e-mail submissions. "See website for details." Cover letter is required. Reads submissions September 15-December 15; January 15-March 15 only. Publishes theme issue every other issue. Guidelines available in magazine or on website. Responds in 3 weeks to 3 months. Acquires first North American serial rights.

☑ HAIGHT ASHBURY LITERARY JOURNAL

558 Joost Ave., San Francisco CA 94127. (415)584-8264. E-mail: poetship@comcast.net. **Contact:** Indigo Hotchkiss, Alice Rogoff, Gail Mitchell, and Cesar Love, editors.

Magazines Needs *Haight Ashbury Literary Journal*, published 1-2 times/year, is a newsprint tabloid that uses "all forms of poetry. Subject matter sometimes political, but open to all subjects. Poems of background—prison, multi-cultural experience—often published, as well as poems of protest. Few rhymes." Has published poetry by Dan O'Connell, Diane Frank, Dancing Bear, Lee Herrick, Al Young, and Laura Beausoleil. *Haight Ashbury* is 16 pages, includes ads. Includes fiction under 20 pages, one story/issue, and b&w drawings. Press run is 2,500. Subscription: $16 for 4 issues; $40 for a lifetime subscription (all future and 9 back issues). Sample: $3.

How to Contact Submit up to 6 poems at a time. Submit only once/6 months. No e-mail submissions; postal submissions only (will accept e-mail submissions from overseas ONLY). "Please type 1 poem to a page, put name and address on every page, and include SASE. No bio." Sometimes publishes theme issues (each issue changes its theme and emphasis). Guidelines available for SASE. Responds in 4 months. Pays 3 contributor's copies, plus small monetary amount to featured writers. Rights revert to author.

Additional Information An anthology of past issues, *This Far Together*, is available for $15.

Tips "Do not send work that is longer than our magazine!"

$ ☑ HANGING LOOSE

Hanging Loose Press, 231 Wyckoff St., Brooklyn NY 11217. E-mail: PRINT225@aol.com. Website: www.hangingloosepress.com. **Contact:** Robert Hershon, Dick Lourie, and Mark Pawlak, poetry editors.

Magazines Needs *Hanging Loose*, published in April and October, "concentrates on the work of new writers." Wants "excellent, energetic" poems. Considers poetry by teens ("one section contains poems by high-school-age poets"). Has published poetry by Sherman Alexie, Paul Violi, Donna Brook, Kimiko Hahn, Harvey Shapiro, and Ha Jin. *Hanging Loose* is 120 pages, offset-printed on heavy stock, flat-spined, with 4-color glossy card cover. Sample: $12.

How to Contact Submit 4-6 poems at a time. No simultaneous submissions. "Would-be contributors should read the magazine first." Responds in 3 months. Pays small fee and 2 contributor's copies.

Additional Information Hanging Loose Press does not consider unsolicited book mss or artwork.

☑ HARPUR PALATE

Dept. of English, Binghamton University, P.O. Box 6000, Binghamton NY 13902-6000. E-mail: harpurpalate@gmail.com. Website: http://harpurpalate.binghamton.edu. **Contact:** Barrett Bowlin, editor-in-chief.

Magazines Needs *Harpur Palate*, published biannually, is "dedicated to publishing the best poetry and prose, regardless of style, form, or genre." Has published poetry by Sherman Alexie, Tess Gallagher, Alex Lemon, Marvin Bell, Ryan G. Van Cleave, Sascha Feinstein, Allison Joseph, Neil Shepard, and Ruth Stone. *Harpur Palate* is 180-220 pages, digest-sized, offset-printed, perfect-bound, with matte or glossy cover. Receives about 1,000 poems/year, accepts about 50. Press run is 800. Single copy: $10; subscription: $16/year (2 issues). Sample: $6. Make checks payable to *Harpur Palate*.

How to Contact Submit 3-5 poems at a time. Lines/poem: "No restrictions; entire submission must be 10 pages or fewer." Considers simultaneous submissions, "but we must be notified immediately if the piece is taken somewhere else"; no previously published poems. No e-mail submissions. Cover letter and SASE is required. Reads submissions year round. Time between acceptance and publication is 2 months. Poems are circulated to an editorial board. Seldom comments on rejected poems. Guidelines available in magazine, for SASE, or on website. Responds in up to 8 months. Pays 2 contributor's copies. Acquires first North American serial rights.

Contest/Award Offerings The Milton Kessler Memorial Prize for Poetry.

Tips "We have no restrictions on subject matter or form. Quite simply, send us your highest-quality poetry. Read through all of our submission instructions very carefully before sending your work (manuscripts that are not properly submitted will be discarded unread). Almost every literary magazine already says this, but it bears repeating: look at a copy of our publication (and other publications as well) to get an idea of the kind of writing published. Do an honest (perhaps even ruthless) assessment of your work to see if it's indeed ready to be submitted."

N ☯ HARVARD REVIEW

Lamont Library, Harvard University, Cambridge MA 02138. E-mail: harvrev@fas.harvard. edu. Website: hcl.harvard.edu/harvardreview. **Contact:** Christina Thompson, editor; Major Jackson, poetry editor.

Magazines Needs *Harvard Review*, published semiannually, "has emerged as a major American literary journal with an eclectic mix of contributors in a wide variety of genres and styles. "Does not want genre fiction. Seamus Heaney, John Ashbery, and Jorie Graham. Single: $13; Subscription: $16/year.

How to Contact Submit up to 5 poems. Considers simultaneous submissions. Accepts submissions by mail only (overseas only can submit by e-mail). Cover letter is required citing recent publications or awards. "Please include a SASE. Manuscripts must be paginated and clearly labeled with author's name on every page." Reads submissions year round. Guidelines available on website. Responds in up to 6 months. Pays 2 contributor's copies; additional copies $7. Acquires first North American serial rights.

Tips "We highly recommend that you familiarize yourself with *Harvard Review* before you submit your work. You can find both previous issues and subscription information online."

☯ HAWAI'I PACIFIC REVIEW

1060 Bishop St., Honolulu HI 96813. (808)544-1108. E-mail: pwilson@hpu.edu. Established 1987. **Contact:** Patrice M. Wilson, editor.

Magazines Needs *Hawai'i Pacific Review*, published annually in September by Hawai'i Pacific University, prints "quality poetry, short fiction, and personal essays from writers worldwide. Our journal seeks to promote a world view that celebrates a variety of cultural themes, beliefs, values, and viewpoints. We wish to further the growth of artistic vision and talent by encouraging sophisticated and innovative poetic and narrative techniques." Has published poetry by Wendy Bishop, Rick Bursky, Virgil Suárez, Bob Hicok, Daniel Gutstein, and Linda Bierds. *Hawai'i Pacific Review* is 80-120 pages, digest-sized, professionally printed on quality paper, perfect-bound, with coated card cover. Receives 800-1,000 poems/year, accepts up to 30-40. Press run is about 500 (100 shelf sales). Single copy: $8.95. Sample: $5.

How to Contact Submit up to 5 poems at a time. Lines/poem: 100 maximum. No previously published poems or simultaneous submissions. No fax or e-mail submissions. Cover letter is required. Include 5-line professional bio including prior publications. SASE required. "One submission per issue. No handwritten manuscripts. Include name on all pages." Reads submissions September 1-December 31 annually. Seldom comments on rejected poems. Guidelines available for SASE, by e-mail, or on website. Responds within 3 months. Pays 2 contributor's copies. Acquires first North American serial rights. Rights revert to poet upon publication. "Must acknowledge *Hawai'i Pacific Review* as first publisher."

Tips "We'd like to receive more experimental verse. Good poetry is eye-opening; it investigates the unfamiliar or reveals the spectacular in the ordinary. Good poetry does more than simply express the poet's feelings; it provides both insight and unexpected beauty. Send us your best work!"

$ ✓ ◎ HIGHLIGHTS FOR CHILDREN

Manuscript Coordinator, 803 Church St., Honesdale PA 18431. Website: www.highlights. com. **Contact:** Manuscript Coordinator. *Highlights*, published monthly, contains poetry for children ages 2-12. Wants "meaningful and/or fun poems accessible to children of all ages. Welcome light, humorous verse." Does not want "poetry that is unintelligible to children; poems containing sex, violence, or unmitigated pessimism." Considers poetry by children and teens (pays only if 16 years or older). Has published poetry by Ruskin Bond, Aileen Fisher, Eileen Spinelli, and Carl Sandburg. *Highlights* is generally 42 pages, magazine-sized, full-color throughout. Receives about 300 submissions/year, accepts up to 30. Press run is 2.5 million (about 2.2 million subscribers). Subscription: $29.64/year (reduced rates for multiple years).

How to Contact Lines/poem: 16 or less ("most poems are shorter"). Considers simultaneous submissions ("please indicate"); no previously published poetry. No e-mail submissions. "Submit typed manuscript with very brief cover letter." Occasionally comments on submissions "if manuscript has merit or author seems to have potential for our market." Guidelines available for SASE. Responds "generally within one month." Always sends prepublication galleys. Pays 2 contributor's copies; "money varies." Acquires all rights.

Tips "Verse is purchased sparingly. We may use the verse as 'filler,' or illustrate the verse with a full-page piece of art. Please note that we do not buy material from anyone under 16 years old." Payment: $25 and up.

✓ HIRAM POETRY REVIEW

P.O. Box 162, Hiram OH 44234. (330)569-7512. Fax: (330)569-5166. E-mail: greenwoodwp@ hiram.edu. **Contact:** Willard Greenwood, poetry editor. Established 1966.

Magazines Needs *Hiram Poetry Review*, published annually in spring, features "distinctive, beautiful, and heroic poetry." Wants "works of high and low art. We tend to favor poems that are pockets of resistance in the undeclared war against 'plain speech,' but we're interested in any work of high quality." Press run is 400 (300 subscribers, 150 libraries). Subscription: $9/year; $23/3 years.

How to Contact Send 3-5 poems at a time. Lines/poem: under 50 (3 single-spaced pages or less). Considers simultaneous submissions. No e-mail submissions, however, "we accept electronic submissions from international writers." Cover letter is required. Include brief bio. Reads submissions year round. Responds in up to 6 months. Pays 2 contributor's copies. Acquires first North American serial rights. Rights return to poets upon publication. Reviews books of poetry in single- or multi-book format, no set length. Send materials for review consideration.

$ ✓ THE HOLLINS CRITIC

P.O. Box 9538, Hollins University, Roanoke VA 24020-1538. (540)362-6275. Website: www. hollins.edu/grad/eng_writing/critic/critic.htm. **Contact:** Cathryn Hankla, poetry editor.

Magazines Needs *The Hollins Critic*, published 5 times/year, prints critical essays, poetry, and book reviews. Uses a few short poems in each issue, interesting in form, content, or both. Has published poetry by William Miller, R.T. Smith, David Huddle, Margaret

Gibson, and Julia Johnson. *The Hollins Critic* is 24 pages, magazine-sized. Press run is 500. Subscription: $10/year ($15 outside U.S.). Sample: $3.

How to Contact Submit up to 5 poems at a time using the online submission form at www. hollinscriticsubmissions.com, available from September 1-December 15. Submissions received at other times will be returned unread. Responds in 6 weeks. Pays $25/poem plus 5 contributor's copies.

▣ ▨ ◎ HOLLY ROSE REVIEW

E-mail: editor@hollyrosereview.com. Website: www.hollyrosereview.com. **Contact:** Theresa Senato Edwards, MA, MFA; founder, editor, and publisher.

Magazines Needs *Holly Rose Review*, published biannually online, publishes two themed issues per year in June and December. "We are interested in poems and photos of tattoos that reach around the corner of life (or death) and grab. Both established and emerging artists from around the world are always welcome here."

How to Contact Submit four poems via e-mail. Considers simultaneous submissions; no previously published poems unless invited. See website for submission periods and themed issues. Regularly publishes theme issues. Guidelines on website. Acquires first North American electronic publication rights, archival rights. "All other rights remain the artist's at publication."

▨ HOME PLANET NEWS

P.O. Box 455, High Falls NY 12440. E-mail: homeplanetnews@yahoo.com. Website: www. homeplanetnews.org. **Contact:** Donald Lev, Editor.

Magazines Needs *Home Planet News*, published 3 times/year, aims "to publish lively and eclectic poetry, from a wide range of sensibilities, and to provide news of the small press and poetry scenes, thereby fostering a sense of community among contributors and readers." Wants "honest, well-crafted poems, open or closed form, on any subject." Does not want "any work which seems to us to be racist, sexist, ageist, anti-Semitic, or imposes limitations on the human spirit." Considers poetry by children and teens. Has published poetry by Enid Dame, Antler, Lyn Lifshin, Gerald Locklin, Hal Sirowitz, and Janine Pommy Vega. *Home Planet News* is 24 pages, tabloid, Web offset-printed, includes ads. Receives about 1,000 poems/year, accepts up to 3%. Press run is 1,000 (300 subscribers). Single copy: $5; subscription: $12/3 issues, $18/6 issues.

How to Contact Submit 3-6 poems at a time. Lines/poem: no limit on length, "but shorter poems (under 30 lines) stand a better chance." No previously published poems or simultaneous submissions. Cover letter is preferred. "SASE is a must." Time between acceptance and publication is 1 year. Seldom comments on rejected poems. Occasionally publishes theme issues. Upcoming themes available in magazine. Guidelines available for SASE or on website; "however, it is usually best to simply send work." Responds in 4 months. Pays one-year gift subscription plus 3 contributor's copies. Acquires first rights. Rights revert to poet upon publication. Reviews books/chapbooks of poetry and other magazines in 1,200 words, single- and multi-book format. Send materials for review consideration to Donald Lev. "Note: we do have guidelines for book reviewers; please write for them or check website. Magazines are reviewed by a staff member."

Tips "Read many publications, attend readings, feel yourself part of a writing community, learn from others."

Ⓝ ▣ ◻ ◉ HOSPITAL DRIVE

Hospital Drive, PO Box 800761, Charlottesville VA 22908-0761. E-mail: query@ hospitaldrive.med.virginia.edu. *Note: We do not accept submissions in the mail. Submissions to the journal are all handled on-line via the Submit page of our website. Website: http://hospitaldrive.med.virginia.edu. **Contact:** Dr. Daniel Becker, Editor. *Hospital Drive*, published irregularly, "encourages original creative work that examines themes of health, illness, and healing. Submissions will be accepted from anyone, but preference is given to those involved in providing, teaching, studying, or researching patient care. All work will be judged anonymously by reviewers and the editorial board. Poems, short fiction, personal essays, reviews, photography, and visual art (painting, drawing, sculpture, mixed media) will be considered. Issues will be released at least once/year, and include invited work." Please review our website thoroughly, and direct any additional questions to: query@hospitaldrive.med.virginia.edu.

How to Contact Submit up to 5 poems at a time. Considers simultaneous submissions. Accepts e-mail submissions as attachment); no fax or disk submissions. Cover letter is unnecessary. All works must be submitted by e-mail, accompanied by basic contact information and the titles of each piece. Attach each poem as a separate document to 1 e-mail. Put "poetry submission" in the e-mail subject line. Reads submissions year round. Time between acceptance and publication is 3-6 months. "All submissions will be reviewed anonymously by the editorial board, and only the highest quality work will be published. Never comments on rejected poems." Guidelines available on website.

◖ HUBBUB

5344 SE 38th Ave., Portland OR 97202. E-mail: lisa.steinman@reed.edu. Website: www. reed.edu/hubbub/. J. Shugrue, Co-Editor. **Contact:** Lisa M. Steinman. *Hubbub*, published once/year in the spring, is designed "to feature a multitude of voices from interesting contemporary American poets." Wants "poems that are well-crafted, with something to say. We have no single style, subject, or length requirement and, in particular, will consider long poems." Does not want light verse. Has published poetry by Madeline DeFrees, Cecil Giscombe, Carolyn Kizer, Primus St. John, Shara McCallum, and Alice Fulton. *Hubbub* is 50-70 pages, digest-sized, offset-printed, perfect-bound, with cover art. Receives about 1,200 submissions/year, accepts up to 2%. Press run is 350. Subscription: $7/year. Sample: $3.35 (back issues), $7 (current issue).

How to Contact Submit 3-6 typed poems at a time. No previously published poems or simultaneous submissions. Include SASE. Guidelines available for SASE. Responds in 4 months. Pays 2 contributor's copies. Acquires first North American serial rights. "We review 2-4 poetry books/year in short (3-page) reviews; all reviews are solicited. We do, however, list books received/recommended." Send materials for review consideration.

Contest/Award Offerings Outside judges choose poems from each volume for 3 awards: Vi Gale Award ($100), Stout Award ($50), and Kenneth O. Hanson Award ($75). There are no special submission procedures or entry fees involved.

$ ◉ HUMPTY DUMPTY'S MAGAZINE

Children's Better Health Institute, 1100 Waterway Blvd., Indianapolis IN 46202. Website: www.humptydumptymag.org. Although our emphasis is on health, we certainly use material with more general themes, including holiday and seasonal poems. Please avoid reference to sugary foods, such as candy, cakes, cookies, and soft drinks. Please send seasonal material at least eight months in advance. Reading our editorial guidelines is not enough. Careful study of current issues will acquaint writers with each title's "personality," various departments, and regular features. Sample copies are $3.99 each (U.S. currency) from U.S.Kids, P.O. Box 567, Indianapolis, IN 46206. *Humpty Dumpty's Magazine*, published bimonthly by he Better Health Institute, is for ages 4-6. "Designed to keep young minds growing and active bodies healthy and fit." Wants light-hearted poetry appropriate for the age group. Reviews submissions for possible use in all Children's Better Health Institute publications. Although our emphasis is on health, we certainly use material with more general themes, including holiday and seasonal poems. Please avoid reference to sugary foods, such as candy, cakes, cookies, and soft drinks. Please send seasonal material at least 8 months in advance.

How to Contact Manuscripts must be typewritten with poet's contact information in upper right-hand corner of each poem's page. SASE required. Guidelines available for SASE or on website. Responds in about 3 months. Pays $25 minimum for poetry. Acquires all rights.

Tips "We receive too many poetry submissions that are about kids, not for kids. Or, the subject matter is one that adults think children would or should like. Reading our guidelines is not enough. Careful study of current issues will acquaint writers with each title's 'personality', various departments, and regular features." Sample copies are $3.99 each (U.S. currency) from U.S.Kids, P.O. Box 567, Indianapolis, IN 46206.

$ ⊘ HUNGER MOUNTAIN

Vermont College, 36 College St., Montpelier VT 05602. (802)828-8517. E-mail: hungermtn@ vermontcollege.edu. Website: www.hungermtn.org. **Contact:** Caroline Mercurio, founding editor. Member: CLMP.

Magazines Needs *Hunger Mountain, The Vermont College Journal of Arts & Letters*, published semiannually, prints "high-quality poetry, prose, and artwork selected by guest editors from the Vermont College MFA in Writing Program." Wants poems "ready for publication." Does not want entire mss, or children's or young adult poetry. Has published poetry by Hayden Carruth, Mark Doty, Carol Muske-Dukes, Maxine Kumin, Charles Simic, and Ruth Stone. *Hunger Mountain* is about 200 pages, 7x10, professionally printed, perfect-bound, with full-bleed color artwork on cover, includes ads (only in back). Receives about 600 poems/year, accepts about 5%. Press run is 1,500 (700 subscribers, 50 libraries, 200 shelf sales); 100 distributed free to writing centers, book fairs, and other journals. Single copy: $10; subscription: $17/year, $32 for 2 years, $60 for 4 years. Make checks payable to *Hunger Mountain*.

How to Contact Submit 3-10 poems at a time. Considers simultaneous submissions; no previously published poems. No fax, e-mail, or disk submissions; please use online submissions manager. Cover letter is preferred. "**Include double copies of everything**, including cover letter." Reads submissions year round. Time between acceptance and publication is 6 months. Poems are circulated to an editorial board. Occasionally comments on rejected poems. Guidelines available for SASE, by fax, e-mail, or on website. Responds in 4 months. Always sends prepublication galleys. Pays $5/page (minimum $30) and 2 contributor's copies. Acquires first North American serial rights.

Contest/Award Offerings The annual Ruth Stone Prize in Poetry.

Tips "Always read submission guidelines and make sure your poems are appropriate for the magazine or journal!"

$ ▢ ◎ HUNGUR MAGAZINE

(Specialized: vampires), P.O. Box 782, Cedar Rapids IA 52406-0782. E-mail: hungurmagazine@ yahoo.com. Website: www.samsdotpublishing.com. Member: The Speculative Literature Foundation (http://SpeculativeLiterature.org).

Magazines Needs *Hungur Magazine*, published biannually, features "stories and poems about vampires, and especially about vampires on other worlds." Prefers a "decadent literary style." Does not want "horror with excessive blood and gore." *Hungur Magazine* is 32 pages, magazine-sized, offset-printed, saddle-stapled, with paper cover with color art, includes ads. Receives about 200 poems/year, accepts about 20 (10%). Press run is 100/ issue. Single copy: $8; subscription: $14/year. Make checks payable to Tyree Campbell/ Sam's Dot Publishing.

How to Contact Submit up to 5 poems at a time. Lines/poem: prefers less than 200. No previously published poems or simultaneous submissions. Accepts e-mail submissions (pasted into body of message); no disk submissions. "Submission should include snail mail address and a short (1-2 lines) bio." Reads submissions year round. Submit seasonal poems 6 months in advance. Time between acceptance and publication is 3-4 months. Editor: Terrie Leigh Relf. Often comments on rejected poems. Guidelines available on website. Responds in 4-6 weeks. Pays $4/poem and 1 contributor's copy. Acquires first North American serial rights. Reviews books and chapbooks of poetry. Send materials for review consideration to Tyree Campbell.

Tips "It's up to the writer to take the first step and submit work. Some of our best poems have come from poets who weren't sure if they were good enough."

▢ THE HURRICANE REVIEW: A NATIONAL JOURNAL OF POETRY AND SHORT FICTION

English/Comm Dept., Pensacola Junior College, 1000 College Blvd., Pensacola FL 32504. (850)484-1447. Fax: (850)484-1149. E-mail: mwernicke@pjc.edu. Website: www.pjc.edu/ academics/departments/english/hurricane.html. **Contact:** Mike Will, faculty advisor.

Magazines Needs *The Hurricane Review, A National Journal of Poetry and Short Fiction*, published annually in the fall, features poetry and short fiction. Wants poetry of "any style, any length. No biases other than quality." Does not want "inspirational or greeting card verse." Has published poetry by R.T. Smith, Sue Walker, Larry Rubin, Cornelius Eady, and Simon Perchik. *The Hurricane Review* is 100 pages, digest-sized, professionally printed, perfect-bound, with matte card cover. Receives about 1,000 poems/year, accepts about 50-60. Press run is 500. Subscription: $4. Sample: $4.

How to Contact Submit 3-5 poems at a time. No previously published poems or simultaneous submissions. Cover letter is preferred. Include bio and/or publication history. SASE required.

Reads submissions August 1-May 15 only. Responds in 3 months, faster when possible. Pays 3 contributor's copies. Acquires first rights.

Tips "As David Kirby says, a poem should be well punctuated and give evidence of careful proofreading. It should be understandable to a reader who is not the poet."

◙ ◎ THE HYCO REVIEW

P.O. Box 1197, Roxboro NC 27573. E-mail: langled@piedmontcc.edu; reflect@piedmontcc.edu. **Contact:** Dawn Langley, Editor. The Hyco Review, an online arts and literary magazine, published by Piedmont Community College, proudly announces the publication of its first online version. The magazine, originally titled Reflections and published in the traditional manner (paper), focuses on showcasing the works of artists and writers from Person and Caswell counties, North Carolina, as well as of alumni from the College. We publish annually and welcome quality submissions in any of the formats listed on our submission page. **Accepts submissions from NC authors only (residents or natives).** "If time and space permit, we'll consider submissions from southeastern U.S. authors and from authors we've previously published." Has published poetry by Robert Cooperman, Fredrick Zydek, Bruce Bennett, Fred Chappell, Shari O'Brien, and Daniel Green.

How to Contact Submit 5 poems maximum at a time. Lines/poem: no longer than 1 page (single-spaced). Considers previously published poems and simultaneous submissions (if notified). Accepts e-mail submissions (pasted into body of message or as attachment in MS Word). "Include a 25-word bio with submission. Include 2 copies of each poem—1 with name and address, 1 without. Affix adequate postage to SAE for return of manuscript if desired, or use First-Class stamps on SAE for notification. Poems are read by an 8- to 12-member editorial board who rank submissions through 'blind' readings. Board members refrain from ranking their own submissions." Sometimes comments on rejected poems. Guidelines available in magazine, for SASE, or by e-mail. Responds in up to 9 months (in March or April). Pays 1 contributor's copy. Acquires first North American serial rights (if poem is unpublished) or one-time rights (if poem is previously published).

◙ IBBETSON ST. PRESS

25 School St., Somerville MA 02143-1721. (617)628-2313. E-mail: dougholder@post.harvard.edu. Website: http://homepage.mac.com/rconte. Established 1999. **Contact:** Doug Holder, editor; submissions editor: Mary Rice, Harris Gardner; copy editor: Dorian Brooks.

Magazines Needs *Ibbetson St. Press*, published semiannually in June and November, prints "'down to earth' poetry that is well-written; has clean, crisp images; with a sense of irony and humor." Wants "mostly free verse, but are open to rhyme." Does not want "maudlin, trite, overly political, vulgar for vulgar's sake work." Has published poetry by Miriam Goodman, Elizabeth Swados, Sarah Hannah, Gloria Mindock, Harris Gardner, Diana-der Hovanessian, Robert K. Johnson, Gary Metras, and others. *Ibbetson St. Press* is 50 pages, magazine-sized, desktop-published, with glossy white cover, includes ads. Receives about 1,000 poems/year, accepts up to 30%. Press run is 200. Also archived at Harvard, Brown, University of Wisconsin, Poets House-NYC, and Buffalo University Libraries. Single copy: $7; subscription: $13. Make checks payable to *Ibbetson St. Press*.

How to Contact Submit 3-5 poems at a time. Considers previously published poems; no simultaneous submissions. No e-mail submissions; postal submissions only. Cover letter is required. Time between acceptance and publication is up to 5 months. "3 editors comment on submissions." Guidelines available for SASE. Responds in 2 months or more. Pays 1 contributor's copy. Acquires one-time rights. Reviews books/chapbooks of poetry and other magazines in 250-500 words. Send materials for review consideration.

Additional Information *Does not accept unsolicited chapbook mss*

Tips "Please buy a copy of the magazine you submit to—support the small press. In your work, be honest."

⊞ ▢ ◎ IDIOM 23

Regional Centre of the Arts, Central Queensland University, Rockhampton 4702, Australia. E-mail: l.hawryluk@cqu.edu.au. **Contact:** Dr. Lynda Hawryluk, Editorial Board.

Magazines Needs *Idiom 23*, published annually, is "named for the Tropic of Capricorn and is dedicated to developing the literary arts throughout the Central Queensland region. Submissions of original short stories, poems, articles, and black-and-white drawings and photographs are welcomed by the editorial collective. *Idiom 23* is not limited to a particular viewpoint but, on the contrary, hopes to encourage and publish a broad spectrum of writing. The collective seeks out creative work from community groups with as varied backgrounds as possible. The magazine hopes to reflect and contest idiomatic fictional representations of marginalized or non-privileged positions and values." Considers poetry written by children and teens (10 years of age and older). *Idiom 23* is about 140 pages, 7¾ × 10, professionally printed, perfect-bound, with 4-color cover, includes ads. Single copy: $15.

How to Contact Considers previously published poems. Cover letter is required. Poems are circulated to an editorial board. Reviews books of poetry in single-book format. Send materials for review consideration to Dr. Lynda Hawryluk.

▣ ▢ ILLOGICAL MUSE

P.O. Box 63, 313 Fulton St., Buchanan MI 49107. E-mail: illogicalmuse@yahoo.com. Website: www.geocities.com/illogicalmuse. Established 2004. **Contact:** Amber Rothrock, editor. *Illogical Muse*, an internet quarterly, welcomes "submissions of poetry, fiction, essays and artwork. Looks for well-crafted, intelligent verse in any form and on any subject." Does not want "anything overly graphic or explicit in content." Considers poetry written by children and teens. Has published poetry by Michael Lee Johnson, Sandra Hedin, B.Z. Niditch, Sara Crawford, and Marianne Lavalle-Vincent. Accepts 90% of the material received. Simultaneous submissions and previously published material are welcome as long as you keep me informed on the status of your submission. A brief bio and cover letter is preferred but not necessary, and a link to your personal website or blog is also acceptable. Response time can be 6months or longer and you may have to wait one year before your accepted ms appears. Responds to postal submissions faster than e-mail submissions.

How to Contact Submit up to 6 poems at a time. Lines/poem: no more than 100. Considers previously published poems and simultaneous submissions. Absolutely no multiple submissions. Accepts e-mail submissions (pasted into body of message); no disk submissions. Cover letter is preferred. Include SASE, IRC's or valid e-mail for response. Work will be returned if proper postage is provided. Reads submissions year-round. Submit seasonal poems 6 months in advance. Time between acceptance and publication is up to 1 year. Sometimes comments on rejected poems. "Current theme is Nature but there are special requirements for this issue so check guidelines before submitting. Guidelines available for SASE or on website. Responds in 6 months. Reviews books/chapbooks of poetry and fiction and other magazine/journals. Send materials for review consideration. Acquires one-time rights and electronic/archival rights for website. All rights remain with poet.

Tips Quarterly writing contest. More information available on the blog. Link from the website.

✪ ILLUMINATIONS

Dept. of English, College of Charleston, 66 George St., Charleston SC 29424-0001. Fax: (843)953-3180. E-mail: lewiss@cofc.edu. Website: www.cofc.edu/Illuminations. **Contact:** Simon Lewis, editor.

Magazines Needs *Illuminations: An International Magazine of Contemporary Writing*, published annually, provides "a forum for new writers alongside already established ones." Open as to form and style, and to translations. Does not want to see anything "bland or formally clunky." Has published poetry by Brenda Marie Osbey, Geri Doran, Dennis Brutus, and Carole Satyamurti. *Illuminations* is 64-88 pages, digest-sized, offset-printed, perfect-bound, with 2-color card cover. Receives about 1,500 poems/year, accepts up to 5%. Press run is 400. Subscription: $15/2 issues. Sample: $10.

How to Contact Submit up to 6 poems at a time. No previously published poems or simultaneous submissions. Accepts fax, e-mail (pasted into body of message, no attachments), and mail. Cover letter is preferred (brief). Time between acceptance and publication "depends on when received. Can be up to a year." Occasionally publishes theme issues. Guidelines available by e-mail or on website. Responds within 2 months. Pays 2 contributor's copies plus 1 subsequent issue. Acquires all rights. Returns rights on request.

✪ ◎ INDEFINITE SPACE

P.O. Box 40101, Pasadena CA 91114. Website: www.indefinitespace.net. Established 1992. "Published annually. From minimalist to avant-garde—-open to innovative, imagistic, philosophical, experimental creations—-poetry drawings, collage photography; reads year round. Guidelines do not exist. Contributors receive one copy. Has published poetry by Marthe Reed, Anne Blonstein, Kevin Magee, Petra Backonja, Peter Layton, and Jill Magi. *Indefinite Space* is 48 pages, digest-sized. Single copy: $7; subscription: $12 for 2 issues. Make checks payable to Marcia Arrieta. Seldom comments on rejected poems."

Magazine Needs Needs experimental, visual and minimalistic poetry. No rhyming poetry. No previously published poems.

$ ✪ INDIANA REVIEW

Ballantine Hall 465, 1020 E. Kirkwood Ave., Bloomington IN 47405-7103. (812)855-3439. E-mail: inreview@indiana.edu. Website: www.indiana.edu/~inreview. **Contact:** Nina Mamikunian, editor.

- Poetry published in *Indiana Review* has been included in *The Best American Poetry* and *The Pushcart Prize*.

Magazines Needs *Indiana Review*, published semiannually, includes prose, poetry, creative nonfiction, book reviews, and visual art. "We look for an intelligent sense of form and language, and admire poems of risk, ambition, and scope." Wants "all types of poems—free verse, traditional, experimental. Reading a sample issue is the best way to determine if *Indiana Review* is a potential home for your work. Any subject matter is acceptable if it is written well. Translations are welcome." Has published poetry by Denise Duhamel, Sherman Alexie, Marilyn Chin, Julianna Baggott, and Alberto Rios. *Indiana Review* is 160 pages, digest-sized, professionally printed, flat-spined, with color matte cover. Receives more than 9,000 submissions/year, accepts up to 60. Has 2,000 subscribers. Subscription: $17/year, $28 for 2 years. Sample: $9.

How to Contact Submit 4-6 poems at a time. Lines/poem: "do not send more than 10 pages of poetry per submission." Considers simultaneous submissions with notification; no previously published poems. Cover letter with brief bio is desired. SASE is mandatory for response. Guidelines available on website. "We try to respond to manuscripts in 3-4 months. Reading time is often slower during summer and holiday months." Pays $5/page ($10 minimum), 2 contributor's copies, and remainder of year's subscription. Acquires first North American serial rights only. Reviews books of poetry. Send materials for review consideration.

Contest/Award Offerings Holds yearly poetry and prose-poem contests. Guidelines available for SASE or on website.

$ ○ INKWELL

Manhattanville College, 2900 Purchase St., Purchase NY 10577. (914)323-7239. Fax: (914)323-3122. **Contact:** Poetry Editor. *Inkwell*, published semiannually, features "emerging writers, high quality poems and short stories, creative nonfiction, artwork, literary essays, memoir and interviews on writing by established figures, and yearly compeitions in poetry and fiction." Wants "serious work—very well made verse, any form, any genre." Does not want "doggerel, light or humorous verse." Please review archives online or send for sample copy. *Inkwell* is 150 pages, digest-sized, press-printed, perfect-bound, with cover with illustration/photography. Receives about 2,500 poems/year, accepts about 30. Press run is 700. Single copy: $10; subscription: $18/year. Sample: $6 (back issue). Make checks payable to Manhattanville College—*Inkwell*.

INNISFREE POETRY JOURNAL

E-mail: editor@innisfreepoetry.org. **Contact:** Greg McBride. "Our journal continues the series of Closer Looks at the poetry of a leading contemporary poet (Marianne Boruch)."

How to Contact Submit up to 5 poems by e-mail; single Word attachment. Include your name, as you would like it to appear in Innisfree, in the subject line of your submission. Format all poems flush with the left margin—no indents other than any within the poem itself. Simultaneous submissions are welcome. "If a poem is accepted elsewhere, however, please be sure to notify us immediately." Does not accept previously published poetry.

Additional Information Acquires first publication rights, including the right to publish it online and maintain it there as part of the issue in which it appears, to make it available in a printer-friendly format, to make the issue of *Innisfree* in which it appears downloadable as a PDF document and available as a printed volume. All other rights revert to the poet after online publication of the poem in *The Innisfree Poetry Journal.*

🖳 ☑ IN OUR OWN WORDS

Burning Bush Publications, P.O. Box 4658, Santa Rosa CA 95402. Website: www.bbbooks. com. **Contact:** Amanda Majestie, editor.

Magazines Needs *In Our Own Words*, published annually online, seeks poetry and prose poems for its literary e-zine. Wants "thought-provoking, creative, alternative writing. We choose work that inspires compassion, peace, and respect for diversity in original and unexpected ways." Does not want "manuscripts of full-length books." Sample: past issues available on website.

How to Contact Cover letter is required. "Send submissions to us by U.S. mail only. Include SASE. If you want us to reply your letter via e-mail, include your e-mail address! We will ask you for a digital file via e-mail, if we want to publish your submission." Reads submissions according to the following deadline: Annual Edition, June 1st. Guidelines available on website. Rights revert to poet upon publication.

Contest/Award Offerings The Burning Bush Poetry Prize.

Tips "Our readers are interested in love, the natural world, social and economic justice, liberation movements, spirituality and improving the quality of life in all communities."

🌐 ☑ INTERPRETER'S HOUSE

19 The Paddox, Oxford OX2 7PN, England. Website: www.interpretershouse.org.uk. **Contact:** Merryn Williams, Editor. *Interpreter's House*, published 3 times/year in February, June, and October, prints short stories and poetry. Wants "good poetry, not too long." Does not want "Christmas-card verse or incomprehensible poetry." Has published poetry by Dannie Abse, Tony Curtis, Pauline Stainer, Alan Brownjohn, Peter Redgrove, and R.S. Thomas. *Interpreter's House* is 74 pages, A5, with attractive cover design. Receives about 1,000 poems/year, accepts up to 5%. Press run is 300 (200 subscribers). Single copy: £3 plus 55p. postage; subscription: £12 for 3 issues. Sample: £3.50.

How to Contact All work is dealt with swiftly. Usually no more than one poem is accepted, and writers who have already appeared in the magazine are asked to wait for at least a year before submitting again. Submit 5 poems at a time. No previously published poems or simultaneous submissions. Cover letter is preferred. Time between acceptance and publication is 2 weeks to 3 months. Often comments on rejected poems. Guidelines available for SASE (or SAE and IRC). Responds "fast." Pays 1 contributor's copy.

Contest/Award Offerings Sponsors the Bedford Open Poetry Competition. Send SAE and IRC for details. The 2009/10 Bedford Open Poetry competition is now closed.

☑ ◎ INVERTED-A HORN

Inverted-A, Inc., P.O. Box 267, Licking MO 65542. E-mail: amnfn@well.com. **Contact:** Nets Katz, and Aya Katz, editors.

Magazines Needs *Inverted-A Horn*, published irregularly, welcomes political topics, social issues, and science fiction. Wants traditional poetry with meter and rhyme. Does not want to see anything "modern, formless, existentialist." *Inverted-A Horn* is usually 9 pages, magazine-sized, offset-printed. Press run is 300. Sample: SASE with postage for 2 ounces (subject to availability).

How to Contact Considers simultaneous submissions. Accepts e-mail submissions (as attachment, ASCII). Responds in 4 months. Pays 1 contributor's copy; offers 40% discount on additional copies.

Additional Information Inverted-A, Inc. is a very small press that evolved from publishing technical manuals for other products. "Our interests center on freedom, justice, and honor." Publishes 1 chapbook/year.

Tips "I strongly recommend that would-be contributors avail themselves of this opportunity to explore what we are looking for. Most of the submissions we receive do not come close."

☑ IODINE POETRY JOURNAL

P.O. Box 18548, Charlotte NC 28218-0548. (704)595-9526. E-mail: iodineopencut@aol.com. Website: www.iodinepoetryjournal.com. **Contact:** Jonathan K. Rice, editor/publisher.

• Poetry published in *Iodine Poetry Journal* has been selected for inclusion in *The Best American Poetry*.

Magazines Needs *Iodine Poetry Journal*, published semiannually, provides "a venue for both emerging and established poets." Wants "good poetry of almost any style, including form (e.g., pantoum and sestina) and experimental." Does not want rhyme, religion, or pornography. Has published poetry by Fred Chappell, Colette Inez, Ron Koertge, Dorianne Laux, and R.T. Smith. *Iodine Poetry Journal* is 84 pages, digest-sized, perfect-bound, with full-color laminated cover, includes ads. Receives about 2,000 poems/year, accepts about 75 poems/issue. Press run is 350. Single copy: $7; subscription: $12/year (2 issues) $22 for 2 years (4 issues). Sample: "Back issues vary in price." Make checks payable to *Iodine Poetry Journal*.

How to Contact Submit 3-5 poems at a time. Lines/poem: 40 or less preferred, "but not totally averse to longer poems." No previously published poems or simultaneous submissions. Accepts e-mail submissions from international poets only; no disk submissions. Cover letter is preferred. "Always include SASE, and specify if SASE is for return of manuscript or reply only. I like a brief introduction of yourself in the cover letter." Reads submissions year round. Submit seasonal poems 6 months in advance. Time between acceptance and publication is 6 months to 1 year. Poems are circulated to an editorial board. "I occasionally have other readers assist in the selection process, but editor makes the final decision." Sometimes comments on rejected poems. Guidelines available in magazine, for SASE, or on website. Responds in 2-3 months. Sometimes sends prepublication galleys. Pays 1 contributor's copy and discounts extra copies of the issue in which work appears. Acquires first North American serial rights.

Also Offers "We no longer publish our broadside, *Open Cut*."

$ ☑ THE IOWA REVIEW

308 EPB, University of Iowa, Iowa City IA 52242. (319)335-0462. E-mail: iowa-review@ uiowa.edu. Website: www.iowareview.org. **Contact:** Russell Valentino, Editor.

• Poetry published in *The Iowa Review* has appeared often in *The Best American Poetry* and *The Pushcart Prize*.

Magazines Needs *The Iowa Review*, published 3 times/year, prints fiction, poetry, essays, reviews, and, occasionally, interviews. "We simply look for poems that, at the time we read and choose, we find we admire. No specifications as to form, length, style, subject matter, or purpose. Though we print work from established writers, we're always delighted when we discover new talent." *The Iowa Review* is 192 pages, professionally printed, flat-spined. Receives about 5,000 submissions/year, accepts up to 100. Press run is 2,900; 1,500 distributed to stores. Subscription: $25. Sample: $9.

How to Contact Submit 3-6 poems at a time. No e-mail submissions. Cover letter (with title of work and genre) is encouraged. SASE required. Reads submissions "only during the Fall semester, September through November, and then contest entries in the spring." Time between acceptance and publication is "around a year." Occasionally comments on rejected poems or offers suggestions on accepted poems. Responds in up to 4 months. Pays $1.50/line of poetry, $40 minimum. Acquires first North American serial rights, non-exclusive anthology rights, and non-exclusive electronic rights.

Contest/Award Offerings *The Iowa Review* Award in Poetry, Fiction, and Essay.

☑ ◎ IRIS: A JOURNAL ABOUT WOMEN

UVA Women's Center, P.O. Box 800588, Charlottesville VA 22908. E-mail: irismagazine@gmail.com. Website: http://iris.virginia.edu. **Contact:** Katy Shively, submissions.

How to Contact Submit no more than 5 poems at a time. Considers simultaneous submissions if notified immediately of acceptance elsewhere. Accepts e-mail submissions (pasted into body of message; no attachments); no fax submissions. For E-mail submissions, include "Submission Poetry" in subject line; for postal submissions, include SASE. Cover letter is required. "Include list of poems submitted and a brief bio. Name, address, and phone number should be listed on every poem." Publishes theme issues. Upcoming themes available in magazine, for SASE, or on website. Guidelines available for SASE or on website. Responds in 6 months. Pays 5 contributor's copies. Acquires first rights. Email submissions to irissubmissions@gmail.com with subject line containing the genre of your submission, i.e. Submission-Poetry. Please both paste your submission in the body of the email and attach a copy. Include contact information and a short bio with each. We normally respond to online submissions within several months. We accept simultaneous submissions, but please let us know immediately if the manuscript is accepted elsewhere. We are unable to offer payment for online submissions at this time.

Tips "The poetry staff at *iris* is interested in pieces exploring all aspects of women's lives—especially the lives of younger women. Because many poems are on similar topics, freshness of imagery and style are even more important."

◎ ITALIAN AMERICANA

URI/FCCE, 80 Washington St., Providence RI 02908-1803. (401)277-5306. E-mail: bonomoal@ital.uri.edu. Website: http://www.uri.edu/prov/research/italianamericana/italianamericana.html. **Contact:** Michael Palma, Poetry Editor. *Italian Americana*, published twice/year, uses 16-20 poems of "no more than 3 pages." Does not want "trite nostalgia about grandparents." Has published poetry by Mary Jo Salter and Jay Parini. *Italian Americana* is 150-200 pages, digest-sized, professionally printed, flat-spined, with glossy card cover. Press run is 1,000. Singly copy: $10; subscription: $20/year, $35 for 2 years. Sample: $7.

How to Contact Submit no more than 3 poems at a time. "Single copies of poems for submissions are sufficient." No previously published poems or simultaneous submissions. Cover letter is not required "but helpful." Name on first page of ms only. Occasionally comments on rejected poems. Responds in 6 weeks. Acquires first rights. Reviews books of poetry in 600 words, multi-book format. Send materials for review consideration to Prof. John Paul Russo, English Dept., University of Miami, Coral Gables, FL 33124.

Contest/Award Offerings Along with the National Italian American Foundation, *Italian Americana* co-sponsors the annual $1,000 John Ciardi Award for Lifetime Contribution to Poetry. *Italian Americana* also presents $250 fiction or memoir award annually; and $1,500 in history prizes.

JERRY JAZZ MUSICIAN

2207 NE Broadway, Portland OR 97232. (503)287-5570. Fax: (801)749-9896. E-mail: jm@jerryjazz.com. Website: www.jerryjazz.com.

Magazines Needs *Jerry Jazz Musician*, published monthly online, "celebrates mid-20th century America, with an emphasis on jazz, film, literature, art, civil rights history, and politics of the era. Open to all topics and poetic forms." Considers poetry by children and teens. Has published poetry by Pablo Neruda, Jim Harrison, Kenneth Rexroth, Golda Soloman, and Bunny M. Receives about 300 poems/year, accepts about 50. Has 4,000 subscribers; distributed free to 150,000 unique Internet visitors/month.

How to Contact Submit 1-2 poems at a time. Lines/poem: 6-100. Considers previously published poems and simultaneous submissions. Accepts e-mail submissions. "Would prefer e-mail submissions pasted into message; however, if font and style are essential to the poem's success, will accept a Microsoft Word attachment." Cover letter is preferred. Reads submissions year round. Submit seasonal poems 4 months in advance. Time between acceptance and publication is 1 month. "Editor consults with a variety of readers, or may make choice on his own." Often comments on rejected poems. Guidelines available on website. Responds in 1 month. Poet retains all rights.

JEWISH CURRENTS

POB 111, Accord NY 12404. (212)889-2523. E-mail: jewishcurrents@circle.org. Website: www.jewishcurrents.org. **Contact:** Lawrence Bush, editor.

Magazines Needs *Jewish Currents*, published 4 times/year, prints articles, reviews, essays, visual art, and poetry "about Jewish subjects or presenting a Jewish point of view on an issue of interest, including translations from Yiddish (original texts should be submitted with translations)." *Jewish Currents* is 48 pages, magazine-sized, offset-printed, saddle-stapled with a full-color arts section, "Jcultcha & Funny Pages." Press run is 700. Subscription: $25/year. Sample: $5.

How to Contact Submit 4 poems at a time with a cover letter. No previously published poems or simultaneous submissions. Cover letter is required. "Include brief bio with author's publishing history." Poems should be typed, double-spaced; include SASE. Time between acceptance and publication is up to 2 years. Often comments on rejected poems.

Responds within 3 months. Always sends prepublication galleys. Pays 3 contributor's copies. Reviews books of poetry.

Tips "Be intelligent, original, unexpected, comprehensible."

$ ☑ ◎ JEWISH WOMEN'S LITERARY ANNUAL

NCJW Women New York Section, 820 Second Ave., New York NY 10017. (212)751-9223. E-mail: info@ncjwny.org. *Jewish Women's Literary Annual*, published in April, prints poetry and fiction by Jewish women. Wants "poems by Jewish women on any topic, but of the highest literary quality." Has published poetry by Linda Zisquit, Merle Feld, Helen Papell, Enid Dame, Marge Piercy, and Lesléa Newman. *Jewish Women's Literary Annual* is 230 pages, digest-sized, perfect-bound, with laminated card cover. Receives about 1,500 poems/year, accepts about 10%. Press run is 1,500. Subscription: $18 for 3 issues. Sample: $7.50.

How to Contact No previously published poems. Poems are circulated to an editorial board. Often comments on rejected poems. Guidelines available for SASE. Responds in up to 5 months. Pays 1 contributor's copy plus a small honorarium. Rights remain with the poet.

Tips "Send only your very best. We are looking for humor, as well as other things, but nothing cutesy or smart-aleck. We do no politics; prefer topics other than 'Holocaust'."

☑ ◎ JOEL'S HOUSE PUBLICATIONS

New Beginning Ministry, Inc., P.O. Box 328, Beach Lake PA 18405-0328. (570)729-8709. E-mail: newbeginmin@ezaccess.net. Website: http://newbeginningmin.org. *Joel's House Publications*, published annually in December, is a newsletter produced by New Beginning Ministry, Inc., a nonprofit corporation. New Beginning's publication is utilized to promote literacy, creativity, spirituality, recovery, and the arts. Wants "poetry that is related to recovery, spirituality; also Christian poetry. Will consider any length, positive topic, and structure. No poetry that is inappropriately sexually graphic or discriminatory in nature." Considers poetry by children and teens. Has published poetry by Cynthia Brackett-Vincent, John Waddington-Feather, Wendy Apgar, K.F. Homer, Melanie Schurr, and William DeWitt Romig. *Joel's House Publications* is 10-20 pages, digest-sized, offset-printed, saddle-stapled, with cardstock cover. Receives about 25-50 poems/year, accepts about 25%. Press run is 1,000 (100 subscribers); 200 distributed free to mailing list. Subscription: $5/year (one issue). Sample: $2 plus p&h. Make checks payable to New Beginning Ministry, Inc.

How to Contact Submit 3-5 poems at a time, typed, with name and address on each poem. No previously published poems or simultaneous submissions. Accepts fax, e-mail, or disk submissions. Cover letter is preferred. "Always include a SASE." Reads submissions year round. Time between acceptance and publication is up to one year. Seldom comments on rejected poems. Guidelines available for SASE. Responds in up to 6 weeks. Always sends prepublication galleys. Pays 2 contributor's copies. Acquires first rights. "Held every December, the William DeWitt Romig Poetry Award will be given to the poet who best demonstrates life through the art of poetry." Guidelines available for SASE. Writing retreats (check website for details).

Tips "Keep writing—revise, revise, revise! If you write poetry, you are a poet. Be true to your craft."

⚡ ✅ JONES AV.

OEL Press, 88 Dagmar Ave., Toronto ON M4M 1W1, Canada. (416)461-8739. E-mail: oel@interlog.com. Website: www.interlog.com/~oel. **Contact:** Pual Schwartz, Editor/Publisher.

Magazines Needs *Jones Av.*, published quarterly, contains "poems from the lyric to the ash can; starting poets and award winners." Wants poems "concise in thought and image. Prose poems sometimes. Rhymed poetry is very difficult to do well these days; it better be good." Has published poetry by Bert Almon, Michael Estabrook, John Grey, Bernice Lever, B.Z. Niditch, and Elana Wolff. *Jones Av.* is 24 pages, digest-sized, photocopied, saddle-stapled, with card cover. Receives about 300 poems/year, accepts 30-40%. Press run is 100. Subscription: $12. Sample: $3. Make checks payable to Paul Schwartz .

How to Contact Submit 3-5 poems at a time. Lines/poem: up to 30. No previously published poems or simultaneous submissions. Accepts e-mail submissions (pasted into body of message). Cover letter is required. Include bio and SASE (or SAE with IRCs). "Remember, U.S. stamps cannot be used in Canada." Time between acceptance and publication is up to 1 year. Often comments on rejected poems. Occasionally publishes theme issues. Upcoming themes available in magazine. Guidelines available for SASE or on website. Responds in 3 months. Pays 1 contributor's copy. Acquires first rights. Staff reviews books/chapbooks of poetry and other magazines/journals in 50-75 words, multi-book format. Send materials for review consideration.

Tips "Request and study a sample issue of the publication if you are not familiar with the editor's taste."

🌐 ✅ ◎ THE DAVID JONES JOURNAL

(Specizlied: David Jones; the Great War; mythology; visual arts), The David Jones Society, 22 Gower Rd., Sketty, Swansea, W. Glam SA2 9BY Wales. (44)(179)220-6144. Fax: (44)(179)247-5037. E-mail: anne.price-owen@smu.ac.uk. Established 1997. **Contact:** Anne Price-Owen, editor.

Magazines Needs *The David Jones Journal*, published annually, features "material related to painter-poet David Jones, War, mythology, religion, poetry, and the visual arts." Wants "anything in the spirit of David Jones." Has published poetry by Seamus Heaney, John Mole, John Montague, R.S. Thomas, Rowan Williams. *The David Jones Journal* is about 200 pages, digest-sized, camera ready-printed, perfect-bound, with full-color card cover. Receives about 30 poems/year, accepts about 12%. Press run is 400 (300 subscribers). Single copy: £10/$25; subscription: £20/$35. Make checks payable to The David Jones Society.

How to Contact Submit 1 poem at a time. Considers simultaneous submissions; no previously published poems. Accepts e-mail and disk submissions. Cover letter is preferred. Time between acceptance and publication is 6 months. "Two editors agree on publication." Occasionally publishes theme issues. Guidelines available by e-mail. Responds in 6 weeks. Sometimes sends prepublication galleys. Pays 2 contributor's copies. Acquires first rights. Reviews books/chapbooks of poetry and other magazines in 750 words, single-book format. Open to unsolicited reviews. Send materials for review consideration.

$ ⬭ ◎ THE JOURNAL

Dept. of English, The Ohio State University, 164 W. 17th Ave., Columbus OH 43210. (614)292-4076. Fax: (614)292-7816. E-mail: thejournalmag@gmail.com. Website: http://english.osu.edu/research/journals/thejournal/. **Contact:** Kathy Fagan, Editor. *The Journal*, published twice/year, includes reviews, quality fiction and nonfiction, and poetry. "We're open to all forms; we tend to favor work that gives evidence of a mature and sophisticated sense of the language." Has published poetry by Beckian Fritz Goldberg, Terrance Hayes, Bob Hicok, and Linda Bierds. *The Journal* is 128-144 pages, digest-sized, professionally printed on heavy stock. Receives about 4,000 submissions/year, accepts about 200. Press run is 1,900. Subscription: $12. Sample: $7.

How to Contact Considers simultaneous submissions, "but please notify us of this at time of submission." No fax or e-mail submissions. Occasionally comments on rejected poems. Occasionally publishes theme issues. Guidelines available on website. Responds in up to 3 months. Pays 2 contributor's copies "and an honorarium of $20-50 when funds are available." Acquires first North American rights and electronic rights. Returns rights on publication. Reviews books of poetry.

Contest/Award Offerings Chooses the winning ms in the Ohio State University Press/*The Journal Award* (see separate listing in Contests & Awards).

Tips "However else poets train or educate themselves, they must do what they can to know our language. Too much of the writing we see indicates poets do not, in many cases, develop a feel for the possibilities of language, and do not pay attention to craft. Poets should not be in a rush to publish—until they are ready."

🌐 ⬭ THE JOURNAL

Original Plus Press, 17 High St., Maryport, Cumbria CA15 6BQ England. E-mail: smithsssj@aol.com. Website: http://thesamsmith.webs.com. Established 1994. **Contact:** Sam Smith.

Magazines Needs *The Journal*, published 3 times a year, features English poetry/translations, reviews, and articles. Wants "new poetry howsoever it comes; translations and original English-language poems." Does not want "staid, generalized, all form/no content." Has published poetry by David H. Grubb, Gary Allen, and Ozdemir Asaf. *The Journal* is 40 pages, A4, offset-printed, stapled. Receives about 1,000 poems/year, accepts about 5%. Press run is 100-150. Single copy: £4; subscription: £11 for 3 issues. Outside UK, single copy: £5; subscription: £14 for 3 issues. Make checks payable to Sam Smith or through PayPal. Back issues £2.

How to Contact Submit up to 6 poems at a time. Considers previously published poems and simultaneous submissions. Accepts e-mail submissions. Cover letter is preferred. "Please send 2 IRCs with hard-copy submissions." Time between acceptance and publication is up to 1 year. Often comments on rejected poems. Guidelines available for SASE (or SAE and IRC). Responds in 1 month. Always sends prepublication galleys. Pays 1 contributor's copy.

Additional Information Since 1997, Original Plus Press has been publishing collections of poetry. Has recently published books by Chris Hardy, Brian Daldorph, Siobhan Logan, Alice Lenkiewics and Helen Bunkingham. But from now will be publishing only chapbooks. Send SASE (or SAE and IRC) or e-mail for details.

Tips "I prefer poetry that has been written with thought—both to what it is saying and how it is being said."

☑ ◎ JOURNAL OF NEW JERSEY POETS

English Dept., County College of Morris, 214 Center Grove Rd., Randolph NJ 07869-2086. (973)328-5471. Fax: (973)328-5425. E-mail: szulauf@ccm.edu. **Contact:** Sander Zulauf, editor. Debra Demattio, Emily Birx, Matt Ayres, and Philip Chase, associate editors. (Specialized: of, by, for NJ poets)

Magazines Needs *Journal of New Jersey Poets*, published annually in April, is "not necessarily about New Jersey—but of, by, and for poets from New Jersey." Wants "serious work that conveys the essential, real, whole emotional moment of the poem to the reader without sentimentality." Has published poetry by Joe Weil, X.J. Kennedy, Marvin Silbersher, Tina Kelley, Gerald Stern, Kenneth Burke, and Catherine Doty. *Journal of New Jersey Poets* is about 90 pages, perfect-bound, offset-printed on recycled stock. Press run is 600. Single copy: $10; subscription: $16 for 2 issues ($16/issue for institutions). Sample: $5.

How to Contact Poets who live or work in New Jersey (or who formerly lived or worked here) are invited to submit up to 3 poems with their New Jersey bio data mentioned in the cover letter. Accepts fax and e-mail submissions, "but they will not be acknowledged nor returned. Include SASE with sufficient postage for return of manuscript, or provide instructions to recycle." Annual deadline for submissions: September 1. Time between acceptance and publication is within 1 year. Guidelines available for SASE or by e-mail. Responds in up to 1 year. Pays 2 contributor's copies and a one-year subscription. Acquires first North American serial rights. All reviews are solicited. Send 2 copies of books for review consideration.

Additional Information Awarded first New Jersey poets prize to Stephen Dobyns in 2010. For prize guidelines, e-mail editor Sander Zulauf.

Tips "Read the *Journal* before submitting. Realize we vote on everything submitted, and rejection is mostly an indication of the quantity of submissions received and the enormous number of New Jersey poets submitting quality work."

☑ JOURNAL OF REGIONAL CRITICISM

Arjuna Library Press, 1025 Garner St., D, Space 18, Colorado Springs CO 80905-1774. E-mail: pfuphoff@earthlink.net. Website: http://home.earthlink.net/ ~ pfuphoff/. **Contact:** CT. Pf. Joseph A. Uphoff, Jr., Executive Director.

Magazines Needs *Journal of Regional Criticism*, published frequently in varied format, features "surrealist prose poetry, visual poetry, dreamlike, short and long works; no obscene, profane (will criticize but not publish), unpolished work." Has published work by Aliya Mehdi, Gaia Experiment, Acid Jazz Jam, Randall Brock, and Ronald Orszag. *Journal of Regional Criticism* is published in JPG files (on CD-ROM) of collage, photography, writing, mathematical, fine art theory, and criticism.

How to Contact Send 1 or 2 short poems at a time. "Upon request will treat material as submitted for reprint, one-time rights." Accepts submissions by postal mail only, including CD-ROM: PDF or JPG, ASF. Cover letter is required. Include SASE. Guidelines (on sample CD) available for SASE. Reviews books of poetry "occasionally." Send materials for review consideration.

Additional Information "The Arjuna Library Press is avant-garde, designed to endure the transient quarters and marginal funding of the literary phenomenon (as a tradition) while presenting a context for the development of current mathematical ideas in regard to theories of art, literature, and performance; publication is now by CD-ROM, JPG, and ASF files. Each disk is unique. The poet is sent a color Xerox hard copy, poems illustrated by photographic and artistic experiments in an irregular format. Photocopy printing allows for very limited editions and irregular format. Quality is maintained as an artistic materialist practice." Publishes 6-12 disks/year, averaging 600 MB (50 pages) each. Sample: $10.

Also Offers "The Arjuna Library Digital Visual Dream Laboratory and Acoustic Studio is extending publication beyond photocopy printing while maintaining respect for artistic relics such as manuscript copies and original photographs or papers. The format will remain varied and irregular (poetic, stream of consciousness production). Poetry is published in writing and with video of poets reading their works. Austerity is due to limited resources and expense of equipment and supplies. Works are now illustrated in color. Development work is continuing of the publication of poetry by the writers listed (Mehdi, Ponce-Melendez, et. al.)."

Tips "Website exhibition of visual poetics and literature has proceeded through the Mail Art phenomenon. This is an excellent means of contacting the public in an impersonal way; it remains true that there are other venues to develop the commercial profile. As a general rule, we should use principles of scientific observation (minimum interference) such that the proferred dimensions are not strained or reconfigured. If the membership grows too large, rather than excluding contributors by pyramidal elitism, more organization can be founded. In this way, an accurate assessment can be maintained as to how many individuals are requesting service. Instead of redesigned organization, the pyramidal elitism can be established by supplemental organization. It follows that acceptance then rises to the level of competency of the artist or writer within a system that provides continuing adequate support for newcomers and advancing practitioners. Thus, we do not need a surrender by vulgar insults: irony can be separated from the other reputable constructs. The audience can gravitate to protected interests. Some of the *Journal of Regional Criticism* will be published and exhibited by the internet including sites such as Creative Thinkers International, csfreshink. com, KKFM Colorado Springs (Community Photographs), eSnips, and Open Fluxus."

☑ ◎ JOURNAL OF THE AMERICAN MEDICAL ASSOCIATION (JAMA)

(Specialized: poetry related to a medical experience), 515 N. State St., Chicago IL 60654. (312)464-2428. Fax: (312)464-5824. E-mail: jamams@jama-archives.org. Website: www. jama.com. Established 1883. **Contact:** Charlene Breedlove, associate editor.

Magazines Needs *Journal of the American Medical Association (JAMA)*, published weekly, includes a poetry and medicine column and publishes poetry "in some way related to a medical experience, whether from the point of view of a health care worker or patient, or simply an observer. No unskilled poetry." Has published poetry by Jack Coulehan, Floyd Skloot, and Walt McDonald. *JAMA* is magazine-sized, flat-spined, with glossy paper cover. Receives about 750 poems/year, accepts about 7%. Has 360,000 subscribers (369 libraries). Subscription: $66. Sample: free, "no SASE needed."

How to Contact No previously published poems or simultaneous submissions. Accepts submissions by fax or through *JAMA*'s Web-based submissions and review system at http:// manuscripts.jama.com (or click the "Information for Authors/Reviewers" button on the www.jama.com home page). "I appreciate inclusion of a brief cover letter; mention of other publications and special biographical notes are always of interest." Publishes theme issues (i.e., in 2007: access to care; malaria; chronic diseases of children; violence/human rights; medical education; poverty and human development). "However, we would rather that poems relate obliquely to the theme." Guidelines available on website. Pays 1 contributor's copy, more by request. "We ask for a signed copyright release, but publication elsewhere is consistently granted."

☑ ◎ KAIMANA: LITERARY ARTS HAWAI'I

Hawai'i Literary Arts Council, P.O. Box 11213, Honolulu HI 96828. E-mail: reimersa001@ hawaii.rr.com. Website: www.hawaii.edu/hlac. **Contact:** Poetry Editor. *Kaimana: Literary Arts Hawai'i*, published annually, is the magazine of the Hawai'i Literary Arts Council. Wants poems with "some Pacific reference—Asia, Polynesia, Hawai'i—but not exclusively." Has published poetry by Kathryn Takara, Howard Nemerov, Anne Waldman, Reuel Denney, Haunani-Kay Trask, and Simon Perchik. *Kaimana* is 64-76 pages, 7½ × 10, saddle-stapled, with high-quality printing. Press run is 1,000. Subscription: $15, includes membership in HLAC. Sample: $10.

How to Contact Cover letter is preferred. Sometimes comments on rejected poems. Guidelines available in magazine or on website. Responds with "reasonable dispatch." Pays 2 contributor's copies."Hawai'i gets a lot of 'travelling regionalists,' visiting writers with inevitably superficial observations. We also get superb visiting observers who are careful craftsmen anywhere. *Kaimana* is interested in the latter, to complement our own best Hawai'i writers."

Tips "Poets published in Kaimana have received the Pushcart Prize, the Hawaii Award for Literature, the Stefan Baciu Award, the Cades Award, and the John Unterecker Award."

$ ◎ KALEIDOSCOPE: EXPLORING THE EXPERIENCE OF DISABILITY THROUGH LITERATURE AND THE FINE ARTS

701 S. Main St., Akron OH 44311-1019. (330)762-9755. Fax: (330)762-0912. E-mail: mshiplett@udsakron.org. Website: www.udsakron.org/kaleidoscope.htm. **Contact:** Gail Willmett, editor-in-chief.

Magazines Needs *Kaleidoscope: Exploring the Experience of Disability through Literature and the Fine Arts*, published twice/year in January and July, is based at United Disability Services, a not-for-profit agency. Distributed by University of Akron Press. Poetry should deal with the experience of disability, but is not limited to that experience when the writer has a disability. Wants high-quality poetry with vivid, believable images and evocative language. Does not want "stereotyping, patronizing, or offending language about disability." Has published poetry by Gerald Wheeler, Jeff Worley, Barbara Crooker, and Sheryl L. Nelms. *Kaleidoscope* is 64 pages, magazine-sized, professionally printed, saddle-stapled, with 4-color semigloss card cover. Press run is 1,500 (for libraries, social service agencies, health care professionals, universities, and individual subscribers). Single copy: $6; subscription: $10 individual, $20 agency. Contact University of Akron Press @uapress@uakron.edu.

How to Contact Submit up to 6 poems at a time. Considers previously published poems and simultaneous submissions "as long as we are notified in both instances." Accepts fax and e-mail submissions. Cover letter is required. Send photocopies with SASE for return of work. "All submissions must be accompanied by an autobiographical sketch and should be double-spaced, with pages numbered and author's name on each page." Reads submissions by March 1 and August 1 deadlines. Publishes theme issues. Upcoming themes available in magazine, for SASE, by fax, e-mail, or on website. Guidelines available for SASE, by fax, e-mail, and on website. Responds within 3 weeks; acceptance or rejection may take 6 months. Pays $10-25 plus 2 contributor's copies. Rights revert to author upon publication. Staff reviews books of poetry. Send materials for review consideration.

☑ KARAMU

Dept. of English, Eastern Illinois University, Charleston IL 61920. Website: www.eiu. edu/~karamu. **Contact:** Olga Abella, Editor.

- *Karamu* has received grants from the Illinois Arts Council, and has won recognition and money awards in the IAC Literary Awards competition.

Magazines Needs *Karamu*, published annually in May or June, aims to "provide a forum for the best contemporary poetry and fiction that comes our way. We especially like to print the works of new writers. We like to see poetry that shows a good sense of what's being done with poetry currently." Wants "poetry that builds around real experiences, real images, and real characters, and that avoids abstraction, overt philosophizing, and fuzzy pontifications. We prefer well-structured free verse, poetry with an inner, sub-surface structure as opposed to, let's say, the surface structure of rhymed quatrains. We have definite preferences in terms of style and form, but no such preferences in terms of length or subject matter." Does not want "the openly didactic poem. We don't want poems that preach against or for some political or religious viewpoint. The poem should first be a poem." Has published poetry by Lauren Lawrence, Susan Johnson, James Hoggard, Christopher Zuver, John Grey, and Elizabeth Johnson-Miller. *Karamu* is 150 pages, digest-sized, handsomely printed (narrow margins), with matte cover. Receives submissions from about 300 poets each year, accepts 40-50 poems. Press run is 500 (300 subscribers, 15 libraries). Single copy: $8. Sample: $6 for 2 back issues.

How to Contact Submit no more than 5 poems at a time. No previously published poems or simultaneous submissions. "Always include a SASE for reply and return of material. Sufficient postage is necessary for return of work." Reads submissions September 1-February 15 only; "for fastest decision, submit January through February 15." Critiques "a few of the better poems. We want the poet to consider our comments and then submit new work." Time between acceptance and publication is up to 1 year. Occasionally publishes theme issues. Guidelines available for SASE. Pays 1 contributor's copy. Acquires first serial rights.

Tips "Follow the standard advice: Know your market. Read contemporary poetry and the magazines you want to be published in. Be patient."

◻ ◎ KELSEY REVIEW

Liberal Arts Division, Mercer County Community College, P.O. Box B, Trenton NJ 08690. E-mail: kelsey.review@mccc.edu. Website: www.mccc.edu/community_kelsey-review. shtml. **Contact:** Holly-Katharine Matthews. *Kelsey Review*, published annually in September by Mercer County Community College, serves as "an outlet for literary talent of people living and working in Mercer County, New Jersey only." Has no specifications as to form, length, subject matter, or style. Fiction: 4,000 word limit. Poetry: Not more than 6 pages.

Nonfiction: 2,500 word limit. Black and White art. Does not want to see poetry "about kittens and puppies." Has published poetry by Vida Chu, Carolyn Foote Edelmann, and Mary Mallery. *Kelsey Review* is about 90 glossy pages, 7x11, with paper cover. Receives 100+ submissions/year, accepts 10. Press run is 2,000; all distributed free to contributors, area libraries, bookstores, and schools.

How to Contact Submit up to 6 poems at a time. No previously published poems or simultaneous submissions. No fax or e-mail submissions. Manuscripts must be typed. Submit poems by May 15 deadline. Send SASE for returns. Guidelines available by e-mail. Responds in August of each year. Pays 3 contributor's copies. All rights revert to authors.

$ ☑ THE KENYON REVIEW

Finn House, Kenyon College, Gambier OH 43022. (740)427-5208. Fax: (740)427-5417. E-mail: kenyonreview@kenyon.edu. Website: KenyonReview.org. **Contact:** David Lynn, editor.

Magazines Needs *The Kenyon Review*, published quarterly, contains poetry, fiction, essays, criticism, reviews, and memoirs. Features all styles, forms, lengths, and subject matters. Considers translations. Has published poetry by Billy Collins, Diane Ackerman, John Kinsella, Carol Muske-Dukes, Diane di Prima, and Seamus Heaney. *The Kenyon Review* is 180 pages, digest-sized, flat-spined. Receives about 6,000 submissions/year. Press run is 6,000. Also now publishes *KR Online*, a separate and complementary literary magazine. Sample: $12 (includes postage).

How to Contact Submit up to 6 poems at a time. No previously published poems or simultaneous submissions. Accepts submissions through online registration only at www. kenyon-review.org/submissions (group poems in a single document; do not submit poems individually). Reads submissions September 15-January 15. Guidelines available on website. Responds in up to 4 months. Payment for accepted work is made upon publication. Author retains rights and will receive a contract upon acceptance. Does not consider unsolicited reviews.

Tips "Read recent issues of the *Review* to become familiar with the type and quality of writing being published before submitting your work."

☑ ◎ THE KERF

College of the Redwoods, 883 W. Washington Blvd., Crescent City CA 95531. (707) 476-4370. E-mail: ken-letko@redwoods.edu. Website: http://www.redwoods.edu/Departments/english/poets&writers/clm.htm. **Contact:** Ken Letko, editor.

Magazines Needs *The Kerf*, published annually in fall, features "poetry that speaks to the environment and humanity." Wants "poetry that exhibits an environmental consciousness." Considers poetry by children and teens. Has published poetry by Ruth Daigon, Alice D'Alessio, James Grabill, George Keithley, and Paul Willis. *The Kerf* is 54 pages, digest-sized, printed via Docutech, saddle-stapled, with CS2 coverstock. Receives about 2,000 poems/year, accepts up to 3%. Press run is 400 (150 shelf sales); 100 distributed free to contributors and writing centers. Sample: $5. Make checks payable to College of the Redwoods.

How to Contact Submit up to 5 poems (7 pages maximum) at a time. No previously published poems or simultaneous submissions. Reads submissions January 15-March 31 only. Time between acceptance and publication is 3-4 months. "Our editors debate (argue for or against) the inclusion of each manuscript." Seldom comments on rejected poems. Guidelines available for SASE. Responds in 2 months. Sometimes sends prepublication galleys. Pays one contributor's copy. Acquires first North American serial rights.

Tips "Provide insights."

$ ☑ THE KIT-CAT REVIEW

244 Halstead Ave., Harrison NY 10528-3611. (914)835-4833. E-mail: kitcatreview@gmail. com. *The Kit-Cat Review*, published quarterly, is named "after the 18th-century Kit-Cat Club whose members included Addison, Steele, Congreve, Vanbrugh, and Garth. Its purpose is to promote/discover excellence and originality." Wants quality work—traditional, modern, experimental. Has published poetry by Coral Hull, Virgil Suaárez, Margret J. Hoehn, Louis Phillips, Chayym Zeldis, and Marin Sorescu. *The Kit-Cat Review* is 75 pages, digest-sized, laser-printed/photocopied, saddle-stapled, with colored card cover. Receives about 1,000 poems/year. Press run is 500. "*The Kit-Cat Review* is part of the collections of the University of Wisconsin (Madison) and the State University of New York (Buffalo)." Subscription: $25. Sample: $7. Make checks payable to Claudia Fletcher.

How to Contact Submit any number of poems at a time. Considers previously published poems and simultaneous submissions. "Cover letter should contain any relevant bio." Time between acceptance and publication is 2 months. Responds within 6 months. Pays up to $100/poem plus 2 contributor's copies. Acquires first or one-time rights.

▣ ◯ KOTAPRESS LOSS JOURNAL

(206)251-6706. E-mail: editor@kotapress.com. Website: www.kotapress.com; www. kotapress.blogspot.com. **Contact:** Kara L.C. Jones, editor.

Magazines Needs *KotaPress Loss Journal*, published quarterly online with blogs almost daily, provides support "of the grief and healing process after the death of a child. We publish *only* nonfictional poetry that somehow relates to grief and healing in relation to the death of a child. Please do not make up poems about this kind of loss and send them just to get in the magazine; it is insulting to many of our readers who are living this reality. As always, our interest is more in the content and story rather than one's ability to write in form; more in the ideas of poetry therapy rather than the academic, critique, competitive ideas normally fostered in universities." Has published poetry by John Fox, Poppy Hullings, Patricia Wellingham-Jones, Carol Jo Horn, and Sarah Bain.

How to Contact "Please read the *Loss Journal* site and blog before sending anything. Then send a letter explaining your interest in contributing. We are interested in knowing how your personal experiences with death, dying, grief, and healing are playing out in the specific poems you are submitting. Include a bio if you wish to see one published with your poems after acceptance. Send your letter, poems, and bio as text all in one e-mail. Multiple e-mails will be ignored. File attachments will be deleted without ever being opened or acknowledged. Submissions without letter explaining your interest will be ignored. Make sure the subject line of your e-mail says 'Loss Journal Submission'—we get over 600 e-mails a day, most of them spam, so we sort and read based on the subject line." Reads submissions year round on a rolling basis. Time between acceptance and publication is up to 6 months. Guidelines available on website. Responds in 2-6 months. Acquires one-time electronic rights and archive rights. "We do not remove works from our archives. Please see our website to find out more about us and about what we offer. We look forward to hearing from you and reading your poetry."

Tips "If you are interested in contributing to our *Loss Journal*, it is really important that you read the journal first. This will tell you a lot about the voice of the work we publish and how your poems might 'fit the bill' for us. Please understand that while we acknowledge that all losses are difficult, we do not equate pet loss with child loss—and we do not equate fictional ideas about loss with the reality of death and dying. Read the journal first. Then submit your poems if you feel they fit the mission of our journal."

⊕ ☑ KRAX

63 Dixon Lane, Leeds, Yorkshire LS12 4RR, England. **Contact:** Andy Robson, Editor. *Krax*, published annually in the summer, prints contemporary poetry from England and America. Wants "poetry that is light-hearted and witty; original ideas." All forms and styles considered. Does not want "haiku, religious, or topical politics." Has published poetry by Dean Blehert, Gail Holmes, and Salena Godden. *Krax* is 72 pages, digest-sized, offset-printed, saddle-stapled. Receives up to 700 submissions/year, accepts about 10%. Single copy: £3.50 ($7); subscription: £10 ($20). Sample: $1 (75p). Cheques payable to A. Robson.

How to Contact Submit 6 poems maximum at a time. Lines/poem: 2,000 words maximum. No previously published poems or simultaneous submissions. No disk submissions. Cover letter is preferred. "Writer's name on same sheet as poem. SASE or SAE with IRC encouraged but not vital." Responds in 2 months. Pays 1 contributor's copy. Reviews books of poetry ("brief, individual comments; no outside reviews"). Send materials for review consideration.

Tips "Rewrite only to improve structure or format—unnecessary rewriting usually destroys the original spontaneity and rhythm."

☑ LAKE EFFECT: A JOURNAL OF THE LITERARY ARTS

School of Humanities & Social Sciences, Penn State Erie, 4951 College Dr., Erie PA 16563-1501. (814)898-6281. Fax: (814)898-6032. E-mail: gol1@psu.edu. Website: www.pserie.psu.edu/lakeeffect. **Contact:** George Looney, editor-in-chief. Member: CLMP.

Magazines Needs *Lake Effect*, published annually in March/April, provides "an aesthetic venue for writing that uses language precisely to forge a genuine and rewarding experience for our readers. *Lake Effect* wishes to publish writing that rewards more than 1 reading, and to present side-by-side the voices of established and emerging writers." Wants "poetry aware of, and wise about, issues of craft in forming language that is capable of generating a rich and rewarding reading experience." Does not want "sentimental verse reliant on clichés." Has published poetry by Jim Daniels, Beckian Fritz Goldberg, David Kirby, Susan Ludvigson, Harry Humes, and Chase Twichell. *Lake Effect* is 180 pages, digest-sized, offset-printed, perfect-bound, with gloss-by-flat film lamination cover. Receives about 3,000 poems/year, accepts about 1%. Press run is 800 (300 shelf sales); 300 distributed free to contributors and writing programs. Single copy: $6; subscription: $6. Make checks payable to The Pennsylvania State University.

How to Contact Submit 3-5 poems at a time. Considers simultaneous submissions; no previously published poems. No fax, e-mail, or disk submissions. Cover letter is required. Reads submissions year round. Time between acceptance and publication is up to 4 months. "The poetry staff reads the poems, meets and discusses them to come to a consensus. Poetry editor, along with editor-in-chief, makes final decisions." Occasionally comments on rejected poems. Guidelines available in magazine or on website. Responds in up to 4 months. Pays 2 contributor's copies. Acquires first North American serial rights.

Tips "*Lake Effect* strives to provide an attractive venue for the good work of both established and emerging writers. We care about the integrity of poetry, and care for the poems we accept."

⊕ ◎ LANDFALL: NEW ZEALAND ARTS AND LETTERS

Otago University Press, P.O. Box 56, Dunedin , New Zealand. (64)(3)479-8807. Fax: (64) (3)479-8385. E-mail: landfall@otago.ac.nz. Website: www.otago.ac.nz/press/landfall. **Contact:** Richard Reeve, coordinator.

Magazines Needs *Landfall: New Zealand Arts and Letters*, published twice/year in May and November, focuses "primarily on New Zealand literature and arts. It publishes new fiction, poetry, commentary, and interviews with New Zealand artists and writers, and reviews of New Zealand books." Single issue: $29.95 NZD; subscription: $45 NZD (2 issues) for New Zealand subscribers, $30 AUD for Australian subscribers, $30 USD for other overseas subscribers.

How to Contact No fax or e-mail submissions. "Once accepted, contributions should, if possible, also be submitted on disk." Submissions must be typed and include SASE. Publishes theme issues. Guidelines available for SASE. New Zealand poets should write for further information.

▣ ▢ LANGUAGEANDCULTURE.NET

4000 Pimlico Dr., Suite 114-192, Pleasanton CA 94588. E-mail: review@languageandculture. net. Website: www.languageandculture.net. **Contact:** Liz Fortini, editor.

Magazines Needs *Languageandculture.net*, published twice/year online, prints contemporary poetry in English. Also accepts translations of Spanish, French, German, Italian, and Russian; "other languages under review." No restrictions on form. Considers poetry by teens. Publishes 20-40 poems/issue.

How to Contact Submit up to 5 poems at a time. Lines/poem: 70 maximum. Considers previously published poems and simultaneous submissions. Accepts e-mail submissions; no disk submissions. "Return e-mail address must be included." Cover letter is preferred. Include brief bio. Reads submissions "yearly." Time between acceptance and publication "varies; no longer than 6-8 months." Poems are circulated to an editorial board. Rarely comments on rejected poems. No payment. Acquires one-time electronic rights.

Tips "Enrich your lives with different perspectives and poetry styles."

$ ▢ ◉ LEADING EDGE

4087 JKB, Provo UT 84602. E-mail: fiction@leadingedgemagazine.com. Website: www. leadingedgemagazine.com. **Contact:** poetry director. (Specialized: science fiction/fantasy only)

Magazines Needs *Leading Edge*, published biannually, is a journal of science fiction and fantasy. Wants "high-quality poetry reflecting both literary value and popular appeal. We accept traditional science fiction and fantasy poetry, but we like innovative stuff." Does not want "graphic sex, violence, or profanity." Considers poetry by children and teens. Has published poetry by Michael Collings, Tracy Ray, Susan Spilecki, and Bob Cook. *Leading Edge* is digest-sized. Receives about 60 poems/year, accepts about 6. Single copy: $5.95; subscription: $10 (2 issues), $20 (4 issues), $27.50 (6 issues).

How to Contact Submit 1 or more poems at a time. No simultaneous submissions or previously published poems. No e-mail submissions. Cover letter is preferred. "Include name, address, phone number, length of poem, title, and type of poem at the top of each page. Please include SASE with every submission." Guidelines available in magazine, for SASE, or on website. Responds in 2-4 months. Always sends prepublication galleys. Pays $10 for the first 4 typeset pages, $1.50 for each additional page, plus 2 contributor's copies. Acquires first North American serial rights.

Tips "Poetry is given equal standing with fiction; it is not treated as filler, but as art."

◪ THE LEAGUE OF LABORING POETS

P.O. Box 1266, San Clemente CA 91724. (626)807-0697. E-mail: laboringpoets@yahoo.com. **Contact:** Tom Conroy, publisher/editor.

Magazines Needs *The League of Laboring Poets*, published quarterly, "includes chapbook reviews, interviews with poets, some photography." Wants "all types of poetry, favors free verse, haiku, and tanka." Does not want "religious, sentimental, defamatory or bigoted poems." *The League of Laboring Poets* is 28 pages, digest-sized, offset, stiched binding, with color photograph cover. Receives about 600 poems/year, accepts about 10%. Press run is 250; distributed free to 22. Single copy: $3.50; subscription: $10/year. Make checks payable to Tom Conroy.

How to Contact Submit 3-5 poems at a time, maximum 80 lines, though will go over for a great poem. Considers previously published poems and simultaneous submissions. Considers poetry posted on a public website/blog/forum and poetry posted on a private, password-protected forum as published. Accepts e-mail submissions; no fax or disk submissions. Cover letter is preferred. Reads submissions year round. Time between acceptance and publication is up to 8 weeks. Poems are circulated to an editorial board. Never comments on rejected poems. Guidelines available in magazine or for SASE. Responds in 2 weeks. Pays 2 contributor copies, 1 poem in the Best Of issue awarded $25. Acquires one-time rights. Rights revert to poets upon publication. Reviews books and chapbooks of poetry in 600-800 words.

Additional Information Also seeking submissions for a trifold insert included with each issue featuring haiku and tanka.

Contest/Award Offerings Best of Issue offered quarterly offers a $25 prize for best poem in each issue. All poems submitted are considered. No entry fee. Deadline: January 1, April 1, August 1, and October 1.

Tips "Strong imagery and well crafted words/sounds are appreciated. No gimmicky poetry accepted."

◪ THE LEDGE

40 Maple Ave., Bellport NY 11713. E-mail: tkmonaghan@aol.com. Website: www. theledgemagazine.com. **Contact:** Timothy Monaghan, editor-in-chief/publisher.

Magazines Needs *The Ledge* seeks "passionate poems that utilize language and imagery in a fresh, original fashion. We favor visceral poems that speak to the human experience. We want inspired, imaginative, well-crafted verse and we are open to all styles and schools of writing, including formal poems. Each issue of The Ledge features a diverse and eclectic group of poets from all backgrounds and persuasions. Excellence is the ultimate criterion." Has published poetry by Michael Colonnese, Moira Egan, Elizabeth Harrington, Melody Lacina, Rick Lott, and Jennifer Perrine. *The Ledge* is 240 pages, 6x9, typeset, perfect-bound, with glossy cover. Accepts 3% of poetry received. Press run is 1,000. Single copy: $10; subscription: $20 for 2 issues, $36 for 4 issues, $48 for 6 issues.

How to Contact Submit 3-5 poems at a time. Considers simultaneous submissions; no previously published poems. Include SASE. Reads submissions October-March. Responds in 4-6 months. Pays 1 contributor's copy; $6 each additional copy. Acquires one-time rights.

Contest/Award Offerings *The Ledge* Poetry Awards Competition and *The Ledge* Poetry Chapbook Contest.

◪ ◎ LEFT CURVE

P.O. Box 472, Oakland CA 94604-0472. (510)763-7193. E-mail: editor@leftcurve.org. Website: www.leftcurve.org. **Contact:** Csaba Polony, editor.

Magazines Needs *Left Curve*, published "irregularly, about every 10 months," addresses the "problem(s) of cultural forms, emerging from the crisis of modernity, that strives to be independent from the control of dominant institutions, and free from the shackles of instrumental rationality." Wants poetry that is "critical culture, social, political, 'post-modern.' We will look at any form of poetry, from experimental to traditional." Does not want "purely formal, too self-centered, poetry that doesn't address in sufficient depth today's problems." Has published poetry by John Berger, Vincent Ferrini, Devorah Major, Jack Hirschman, and Lawrence Ferllinghetti. *Left Curve* is 144 pages, magazine-sized, offset-printed, perfect-bound, with 4-color Durosheen cover, includes ads. Press run is 2,000 (250 subscribers, 100 libraries, 1,600 shelf sales). Subscription: $35/3 issues (individuals) , $50/3 issues (institutions). Sample: $12.

How to Contact Submit up to 5 poems at a time. Lines/poem: "most of our published poetry is 1 page in length, though we have published longer poems of up to 8 pages." Accepts e-mail or disk submissions. Cover letter is required. "Explain why you are submitting." Publishes theme issues. Guidelines available for SASE, by e-mail, or on website. Responds in up to 6 months. Pays 2-3 contributor's copies. Send materials for review consideration.

◪ ◎ LIGHT

P.O. Box 7500, Chicago IL 60680. Website: www.lightquarterly.com. Lisa Markwart, Managing Editor. **Contact:** John Mella, Editor. *Light*, published quarterly, prints "light and occasional verse, satire, wordplay, puzzles, cartoons, and line art." Does not want "greeting card verse, cloying or sentimental verse." *Light* is 64 pages, perfect-bound. Single copy: $6; subscription: $22/year, $34 for 2 years, $38/year international ($28/year, $46 for 2 years for institutions). Sample (back issue): $5 plus $2 for first-class postage.

How to Contact No previously published poems or simultaneous submissions. Submit 1 poem/page. Include name, address, poem title, and page number on each page. Seldom comments on rejected poems. Guidelines available for #10 SASE. Responds in 6 months or less. Always sends prepublication galleys. Pays 2 contributor's copies to domestic contributors, 1 to foreign contributors. Send materials for review consideration.

◎ LILITH MAGAZINE: INDEPENDENT, JEWISH & FRANKLY FEMINIST

250 W. 57th St., Suite 2432, New York NY 10107. (212)757-0818. Fax: (212)757-5705. E-mail: info@lilith.org. Website: www.lilith.org. Susan Weidman Schneider, editor-in-chief. **Contact:** Poetry Editor. *Lilith Magazine: Independent, Jewish & Frankly Feminist*, published quarterly, is "an independent magazine with a Jewish feminist perspective" that uses poetry by Jewish women "about the Jewish woman's experience." Does not want poetry on other subjects. "Generally we use short rather than long poems." Has published poetry by Irena Klepfisz, Lyn Lifshin, Marcia Falk, Adrienne Rich, and Muriel Rukeyser. *Lilith Magazine* is 48 pages, magazine-sized, with glossy color cover. Publishes about 4 poems/year. Press run is about 10,000 (about 6,000 subscribers). Subscription: $26/year. Sample: $7.

How to Contact Send up to 3 poems at a time. No simultaneous submissions or e-mail submissions. "Please put name and contact info on each sheet submitted. Copy should be neatly typed and proofread for typos and spelling errors. Short cover letters only." Sometimes comments on rejected poems. Guidelines available for SASE or on website. Responds in up to 6 months.

Tips "Read a copy of the publication before you submit your work. Please be patient."

Ⓝ LIMP WRIST MAGAZINE

E-mail: dustin@limpwristmag.com. "We offer a creative writing scholarship ($150) for gay high school seniors. The winner will also win a spot at the 2009 Juniper Summer Writing Institute. We plan to offer a yearly chapbook competition open."

How to Contact Submit a maximum of five poems by e-mail only in the body of the message to Dustin Brookshire (dustin@limpwristmag.com). No attachments. "We can't handle anything bigger than five! All submissions should be a final version ready for publication—it is not the responsibility of the *Limp Wrist* staff to correct your errors or revise submissions. Please include the following statement (and mean it!) with your submissions: 'The poems submitted are my own original work and have not been previously published.'"

Ⓝ ◯ LINEBREAK

333 Kimpel Hall, University of Arkansas, Fayetteville AR 72701. E-mail: editors@linebreak. org. Website: http://linebreak.org. **Contact:** Johnathon Williams, founding editor.

- Poems published on *Linebreak* have been selected for the Best New Poets anthology and nominated for the Pushcart Prize.

Magazines Needs all styles. Has published Dorianne Laux, Bob Hicok, D.A. Powell, C. Dale Young, Richard Siken, Sandra Beasley. Receives about 2,200 poems/year; accepts about 52.

Averages 3,000 unique visitors per month, with 220 additional subscribers to RSS feed, and 250 subscribers to weekly newsletter.

How to Contact Submit up to 5 poems at a time through upload form on website. Considers simultaneous submissions. Reads submissions year round. Time between acceptance and publication is 2-16 weeks. Poems are circulated to an editorial board. Sometimes comments on rejected poems. Guidelines available on website. Responds in 6 weeks. Sometimes sends prepublication galleys. Acquires electronic rights: "We require the rights to publish and archive the work indefinitely on our website, and the right to create an audio recording of each poem, which is also archived indefinitely. Copyright remains with the author."

Tips "The best advice for submitting to *Linebreak* is to read our archives. We publish only 52 poems per year, which requires us to be incredibly selective. That said, nothing makes us happier than discovering new voices."

☑ LIPS

7002 Blvd. East, #2-26G, Guttenberg NJ 07093. (201)662-1303. E-mail: LBoss79270@aol. com. **Contact:** Laura Boss, Poetry Editor.

Magazines Needs *Lips*, published twice/year, takes pleasure "in publishing previously unpublished poets as well as the most established voices in contemporary poetry. We look for quality work: the strongest work of a poet; work that moves the reader; poems that take risks that work. We prefer clarity in the work rather than the abstract. Poems longer than 6 pages present a space problem." Has published poetry by Robert Bly, Allen Ginsberg, Michael Benedikt, Maria Gillan, Stanley Barkan, Lyn Lifshin, and Ishmael Reed. *Lips* is about 150 pages, digest-sized, flat-spined. Receives about 16,000 submissions/year, accepts about 1%. Press run is 1,000 (200 subscribers, 100 libraries). Sample: $10 plus $2 for postage.

How to Contact Submit 6 pages maximum at a time. Poems should be typed. Reads submissions September-March only. Guidelines available for SASE. Responds in 1 month (but has gotten backlogged at times). Sometimes sends prepublication galleys. Pays 1 contributor's copy. Acquires first rights.

Tips "Remember the 2 T's: Talent and Tenacity."

☑ THE LISTENING EYE

Kent State Geauga Campus, 14111 Claridon-Troy Rd., Burton OH 44021. E-mail: grace_butcher@msn.com. Website: http://reocities.com/athens/3716/eye.htm. **Contact:** Grace Butcher, Editor.

Magazine Needs *The Listening Eye*, published annually in early fall, prints poetry, short fiction, creative nonfiction, and art. Wants "high literary-quality poetry. Any subject, any style." Does not want "trite images or predictable rhyme." Considers poetry by children and teens if high literary quality. Has published poetry by Alberta Turner, Virgil Suaárez, Walter McDonald, and Simon Perchik. *The Listening Eye* is 52-60 pages, digest-sized, professionally printed, saddle-stapled, with card stock cover with b&w or color art. Receives about 200 poems/year, accepts about 5%. Press run is 200. Single copy: $4. Make checks payable to Kent State University.

How to Contact Submit up to 4 poems at a time. Lines/poem: "prefer shorter poems (less than 2 pages), but will consider longer if space allows." Accepts previously published poems "occasionally"; no simultaneous submissions. No e-mail submissions "unless from overseas." Cover letter is required. Poems should be typed, single-spaced, 1 poem/page—name, address, phone number, and e-mail address in upper left-hand corner of each page—with SASE for return of work. Reads submissions January 1-April 15 only: max four poems/ four pages. Time between acceptance and publication is up to 6 months. Poems are circulated to the editor and 2 assistant editors who read and evaluate work separately, then meet for final decisions. Occasionally comments on rejected poems. Guidelines available in magazine or for SASE. Responds in 1 month. Pays 2 contributor's copies. Acquires first or one-time rights. Awards $30 to the best sports poem in each issue.

Tips "I look for tight lines that don't sound like prose; unexpected images or juxtapositions; the unusual use of language; noticeable relationships of sounds; a twist in viewpoint; an ordinary idea in extraordinary language; an amazing and complex idea simply stated; play on words and with words; an obvious love of language. Poets need to read the 'Big 3'—Cummings, Thomas, Hopkins—to see the limits to which language can be taken. Then read the 'Big 2'—Dickinson to see how simultaneously tight, terse, and universal a poem can be, and Whitman to see how sprawling, cosmic, and personal. Then read everything you can find that's being published in literary magazines today, and see how your work compares to all of the above."

▣ ◪ LITERAL LATTÉ

200 E. 10th St., Suite 240, New York NY 10003. (212)260-5532. E-mail: litlatte@aol.com. Website: www.literal-latte.com. **Contact:** Dorie Davidson, Associate Editor.

Magazines Needs *Literal Latté*, published continually online, is a literary journal of "pure prose, poetry, and art. Open to all styles of poetry—quality is the determining factor." Has published poetry by Allen Ginsberg, Carol Muske, Amy Holman, and John Updike. Receives about 3,000 poems/year, accepts 1%.

How to Contact Considers simultaneous submissions; no previously published poems. No e-mail submissions; postal submissions only. Cover letter is required. Include bio and e-mail address for response only. Time between acceptance and publication is within 1 year. Often comments on rejected poems. Guidelines available by e-mail or on website. Responds in 5 months.

Additional Information "We will publish an anthology in book form at the end of each year, featuring the best of our Web magazine."

Contest/Award Offerings *Literal Latté* Poetry Awards and *Literal Latté* Food Verse Awards.

▣ ◪ ◎ LITERARY MAMA

E-mail: poetry@literarymama.com (submissions); info@literarymama.com (inquiries). Website: www.literarymama.com. **Contact:** Sharon Kraus, poetry editor.

Magazines Needs *Literary Mama*, published monthly online, prints fiction, poetry, and creative nonfiction by writers of all ages who are "self-identified" mothers. "We also publish literary criticism, book reviews, and profiles about mother writers. *Literary Mama* is doing something for mama-centric literature that no one else is doing. The poetry, fiction, and creative nonfiction that may be too long, too complex, too ambiguous, too deep, too raw, too edgy, too irreverent, too ironic, too body-conscious, and too full of long words for the general reader will find a home with us. While there are plenty of online literary magazines that publish writing like this, none devote themselves exclusively to writing about motherhood." Wants poems of any form that are "extraordinary for their vision, craft, integrity, and originality; centered around parenting; written by writers who are also self-identified mothers: biological, non-biological, step, transgender, adoptive." Receives about 70 poems/month, accepts about 3%.

How to Contact Submit 4 poems maximum at a time. Considers previously published poems (if they are not otherwise available on the Web) and simultaneous submissions. Accepts e-mail submissions (pasted into body of message; no attachments); no disk submissions. Include full name plus the word "submission" in your subject line. Cover letter is required. "Please include name, brief bio, and contact information." Reads submissions year round except for December and June. Time between acceptance and publication is 2-16 weeks. "The final decision about all poetry submissions is made by the poetry editor." Guidelines available on website. Responds in 6-9 months. No payment. Acquires first rights for previously unpublished work, non-exclusive one-time rights for reprints. Reviews books/chapbooks of poetry. Query via e-mail prior to sending materials for review consideration.

◪ THE LITERARY REVIEW: AN INTERNATIONAL JOURNAL OF CONTEMPORARY WRITING

Fairleigh Dickinson University, 285 Madison Ave., Madison NJ 07940. (973)443-8564. Fax: (973)443-8364. E-mail: tlr@fdu.edu. Established 1957. **Contact:** Minna Proctor, editor-in-chief.

Magazines Needs *The Literary Review*, published quarterly, seeks "work by new and established poets that reflects a sensitivity to literary standards and the poetic form." No specifications as to form, length, style, subject matter, or purpose. Has published poetry by David Citino, Rick Mulkey, Virgil Suárez, Gary Fincke, and Dale M. Kushner. *The Literary Review* is about 180 pages, digest-sized, professionally printed, flat-spined, with glossy color cover. Receives about 1,200 submissions/year, accepts 100-150. Press run is 2,000 (800 subscribers, one-third are overseas). Sample: $7 domestic, $8 outside U.S.; request a "general issue."

How to Contact Submit up to 5 typed poems at a time. Accepts only online submissions at www.theliteraryreview.org/submit.html. No mail, fax, or e-mail submissions. Considers simultaneous submissions. **Read-time September 1 through May 31**. Sometimes comments on rejected poems. Publishes theme issues. Responds in 4-6 months. Always sends prepublication galleys. Pays 2 contributor's copies. Acquires first rights. Reviews books of poetry in 500 words, single-book format. Send materials for review consideration.

Also Offers *TLR Online*, available on the website, features original work not published in the print edition. Has published poetry by Renée Ashley and Catherine Kasper.

Tips "Read a general issue of the magazine carefully before submitting."

⊕ ▣ ◯ LIVING POETS MAGAZINE

Dragonheart Press, 11 Menin Rd., Allestree, Derby DE22 2NL England. E-mail: submissions@dragonheartpress.com. Website: www.dragonheartpress.com. Established 1995. **Contact:** Sean Woodward, executive editor.

Magazines Needs *Living Poets Magazine*, published irregularly online, provides a showcase for poetry. Wants "crafted poetry with strong imagery." Does not want "constrained rhyming structures." Receives about 400 poems/year, accepts about 20%. Digital sample: $10 (printable from PDF). Make checks payable to S. Woodward or via PayPal.

How to Contact Submit 3 poems at a time no longer than 40 lines. Considers previously published poems and simultaneous submissions. Prefers e-mail submissions. Cover letter is preferred. Include bio and publication credits. Time between acceptance and publication is 1-2 months. Often comments on rejected poems. Publishes theme issues. Guidelines available on website or for SASE, by e-mail, or on website. Responds in 3 months. Pays 1 contributor's copy. Reviews books/chapbooks of poetry or other magazines in single-book format. Send materials for review consideration to Review Editor, Dragonheart Press.

Contest/Award Offerings Sponsors Dragonheart Press Annual Poetry Competition. **Deadline:** December 31. Guidelines available for SASE (or SAE and IRC) or by e-mail (competition@dragonheartpress.com).

☑ LONE STARS MAGAZINE

4219 Flint Hill St., San Antonio TX 78230-1619. E-mail: lonestarsmagazine@yahoo.com. Website: www.lonestarsmagazine.net. **Contact:** Milo Rosebud, Editor/Publisher.

Magazines Needs *Lone Stars*, published 3 times/year, features "contemporary poetry." Wants poetry "that holds a continuous line of thought." Does not want "profanity." Considers poetry by children and teens. Has published poetry by Terry Lee, Eve Blohm, Larry Granger, Deirdre Cafferty, & Rex Sexton. *Lone Stars* is 25 pages, magazine-sized, photocopied, saddle-stapled, bound with tape. Press run is 200. Single copy: $6; subscription: $20 for 4 issues. Sample: $5.50. Past issues: $2.

How to Contact Submit 3-5 poems at a time. Considers previously published poems and simultaneous submissions. Cover letter is preferred. Submit poems on any subject, formatted and "typed the way you want them in print." **Charges reading fee of $1 per poem.** Time between acceptance and publication is 3-6 months. Guidelines available for SASE. Responds within 3 months. Acquires one-time rights.

Contest/Award Offerings Sponsors annual "Light of the Stars" open poetry Contest. Sponsors annual "Songbook" lyric poetry contest. Details available for SASE, or on website.

Tips "Submit poetry that expresses a rational idea."

▣ LONG ISLAND QUARTERLY

P.O. Box 114, Northport NY 11768. E-mail: Liquarterly@aol.com. Website: www.poetrybay. com. **Contact:** George Wallace, editor/publisher.

Magazines Needs *Long Island Quarterly*, published online, is a journal of poetry (mostly lyric free verse) by people on or from Long Island. "Surprise us with fresh language. No conventional imagery, self-indulgent confessionalism, compulsive article-droppers." Has published poetry by Edmund Pennant and David Ignatow.

How to Contact Submit 3 poems at a time. Accepts e-mail submissions (preferred; pasted into body of message; "no attachments will be opened"). Include name and address on each page for postal entries; submissions without SASE are not returned. Cover letter with brief bio stating connection to Long Island region is required. Responds in 3 months.

Tips "1) Go beyond yourself; 2) Don't be afraid to fictionalize; 3) Don't write your autobiography—if you're worth it, maybe someone else will."

☑ LONG STORY SHORT, AN E-ZINE FOR WRITERS

P.O. Box 475, Lewistown MT 59457. E-mail: dencassino@gmail.com. Website: www.alongstoryshort.net. **Contact:** Denise Cassino; Linda Barnett-Johnson, editors; Marie Delgado Travis, poetry editor.

Magazines Needs *Long Story Short, An E-zine for Writers*, published monthly online, is "eclectic—open to all forms and styles" of poetry. Does not want "profanity; overly explicit sex." Considers poetry by children (ages 10 and up) and teens. Has published poetry by Michael Lee Johnson, Maria Ercilla, Shonda Buchanan, Patricia Wellingham-Jones, Floriana Hall, and Russell Bittner.

How to Contact Submit up to 3 poems at a time. Short, concise poems are preferred. Considers previously published poems and simultaneous submissions. Accepts e-mail submissions only ("paste poems in the body of your e-mail; no attachments will be opened"). Include a brief biography and permission to use e-mail address for reader contact. Reads submissions year round. Submit seasonal poems 6 months in advance. Time between acceptance and publication is up to 6 months, depending on theme. "Poems are reviewed and chosen by the poetry editor." Often comments on rejected poems. Guidelines available on website. ("Read them!") All rights reserved by author.

Also Offers Free newsletter with poetry of the month chosen by poetry editor; includes author's bio and Web page listed in the e-zine. Also provides resource page on website. Offers light critique of submissions upon request, and a free writing forum.

Tips "*Long Story Short* is an e-zine dedicated to the advancement of writers. It has been voted one of the 101 Best Websites for Writers by the readers of *Writer's Digest Magazine*."

☑ LOS

150 N. Catalina St., No. 2, Los Angeles CA 90004. E-mail: lospoesy@earthlink.net. Website: http://home.earthlink.net/~lospoesy.

Magazines Needs *Los*, published 4 times/year, features poetry. Has published poetry by John P. Campbell, Jean Esteve, Mary Kasimor, Bill Knott, Paul Lowe, and Charles Wuest. *Los* is digest-sized and saddle-stapled. Press run is 100.

How to Contact Accepts e-mail submissions (pasted into body of message or as attachment). Time between acceptance and publication is up to 1 month. Guidelines available on website. Responds in 3 months. Pays 1 contributor's copy.

☑ LOUISIANA LITERATURE

SLU Box 10792, Southeastern Louisiana University, Hammond LA 70402. (504)549-5022. E-mail: lalit@selu.edu. Website: http://www.louisianaliterature.org/press/. **Contact:** Jack Bedell, Editor.

Magazines Needs *Louisiana Literature*, published twice/year, considers "creative work from anyone, though we strive to showcase our state's talent. We appreciate poetry that shows firm control and craft; is sophisticated yet accessible to a broad readership. We don't use highly experimental work." Has published poetry by Claire Bateman, Elton Glaser, Gray Jacobik, Vivian Shipley, D.C. Berry, and Judy Longley. *Louisiana Literature* is 150 pages, 634x934, handsomely printed on heavy matte stock, flat-spined, with matte card cover. Single copy: $8 for individuals; subscription: $12 for individuals, $12.50 for institutions.

How to Contact Submit 3-5 poems at a time. No simultaneous submissions. No fax or e-mail submissions. "Send cover letter, including bio to use in the event of acceptance. Enclose SASE and specify whether work is to be returned or discarded." Reads submissions year round, "although we work more slowly in summer." Publishes theme issues. Guidelines available for SASE or on website. Sometimes sends prepublication galleys. Pays 2 contributor's copies. Send materials for review consideration; include cover letter.

Tips "It's important to us that the poets we publish be in control of their creations. Too much of what we see seems arbitrary."

☑ ◎ THE LOUISIANA REVIEW

Louisiana State University at Eunice, P.O. Box 1129, Eunice LA 70535. (337)550-1315. E-mail: malleman@lsue.edu. Website: www.lsue.edu/LA-Review/. **Contact:** Dr. Michael Alleman, poetry editor. (Specialized: LA poets, LA-related poetry)

Magazines Needs *The Louisiana Review*, published annually during the fall or spring semester, offers "Louisiana poets, writers, and artists a place to showcase their most beautiful pieces. Others may submit Louisiana- or Southern-related poetry, stories, and b&w art, as well as interviews with Louisiana writers. We want to publish the highest-quality poetry, fiction, and art." Wants "strong imagery, metaphor, and evidence of craft." Does not want "sing-song rhymes, abstract, religious, or overly sentimental work." Has published poetry by Gary Snyder, Antler, David Cope, and Catfish McDaris. *The Louisiana Review* is 100-200 pages, digest-sized, professionally printed, perfect-bound. Receives up to 2,000 poems/year, accepts 40-50. Press run is 300-600. Single copy: $5.

How to Contact Submit up to 5 poems at a time. No previously published poems. No fax or e-mail submissions. "Include cover letter indicating your association with Louisiana, if any. Name and address should appear on each page." Reads submissions year round. Time between acceptance and publication is up to 2 years. Pays one contributor's copy. Poets retain all rights.

Tips "Be true to your own voice and style."

☑ THE LOUISVILLE REVIEW

Spalding University, 851 S. Fourth St., Louisville KY 40203. (502)585-9911, ext. 2777. E-mail: louisvillereview@spalding.edu. Website: www.louisvillereview.org. **Contact:** Kathleen Driskell, Associate Editor.

Magazines Needs *The Louisville Review*, published twice/year, prints all kinds of poetry. Has a section devoted to children's poetry (grades K-12) called The Children's Corner. Considers poetry by children and teens. Has published poetry by Wendy Bishop, Gary Fincke, Michael Burkard, and Sandra Kohler. *The Louisville Review* is 150 pages, digest-sized, flat-spined. Receives about 700 submissions/year, accepts about 10%. Single copy: $8; subscription: $14/year, $27/2 years, $40/3 years (foreign subscribers add $6/year for s&h). Sample: $5.

How to Contact Considers simultaneous submissions; no previously published poems. Accepts submissions via online manager; please see website for more information. "Poetry by children must include permission of parent to publish if accepted. Address those submissions to The Children's Corner." Reads submissions year round. Time between acceptance and publication is up to 4 months. Submissions are read by 3 readers. Guidelines available on website. Responds in 4-6 months. Pays in contributor's copies.

Tips "We look for the striking metaphor, unusual imagery, and fresh language."

☑ LULLWATER REVIEW

Emory University, P.O. Box 122036, Atlanta GA 30322. (404)727-6184. E-mail: LullwaterReview@yahoo.com. **Contact:** Arina Korneva, editor in chief.

Magazines Needs *Lullwater Review*, published in May and December, prints poetry, short fiction, and artwork. Wants poetry of any genre with strong imagery, original voice, on any subject. Does not want profanity or pornographic material. Has published poetry by Amy Greenfield, Peter Serchuk, Katherine McCord, and Ha Jin. *Lullwater Review* is 60-80 pages, magazine-sized, with full-color cover, includes b&w and color pictures. Press run is 1,200. Subscription: $8 for individuals, $10 for institutions. Sample: $5.

How to Contact Submit 6 or fewer poems at a time. Considers simultaneous submissions; no previously published poems. Cover letter is preferred. Prefers poems single-spaced with name and contact info on each page. "Poems longer than 1 page should include page numbers. We must have a SASE with which to reply." Reads submissions September 1-May 15 only. Time between acceptance and publication is up to 6 months. Poems are circulated to an editorial board. Seldom comments on rejected poems. Guidelines available for SASE. Responds in 5 months maximum. Pays 3 contributor's copies. Acquires first North American serial rights.

Tips "Keep writing, find your voice, don't get frustrated. Please be patient with us regarding response time. We are an academic institution."

☑ LUNGFULL!MAGAZINE

316 23rd St., Brooklyn NY 11215. E-mail: lungfull@rcn.com. Website: http://lungfull.org. **Contact:** Brendan Lorber, editor/publisher.

- *LUNGFULL!* was the recipient of a grant from the New York State Council for the Arts.

Magazines Needs *LUNGFULL!magazine*, published annually, prints "the rough draft of each poem, in addition to the final, so that the reader can see the creative process from start to finish. People who have not read the journal will be obvious and at a disadvantage." Wants "any style as long as it's urgent, immediate, playful, probing, showing great thought while remaining vivid and grounded. Poems should be as interesting as conversation." Does not want "empty poetic abstractions." Has published poetry by Alice Notley, Lorenzo Thomas, Tracie Morris, Hal Sirowitz, Eileen Myles, and John Ashbery. *LUNGFULL!* is 200 pages, 8½ × 7, offset-printed, desktop-published, perfect-bound, with glossy waterproof 2-color cover, includes ads. Receives about 1,000 poems/year, accepts 3%. Press run is 3,000 (600 subscribers, 2300 shelf sales); 100 distributed free to contributors. Single copy: $9.95; subscription: $39.80 for 4 issues, $19.90 for 2 issues. Sample: $13.95. Make checks payable to Brendan Lorber, or order online.

How to Contact Submit up to 6 poems at a time. Considers previously published poems and simultaneous submissions (with notification; "however, other material will be considered first and stands a much greater chance of publication"). Accepts e-mail submissions. "We prefer hard copy by USPS—but e-submissions can be made in the body of the e-mail itself; submissions with attachments will be deleted unread." Cover letter is preferred. Time between acceptance and publication is up to 8 months. "The editor looks at each piece for its own merit and for how well it will fit into the specific issue being planned based on other accepted work." Guidelines available by e-mail. Responds in 1 year. Pays 2 contributor's copies. "Read the magazine before submitting and mention why you want to be published in LUNGFULL! in your cover letter."

Also Offers "Each copy of *LUNGFULL!magazine* contains a Cultural Attache Sticker—they can be removed from the magazine and placed on any flat surface to make it a little less flat. Previous stickers contain statements like 'Together we can keep the poor poor' and 'You only live once—just not as long as in countries with free healthcare.'"

Tips "Failure demands a certain dedication. Practice makes imperfection, and imperfection makes room for the amazing. Only outside the bounds of acceptable conclusions can the astounding transpire, can writing contain anything beyond twittering snack food logic and the utilitarian pistons of mundane engineering."

☑ ◎ THE LUTHERAN DIGEST

P.O. Box 4250, Hopkins MN 55343. (952)933-2820. Fax: (952)933-5708. E-mail: tldi@ lutherandigest.com. Website: www.lutherandigest.com. **Contact:** David Tank, editor.

Magazines Needs *The Lutheran Digest,* published quarterly, aims to "entertain and encourage believers and to subtly persuade non-believers to embrace the Lutheran-Christian faith. We publish short poems that will fit in a single column of the magazine. Most are inspirational, but that doesn't necessarily mean religious." Does not want "avant-garde poetry." Considers poetry by children and teens. Has published poetry by Kathleen A. Cain, William Beyer, Margaret Peterson, Florence Berg, and Erma Boetkher. *The Lutheran Digest* is 64 pages, digest-sized, offset-printed, saddle-stapled, with 4-color paper cover, includes local ads. Receives about 200 poems/year, accepts 10-20%. Press run is 60,000-65,000; most distributed free to Lutheran churches. Subscription: $16/year, $22/2 years. Sample: $3.50.

How to Contact Submit 3 poems at a time. Lines/poem: 25 maximum. Considers previously published poems and simultaneous submissions. Accepts fax and e-mail (as attachment) submissions. Cover letter is preferred. "Include SASE if return is desired." Time between acceptance and publication is up to 9 months. "Poems are selected by editor and reviewed by publication panel." Guidelines available for SASE or on website. Responds in 3 months. Pays credit and 1 contributor's copy. Acquires one-time rights.

Tips "Poems should be short and appeal to senior citizens. We also look for poems that can be sung to traditional Lutheran hymns."

☑ ◎ THE LYRIC

P.O. Box 110, Jericho Corners VT 05465. E-mail: themuse@thelyricmagazine.com. Website: www.thelyricmagazine.com. Established 1921. *The Lyric,* published quarterly, is "the oldest magazine in North America in continuous publication devoted to traditional poetry." Prints about 55 poems/issue. Wants "rhymed verse in traditional forms, for the most part, with an occasional piece of blank or free verse. Our themes are varied, ranging from religious ecstasy to humor to raw grief, but we feel no compulsion to shock, embitter, or confound our readers. We also avoid poems about contemporary political or social problems—'grief but not grievances,' as Frost put it. Frost is helpful in other ways: If yours is more than a lover's quarrel with life, we are not your best market. And most of our poems are accessible on first or second reading. Frost again: 'Don't hide too far away.'" Has published poetry by Rhina P. Espaillat, Gail White, Joseph Awad, Alfred Dorn, Barbara Loots, and Glenna Holloway. *The Lyric* is 32 pages, digest-sized, professionally printed with varied typography, with matte card cover. Press run is 750 (600 subscribers, 40 libraries). Receives about 3,000 submissions/year, accepts 5%. Subscription: $15/year, $28/2 years, $38/3 years (U.S.), $17/year for Canada and other countries (in U.S. funds only). Sample: $4.

How to Contact Submit up to 6 poems at a time. Lines/poem: 40 maximum. Considers simultaneous submissions (although "not preferred"); no previously published poems. Cover letter is "often helpful, but not required. Subscription will not affect publication of submitted poetry." Guidelines available for SASE or by e-mail. Responds in 3 months ("average; inquire after 6 months"). Pays 1 contributor's copy.

Contest/Award Offerings All contributors are eligible for quarterly and annual prizes totaling $650. Also offers the Lyric College Contest, open to undergraduate students. Awards prize of $400. Deadline: December 15. Send entries to Tanya Cimonetti, 1393 Spear St., S., Burlington VT 05403.

Tips "Our *raison d'etre* has been the encouragement of form, music, rhyme, and accessibility in poetry. As we witness the growing tide of appreciation for traditional/lyric poetry, we are proud to have stayed the course for 89 years, helping keep the roots of poetry alive."

▣ ⊘ LYRIC POETRY REVIEW

P.O. Box 2494, Bloomington IN 47402. E-mail: lyric@lyricreview.org. Website: www. lyricreview.org. **Contact:** Nathaniel Perry, Editor. *We hope to begin reading again in Spring 2010 - Please check our website for updates.* In the meantime, keep an eye out for Lyric #12, due out soon, featuring long poems by Forrest Gander, Linda Zisquit, George Scarbrough and others. *Lyric Poetry Review*, published semiannually, presents "poetry by Americans and translations of both little-known and celebrated poets from around the world." Also publishes interviews and literary essays on poetry or poetics. Wants "poetry that has strong musicality and lyricism. We are open to all styles, including longer poems and lyrical narratives. We tend to publish more than 1 poem by any given author and try to find a group of poems that demonstrates both range and consistency of voice." Has published poetry by Marilyn Hacker, Maurice Manning, Czeslaw Milosz, Jean Valentine, Alicia Ostriker, and Gerald Stern. *Lyric Poetry Review* is 96 pages, digest-sized, perfect-bound, with full-color cover with original artwork. Receives about 2,500 poems/year, accepts about 5%. Press run is 1,000. Single copy: $16; subscription: $30/year (subscribers outside U.S. add $10/year, $15/2 years' postage). Make checks payable to *Lyric Poetry Review*.

How to Contact Submit 3-6 poems at a time. Considers simultaneous submissions if notified; no previously published poems. No e-mail or disk submissions. Cover letter is required. Reads submissions year round. Response time may be considerably slower in the summer months. Time between acceptance and publication is up to 1 year. "We strongly advise that those submitting work read a recent issue first." Seldom comments on rejected poems. Occasionally publishes theme issues. Upcoming themes available by e-mail. Guidelines available in magazine, for SASE, or on website. Responds in up to 4 months. Always sends prepublication galleys. Pays 2 contributor's copies. Acquires first rights. Solicits reviews.

☑ THE MACGUFFIN

Schoolcraft College, 18600 Haggerty Rd., Livonia MI 48152-2696. (734)462-4400, ext. 5327. Fax: (734)462-4679. E-mail: macguffin@schoolcraft.edu. **Contact:** Carol Was, poetry editor.

Magazines Needs *The MacGuffin*, published 3 times/year, prints "the best poetry, fiction, nonfiction, and artwork we receive. We have no thematic or stylistic biases. We look for well-crafted poetry." Does not want "pornography, triteness, and sloppy poetry. We do not publish haiku, concrete, or light verse." Has published poetry by Thomas Lynch, Gabriel Welsch, Linda Nemec Foster, Conrad Hilberry, and Laurence Lieberman. *The MacGuffin* is 160 pages, 6x9, perfect-bound, with color cover. Press run is 500. Subscription: $22/year. Sample: $6/copy.

How to Contact Submit no more than 5 poems at a time. Lines/poem: 400 maximum. Considers simultaneous submissions if informed; no previously published poems. Accepts fax, e-mail (as Word attachment only), and hard copy submissions via mail (SASE for reply only). Cover letter is required. "List titles and brief bio in cover letter. Do not staple work." Poems should be typed, single-spaced, 1 per page. Poet's name, address, and e-mail should appear on each page. Include SASE. Guidelines available for SASE, by fax, e-mail, or on website. Responds in 2-6 months. Pays 2 contributor's copies plus discount on additional copies. Acquires first rights if published; rights revert to poets upon publication.

Contest/Award Offerings The National Poet Hunt Contest.

☑ THE MADISON REVIEW

University of Wisconsin, Dept. of English, Helen C. White Hall, 600 N. Park St., Madison WI 53706. E-mail: madisonrevw@gmail.com. Website: themadisonreview.blogspot.com. **Contact:** Poetry Editor.

Magazines Needs *The Madison Review*, published semiannually in May and December, seeks poems that are "smart and tight, that fulfill their own propositions." Does not want "religious or patriotic dogma and light verse." Has published poetry by Simon Perchik, Amy Quan Barry, Mitch Raney, Erica Meitner, and Henry B. Stobbs. Selects 15-20 poems from a pool of 750. Subscription: $15/year, $25 for 2 years. Sample: $8.

How to Contact Submit up to 5 poems at a time. No simultaneous submissions. No e-mail submissions. Cover letter is preferred. Include SASE. Submissions must be typed. Guidelines available in magazine, for SASE, by e-mail, or on website. Usually responds in 9 months. Pays 2 contributor's copies.

Tips "Contributors: Know your market! Read before, during, and after writing. Treat your poems better than job applications!"

$ ☑ ◎ THE MAGAZINE OF FANTASY & SCIENCE FICTION

P.O. Box 3447, Hoboken NJ 07030. E-mail: FandSF@aol.com. Website: www.fsfmag.com. **Contact:** Gordon Van Gelder, editor.

- *The Magazine of Fantasy & Science Fiction* is a past winner of the Hugo Award and World Fantasy Award.

Magazines Needs *The Magazine of Fantasy & Science Fiction*, published bimonthy, is "one of the longest-running magazines devoted to the literature of the fantastic." Wants only poetry that deals with the fantastic or the science-fictional. Has published poetry by Rebecca Kavaler, Elizabeth Bear, Sophie M. White, and Robert Frazier. *The Magazine of Fantasy & Science Fiction* is 240 pages, digest-sized, offset-printed, perfect-bound, with glossy cover, includes ads. Receives about 20-40 poems/year, accepts about 1%. Press run is 35,000 (20,000 subscribers). Single copy: $7; subscription: $34.97. Sample: $6. Make checks payable to *The Magazine of Fantasy & Science Fiction*.

How to Contact Submit 1-3 poems at a time. No previously published poems or simultaneous submissions. No e-mail or disk submissions. Time between acceptance and publication is up to 2 years, but usually about 9 months. "I buy poems very infrequently—just when one hits me right." Seldom comments on rejected poems. Guidelines available for SASE or on website. Responds in up to 1 month. Always sends prepublication galleys. Pays $50/poem and 2 contributor's copies. Acquires first North American serial rights.

$ ◑ ◎ THE MAGAZINE OF SPECULATIVE POETRY

Website: http://www.sff.net/people/roger-dutcher/#mspgdln. **Contact:** Roger Dutcher, Editor. *The Magazine of Speculative Poetry*, published biannually, features "the best new speculative poetry. We are especially interested in narrative form, but open to any form, any length (within reason); interested in a variety of styles. We're looking for the best of the new poetry utilizing the ideas, imagery, and approaches developed by speculative fiction, and will welcome experimental techniques as well as the fresh employment of traditional forms." Has published poetry by Joanne Merriam, Jeannine Hall Gailey, Ann K. Schwader, and Kendall Evans. *The Magazine of Speculative Poetry* is 24-28 pages, digest-sized, offset-printed, saddle-stapled, with matte card cover. Receives about 500 poems/year, accepts less than 5%. Press run is 150-200. Subscription: $19 for 4 issues. Sample: $5.

▦ MAGMA POETRY MAGAZINE

43 Keslake Rd., London NW6 6DH England. E-mail: contributions@magmapoetry.com. Website: www.magmapoetry.com. **Contact:** Laurie Smith, editor. Established 1994.

Magazines Needs *Magma* appears 3 times/year and contains "modern poetry, reviews and interviews with poets." Wants poetry that is "modern in idiom and shortish (2 pages maximum). Nothing sentimental or old fashioned." Has published poetry by Thomas Lynch, Thom Gunn, Michael Donaghy, John Burnside, Vicki Feaver, and Roddy Lumsden. *Magma* is 64 pages, 8 × 8, photocopied and stapled, includes b&w illustrations. Receives about 3,000 poems/year, accepts 4-5%. Press run is about 500. Single copy: £5.70 UK and Ireland, £6.15 rest of Europe, £7.50 airmail ROW. Subscription: £14.50 UK and Ireland, £18 rest of Europe, £20.50 airmail ROW. Make checks payable to *Magma*. For subscriptions, contact Helen Nicholson, distribution secretary, Flat 2, 86 St. James's Dr., London SW17 7RR England.

How to Contact Submit up to 6 poems at a time. Accepts simultaneous submissions. Accepts submissions by post (with SAE and IRCs) and by e-mail (preferably pasted into body of message; if attachment, only 1 file). Cover letter is preferred. Deadlines for submissions: end of February, mid-July, end of October. "Poems are considered for one issue only." Time between acceptance and publication is maximum 3 months. "Each issue has an editor who submits his/her selections to a board for final approval. Editor's selection very rarely changed." Occasionally publishes theme issues. Responds "as soon as a decision is made." Always sends prepublication galleys. Pays one contributor's copy.

Also Offers "We hold a public reading in London three times/year, to coincide with each new issue, and poets in the issue are invited to read."

⚡ ◯ MAGNAPOETS

13300 Tecumseh Road East Ste 226, Tecumseh ON N8N 4R8, Canada. E-mail: Magnapoets@gmail.com. Website: www.magnapoets.com. **Contact:** Aurora Antonovic, editor-in-chief.

Magazines Needs *Magnapoets*, published semiannually in January and July, prints "all forms of poetry, as well as short stories and articles." Wants all forms of poetry, including free verse, formal poetry, tanka, haiku, senryu. Does not want "anything hateful, racist, bigoted, or overtly partisan. Considers poetry by teens. Has published poetry by Robert Pinsky, Kirsty Karkow, Elisha Porat, Peggy Lyles Wills, Curtis Dunlap, an'ya. *Magnapoets* is 36-40 pages, magazine-sized, digital press print format, saddle-stitched, with a glossy cover with full-sized color photograph or art. Single copy: $5 CAN; subscription: $10 CAN. Make checks payable to Aurora Antonovic.

How to Contact Follow submissions guidelines properly and be sure to submit to the appropriate editor and include "Magnapoets" in the subject line. E-mail submissions only. Submit up to 3 poems of free verse and formal poetry, maximum 48 lines including title, to Ursula Gibson at UrsulaTG1@aol.com; for haiku and tanka, send up to 10 poems at a time, to Aurora Antonovic at Magnapoets@gmail.com; for short stories, submit ONE prose piece, Word length: 250 - 2,500 words to Marie Lecrivain at marie@poeticdiversity.org . Cover letter is preferred. Include a 25-word (or less) bio. Reads submissions in the months of May and October. Time between acceptance and publication is 2-3months. "Each editor edits his/her own section separately. Send submissions to each individual editor as specified. Currently, we have 5 editors: Ursula T. Gibson (free verse and form), Marie Lecrivain (short stories), David Herrle (special features), Guest Editor(haiku and senryu), Aurora Antonovic (tanka)." Never comments on rejected poems. Never publishes theme issues. Guidelines available in magazine and on website. Responds in 2 months. Pays 1 contributor's copy. Acquires first serial rights (magazine is distributed internationally). Rights revert to poets upon publication.

Additional Information "We publish themed anthologies twice a year. For information, see the website."

Tips "Send your best work. Follow the guidelines as detailed on the site."

◯ ◎ THE MAGNOLIA QUARTERLY

P.O. Box 10294, Gulfport MS 39506. E-mail: gcwriters@aol.com. Website: www.gcwriters. org. **Contact:** Phil Levin, editor; John Freeman, poetry editor. Publication of the Gulf Coast Writers Association.

Magazines Needs *The Magnolia Quarterly* publishes poetry, fiction, nonfiction, reviews, and photography. **Membership required to submit to magazine** (exception: each issue features a non-member poet chosen by the poetry editor). Will consider all styles of poetry. Does not want "pornography, racial or sexist bigotry, far-left or far-right political poems." Has published poetry by Leonard Cirino, Catharine Savage Brosman, Angela Ball, Jack

Bedell, and Larry Johnson. *The Magnolia Quarterly* is 40 pages, pocket-sized, stapled, with glossy cover, includes ads. Single copy: $5; subscription: included in $30 GCWA annual dues. Make checks payable to Gulf Coast Writers Assocation. Editing service offered on all prose.

How to Contact Submit 1-5 poems at a time. Lines/poem: open. Considers previously published poems and simultaneous submissions. Prefers e-mail submissions. Cover letter is preferred. Reads submissions year round. Time between acceptance and publication varies. Guidelines available in magazine, for SASE, by e-mail, or on website. No payment. Returns rights to poet upon publication.

Contest/Award Offerings "Let's Write" contest, with cash prizes for poetry and prose. Additional information available on website.

Also Offers The Gulf Coast Writers Association, "a nationally recognized organization dedicated to encouraging all writers."

☑ THE MAIN STREET RAG

P.O. Box 690100, Charlotte NC 28227-7001. (704)573-2516. E-mail: editor@mainstreetrag. com. **Contact:** M. Scott Douglass, Editor/Publisher.

Magazines Needs *The Main Street Rag*, published quarterly, prints "poetry, short fiction, essays, interviews, reviews, photos, art. We like publishing good material from people who are interested in more than notching another publishing credit, people who support small independent publishers like ourselves." Will consider "almost anything," but prefers "writing with an edge—either gritty or bitingly humorous. Contributors are advised to visit our website prior to submission to confirm current needs." Has published poetry by Silvia Curbelo, Sean Thomas Dougherty, Denise Duhamel, Cathy Essinger, Ishle Yi Park, and Dennis Must. *The Main Street Rag* is about 130 pages, digest-sized, perfect-bound, with 12-pt laminated color cover. Receives about 5,000 submissions/year; publishes 35-50 poems and 2-4 short stories per issue. Press run is about 600 (300 subscribers, 15 libraries). Single copy: $8; subscription: $24/year, $45 for 2 years.

How to Contact Submit 6 pages of poetry at a time. No previously published poems or simultaneous submissions. **Accepts e-mail submissions from subscribers only**. Cover letter is preferred. "No bios or credits—let the work speak for itself." Time between acceptance and publication is up to 1 year. Guidelines available for SASE, by e-mail, or on website. Responds within 6 weeks. Pays 1 contributor's copy. Acquires first North American print rights.

Contest/Award Offerings Main Street Rag's Annual Poetry Book Award and Main Street Rag's Annual Chapbook Contest.

Tips "Small press independents exist by and for writers. Without their support (and the support of readers), we have no reason to exist. Sampling first is always appreciated."

▧ $ ☑ THE MALAHAT REVIEW

University of Victoria, P.O. Box 1700, STN CSC, Victoria BC V8W 2Y2, Canada. (250)721-8524. Fax: (250)472-5051. E-mail: malahat@uvic.ca. Website: www.malahatreview.ca. **Contact:** John Barton, editor.

Magazines Needs *The Malahat Review*, published quarterly, is "a high-quality, visually appealing literary journal that has earned the praise of notable literary figures throughout North America. Its purpose is to publish and promote poetry, and fiction, and creative nonfiction of a very high standard, both Canadian and international." Wants "various styles, lengths, and themes. The criterion is excellence." Has published poetry by Steven Heighton, George Elliot Clarke, Daryl Hine, and Jan Zwicky. Receives about 2,000 poems/year, accepts about 100. Subscription: $35 CAD for individuals, $50 USD for individuals in the United States, or $20CAD for online subscription, $50 CAD for institutions (or U.S. equivalent). Sample: $16.45 USD.

How to Contact Submit 5-10 poems at a time. No previously published poems or simultaneous submissions. No e-mail submmissions; postal submissions only. Include SASE with Canadian stamps or IRC with each submission. Guidelines available for SASE (or SAE and IRC). Responds usually within 3 months. Pays $40 CAD per printed page, 2 contributor's copies, and 1 year's subscription. Acquires first world serial rights. Reviews Canadian books of poetry.

Contest/Award Offerings Presents the P.K. Page Founders' Award for Poetry, a $1,000 prize to the author of the best poem or sequence of poems to be published in *The Malahat Review*'s quarterly issues during the previous calendar year. Also offers the Open Season Awards, biennial Long Poem Prize, and Far Horizons Award for Poetry.

◐ ◎ THE MANHATTAN REVIEW

440 Riverside Dr., Apt. 38, New York NY 10027. (212)932-1854. Established 1980. **Contact:** Philip Fried, poetry editor.

Magazines Needs *The Manhattan Review*, published annually "with ambitions to be semiannual," prints "American writers and foreign writers with something valuable to offer the American scene. We like to think of poetry as a powerful discipline engaged with many other fields." Wants to see "ambitious work. Interested in both lyric and narrative. We select high-quality work from a number of different countries, including the U.S." Does not want "mawkish, sentimental poetry." Has published poetry by Zbigniew Herbert, D. Nurkse, Baron Wormser, Penelope Shuttle, Marilyn Hacker, and Peter Redgrove. *The Manhattan Review* is 208 pages, digest-sized, professionally printed, with glossy card cover. Receives about 400 submissions/year, accepts few ("but I do read everything submitted carefully and with an open mind"). Press run is 500 (400 subscribers, 250 libraries). Single copy: $7.50; subscription: $15. Sample: $9 and 7 × 10 envelope.

How to Contact Submit 3-5 pages of poetry at a time. Simultaneous submissions "discouraged; notification required." Cover letter is required. Include short bio and publication credits. Sometimes comments on poems, "but don't count on it." Responds in 3 months, if possible. Pays in contributor's copies. Staff reviews books of poetry. Send materials for review consideration.

Tips "Always read the magazine first to see if your work is appropriate."

$ ◐ MANOA

1733 Donaghho Rd., Honolulu HI 96822. (808)956-8805. Fax: (808)956-3083. E-mail: mjournal-l@hawaii.edu. Website: http://manoajournal.hawaii.edu. **Contact:** Frank Stewart, poetry editor.

- Poetry published in *Manoa* has also appeared in volumes of *The Best American Poetry*.

Magazines Needs *Manoa*, published twice/year, is a general interest literary magazine that considers work "in many forms and styles, regardless of the author's publishing history. However, we are not for the beginning writer. It is best to look at a sample copy of the journal before submitting." Has published poetry by Arthur Sze, Ai, Linda Gregg, Jane Hirshfield, and Ha Jin. *Manoa* is 240 pages, 7x10, offset-printed, flat-spined. Receives about 1,000 poems/year, accepts 1%. Press run is more than 2,500 (several hundred subscribers, 130 libraries, 400 shelf sales). "In addition, *Manoa* is available through Project Muse to about 900 institutional subscribers throughout the world." Subscription: $22/year. Sample: $10.

Tips "We are not a regional journal, but each issue features a particular part of Asia or the Pacific; these features, which include poetry, are assembled by guest editors. The rest of each issue features work by poets from the U.S. and elsewhere. We welcome the opportunity to read poetry from throughout the country, but we are not interested in genre or formalist writing for its own sake, or in casual impressions of the Asia-Pacific region."

☑ MANY MOUNTAINS MOVING

Literary Journal of Diverse Contemporary Voices, 1705 Lombard St., Philadelphia PA 19146. E-mail: editors@mmminc.org. Website: www.mmminc.org. **Contact:** Poetry Editors: Erik Nilsen, Patrick Lawler, Malinda Miller, & Debra Bokur. TRADITIONAL PAPER SUBMISSIONS will only be read until Apr. 2010. NEW: mmm-submissions.org is closed until we work through the very large backlog! 05/02/2010. Many Mountains Moving: a literary journal of diverse contemporary voices, published annually in the fall, welcomes "previously unpublished poetry, fiction, nonfiction, reviews, and art from writers and artists of all walks of life." Wants "all forms of poetry, welcoming writing with intelligence, wit, craft, and guile. We look for any form of excellent writing, and also appreciate work that reflects the diversity of our culture. Translations and book reviews are welcome." Has published Robert Bly, Lorna Dee Cervantes, Amiri Baraka, Allen Ginsberg, Yusef Komunyakaa, and Adrienne Rich. Many Mountains Moving is over 200 pages, digest-sized, with 4-color glossy cover. Receives 5,000 poems/year, accepts 1%. Press run is 600. Single copy: $12; subscription: $12/year.

☑ MARGIE/THE AMERICAN JOURNAL OF POETRY

P.O. Box 250, Chesterfield MO 63006-0250. Fax: (636)532-0539. E-mail: margiereview@aol.com. Website: www.margiereview.com. **Contact:** Robert Nazarene, Founding Editor.

- Multiple selections from *MARGIE* have appeared in *The Best American Poetry*.

Magazines Needs *MARGIE/The American Journal of Poetry*, published annually in the fall, features "superlative poetry. No limits as to school, form, or subject matter. Imaginative, risk-taking poetry which disturbs and/or consoles is of paramount interest. A distinctive voice is prized." Has published poetry by Billy Collins, Molly Peacock, Emmylou Harris, Charles Simic, Paul Muldoon, Ted Kooser, Maxine Kumin, Sally VanDoren, David Wagoner, and Robert Wrigley. *MARGIE* is about 450+ pages, digest-sized, professionally printed, perfect-bound, with glossy cover with art/graphics, includes ads. Receives about 40,000-

50,000 poems/year, accepts less than 1%. **Available by subscription only.** Single copy: $19.95 for individuals (1 copy, shipping included), $24.95 for institutions and foreign

How to Contact Submit 3-5 poems at a time. Considers simultaneous submissions (notify in cover letter). Reads submissions according to the following schedule: open reading period is June 1-July 15 (one submission/poet during this time); **subscribers only** may submit up to 4 times annually, year round ("please mark 'Subscribe' on the outside of submission envelope"). Time between acceptance and publication is up to 1 year. Editor makes final decision. Sometimes comments on rejected poems. Guidelines available in magazine, for SASE, or on website. Responds in 1-3 weeks. Pays 1 contributor's copy. Acquires first rights. All rights revert to poet upon publication.

Tips "Read, read, read. Then: write. Be audacious, innovative, unafraid, distinctive. Finally, give generously to human and animal rights organizations."

$ ◪ THE MASSACHUSETTS REVIEW

South College, University of Massachusetts, Amherst MA 01003. (413)545-2689. E-mail: massrev@external.umass.edu. Website: www.massreview.org.

• Work published in *The Massacusetts Review* has been included frequently in *The Best American Poetry*.

Magazines Needs *The Massachusetts Review*, published quarterly, prints "fiction, essays, artwork, and excellent poetry of all forms and styles." Has published poetry by Catherine Barnett, Billy Collins, and Dara Wier. *The Massachusetts Review* is digest-sized, offset-printed on bond paper, perfect-bound, with color card cover. Receives about 2,500 poems/year, accepts about 25. Press run is 1,600 (1,100-1,200 subscribers, 1,000 libraries, the rest for shelf sales). Subscription: $27/year U.S., $35 outside U.S., $37 for libraries. Sample: $9 U.S., $12 outside U.S.

How to Contact No previously published poems or simultaneous submissions. Reads submissions October 1-May 31 only. "Guidelines are available online at our website, as is our new online submission manager." Responds in 2 months. Pays $25 plus 2 contributor's copies.

$ ◪ ◎ MATURE YEARS

P.O. Box 801, 201 Eighth Ave. S., Nashville TN 37202. (615)749-6292. Fax: (615)749-6512. E-mail: matureyears@umpublishing.org. **Contact:** Marvin W. Cropsey, editor.

Magazines Needs *Mature Years*, published quarterly, aims to "help persons understand and use the resources of Christian faith in dealing with specific opportunities and problems related to aging. Poems may or may not be overtly religious. Poems should not poke fun at older adults, but may take a humorous look at them." Does not want "sentimentality and saccharine. If using rhymes and meter, make sure they are accurate." *Mature Years* is 112 pages, magazine-sized, perfect-bound, with full-color glossy paper cover. Press run is 55,000. Sample: $6.

How to Contact Lines/poem: 16 lines of up to 50 characters maximum. Accepts fax and e-mail submissions (e-mail preferred). Submit seasonal and nature poems for spring from December through February; for summer, March through May; for fall, June through August; and for winter, September through November. Time between acceptance and publication is up to 1 year. Guidelines available for SASE or by e-mail. Responds in 2 months. Pays $1/line upon acceptance.

☑ ◎ MEASURE: A REVIEW OF FORMAL POETRY

Dept. of English, The University of Evansville, 1800 Lincoln Ave., Evansville IN 47722. (812)488-2963. E-mail: measure@evansville.edu.

Magazines Needs *Measure: A Review of Formal Poetry* is "dedicated to publishing the best metrical, English-language verse from both the United States and abroad. In each issue we strive to bring you the best new poetry from both established and emerging writers, and we also reprint a small sampling of poems from the best books of metrical poetry published the previous year. Likewise, each issue includes interviews with some of our most important contemporary poets and offers short critical essays on the poetry that has helped to shape the craft." Wants "English-language metrical poetry with no particular stanza preference. See our website or a back issue for examples. *Measure* also reprints poems from books; send copy for consideration." Does not want "fixed forms written in free verse; syllabics; quantitative." Has published poetry by Timothy Steele, R.S. Gwynn, Philip Dacey, X.J. Kennedy, Rachel Hadas, and Charles Rafferty. *Measure* is 180 pages, digest-sized, perfect-bound, with glossy cover with color artwork. Receives about 1,500 poems/year, accepts about 10%. Press run is 1,000. Single copy: $10; subscription: $18 for one year, $34 for 2 years, $50 for 3 years. Make checks payable to *Measure*.

How to Contact Submit 3-5 poems at a time. Lines/poem: no minimum or maximum. No previously published poems or simultaneous submissions. No e-mail or disk submissions. Cover letter is preferred. "All submissions should be typed. Each poem should include the poet's name and phone number. A self-addressed stamped envelope must accompany the submission." Reads submissions year round. Time between acceptance and publication "depends." Never comments on rejected poems. Guidelines available in magazine, for SASE, or on website. Responds in 3 months, longer in summer. Pays 2 contributor's copies. Acquires one-time rights. Rights revert to poet upon publication.

Additional Information Prints the winners of the annual Howard Nemerov Sonnet Award.

◎ THE MENNONITE

722 Main St., Newton KS 67114-1819. (866)866-2872 ext. 34398. Fax: (316)283-0454. E-mail: gordonh@themennonite.org. Website: www.themennonite.org. **Contact:** Gordon Houser, associate editor.

Magazines Needs *The Mennonite*, published monthly, seeks "Christian poetry—usually free verse, not too long, with multiple layers of meaning." Does not want "sing-song rhymes or poems that merely describe or try to teach a lesson." Has published poetry by Jean Janzen and Julia Kasdorf. *The Mennonite* is 64 pages, magazine-sized, with full-color cover, includes ads. Receives about 200 poems/year, accepts about 5%. Press run is 10,000 (9,665 subscribers). Single copy: $3; subscription: $43.95. Sample: $3.

How to Contact Submit up to 4 poems at a time. Considers previously published poems and simultaneous submissions. Accepts e-mail submissions (preferred). Cover letter is preferred. Time between acceptance and publication is up to 1 year. Seldom comments on rejected poems. Occasionally publishes theme issues. Guidelines available for SASE. Responds in 2 weeks. Pays 1 contributor copy. Acquires first or one-time rights.

◻ MERIDIAN ANTHOLOGY OF CONTEMPORARY POETRY

904 Rose Way, Naples FL 34104. E-mail: LetarP@aol.com. Website: www.MeridianAnthology. com. **Contact:** Phyliss L. Geller, editor/publisher; Marylin Krepf, literary editor.

Magazines Needs *Meridian Anthology of Contemporary Poetry*, next published in 2010, seeks "poetry that is contemporary, insightful, and illuminating; that touches the nerves. It should have color, content, and be deciphering of existence." Does not want vulgarity, clichés. Has published poetry by Elizabeth Swados, Ann McGovern, Gladys Justin Carr, Alan Britt, and Doug Ramspeck. Has reprinted poetry (with poet's permission) by Philip Levine and Jane Hirshfield, Dorianne Laux, Marie Howe and Thomas Lux. Sample copy $10, includes postage. Make checks payable to *Meridian Anthology of Contemporary Poetry*.

How to Contact Submit 1-5 poems at a time. Lines/poem: 78 maximum. Considers previously published poems and simultaneous submissions. No e-mail or disk submissions. Cover letter is preferred. Must include SASE with sufficient postage if you want your poems returned. Reads submissions March-December. Time between acceptance and publication is up to one year. Seldom comments on rejected poems. Guidelines available for SASE or on website. Responds in 2-6 months, "depending on backlog." Acquires one-time rights. Please include consent to publish, form is available on website.

Additional Information "Volume 5, anniversary issue featured reprinted poems by Dorianne Laux, Jane Hirshfield, and Marie Howe. Volume 4 featured Jane Hirshfield, Volume 3 featured Philip Levine). Editing services available: please go to our website for information."

Tips "A poem must have a reason for existence, some universal tendril."

$ ☑ MICHIGAN QUARTERLY REVIEW

University of Michigan, 3574 Rackham Bldg., 915 E. Washington St., Ann Arbor MI 48109. (734)764-9265. E-mail: mqr@umich.edu. Website: www.umich.edu/~mqr. **Contact:** Vicki Lawrence, managing editor.

- Poetry published in *Michigan Quarterly Review* is included frequently in volumes of *The Best American Poetry* and *The Pushcart Prize* anthologies.

Magazines Needs *Michigan Quarterly Review* is "an interdisciplinary, general interest academic journal that publishes mainly essays and reviews on subjects of cultural and literary interest." Wants all kinds of poetry except light verse. No specifications as to form, length, style, subject matter, or purpose. Has published poetry by Susan Hahn, Campbell McGrath, Carl Phillips, and Cathy Song. *Michigan Quarterly Review* is 160 pages, digest-sized, professionally printed, flat-spined, with glossy card cover. Receives about 1,400 submissions/year, accepts about 30. Press run is 2,000 (1,200 subscribers, half are libraries). Single copy: $7; subscription: $25. Sample: $4.

How to Contact No previously published poems or simultaneous submissions. No e-mail submissions. Cover letter is preferred. "It puts a human face on the manuscript. A few sentences of biography is all I want, nothing lengthy or defensive." Prefers typed mss. Publishes theme issues. Upcoming themes available in magazine and on website. Guidelines available for SASE or on website. Responds in 6 weeks. Always sends prepublication galleys. Pays $8-12/page. Acquires first rights only. Reviews books of poetry. "All reviews are commissioned."

Contest/Award Offerings The Laurence Goldstein Poetry Award, an annual cash prize of $1,000, is given to the author of the best poem to appear in *Michigan Quarterly* during the calendar year. "Established in 2002, the prize is sponsored by the Office of the President of the University of Michigan."

Tips "There is no substitute for omnivorous reading and careful study of poets past and present, as well as reading in new and old areas of knowledge. Attention to technique, especially to rhythm and patterns of imagery, is vital."

MID-AMERICAN REVIEW

Department of English, Box W, Bowling Green State University, Bowling Green OH 43403. (419)372-2725. E-mail: mikeczy@bgsu.edu. Website: www.bgsu.edu/midamericanreview. **Contact:** Michael Czyzniejewski. "We try to put the best possible work in front of the biggest possible audience. We publish serious fiction and poetry, as well as critical studies in contemporary literature, translations and book reviews."

Magazines Needs "Poems should emanate from textured, evocative images, use language with an awareness of how words sound and mean, and have a definite sense of voice. Each line should help carry the poem, and an individual vision must be evident. We encourage new as well as established writers. There is no length limit on individual poems, but please send no more than six poems."

How to Contact Submit by mail with SASE or through online submissions form at website.

☑ THE MIDWEST QUARTERLY

Pittsburg State University, Pittsburg KS 66762. (620)235-4689. Fax: (620)235-4686. E-mail: smeats@pittstate.edu. Website: www.pittstate.edu/engl/mwq/MQindex.html. **Contact:** Stephen Meats, Poetry Editor.

Magazines Needs *The Midwest Quarterly* publishes "articles on any subject of contemporary interest, particularly literary criticism, political science, philosophy, education, biography, and sociology. Each issue contains a section of poetry usually 12 poems in length." Wants "well-crafted poems, traditional or untraditional, that use intense, vivid, concrete, and/or surrealistic images to explore the mysterious and surprising interactions of the natural and inner human worlds." Does not want "'nature poems,' per se, but if a poem doesn't engage nature in a significant way, as an integral part of the experience it is offering, I am unlikely to be interested in publishing it." Has published poetry by Peter Cooley, Jim Daniels, Naomi Shihab Nye, Jonathan Holden, William Kloefkorn, and Jeanne Murray Walker. *The Midwest Quarterly* is 130 pages, digest-sized, professionally printed, flat-spined, with matte cover. Press run is 650 (600 subscribers, 500 libraries). Receives about 4,000 poems/year, accepts about 50. Subscription: $15. Sample: $5.

How to Contact Submit no more than 5 poems at a time. Lines/poem: 60 maximum ("occasionally longer if exceptional"). Considers simultaneous submissions; no previously published poems. No fax or e-mail submissions. "Manuscripts should be typed with poet's name on each page. Submissions without SASE cannot be acknowledged." Comments on rejected poems "if the poet or poem seems particularly promising." Occasionally publishes theme issues or issues devoted to the work of a single poet. Guidelines available on website. Responds in 2 months. Pays 2 contributor's copies. Acquires first serial rights. Reviews books of poetry by *Midwest Quarterly*-published poets only.

Tips "Keep writing; read as much contemporary poetry as you can lay your hands on; don't let rejection discourage you from sending your work out to editors."

$ ☑ MILLER'S POND

(570)376-3361. Fax: (570)376-2674. E-mail: publisher@millerspondpoetry.com. Website: http://millerspondpoetry.com. **Contact:** C.J. Houghtaling, Publisher; Julie Damerell, Editor.

Magazines Needs *miller's pond*, published online, features contemporary poetry, interviews, reviews, and markets. Wants "contemporary poetry that is fresh, accessible, energetic, vivid, and flows with language and rhythm." Does not want "religious, horror, pornographic, vulgar, rhymed, preachy, lofty, trite, or overly sentimental work." Has published poetry by Vivian Shipley, Barbara Crooker, Philip Memmer, and Shoshauna Shy.

How to Contact As of 2009 *miller's pond* will be exclusively an e-zine and will not publish in hard copy format. "All submissions must be sent electronically from our website. Mail sent through the post office will be returned. No payment for accepted poems or reviews. Current guidelines, updates, and changes are always available on our website. Check there first before submitting anything."

Additional Information Books are available for sale via website, phone, or fax.

Tips "Believe in yourself. Perseverance is a writer's best 'tool.' Study the contemporary masters: Vivian Shipley, Billy Collins, Maxine Kumin, Colette Inez, Hayden Carruth. Please check our website before submitting."

☑ ◎ THE MINNESOTA REVIEW

Aspect, Virginia Tech, 202 Major Williams Hall (0192), Blacksburg VA 24061. E-mail: submissions@theminnesotareview.org. **Contact:** Janell Watson, Editor.

Magazines Needs *The Minnesota Review*, published biannually, features quality poetry, short fiction, and critical essays. Each issue is about 200 pages, digest-sized, flat-spined, with glossy card cover. Press run is 1,000 (400 subscribers). Also available online. Subscription: $30/2 years for individuals, $60/year for institutions. Sample: $15.

How to Contact Submit up to 5 poems every 3 months online. Reads poetry August 1-April 1. Payment is 2 contributor's copies.

MISSISSIPPI REVIEW

Univ. of Southern Mississippi, 118 College Dr., #5144, Hattiesburg MS 39406-0001. (601)266-4321. Fax: (601)266-5757. Website: www.mississippireview.com. "Literary publication for those interested in contemporary literature—writers, editors who read to be in touch with current modes."

How to Contact "Literary publication for those interested in contemporary literature—writers, editors who read to be in touch with current modes. We do not accept unsolicited manuscripts except under the rules and guidelines of the *Mississippi Review* Prize Competition. See website for guidelines."

☑ ◎ THE MOCCASIN

The League of Minnesota Poets, 427 N. Gorman St., Blue Earth MN 56013. (507)526-5321. Website: www.mnpoets.org. *The Moccasin*, published annually in October, is the literary magazine of The League of Minnesota Poets. **Membership is required to submit work.** Wants "all forms of poetry. Prefer strong short poems." Does not want "profanity or obscenity." Considers poetry by children and teens who are student members of The League of Minnesota Poets (write grade level on poems submitted). Has published poetry by Diane Glancy, Laurel Winter, Susan Stevens Chambers, Doris Stengel, Jeanette Hinds, and Charmaine Donovan. *The Moccasin* is 40 pages, digest-sized, offset-printed, stapled, with 80 lb. linen-finish text cover with drawing and poem. Receives about 190 poems/year, accepts about 170. Press run is 200. Single copy: $5.25; subscription: free with LOMP membership.

Also Offers To become a member of The League of Minnesota Poets, send $20 ($10 if high school student or younger) to Angela Foster, LOMP Treasurer, 30036 St. Croix Rd, Pine City MN 55063. Make checks payable to LOMP. You do not have to live in Minnesota to become a member of LOMP. "Membership in LOMP automatically makes you a member of the National Federation of State Poetry Societies, which makes you eligible to enter its contests at a cheaper (members') rate."

$ ☑ ◎ MODERN HAIKU

(Specialized: haiku/senryu/haiga only; translations), P.O. Box 33077, Santa Fe, NM 87549-3077. E-mail: trumbullc@comcast.net. Website: www.modernhaiku.org. Established 1969. **Contact:** Charles Trumbull, editor.

Magazines Needs *Modern Haiku*, published 3 times/year in February, June, and October, is "the foremost international journal of English-language haiku and criticism. We are devoted to publishing only the very best haiku. We also publish articles on haiku and have the most complete review section of haiku books." Wants "haiku in English (including translations into English) that incorporate the traditional aesthetics of the haiku genre, but which may be innovative as to subject matter, mode of approach or angle of perception, and form of expression. No tanka or renku. No special consideration given to work by children and teens." Has published haiku by Roberta Beary, Billy Collins, Lawrence Ferlinghetti, Carolyn Hall, Sharon Olds, Gary Snyder, John Stevenson, George Swede, and Cor van den Heuvel. *Modern Haiku* is 120 pages (average), digest-sized, printed on heavy quality stock, with full-color cover illustrations 4-page full-color art sections. Receives about 15,000-14,000 submissions/year, accepts about 1,000. Press run is 650. Subscription: $30 ppd. Sample: $13 ppd in the U.S.

How to Contact Submit "a maximum of 20 haiku on one or two letter-sized sheets." No e-mail submissions from North America. No previously published haiku or simultaneous submissions. Put name and address on each sheet. Include SASE. Guidelines available for SASE or on website. Responds in 4-6 weeks. Pays $1/haiku; no contributor's copies. Acquires first international serial rights. Reviews of books of haiku by staff and freelancers by invitation in 350-1,000 words, usually single-book format. Send materials for review consideration with complete ordering information.

Contest/Award Offerings Sponsors the annual Robert Spiess Memorial Haiku Competition. Guidelines available for SASE or on website.

Tips "Take the time to find out what haiku really are. We do not want sentimentality, pretty-pretty, or pseudo-Japanese themes. Five-seven-five syllable count, rhyme, ego, and intellectualizations are viewed with suspicion."

◻ MUDFISH

Box Turtle Press, 184 Franklin St., New York NY 10013. (212)219-9278. E-mail: mudfishmag@aol.com. Website: www.mudfish.org. **Contact:** Jill Hoffman, editor.

Magazines Needs *Mudfish*, published annually by Box Turtle Press, is an annual journal of poetry and art. Wants "free verse with energy, intensity, and originality of voice, mastery of style, the presence of passion." Has published poetry by Charles Simic, Jennifer Belle, Stephanie Dickinson, Ronald Wardall, Doug Dorph, and John Ashberry. Press run is 1,200. Single copy: $12 plus $3.50 subscription: $24 for 2 years (price includes s&h).

How to Contact Submit 4-6 poems at a time. No previously published poems or simultaneous submissions. No e-mail submissions; postal submissions only. Responds "immediately to three months." Pays one contributor's copy.

Contest/Award Offerings Sponsors the Mudfish Poetry Prize Award of $1,000. **Entry fee:** $15 for up to 3 poems, $3 for each additional poem. **Deadline:** varies. Guidelines available for SASE.

Also Offers Also publishes Mudfish Individual Poet Series #6 marbles, by Mary Du Passage.

Tips "Send your best poems—those with heart and craft."

▣ ◪ MUDLARK: AN ELECTRONIC JOURNAL OF POETRY & POETICS

Dept. of English, University of North Florida, Jacksonville FL 32224-2645. (904)620-2273. Fax: (904)620-3940. E-mail: mudlark@unf.edu. Website: www.unf.edu/mudlark. **Contact:** William Slaughter, editor.

Magazines Needs *Mudlark: An Electronic Journal of Poetry & Poetics*, published online "irregularly, but frequently," offers 3 formats: issues of *Mudlark* "are the electronic equivalent of print chapbooks; posters are the electronic equivalent of print broadsides; and flash poems are poems that have news in them, poems that feel like current events. The poem is the thing at *Mudlark*, and the essay about it. As our full name suggests, we will consider accomplished work that locates itself anywhere on the spectrum of contemporary practice. We want poems, of course, but we want essays, too, that make us read poems (and write them?) differently somehow. Although we are not innocent, we do imagine ourselves capable of surprise. The work of hobbyists is not for *Mudlark*." Has published poetry by John Allman, Denise Duhamel, Taylor Graham, Susan Kelly-Dewitt, Frederick Pollack, and Peter Waldor. *Mudlark* is archived and permanently on view at www.unf.edu.

How to Contact Submit any number of poems at a time. Considers previously published poems ("inasmuch as issues of *Mudlark* are the electronic equivalent of print chapbooks, some of the individual poems in them might, or might not, have been previously published; if they have been, that previous publication must be acknowledged"); no simultaneous submissions ("because of our short turn-around time"). "Only poems that have not been previously published will be considered for *Mudlark* posters, the electronic equivalent of print broadsides, or for *Mudlark* flash poems." Accepts e-mail submissions; no fax submissions. Cover letter is optional. Time between acceptance and publication is up to 3 months. Seldom comments on rejected poems. Guidelines available for SASE, by e-mail, or on website. Responds in "1 day to 1 month, depending.." Always sends prepublication galleys "in the form of inviting the author to proof the work on a private website that *Mudlark* maintains for that purpose." No payment; however, "one of the things we can do at *Mudlark* to 'pay' our authors for their work is point to it here and there. We can tell our readers how to find it, how to subscribe to it, and how to buy it—if it is for sale. Toward that end, we maintain A-Notes (on the authors) we publish. We call attention to their work." Acquires one-time rights.

Tips "*Mudlark* has been reviewed well and often. At this point in its history, *Mudlark* has established itself, arguably, as one of the few serious rivals in the first generation of the electronic medium, to print versions of its kind. Look at *Mudlark*, visit the website, spend some time there. Then make your decision: to submit or not to submit."

$ ☑ ◎ MYTHIC DELIRIUM

3514 Signal Hill Ave. NW, Roanoke VA 24017-5148. E-mail: mythicdelirium@gmail.com. Website: www.mythicdelirium.com. **Contact:** Mike Allen, Editor. *Mythic Delirium*, published biannually, is "a journal of speculative poetry for the new millennium. All forms considered. Must fit within the genres we consider, though we have published some mainstream verse." Does not want "forced rhyme, corny humor, jarringly gross sexual material, gratuitous obscenity, handwritten manuscripts." Has published poetry by Sonya Taaffe, Theodora Goss, Joe Haldeman, Ursula K. Le Guin, Ian Watson, and Jane Yolen. *Mythic Delirium* is 32 pages, digest-sized, saddle-stapled, with color cover art, includes house ads. Receives about 750 poems/year, accepts about 5%. Press run is 150. Subscription: $9/year, $16/2 years. Sample: $5. Make checks payable to Mike Allen. Member: Science Fiction Poetry Association, Science Fiction & Fantasy Writers of America.

$ ☑ THE NATION

33 Irving Place, New York NY 10003. Website: www.thenation.com/about/poetry_guidelines.mhtml. **Contact:** Peter Gizzi, Poetry Editor. *The Nation*, published weekly, is a journal of left/liberal opinion, with arts coverage that includes poetry. The only requirement for poetry is "excellence." Has published poetry by W.S. Merwin, Maxine Kumin, James Merrill, May Swenson, Edward Hirsch, and Charles Simic. Submit up to 3 poems at a time, no more than 8 poems within the calendar year. No simultaneous submissions. No fax, e-mail, or disk submissions; send by first-class mail only. No reply without SASE.

☑ NATURAL BRIDGE

Dept. of English, University of Missouri-St. Louis, One University Blvd., St. Louis MO 63121. E-mail: natural@umsl.edu. Website: www.umsl.edu/~natural. **Contact:** Jamie Nelson. *Natural Bridge*, published biannually, seeks "fresh, innovative poetry, both free and formal, on any subject. We want poems that work on first and subsequent readings—poems that entertain and resonate and challenge our readers. *Natural Bridge* also publishes fiction, essays, and translations." Has published poetry by Ross Gay, Beckian Fritz Goldberg, Joy Harjo, Bob Hicok, Sandra Kohler, and Timothy Liu. *Natural Bridge* is 150-200 pages, digest-sized, printed on 60 lb. opaque recycled, acid-free paper, true binding, with 12 pt. coated glossy or matte cover. Receives about 1,200 poems/year, accepts about 1%. Press run is 1,000 (200 subscribers, 50 libraries). Single copy: $10; subscription: $15/year, $25/2 years. Make checks payable to *Natural Bridge*. Member: CLMP.

How to Contact Submit 4-6 poems at a time. Lines/poem: no limit. Considers simultaneous submissions; no previously published poems. No e-mail or disk submissions. "Submissions should be typewritten, with name and address on each page. Do not staple manuscripts. Send SASE." Reads submissions July 1-August 31 and November 1-December 31. Time between acceptance and publication is 9 months. "Work is read and selected by the guest-editor and editor, along with editorial assistants made up of graduate students in our MFA program. We publish work by both established and new writers." Sometimes comments on rejected poems. Sometimes publishes theme issues. Upcoming themes available on website. Guidelines available in magazine or on website. Responds in 6 months after the close of the submission period. Sometimes sends prepublication galleys. Pays 2 contributor's copies plus one-year subscription. Rights revert to author upon publication.

NAUGATUCK RIVER REVIEW

P.O. Box 368, Westfield MA 01085. E-mail: naugatuckriver@aol.com. Website: http:// naugatuckriverreview.wordpress.com/. **Contact:** Lori Desrosiers, Publisher.

Magazines Needs The *Naugatuck River Review*, published semiannually, "is a literary journal for great narrative poetry looking for narrative poetry of high caliber, where the narrative is compressed with a strong emotional core." Considers poetry by teens. Has published poetry by Edward Byrne, Sheila Nickerson, Leslea Newman, Jeff Friedman, Roderick Bates, Frederick Lord, Derek Sheffield, and Allen Braden. *Naugatuck River Review* is 100 pages, digest-sized, perfect-bound with paper and artwork cover. Receives about 1,600 poems/year, accepts about 120. Press run is print-on-demand. Single copy: $15; Subscription (starting with next issue): $20/year. Make checks payable to *Naugatuck River Review*.

How to Contact Submit 3 poems at a time. Lines/poem: 50. Prefers unpublished poems but will consider simultaneous submissions. Accepts online submissions through submission manager; no fax or disk. Include a brief bio and mailing information. Reads submissions January 1-March 1 and July 1-September 1 for contest. Time between acceptance and publication is 2-3 months. "We have four poetry editors on staff and submissions are blind-read." Never comments on rejected poems. Sometimes publishes theme issues. Guidelines available in magazine and on website. Responds in 2-12 weeks. Always sends prepublication galleys. Pays 1 contributor's copy. Acquires first North American serial rights.

▧ ▣ ◯ NECROLOGY SHORTS: TALES OF MACABRE AND HORROR

Isis International, P.O. Box 510232, Saint Louis MO 63151. E-mail: editor@necrologyshorts. com; submit@necrologyshorts.com. Website: www.necrologyshorts.com. **Contact:** John Ferguson, Editor. Consumer publication published online daily and through Amazon Kindle. Also offers an annual collection. "*Necrology Shorts* is an online publication which publishes fiction, articles, cartoons, artwork, and poetry daily. Embracing the internet, e-book readers, and new technology, we aim to go beyond the long time standard of a regular publication to bringing our readers a daily flow of entertainment. We will also be publishing an annual collection for each year in print, e-book reader, and Adobe PDF format. Our main genre is suspense horror similar to H.P. Lovecraft and/or Robert E. Howard. We also publish science fiction and fantasy. We would love to see work continuing the Cthulhu Mythos, but we accept all horror. We also hold contests, judged by our readers, to select the top stories and artwork. Winners of contests receive various prizes, including cash."

Magazines Needs *Necrology Shorts*, published online daily and through Amazon Kindle, is seeking avante-garde, free verse, haiku, light-verse, and traditional poetry in the genres of horror, fantasy, and science fiction. "We will also be publishing an annual collection for each year in print, e-book reader, and Adobe PDF format. Our main genre is suspense horror similar to H.P. Lovecraft and/or Robert E. Howard. We also publish science fiction and fantasy. We would love to see work continuing the Cthulhu Mythos, but we accept all horror." Buys 500 poems/year.

How to Contact Submit up to 5 poems at one time. Length: 4-100 lines.

Tips "*Necrology Shorts* is looking to break out of the traditional publication types to use the internet, e-book readers, and other technology. We not only publish works of authors and artists, we let them use their published works to brand themselves and further their profits of their hard work. The best way to get to us is to let your creative side run wild and not send us the typical fare. Don't forget that we publish horror, sci-fi, and fantasy. We expect deranged, warped, twisted, strange, sadistic, and things that question sanity and reality."

Ⓝ NEW COLLAGE

New College of Florida, New College of Florida, c/o WRC, 5800 Bayshore Rd., Sarasota FL 34243. E-mail: newcollagemag@gmail.com. Website: newcollagemag.wordpress.com. **Contact:** Alexis Orgera, editor. "*New CollAge* accepts unsolicited submissions of previously unpublished poetry, short fiction (short shorts, fewer than 1,500/words), creative nonfiction, artwork (especially that of the collage-inspired variety), and hybrids thereof from August-May each year for both our print issue and web exclusives. Submissions received in June and July will not be read. Note that we publish primarily poetry."

Magazines Needs *New CollAge*, published annually, is a "journal of new writing and visual art produced by a general editor alongside a staff of New College of Florida undergraduates who subscribe to the notion that a collage is an assemblage of different voices that merge to create new conversations."

How to Contact E-mail no more than 1500 words in a single Word document. "Do not submit again until you've heard back." Note "submission" in the subject line, as well as the type of work you're submitting." Accepts simultaneous submissions. Reads September-May. Responds in 2-6 months.

Additional Information Acquires first serial rights, print and online. All rights revert to author upon publication. Author receives 2 contributor copies.

$ ☑ NEW ENGLAND REVIEW

Middlebury College, Middlebury VT 05753. (802)443-5075. E-mail: nereview@middlebury. edu. Website: www.nereview.com. **Contact:** Poetry Editor.

• Work published in *New England Review* is frequently included in *The Best American Poetry*.

Magazines Needs *New England Review*, published quarterly, is a prestigious, nationally distributed literary journal. Has published poetry by Carl Phillips, Lucia Perillo, Linda Gregerson, and Natasha Trethewey. *New England Review* is 200+ pages, 7x10, printed on heavy stock, flat-spined, with glossy cover with art. Receives 3,000-4,000 poetry submissions/year, accepts about 70-80 poems/year. Subscription: $30. Sample: $10. Overseas shipping fees add $25 for subscription, $12 for Canada; international shipping $5 for single issues.

How to Contact Submit up to 6 poems at a time. No previously published poems or simultaneous submissions. Accepts submissions by postal mail only; accepts questions by e-mail. "Cover letters are useful." Address submissions to "Poetry Editor." Reads submissions postmarked September 1-May 31 only. Time between acceptance and publication is 3-6 months. Responds in up to 3 months. Always sends prepublication galleys. Pays $10/page ($20 minimum) plus 2 contributor's copies. Send materials for review consideration.

Tips "Read a few copies of the magazine before submitting work. Our response time is reasonable, so please do not send simultaneous submissions."

☑ THE NEW LAUREL REVIEW

828 Lesseps St., New Orleans LA 70117. Fax: (504)948-3834. Website: http://www. nathanielturner.com/newlaurelreview.htm. **Contact:** Lewis Schmidt, Managing Editor. *The New Laurel Review*, published annually, is "an independent nonprofit literary magazine dedicated to fine art. The magazine is meant to be eclectic, and we try to publish the best we receive, whether the submission is poem, translation, short story, essay, review, or interview. We have no domineering preferences regarding style, and we do consult with invited readers and writers for their opinions. We are seeking original work without hackneyed phrases, indulgent voices, or tired thinking. We love surprises and to see a writer or artist enliven our too often dull, editorial worlds." Has published poetry by Gerald Locklin, Roland John (British), Joyce Odam, Ryan G. Van Cleave, Robert Cooperman, and Jared Carter. *The New Laurel Review* is about 115-130 pages, 6 × 9, laser-printed, perfect-bound, with original art on laminated cover. Receives 400-600 submissions/year, accepts about 30-40 poems. Press run is about 500. Single copy: $12 for individuals, $14 for institutions. Sample (back issue): $5.

☑ NEW MEXICO POETRY REVIEW

44 Via Punto Nuevo, Santa Fe NM 87508. E-mail: nmpr@live.com. Website: newmexicopoetryreview.com. **Contact:** Kathleen Johnson, editor.

Magazines Needs *New Mexico Poetry Review*, published semiannually in April and October, is dedicated to publishing strong, imaginative, well-crafted poems by both new talents and established writers. Wants "poems, prose poems, poetry-related essays, and interviews." Does not want "dull or pretentious writing." *New Mexico Poetry Review* is 80-120 pages, digest-sized, professionally printed, perfect-bound, with a full-color glossy card with art, includes ads. Press run is 500. Single copy: $8; subscription: $15/year. Make checks payable to New Mexico Poetry Review.

How to Contact Submit up to 5 poems at a time of no more than 70 lines. Does not consider simultaneous submissions; no previously published poems. Accepts e-mail submissions pasted into body of e-mail message; no fax or disk submissions. Cover letter is not required. Reads submissions year round. Time between acceptance and publication is 4-6 months. Sometimes comments on rejected poems. Sometimes publishes theme issues. Guidelines available for SASE, by e-mail, or on website. Responds in 1-3 months. Sometimes sends prepublication galleys. Pays 1 contributor's copy. Acquires first North American serial rights. Reviews books and chapbooks of poetry by New Mexico poets in 500-700 words, single and multi-book format.

Additional Information Publishes occasional books and chapbooks, but does not accept unsolicited book/chapbook submissions.

Tips "Read as much good poetry as you can. Learn from the best. Take chances."

☑ NEW OHIO REVIEW

English Dept., 360 Ellis Hall, Ohio University, Athens OH 45701. *NOR*, published biannually in Spring and Fall, publishes fiction, nonfiction, and poetry. Wants "literary submissions in any genre. Translations are welcome if permission has been granted." Billy Collins, Stephen Dunn, Stuart Dybek, Eleanor Wilner, Yusef Komunyakaa, Kim Addonizio, William Olson. Single: $9; Subscription: $16. Member: CLMP.

How to Contact Submit up to 6 poems at a time. "Do not submit more than once every six months. "Considers simultaneous submissions. "Notify immediately if work is accepted elsewhere. "Accepts mail only. Include SASE or IRC, or provide a valid e-mail address (international submissions only). Primary reading period is September through May, but will accept submissions from subscriber e-mail address (international submissions only).

$ ☑ NEW ORLEANS REVIEW

Box 195, Loyola University, New Orleans LA 70118. Website: neworleansreview.org. **Contact:** Mark Yakich, poetry editor.

Magazines Needs *New Orleans Review*, published twice/year, is an international journal of poetry, fiction, essays, book reviews, and interviews. Wants "dynamic writing that demonstrates attention to the language and a sense of the medium; writing that engages, surprises, moves us. We subscribe to the belief that in order to truly write well, one must first master the rudiments: grammar and syntax, punctuation, the sentence, the paragraph, the line, the stanza." Has published poetry by Chrisopher Howell, Martha Zweig, Lee Upton, Jeffrey Levine, Carlie Rosemurgy, and D.C. Berry. *New Orleans Review* is 200 pages, elegantly printed, perfect-bound, with glossy card cover. Receives about 3,000 mss/year. Press run is 1,500. Single copy: $10. Sample: $6.

How to Contact Submit 1-5 pages of poems at a time "using our electronic submission system on our website. We no longer accept poetry submissions via air mail." Reading period August 15-May 15. Considers simultaneous submissions "if we're notified immediately upon acceptance elsewhere"; no previously published poems. No fax submissions. Brief cover letter is preferred. Guidelines available on website. Responds in 2-4 months. Pays 2 contributor's copies and honorarium. Acquires first North American serial rights.

$ ☑ THE NEW RENAISSANCE

26 Heath Rd. #11, Arlington MA 02474-3645. E-mail: marccreate@aol.com. Website: www. tnrlitmag.net.

Magazines Needs *the new renaissance*, published spring and fall ("resources permitting'), is "intended for the 'renaissance' person—the generalist, not the specialist. We publish the best new writing and translations and offer a forum for articles on political, sociological topics; feature established as well as emerging visual artists and writers; highlight reviews of small press; and offer essays on a variety of topics from visual arts and literature to science. Open to a variety of styles, including traditional." Has published poetry by Anita Susan Brenner, Anne Struthers, Marc Widershien, Miguel Torga (trans. Alexis Levetin), Stephen Todd Booker, and Rabindranath Togore (trans. Wendy Barker and S. Togore). *the new renaissance* is 144-182 pages, digest-sized, professionally printed on heavy stock, flat-spined, with glossy color cover. Receives about 650 poetry submissions/year, accepts about 40. Press run is 1,500 (760 subscribers, 132 libraries). Single copy: $12.50 (current), $11.50 (recent), $7.50 (back issue); subscription: $30 for 3 issues in U.S., $35 in Canada, $38 all others. "All checks in U.S. dollars. A 3-issue subscription covers 18-22 months."

How to Contact Submit 3-6 poems at a time, "unless a long poem—then 1." Considers simultaneous submissions, if notified; no previously published poems "unless magazine's circulation was under 250." Always include SASE or IRC. Accepts submissions by postal mail only; "when accepted, we ask if a disk is available, and we prefer accepted translations to be available in the original language on disk. **All poetry submissions are tied to our Awards Program for poetry published in a 3-issue volume; judged by independent judges.**" Entry fee: $16.50 for nonsubscribers, $11.50 for subscribers, "for which they receive 2 back issues or a recent issue or an extension of their subscription. Submissions without entry fee are returned unread." Reads submissions January 2-June 30. Guidelines available for SASE. Responds in 5 months. Pays $21-40 (more for the occasional longer poem), plus 1 contributor's copy/poem. Acquires all rights but returns rights provided *the new renaissance* retains rights for any *the new renaissance* collection. Reviews books of poetry.

Contest/Award Offerings The Awards Program offers 3 prizes of $250, $125, and $50, with 3-4 Honorable Mentions of $25 each; all submissions are tied to the Awards Program.

Tips "Read, read, read! And support the literary magazines that support serious writers and poets. In 2002, more than 350 separate submissions came in, all without the required fee. Since our Poetry Awards Program has been in effect since 1995, and since we've notified all markets about our guidelines and entry fee, this just shows an indifferent, careless reading of our magazine's requirements."

☑ NEW SOUTH

Georgia State University, Campus Box 1894, Atlanta GA 30303. E-mail: gsu_review@langate. gsu.edu. Website: www.review.gsu.edu.

Magazines Needs *New South*, published semiannually, prints fiction, poetry, nonfiction, and visual art. Wants "original voices searching to rise above the ordinary. No subject or form biases." Does not want pornography or Hallmark verse. *New South* is 160+ pages. Press run is 2,000; 500 distributed free to students. Single copy: $5; subscription: $8/year; $14 for 2 issues. Sample: $3 (back issue).

How to Contact Submit up to 3 poems at a time. Considers simultaneous submissions (with notification in cover letter); no previously published poems. No e-mail submissions. Name, address, and phone/e-mail must appear on each page of ms. Cover letter is required. Include "a 3-4 line bio, a list of the work(s) submitted in the order they appear, and your name, mailing address, phone number, and e-mail address." Include SASE for notification. Time between acceptance and publication is 3-5 months. Seldom comments on rejected poems. Guidelines available for SASE, by e-mail, or on website. Pays 2 copies. Rights revert to poets upon publication.

Contest/Award Offerings The *New South* Annual Writing Contest offers $1,000 for the best poem; copy of issue to all who submit. Submissions must be unpublished. Submit up to 3 poems on any subject or in any form. "Specify 'poetry' on outside envelope." Guidelines available for SASE, by e-mail, or on website. **Deadline:** March 4. Competition receives 200 entries. Past judges include Sharon Olds, Jane Hirschfield, Anthony Hecht, Phillip Levine and Jake Adam York. Winner will be announced in the Spring issue.

Tips "Avoid clichéd and sentimental writing but as all advice is filled with paradox—write from the heart. We look for a smooth union of form and content."

🌐 🖥 ✒ ◎ THE NEW VERSE NEWS

E-mail: nvneditor@yahoo.com; nvneditor@gmail.com. Website: www.newversenews. com. **Contact:** James Penha, Editor. *The New Verse News*, published online and updated "every day or 2," has "a clear liberal bias, but will consider various visions and views." Wants "poems, both serious and satirical, on current events and topical issues; will also consider prose poems and short-short stories and plays." Does not want "work unrelated to the news." Receives about 700 poems/year, accepts about 300.

How to Contact Submit 1-5 poems at a time. Lines/poem: no length restrictions. No previously published poems or simultaneous submissions. Accepts e-mail submissions (pasted into body of message); use "Verse News Submission" as the subject line; no disk submissions. Send brief bio. Reads submissions year-round. Submit seasonal poems 1 month in advance. "Normally, poems are published immediately upon acceptance." Poems are circulated to an editorial board. Sometimes comments on rejected poems. Guidelines available on website. Responds in 1-3 weeks. No payment. Acquires first rights. Rights revert to poet upon publication.

🌐 $ ✒ THE NEW WRITER

P.O. Box 60, Cranbrook, Kent TN17 2ZR, England. (44)(1580)212626. Fax: (44)(1580)212041. E-mail: admin@thenewwriter.com. Website: www.thenewwriter.com. **Contact:** Sarah Jackson, poetry editor.

Magazines Needs *The New Writer*, published 6 times/year, is "aimed at writers with a serious intent, who want to develop their writing to meet the high expectations of today's editors. The team at *The New Writer* is committed to working with its readers to increase the chances of publication through masses of useful information and plenty of feedback. More than that, we let you know about the current state of the market with the best in contemporary fiction and cutting-edge poetry, backed up by searching articles and in-depth features." Wants "short and long unpublished poems, provided they are original and undeniably brilliant. No problems with length/form, but anything over 2 pages (150 lines) needs to be brilliant. Cutting edge shouldn't mean inaccessible. The poetry editor prefers poems which provide a good use of language, offering challenging imagery." *The New Writer* is 56 pages, A4, professionally printed, saddle-stapled, with paper cover. Press run is 1,500 (1,350 subscribers); 50 distributed free to publishers, agents. Single copy: £6.25 in U.S. (5 IRCs required); subscription: £37.50 in U.S. "We have a secure server for subscriptions and entry into the annual Prose and Poetry Prizes on the website. Monthly e-mail newsletter included free of charge in the subscription package."

How to Contact Submit up to 3 poems at a time. Lines/poem: 150 maximum. Does not consider previously published poems. Accepts e-mail submissions (pasted into body of message). Time between acceptance and publication is up to 6 months. Often comments on rejected poems. Guidelines available for SASE (or SAE with IRC) or on website. Pays £3 voucher plus 1 contributor's copy. Acquires first British serial rights.

Contest/Award Offerings Sponsors *The New Writer* Prose & Poetry Prizes annually. "All poets writing in the English language are invited to submit an original, previously unpublished poem or a collection of 6-10 poems. Up to 25 prizes will be presented, as well as publication for the prize-winning poets in an anthology, plus the chance for a further 10 shortlisted poets to see their work published in *The New Writer* during the year." Guidelines available by e-mail or on website.

$ ◙ THE NEW YORKER

4 Times Square, New York NY 10036. Website: www.newyorker.com. **Contact:** Poetry Editor.

• Poems published in *The New Yorker* often have been included *The Best American Poetry*.

Magazines Needs *The New Yorker*, published weekly, prints poetry of the highest quality (including translations). Subscription: $47/year (47 issues), $77 for 2 years (94 issues).

How to Contact Submit no more than 6 poems at a time. No previously published poems or simultaneous submissions. Use online e-mail source and upload as pdf attachment. Include poet's name in the subject line and as the title of attached document. "We prefer to receive no more than two submissions per writer per year." Pays top rates.

◙ NEW YORK QUARTERLY

P.O. Box 693, Old Chelsea Station, New York NY 10113. Website: www.nyquarterly.com. **Contact:** Raymond Hammond, editor.

Magazines Needs *New York Quarterly*, published 3 times/year, seeks to print "a most eclectic cross-section of contemporary American poetry." Has published poetry by Charles Bukowski, James Dickey, Lola Haskins, Lyn Lifshin, Elisavietta Ritchie, and W.D. Snodgrass. *New York Quarterly* is digest-sized, elegantly printed, flat-spined, with glossy color cover. Subscription: $35.

How to Contact Submit 3-5 poems at a time. No e-mail submissions, but accepts electronic submissions on website. Considers simultaneous submissions with notification. No previously published poems. Include your name and address on each page. "Include SASE; no international postage coupons." Guidelines available on website. Responds within 6 weeks. Pays in contributor's copies.

☑ NEXUS LITERARY JOURNAL

W104 Student Union, Wright State University, Dayton OH 45435. Website: www.wsunexus. com. **Contact:** Max Lake, Editor. *Nexus Literary Journal*, published 3 times/year in fall, winter, and spring, is a student-operated magazine of mainstream and street poetry. Wants "truthful, direct poetry. Open to poets anywhere. We look for contemporary, imaginative work." *Nexus* is 80-96 pages. Receives about 1,000 submissions/year, accepts about 50-70. Circulation is 3,000. Sample: free for 10x15 SAE with 5 first-class stamps.

☐ NIBBLE

1714 Franklin St., Suite 100-231, Oakland CA 94612. E-mail: nibblepoems@gmail.com. Website: http://nibblepoems.wordpress.com. **Contact:** Jeff Fleming, editor. *nibble*, published bimonthly, is a journal of poetry "focusing on short poems (less than 20 lines)." Does not want "inaccessible, self-important poems." *nibble* is 32 pages, digest-sized, laser-printed, side-stapled, with a cardstock, imaged cover. Receives about 1,500 poems/year, accepts about 250. Press run is 250; 50 distributed free to schools. Single copy: $6; Subscription: $24/6 issues. Make checks payable to Jeff Fleming.

How to Contact Prefers e-mail submissions. Submit 3-5 poems at a time. SASE required for mail submissions; cover letter is required. Reads submissions year round. Time between acceptance and publication is 2 months. Often comments on rejected poems. Sometimes publishes theme issues. Upcoming themes available by e-mail. Guidelines available for SASE and by e-mail. Responds in 2-4 weeks. Pays 1 contributor's copy. Acquires one-time rights. Reviews books and chapbooks of poetry.Occasionally will publish chapbooks.

☑ NIMROD: INTERNATIONAL JOURNAL OF POETRY AND PROSE

University of Tulsa, 800 S. Tucker Dr., Tulsa OK 74104-3189. (918)631-3080. Fax: (918)631-3033. E-mail: nimrod@utulsa.edu. Website: www.utulsa.edu/nimrod. **Contact:** Lisa Ransom and Ann Stone, poetry editors.

• Poetry published in *Nimrod* has been included in *The Best American Poetry*.

Magazines Needs *Nimrod: International Journal of Poetry and Prose*, published 2 times/year, is "an active 'little magazine,' part of the movement in American letters which has been essential to the development of modern literature." Publishes an awards issue in the fall, featuring the prizewinners of its national competition, and a thematic issue each spring. "Poems in non-award issues range from formal to freestyle with several translations." Wants "vigorous writing that is neither wholly of the academy nor the streets; typed manuscripts." Has published poetry by Diane Glancy, Judith Strasser, Steve Lautermilch, Virgil Suaárez, and Jen-Mark Sens. *Nimrod* is about 200 pages, digest-sized, professionally printed on coated stock, perfect-bound, with full-color glossy cover. Receives about 2,000 submissions/year, accepts 1%. Press run is 2,500. Subscription: $18.50/year U.S., $20 foreign. Sample: $11. "Specific back issues available. Please send check or money order."

How to Contact Submit 5-10 poems at a time. No fax or e-mail submissions. Open to general submissions from January 1-November 30. Publishes theme issues. Guidelines available for SASE, by e-mail, or on website. Responds in up to 3 months. "During the months that the *Nimrod* Literary Awards competition is being conducted, reporting time on non-contest manuscripts will be longer." Pays 2 contributor's copies, plus reduced cost on additional copies.

Contest/Award Offerings The annual *Nimrod* Literary Awards, including The Pablo Neruda Prize for Poetry.

Also Offers Sponsors the *Nimrod* workshop for readers and writers, a one-day workshop held annually in October. Cost is about $50. Send SASE for brochure and registration form.

$ ◢ NINTH LETTER

Dept. of English, University of Illinois, 608 S. Wright St., Urbana IL 61801. (217)244-3145. E-mail: poetry@ninthletter.com. Website: www.ninthletter.com. *Ninth Letter*, published semiannually, is "dedicated to the examination of literature as it intersects with various aspects of contemporary culture and intellectual life." Open to all forms of poetry. Wants "exceptional literary quality." Has published poetry by Cate Marvin, L.S. Asekoff, Patricia Smith, Bob Hicok, Sharmila Voorakkara, Geri Doran, and Angie Estes. *Ninth Letter* is 176 pages, 9x12, offset-printed, perfect-bound, with 4-color cover with graphics. Receives about 9,000 poems/year, accepts about 40. Press run is 2,500 (500 subscribers, 1,000 shelf sales); 500 distributed free, 500 to contributors, media, and fundraising efforts. Single copy: $14.95; subscription: $21.95/year. Sample: $8.95 (back issue). Make checks payable to *Ninth Letter*.Member: CLMP; CELJ.

How to Contact Submit no more than 6 poems or 10 pages at a time. No previously published poems. Electronic submissions accepted through website. No e-mail or disk submissions. Cover letter is preferred. "SASE must be included for reply." Reads submissions September 1- April 30 (inclusive postmark dates). Time between acceptance and publication is 5-6 months. Poems are circulated to an editorial board. Sometimes comments on rejected poems. Guidelines available for SASE, by e-mail, or on website. Responds in 2 months. Always sends prepublications galleys. Pays $25/page and 2 contributor's copies. Acquires first North American serial rights. Rights revert to poet upon publication.

◢ ◎ THE NOCTURNAL LYRIC

P.O. Box 542, Astoria OR 97103. **Contact:** Susan Moon, Editor. *The Nocturnal Lyric, Journal of the Bizarre*, published annually, features "bizarre fiction and poetry, primarily by new writers." Wants "poems dealing with the bizarre: fantasy, death, morbidity, horror, gore, etc. Any length" Does not want "boring poetry." Has published poetry by Eric Martin, Michael J. Frey, David L. Paxton, Herbert Jerry Baker, Debbie Berk, and Kenneth C. Wickson. *The Nocturnal Lyric* is 40 pages, digest-sized, photocopied, saddle-stapled, includes ads. Receives about 200 poems/year, accepts about 35%. Press run is 400 (40 subscribers). Single copy: $3 U.S., $5 foreign. Make checks payable to Susan Moon.

How to Contact *The Nocturnal Lyric, Journal of the Bizarre*, published annually, features "bizarre fiction and poetry, primarily by new writers." Wants "poems dealing with the bizarre: fantasy, death, morbidity, horror, gore, etc. Any length" Does not want "boring poetry." Has published poetry by Eric Martin, Michael J. Frey, David L. Paxton, Herbert Jerry Baker, Debbie Berk, and Kenneth C. Wickson. *The Nocturnal Lyric* is 40 pages, digest-sized, photocopied, saddle-stapled, includes ads. Receives about 200 poems/year, accepts about 35%. Press run is 400 (40 subscribers). Single copy: $3 U.S., $5 foreign. Make checks payable to Susan Moon.

Tips "Don't follow the trends. We admire the unique."

☑ NOMAD'S CHOIR

30-15 Hobart St., F4H, Woodside NY 11377. **Contact:** Joshua Meander, Editor. *Nomad's Choir*, published quarterly, seeks "love poems, protest poems, mystical poems, nature poems, poems of humanity, poems with solutions to world problems and inner conflict, poems with hope; simple words, careful phrasing." Wants "free verse, rhymed poems, sonnets." Does not want "curse words in poems; little or no name-dropping; no naming of consumer products; no 2-page poems; no humor, no bias writing, no poems untitled." Has published poetry by Steven Baker, Angela Castillo, Murry Kaufman, and Joan Kitcher-White. *Nomad's Choir* is 12 pages, magazine-sized, typeset, saddle-stapled. Receives about 150 poems/year, accepts 50. Press run is 400; all distributed free. Subscription: $5. Sample: $1.50. Make checks payable to Joshua Meander.

How to Contact Submit 4 poems at a time, each on a different topic. Lines/poem: 9 minimum, 30 maximum. Responds in 2 months. Pays 1 contributor's copy.

Tips "Social commentary with beauty and hope gets first consideration."

$ ☑ NORTH AMERICAN REVIEW

University of Northern Iowa, 1222 West 27th St., Cedar Falls IA 50614-0516. (319)273-6455. Fax: (319)273-4326. E-mail: nar@uni.edu. Website: northamericanreview.org. **Contact:** Poetry Editor.

Magazines Needs *North American Review*, published 5 times/year, is "the oldest literary magazine in America." Wants "poetry of the highest quality; poems that are passionate about subject, language, and image. Especially interested in work that addresses contemporary North American concerns and issues, particularly with the environment, race, ethnicity, gender, sexual orientation, and class." Has published poetry by Debra Marquart, Nick Carboó, Yusef Komunyakaa, Virgil Suaárez, Nance Van Winckel, and Dara Wier. *North American Review* is about 48 pages, magazine-sized, professionally printed, saddle-stapled, with glossy full-color paper cover. Receives about 10,000 poems/year, accepts 100. Press run is 2,500 (1,500 subscribers, 1,000 libraries). Subscription: $22 in U.S., $29 in Canada, $32 foreign. Sample: $5.

How to Contact Submit 6 poems at a time. No previously published poems or simultaneous submissions. No fax, e-mail, or disk submissions. Cover letter is preferred. Include brief bio and list poem titles. Include SASE. Time between acceptance and publication is up to 1 year. Guidelines available in magazine, for SASE, by e-mail, or on website. Responds in 4 months. Always sends prepublication galleys. Pays $1/line ($20 minimum, $100 maximum) and 2 contributor's copies. Acquires first North American serial rights only. Rights revert to poets upon publication.

Contest/Award Offerings The annual James Hearst Poetry Prize.

$ ◎ NORTH CAROLINA LITERARY REVIEW

East Carolina University and the North Carolina Literary & Historical Association, Dept. of English, East Carolina University, Greenville NC 27858-4353. **Contact:** Submissions Manager. *North Carolina Literary Review*, published annually in the summer, contains "articles and other works about North Carolina topics or by North Carolina authors." Wants "poetry by writers currently living in North Carolina, those who have lived in North Carolina, or those using North Carolina for subject matter." Has published poetry by Betty Adcock, James

Applewhite, and A.R. Ammons. *North Carolina Literary Review* is 200 pages, magazine-sized. Receives about 100 submissions/year, accepts about 10%. Press run is 1,000 (350 subscribers, 100 libraries, 100 shelf sales); 100 distributed free to contributors. Subscription: $20 for 2 years, $36 for 4 years. Sample: $15.

◯ ◎ NORTH CENTRAL REVIEW

North Central College, CM #235, 30 N. Brainard St., Naperville IL 60540. (630)637-5291. E-mail: nccreview@noctrl.edu. Website: http://orgs.northcentralcollege.edu/review. *North Central Review,* published semiannually, considers "work in all literary genres, including occasional interviews, from undergraduate writers globally. The journal's goal is for college-level, emerging creative writers to share their work publicly and create a conversation with each other. ALL styles and forms are welcome as submissions. The readers tend to value attention to form (but not necessarily fixed form), voice, and detail. Very long poems or sequences (running more than 4 or 5 pages) may require particular excellence because of the journal's space and budget constraints." Does not want "overly sentimental language and hackneyed imagery. These are all-too-common weaknesses that readers see in submissions; we recommend revision and polishing before sending work." Considers poetry by teens (undergraduate writers only). *North Central Review* is 120 pages, digest-sized, perfect-bound, with cardstock cover with 4-color design. Press run is about 750, distributed free to contributors and publication reception attendees. Single copy: $5; subscription: $10. Make checks payable to North Central College.

How to Contact Submit up to 5 poems at a time. Lines/poem: "no limit, but poems running more than 4-5 pages may undergo particular scrutiny." No previously published poems or simultaneous submissions. Accepts e-mail submissions (as Word attachments only); no fax submissions. Cover letter is preferred. Include name, postal address, phone number, and e-mail address (.edu address as proof of student status). If necessary (i.e., .edu address not available), include a photocopy of student ID with number marked out as proof of undergraduate status. Reads submissions September-March, with deadlines of February 15 and October 15. Time between acceptance and publication is 1-4 months. Poems are circulated to an editorial board. "All submissions are read by at least 3 staff members, including an editor." Rarely comments on rejected poems. Guidelines available on website, in magazine, for SASE, or by e-mail. Responds in 1-4 months. Pays 2 contributor's copies. Acquires one-time rights. Rights revert to poet upon publication.

Tips "Don't send anything you just finished moments ago—rethink, revise, and polish. Avoid sentimentalitity and abstraction. That said, the *North Central Review* publishes beginners, so don't hesitate to submit and, if rejected, submit again."

◉ NORTH DAKOTA QUARTERLY

Merrifield Hall Room 110, 276 Centennial Dr. Stop 7209, Grand Forks ND 58202-7209. E-mail: ndq@und.nodak.edu. Website: www.und.nodak.edu/org/ndq. Established 1910. **Contact:** Robert Lewis, editor.

Magazines Needs *North Dakota Quarterly* is published by the University of North Dakota. Seeks material related to the arts and humanities—essays, fiction, interviews, poems, reviews, and visual art. Wants poetry "that reflects an understanding not only of the difficulties of the craft, but of the vitality and tact that each poem calls into play." Has published poetry by Maxine Kumin, Paul Muldoon, Robert Bagg, James Scully, Patricia Schneider, and Marianne Boruch. *North Dakota Quarterly* is about 200 pages, digest-sized, professionally designed and printed, perfect-bound, with full-color artwork on white card cover. Has 550 subscribers. Subscription: $25/year. Sample: $8.

How to Contact Submit 5 poems at a time. No previously published poems or simultaneous submissions. No e-mail submissions; accepts only typed hard-copy submissions by postal mail. Time between acceptance and publication varies. Responds in up to 6 weeks. Always sends prepublication galleys. Pays 2 contributor's copies. Acquires first serial rights.

Tips "We look to publish the best fiction, poetry, and essays that, in our estimation, we can. Our tastes and interests are best reflected in what we have been recently publishing, and we suggest that you look at some current numbers."

✉ NORTHWEST REVIEW

5243 University of Oregon, Eugene OR 97403. (541)346-3957. Fax: (541)346-0537. E-mail: nweditor@uoregon.edu. Website: http://nwr.uoregon.edu. **Contact:** Daniel Anderson, general editor. Established 1957. *Northwest Review*, published 2 times/year is "looking for smart, crisp writing about poetry and poetics. The only criterion for acceptance of material for publication is excellence." Has published poetry and essays by AI, Yusef Komunyakaa, Charles Wright, Brenda Hillman, Eavan Boland, and Marilyn Chin. *Northwest Review* is digest-sized, flat-spined. Receives about 3,500 submissions/year, accepts about 4%. Press run is 1,300. Single copy: $8-10; subscription: $20/year (two issues). Sample: $8-10.

Tips "Persist."

$ ✉ NOTRE DAME REVIEW/ND[RE]VIEW

840 Flanner Hall, University of Notre Dame, Notre Dame IN 46556. (574)631-6952. Fax: (574)631-4795. E-mail: english.ndreview.1@nd.edu. Website: www.nd.edu/~ndr/review. htm. **Contact:** Managing Editor.

Magazines Needs *Notre Dame Review*, published semiannually, aims "to present a panoramic view of contemporary art and literature—no one style is advocated over another. We are especially interested in work that takes on big issues by making the invisible seen." Has published poetry by W.S. Merwin, R.T. Smith, Moira Egan, Michael Harper, Floyd Skloot, and Kevin Ducey. *Notre Dame Review* is 170 pages, magazine-sized, perfect-bound, with 4-color glossy cover, includes ads. Receives about 400 poems/year, accepts 10%. Press run is 2,000 (500 subscribers, 150 libraries, 1,000 shelf sales); 350 distributed free to contributors, assistants, etc. Single copy: $8; subscription: $15/year. Sample: $6 (back issue).

How to Contact Submit 3-5 poems at a time. Considers simultaneous submissions; no previously published poems. Cover letter is required. Reads submissions September-November and January-March only. Time between acceptance and publication is 3 months. Seldom comments on rejected poems. Publishes theme issues. Guidelines available on website. Responds in 3 months. Always sends prepublication galleys. Pays small gratuity on publication, plus 2 contributor's copies. Acquires first rights. Staff reviews books of poetry in 500 words, single- and multi-book format. Send materials for review consideration.

Additional Information *nd[[re]]view* is the online companion to *Notre Dame Review*, offering "interviews, critique, and commentary on authors and artists showcased within the pages of the print magazine." See website for more details.

Contest/Award Offerings The Ernest Sandeen Prize in Poetry.

Tips "Read magazine before submitting."

⊕ ▣ ☻ NTHPOSITION

E-mail: rquintav@gmail.com. Website: www.nthposition.com. **Contact:** Rufo Quintavalle, Poetry Editor.

Magazines Needs *nthposition*, published monthly online, is an eclectic, London-based journal dedicated to poetry, fiction, and nonfiction "with a weird or innovative edge." Wants "all kinds of poetry—from spoken word to new formalist to linguistically innovative. We also publish political poetry." Has published poetry by Charles Bernstein, George Szirtes, Stephanie Bolster, and Mimi Khalvati. Receives about 2,000 poems/year, accepts about 10%.

How to Contact Submit 2-6 poems at a time. No previously published poems or simultaneous submissions. Accepts e-mail submissions only (pasted into body of message, no attachments). Cover letter is required. "A brief author's bio is appreciated." Reads submissions throughout the year. Time between acceptance and publication is 4 months. "Poems are read and selected by the poetry editor, who uses his own sense of what makes a poem work online to select." Never comments on rejected poems. Occasionally publishes theme issues. Guidelines available by e-mail or on website. Responds in 6 weeks. No payment. Does not request rights but expects proper acknowledgement if poems reprinted later.

Also Offers Publishes special theme e-books from time to time, such as *100 Poets Against the War*.

Tips "Never give up; keep writing. Poetry is a life's work."

⊕ ◯ OBSESSED WITH PIPEWORK

8 Abbot's Way, Pilton, Somerset BA4 4BN, England. E-mail: cannula.dementia@virgin.net. **Contact:** Charles Johnson, Editor. 8 Abbot's Way, Pilton, Somerset BA4 4BN England. (44)(1749)890019. E-mail: cannula.dementia@virgin.net. Established 1995. **Contact:** Charles Johnson, editor.

Magazines Needs *Obsessed with Pipework*, published quarterly, is "very keen to publish strong new voices—'new poems to surprise and delight' with somewhat of a high-wire aspect." Wants "original, exploratory poems—positive, authentic, oblique maybe—delighting in image and in the dance of words on the page." Does not want "the predictable, the unfresh, the rhyme-led, the clever, the didactic, the sure-of-itself. No formless outpourings, please." Has published poetry by David Hart, Jennifer Compton, Susan Wicks, Carol Burns, Lucille Gang Shulklapper, and Maria Jastrzebska. *Obsessed with Pipework* is 49 pages, A5, stapled, with card cover. Receives about 1,500 poems/year, accepts about 10%. Press run is 70-100. Single copy: £3.50; subscription: £12. Sample: £2 if available. Make checks payable in pounds to Flarestack Publishing. Back issues are also available online at www.poetrymagazines.org.uk.

How to Contact Submit maximum of 6 poems at a time. No previously published poems or simultaneous submissions. Does not accept e-mail submissions. Cover letter is preferred. Often comments on rejected poems. Guidelines available for SASE or by e-mail. Responds in 2 months. Pays 1 contributor's copy. Acquires first rights.

Tips "Most beginning poets show little evidence of reading poetry before writing it! Join a poetry workshop."

☑ OFF THE COAST

P.O. Box 14, Robbinston ME 04671. (207)454-8026. E-mail: poetrylane2@gmail.com. Website: www.off-the-coast.com. Michael Brown, Editor/Publisher. **Contact:** Valerie Lawson, Editor/Publisher. OTC is accepting submissions of poetry (any subject or style, e-mail submissions preferred, postal submissions OK with SASE), graphics, and books for review (books only, no chapbooks). Subscriptions are $35. Single issue: $10. *Off the Coast*, prints all styles and forms of poetry. Does not want pornography or profanity. Considers poetry by children and teens. Has published poetry by Kate Barnes, Henry Braun, Wesley McNair, Baron Wormser, Betsy Sholl, and Robert Cording. *Off the Coast* is 68+ pages, digest-sized, copied, perfect-bound, with stock cover with original art. Receives about 1,500 poems/year, accepts about 175. Press run is 300 (247 subscribers, 6 shelf sales); occasional complimentary copies offered. Make checks payable to *Off the Coast*.

How to Contact Submit 4-6 poems at a time. Lines/poem: prefers 32 maximum. Considers previously published poems. No e-mail or disk submissions. Cover letter is preferred. "Put name and address on every page; include SASE." Reads submissions year-round. Time between acceptance and publication is 3-6 months. Sometimes comments on rejected poems. Guidelines available in magazine. Responds in 1-3 months. Pays one contributor's copy. "The rights to each individual poem and print are retained by each individual artist." Deadlines for Off the Coast are March, June, September and December 15. Reviews books/chapbooks of poetry and other magazines/journals in 500 words.

◻ THE OLD RED KIMONO

Georgia Highlands College, 3175 Cedartown Highway SE, Rome GA 30161. E-mail: napplega@highlands.edu. Website: www.highlands.edu/ork/default.htm. **Contact:** Dr. Nancy Applegate, Jesse Bishop, Thad Dittmer, and Ashley Hill, editors.

Magazines Needs *The Old Red Kimono*, published annually, prints original, high-quality poetry and fiction. Has published poetry by Walter McDonald, Peter Huggins, Ruth Moon Kempher, John Cantey Knight, Kirsten Fox, and Al Braselton. *The Old Red Kimono* is 72 pages, magazine-sized, professionally printed on heavy stock, with colored matte cover with art. Receives about 500 submissions/year, accepts about 60-70. Sample: $3.

How to Contact Submit 3-5 poems at a time. Accepts e-mail submissions. Reads submissions September 1-March 1 only. Guidelines available for SASE or on website for more submission information. Responds in 3 months. Pays 2 contributor's copies. Acquires first publication rights.

⬍ ◎ OPEN MINDS QUARTERLY

The Writer's Circle, 680 Kirkwood Dr., Building 1, Sudbury ON P3E 1X3, Canada. (705)675-9193, ext. 8286. E-mail: openminds@nisa.on.ca. Website: www.nisa.on.ca. **Contact:** Dinah Laprairie, editor. (Specialized: writing by those who have experienced mental illness)

Magazines Needs *Open Minds Quarterly* provides a "venue for individuals who have experienced mental illness to express themselves via poetry, short fiction, essays, first-person accounts of living with mental illness, book/movie reviews." Wants "unique, well-written, provocative poetry." Does not want overly graphic or sexual violence. Considers poetry by children and teens. Has published poetry by Pamela MacBean, Sophie Soil, Alice Parris, and Kurt Sass. *Open Minds Quarterly* is 24 pages, magazine-sized, saddle-stapled, with 100 lb. stock cover with original artwork, includes ads. Receives about 300 poems/year, accepts about 30%. Press run is 750; 400 distributed free to potential subscribers, published writers, advertisers, and conferences and events. Single copy: $5.40 CAD, $5 USD; subscription: $35 CAD, $28.25 USD (special rates also available). Make checks payable to NISA/Northern Initiative for Social Action.

How to Contact Submit 1-5 poems at a time. Considers previously published poems and simultaneous submissions. Accepts e-mail and disk submissions. Cover letter is required. "Info in cover letter: indication as to 'consumer/survivor' of the mental health system status." Reads submissions year round. Submit seasonal poems at least 8 months in advance. Time between acceptance and publication is 6-18 months. "Poems are first reviewed by poetry editor, then accepted/rejected by the editor. Sometimes, submissions are passed on to a third party for input or a third opinion." Seldom comments on rejected poems. Guidelines available for SASE, by fax, e-mail, or on website. Responds in up to 4 months. "Rarely" sends prepublication galleys. "All authors own their work—if another publisher seeks to reprint from our publication, we request they cite us as the source."

Contest/Award Offerings "The Brainstorm Poetry Contest runs in first 2 months of each year. Contact the editor for information."

Also Offers "All material not accepted for our journal will be considered for The Writer's Circle Online, our Internet publication forum. Same guidelines apply. Same contact person."

Tips "We are unique in that our outlets help to reduce the stigma surrounding mental illness by illustrating the creative talents of individuals suffering from mental illness."

⊞ ○ ORBIS: AN INTERNATIONAL QUARTERLY OF POETRY AND PROSE

17 Greenhow Ave., West Kirby, Wirral CH48 5EL England. Website:www.kudoswritingcompetitions.com. E-mail: baldock.carole@google-mail.com. Established 1968. **Contact:** Carole Baldock, editor.

Magazines Needs *Orbis: An International Quarterly of Poetry and Prose* features "news, reviews, views, letters, prose, and quite a lot of poetry." Wants "more work from young people (this includes 20-somethings) and women writers." *Orbis* is 84 pages, digest-sized, professionally printed, flat-spined, with full-color glossy card cover. Receives "thousands" of submissions/year. Single copy: £5 UK, £6 overseas (10, $14 USD); subscription: £17 UK, £23 overseas (30, $46 USD).

How to Contact Submit up to 4 poems at a time. Accepts e-mail submissions "from outside UK only;Send press release in first instance not review copy: nessaomahony@iol.ie. For postal submissions; enclose SASE (or SAE and 3 IRCs) with all correspondence." Responds in up to 1 month. Reviews books and other magazines.

Contest/Award Offerings Prizes in each issue: £50 for featured writer (3-4 poems); £50 Readers' Award for piece receiving the most votes; £50 split among 4 (or more) runners-up.

☑ OSIRIS

P.O. Box 297, Deerfield MA 01342-0297. E-mail: amoorhead@deerfield.edu. **Contact:** Andrea Moorhead, poetry editor.

Magazines Needs *Osiris*, published semiannually, prints contemporary poetry in English, French, and Italian without translation, and in other languages with translation, including Polish, Danish, and German. Wants poetry that is "lyrical, non-narrative, multi-temporal, post-modern, well-crafted. Also looking for translations from non-IndoEuropean languages." Has published poetry by Abderrahmane Djelfaoui (Algeria), George Moore (USA), Flavio Ermini (Italy), Mylene Durand (Quebec), Anne Blonstein (Switzerland), Astrid Cabral (Brazil), and Rob Cook (USA). *Osiris* is 48-56 pages, digest-sized, perfect-bound. Press run is 500 (50 subscription copies sent to college and university libraries, including foreign libraries). Receives 200-300 submissions/year, accepts about 12. Single copy: $10; subscription: $18. Sample: $6.

How to Contact Submit 4-6 poems at a time. "Poems should be sent by postal mail. Include short bio and SASE with submission. Translators should include a letter of permission from the poet or publisher as well as copies of the original text." Responds in 1 month. Sometimes sends prepublication galleys. Pays 5 contributor's copies.

Tips "It is always best to look at a sample copy of a journal before submitting work, and when you do submit work, do it often and do not get discouraged. Try to read poetry and support other writers."

☑ OVER THE TRANSOM

825 Bush St. #203, San Francisco CA 94108. (415)928-3965. E-mail: jsh619@earthlink.net. **Contact:** Jonathan Hayes, Editor.

Magazines Needs *Over The Transom*, published 2 times/year, is a free publication of poetry and prose. Open to all styles of poetry. "We look for the highest quality writing that best fits the issue." Considers poetry by children and teens. Has published poetry by Garrett Caples, Richard Lopez, Glen Chesnut, Daniel J. Langton. *Over The Transom* is 32 pages, magazine-sized, saddle-stapled, with cardstock cover. Receives about 1,000 poems/year, accepts about 5%. Press run is 300 (100 subscribers); 150 distributed free to cafes, bookstores, universities, and bars. Single copy: free. Sample: $3. Make checks payable to Jonathan Hayes.

How to Contact Submit 5 poems at a time. Considers previously published poems and simultaneous submissions. Accepts e-mail submissions; no disk submissions. Must include a SASE with postal submissions. Reads submissions year round. Time between acceptance and publication is 2-6 months. Never comments on rejected poems. Occasionally publishes theme issues. Guidelines available for SASE or by e-mail. Responds in 2 months. Sometimes sends prepublication galleys. Pays 1 contributor's copy. Acquires first rights.

Tips "Editors have differing tastes, so don't be upset by rejection. Always send a SASE for response."

☑ OYEZ REVIEW

School of Liberal Studies, Roosevelt University, 430 S. Michigan Ave., Chicago IL 60605. *Oyez Review*, published annually in January by Roosevelt University's MFA Program in Creative Writing, receives "submissions from across the nation and around the world. We're open to poetic sequences and longer poems provided they hold the reader's attention. We welcome skilled and polished work from newcomers as well as poems from established authors. The quality of the individual poem is key, not the poet's reputation." Has published poetry by Gary Fincke, Moira Egan, Gaylord Brewer, Barbara De Cesare, Prairie Markussen, Gary Held. *Oyez Review* is 90 pages, digest-sized. Accepts 5% of poems received. Press run is 800. Single copy: $5.

How to Contact Submit up to 5 poems, no more than 10 pages of poetry at a time. No simultaneous submissions. No fax, e-mail, or disk submissions. Cover letter is required. "Be sure to include a three- to five-sentence biography and complete contact information, including phone and e-mail." Reads submissions August 1-October 1 only. Time between acceptance and publication is 2 months. Guidelines available on website. Responds in 3 months. Pays 2 contributor's copies. Acquires first North American serial rights.

☑ PACIFIC COAST JOURNAL

P.O. Box 56, Carlsbad CA 92018. E-mail: pcj@frenchbreadpublications.com. Website: www.frenchbreadpublications.com/pcj. **Contact:** Stillson Graham, editor.

Magazines Needs *Pacific Coast Journal*, published quasi-quarterly, is an "unprofessional literary magazine. Whatever you think that means, go with it." Has published poetry by Michael Meinhoff, Guy R. Beining, and A.D. Winans. *Pacific Coast Journal* is 40 pages, digest-sized, photocopied, saddle-stapled, with cardstock cover. Receives 750 poems/year, accepts about 3%. Press run is 200. Single copy: $4; subscription: $14. Sample: $3.

How to Contact Submit up to 6 poems or 12 pages at a time. Considers simultaneous submissions; no previously published poems. No e-mail submissions. Cover letter is preferred. Encourages the inclusion of e-mail address in lieu of SASE for response. Time between acceptance and publication is 3-18 months. Sometimes comments on rejected poems. Guidelines available for SASE, by e-mail, or on website. Responds in 6-9 months (usually). Pays 1 contributor's copy. Acquires one-time rights.

Tips "We like experiments."

☑ PACKINGTOWN REVIEW

English Department, UH 2027, University of Illinois at Chicago, 601 S. Morgan, Chicago IL 60607. (908)745-1547. E-mail: editors@packingtownreview.com. Website: www.packingtownreview.com. **Contact:** Jennifer Moore and Matthew Corey, Editors-in-Chief.

Magazines Needs *Packingtown Review*, published annually in March, prints creative writing and critical prose by emerging and established writers. "We welcome submissions of poetry, scholarly articles, drama, creative nonfiction, fiction, and literary translation, as well as genre-bending pieces." Wants "well-crafted poetry. We are open to most styles and forms. We are also looking for poetry that takes risks and does so successfully. We will consider articles about poetry." Does not want "uninspired or unrevised work." *Packingtown Review* is 250 pages, magazine-sized. Press run is 500. Single copy: see website for prices.

How to Contact Submit 3-5 poems at a time. Considers simultaneous submissions (with notification); no previously published poems (considers poems posted on a public website/blog/forum previously published, but not those posted on a private, password-protected forum). No e-mail or disk submissions. Cover letter is required. "Please include a SASE. If you have simultaneously submitted these poems, please indicate in the cover letter and let us know ASAP if a poem is accepted elsewhere." Reads submissions year round. Poems are circulated to an editorial board. Sometimes comments on rejected poems. Sometimes publishes theme issues. Guidelines available on website. Responds in 3 months. Always sends prepublication galleys. Pays 2 contributor's copies. Acquires first North American serial rights. Rights revert to poets upon publication. Review books/chapbooks of poetry and other magazines/journals. Send materials for review consideration to Lucas Johnson.

▣ $ ☑ PAINTED BRIDE QUARTERLY

Drexel University, Dept. of English & Philosophy, 3141 Chestnut St., Philadelphia PA 19104. E-mail: pbq@drexel.edu. Website: pbq.drexel.edu. **Contact:** Poetry Editors.

Magazines Needs *Painted Bride Quarterly*, published online, "aims to be a leader among little magazines published by and for independent poets and writers nationally. We have no specifications or restrictions. We'll look at anything." Has published poetry by Robert Bly, Charles Bukowski, S.J. Marks, and James Hazen. *Painted Bride Quarterly* is printed as one hardcopy anthology annually. Single copy: $15.

How to Contact Submit up to 5 poems at a time. Lines/poem: any length. No previously published poems. No e-mail submissions. "Submissions must be original, typed, and should include a short bio." Time between acceptance and publication is 6-9 months. Seldom comments on rejected poems. Occasionally publishes theme issues. Guidelines available on website. Pays one-year subscription, one half-priced contributor's copy, and $5/accepted piece. Publishes reviews of poetry books.

Contest/Award Offerings Sponsors an annual poetry contest and a chapbook competition. **Entry fee:** required for both. Guidelines available for SASE or on website.

◎ PARADOXISM

University of New Mexico, Gallup NM 87301. E-mail: smarand@unm.edu. Website: www. gallup.unm.edu/ ~ smarandache/a/Paradoxism.htm. **Contact:** Florentin Smarandache, Editor.

Magazines Needs *Paradoxism*, published annually, prints "avant-garde poetry, experiments, poems without verses, literature beyond the words, anti-language, non-literature and its literature, as well as the sense of the non-sense; revolutionary forms of poetry. Paradoxism, a 1980s movement of anti-totalitarian protest, is based on excessive use of antitheses, antinomies, contradictions, paradoxes in creation." Wants "avant-garde poetry, 1-2 pages, any subject, any style (lyrical experiments)." Does not want "classical, fixed forms." Has published poetry by Paul Georgelin, Mircea Monu, Ion Rotaru, Michéle de LaPlante, and Claude LeRoy. *Paradoxism* is 52 pages, digest-sized, offset-printed, with soft cover. Press run is 500; distributed "to its collaborators, U.S. and Canadian university libraries, and the Library of Congress as well as European, Chinese, Indian, and Japanese libraries."

How to Contact No previously published poems or simultaneous submissions. Do not submit during the summer. "We do not return published or unpublished poems or notify the author of date of publication." Responds in up to 3 weeks. Pays 1 contributor's copy.

Additional Information Paradoxism Association also publishes 2 poetry paperbacks and 1-2 chapbooks/year, including translations. "The poems must be unpublished and must meet the requirements of the Paradoxism Association." Responds to queries in 2 months; to mss in up to 3 weeks. Pays 50 author's copies. Sample e-books available on website at www. gallup.unm.edu/ ~ smarandache/eBooksLiterature.htm.

Tips "We mostly receive traditional or modern verse, but not avant-garde (very different from any previously published verse). We want anti-literature and its literature, style of the non-style, poems without poems, non-words and non-sentence poems, very upset free verse, intelligible unintelligible language, impersonal texts personalized, transformation of the abnormal to the normal. Make literature from everything; make literature from nothing!"

THE PARIS REVIEW

62 White Street, New York NY 10013. (212)343-1333. E-mail: queries@theparisreview.org. "Fiction and poetry of superlative quality, whatever the genre, style or mode. Our contributors include prominent, as well as less well-known and previously unpublished writers. Writers at Work interview series includes important contemporary writers discussing their own work and the craft of writing."

How to Contact Submit no more than six poems at a time. Poetry can be sent to the Poetry Editor at the above address (please include a self-addressed, stamped envelope), or submitted online at http://www.theparisreview.org/poetry/. Pays $35 minimum varies according to length. Buys all rights, buys first English-language rights.

Contest/Award Offerings Awards $1,000 in Bernard F. Conners Poetry Prize contest.

☑ PATERSON LITERARY REVIEW

Poetry Center, Passaic County Community College, Cultural Affairs Dept., One College Blvd., Paterson NJ 07505-1179. (973)684-6555. Fax: (973)523-6085. E-mail: mgillan@pccc. edu. Website: www.pccc.edu/poetry. **Contact:** Maria Mazziotti Gillan, editor/executive director.

- The Poetry Center Library at Passaic County Community College has an extensive collection of contemporary poetry and seeks small press contributions to help keep it abreast.

Magazines Needs *Paterson Literary Review*, published annually, is produced by the The Poetry Center at Passaic County Community College. Wants poetry of "high quality; clear, direct, powerful work." Has published poetry by Diane di Prima, Ruth Stone, Marge Piercy, and Laura Boss. *Paterson Literary Review* is 300-400 pages, magazine-sized, professionally printed, saddle-stapled, with glossy 4-color card cover. Press run is 2,500. Sample: $13.

How to Contact Submit up to 5 poems at a time. Lines/poem: 100 maximum. Considers simultaneous submissions. Reads submissions December 1-March 31 only. Responds within 1 year. Pays 1 contributor's copy. Acquires first rights.

Contest/Award Offerings The Allen Ginsberg Poetry Awards and The Paterson Poetry Prize.

Also Offers Publishes *The New Jersey Poetry Resource Book* ($5 plus $1.50 p&h) and *The New Jersey Poetry Calendar*. The Distinguished Poets Series offers readings by poets of international, national, and regional reputation. Poetryworks/USA is a series of programs produced for UA Columbia-Cablevision. See website for details about these additional resources.

⊕ ◖ PATTAYA POETRY REVIEW

Classic Village, 95/31 Moo 10 Nong Phrue, Banglamung, Chonburi 20260, Thailand. (6681)7177 941. E-mail: jsutta@yahoo.com. **Contact:** Jiraporn Sutta, Editor.

Magazines Needs *Pattaya Poetry Review*, published quarterly, prints poetry. Wants "all types and styles, especially traditional forms." *Pattaya Poetry Review* is 16 pages, digest-sized, with cardstock cover. Receives about 200 poems/year, accepts about 20%. Press run is 70. Single copy: $9; subscription: $16.

How to Contact Submit no more than 3 poems at a time. Considers previously published poems and simultaneous submissions. Accepts e-mail submissions only. Reads submissions year round. Time between acceptance and publication is 3 months. Sometimes comments on rejected poems. Guidelines available. Responds in 3 months. Sometimes sends prepublication galleys. Pays 1 contributor's copy. Returns rights upon written request. Send materials for review consideration to Jiraporn Sutta.

☑ PAVEMENT SAW

Pavement Saw Press, 321 Empire Street, Montpelier OH 43543. E-mail: info@pavementsaw. org. Website: http://pavementsaw.org. **Contact:** David Baratier, editor.

Magazines Needs *Pavement Saw*, published annually in August, wants "letters and short fiction, and poetry on any subject, especially work." Does not want "poems that tell; no work by a deceased writer, and no translations." Dedicates 15-20 pages of each issue to a featured writer. Has published poetry by Simon Perchik, Sofia Starnes, Alan Catlin, Adrianne Kalfopoulou, Jim Daniels, and Mary Weems. *Pavement Saw* is 88 pages, digest-sized, perfect-bound. Receives about 9,000 poems/year, accepts less than 1%. Press run is 550. Single copy: $8; subscription: $14. Sample: $7. Make checks payable to Pavement Saw Press.

How to Contact Submit 5 poems at a time. Lines/poem: 1-2 pages. Considers simultaneous submissions, "as long as poet has not published a book with a press run of 1,000 or more"; no previously published poems. No e-mail submissions; postal submissions only. Cover letter is required. "No fancy typefaces." Seldom comments on rejected poems. Guidelines available in magazine or for SASE. Responds in 4 months. Sometimes sends prepublication galleys. Pays at least 2 contributor's copies. Acquires first rights.

Additional Information Pavement Saw Press also publishes books of poetry. "Most are by authors who have been published in the journal." Published "7 titles in 2005 and 7 titles in 2006; 5 were full-length books ranging from 80 to 240 pages."

Contest/Award Offerings Transcontinental Poetry Award and Pavement Saw Press Chapbook Award.

⊕ ◻ ◎ PEACE & FREEDOM

Peace & Freedom Press, 17 Farrow Rd., Whaplode Drove, Spalding, Lincs PE12 0TS, England. Published semiannually; emphasizes social, humanitarian, and environmental issues. **Considers submissions from subscribers only.** "Those new to poetry are welcome. The poetry we publish is pro-animal rights/welfare, anti-war, environmental; poems reflecting love; erotic, but not obscene; humorous; spiritual, humanitarian; with or without rhyme/meter." Considers poetry by children and teens. Has published poetry by Dorothy Bell-Hall, Freda Moffatt, Bernard Shough, Mona Miller, and Andrew Savage. *Peace & Freedom* has a varied format. Subscription: $20 U.S., £10 UK for 6 issues. Sample: $5 U.S., £1.75 UK. "Sample copies can be purchased only from the above address. Advisable to buy a sample copy before submitting. Banks charge the equivalent of $5 to cash foreign checks in the UK, so please only send bills, preferably by registered post."

How to Contact Lines/poem: 32 maximum. No previously published poems or simultaneous submissions. Accepts e-mail submissions (pasted into body of message, no attachments; no more than 3 poems/e-mail); no fax submissions. Include bio. Reads submissions year round. Publishes theme issues. Upcoming themes available in magazine, for SAE with IRC, by e-mail, or on website. Responds to submissions in less than a month ("usually"), with SAE/IRC. "Work without correct postage will not be responded to or returned until proper postage is sent." Pays one contributor's copy. Reviews books of poetry.

Contest/Award Offerings "*Peace & Freedom* holds regular poetry contests as does one of our other publications, *Eastern Rainbow*, which is a magazine concerning 20th-century popular culture using poetry up to 32 lines." Subscription: $20 U.S., £10 UK for 6 issues. Further details of competitions and publications available for SAE with IRC or on website.

Also Offers Publishes anthologies. Guidelines and details of upcoming anthologies available in magazine, for SAE with IRC, by e-mail, or on website.

☑ PEARL

Pearl Editions, 3030 E. Second St., Long Beach CA 90803-5163. (562)434-4523 or (714)968-7530. E-mail: pearlmag@aol.com. Website: www.pearlmag.com. **Contact:** Joan Jobe Smith, Marilyn Johnson, and Barbara Hauk, poetry editors.

Magazines Needs *Pearl*, published semiannually in May and November, is interested "in accessible, humanistic poetry that communicates and is related to real life. Humor and wit are welcome, along with the ironic and serious. No taboos, stylistically or subject-wise." Does not want "sentimental, obscure, predictable, abstract, or cliché-ridden poetry. Our purpose is to provide a forum for lively, readable poetry that reflects a wide variety of contemporary voices, viewpoints, and experiences—that speaks to real people about real life in direct, living language, profane or sublime. Our Fall/Winter issue is devoted exclusively to poetry, with a 12- to 15-page section featuring the work of a single poet." Has published poetry by Christopher Buckley, Fred Voss, David Hernandez, Lisa Glatt, Jim Daniels, Nin Andrews, and Frank X. Gaspar. *Pearl* is 112-136 pages, digest-sized, offset-printed, perfect-bound, with glossy cover. Press run is 700. Subscription: $21/year (includes a copy of the Pearl Poetry Prize-winning book). Sample: $8.

How to Contact Submit 3-5 poems at a time. Lines/poem: no longer than 40 lines preferred, each line no more than 10-12 words, to accommodate page size and format. Considers simultaneous submissions ("must be acknowledged as such"); no previously published poems. No e-mail submissions; postal submissions only. Cover letter is appreciated. "Handwritten submissions and unreadable printouts are not acceptable." Reads submissions January-June only. Time between acceptance and publication is up to 1 year. Guidelines available for SASE or on website. Responds in 2 months. Sometimes sends prepublication galleys. Pays 1 contributor's copy. Acquires first serial rights.

Additional Information Pearl Editions publishes the winner of the Pearl Poetry Prize only. All other books and chapbooks are by invitation only.

Tips "Advice for beginning poets? Just write from your own experience, using images that are as concrete and sensory as possible. Keep these images fresh and objective. Always listen to the music."

▣ $ ☑ THE PEDESTAL MAGAZINE

E-mail: pedmagazine@carolina.rr.com. Website: www.thepedestalmagazine.com. **Contact:** John Amen, editor-in-chief. Member: CLMP.

Magazines Needs *The Pedestal Magazine*, published bimonthly online, prints "12-15 poems per issue, as well as fiction, interviews, and book reviews. We are open to a wide variety of poetry, ranging from the highly experimental to the traditionally formal." Receives about 5,000 poems/year, accepts about 1%. "We have a readership of approximately 15,000 per month."

How to Contact Submit up to 6 poems at a time. Lines/poem: open. Considers simultaneous submissions; no previously published poems. No e-mail or disk submissions. "Submissions are accepted via a submission form provided in the 'Submit' section of the website. Our submissions schedule is posted in the guidelines section." Time between acceptance and publication is 2-4 weeks. Poems are circulated to an editorial board. Sometimes comments on rejected poems. Sometimes publishes theme issues. Guidelines available on website. Responds in 4-6 weeks. Always sends prepublication galleys (by e-mail). Pays $40/poem. Acquires first rights. Reviews books/chapbooks of poetry in 850-1,000 words. "Please query via e-mail prior to sending books or related materials."

☐ ◎ THE PEGASUS REVIEW

P.O. Box 88, Henderson MD 21640-0088. (410)482-6736. E-mail: Pegasus.sgc.edu. Dr. William Webster, faculty adviser. *The Pegasus Review*, now a quarterly, focuses on a specific theme for each issue and issued in calligraphic format. "Since themes might change it is advisable to contact editor about current themes. With us, brevity is the key. Themes may be submitted in the way of poetry, short-short fiction and essays." Has published work by Jane Stuart, Ed Galing, John Grey, and Burton R. Hoffman. Press run is 120 (100 subscribers, 2 libraries). Subscription: $12. Sample: $2.50, including shipping and handling. "We are currently accepting original poetry, prose, and artwork for consideration. Poetry and prose should be submitted electronically. Simply cut and paste it directly into an e-mail sent to: pegasus@sgc.edu."

⊕ ◪ PENNINE INK MAGAZINE

Mid Pennine Arts, The Gallery, Yorke St., Burnley BB11 1HD, England. E-mail: sheridansdandl@yahoo.co.uk. **Contact:** Laura Sheridan, Editor.

Magazines Needs *Pennine Ink*, published annually in January, prints poems and short prose pieces. *Pennine Ink* is 48 pages, A5, with b&w illustrated cover. Receives about 400 poems/year, accepts about 40. Press run is 200. "Contributors wishing to purchase a copy of *Pennine Ink* should enclose £2 ($4 USD) per copy."

How to Contact Submit up to 6 poems at a time. Lines/poem: 40 maximum; prose: no longer than 1,000 words. Considers previously published poems and simultaneous submissions. Accepts e-mail submissions. Seldom comments on rejected poems. Responds in 3 months. Pays 1 contributor's copy.

Tips "Submissions should be accompanied by an e-mail address so we can contact you and a mailing address so we can send your copy of the magazine or a suitable SASE (or SAE with IRCs)."

◪ PENNSYLVANIA ENGLISH

Penn State DuBois, DuBois PA 15801-3199. (814)375-4814. E-mail: ajv2@psu.edu. **Contact:** Antonio Vallone, Editor.

Magazines Needs *Pennsylvania English*, published annually, is "sponsored by the Pennsylvania College English Association." Wants poetry of "any length, any style." Has published poetry by Liz Rosenberg, Walt MacDonald, Amy Pence, Jennifer Richter, and Jeff Schiff. *Pennsylvania English* is up to 200 pages, digest-sized, perfect-bound, with full-color cover. Press run is 500. Subscription: $10/year.

How to Contact Submit 3 or more poems at a time. Considers simultaneous submissions; no previously published poems. No e-mail submissions. Submissions must be typed. Include SASE. Guidelines available for SASE. Responds in 6 months. Pays 2 contributor's copies.

Tips "Poetry does not express emotions; it evokes emotions. Therefore, it should rely less on statements and more on images."

☑ ◎ THE PENWOOD REVIEW

P.O. Box 862, Los Alamitos CA 90720-0862. E-mail: lcameron65@verizon.net. Website: www.penwoodreview.com. **Contact:** Lori Cameron, editor.

Magazines Needs *The Penwood Review*, published semiannually, seeks "to explore the spiritual and sacred aspects of our existence and our relationship to God." Wants "disciplined, high-quality, well-crafted poetry on any subject. Rhyming poetry must be written in traditional forms (sonnets, tercets, villanelles, sestinas, etc.)." Does not want "light verse, doggerel, or greeting card-style poetry. Also, nothing racist, sexist, pornographic, or blasphemous." Has published poetry by Kathleen Spivack, Anne Babson, Hugh Fox, Anselm Brocki, Nina Tassi, and Gary Guinn. *The Penwood Review* is about 40 pages, magazine-sized, saddle-stapled, with heavy card cover. Press run is 50-100. Single copy: $8; subscription: $16.

How to Contact Submit 3-5 poems at a time. Lines/poem: less than 2 pages preferred. No previously published poems or simultaneous submissions. Accepts e-mail submissions (pasted into body of message). Cover letter is preferred. 1 poem to a page with the author's full name, address, and phone number in the upper right corner. Time between acceptance and publication is up to 1 year. "Submissions are circulated among an editorial staff for evaluations." Never comments on rejected poems. Responds in up to 4 months. Pays with subscription discount of $10 and, with subscription, 1 additional contributor's copy. Acquires one-time rights.

☑ PEREGRINE

Amherst Writers & Artists Press, P.O. Box 1076, Amherst MA 01004. E-mail: peregrine@amherstwriters.com. Website: www.amherstwriters.com. **Contact:** Nancy Rose, editor.

Magazines Needs *Peregrine*, published annually, features poetry and fiction. Open to all styles, forms, and subjects except greeting card verse. "*Peregrine* has provided a forum for national and international writers since 1983, and is committed to finding excellent work by emerging as well as established authors. We publish what we love, knowing that all editorial decisions are subjective." Has published poetry by Willie James King, Virgil Suaárez, Susan Terris, Myron Ernst, Pat Schneider, Edwina Trentham, Sacha Webley, Fred Yannantuono, and Ralph Hughes. *Peregrine* is 104 pages, digest-sized, professionally printed, perfect-bound, with glossy cover. Press run is 1,000. Single copy: $15. Sample: $12. Make checks payable to AWA Press.

How to Contact Submit 3-5 poems at a time. Lines/poem: 60 maximum (including spaces). Considers simultaneous submissions; no previously published poems. No e-mail submissions. Include cover letter with bio, 40 words maximum; indicate line count for each poem. Enclose sufficiently stamped SASE for return of mss; if disposable copy, enclose #10 SASE for response. Reads submissions January 2-March 31 (postmark) only. Each ms read by several readers; final decisions made by the editor. Guidelines available for #10 SASE or on website. Pays 2 contributor's copies. Acquires first rights.

Tips "Check guidelines before submitting your work. Familiarize yourself with *Peregrine*."

◩ PERMAFROST: A LITERARY JOURNAL

c/o English Dept., University of Alaska Fairbanks, P.O. Box 755720, Fairbanks AK 99775. *Permafrost: A Literary Journal*, published in May/June, contains poems, short stories, creative nonfiction, b&w drawings, photographs, and prints. "We survive on both new and established writers, hoping and expecting to see the best work out there. We publish any style of poetry provided it is conceived, written, and revised with care. While we encourage submissions about Alaska and by Alaskans, we also welcome poems about anywhere, from anywhere. We have published work by E. Ethelbert Miller, W. Loran Smith, Peter Orlovsky, Jim Wayne Miller, Allen Ginsberg, and Andy Warhol." *Permafrost* is about 200 pages, digest-sized, professionally printed, flat-spined. Subscription: $9/year, $16/2 years, $22/3 years. Back-issues $5.

◻ ◎ PHILADELPHIA STORIES

93 Old York Road, Ste 1/#1-753, Jenkintown PA 19046. E-mail: info@philadelphiastories. org. Website: www.philadelphiastories.org. **Contact:** Conrad Weister, co-publisher. Member: CLMP.

Magazines Needs *Philadelphia Stories*, published quarterly, publishes "literary fiction, poetry, and art from Pennsylvania, New Jersey, and Delaware—and provide it to the general public free of charge." Wants "polished, well crafted poems." Does not want "first drafts." Considers poetry by teens. Has published poetry by Daniel Abdal-Hayy Moore, Scott Edward Anderson, Sandy Crimmins, Liz Dolan, Alison Hicks, and Margaret A. Robinson. *Philadelphia Stories* is 24 pages, magazine-sized, saddle-stapled, with 4-color cover with original art, includes ads. Receives about 600 poems/year, accepts about 15%. Press run is 12,000 per quarter, distributed free. Subscription: "we offer $20 memberships that include home delivery." Make checks payable to *Philadelphia Stories*.

How to Contact Submit 3 poems at a time. Lines/poem: 36. Considers simultaneous submissions; no previously published poems. Accepts submissions through online submission form at www.philadelphiastories.org/submissions; no disk submissions. Cover letter is preferred. Reads submissions year round. Time between acceptance and publication is 3 months. Poems are circulated to an editorial board. "Each poem is reviewed by a preliminary board that decides on a final list; the entire board discusses this list and chooses the mutual favorites for print and Web." Guidelines available on website. Responds in 3 months. "We send a layout proof to check for print poems." Acquires one-time rights. Rights revert to poets upon publication. Reviews books of poetry.

☑ THE PINCH

Dept. of English, University of Memphis, Memphis TN 38152-6176. (901)678-4591. Fax: (901)678-2226. E-mail: thepinch@memphis.edu. Website: www.thepinchjournal.com. **Contact:** Kristen Iversen, editor in chief.

Magazines Needs *The Pinch* (previously *River City*), published semiannually (fall and spring), prints fiction, poetry, interviews, creative nonfiction, and visual art. Has published poetry by Albert Goldbarth, Maxine Kumin, Jane Hirshfield, Terrance Hayes, S. Beth Bishop, and Naomi Shahib Nye. *The Pinch* is 160 pages, 7x10, professionally printed, perfect-bound, with colorful glossy cover and color art and photography. Press run is 2,500. Sample: $12.

How to Contact Submit no more than 5 poems at a time. No e-mail submissions. Include SASE. "We do not read in the summer months." Reads submissions according to these deadlines only: August 15-November 1 (Spring issue) and January 15-March 15 (Fall issue). Guidelines available for SASE, by e-mail, or on website. Responds in up to 3 months. Pays 2 contributor's copies.

Contest/Award Offerings Offers an annual award in poetry. 1st Prize: $1,000 and publication; 2nd- and 3rd-Prize poems may also be published. Any previously unpublished poem of up to 2 pages is eligible. No simultaneous submissions. Poems should be typed and accompanied by a cover letter. Author's name should not appear anywhere on ms. Manuscripts will not be returned. Guidelines available for SASE, by e-mail, or on website. **Entry fee:** $15 for up to 3 poems (includes one-year subscription). **Deadline:** January 15-March 15 (inclusive postmark dates). Winners will be notified in July; published in subsequent issue.

▣ ○ THE PINK CHAMELEON—ONLINE

E-mail: dpfreda@juno.com. Website: www.thepinkchameleon.com. **Contact:** Mrs. Dorothy P. Freda, editor/publisher.

Magazines Needs *The Pink Chameleon Online* published annually online, contains "family-oriented, upbeat poetry, any genre in good taste that gives hope for the future." Wants "poems about nature, loved ones, rare moments in time." Does not want "pornography, cursing, swearing; nothing evoking despair." Also considers poetry by children and teens. Receives about 50 poems/year, accepts about 50%.

How to Contact Submit 1-4 poems at a time. Lines/poem: 6 minimum, 24 maximum. Considers previously published poems; no simultaneous submissions. Accepts e-mail submissions only (pasted into body of message; "please, no attachments"). Use plain text and include a brief bio. Reads submissions January-April 30th and September-October 31st. Time between acceptance and publication is up to 1 year depending on date of acceptance. "As editor, I reserve the right to edit for grammar, spelling, sentence structure, flow; omit redundancy and any words or material I consider in bad taste." Often comments on rejected poems. Guidelines available by e-mail or on website. Responds in 1 month. No payment. Acquires one-time, one-year publication rights. All rights revert to poet in 6 months to a year, depending on date of acceptance.

Tips "Always keep a typed hard copy or a back-up disk of your work for your files. Mail can go astray. And I'm human, I can accidentally delete or lose the submission."

☑ PINYON

Dept. of Languages, Literature & Communications, Mesa State College, 1100 North Ave., Grand Junction CO 81051. E-mail: pinyonpoetry@hotmail.com. **Contact:** Randy Phillis, editor.

Magazines Needs *Pinyon*, published annually in June, prints "the best available contemporary American poetry and fiction. No restrictions other than excellence. We appreciate a strong voice." Does not want "inspirational, light verse, or sing-song poetry." Has published poetry by Mark Cox, Barry Spacks, Wendy Bishop, and Anne Ohman Youngs. *Pinyon* is about 120 pages, magazine-sized, perfect-bound. Receives about 4,000 poems/year, accepts 2%. Press run is 300; 100 distributed free to contributors, friends, etc. Subscription: $8/year. Sample: $4.50. Make checks payable to Pinyon, MSC.

How to Contact Submit 3-5 poems at a time. No previously published poems or simultaneous submissions. Cover letter is preferred. "Name, address, e-mail, and phone number on each page. SASE required." Reads submissions August 1-December 1. "3 groups of assistant editors, led by an associate editor, make recommendations to the editor." Seldom comments on rejected poems. Guidelines available for SASE. Responds in February. Pays 2 contributor's copies. Acquires one-time rights.

Tips "Send us your best work!"

☑ PIRENE'S FOUNTAIN

3616 Glenlake Dr, Glenview IL 60026. E-mail: pirenesfountain@gmail.com. Submissions editors: Oliver Lodge, Charles Morrison; Senior editor: Tony Walbran; Magazine editor: Lark Vernon; Publisher: Ami Kaye. **Contact:** Submissions editor. *Pirene's Fountain* is published online 2 times per year in April and October. Does not want "blatantly religious/political themes, anything obscene, pornographic, or discriminatory in nature." Has published work by Lisel Mueller, Alison Croggan, Dorianne Laux, Rebecca Seiferle, Joseph Millar, Kim Addonizio, Dimitris Varos, Cynthia Bracket-Vincent, Aine MacAodha, and Mary Hutchins Harris. Receives about 1,000 poems/year, accepts about 15%.

How to Contact Submit 3-8 poems at a time. Considers previously published poems and simultaneous submissions. Considers poetry posted on a public website/blog/forum and poetry posted on a private, password-protected forum as published. Accepts e-mail submissions pasted into body of message; no postal, fax or disk submissions. Cover letter is unnecessary but 50-100 word bio is required. Reads submissions during the months of November, April, and September. Submit seasonal poems anytime. Time between acceptance and publication is 4 to 6 weeks. Poems are circulated to an editorial board. Never comments on rejected poems. Sometimes publishes theme issues. Guidelines available on website. Responds in 4 to 5 weeks. Poets retain copyright to their own work, rights revert to poets upon publication.

Tips "We offer a poetry discussion group on Facebook, entitled 'PF Poetry.' Membership on Facebook is free and approval from a PF officer is required. E-mail publisher for details if interested." "Please read submission guidelines carefully and send in *at least* 3 poems."

☑ ◎ PLAINSONGS

Dept. of English, Hastings College, Hastings NE 68901. (402)461-7352. Fax: (402)461-7756. E-mail: plainsongs@hastings.edu. **Contact:** Laura Marvel Wunderlich, editor.

Magazines/Journals

Magazines Needs *Plainsongs*, published 3 times/year, considers poems "on any subject, in any style, but free verse predominates. Plains region poems encouraged." *Plainsongs'* title suggests not only its location on the Great Plains, but its preference for the living language, whether in free or formal verse. "*Plainsongs* is committed to poems only, to make space without visual graphics, bios, reviews, or critical positions." Has published poetry by Judith Tate O'Brien, Andrew H. Oerke, Lyn Lifshin, Larsen Bowker, and Louis Daniel Brodsky. *Plainsongs* is 40 pages, digest-sized, laser-set, printed on thin paper, saddle-stapled, with one-color matte card cover with generic black logo. "Published by the English department of Hastings College, the magazine is partially financed by subscriptions. Although editors respond to as many submissions with personal attention as they have time for, the editor offers specific observations to all contributors who also subscribe." Subscription: $15 for 3 issues. Sample: $5.

How to Contact Submit up to 6 poems at a time, with name and address on each page. No fax, e-mail, or disk submissions; postal submissions only. Reads submissions according to the following deadlines: August 15 for Winter issue; November 15 for Spring issue; March 15 for Fall issue. Responds 7-8 weeks after deadline. Guidelines available for SASE. Pays 2 contributor's copies and one-year subscription. Acquires first rights.

Contest/Award Offerings 3 poems in each issue receive a $25 prize. "A short essay in appreciation accompanies each award poem."

Tips "We like poems that seem to be aware of modernist and post-modernist influences during the last hundred years, not necessarily by imitation or allusion, but by using the tools provided by that rich heritage. Poets need to read and absorb the work of other poets."

✪ PLAIN SPOKE

6199 Steubenville Road SE, Amsterdam OH 43903. (740)543-4333. E-mail: plainspoke@gmail.com. Website: www.plainspoke.net. **Contact:** Cindy Kelly, editor.

Magazines Needs *Plain Spoke*, published quarterly, publishes "poetry heavy in sense images and with a clear, plain-spoken voice." Wants "Americana, nostalgia, narrative." Does not want "esoteric, universal, cliché." Has published poetry by Claudia Burbank, Deborah Bogen, Doug Ramspeck, Amy Sargent. *Plain Spoke* is 36-60 digest-sized, laser-printed, saddle-stitched, with a color art on cardstock cover. Receives about 2,500 poems/year, accepts about 5%. Press run is 300. Single copy: $8; subscription: $25. Make checks payable to Amsterdam Press.

How to Contact Submit up to 6 poems at a time, preferably under 40 lines. Considers simultaneous submissions, no previously published poems (considers poetry posted on a public website/blog/forum). Accepts e-mail submissions (following guidelines on website at www.plainspoke.net. Cover letter is required. Paper submissions require an SASE. Submissions received without an SASE are recycled. No postcards. Reads submissions year round. Submit seasonal poems 3 months in advance. Time between acceptance and publication is 1-4 months. Poems are circulated to an editorial board. Sometimes comments on rejected poems. Never publishes theme issues. Guidelines available for SASE, by e-mail, and on website. Responds in 1 week. Pays 1 contributor's copy. Acquires first North American serial rights. Rights revert to poets upon publication. Reviews books and chapbooks of poetry in single-book format. Send cover letter and materials for review consideration to Reviews Editor, *Plain Spoke*.

▦ $ ☑ ◎ PLANET: THE WELSH INTERNATIONALIST

P.O. Box 44, Aberystwyth, Ceredigion SY23 3ZZ, Wales. E-mail: Planet.enquiries@ Planetmagazine.org.uk; helle.michelsen@planetmagazine.org.uk. Website: www. planetmagazine.org.uk. **Contact:** Helle Michelsen, Editor. *Planet: The Welsh Internationalist*, published quarterly, is a cultural magazine "centered on Wales, but with broader interests in arts, sociology, politics, history, and science." Wants "good poetry in a wide variety of styles. No limitations as to subject matter; length can be a problem." Has published poetry by Nigel Jenkins, Anne Stevenson, and Les Murray. *Planet* is 128 pages, A5, professionally printed, perfect-bound, with glossy color card cover. Receives about 500 submissions/year, accepts about 5%. Press run is 1,550 (1,500 subscribers, about 10% libraries, 200 shelf sales). Single copy: £6.75; subscription: £22 (£38 overseas). Sample available.

$ ☑ PLEIADES

Pleiades Press, Dept. of English,Central Missouri State University, Warrensburg MO 64093. (660)543-8106. E-mail: pleiades@ucmo.edu. Website: www.ucmo.edu/englphil/pleiades. **Contact:** Kevin Prufer, editor.

• Poems published in *Pleiades* have appeared in *The Best American Poetry* and *The Pushcart Prize*.

Magazines Needs *Pleiades*, published semiannually in April and October, prints poetry, fiction, literary criticism, belles lettres (occasionally), and reviews. Open to all writers. Wants "avant-garde, free verse, and traditional poetry, and some quality light verse." Does not want anything "pretentious, didactic, or overly sentimental." Has published poetry by James Tate, Joyce Carol Oates, Brenda Hillman, Wislawa Szymborska, Carl Phillips, and Jean.Valentine. *Pleiades* is 160 pages, digest-sized, perfect-bound, with heavy coated cover with color art. Receives about 9,000 poems/year, accepts fewer than 1%. Press run is 2,500-3,000; about 200 distributed free to educational institutions and libraries across the country. Single copy: $6; subscription: $12. Sample: $5. Make checks payable to Pleiades Press.

How to Contact Submit 3-5 poems at a time. Considers simultaneous submissions with notification; no previously published poems. Cover letter is preferred. Include brief bio. Time between acceptance and publication "can be up to 1 year. Each poem published must be accepted by 2 readers and approved by the poetry editor." Seldom comments on rejected poems. Guidelines available for SASE or on website. Responds in up to 3 months. Payment varies. Acquires first and second serial rights.

$ ☑ PLOUGHSHARES

Emerson College, *Ploughshares*, 120 Boylston St., Boston MA 02116. E-mail: pshares@ emerson.edu. Website: www.pshares.org. **Contact:** Poetry Editor. *Ploughshares*, published 3 times/year, is "a journal of new writing guest-edited by prominent poets and writers to reflect different and contrasting points of view. Translations are welcome if permission has been granted." Editors have included Carolyn Forché, Gerald Stern, Rita Dove, Chase Twichell, and Marilyn Hacker. Has published poetry by Donald Hall, Li-Young Lee, Robert

Pinsky, Brenda Hillman, and Thylias Moss. *Ploughshares* is 200 pages, digest-sized. Receives about 4,500 poetry submissions/year. Press run is 6,000. Subscription: $30 domestic, $30 plus shipping (see website) foreign. Sample: $14 current issue, $10.95 back issue.

How to Contact Submit 1-3 poems at a time. Considers simultaneous submissions if indicated as such; no previously published poems. We do accept electronic submissions — there is a $3 fee per submission, which is waived if you are a subscriber. Postal submissions: include SASE. Cover letter is preferred. Reads submissions June 1-January 15 (postmark); mss submitted January 16-May 31 will be returned unread. "We suggest you read a few issues (online or in print) before submitting. Check our website for any special guidelines." Responds in up to 5 months. Always sends prepublication galleys. Pays $25/printed page ($50 minimum, $250 maximum), plus 2 contributor's copies and a 1-year subscription.

☑ POEM

Huntsville Literary Association, P.O. Box 2006, Huntsville AL 35804. **Contact:** Rebecca Harbor, Editor. *Poem*, published twice/year in May and November, consists entirely of poetry. "We publish both traditional forms and free verse." Wants poems "characterized by compression, rich vocabulary, significant content, and evidence of 'a tuned ear and practiced pen.' We want coherent work that moves through the particulars of the poem to make a point. We equally welcome submissions from established poets as well as from less-known and beginning poets." Does not want translations. Has published poetry by Kathryn Kirkpatrick, Peter Serchuk, and Kim Bridgford. *Poem* is 90 pages, digest-sized, flat-spined, printed on good stock paper, with a clean design and a matte cover. Prints more than 60 poems/issue, generally featured 1 to a page. Press run is 500. Single copy: $10; subscription: $20. Sample: $7 (back issue).

How to Contact Send 3-5 poems at a time. No previously published poems or simultaneous submissions. Include SASE. Reads submissions year-round. Guidelines available for SASE or on website. Responds in 1-2 months. Pays 2 contributor's copies. Acquires first serial rights.

☑ POEMS & PLAYS

English Dept., Middle Tennessee State University, Murfreesboro TN 37132. **Contact:** Gaylord Brewer, Editor. *Poems & Plays*, published annually in the spring, is an "eclectic publication for poems and short plays." No restrictions on style or content of poetry. Has published poetry by Naomi Wallace, Kate Gale, James Doyle, and Ron Koertge. *Poems & Plays* is 88 pages, digest-sized, professionally printed, perfect-bound, with coated color card cover. Receives 1,500 poems per issue, publishes 30-35 "typically." Press run is 800. Subscription: $10 for 2 issues. Sample: $6.

How to Contact No previously published poems or simultaneous submissions. Reads submissions October-November only. "Work is circulated among advisory editors for comments and preferences. All accepted material is published in the following issue." Sometimes comments on rejected poems. Responds in 2 months. Pays 1 contributor's copy. Acquires first publication rights only.

Tips Considers chapbook mss (poems or short plays) of 20-24 pages for The Tennessee Chapbook Prize. "Any combination of poems or plays, or a single play, is eligible. The winning chapbook is printed within *Poems & Plays*." Winning author receives 50 copies of the issue. SASE required. Entry fee: $15 (includes 1 copy of the issue). Deadline: same as for the magazine (October-November). Past winners include Tammy Armstrong and Judith Sornberger. "The chapbook competition annually receives over 150 manuscripts from the U.S. and around the world."

☑ ◎ POESY MAGAZINE

P.O. Box 7823, Santa Cruz CA 95061. (831)239-4419. E-mail: brian@poesy.org. Website: www.poesy.org. **Contact:** Brian Morrisey, Editor/Publisher. *POESY Magazine*, published biannually, is "an anthology of American poetry. *POESY*'s main concentrations are Boston, Massachusetts and Santa Cruz, California, 2 thriving homesteads for poets, beats, and artists of nature. Our goal is to unite the 2 scenes, updating poets on what's happening across the country." Wants to see "original poems that express observational impacts with clear and concise imagery. Acceptence is based on creativity, composition, and relation to the format of *POESY*." Does not want "poetry with excessive profanity. We would like to endorse creativity beyond the likes of everyday babble." Has published poetry by Lawrence Ferlinghetti, Jack Hirschman, Edward Sanders, Todd Moore, Diane Di Prima, and Julia Vinograd. *POESY* is 16 pages, magazine-sized, newsprint, glued/folded, includes ads. Receives about 1,000 poems/year, accepts about 10%. Press run is 1,000; most distributed free to local venues. Single copy: $1; subscription: $12/year. Sample: $2. Make checks payable to Brian Morrisey.

How to Contact Submit 3-5 poems at a time. Lines/poem: 32 maximum. No previously published poems or simultaneous submissions. Accepts e-mail (submissions@poesy.org) and disk submissions. "Snail mail submissions are preferred with a SASE." Cover letter is preferred. Reads submissions year round. Time between acceptance and publication is 1 month. "Poems are accepted by the Santa Cruz editor/publisher based on how well the poem stimulates our format." Guidelines available in magazine, for SASE, by e-mail, or on website. Responds in 1 month. Sometimes sends prepublication galleys. Pays 3 contributor's copies. Acquires one-time rights. Reviews books/chapbooks of poetry and other magazines/journals in 1,000 words, single-book format. Send materials for review consideration to *POESY*, c/o Brian Morrisey.

Tips "Stay away from typical notions of love and romance. Become one with your surroundings and discover a true sense of natural perspective."

☑ POETALK

Bay Area Poets Coalition, P.O. Box 11435, Berkeley CA 94712-2435. E-mail: poetalk@aol.com. **Contact:** Maggie Morley, Editor. *POETALK*, currently published 1-2 issues/year, is the poetry journal of the Bay Area Poets Coalition (BAPC) and publishes about 65 poets in each issue. "*POETALK* is open to all. No particular genre. Rhyme must be well done." *POETALK* is 36 pages, digest-sized, photocopied, saddle-stapled, with heavy card cover. Press run is 400. Subscription: $5/2 issues. Sample: $2.

How to Contact Submit 3-5 poems at a time, no more than twice/year. Lines/poem: under 35 preferred; longer poems of outstanding quality considered. Considers previously published poems and simultaneous submissions, but must be noted. Cover letter is preferred. Include SASE. "Manuscripts should be clearly typed, single-spaced, and include author's name and mailing address on every page. Include e-mail address if you have one." Usually responds in up to 6 months. Pays 1 contributor's copy. All rights revert to author upon publication.

Sponsors yearly contest. Deadline: submit October 1-November 15 (postmark). Guidelines available in early September for SASE, by e-mail, or see posting on website.

Tips "If you don't want suggested revisions, you need to say so clearly in your cover letter or indicate on each poem submitted." Also Offers Bay Area Poets Coalition which holds monthly readings (in Berkeley, CA). BAPC has 150 members. BAPC Membership: $15/year (includes subscription to POETALK and other privileges); extra outside U.S.

◎ POETICA MAGAZINE, REFLECTIONS OF JEWISH THOUGHT

P.O. Box 11014, Norfolk VA 23517. Fax: (757)399-3936. E-mail: poeticamag@aol.com. Website: www.poeticamagazine.com. Established 2002. **Contact:** Michal Mahgerefteh, publisher/editor.

Magazines Needs *Poetica Magazine, Reflections of Jewish Thought*, published 3 times/year, offers "an outlet for the many writers who draw from their Jewish backgrounds and experiences to create poetry/prose/short stories, giving both emerging and recognized writers the opportunity to share their work with the larger community." Does not want long pieces, haiku, rhyming poetry. Considers poetry by children and teens, grades 6-12. *Poetica* is 70pages, perfect bound, full color cover, includes some ads. Receives about 500 poems/year, accepts about 60%. Press run is 350. Single copy: $10; subscription: $19.50.

How to Contact Submit 3 poems at a time. Lines/poem: 2 pages maximum. Considers simultaneous submissions. No e-mail or disk submissions. Cover letter is optional. Reads submissions year round. Time between acceptance and publication is 1 year. Seldom comments on rejected poems. Occasionally publishes theme issues. Guidelines available for SASE or on website. Responds in 1 month. Pays 1 contributor's copy. Poet retains all rights.

Contest/Award Offerings Offers annual poetry contest with up to $50 awarded for First Prize; up to 5 Honorable Mentions. Selected poems will be published in future issues of *Poetica*. Accepts simultaneous submissions. No limit on number of entries (3 poems constitute an entry). Submit 2 copies of each poem, single-spaced, no more than 1 poem/page. Include poet's name on all pages. No e-mail submissions. Include SASE for results only; mss will not be returned. Guidelines available on website. **Entry fee:** $15 for up to 3 poems. **Deadline:** March 31 annually. Judge: Jane Ellen Glasser. Notifies winners by June. Other contests include the Poet of the Month Award, Annual Chapbook Award, and annual anthology centered on a theme.

⊕ ◻ ◎ POETIC HOURS

43 Willow Rd., Carlton, Nolts NG4 3BH, England. E-mail: erranpublishing@hotmail.com. Website: http://poetichours.homestead.com/contactpage.html. **Contact:** Nicholas Clark, Editor. *Poetic Hours* is an online publication, published semiannually, that aims "to encourage and publish new poets, i.e., as a forum where good but little known poets can appear in print; and **to raise money for third world and other charities**. *Poetic Hours* features poetry by invited poets and others." Wants "any subject; rhyme preferred but not essential; suitable for wide-ranging readership." Does not want "gothic, horror, extremist, political, self-interested." *Poetic Hours* is an online publication. Receives about 500 poems/year, accepts about 40%. Free to read on magazines website but accepted poets asked to make a contrbution towards nominated charities if accepted.

■ ☑ POETIC MATRIX, A PERIODIC LETTER

P.O. Box 1223, Madera CA 93639. E-mail: poeticmatrix@yahoo.com. Website: www. poeticmatrix.com. **Contact:** John Peterson, Editor. *Poetic Matrix, a periodic letteR*, published 2 times/year online, seeks poetry that "creates a 'place in which we can live' rather than telling us about the place; poetry that draws from the imaginal mind and is rich in the poetic experience—hence the poetic matrix." Does not want poetry that talks about the experience. Has published poetry by Lyn Lifshin, Tony White, Gail Entrekin, James Downs, Joan Michelson, and Brandon Cesmat.

How to Contact Accepts e-mail submissions (pasted into body of message, no attachments). Guidelines available by e-mail or on website. Acquires one-time rights."*Poetic Matrix* has a call for manuscripts for the Slim Volume Series' every 2 years. See website for when reading dates are set and for additional guidelines and awards. The Slim Volume Series is for manuscripts of 65-75 pages." **Charges reading fee of $17.**

Tips "We seek writing of quality, with passion and intelligence."

☑ POET LORE

The Writer's Center, 4508 Walsh St., Bethesda MD 20815. E-mail: postmaster@writer.org. E. Ethelbert Miller, Editor. **Contact:** Jody Bolz, Editor. *Poet Lore*, published semiannually, is "dedicated to the best in American and world poetry as well as timely reviews and commentary." Wants "fresh uses of traditional forms and devices, but any kind of excellence is welcome." Has published poetry by Ai, Denise Duhamel, Jefferey Harrison, Eve Jones, Carl Phillips, and Ronald Wallace. *Poet Lore* is 144 pages, digest-sized, professionally printed, perfect-bound, with glossy card cover. Receives about 4,200 poems/year, accepts 125. Press run is at least 800. Single copy: $8; subscription: $18/nonmember, $12/member. "Add $1/single copy for shipping; add $5 postage for subscriptions outside U.S."

How to Contact Considers simultaneous submissions "with notification in cover letter." No e-mail or disk submissions. "Submit typed poems (up to 5), with author's name and address on each page; SASE is required." Guidelines available for SASE or on website. Responds in 3 months. Pays 2 contributor's copies and a one-year subscription. Reviews books of poetry. Send materials for review consideration.

$ ☑ POETRY

444 N. Michigan Ave., Suite 1850, Chicago IL 60611. E-mail: poetry@poetrymagazine.org. Website: www.poetryfoundation.org.

• Work published in Poetry is frequently included in *The Best American Poetry* and *The Pushcart Prize: Best of the Small Presses*.

Magazines Needs *Poetry*, published monthly by The Poetry Foundation (see separate listing in Organizations), "has no special manuscript needs and no special requirements as to form or genre: We examine in turn all work received and accept that which seems best." Has published poetry by the major voices of our time as well as new talent. *Poetry* is 5½ × 9, elegantly printed, flat-spined. Receives 90,000 submissions/year, accepts about 300-350. Press run is 16,000. Single copy: $3.75; subscription: $35 ($38 for institutions). Sample: $5.50.

How to Contact Submit no more than 4 poems at a time. No previously published poems or simultaneous submissions. Electronic submission preferred. When submitting by post put return address on outside of envelope; include SASE. Submissions must be typed, single-spaced, with poet's name and address on every page. Guidelines available for SASE. Responds in 1-2 months. Pays $10/line (with a minimum payment of $300). Reviews books of poetry in multi-book formats of varying lengths. Does not accept unsolicited reviews.

Contest/Award Offerings 7 prizes (Bess Hokin Prize, Levinson Prize, Frederick Bock Prize, J. Howard and Barbara M.J. Wood Prize, John Frederick Nims Memorial Prize, Friends of Literature Prize, Union League Civic and Arts Poetry Prize) ranging from $300 to $5,000 are awarded annually to poets whose work has appeared in the magazine that year. Only verse already published in *Poetry* is eligible for consideration; no formal application is necessary.

Also Offers *Poetry*'s website offers featured poems, letters, reviews, interviews, essays, and web-exclusive features.

POETRYBAY

P.O. Box 114, Northport NY 11768. (631)427-1950. E-mail: poetrybay@aol.com. Website: www.poetrybay.com. **Contact:** George Wallace, Editor.

Magazines Needs *Poetrybay*, published semiannually online, seeks "to add to the body of great contemporary American poetry by presenting the work of established and emerging writers. Also, we consider essays and reviews." Has published poetry by Robert Bly, Yevgeny Yevtushenko, Marvin Bell, Diane Wakoski, Cornelius Eady, and William Heyen.

How to Contact Submit 5 poems at a time. Considers simultaneous submissions; no previously published poems. Accepts e-mail submissions (pasted into body of message); no disk submissions. Time between acceptance and publication is 6-12 months. Seldom comments on rejected poems. Occasionally publishes theme issues. Guidelines available on website. Sometimes sends prepublication galleys. Acquires first-time electronic rights. Reviews books/chapbooks of poetry and other magazines/journals. Send materials for review consideration.

THE POETRY CHURCH MAGAZINE

Moorside Words and Music, Eldwick Crag Farm, High Eldwick, Bingley,, W. Yorkshire BD16 3BB, England. E-mail: reavill@globalnet.co.uk. **Contact:** Tony Reavill, editor. (Specialized: subscribers only; Christian)

Magazines Needs *The Poetry Church Magazine*, published quarterly, contains Christian poetry, prayers, and hymns. Wants "Christian or good religious poetry." Does not want "unreadable blasphemy." **Publishes subscribers' work only.** Considers poetry by children over age 10. Has published poetry by Laurie Bates, Joan Sheridan Smith, Idris Caffrey, Isabella Strachan, Walter Nash, and Susan Glyn. *The Poetry Church Magazine* is 40 pages, digest-sized, photocopied, saddle-stapled, with illustrated cover. Receives about 1,000 poems/year, accepts about 500. Press run is 1,000. Single copy: free; subscription: £12 for 4 issues ($20 USD). Make checks payable in sterling to Feather Books. Payment can also be made through website.

How to Contact Submit 2 poems at a time. Lines/poem: usually around 20, "but will accept longer." Considers previously published poems and simultaneous submissions. Cover letter is preferred (with information about the poet). No e-mail submissions; postal submissions only. Include SASE, or SAE and IRC. Submissions must be typed. **Publishes "only**

subscribers' poems as they keep us solvent." Time between acceptance and publication is 4 months. "The editor does a preliminary reading, then seeks the advice of colleagues about uncertain poems." Responds within 1 week. Poets retain copyright.

Additional Information Feather Books publishes the Feather Books Poetry Series, collections of around 20 Christian poems and prayers. Has recently published the Glyn family, Walter Nash, David Grieve, and Rosie Morgan Barry. "We have now published 300 poetry collections by individual Christian poets." Books are usually photocopied, saddle-stapled, with illustrated covers. "We do not insist, but **most poets pay for their work. Enquire for current costs.** If they can't afford it, but are good poets, we stand the cost. We expect poets to read *The Poetry Church Magazine* to get some idea of our standards."

Also Offers Each winter and summer, selected poems appear in *The Poetry Church Collection*, the leading Christian poetry anthology used in churches and schools.

Tips "We find it better for poets to master rhyme and rhythm before trying free verse. Many poets seem to think that if they write 'down' a page they're writing poetry, when all they're doing is writing prose in a different format. But good free verse is accpted."

☑ POETRY INTERNATIONAL

Dept. of English & Comparative Literature, SDSU, Arts & Letters Bldg., second fl, rm 262, 5500 Campanile Dr., San Diego CA 92182-8140. E-mail: poetry.international@yahoo.com; fmoramar@mail.sdsu.edu. Website: http://poetryinternational.sdsu.edu. **Contact:** Fred Moramarco, Editor. *Poetry International*, published annually in November, is "an eclectic poetry magazine intended to reflect a wide range of poetry being written today." Wants "a wide range of styles and subject matter. We're particularly interested in translations." Does not want "cliché-ridden, derivative, or obscure poetry." Has published poetry by Adrienne Rich, Robert Bly, Hayden Carruth, Kim Addonizio, Maxine Kumin, and Gary Soto. *Poetry International* is 200 pages, perfect-bound, with coated cardstock cover. Press run is 1,500. Single copy: $12; subscription: $24/2 years (plus s&h).

How to Contact Submit up to 5 poems at a time. Considers simultaneous submissions, "but prefer not to"; no previously published poems. No fax or e-mail submissions. Reads submissions September 1-30 only. Time between acceptance and publication is 8 months. Poems are circulated to an editorial board. Seldom comments on rejected poems. Responds in up to 4 months. Pays 2 contributor's copies. Acquires all rights. Returns rights "50/50," meaning they split with the author any payment for reprinting the poem elsewhere. "We review anthologies regularly."

Tips "We're interested in new work by poets who are devoted to their art. We want poems that matter—that make a difference in people's lives. We're especially seeking good translations and prose by poets about poetry."

🌐 ☑ POETRY KANTO

Kanto Gakuin University, Kamariya-cho 3-22-1, Kanazawa-ku, Yokohama 236-8502, Japan. E-mail: alan@kanto-gakuin.ac.jp. Website: http://home.kanto-gakuin.ac.jp/~kg061001/. **Contact:** Alan Botsford, Editor.

Magazines Needs *Poetry Kanto*, published annually in November by the Kanto Gakuin University, is a journal bridging east and west, featuring "outstanding poetry that navigates the divide of ocean and language from around the world. We seek exciting, well-crafted contemporary poetry in English, and also encourage and publish high-quality English translations of modern and emerging Japanese poets. All translations must be accompanied by the original poems." See website for sample poems. Has published poetry by Jane Hirschfield, Ilya Kaminsky, Beth Ann Fennelly, Vijay Seshadri, Michael S. Collins, Mari L'Esperance, Michael Sowder, and Sarah Arvio. *Poetry Kanto* is 120 pages, 6x9, professionally printed on coated stock, perfect-bound, with glossy cover. Press run is 1,000; many are distributed free worldwide to schools, poets, and presses. The magazine is unpriced. Sample: send SAE with IRCs.

How to Contact Submit 5 poems at a time maximum. Queries welcome. No previously published poems or simultaneous submissions. Prefers e-mail submissions (as attachment in Word). Cover letter is required. Include brief bio. All postal submissions require SAE and IRCs. Reads submissions December - April. Guidelines available on website. Pays 3-5 contributor's copies.

Tips "From forebears, learn; from the future, write; in the present, live."

▣ ☑ POETRY MIDWEST

E-mail: submit@poetrymidwest.org. Website: www.poetrymidwest.org. *Poetry Midwest*, published 3 times/year online (winter, spring/summer, fall), features poetry, nongenre microfiction, and brief creative nonfiction from new and established writers. Wants free verse, traditional Western forms, traditional Asian forms other than haiku and senryu, prose poems, long poems, nongenre microfiction (up to 300 words), and brief creative nonfiction (up to 300 words). Does not want science fiction, fantasy, inspirational, religious, or children's verse or fiction; anything of an overtly political or religious nature; or spoken word poetry. Has published poetry by Philip Dacey, Cherryl Floyd-Miller, Rhoda Janzen, J. Patrick Lewis, Adrian Matejka, and Matt Rasmussen. *Poetry Midwest* is 20-100 pages, published online as a (free) downloadable Adobe Acrobat PDF file. Receives about 1,500 poems/year, accepts about 7%.

How to Contact Submit 3 poems at a time. Lines/poem: 3 minimum, 10 pages maximum. Considers simultaneous submissions; no previously published poems. "Submit via e-mail only. Submissions should be pasted into the body of an e-mail message with 'Poetry Midwest Submission' in subject line (omit quotation marks). Absolutely no e-mail file attachments. E-mail messages containing attachments will be deleted upon receipt. Do not send submissions via postal mail; they will be returned unread." Reads submissions year-round. Submit seasonal poems 3-6 months in advance. Time between acceptance and publication is 3 months to one year. "I read submissions as they are received, deciding whether or not to use a piece based on its own literary merits and whether it fits in with other poems selected for an issue in progress." Seldom comments on rejected poems. Guidelines available by e-mail or on website. Responds in up to 6 months. Acquires first rights or first North American serial rights as well as first electronic rights, reprint rights, and electronic archival rights.

Tips "Submissions to online journals should reflect the same attention to detail that goes into submissions to traditional print journals. Fancy display fonts, distracting animated graphics, and pictures of you and/or your significant other and/or pets do not increase the likelihood of a piece being accepted; in fact, they almost ensure your piece will be automatically rejected. There are professional standards for submitting to literary journals which can be found on many websites and in most handbooks for creative writers. Follow those guidelines and any market-specific requests if you want your submission seriously considered."

☑ POETRY NORTHWEST

Everett Community College, 2000 Tower Street, Everett WA 98103. (425)388-9395. E-mail: editors@poetrynw.org. Website: www.poetrynw.org. **Contact:** Kevin Craft, editor.

Magazines Needs *Poetry Northwest* is published semiannually in April and October. "The mission of *Poetry Northwest* is to publish the best poetry written or translated into English. In the words of founding editor Carolyn Kizer, we aim to 'encourage the young and the inexperienced, the neglected mature, and the rough major talents and the fragile minor ones.' All styles and aesthetics will find consideration." Has published poetry by Theodore Roethke, Czeslaw Milosz, Anne Sexton, Harold Pinter, Thom Gunn, and Philip Larkin. *Poetry Northwest* is 40+ pages, magazine-sized, Web press-printed, saddle-stapled, with 4-color cover, includes ads. Receives about 10,000 poems/year, accepts about 1%. Press run is 2,000. Single copy: $8. Sample: $9. Make checks payable to *Poetry Northwest*.

How to Contact Submit 3-5 poems at a time once per submission period. No previously published poems; simultaneous submissions ok with notice. Regular mail or online submission form only. No e-mail or disk submissions. Cover letter is required. Time between acceptance and publication is 2-3 months. Sometimes comments on rejected poems. Sometimes publishes theme issues. Upcoming themes available in magazine or on website. Guidelines available on website. Responds in 8-12 weeks. Reading period September-April. Mss sent outside reading period will be returned unread. Always sends prepublication galleys. Pays 2 contributor's copies. Acquires all rights. Returns rights to poets upon request. Reviews books of poetry in single- and multi-book format.

POETRY NOW

1719 25th Street, Sacramento CA 95816. Richard Hansen, design/layout. **Contact:** Trian Drotar, Managing editor. *Poetry Now* is now published bimonthly with more online content, in newsletter style, with some graphic art design work. The publication serves the members of the Sacramento Poetry Center and other interested readers. Poetry now is frequently available on the poetry center's website in a downloadable format. The newsletter includes a calendar of local events, reviews, interviews, and poetry. Wants all styles and forms of poetry. Accepts work primarily from the Northern California poets, but will take a look at poets elsewhere. Has published poetry by Francisco Alarcon, Alice Anderson, Quinton Duvall, Bob Stanley, Joyce Odam, and Allegra Silberstein. Receives about 300 poems/year, accepts about 40%. Press run suits the demand of membership with some extra copies for bookstore distribution. Membership to the Poetry Center, with a subscription of *Poetry Now* and its sister publication, *Tule Review*, is $30.

How to Contact Submit a few poems at a time, generally no more than 1-page poems. Looking for unpublished work, but will consider previously published work by writers with a published collection or book of poems. Prefer to receive e-mail submissions with a brief bio, no cover letter necessary. Reads submissions year round. Time of acceptance is up to 60 days.SPC has an annual poetry contest: deadline is usually in January/February. Check with the newsletter to find details.

Tips "Study the works of poets you love. Attend a group meeting of experienced and published poets, like Sacramento Poetry Center's workshop. Find your genre, submit often, and keep the faith."

◻ POETRY OF THE PEOPLE

3341 SE 19th Ave., Gainesville FL 32641. (352)231-3171. E-mail: poetryforaquarter@yahoo. com. **Contact:** Paul Cohen, Editor. *Poetry of the People*, a pamphlet published occasionally, is open to all forms of poetry. Wants "humorous poetry, love poetry, nature poetry, and fantasy." Does not want "racist or highly ethnocentric poetry. We do not like poetry that lacks images or is too personal or contains rhyme to the point that the poem has been destroyed." Also considers poetry written in French and Spanish. Considers poetry by children and teens. Has published poetry by Laura Stamps, Dan Matthews, Jenica Deer, Shannon Dixon, Kristi Castro, and Peggy C. Hall. *Poetry of the People* is 4 pages, magazine-sized. Sample: $4 for 11 pamphlets.

How to Contact Submit "as many poems as you want" at a time. Accepts e-mail and disk submissions. Include SASE with postal submissions. Cover letter is required (often publishes the cover letter). Include bio. "Autobiographical information is important in understanding the poetry." Often comments on rejected poems. No racism, sexism, or ethnocentracism. Guidelines available by e-mail or on website. Responds within 18 months. Pays 5 contributor's copies. Acquires first rights.

Tips "You should appeal to as broad an audience as possible. Nature makes people happy."

▦ ◻ POETRY SALZBURG REVIEW

University of Salzburg, Dept. of English, Akademiestrasse 24, Salzburg A-5020, Austria. (43)(662)8044-4422. Fax: (43)(662)8044-167. E-mail: editor@poetrysalzburg.com. Website: www.poetrysalzburg.com. **Contact:** Dr. Wolfgang Goertschacher, Andreas Schachermayr, editors.

Magazines Needs *Poetry Salzburg Review*, published twice/year, contains "articles on poetry, mainly contemporary, and 60 percent poetry. Also includes essays on poetics, review-essays, interviews, artwork, and translations. We tend to publish selections by authors who have not been taken up by the big poetry publishers. Nothing of poor quality." Has published poetry by Paul Muldoon, Alice Notley, Samuel Menashe, Jerome Rothenberg, Michael Heller. *Poetry Salzburg Review* is about 200 pages, A5, professionally printed, perfect-bound, with illustrated card cover. Receives about 5,000 poems/year, accepts 5%. Press run is 500. Single copy: $12; subscription: $22 (cash preferred; subscribers can also pay with PayPal). Make checks payable to Wolfgang Goertschacher. "No requirements, but it's a good idea to subscribe to *Poetry Salzburg Review*."

How to Contact No previously published poems or simultaneous submissions. Accepts e-mail submissions (as attachment). Time between acceptance and publication is 6 months. Seldom comments on rejected poems. Occasionally publishes theme issues. Responds in 2 months. No payment. Acquires first rights. Reviews books/chapbooks of poetry as well as books on poetics. Send materials for review consideration.

▨ POETS AND ARTISTS (O&S)

E-mail: ospoetry&yahoo.com. Website: www.poetsandartists.com. **Contact:** Didi Menendez, publisher. "Reviews books of poetry, chapbooks of poetry, and other magazines/journals. Reads poetry submissions year round. Sometimes upcoming themes are available online at website.

How to Contact Buys 300 poems/year. Submit maximum 5 poems.

Tips "Publisher also publishes MiPOesias Magazine, which has been featured in Best American Poetry, and OCHO, which has received Pushcart Prize and has been featured in Best American Poetry."

☑ THE POET'S ART

171 Silverleaf Lane, Islandia NY 11749. (631)439-0427. E-mail: davidirafox@yahoo.com. **Contact:** David Fox, editor.

Magazines Needs *The Poet's Art*, published quarterly, is "a family-style journal, accepting work from the unpublished to the well known and all levels in between." Wants "family-friendly, positive poetry; any form considered. Topics include humor, nature, inspirational, children's poetry, or anything else that fits the family-friendly genre." Does not want "violent, vulgar, or overly depressing work. Work is read and accepted by the mentally-ill population, but they should keep in mind this is a family-friendly journal." Considers poetry by children and teens, "any age, as long as it's good quality; if under 18, get parents' permission." Has published poetry by Susan Marie Davniero, Ken Fisher, Dolores Patitz, James Webb Wilson, and Andy Roberts. *The Poet's Art* is 40 or more pages, magazine-sized, photocopied, paper-clipped or stapled, with computer cover, includes ads. Receives about 100 poems a year, accepts about 50%. Press run is 30+. "Due to limited supplies, only those who submit or whose review is accepted receive a copy; foreign contributors must pay for a copy. (There are no samples or subscriptions offered by this magazine.)"

How to Contact Submit "as many poems that will fit on 1 page" at a time ("you can submit more, if compelled to do so; extra accepted pieces will be spread over a few issues"). Lines/poem: rarely accepts anything over 1 page. Considers simultaneous submissions ("list any other small press journals (if any) poems titles"). No e-mail or disk submissions; postal submissions only. Cover letter is preferred. "It's only polite. And include a SASE—a must! (I have been lax in this rule about SASEs, but I will now throw any submissions without a SASE away!)" Reads submissions year round, "but poets should be aware we are currently backlogged into June 2011, as of this listing. I review all poems submitted and then decide what I wish to publish." Always comments on rejected poems. Reviews chapbooks of poetry and other magazines/journals, "but editors and authors must write reviews themselves. After all, who knows your magazine/journal or chapbook better than you? (Little-known/newer journals sent in by editors or contributors get first consideration for reviews)." Send to David Fox.

Tips "We enjoy and value loyalty, but remember to send your work out to as many magazines/journals as you can. Poetry is meant to be shared. Family-friendly poetry for this journal, please! Also, I am NOT a book publisher, or an agent. Please do not send book-length mss to be published or to find a publisher. You may send chapbooks for review only."

▣ ☺ POETSESPRESSO

1426 Telegraph Ave. #4, Stockton CA 95204. E-mail: poetsespresso@gmail.com. Website: www.poetsespresso.com. **Contact:** Donald R. Anderson, editor-in-chief.

Magazines Needs *poetsespresso*, published bimonthly online and in print, is "a small black and white publication of poetry, art, photography, recipes, and local events." Sponsored by the Writers' Guild, a club of San Joaquin Delta College. "We value variety, appropriateness for most age groups, and poetry that goes well with the season of the issue, visual and bilingual poetry (side by side with translation), and of length that will fit on our half-sheet pages." Does not want "profanity, racially prejudiced, otherwise offensive material, porn, submissions that are excessively long, illegible writing, nor your only copy of the poem." Considers poetry by all ages. "Please include contact info of parent if from a minor." Has published poetry by David Humphreys, Nikki Quismondo, Susan Richardson Harvey, Marie J. Ross, Christine Stoddard, Michael C. Ford, and Allen Field Weitzel. *poetsespresso* (print edition) is 24-28 pages, digest-sized, printed "on College's industrial printers," stapled, with colored paper cover with b&w photograph/artwork, might include ads. Accepts about 100 poems/year. Number of unique visitors (online): "small count with rapid growth." Single copy: $2; subscription: $12/year (6 issues). Sample: free in return for review or swap for a desired publication. Make checks payable to Donald Anderson.

How to Contact Submit "as many poems as you wish" at a time. Lines/poem: "from quote-size up to 80." Considers previously published poems and simultaneous submissions with notification. Accepts e-mail (as attachment in MS Word, MS Works, rich text, InDesign Interchange, or notepad formats) and disk submissions; no fax submissions. ."If postal submissions, submit copies, not originals of works, bio, optional photo. Pieces will not be returned, will respond if accepted with copy of publication. Text must be typed/printed without illegible markings. " "In any submission except ads, 2 to 4 line biography about the poet/artist is required, written in third person. Biography photo is optional. You may include info for readers to contact you, if you wish." Reads submissions year round. "Deadline for submissions are on or before the 25th of the month prior to the issue." Jan. 25 deadline for Feb-Mar, Mar. 25 for Apr-May, May 25 for Jun-Jul, Jul. 25 for Aug-Sep, Sep. 25 for Oct-Nov, Nov. 25 for Dec-Jan. Submit seasonal poems at least 1 week in advance. Time between acceptance and publication is 1 to 12 months. "Include SASE with cover requesting response if want release from publishing consideration of works after submission. Otherwise may publish up to 12 months after submission. The editor bases acceptance upon space available, interest and meeting the guidelines." Sometimes comments on rejected poems. Regularly publishes (seasonal) theme issues. Guidelines available for SASE with cover letter request, by e-mail, or on website. Responds in up to 2 months. Sometimes sends prepublication galleys (upon request). Pays 1 contributor's copy (extra copies at $2 postage per copy). Acquires one-time rights for print edition; acquires electronic rights "to keep an archived issue available online indefinitely in the future." "Rights remain with author to publish in any way; rights are given to *poetsespresso* for indefinite archive on website and 1 issue of the newsletter". Send materials for review consideration by e-mail or to Donald R. Anderson by postal mail with cover letter.

Additional Information "We occasionally publish anthologies. For info on other works we have published, please visit the website for the book *Sun Shadow Mountain* and other projects linked on the project page at www.rainflowers.org."

Tips "Be definitive, stand out, and yet link to a common experience."

▣ ◻ THE POET'S HAVEN

Website: www.PoetsHaven.com. **Contact:** Vertigo Xavier, Publisher.

Magazines Needs *The Poet's Haven* is a website "featuring poetry, artwork, stories, essays, and more." Wants work that's "emotional, personal, and intimate with the author or subject. Topics can cover just about anything." Does not publish religious material. Has published poetry by Robert O. Adair, Christopher Franke, T.M. Göttl, Mary I. Huang, and Anne McMillen. Work published on *The Poet's Haven* is left on the site permanently. Receives about 1,000 poems/year, accepts about 70%.

How to Contact Considers previously published poems and simultaneous submissions. Accepts submissions through online form only. Time between acceptance and publication is about 2 weeks. Never comments on rejected poems. Guidelines available on website. No payment for online publication. Acquires rights to publish on the website permanently and in any future print publications. Poet retains rights to have poems published elsewhere, "provided the other publishers do not require first-time or exclusive rights."

Additional Information Publishes audio podcast as "Saturday Night With *The Poet's Haven*." Check website for submission information or to download sample episodes.

Also Offers Publisher's blog, and open-mic events.

▣ ◻ POET'S INK

E-mail: poet_Kelly@yahoo.com. Website: www.PoetsInk.com. **Contact:** Kelly Morris, editor.

Magazines Needs *Poet's Ink*, published monthly online, seeks "poetry of all kinds. Work by new poets is published alongside that of more experienced poets." Does not want "bad rhyme, clichés, poetry riddled with abstractions." Considers poetry by teens. "Will be judged by the same standards as poetry by adults." Has published poetry by Alexandria Webb, David Waite, Colin Baker, Megan Arkenburg, and Robert Demaree. Receives about 500 poems/year, accepts about 10%.

How to Contact Submit 3-5 poems at a time. Lines/poem: 2 minimum, 100 maximum ("longer poems better not be long-winded!"). Considers previously published poems and simultaneous submissions. Accepts e-mail submissions (as attachment); no disk submissions. Cover letter is preferred. "No funky formatting of poems!" Reads submissions year round. Time between acceptance and publication is 2 months. Often comments on rejected poems. Sometimes publishes theme issues. Guidelines available by e-mail or on website. Responds in 1 month. Acquires one-time rights. Rights revert to poets upon publication.

Tips "Read guidelines carefully before submitting. Take advantage of all the advice you get, but also follow your heart."

◪ THE POET'S PEN

The Society of American Poets (SOAP), 6500 Clito Road, Statesboro GA 30461. 912-587-4400. Website: http://ihspub.com. **Contact:** Dr. Charles E. Cravey, editor.

Magazines Needs *The Poet's Pen*, published quarterly by The Society of American Poets, is "open to all styles of poetry and prose—both religious and secular." Does not want "gross or 'X-rated' poetry without taste or character." Has published poetry by Najwa Salam Brax, Henry Goldman, Henry W. Gurley, William Heffner, Linda Metcalf, and Charles Russ, among others. *The Poet's Pen* uses poetry **primarily by members and subscribers**, but outside submissions are also welcome. Subscription: included in membership, $30/year ($25 for students). Sample: $10.

How to Contact Submit 3 poems at a time/quarter. Considers simultaneous submissions and previously published poems, if permission from previous publisher is included. Include name and address on each page. "Submissions or inquiries will not be responded to without a #10 business-sized SASE. We do stress originality and have each new poet and/or subscriber sign a waiver form verifying originality." Publishes seasonal/theme issues. Guidelines available in magazine, for SASE, or by e-mail. Sometimes sends prepublication galleys. Always comments on rejected poems.

Contest/Award Offerings Sponsors several contests each quarter, with prizes totaling $100-250. Also offers Editor's Choice Awards each quarter. The President's Award for Excellence is a prize of $50. **Deadline:** November 1. Also publishes a quarterly anthology from poetry competitions in several categories with prizes of $25-100. Guidelines available for SASE or by e-mail.

Tips "Be honest with yourself above all else. Read the greats over and again and study styles, grammar, and what makes each unique. Meter, rhythm, and rhyme are still the guidelines that are most acceptable today."

⬚ ▢ POETS' PODIUM

2-3265 Front Rd., E. Hawkesbury ON K6A 2R2, Canada. Ken Elliott, Catherine Heaney Barrowcliffe, Robert Piquette, or Ron Barrowcliffe, associate editors. **Contact:** Ken Elliot. *Poets' Podium*, published quarterly, is a newsletter that aims "to promote the reading and writing of the poetic form, especially among those being published for the first time." Poetry specifications are open. "**Priority is given to valued subscribers.** Nevertheless, when there is room in an issue, we will publish nonsubscribers." Does not want poetry that is "gothic, erotic/sexual, gory, bloody, or that depicts violence." Subscription: $15 USD. Sample: $3 USD.

How to Contact Submit 3 poems at a time. Lines/poem: 4 minimum, 25 maximum. Considers previously published poems and simultaneous submissions. Cover letter is required. Include SASE (or SAE and IRC), name, address, and telephone number; e-mail address if applicable. Time between acceptance and publication varies. Guidelines available for SASE (or SAE and IRC), or by fax or by e-mail. Pays 3 contributor's copies. All rights remain with the author.

Tips "Poetry is a wonderful literary form. Try your hand at it. Send us the fruit of your labours."

▨ THE PORTLAND REVIEW

Portland State University, P.O. Box 347, Portland OR 97207-0347. E-mail: theportlandreview@gmail.com. Website: www.portlandreview.org. **Contact:** Chris Cottrell, editor. Portland State University, P.O. Box 347, Portland OR 97207-0347. (503)725-4533. Fax: (503)725-4534. Website: www.portlandreview.org. Established 1956. **Contact:** Chris Cottrell, editor.

Magazines Needs *The Portland Review*, published 3 times/year by Portland State University, seeks "submissions exhibiting a unique, compelling voice and content of substance. Experimental poetry welcomed." Has published poetry by Gaylord Brewer, Richard Bentley, Charles Jensen, Mary Biddinger, and Jerzy Gizella. *The Portland Review* is about 130 pages. Receives about 1,000 poems/year, accepts about 30. Press run is 1,000 for subscribers, libraries, and bookstores nationwide. Single copy: $9; subscription: $28/year, $54/2 years. Sample: $8.

How to Contact Submit up to 5 poems at a time. Considers simultaneous submissions; no previously published poems. Accepts postal submissions only. Include phone number, e-mail address, and other contact information on ms. Indicate whether you wish ms returned; if so, include SASE (otherwise mss will be recycled automatically). Reads submissions year round except during the months of June, July, and August. Guidelines available for SASE or on website. "Our website is a general introduction to our magazine, with samples of our poetry, fiction, and art." Responds in up to 4 months. Pays 1 contributor's copy. Acquires first North American rights.

Tips "Include a SASE and specify if submissions need to be returned. Otherwise, they will be recycled."

▣ ☑ THE POTOMAC

E-mail: charles.rammelkamp@ssa.gov. Website: http://thepotomacjournal.com. **Contact:** Charles Rammelkamp, Editor. Member: Web del Sol.

Magazines Needs *The Potomac*, published semi-annually online, features political commentary, cutting-edge poetry, flash fiction, and reviews. Open to all forms of poetry by new and established writers. Has published poetry and fiction by Robert Cooperman, Michael Salcman, Joanne Lowery, Roger Netzer, Pamela Painter, and L.D. Brodsky. Receives a "variable" number of poems/year, accepts about 50-60. Sample: free online.

How to Contact Submit any number of poems at a time. Considers simultaneous submissions; no previously published poems. Accepts e-mail submissions (as attachment) only; no postal or disk submissions. Cover letter is preferred. Reads submissions year round. Time between acceptance and publication is 3 months. Often comments on rejected poems. Guidelines available on website. Responds in 2 months. Sometimes sends prepublication galleys. No payment. Acquires one-time rights. Reviews books/chapbooks of poetry and other magazines/journals in up to 2,000 words, single- and multi-book format. Send materials for review consideration.

Tips "We welcome the opportunity to read work from new writers."

☑ POTOMAC REVIEW: A JOURNAL OF ARTS & HUMANITIES

Montgomery College, Paul Peck Humanities Institute, 51 Mannakee St., Rockville MD 20850. (240)567-4100. E-mail: PotomacReviewEditor@montgomerycollege.edu. Website: www.montgomerycollege.edu/potomacreview. **Contact:** Julie Wakeman-Linn, editor.

Magazines Needs *Potomac Review: A Journal of Arts & Humanities*, published semiannually in November and May, "welcomes poetry, from across the spectrum, both traditional and nontraditional poetry, free verse and in-form (translations accepted). Essays and creative nonfiction are also welcome." Has published work by David Wagoner, Elizabeth Spires, Ramola D, Amy Holman, and Luke Johnson. *Potomac Review* is 150 pages, digest-sized, 50 lb paper; 65 lb cover stock. Receives about 2,500 poems/year, accepts 3%. Subscription: $18/year (includes 2 issues). Sample: $10.

How to Contact Submit up to 3 poems (5 pages maximum) at a time. Considers simultaneous submissions; no previously published poems. Cover letter is preferred. Include brief bio; enclose SASE. Time between acceptance and publication is up to 1 year. Poems are read "in house," then sent to poetry editor for comments and dialogue. Often comments on rejected poems. Does not publish theme issues. Guidelines available on website. Responds within 3 months. Pays 2 contributor's copies and offers 40% discount on additional copies.

Contest/Award Offerings Sponsors an annual poetry contest and annual fiction contest. Guidelines available in magazine (fall/winter issue), for SASE.

Tips "Read a current issue to see what kind of work delights us. We like a wide variety of subjects, and we especially love memorable characters and evocative imagery. Keep checking website for updates and changes."

⚃ $ ☑ ◎ THE PRAIRIE JOURNAL

Prairie Journal Press, P.O. Box 68073, 28 Crowfoot Terrace NW, Calgary AB T3G 3N8, Canada. E-mail: prairiejournal@yahoo.com. Website: prairiejournal.org. **Contact:** A. Burke, Editor. *The Prairie Journal*, published twice/year, seeks poetry "of any length; free verse, contemporary themes (feminist, nature, urban, non-political), aesthetic value, a poet's poetry." Does not want to see "most rhymed verse, sentimentality, egotistical ravings. No cowboys or sage brush." Has published poetry by Liliane Welch, Cornelia Hoogland, Sheila Hyland, Zoe Lendale, and Chad Norman. *The Prairie Journal* is 40-60 pages, digest-sized, offset-printed, saddle-stapled, with card cover, includes ads. Receives about 1,000 poems/year, accepts 10%. Press run is 600; the rest are sold on newsstands. Subscription: $10 for individuals, $18 for libraries. Sample: $8 ("use postal money order"). No U.S. stamps.

How to Contact No previously published poems or simultaneous submissions. No e-mail submissions. "We will not be reading submissions until such time as an issue is in preparation (twice yearly), so be patient and we will acknowledge, accept for publication, or return work at that time." Guidelines available for postage ("no U.S. stamps, please"; get IRCs from USPS) or on website. Sometimes sends prepublication galleys. Pays $10-50 and 1 contributor's copy. Acquires first North American serial rights. Reviews books of poetry, "but must be assigned by editor. Query first."

Tips For chapbook publication by Prairie Journal Press, Canadian poets only (preferably from the plains region). Has published *Voices From Earth*, selected poems by Ronald Kurt and Mark McCawley, and *In the Presence of Grace* by McCandless Callaghan. "We also publish anthologies on themes when material is available." Query first, with 5 sample poems and cover letter with brief bio and publication credits. Responds to queries in 2 months; to mss in 6 months. Payment in modest honoraria. Publishes "Poems of the Month" online. Submit up to 4 poems with $1 reading fee by postal mail."Read recent poets! Experiment with line length, images, metaphors. Innovate."

☑ PRAIRIE SCHOONER

201 Andrews hall, P.O. Box 880334, University of Nebraska, Lincoln NE 68588-0334. (402)472-0911. Fax: (402)472-9771. E-mail: jengelhardt2@unl.edu. Website: http://prairieschooner.

unl.edu. **Contact:** Contest Director. Poetry published in Prairie Schooner has been selected for inclusion in *The Best American Poetry* and *The Pushcart Prize*.

Magazines Needs *Prairie Schooner*, published quarterly, prints poetry, fiction, personal essays, interviews, and reviews. Wants "poems that fulfill the expectations they set up." No specifications as to form, length, style, subject matter, or purpose. Has published poetry by Alicia Ostriker, Marilyn Hacker, D.A. Powell, Stephen Dunn, and David Ignatow. *Prairie Schooner* is about 200 pages, digest-sized, flat-spined. Receives about 5,500 submissions/year, uses about 300 pages of poetry. Press run is 2,500. Single copy: $9; subscription: $28. Sample: $6.

How to Contact Submit 5-7 poems at a time. No simultaneous submissions. No fax or e-mail submissions; postal submissions only. Reads submissions September 1-May 1 (mss must be received during that period). Guidelines available for SASE or on website. Responds in 4 months, "sooner if possible." Always sends prepublication galleys. Pays 3 contributor's copies. Acquires all rights. Returns rights upon request without fee. Reviews books of poetry. Send materials for review consideration.

Contest/Award Offerings "All manuscripts published in *Prairie Schooner* automatically will be considered for our annual prizes." These include The Strousse Award for Poetry ($500), the Bernice Slote Prize for Beginning Writers ($500), the Hugh J. Luke Award ($250), the Edward Stanley Award for Poetry ($1,000), the Virginia Faulkner Award for Excellence in Writing ($1,000), the Glenna Luschei Prize for Excellence ($1,500), and the Jane Geske Award ($250). Also, each year 10 Glenna Luschei Awards ($250 each) are given for poetry, fiction, and nonfiction. All contests are open only to those writers whose work was published in the magazine the previous year. Editors serve as judges. Also sponsors The *Prairie Schooner* Book Prize.

Also Offers Editor-in-Chief Hilda Raz also promotes poets whose work has appeared in her pages by listing their continued accomplishments in a special section (even when their work does not concurrently appear in the magazine).

◯ ◎ PRAYERWORKS

P.O. Box 301363, Portland OR 97294-9363. (503)761-2072. E-mail: jay4prayer@aol.com. **Contact:** V. Ann Mandeville, Editor. *PrayerWorks*, published weekly, is a newsletter "encouraging elderly people to recognize their value to God as prayer warriors." Established as a ministry to people living in retirement centers, *PrayerWorks* features "prayers, ways to pray, stories of answered prayers, teaching on a Scripture portion, articles that build faith, and poems." *PrayerWorks* is 4 pages, digest-sized, desktop-published, photocopied, folded. Receives about 50 poems/year, accepts about 25%. Press run is 1,000. Subscription: free.

How to Contact Submit 5 poems at a time. Considers previously published poems and simultaneous submissions. Accepts e-mail submissions (WordPerfect or Microsoft Word attachments). Cover letter is preferred. 1 poem/page. Time between acceptance and publication is usually within 1 month. Seldom comments on rejected poems. Publishes theme issues relating to the holidays (submit holiday poetry 2 months in advance). Guidelines available for SASE. Responds in 3 weeks. Pays 5 or more contributor's copies.

☑ PRESA

P.O. Box 792, Rockford MI 49341.E-mail: presapress@aol.com. Website: www.presapress. com. Established 2003. **Contact:** Roseanne Ritzema, editor.

Magazines Needs *Presa*, published twice/year, prints poems, reviews, essays, photos, criticism, and prose. Wants imagistic, surreal, experimental, and personal poetry. Dedicates 6-8 pages of each issue to a featured poet. Does not want political or didactic poetry. Has published poetry by John Amen, Kirby Congdon, Erick Greinke, Richard Kostelanetz, Donald Lev, Lyn Lifshin, Sion Perchik. *Presa* is 48-64 pages, digest-sized laser printed on 20-24 lb. paper, pefect bound with a laminated color cover artwork on card stock; includes ads. Receives about 2,500 poems/year, accepts about 5%. Press run is 500. Single copy: $8.50; subscription: $15. Make checks payable to Presa Press.

How to Contact Submit 3-5 poems at a time. Considers previously published poems. (Considers poetry posted on a public website/blog/forum and poetry posted on a private, password-protected forum as published.) Accepts postal submissions only. Cover letter is preferred. Reads submissions year round. Time between acceptance and publication is 8-12 weeks. Poems are circulated to an editorial board. Never comments on rejected poems. Never publishes theme issues. Guidelines available in magazine, for SASE, and by e-mail. Responds in 4-8 weeks. Pays in contributor copies. Acquires first North American serial rights and the right to reprint in anthologies. Rights revert to poets upon publication. Reviews books and chapbooks of poetry. Send materials for review consideration to Roseanne Ritzema.

Tips "Read an issue or check our website."

☑ PRISM QUARTERLY

(217)529-5933. E-mail: prism@daybreakpoetry.com. Website: http://www.pwlf.com/ prism_quarterly.htm. **Contact:** Michelle Delheimer. *Prism Quarterly*, published by Daybreak Press, a division of Pitch-Black LLC, considers "all styles and forms of poetry." Does not want poems over 100 lines long. Considers poetry by children and teens. Has published poetry by Marge Piercy, Marcellus Leonard, Barb Robinette, and Siobhan. *Prism Quarterly* is 128 pages, digest-sized, laser-printed, perfect-bound, with cardstock cover with original artwork, includes ads. Receives about 800 poems/year, accepts about 200. Press run is 200; 25 distributed free to contributors and reviewers. Single copy: $7.95; subscription: $29.95. Make checks payable to Pitch-Black LLC.

How to Contact Submit no more than 3 poems at a time. Lines/poem: 100 maximum. No previously published poems or simultaneous submissions. Accepts e-mail submissions (pasted into body of message or as attachment in Rich Text Format); no disk submissions. Cover letter is required. "Please include SASE and e-mail address (if available) if response is desired for any submission." Reads submissions year-round. Submit seasonal poems 3 months in advance. Time between acceptance and publication is 2-3 months. Poems are circulated to an editorial board. Always comments on rejected poems. Guidelines available on website. Responds in 1-3 months. Pays one contributor's copy. Acquires first rights. Rights revert to poet upon publication.

Contest/Award Offerings "Intermittent contests are announced at our website. Please see site for frequent updates."

Tips "*Prism Quarterly* is a superlative journal of eclectic literature. The publishers welcome poets and writers in all (publishable) stages of their careers and seek a variety of themes, forms, and styles."

☐ THE PUCKERBRUSH REVIEW

E-mail: sanphip@aol.com. Website: http://puckerbrushreview.com. **Contact:** Sanford Phippen, Poetry Editor. *The Puckerbrush Review*, a print-only journal published twice/ year, looks for "freshness and simplicity." Does not want to see "confessional, religious, sentimental, dull, feminist, incompetent, derivative" poetry. Has published poetry by Wolly Swist and Muska Nagel. Submit 5 poems at a time. Guidelines available for SASE. Pays 2 contributor's copies.

⊞ ☑ PULSAR POETRY MAGAZINE

Ligden Publishers, 34 Lineacre, Grange Park, Swindon, Wiltshire SN5 6DA, England. E-mail: pulsar.ed@btopenworld.com. Website: www.pulsarpoetry.com. **Contact:** David Pike, Editor. *Pulsar Poetry Magazine* changed and is now a web-zine only. We will publish poems on the Pulsar web on a quarterly basis, i.e. March, June, September and December. The selection process for poems will not alter and we will continue to publish on a merit basis only, be warned the editor is very picky! See poem submission guidelines online. We encourage the writing of poetry from all walks of life. Wants "hard-hitting, thought-provoking work; interesting and stimulating poetry." Does not want "racist material. Not keen on religious poetry." Has published poetry by A.C. Evans, Chris Hardy, Kate Edwards, Elizabeth Birchall, and Michael Newman.

How to Contact Submit 3 poems at a time. No previously published poems or simultaneous submissions. Accepts e-mail submissions (pasted into body of message). "Send no more than 2 poems via e-mail; file attachments will not be read." Cover letter is preferred. Include SAE with adequate IRCs for a reply only (mss not returned if non-UK). Manuscripts should be typed. Time between acceptance and publication is about 1 month. "Poems can be published in next edition if it is what we are looking for. The editor and assistant read all poems." Seldom comments on rejected poems. Guidelines available for SASE (or SAE and IRC) or on website. Responds within 1 month. Pays 1 contributor's copy. Acquires first rights. "Originators retain copyright of their poems." Staff reviews poetry books and CDs (mainstream); word count varies. Send materials for review consideration.

Tips "Give explanatory notes if poems are open to interpretation. Be patient and enjoy what you are doing. Check grammar, spelling, etc. (should be obvious). Note: we are a nonprofit-making society."

☐ PULSE ONLINE LITERARY JOURNAL

12 Center St., Rockland ME 04841. (760)243-8034. E-mail: mainepoet@mac.com. Website: www.heartsoundspressliterary.com. **Contact:** Carol Bachofner, Poetry Editor.

Magazines Needs *Pulse Online Literary Journal* is open to formal poetry as well as free verse. Wants "your best. Send only work revised and revised again! Translations welcome with submitted original language piece." Does not want "predictable, sentimental, greeting card verse. No gratuitous sexuality or violence. No religious verse or predictable rhyme."

Has published poetry by Walt McDonald and Lyn Lifshin. Receives about 400 poems/year, accepts about 30-45%.

How to Contact Submit 3-5 poems at a time. Lines/poem: up to 120. Considers previously published poems. Only accepts e-mail submissions (pasted into body of e-mail); no disk submissions. Cover letter is required. "Send bio of 50-100 words with submission." Reads submissions year round; publishes February, April, June, August, September, October, December. Submit seasonal poems 2 months in advance. Time between acceptance and publication is 3-4 weeks. Sometimes comments on rejected poems. Sometimes publishes theme issues. Themes for 2009 were April-September: Urban Landscape; September-December: Movements. Guidelines available on website. Responds in 3-4 weeks. Acquires first rights. Reviews books/chapbooks of poetry.

Contest/Award Offerings Larry Kramer Memorial Chapbook Award; William Dunbar Book-length poetry contest. Submission ofr the contest is by USPS. See website for guidelines and deadlines. Entry fee: varies with contest (multiple entries okay with additional fee for each). Deadline: April 1.

Tips "Be relentless in the revision process. Read widely. Write *something* every day."

⊞ ☑ PURPLE PATCH

25 Griffiths Rd., West Bromwich B7I 2EH, England. E-mail: ppatch66@hotmail.com. Website: www.purplepatchpoetry.co.uk. **Contact:** Geoff Stevens, editor.

Magazines Needs *Purple Patch*, published quarterly, is a poetry and short prose magazine with reviews, coments, and illustrations. "All good examples of poetry considered." Does not want "poor rhyming verse, non-contributory swear words or obscenities, hackneyed themes." Has published poetry by Raymond K. Avery, Bryn Fortey, Bob Mee, B.Z. Niditch, and Steve Sneyd. *Purple Patch* is 24 pages, digest-sized, photocopied, side-stapled, with cover on the same stock with b&w drawing. Receives about 2,500 poems/year, accepts about 8%. Circulation varies. Subscription: £6 UK/3 issues; $12 USD (send dollars). Make checks (sterling only) payable to G. Stevens.

How to Contact Submit 2 or more poems at a time. Lines/poem: 40 maximum. No e-mail submissions; postal submissions only. Cover letter is preferred. Include self-introduction. Submissions must be sent return postage-paid. Reads submissions year round. Time between acceptance and publication is 4 months. Comments on rejected poems. Occasionally publishes theme issues. Upcoming themes available for SASE (or SAE and IRCs). Guidelines available in magazine or on website. Responds in one month to Great Britain; can be longer to U.S. Pays one contributor's copy "to European writers only; overseas contributors must purchase a copy to see their work in print." Acquires first British serial rights. Staff reviews poetry chapbooks, short stories, and tapes in 30-300 words. Send materials for review consideration.

Tips "Don't just send one poem. Send at least two, and I'll try to like them."

$ ◎ PURPOSE

E-mail: purposeeditor@mph.net. Website: www.mpn.net. **Contact:** Editor: Carol Duerksen. *Purpose*, published monthly by Faith & Life Resources, an imprint of the Mennonite Publishing Network (the official publisher for the Mennonite Church in the U.S. and Canada), is a "religious young adult/adult monthly." Focuses on "action-oriented, discipleship living."

Purpose is digest-sized with 4-color printing throughout. Press run is 8,000. Receives about 2,000 poems/year, accepts 150. Sample: (with guidelines) $2 and 9x12 SAE.

How to Contact Lines/poem: up to 12. Considers simultaneous submissions. Prefers e-mail submissions. Postal submissions should be double-spaced, typed on one side of sheet only. Responds in 6 months. Guidelines available electronically or for SASE. Pays $7.50 to $20 per poem plus 2 contributor's copies.

☑ QUARTERLY WEST

Dept. of English/LNCO 3500, University of Utah, 255 S. Central Campus Dr., Salt Lake City UT 84112-9109. (801)581-3938. E-mail: quarterlywest@yahoo.com. Website: www. utah.edu/quarterlywest. **Contact:** Shira Dentz & Julie Gonnering, poetry editors. *Quarterly West*, published semiannually, seeks "original and accomplished literary verse—free or formal." Also considers translations (include originals with submissions). No greeting card or sentimental poetry. Has published poetry by Quan Barry, Medbh McGuckian, Alice Notley, Brenda Shaughnessy, Bob Hicok, David Kirby, and Linh Dinh. *Quarterly West* is 160 pages, digest-sized, offset-printed, with 4-color cover art. Receives 2,500 submissions/year, accepts less than 1%. Press run is 1,500 (500 subscribers, 300-400 libraries). Subscription: $14/year, $25 for 2 years. Sample: $8.50.

How to Contact Submit 3-5 poems at a time. Online submissions only, guidelines available on website. Considers simultaneous submissions, with notification; no previously published poems. Reads submissions September 1-May 1. Seldom comments on rejected poems. Responds in up to 6 months. Pays 2 contributor's copies and money when possible. Acquires first North American serial rights. Returns rights with acknowledgment and right to reprint. Reviews books of poetry in 1,000-3,000 words.

$ ◻ ◉ ELLERY QUEEN'S MYSTERY MAGAZINE

267 Broadway, 4th Floor, New York NY 10007. E-mail: elleryqueen@dellmagazines.com. Website: www.themysteryplace.com. **Contact:** Janet Hutchings.

Magazines Needs *Ellery Queen's Mystery Magazine*, published 10 times/year, uses primarily short stories of mystery, crime, or suspense—little poetry. *Ellery Queen's Mystery Magazine* is 112 pages (double-issue, published twice/year, is 192 pages), digest-sized, professionally printed on newsprint, flat-spined, with glossy paper cover. Single copy: $5.50 by check to publisher, available for $4.99 on newsstands; subscription: $55.90.

How to Contact Considers simultaneous submissions; no previously published poems. No e-mail submissions; postal submissions only. Include SASE with submissions. Guidelines available for SASE or on website. Responds in 3 months. Pays $15-65 and 3 contributor's copies.

☑ QUERCUS REVIEW

Quercus Review Press, Modesto Junior College, Literature & Language Arts, 35 College Ave., Modesto CA 95350. (209)575-6183. E-mail: pierstorffs@mjc.edu. Website: www. quercusreview.com. **Contact:** Sam Pierstorff, editor.

Magazines Needs *Quercus Review*, published annually in May/June, prints high-quality poetry, fiction, and b&w art. "We publish numerous nationally recognized and award-winning writers from across the nation." Wants "writing with a pulse. Writing that reflects a unique voice." Does not want "rhyme, religious, or cliché writing." Considers poetry by children and teens. Has published poetry by X.J. Kennedy, Gerald Locklin, Naomi Shihab Nye, Amiri Baraka, Charles Harper Webb, and Dorianne Laux. *Quercus Review* is 112 pages, digest-sized, professionally printed, perfect-bound, with full-color cover. Receives about 3,500 poems/year, accepts less than 5%. Press run is 500; 100 distributed free to contributors and local bookstores. Single copy: $8; subscription: $20 for 2 years (includes 2 issues of *Quercus Review*, plus annual book award winner). Make checks payable to "MJC (QR)."

How to Contact Submit 3-5 poems at a time. Lines/poem: prefers 40 maximum, but will consider longer. No previously published poems or simultaneous submissions. No e-mail or disk submissions. Cover letter is required. Include brief bio and SASE. Reads submissions August 1-February 1 only. Time between acceptance and publication is usually 3 weeks to 3 months. "Poems are selected by 5-person staff of editors, which rotates annually." Guidelines available on website. Sometimes sends prepublication galleys. Pays 1 contributor's copy, 30% discount on additional copies. Acquires first rights.

Contest/Award Offerings Quercus Review Press Poetry Series Book Award.

Tips "Avoid overusing the world 'soul,' but feel free to drown us in fresh imagery and bold language. We like poems with a pulse. Make us laugh or cry, but don't bore or try too hard to impress us."

☑ QUEST

Lynn's Literary and Arts Journal, Lynn University, 3601 N. Military Trail, Boca Raton FL 33431-5598. Website: www.lynn.edu. **Contact:** John Daily, Editor. Annual literary magazine publishes short fiction, poetry, one-act plays, and art created by and for students, faculty, staff, and friends of Lynn University. "We appreciate fresh voices as much as seasoned work."

Magazines Needs *Quest*, published annually in Autumn, is a literary and arts journal. Wants "poems with a clear voice that use careful diction to create poetry in which sound and sense work together, creating fresh perception." Does not want "poems that rely on profanity or shock value." Receives about 100 poems/year, accepts about 25. Press run is 1,000 (one library subscriber); 150 distributed free to Lynn University faculty, staff, and students. Single copy: $5. Make checks payable to Lynn University.

How to Contact Submit up to 3 poems at a time. No previously published poems or simultaneous submissions. No e-mail or disk submissions. Cover letter is preferred. "Include adequate SASE if you want work returned." Reads submissions mid-September to April 30. Time between acceptance and publication is up to 7 months. "The Lynn English Department faculty and selected students form the Editorial Board to review submissions." Seldom comments on rejected poems. Responds in up to 4 months. Pays 1 contributor's copy. Acquires one-time rights.

Tips "Even the freest of verse has its roots in the formal elements."

☑ QUIDDITY: INTERNATIONAL LITERARY JOURNAL AND PUBLIC-RADIO PROGRAM

1500 N. Fifth St., Springfield IL 62702. (217)525-1420. E-mail: quiddity@sci.edu. Website: www.sci.edu/quiddity. **Contact:** poetry editor. Member: CLMP, AWP.

Magazines Needs *Quiddity*, published semi-annually, is "a print journal and public-radio program featuring poetry, prose, and artwork by new, emerging, and established contributors from around the globe. Please visit the website for guidelines." Has published work by J.O.J. Nwachukwu-Agbada, Kevin Stein, Karen An-Hwei Lee, and Haider Al-Kabi. *Quiddity* is 176 pages, 7X9, perfect-bound, with 60 lb. full color cover. Receives about 3,500 poems/year, accepts about 3%. Press run is 1,000. Single copy: $9; subscription: $15/year. Make checks payable to *Quiddity*.

How to Contact Submit up to 5 poems at a time, no more than 10 pages. Considers simultaneous submissions; no previously published poems (previously published includes work posted on a public website/blog/forum and on private, password-protected forums). Cover letter is preferred. "Address to poetry editor, SASE required (except international). See website for reading dates. Time between acceptance and publication is 6 months to 2 years. Poems are circulated to an editorial board. Never comments on rejected poems. Sometimes publishes theme issues. Upcoming themes and guidelines available on website. Responds in 6 months. Typically sends prepublication galleys. Pays 1 contributor's copy. Acquires first North American serial rights and may request broadcast rights. Print rights revert to poet on publication. Considers reviews for books of poetry only when sent from publisher. Send materials for review consideration to poetry editor.

Contest/Award Offerings Sponsors the annual Teresa A. White Creative Writing Award and the Linda Bromberg Literary Award. **Entry fee**: $12. "See website for guidelines, deadline, and prize information. All entries are considered for publication."

◩ ◎ RADIX MAGAZINE

P.O. Box 4307, Berkeley CA 94704. E-mail: RadixMag@aol.com. Website: www.radixmagazine.com. **Contact:** Luci Shaw, poetry editor; Sharon Gallagher, editor. (Specialized: poetry that expresses a Christian world-view)

Magazines Needs *Radix Magazine*, published quarterly, is named for the Latin word for "root" and "has its roots both in the 'real world' and in the truth of Christ's teachings." Wants poems "that reflect a Christian world-view, but aren't preachy." Has published poetry by John Leax, Czeslaw Milosz, Madeleine L'Engle, and Luci Shaw. *Radix* is 32 pages, magazine-sized, offset-printed, saddle-stapled, with 60-lb. self cover. Receives about 120 poems/year, accepts about 10%. Press run varies. Sample: $5. Make checks payable to *Radix Magazine*.

How to Contact Submit 1-4 poems at a time. No previously published poems or simultaneous submissions. Accepts e-mail submissions only. Submit seasonal poems 6 months in advance. Time between acceptance and publication is 3 months to 3 years. "We have a serious backlog. The poetry editor accepts or rejects poems and sends the accepted poems to the editor. The editor then publishes poems in appropriate issues. If more than one poem is accepted from any poet, there will probably be a long wait before another is published, because of our backlog of accepted poems." Seldom comments on rejected poems. Occasionally publishes theme issues. Responds in 2 months. Pays 2 contributor's copies. Acquires first rights. Returns rights upon request. Reviews books of poetry.

Tips "*Radix* has a distinctive voice and often receives submissions that are completely inappropriate. Familiarity with the magazine is recommended before sending any submissions."

☑ ◎ THE RAINTOWN REVIEW

Central Ave Press, 2132A Central SE #144, Albuquerque NM 87106. E-mail: theraintownreview@gmail.com. Website: www.theraintownreview.com. **Contact:** Anna Evans, Editor. We prefer poems that have NOT been previously published. *The Raintown Review*, published 2 times/year in December and July, contains poetry "and the occasional literary criticism or review." Wants well-crafted poems. "We are primarily a venue for formal/traditional poetry." Has published poetry by William Baer, Joseph S. Salemi, Richard Moore, Annie Finch, Dana Gioia, Daniel Hoffman, A.E. Stallings, Richard Wilbur, and many others. *The Raintown Review* is 120 pages, perfect-bound. Receives about 1,500 poems/year, accepts 10-15%. Press run is 150 (most go to subscribers and contributors). Subscription: $24/year, $45 for 2 years, $65 for 3 years. Sample: $12. Make checks/money orders payable to Central Ave Press

How to Contact Submit 3-5 poems at a time. Lines/poem: no restrictions. Considers simultaneous submissions. Accepts e-mail submissions only (pasted into body of message); no postal submissions. Comments on rejected poems if requested at the time of submission. Guidelines available on website. Usually responds in 2 months, if possible. Pays 1 contributor's copy. Acquires one-time rights.

☑ ◎ RATTAPALLAX

217 Thompson St., Suite 353, New York NY 10012. E-mail: info@rattapallax.com. Website: www.rattapallax.com. **Contact:** Poetry Editor.

Magazines Needs *Rattapallax*, published semiannually, is named for "Wallace Steven's word for the sound of thunder. The magazine includes a DVD featuring poetry films and audio files. *Rattapallax* is looking for the extraordinary in modern poetry and prose that reflect the diversity of world cultures. Our goals are to create international dialogue using literature and focus on what is relevant to our society." Has published poetry by Anthony Hecht, Sharon Olds, Lou Reed, Marilyn Hacker, Billy Collins, and Glyn Maxwell. *Rattapallax* is 112 pages, magazine-sized, offset-printed, perfect-bound, with 12-pt. CS1 cover. Receives about 5,000 poems/year, accepts 2%. Press run is 2,000 (100 subscribers, 50 libraries, 1,200 shelf sales); 200 distributed free to contributors, reviews, and promos. Single copy: $7.95; no subscriptions. Make checks payable to *Rattapallax*.

How to Contact Submit 3-5 poems at a time. Considers simultaneous submissions; no previously published poems. Accepts e-mail submissions (sent as simple text) from outside the U.S. and Canada; all other submissions must be sent via postal mail (SASE required). Cover letter is preferred. Reads submissions year round; issue deadlines are June 1 and December 1. Time between acceptance and publication is 6 months. "The editor-in-chief, senior editor, and associate editor review all the submissions and then decide on which to accept every week. Near publication time, all accepted work is narrowed, and unused work is kept for the next issue." Often comments on rejected poems. Guidelines available by e-mail or on website. Responds in 2 months. Always sends prepublication galleys. Pays 2 contributor's copies. Acquires first rights.

☑ RATTLE

12411 Ventura Blvd., Studio City CA 91604. (818)505-6777. E-mail: timgreen@rattle.com. Website: www.rattle.com. **Contact:** Timothy Green, Editor.

Magazines Needs *RATTLE*, published semiannually in June and December, includes poems, essays, reviews, interviews with poets, and a tribute section dedicated to a specific ethnic or vocational group. Wants "high-quality poetry of any form. Nothing unintelligible." Considers some poetry by children and teens (ages 10-18). Has published poetry by Lucille Clifton, Charles Simic, Mark Doty, Sharon Olds, Billy Collins, and Stephen Dunn. *RATTLE* is 196 pages, digest-sized, neatly printed, perfect-bound, with 4-color coated card cover. Receives about 8,000 submissions/year, accepts 200. Press run is 4,000. Subscription: $18/year, $30/2 years, $36/3 years. Sample: $10. Make checks payable to *RATTLE*.

How to Contact Submit up to 5 poems at a time. Considers simultaneous submissions "if notified immediately by e-mail or phone should they be taken elsewhere." Accepts e-mail submissions (pasted into body of message). Cover letter is required (with e-mail address, if possible). Include bio. For postal submissions, put name, address, and phone number on each page in upper right corner; include SASE. Reads submissions year round. Seldom comments on rejected poems (unless requested by the author). Guidelines available in magazine, by e-mail, or on website. Responds in up to 2 months. Pays 2 contributor's copies. Rights revert to poet upon publication. Publishes reviews of books of poetry online. Send materials for review consideration.

Additional Information Welcomes essays up to 2,000 words on poetry or the writing process. Publishes a biannual electronic issue in March and September, e-mailed as a PDF to 4,000 subscribers, featuring excerpts from poetry collections, chapbooks, reviews, and print issue previews.

Contest/Award Offerings "All submissions are automatically considered for the Neil Postman Award for Metaphor, an annual $500 prize for the best use of metaphor as judged by the editors. No entry fee or special formatting is required, simply follow the regular guidelines." Also, the *RATTLE* Poetry Prize.

▣ $ ☑ ◎ RAVING DOVE

PO Box 28, West Linn OR 97068. E-mail: editor@ravingdove.org. Website: www.ravingdove. org. **Contact:** Jo-Ann Moss, editor. *Raving Dove*, published quarterly, "is an online literary journal that publishes original poetry, nonfiction, fiction, photography, and art with universal anti-violence, anti-hate, human rights, and social justice themes. We share sentiments that oppose physical and psychological violence in all its forms, including war, discrimination against sexual orientation, and every shade of bigotry." Wants free verse only, any length. Has published poetry by Howard Camner, Marguerite Bouvard, John Kay, Harry Youtt. Receives about 750 poems/year, accepts about 30. Number of visitors is "2,000/month and growing."

How to Contact Considers simultaneous submissions. Accepts e-mail submissions only; allows attachments. No fax, disk, or postal submissions. Cover letter is unnecessary. Poetry Submission must appear as the subject of the e-mail; all submissions must include full name, general geographic location, and a third-person bio of 100 words or less. Weblinks are permitted. Reads submissions year round. Time between acceptance and publication is no more than 3 months. Sometimes comments on rejected poems. Guidelines available on website. Always sends prepublication galleys ("the link to the poet's Web page at *Raving Dove* is sent prior to publication"). Responds in 3 months. Payment is based on funding. Acquires first North American and Internet serial rights, exclusive for the duration of the edition in which the poetry appears (see submission guidelines on website for further information). Rights revert to poets at the end of the issue.

N̲ REDHEADED STEPCHILD

E-mail: redheadedstepchildmag@gmail.com. Website: www.redheadedstepchildmag.com/poetry/. **Contact:** Malaika King Albrecht. "The Redheaded Stepchild only accepts poems that have been rejected by other magazines. We publish biannually, and we accept submissions in the months of August and February only. We do not accept previously published work. We do, however, accept simultaneous submissions, but please inform us immediately if your work is accepted somewhere else. We are open to a wide variety of poetry and hold no allegiance to any particular style or school. If your poem is currently displayed online on your blog or website or wherever, please do not send it to us before taking it down, at least temporarily. Submit 3-5 poems that have been rejected elsewhere with the names of the magazines that rejected the poems. We do not want multiple submissions, so please wait for a response to your first submission before you submit again. As is standard after publication, rights revert back to the author, but we request that you credit Redheaded Stepchild in subsequent republications. We do not accept e-mail attachments; therefore, in the body of your e-mail, please include the following: a brief bio; 3-5 poems; the publication(s) that rejected the poems."

• "The *Redheaded Stepchild, published semiannually,* only accepts poems that have been rejected by other magazines. We publish biannually, and we accept submissions in the months of August and February only."

Magazines Needs Wants a wide variety of poetic styles. Does not want previously published poems. Has published poetry by Kathryn Stripling Byer, Alex Grant, Amy King, Diane Lockward, Susan Yount, and Howie Good.

How to Contact Submit 3-5 poems at a time. Considers simultaneous submissions. Accepts e-mail submissions pasted into body of e-mail message. Cover letter is preferred. Time between acceptance and publication is 3 months. Poems are circulated to an editorial board. Sometimes comments on rejected poems. Guidelines on website. Responds in 3 months. Acquires first rights. Rights revert to poets upon publication.

☑ REDIVIDER

Dept. of Writing, Literature, and Publishing, Emerson College, 120 Boylston St., Boston MA 02118. E-mail: poetry@rediverpoetry.com. Website: www.rediverjournal.org. *Redivider*, published semiannually, prints high-quality poetry, art, fiction, and creative nonfiction. Wants "all styles of poetry. Most of all, we look for language that seems fresh and alive on the page, that tries to do something new. Read a sample copy for a good idea." Does not want "greeting card verse or inspirational verse." Has published poetry by Bob Hicok, Billy Collins, Paul Muldoon, Tao Lin, Claudia Emerson, and Bobby Byrd. *Redivider* is 100+ pages, digest-sized, offset-printed, perfect-bound, with 4-color artwork on cover. Receives about 1,000 poems/year, accepts about 30%. Press run is 1,000. Single copy: $6; subscription: $10. Make checks payable to *Redivider* at Emerson College.

How to Contact As of May 1, 2010, we are taking electronic submissions solely through our online submissions manager. Hard copy submissions and inquiries may be sent to the appropriate genre editor. Submit 3-6 poems at a time. Considers simultaneous submissions, but requires notification if your work is taken elsewhere; no previously published poems. Cover letter is required. Reads submissions year-round. Seldom comments on rejected poems. Guidelines available in magazine, for SASE, by e-mail, or on website. Responds in 5 months. Pays 2 contributor's copies. Acquires first North American serial rights. Reviews books of poetry in 500 words, single-book format. Send materials for review consideration, Attn: Review Copies. "Book reviews and interviews are internally generated." Our deadlines are July 1 for the Fall issue, and December 1 for the Spring issue of 2010.

Tips "We want your finished product—don't send your experimental first draft!"

$ ◎ RED LIGHTS

2740 Andrea Drive, Allentown PA 18103-4602. (212)875-9342. E-mail: mhazelton@rcn.com; marilynhazelton@rcn.com. **Contact:** Marilyn Hazelton, Editor. *red lights*, published semiannually in January and June, is devoted to English-language tanka and tanka sequences. Wants "print-only tanka, mainly 'free-form' but also strictly syllabic 5-7-5-7-7; will consider tanka sequences and tan-renga." Considers poetry by children and teens. Has published poetry by Sanford Goldstein, Michael McClintock, Laura Maffei, Linda Jeannette Ward, Jane Reichhold, and Michael Dylan Welch. *red lights* is 28-36 pages, 8½ × 3¾, offset-printed, saddle-stapled, with Japanese textured paper cover; copies are numbered. Receives about 1,200 poems/year, accepts about 20%. Press run is 150. Single copy: $7; subscription: $14 U.S., $15 USD Canada, $17 USD foreign. Make checks payable to "red lights" in the U.S.

How to Contact Submit 10 tanka or 2 sequences at a time (maximum). No previously published poems or simultaneous submissions. Prefers e-mail submissions. Include SASE if mailing. Submissions are due in hand April 15th for the June issue and November 15th for the January issue. Reads submissions year-round. Time between acceptance and publication "depends on submission time." Guidelines available for SASE. Acquires first rights.

Tips "Each issue features a '*red lights* featured tanka' on the theme of 'red lights.' Poet whose poem is selected receives 1 contributor's copy."

$ ◨ ◎ THE RED MOON ANTHOLOGY OF ENGLISH LANGUAGE HAIKU

P.O. Box 2461, Winchester VA 22604-1661. E-mail: jim.kacian@redmoonpress.com. Website: www.redmoonpress.com. **Contact:** Jim Kacian, Editor/Publisher.

Magazines Needs *The Red Moon Anthology of English Language Haiku*, published annually in February, is "a collection of the best haiku published in English around the world." Considers poetry by children and teens. Has published haiku and related forms by Carolyn Hall, Marcus Larsson, Yu Chang, and Harriot West. *The Red Moon Anthology of English Language Haiku* is 184 pages, digest-sized, offset-printed on quality paper, with 4-color heavy-stock cover. Receives several thousand submissions/year, accepts less than 2%. Print run is 1,000 for subscribers and commercial distribution. Subscription: $17 plus $5 p&h. Sample available for SASE or by e-mail.

How to Contact "We do not accept direct submissions to the *Red Moon Anthology*. Rather, we employ an editorial board who are assigned journals and books from which they cull and nominate. Nominated poems are placed on a roster and judged anonymously by the entire editorial board twice a year." Guidelines available for SASE or by e-mail. Pays $1/page. Acquires North American serial rights.

Also Offers *contemporary haibun*, "an annual volume of the finest English-language haibun and haiga published anywhere in the world." (See separate listing in this section.)

Tips "Haiku is a burgeoning and truly international form. It is nothing like what your fourth-grade teacher taught you years ago, and so it is best if you familiarize yourself with what is happening in the genre (and its close relatives) today before submitting. We strive to give all the work we publish plenty of space in which to resonate, and to provide a forum where the best of today's practitioners can be published with dignity and prestige."

▣ ◪ ◎ THE REDNECK REVIEW

P.O. Box 8718, Atlanta GA 31106. E-mail: editor@redneckreview.com. Website: www.redneckreview.com. **Contact:** Penya Sandor, editor.

Magazines Needs *The Redneck Review*, published semiannually online, is "born out of the rich literary tradition of the South." Wants "writing that is interesting, has energy, and doesn't feel like homework." Considers poetry by children and teens. Has published poetry by Denise Duhamel, Marie Howe, Walt McDonald, Hal Sirowitz, Ben Satterfield, and Jean Trounstine. Publishes about 15-20 poems/issue.

How to Contact Submit no more than 5 poems at a time. Considers previously published poems and simultaneous submissions. Accepts e-mail and disk submissions. Cover letter is preferred. "If sending submissions by postal mail, include SASE unless you have an e-mail address. Poems won't be returned." Time between acceptance and publication "depends." Often comments on rejected poems. Guidelines available on website. Response time varies. Sometimes sends prepublication galleys. No payment. "Authors retain rights, but we ask that they mention our journal if they publish the poem again." Send materials for review consideration to *The Redneck Review*.

Tips "There are many respectable literary journals that publish well-written but dull writing. We would prefer to read literature that is electric, not just technically well crafted."

◪ RED ROCK REVIEW

Dept. of English W20E, College of Southern Nevada, 6375 W. Charleston Blvd., Las Vegas NV 89146. (702)651-4094. Fax: (702)651-4639. E-mail: richard.logsdon@csn.edu. Website: http://sites.csn.edu/english/redrockreview/. **Contact:** Dr. Richard Logson, Editor. Poetry Editor: Jeanie French. Associate Editor: Todd Moffett.

Magazines Needs *Red Rock Review*, published semiannually in May and December, prints "the best poetry available," as well as fiction, creative nonfiction, and book reviews. Has published poetry by Dorianne Laux, Kim Addonizio, Ellen Bass, Cynthia Hogue, and Dianne di Prima. *Red Rock Review* is about 130 pages, magazine-sized, professionally printed, perfect-bound, with 10-pt. CS1 cover. Accepts about 15% of poems received/year. Press run is 2350. Sample: $6.50.

How to Contact Submit 2-3 poems at a time by e-mail. Attach Word, RTF, or PDF file to redrockreview@csn.edu. Lines/poem: 80 maximum. Considers simultaneous submissions. Accepts disk submissions. Cover letter and SASE are required. Reads submissions September-May. Time between acceptance and publication is 2-3 months. "Poems go to poetry editor, who then distributes them to 3 readers." Occasionally comments on rejected poems. Guidelines available on website. Responds in 2-3 months. Pays 2 contributor's copies. Acquires first North American serial rights. Reviews books/chapbooks of poetry in 500-1,000 words, multi-book format. Send materials for review consideration.

☑ RED WHEELBARROW

De Anza College, 21250 Stevens Creek Blvd., Cupertino CA 95014. E-mail: weisnerken@ fhda.edu. **Contact:** Ken Weisner. *Red Wheelbarrow*, published annually in spring, is a college-produced, national magazine. Wants "diverse voices." Has published poetry by Nils Peterson, Ellen Bass, Ed Pavlic, Scott Hernandez, Debra Spencer, and Steve Kuusisto. *Red Wheelbarrow* is about 250 pages, book-sized, printed on heavy stock with color cover and occasional b&w graphics, perfect-bound. Press run is on demand. Single copy: $10. Sample: $2.50 (for back issue).Submit up to 5 poems at a time. Accepts e-mail submissions. Include SASE or e-mail address for reply. Reads submissions September-January (January 31 deadline). Responds in 2-6 months, depending on backlog. Pays 1 contributor's copy.

☑ RHINO

P.O. Box 591, Evanston IL 60204. Website: www.rhinopoetry.org. **Contact:** Marcia L. Zuckerman, associate editor. "This eclectic annual journal of more than 30 years accepts poetry, flash fiction (1,000 words or less), and poetry-in-translation that experiments, provokes, compels and/or sings. More than 80 poets are showcased. The regular call for poetry as well as the Founder's Contest submission period is from April 1 to October 1."

- *RHINO* poems have been reprinted in *The Best American Poetry*, nominated for Pushcart Prizes, and won repeated Illinois Arts Council awards.

Magazines Needs *RHINO*, published annually in spring, prints poetry, short-shorts, and translations. Wants "work that reflects passion, originality, engagement with contemporary culture, and a love affair with language. We welcome free verse, formal poetry, innovation, and risk-taking." Has published poetry by Geoffrey Forsyth, Penelope Scambly Schott, F. Daniel Rzicznek, and Ricardo Pau-Llosa. *RHINO* is 150 pages, 7x10, printed on high-quality paper, with card cover with art. Receives 8,000-10,000 submissions/year, accepts 90-100, or 1%. Press run is 800. Single copy: $12. Sample: $5 (back issue).

How to Contact Submit 3-5 poems or 1-3 short-shorts once during reading period. Considers simultaneous submissions with notification; no previously published poems. Include SASE. Expects electronic copy upon acceptance. Reads submissions April 1-October 1. Guidelines available for SASE or on website. Responds in up to 6 months. Pays 2 contributor's copies. Acquires first rights only.

▣ ☑ ◎ RHODE ISLAND ROADS

2 Barber Ave., Warwick RI 02886. (401)480-9355. E-mail: editor@RIRoads.com; asurkont@ local.net. Website: www.riroads.com. Paul Pence, Editor. **Contact:** Amanda Surkont, Poetry Editor. *Rhode Island Roads*, the online monthly magazine of travel, dining, life, and entertainment for people who love Rhode Island, features work with Rhode Island and New England themes. Open to all forms and styles, although "rhyme will have difficulty finding a home here." Considers poetry by children and teens. Has published poetry by Audrey Friedman, Barbara Schweitzer, Michele F. Cooper, Pat Hagneur, Lauri Burke, and Peggy Conti. Receives about 150 poems/year, accepts 12-16/year. Has about

70,000 readers/month. Sample: can view sample pages for free online.(Specialized: RI/ New England themes)E-mail: asurkont@local.net. Website: www.riroads.com. Established 2000. **Contact:** Amanda Surkont, poetry editor.

Tips "Know your market. Read the publication before submitting poems. Get a feel for what we like. We sometimes suggest an alternative market for work. We suggest poets make a commitment to subscribing to five lit mags per year; we have more writers of poetry than readers. This is not a good balance."

⊕ $ ✉ THE RIALTO

P.O. Box 309, Alysham, Norwich NR11 6LN, England. Website: www.therialto.co.uk. **Contact:** Michael Mackmin, Editor. *The Rialto*, published 3 times/year, seeks "to publish the best new poems by established and beginning poets. We seek excellence and originality." Has published poetry by Alice Fulton, Jenny Joseph, Les Murray, George Szirtes, Philip Gross, and Ruth Padel. *The Rialto* is 64 pages, A4, with full-color cover. Receives about 12,000 poems/year, accepts about 1%. Press run is 1,500. Single copy: £7.50; subscription: £23 (prices listed are for U.S. and Canada). Make checks payable to *The Rialto*. "Checks in sterling only, please. Online payment also available on website."

How to Contact Submit up to 6 poems at a time. Considers simultaneous submissions; no previously published poems. Cover letter is preferred. "SASE or SAE with IRCs essential. U.S. readers please note that U.S. postage stamps are invalid in UK." No poetry submissions will be accepted by email or online. Time between acceptance and publication is up to 4 months. Seldom comments on rejected poems. Responds in 5-6 months. Pays £20/poem. Poet retains rights.

Tips "*The Rialto* has recently commenced publishing first collections by poets. Please do not send book-length manuscripts. Query first." Sponsors an annual young poets competition. Details available in magazine and on website. Before submitting, "you will probably have read many poems by many poets, both living and dead. You will probably have put aside each poem you write for at least 3 weeks before considering it afresh. You will have asked yourself, 'Does it work technically?'; checked the rhythm, the rhymes (if used), and checked that each word is fresh and meaningful in its context, not jaded and tired. You will hopefully have read *The Rialto*."

✉ ◎ RIBBONS: TANKA SOCIETY OF AMERICA JOURNAL

David Bacharach, TSA Editor, 5921 Cayutaville Rd., Alpine NY 14805. E-mail: davidb@ htva.net. Website: www.tankasocietyofamerica.com. **Contact:** David Bacharach, Editor. Published quarterly, seeks and regularly prints "the best tanka poetry being written in English, together with reviews, critical and historical essays, commentaries, and translations." Wants "poetry that exemplifies the very best in English-language tanka, which we regard as 'the queen of short form poetry,' having a significant contribution to make to the short poem in English. All schools and approaches are welcome." Tanka should "reflect contemporary life, issues, values, and experience, in descriptive, narrative, and lyrical modes." Does not want "work that merely imitates the Japanese masters." Considers poetry by children and teens. "We have no age restrictions." Has published poetry by Cherie Hunter Day, Marianne Bluger, Sanford Goldstein, Larry Kimmel, John Stevenson, and George Swede. *Ribbons* is 60-72 pages, 6x9 perfect-bound, with color cover and art.

Receives about 2,000 poems/year, accepts about 20%. Press run is 275; 15 distributed free. Single copy: $10; subscription: $30. Make checks payable to Tanka Society of America and contact Carole MacRury, Secretary/Treasurer (e-mail: macrury@whidbey.com; 1636 Edwards Dr., Point Roberts, WA 98281).

Poetry See features. 200 new tanka appear in each issue. McClintock's 'Tanka Cafe' uses up to 45 poems per issue on a given theme, with critical commentary relating to contemporary tanka in English trends, styles, techniques, and subject matter."The annual Tanka Society of America International English-Language Tanka Competition (see separate listing in Contests & Awards). "Additionally, a Members' Choice Award of $25 is given each quarter for a poem appearing in the 'Tanka Cafe' feature; non-cash Editor's Choice Awards are also featured in each issue.". Submit 1-8 poems at a time. Lines/poem: 5 minimum; sequences of up to 50 total lines considered. No previously published poems or simultaneous submissions. Prefers e-mail submissions (pasted into body of message); no disk submissions. "Postal submissions must include SASE." Reads submissions year-round. "See the publication or contact the editor for specific deadlines for each issue." Time between acceptance and publication is 2 months. Sometimes comments on rejected poems. Regularly publishes theme issues. Guidelines available in magazine or on website. Responds in 4-8 weeks. No payment. Acquires one-time rights. Rights revert to poet upon publication. Reviews books/chapbooks of poetry and other magazines/journals in 250-1,200 words, single- or multi-book format. Send materials for review consideration to the editor or to Michael McClintock, President, Tanka Society of America, 9230 N. Stoneridge Lane, Fresno CA 93720.

Tips "Work by beginning as well as established English-language tanka poets is welcome; first-time contributors are encouraged to study the tanka form and contemporary examples before submitting. No particular school or style of tanka is preferred over another; our publications seek to showcase the full range of English-language tanka expression and subject matter through the work of new and established poets in the genre from around the world."

▢ ◎ RIO GRANDE REVIEW

P.M. Box 671, 500 W. University Ave., El Paso TX 79968-0622. E-mail: editors@ riograndereview.com. Website: www.utep.edu/rgr. **Contact:** Poetry Editor. *Rio Grande Review*, published in January and August, is a bilingual (English-Spanish) student publication from the University of Texas at El Paso. Contains poetry; flash, short, and nonfiction; short drama; photography and line art. *Rio Grande Review* is 168 pages, digest-sized, professionally printed, perfect-bound, with card cover with line art. Subscription: $8/year, $15/2 years.

How to Contact Poetry has a limit of 10 pages. No simultaneous submissions. Accepts e-mail submissions only (as attachment or pasted into body of message). Include short bio. Guidelines available for SASE, by e-mail, or on website. The deadline for the Fall 2010 issue is September 10, 2010. Any submissions received after a reception deadline will automatically be considered for the following edition. Pays 2 contributor's copies. "Permission to reprint material remains the decision of the author. However, *Rio Grande Review* does request it be given mention."

☑ RIVER OAK REVIEW

Elmhurst College, 190 Prospect Ave., Elmhurst IL 60126. (630)617-6483. Website: www.riveroakreview.org. **Contact:** Ann Frank Wake, Poetry Editor.

Magazines Needs *River Oak Review*, published annually, prints high-quality poetry, short fiction, and creative nonfiction. "We are a national journal striving to publish midwestern poets in each issue." Has published poetry by Wendy Bishop, Jim Elledge, James Doyle, Ken Meisel, Blair Beacom Deets, and Robin Becker. *River Oak Review* is at least 128 pages, digest-sized, neatly printed, perfect-bound, with glossy color cover with art. Publishes about 5% of poetry received. Press run is 500. Single copy: $10; subscription: $10/year, $20/2 years. Sample: $5. Make checks payable to *River Oak Review*.

How to Contact Submit 4-6 poems at a time. No previously published poems. SASE required. Reads submissions year round. Sometimes comments on rejected poems. Guidelines available for SASE or on website. Tries to respond in 3 months. Pays 2 contributor's copies. Acquires first North American serial rights.

Tips "Mary Oliver suggests that poets should read modern poetry for at least 2 hours for every hour they spend writing. Our experience as editors bears this out." We agree in principle with Stanley Kunitz, who told his poetry students to 'End on an image and don't explain it!' While we don't mean this literally, we do think that a 'less is more' philosophy usually results in better poems."

$ ☑ RIVER STYX MAGAZINE

3547 Olive St., Suite 107, St. Louis MO 63103-1014. E-mail: bigriver@riverstyx.org. Website: www.riverstyx.org. **Contact:** Richard Newman, Editor.

• Poetry published in *River Styx* has been selected for inclusion in past volumes of *The Best American Poetry*, *Beacon's Best*, *Best New Poets* and *The Pushcart Prize*.

Magazines Needs *River Styx Magazine*, published 3 times/year in April, August, and December, is "an international, multicultural journal publishing both award-winning and previously undiscovered writers. We feature poetry, short fiction, essays, interviews, fine art, and photography." Wants "excellent poetry—original, energetic, musical, and accessible." Does not want "chopped prose or opaque poetry that isn't about anything." Has published poetry by Jennifer Perrine, Louis Simpson, Molly Peacock, Marilyn Hacker, Yusef Komunyakaa, Andrew Hudgins, and Catie Rosemurgy. *River Styx Magazine* is 100-120 pages, digest-sized, professionally printed on coated stock, perfect-bound, with color cover, includes ads. Receives about 8,000 poems/year, accepts 60-75. Press run is 2,500 (1,000 subscribers, 80 libraries). Subscription: $20/year, $35/2 years. Sample: $9.

How to Contact Submit 3-5 poems at a time. Manuscripts should be "legible copies with name and address on each page." Reads submissions May 1-November 30 only. No electronic submissions. Time between acceptance and publication is up to 1 year. Sometimes comments on rejected poems. Publishes 1 theme issue/year. Upcoming themes available in magazine or on website. Guidelines available for SASE or on website. Responds in up to 5 months. Pays 2 contributor's copies and one-year subscription, plus $15/page. Acquires one-time rights.

Contest/Award Offerings Sponsors an annual poetry contest. Past judges include Kim Addonizio, Alan Shapiro, Dorianne Laux, Ellen Bryant Voigt, Philip Levine, and Naomi Shihab Nye. **Deadline:** May 31. Guidelines available for SASE or on website.

▣ ◻ ◎ THE ROAD NOT TAKEN: THE JOURNAL OF FORMAL POETRY

E-mail: jimatshs@yahoo.com. Website: www.journalofformalpoetry.com. **Contact:** Dr. Jim Prothero, co-editor.

Magazines Needs *The Road Not Taken: the Journal of Formal Poetry*, published quarterly online, prints formal poetry "in the tradition of Frost, Wordsworth, Tennyson, Hopkins, etc." Wants "formal poetry only. Nature and spiritual poetry always of interest but not required. Also essays/blogs on the topic of formal poetry would be of interest." Does not want free verse. Accepts poetry by children and teens; no age limitations, "it just has to be excellent."

How to Contact Submit 5 poems at a time. Considers previously published poems; no simultaneous submissions. (Considers poetry posted on a public website/blog/forum as published.) Accepts e-mail submissions (pasted into body of message); no fax or disk submissions. Cover letter is unnecessary. Reads submissions year round. Submit seasonal poems 3 months in advance. Time between acceptance and publication is 2 months. Poems are circulated to an editorial board. "There are 2 editors, Dr. Jim Prothero and Dr. Don Williams. Poems must meet both of our approval." Sometimes comments on rejected poems. Never publishes theme issues. Guidelines available by e-mail and on website. Responds in 1 month. Acquires one-time rights. Rights revert to poets upon publication.

Tips "Frost is really our patron here. We like skilled formal poetry and nature or spiritual topics are of interest."

▣ ◻ ◎ ROADRUNNER HAIKU JOURNAL

E-mail: scott@roadrunnerjournal.net; ztemttocs@gmail.com. Website: www.roadrunnerjournal.net. **Contact:** Scott Metz, editor.

Magazines Needs *Roadrunner Haiku Journal*, published quarterly online, is "an international Web journal that publishes the most innovative modern haiku written today." Wants haiku, senryu, and short haiku-like poetry. Does not want tanka, haiga, or haibun. Considers poetry by children and teens. Has published poetry by Fay Aoyagi, Richard Gilbert, Jim Kacian, Dhugal Lindsay, and Dietmar Tauchner. Receives about 5,000 poems/year, accepts about 5%. Distributed free online. Number of unique visitors: 25,000/year.

How to Contact Submit 5-15 poems at a time. Lines/poem: "less than 5 or so." No previously published poems or simultaneous submissions. Accepts e-mail submissions only (pasted into body of message, with "Roadrunner Submission" and poet's name in subject line); no disk submissions. Cover letter is unnecessary. "Please include a short bio." Reads submissions year round. Time between acceptance and publication is less than 3 months. Sometimes comments on rejected poems. Guidelines available on website. Responds in 2 weeks. Sometimes sends prepublication galleys. Acquires first rights. Rights revert to poets upon publication.

◨ ROANOKE REVIEW

English Dept., Roanoke College, 221 College Lane, Salem VA 24153. (540)375-2500. E-mail: review@roanoke.edu. Website: www.roanokereview.wordpress.com. **Contact:** Paul S. Hanstedt, poetry editor. *Roanoke Review*, published annually, uses poetry that is "grounded in strong images and unpretentious language." Has published poetry by Will Wells, Jeff Daniel Marion, and Charles Wright. *Roanoke Review* is 200 pages, digest-sized, professionally printed, with matte card cover with full-color art. Receives 600-1,000 submissions of poetry/year, accepts 20-40. Press run is 250-300 (150 subscribers, 50 libraries). Single copy: $8; subscription: $13/2 years. Sample: $5.

How to Contact Submit original typed mss, no photocopies. Guidelines available on website. Responds in 3-6 months. Pays 2 contributor's copies "plus cash when budget allows."

Tips "Be real. Know rhythm. Concentrate on strong images."

☑ ROSEBUD

N3310 Asje Rd., Cambridge WI 53523. E-mail: jrodclark@smallbytes.net (for questions only). Website: www.rsbd.net. Established 1993. **Contact:** John Smelcer, poetry editor. You can now e-mail up to 3 Poetry submissions to John Smelcer at: jesmelcer@aol.com (or send poems to P.O. Box 234, Binghamton, NY 13905).

Magazines Needs *Rosebud*, published 3 times/year in April, August, and December, has presented "many of the most prominent voices in the nation and has been listed as among the very best markets for writers." Wants poetry that avoids "excessive or well-worn abstractions, not to mention clichés. Present a unique and convincing world (you can do this in a few words!) by means of fresh and exact imagery, and by interesting use of syntax. Explore the deep reaches of metaphor. But don't forget to be playful and have fun with words." *Rosebud* is "elegantly" printed with full-color cover. Press run is 10,000. Single copy: $7.95 U.S., $11.95 Canada; subscription: $20 for 3 issues, $35 for 6 issues (Canadian and foreign subscribers add $10/year for surface mail).

How to Contact Put the letters RFI on the outside of the envelope, and circle it! FOR PROSE ONLY: Include a one-dollar handling fee or check for $1 made out to ROSEBUD. ($1 covers up to three stories). Include 1 to 3 stories and/or 1 to 5 poems; include a self-addressed stamped envelope for our reply (we can recycle manuscripts) and/or manuscript return. Send fiction, essays, and/or poetry with SASE and $1.00 handling fee (if the piece is prose) to Rod Clark at above address. You can now e-mail up to 3 Poetry submissions to John Smelcer at: jesmelcer@aol.com. Cover letter is required. Include brief bio and SASE with sufficient postage. Poems must be typed, single-spaced. Responds in 3 months. Pays 3 contributor's copies. Acquires one-time rights. Rights revert to poets upon publication.

Contest/Award Offerings Sponsors The William Stafford Poetry Award. Deadline: June 15, 2010. And the X.J. Kennedy Award for Creative Nonfiction. Deadline: January 15, 2011. Guidelines for both available on website.

Tips "Let the poems speak for themselves; don't tell the reader what to think or expect. Make your poems accessible to a wide audience—what interests you may not interest others. Avoid rhyming poetry and poems that try to be too deep (heavy allusions to mythological, biblical, and philosophical references). Great writing is often simply told, using the language of the everyday. A mentor once told me not to waste postage sending out my poetry. He was wrong! Keep trying, but learn from the effort."

☑ SALT HILL

English Dept., Syracuse University, Syracuse NY 13244-1170. (315)443-1984. E-mail: salthilljournal@gmail.com. Website: www.salthilljournal.net.

Magazines Needs *Salt Hill*, published semiannually, is "published by a group of writers affiliated with the Creative Writing Program at Syracuse University. Our eclectic taste ranges from traditional to experimental. All we ask is that it's good. Open to most themes. Accepting translations." Has published poetry by Denise Duhamel, Joe Wenderoth, Dorianne Laux, Campbell McGrath, Dean Young, Kim Addonizio, and James Tate. *Salt Hill* is 144-180 pages, digest-sized, includes ads. Receives about 3,000 poems/year, accepts about 2%. Press run is 1,000. Subscription: $15/year. Sample: $10 domestic.

How to Contact Submit 5 poems at a time between August 1-April 1. Submit 3-7 poems at a time. Considers simultaneous submissions; no previously published poems. Cover letter is preferred. Include a brief bio. Time between acceptance and publication is up to 8 months. Enclose SASE for reply. "We recycle mss. and encourage you to use a "forever" stamp on your SASE. Responds in up to 9 months. Pays 2 contributor's copies. Acquires one-time rights.

☑ THE SAME

P.O. Box 494, Mount Union PA 17066. E-mail: riverfrontreadings@yahoo.com. Website: http://tsmag.itgo.com. **Contact:** Philip Miller, editor.

Magazines Needs *The Same*, published semiannually, prints nonfiction (essays, reviews, literary criticism), poetry, and short fiction. Wants "eclectic poetry (formal to free verse,'mainstream' to experimental, all subject matter.)" Considers poetry by children and teens. Has published poetry by Phyllis Becker, Graham Duncan, Patricia Lawson, Holly Posner, Stephen Stepanchev, and Robert Weaver. *The Same* is 50-100 pages, desktop-published, perfect-bound, with cardstock cover. Receives about 2,000 poems/year, accepts about 5%. Press run is 250 (125 subscribers/shelf sales). Single copy: $5; subscription: $10 for 2 issues, $18 for 4 issues. Make checks payable to Philip Miller.

How to Contact Submit 1-7 poems at a time. Lines/poem: 120 maximum. No previously published poems or simultaneous submissions "without query." Prefers e-mail submissions (pasted into body of message). Cover letter is optional. "Include SASE if you want a snail mail response. If you don't want your manuscript returned, you may omit the SASE if we can respond by e-mail." Please query before submitting fiction and nonfiction. Reads submissions year round. Time between acceptance and publication can be up to 11 months. Sometimes comments on rejected poems. Guidelines available for SASE, by e-mail, or on website. Responds within 2 months. Pays one contributor's copy. Acquires first North American serial rights and online rights for up to 9 months; returns rights to poet.

Additional Information Publishes 1-3 chapbooks/year. **Solicited mss only.** Chapbooks are 24-32 pages, desktop-published, saddle-stapled, with cardstock covers. Pays 25 author's copies (out of a press run of 100).

Tips "Our motto is 'Everyone else is different, but we're the same!' We are eclectic and non-doctrinaire."

☐ ◎ SAMSARA: THE MAGAZINE OF SUFFERING

P.O. Box 467, Ashburn VA 20147. E-mail: rdfgoalie@gmail.com. Website: www.samsaramagazine.net. **Contact:** R. David Fulcher, Editor.

Magazines Needs *Samsara, The Magazine of Suffering*, published biannually, prints poetry and fiction dealing with suffering and healing. "Both metered verse and free verse poetry are welcome if dealing with the theme of suffering/healing." Has published poetry by Michael Foster, Nicole Provencher, and Jeff Parsley. *Samsara* is 80 pages, magazine-sized, desktop-published, with color cardstock cover. Receives about 200 poems/year, accepts about 15%. Press run is 300 (200 subscribers). Single copy: $5.50; subscription: $10. Sample: $4.50. Make checks payable to R. David Fulcher.

How to Contact Submit up to 5 poems at a time. Lines/poem: 3 minimum, 100 maximum. Considers simultaneous submissions "if noted as such"; no previously published poems. Cover letter is preferred. No e-mail submissionis; accepts submissions by postal mail only. Time between acceptance and publication is 3 months. Seldom comments on rejected poems. Guidelines available for SASE or on website. Responds in 2 months. Pays 1 contributor's copy. Acquires first North American serial rights. Reviews books/chapbooks of poetry in 500 words, single-book format. Send material for review consideration.

☐ SANSKRIT LITERARY ARTS MAGAZINE

UNC Charlotte, 9201 University City Blvd., Student Union Rm 045, Charlotte NC 28223. (704)687-2326. E-mail: sanskrit@uncc.edu. Website: http://mymedia.uncc.edu/node/41; www.facebook.com/group.php?gid=2201452053. **Contact:** Editor. *Sanskrit*, published annually in April, seeks "to encourage and promote beginning and established artists and writers. No restrictions as to form or genre, but we do look for maturity and sincerity in submissions." Does not want anything "lewd or sentimental." Has published poetry by Kimberleigh Luke-Stallings. *Sanskrit* is 64 pages. Press run is 3,500 (about 100 subscribers, 2 libraries). Sample: $10.

How to Contact Submit up to 15 poems at a time. Considers simultaneous submissions. Accepts e-mail submissions. Cover letter is required. "Include 30- to 70-word bio. Please do not list previous publications as a bio." Reads submissions by the first Friday in November (deadline). Never comments on rejected poems. Guidelines available for SASE or by e-mail. Responds in 2 months. Pays one contributor's copy.

☑ THE SARANAC REVIEW

CVH, Plattsburgh State University, 101 Broad St., Plattsburgh NY 12901. (518)564-2241. E-mail: saranacreview@plattsburgh.edu. CVH, Plattsburgh State University, 101 Broad St., Plattsburgh NY 12901. Established 2004. **Contact:** Poetry Editor.

Magazines Needs *The Saranac Review*, published annually in the fall, wants poetry from both U.S. and Canadian writers. Does not want "amateurish or 'greeting card' poetry." Has published poetry by Donald Revell, Ricardo Pau-Llosa, Jim Daniels, Rustin Larson, Rane Arroyo, Ross Leckie, Diane Swan, T. Alan Broughton, Brian Bartlett, Barry Dempster. *The Saranac Review* is magazine-sized, with color photo or painting on cover, includes ads. Press run is 1,000. Single copy: $12/$14CA; subscription: $15/year, $20 for 2 years, $28 for 3 years, $45 for 5 years ($18/year for institutions—multi-year subscriptions receive 15% discount); all Canadian subscriptions add $3/year. Make checks payable to Subscriptions/ *The Saranac Review*.

How to Contact Submit no more than 3 poems at a time. Considers simultaneous submissions if notified; no previously published poems. No e-mail or disk submissions. Cover letter is appreciated. Include phone and e-mail contact information (if possible) in cover letter. Manuscripts will not be returned without SASE. Reads submissions September 1-February 15 (firm). Poems are circulated to an editorial board. Sometimes comments on rejected poems. Guidelines available on website. Responds in 3-6 months. Pays 2 contributor's copies. Acquires first rights.

☐ ◎ SCIENCE EDITOR

12100 Sunset Hills Road, Suite 130, Reston VA 20190. (703)437-4377. Fax: (703)435-4390. E-mail: mknatterud@surgery.arizona.edu. Website: www.CouncilScienceEditors.org. **Contact:** Mary E. Knatturud, PhD, editor. Member: Council of Science Editors (CSE).

Magazines Needs *Science Editor*, published bimonthly, is "a forum for the exchange of information and ideas among professionals concerned with publishing in the sciences." Wants "up to 90 typeset lines of poetry on the intersection of science (including but not limited to biomedicine) and communication. Geared toward adult scholars, writers, and editors in communication and the sciences." Has published poetry by Mary Knatterud, Judy Meiksin, David Goldblatt, Mary Donnelly, Nancy Overcott, Jyothirmai Gubili, Neil H. Segal, Michele Arduengo. *Science Editor* is approx. 32 pages, magazine-sized, 4-color process, saddle-stitched, with an 80 pd Dull Cover; includes ads. Press run is 1,500. Single copy: $12 US; $15 Int'l. "Journal is a membership benefit; dues are $164 per year; nonmember subscriptions: $55 US; $68 Int'l/year." Make checks payable to Council of Science Editors (CSE).

How to Contact Submit up to 3 poems at a time, maximum 90 lines. Does not consider previously published poems or simultaneous submissions. Accepts e-mail submissions (pasted into the body of message), no fax or disk. "Submit both cover letter and poetry by e-mail only in the body of the same e-mail message, with no attachments." Submit seasonal poems 9 months in advance. Time between acceptance and publication is 3-6 months. Sometimes comments on rejected poems. Guidelines available by e-mail. Responds in 3-6 weeks. Pays 3 contributor's copies. Acquires one-time rights, electronic rights. "Science Editor is posted online. Issues at least one year old are openly displayed accessible. Issues less than one year old can be accessed only by Council of Science Editors members." Rights revert to poet upon publication.

Tips "The cover letter (i.e., the e-mail message preceding the poetry, which must also be in the body of that same e-mail) should include the poet's phone number, current title and workplace, and complete US mail address, as well as a short paragraph about his or her educational and professional background, including whether he or she has had any poetry or other literary work published before; note that this material may be edited for inclusion in the column, if the poetry is accepted."

▣ $ ☐ ◎ SCIFAIKUEST

P.O. Box 782, Cedar Rapids IA 52406-0782. E-mail: gatrix65@yahoo.com. Website: www. samsdotpublishing.com. **Contact:** Tyree Campbell, Managing Editor. (Specialized: scifaiku, horror-ku, tanka, senryu, haibun, and other minimalist poetry forms). Member: The Speculative Literature Foundation.

• Scifaikuest was voted #1 poetry magazine in the 2004 Preditors & Editors poll.

Magazines Needs *Scifaikuest*, published quarterly both online and in print, features "science fiction/fantasy/horror minimalist poetry, especially scifaiku, and related forms. We also publish articles about various poetic forms and reviews of poetry collections. The online and print versions of *Scifaikuest* are different." Wants "artwork, scifaiku and speculative minimalist forms such as tanka, haibun, ghazals, senryu. No 'traditional' poetry." Has published poetry by Tom Brinck, Oino Sakai, Deborah P. Kolodji, Aurelio Rico Lopez III, Joanne Morcom, and John Dunphy. *Scifaikuest* (print edition) is 32 pages, digest-sized, offset-printed, perfect-bound, with color cardstock cover, includes ads. Receives about 500 poems/year, accepts about 160 (32%). Press run is 100/issue; 5 distributed free to reviewers. Single copy: $7; subscription: $20/year, $37 for 2 years. Make checks payable to Tyree Campbell/Sam's Dot Publishing.

How to Contact Submit 5 poems at a time. Lines/poem: varies, depending on poem type. No previously published poems or simultaneous submissions. Accepts e-mail submissions (pasted into body of message). No disk submissions; artwork as e-mail attachment or inserted body of e-mail. "Submission should include snail mail address and a short (1-2 lines) bio." Reads submissions year round. Submit seasonal poems 6 months in advance. Time between acceptance and publication is 1-2 months. "Editor Teri Santitoro makes all decisions regarding acceptances." Often comments on rejected poems. Guidelines available on website. Responds in 6-8 weeks. Pays $1/poem, $4/review or article, and 1 contributor's copy. Acquires first North American serial rights.

Tips "It's up to the writer to take the first step and submit work. Some of our best poems have come from poets who weren't sure if they were good enough. A basic knowledge of writing traditional haiku is helpful."

THE SEATTLE REVIEW

(206)543-2302. E-mail: seaview@u.washington.edu. Includes general fiction, poetry, craft essays on writing, and one interview per issue with a Northwest writer.

How to Contact Submit 3-5 poems via mail, attention: Poetry Editor. Include SASE. Submissions must be typed on white, 8 1/2x11 paper. The author's name and address should appear in the upper right hand corner. No simultaneous submissions. Reading period October 1-May 31.

☑ SENECA REVIEW

Hobart and William Smith Colleges, Geneva NY 14456-3397. (315)781-3392. Fax: (315)781-3348. E-mail: senecareview@hws.edu. Website: www.hws.edu/senecareview/. **Contact:** David Weiss, editor.

• Poetry published in *Seneca Review* has been included in *The Best American Poetry* and The Pushcart Prize anthologies.

Magazines Needs *Seneca Review*, published semiannually, seeks "serious poetry of any form, including translations. Also essays on contemporary poetry and lyrical nonfiction. You'll find plenty of free verse here—some accessible and some leaning toward experimental—with emphasis on voice, image, and diction. All in all, poems and translations complement each other and create a distinct editorial mood in each issue." Does not want "light verse." Has published poetry by Seamus Heaney, Rita Dove, Denise Levertov, Stephen Dunn, and Hayden Carruth. *Seneca Review* is 100 pages, digest-sized, professionally printed on quality stock, perfect-bound, with matte card cover. Receives 3,000-4,000 poems/year, accepts about 100. Press run is 1,000. Subscription: $15/year, $28 for 2 years. Sample: $8 plus $1 shipping.

How to Contact Submit 3-5 poems at a time. No previously published poems or simultaneous submissions. No e-mail submissions; postal submissions only. SASE required. Reads submissions September 1-May 1 only. "Submit only once during the annual reading period." Guidelines available on website. Responds in up to 3 months. Pays 2 contributor's copies and a 2-year subscription.

$ ⊘ THE SEWANEE REVIEW

University of the South, 735 University Ave., Sewanee TN 37383-1000. (931)598-1246. E-mail: lcouch@sewanee.edu. Website: www.sewanee.edu/sewanee_review. George Core, Editor. *Sewanee Review*, published quarterly, is open "to all styles and forms: formal sequences, metered verse, structured free verse, sonnets, and lyric and narrative forms—all accessible and intelligent. Fiction, criticism, and poetry are invariably of the highest establishment standards. Many of our major poets appear here from time to time." Has published poetry by Wendell Berry, George Bilgere, Catherine Savage Brosman, David Mason, Leslie Norris, and Christian Wiman. *The Sewanee Review* is nearly 200 pages, conservatively bound in matte paper, always of the same typography. Press run is 2,600. Subscription: $25/year for individuals, $45/year for institutions. Sample: $8.50 U.S., $9.50 foreign.

How to Contact Submit up to 6 poems at a time. Lines/poem: 40 maximum. No simultaneous submissions. No e-mail submissions; postal submissions only. "Unsolicited works should not be submitted between June 1 and August 31. A response to any submission received during that period will be greatly delayed." Guidelines available in magazine or on website. Responds in 2 months. Pays per line, plus 2 contributor's copies (and reduced price for additional copies). Solicits brief, standard, and essay-reviews.Winners of the Allen Tate Prize and the Aiken Taylor Award for Modern American Poetry are determined by the editorial board and a prize committee; poets cannot apply for these awards.

Tips "Please keep in mind that for each poem published in *The Sewanee Review*, approximately 250 poems are considered."

☐ ◎ SHEMOM

2486 Montgomery Ave., Cardiff CA 92007. E-mail: pdfrench@cox.net. **Contact:** Peggy French, Editor.

Magazines Needs *Shemom*, published 3 times/year, is a zine that "celebrates parenting and the joys and struggles that present themselves on that journey." Includes poetry, essays, book and CD reviews, recipes, art, and children's poetry. Open to any style, but prefers free verse. "We showcase writers of all ages that reflect on life's varied experiences. We often feature haiku." *Shemom* is 10-20 pages. Receives about 200 poems/year, accepts 50%. Press run is 60 (30 subscribers). Single copy: $4; subscription: $12/3 issues. Make checks payable to Peggy French.

How to Contact Submit 3 poems at a time. Considers previously published poems and simultaneous submissions. Accepts e-mail submissions (as attachment or pasted into body of message). "Prefer e-mail submission, but not required; if material is to be returned, please include a SASE." Time between acceptance and publication is 3 months. Guidelines available for SASE or by e-mail. Responds in 2 months. Pays 1 contributor's copy. Acquires one-time rights.

$ ☑ SHENANDOAH

Mattingly House, 2 Lee Ave., Washington and Lee University, Lexington VA 24450-0303. (540)458-8765. Fax: (540)458-8461. E-mail: lleech@wlu.edu. Website: http://shenandoah. wlu.edu. R. T. Smith, Editor - shenandoah@wlu.edu. **Contact:** Lynn L. Leech, Managing Editor. *2010 Reading Moratorium: Unsolicited manuscripts will not be read until October of 2010. All manuscripts received during this period will be recycled unread.* We encourage you to subscribe to Shenandoah and acquaint yourself with the material we publish before submitting your work.

Contest/Award Offerings Sponsors the annual James Boatwright III Prize for Poetry, a $1,000 prize awarded to the author of the best poem published in *Shenandoah* during a volume year. The Shenandoah/Glasgow Prize for Emerging Writers $2,000 awarded for poetry on alternate years.

☑ ◎ THE SHEPHERD

1530 Seventh St., Rock Island IL 61201. (309)788-3980. **Contact:** Betty Mowery, Poetry Editor. *The Shepherd*, published quarterly, features inspirational poetry from all ages. Wants "something with a message but not preachy." Subscription: $12. Sample: $4. Make all checks payable to *The Oak*.

How to Contact Submit up to 5 poems at a time. Lines/poem: 35 maximum. Considers previously published poems. Include SASE with all submissions. Responds in one week. "*The Shepherd* does not pay in dollars or copies, but you need not purchase to be published." Acquires first or second rights. All rights revert to poet upon publication.

Contest/Award Offerings Sponsors poetry contest. Guidelines available for SASE.

☑ SIERRA NEVADA REVIEW

999 Tahoe Blvd., Incline Village NV 89451. E-mail: sncreview@sierranevada.edu. Website: www.sierranevada.edu/800. Established 1990. **Contact:** June Sylvester Saraceno, advisory editor.

Magazines Needs *Sierra Nevada Review*, published annually in May, features poetry and short fiction by new writers. Wants "image-oriented poems with a distinct, genuine voice. Although we don't tend to publish 'light verse,' we do appreciate, and often publish, poems that make us laugh. No limit on length, style, etc." Does not want "sentimental, clichéd, or obscure poetry." Has published poetry by Virgil Suaárez, Simon Perchik, Carol Frith, and Marisella Veiga. *Sierra Nevada Review* is about 75 pages, with art on cover. Receives about 1,000 poems/year, accepts about 50. Press run is 500. Subscription: $10/year. Sample: $5.

How to Contact Submit up to 5 poems at a time. Considers simultaneous submissions; no previously published poems. Accepts e-mail submissions (pasted into body of message, no attachments). Reads submissions September 1-March 1 only. Sometimes comments on rejected poems. Guidelines available for SASE, by e-mail, or on website. Responds in about 3 months. Pays 2 contributor's copies.

Tips "We're looking for poetry that shows subtlety and skill." Guest editor for 2010/2011 Brian Turner.

☑ SKIDROW PENTHOUSE

68 East Third St., Suite 16, New York NY 10003. E-mail: info@skidrowpenthouse.com. Website: http://skidrowpenthouse.com. Stephanie Dickinson, Co-Editor. **Contact:** Rob Cook, Editor. *Skidrow Penthouse* aims to "give emerging and idiosyncratic writers a new forum in which to publish their work. We are looking for deeply felt authentic voices, whether surreal, confessional, New York School, formal, or free verse. Work should be well crafted: attention to line-break and diction." Wants "poets who sound like themselves, not workshop professionals." Does not want "gutless posturing, technical precision with no subject matter, explicit sex and violence without craft, or abstract intellectualizing. We are not impressed by previous awards and publications." Has published poetry by Lisa Jarnot, Christopher Edgar, Aase Berg, Karl Tierney, James Grinwis, and Robyn Art. *Skidrow Penthouse* is 280 pages, 6 × 9, professionally printed, perfect-bound, with 4-color cover. Receives about 500 poems/year, accepts 3%. Press run is 300 (50 subscribers); 10% distributed free to journals for review consideration. Single copy: $12.50; subscription: $20. Make checks payable to Skidrow Penthouse.

How to Contact Submit 3-5 poems at a time. Considers previously published poems and simultaneous submissions. "Include a legal-sized SASE; name and address on every page of your submission. No handwritten submissions will be considered." Time between acceptance and publication is one year. Seldom comments on rejected poems. Responds in 2 months. Pays one contributor's copy. Acquires one-time rights. Reviews books and chapbooks of poetry and other magazines in 1,500 words, single-book format. Send materials for review consideration. "We're trying to showcase a poet in each issue by publishing up to 60-page collections within the magazine." Send query with SASE.

Tips "We get way too many anecdotal fragments posing as poetry; too much of what we receive feels like this morning's inspiration mailed this afternoon. The majority of those who submit do not seem to have put in the sweat a good poem demands. Also, the ratio of submissions to sample copy purchases is 50:1. Just because our name is *Skidrow Penthouse* does not mean we are a repository for genre work or 'eat, shit, shower, and shave' poetry."

☐ SKIPPING STONES: A MULTICULTURAL MAGAZINE

E-mail: editor@skippingstones.org. Website: www.skippingstones.org. **Contact:** Arun Toké, Editor.

- *Skipping Stones,* now in its 22st year, has been the recipient of EdPress, NAME, WRITER, and Parent's Guide Awards, among others.

Magazines Needs *Skipping Stones,* published bimonthly during the school year (5 issues), "encourages cooperation, creativity, and celebration of cultural and ecological richness." Wants "poetry by young writers under age 18, on multicultural and social issues, family, freedom—uplifting. No adult poetry, please." *Skipping Stones* is magazine-sized, saddle-stapled, printed on recycled paper. Receives about 500-1,000 poems/year, accepts 10%. Press run is 2,500. Subscription: $25. Sample: $6.

How to Contact Submit up to 5 poems at a time. Lines/poem: 30 maximum. Considers simultaneous submissions; no previously published poems. Accepts e-mail submissions. Cover letter is preferred. "Include your cultural background, experiences, and the inspiration behind your creation." Time between acceptance and publication is 6-9 months. "A piece is chosen for publication when most of the editorial staff feel good about it." Seldom comments on rejected poems. Publishes multi-theme issues. Guidelines available for SASE. Responds in up to 4 months. Pays 1 contributor's copy, offers 40% discount for morecopies and subscription, if desired. Acquires first serial rights and non-exclusive reprint rights.

Contest/Award Offerings Sponsors Annual Youth Honor Awards for 7- to 17-year-olds. Theme is "Multicultural, Social, International, and Nature Awareness." Guidelines available for SASE or on website. **Entry fee:** $3 (entitles entrant to a free issue featuring the 10 winners). **Deadline:** June 25.

☑ SLANT: A JOURNAL OF POETRY

Box 5063, University of Central Arkansas, 201 Donaghey Ave., Conway AR 72035-5000. (501)450-5107. Website: www.uca.edu/english/poetryjournal/. **Contact:** James Fowler, Editor.

Magazines Needs *Slant: A Journal of Poetry*, published annually in May, aims "to publish a journal of fine poetry from all regions of the United States and beyond." Wants "traditional and 'modern' poetry, even experimental; moderate length, any subject on approval of Board of Readers." Doesn't want "haiku, translations." Has published poetry by Richard Broderick, Susana H. Case, David Jordan, Timothy Martin, Barbara F. Lefcowitz, and Donna Pucciani. *Slant* is 120 pages, professionally printed on quality stock, flat-spined, with matte card cover. Receives about 1,200 poems/year, accepts 70-75. Press run is 175 (70-100 subscribers). Sample: $10.

How to Contact Submit up to 5 poems at a time. Lines/poem: poems should be of moderate length. No previously published poems or simultaneous submissions. Submissions should be typed; include SASE. "Put name, address (including e-mail if available), and phone number at the top of each page." Accepts submissions September 1-November 15. Comments on rejected poems "on occasion." Guidelines available in magazine, for SASE, or on website. Responds in 3-4 months from November 15 deadline. Pays 1 contributor's copy. Poet retains rights.

Tips "We tend to publish those poems whose execution, line by line, does full justice to their conception. Often the decision to accept comes down to the matter of craft, language."

☐ SLATE & STYLE

2704 Beach Dr., Merrick NY 11566. E-mail: LoriStay@aol.com; qobells@roadrunner.com. Website: www.nfb-writers-division.org. **Contact:** Loraine Stayer, poetry editor, and Shelley Alongi, editor.

Magazines Needs *Slate & Style*, published quarterly, is the magazine of the Writers' Division of the National Federation of the Blind. Published for blind writers, *Slate & Style* is available in large print, in Braille, and by e-mail, and includes resources and articles of interest to blind writers. "We prefer contributors be blind writers, or at least writers by profession or inclination. New writers welcome. No obscenities. Will consider all forms of poetry including haiku. Interested in new talent." Considers poetry by children and teens, "but please specify age." Has published poetry by Harriet Barrett, W. Burns Taylor, Chelsea Cook, Jennifer Shields, and David Thomas. *Slate & Style* (print format) is 28-32 pages, magazine-sized, stapled. Press run is 200 (160 subscribers, 4-5 libraries). Subscription/membership: $10/year (regardless of format). Sample: $3. Please specify format when subscribing, and make all checks out to the NFB writers' division.

How to Contact Submit 3 poems at a time once or twice/year. Lines/poem: 5-36. No previously published poems or simultaneous submissions. Accepts submissions by e-mail (pasted into body of message). "On occasion we receive poems in Braille. I prefer print, since Braille slows me down. Typed is best." Cover letter is preferred. Reads submissions according to the following deadlines: February 16, May 15, August 15, November 15; "do not submit manuscripts in July." Comments on rejected poems "if requested." Guidelines available in magazine, for SASE, by e-mail, or on website. Responds in 2 weeks "if I like it." Pays 1 contributor's copy. Reviews books of poetry. Send materials for review consideration.

Contest/Award Offerings Sponsors an annual poetry contest, awarding 1st Prize: $100; 2nd Prize: $50; 3rd Prize: $25. Honorable mentions may also be awarded, and winning poems will be published in magazine. **Entry fee:** $5 for up to 3 poems. Make check or money order payable to NFB Writers' Division. "Include cover letter with title and your identifying information." Opens January 1st; **Deadline: June 1.** We are now sponsoring a poetry contest for blind students, K-12. Guidelines available for SASE, by e-mail, or on website.

Tips "Before you send us a poem, please proofread twice. Thank you."

SLIPSTREAM

Dept. W-1, P.O. Box 2071, Niagara Falls NY 14301-0071. (716)282-2616 (after 5 PM EST). E-mail: editors@slipstreampress.org. Website: www.slipstreampress.org. **Contact:** Dan Sicoli, Robert Borgatti, and Livio Farallo, poetry editors.

Magazines Needs *Slipstream*, published annually in spring, is "about 95% poetry, with some artwork. We like new work with contemporary urban flavor. Writing must have a cutting edge to get our attention. Any length, subject, style. Best to see a sample to get a feel. Like city stuff as opposed to country." Wants "poetry that springs from the gut, screams from dark alleys, inspired by experience." Does not want "pastoral, religious, traditional, rhyming" poetry. Has published poetry by Terry Godbey, Gerald Locklin, David Chorlton, Patrick Carrington, Jim Daniels, Beth Royer, and Mofolasayo Ogundiran. *Slipstream* is 80-100 pages, 7x812, professionally printed, perfect-bound. Receives more than 2,500 poetry submissions/year, accepts less than 10%. Press run is 500 (400 subscribers, 10 libraries). Subscription: $20 for 2 issues and 2 chapbooks. Sample: $10.

How to Contact No e-mail submissions. Sometimes comments on rejected poems. Publishes theme issues. Guidelines available for SASE or on website. Responds in up to 2 months "if SASE included." Pays 1-2 contributor's copies.

Contest/Award Offerings *Slipstream* Poetry Chapbook Contest.

Tips "Do not waste time submitting your work 'blindly.' Sample issues from the small press first to determine which ones would be most receptive to your work."

SMARTISH PACE

P.O. Box 22161, Baltimore MD 21203. E-mail: sreichert@smartishpace.com. Website: www.smartishpace.com. **Contact:** Stephen Reichert, editor.

Magazines Needs *Smartish Pace*, published in April, contains poetry and translations. "*Smartish Pace* is an independent poetry journal and is not affiliated with any institution." No restrictions on style or content of poetry. Has published poetry in the past year by Gerald Stern, Eamon Grennan, Katie Ford, Sherman Alexie, Carol Muske-Dukes, and Aram Saroyan. *Smartish Pace* is about 140 pages, digest-sized, professionally printed, perfect-bound, with full-color cover featuring contemporary artwork. Receives about 5,000 poems/year, accepts 1%. Press run is 1,100. Subscription: $20. Sample: $10.

How to Contact Submit no more than 6 poems at a time via online submission form. Does not accept submissions by mail. Considers simultaneous submissions; no previously published poems. Responds in 1-6 months. Pays 1 contributor's copy. Acquires first rights. Encourages unsolicited reviews, essays, and interviews. Send materials for review consideration. All books received will also be listed in the Books Received section of each issue and on the website along with ordering information and a link to the publisher's website.

Contest/Award Offerings *Smartish Pace* hosts the annual Erskine J. Poetry Prize and the Beullah Rose Poetry Prize (for women).

Also Offers Also available on Poets Q&A, where readers can ask questions of poets and read their responses. Recent participants have included Robert Pinsky, Jorie Graham, Stephen Dunn, Carl Dennis, Eavan Boland, Campbell McGrath, and Robert Hass. "The website has constantly updated poetry news and ever expanding audio and video (poetry readings) section."

Tips "Visit our website. Read a few issues."

🌐 ☑ SMOKE

First Floor, Liver House, 96 Bold St., Liverpool L1 4HY, England. (44)(151)709-3688. E-mail: windows@windowsproject.demon.co.uk. Website: www.windowsproject.demon.co.uk. **Contact:** Dave Ward, Editor. *Smoke*, published semiannually, contains poetry and graphics. Wants "short, contemporary poetry, expressing new ideas through new forms." Has published poetry by Carol Ann Duffy, Roger McGough, Jackie Kay, and Henry Normal. *Smoke* is 24 pages, A5, offset-litho-printed, stapled, with paper cover. Receives about 3,000 poems/year, accepts about 40. Press run is 750 (350 subscribers, 18 libraries, 100 shelf sales); 100 distributed free to contributors/other magazines. Subscription: $10. Sample: $2. Make checks payable to Windows Project (cash preferred—exchange rate on checks not viable).

$ ☑ ◎ SNOWY EGRET

Oldest Independent U.S. Journal of Nature Writing, P.O. Box 29, Terre Haute IN 47808. **Contact:** Poetry Editor. *Snowy Egret*, published in spring and autumn, specializes in work that is "nature-oriented: poetry that celebrates the abundance and beauty of nature or explores the interconnections between nature and the human psyche." Has published poetry by Conrad Hilberry, Lyn Lifshin, Gayle Eleanor, James Armstrong, and Patricia Hooper. *Snowy Egret* is 60 pages, magazine-sized, offset-printed, saddle-stapled. Receives about 500 poems/year, accepts about 30. Press run is 400. Sample: $8; subscription: $15/year, $25 for 2 years.

How to Contact Guidelines available on website. Responds in 1 month. Always sends prepublication galleys. Pays $4/poem or $4/page plus 2 contributor's copies. Acquires first North American and one-time reprint rights.

Tips "First-hand, detailed observation gives poetry authenticity and immediacy."

$ ☑ SOFA INK QUARTERLY

Gray Sunshine, Sofa Ink Quarterly, PO Box 625, American Fork UT 84003. E-mail: acquisitions@sofaink.com. Website: www.sofaink.com. **Contact:** David Cowseret, Editor. *Sofa Ink Quarterly* is a literary magazine "distributed primarily to waiting rooms and lobbies of medical facilities. It has been used in high schools and college classes for supporting creative writing efforts, and a variety of writing groups and conferences. All of our stories and poetry have positive endings. We like to publish a variety of genres with a focus on good storytelling and word-mastery." Wants avant-garde, free verse, haiku, light verse, and traditional. Does not want "swearing, profaning deity, gore, excessive violence, or gratuitous sex." Accepts 9-15 poems/year. Sample: $6.

Poetry Submit 5 poems maximum at a time. Considers simultaneous submissions. Accepts e-mail submissions (as attachment in Word). Submit seasonal poems 4 months in advance. Time between acceptance and publication is about 3 months. Guidelines available for SASE or on website. Responds in 1-3 months. Pays $5 and 3 contributor's copies. Acquires first North American serial rights.

How to Contact "We plan on maintaining an online authors' archive where the public can see brief biographies and pictures of authors and summaries of stories they have published with us, as well as hyperlinks to the authors' personal web pages."

Tips "Follow the content guidelines."

☑ SONG OF THE SAN JOAQUIN

P.O. Box 1161, Modesto CA 95353-1161. E-mail: cleor36@yahoo.com. Website: www. ChaparralPoets.org/SSJ.html. **Contact:** The Editor.

Magazines Needs *Song of the San Joaquin*, published quarterly, features "subjects about or pertinent to the San Joaquin Valley of Central California. This is defined geographically as the region from Fresno to Stockton, and from the foothills on the west to those on the east." Wants all forms and styles of poetry. "Keep subject in mind." Does not want "pornographic, demeaning, vague, or trite approaches." Considers poetry by children and teens. Has published poetry by Joyce Odam, Wilma Elizabeth McDaniel, Margarita Engle, Marnelle White, Frederick Zydek, and Nancy Haskett. *Song of the San Joaquin* is 60 pages, digest-sized, direct-copied, saddle-stapled, with cardstock cover with glossy color photo. Press run is 200 (25 copies to libraries); 40 distributed free to contributors.

How to Contact Submit up to 3 poems at a time. Lines/poem: open ("however, poems under 40 lines have the best chance"). Considers previously published poems; no simultaneous submissions. E-mail submissions are preferred; no disk submissions. Cover letter is preferred. "SASE required. All submissions must be typed on 1 side of the page only. Proofread submissions carefully. Name, address, phone number, and e-mail address should appear on all pages. Cover letter should include any awards, honors, and previous publications for each poem, and a biographical sketch of 75 words or less." Reads submissions "periodically throughout the year." Submit seasonal poems at least 3 months in advance. Time between acceptance and publication is 3-6 months. "Poems are circulated to an editorial board of 7 who then decide on the final selections." Seldom comments on rejected poems. Occasionally publishes theme issues. Upcoming themes available for SASE, by e-mail, or on website. Guidelines available in magazine, for SASE, by e-mail, or on website. Responds in up to 3 months. Pays 1 contributor's copy. Acquires one-time rights.

Additional Information "Poets of the San Joaquin, which sponsors this publication, is a chapter of California Federation of Chaparral Poets, Inc., and publishes an annual anthology of members' works. Information available for SASE or by e-mail."

Contest/Award Offerings Poets of the San Joaquin holds an annual local young poets' contest as well as regular poetry contests. Guidelines available for SASE or by e-mail.

Tips "Know the area about which you write. Poems do not need to be agricultural or nature-oriented but should reflect the lifestyles of the California Central Valley."

☑ SOUL FOUNTAIN

90-21 Springfield Blvd., Queens Village NY 11428. (718)479-2594. Fax: (718)479-2594. E-mail: davault@aol.com. Website: www.TheVault.org. **Contact:** Tone Bellizzi, Editor.

Magazines Needs *Soul Fountain*, published 3 times/year, is produced by The Vault, a not-for-profit arts project of the Hope for the Children Foundation, "committed to empowering young and emerging artists of all disciplines at all levels to develop and share their talents through performance, collaboration, and networking." Prints poetry, art, photography, short fiction, and essays. Open to all. "We publish quality submitted work, and specialize in emerging voices. We favor visionary, challenging, and consciousness-expanding material." Does not want "poems about pets, nature, romantic love, or the occult. Sex and violence themes not welcome." Welcomes poetry by teens. *Soul Fountain* is 28 pages, magazine-sized, offset-printed, saddle-stapled. Subscription: $24. Sample: $7. Make checks payable to Hope for the Children Foundation.

How to Contact Submit 2-3 poems at a time. Lines/poem: 1 page maximum. Considers previously published poems and simultaneous submissions. Accepts e-mail submissions (pasted into body of message). Poems should be camera-ready. "When e-mailing a submission, it is necessary to include your mailing address. Cover letter not needed. SASE with postal mail submissions is not necessary, but $2 in postage is appreciated." Time between acceptance and publication is up to 1 year. Guidelines available for SASE or on website. Pays 1 contributor's copy.

☑ THE SOUTH CAROLINA REVIEW

Center for Electronic & Digital Publishing, Strode Tower Room 611, Box 340522, Clemson SC 29634-0522. Website: http://www.clemson.edu/cedp/cudp/scr/about.htm. **Contact:** The Editor. *The South Carolina Review*, published semiannually, is a literary magazine "recognized by the *New York Quarterly* as one of the top 20 of this type." Wants "any kind of poetry as long as it's good. Interested in seeing more traditional forms." Does not want "stale metaphors, uncertain rhythms, or lack of line integrity." Has published poetry by Stephen Cushman, Alberto Ríos, and Virgil Suaárez. *The South Carolina Review* is 200 pages, digest-sized, professionally printed, flat-spined. Receives about 1,000 submissions of poetry/year, accepts about 100. Press run is 500 (350 subscribers, 250 libraries). Sample: $16.

How to Contact Submit 3-10 poems at a time. No previously published poems or simultaneous submissions. Cover letter is preferred. "Editor prefers a chatty, personal cover letter plus a list of publishing credits. Manuscript format should be according to new MLA Stylesheet." Submissions should be sent "in an 8x10 manila envelope so poems aren't creased." Do not submit during June, July, August, or December. Occasionally publishes theme issues. Responds in 2 months. Pays in 2 contributor's copies. Staff reviews books of poetry.

☑ ◎ SOUTH DAKOTA REVIEW

Dept. of English, University of South Dakota, 414 E. Clark St., Vermillion SD 57069. (605)677-5184 or 677-5966. Fax: (605)677-6409. E-mail: bbedard@usd.edu. Website: www.

usd.edu/sdreview/. **Contact:** Brian Bedard, editor. (Specialized: American West subjects & work by Western authors)

Magazines Needs *South Dakota Review*, published quarterly, prints "poetry, fiction, criticism, and scholarly and personal essays. When material warrants, emphasis is on the American West; writers from the West; Western places or subjects. There are frequent issues with no geographical emphasis; periodic special issues on one theme, one place, or one writer." Wants "originality, sophistication, significance, craft—i.e., professional work." Has published poetry by Allan Safarik, Joanna Gardner, Nathaniel Hansen, and Jeanine Stevens. Press run is 500-600 (450 subscribers, half libraries). Single copy: $10; subscription: $30/year, $45/2 years. Sample: $8.

How to Contact Submit 3-5 poems at a time. No e-mail submissions. Cover letter is required. Must include SASE. Reads submissions year round. Time between acceptance and publication is up to 6 months. Sometimes comments on rejected poems. Publishes theme issues. Guidelines available for SASE or on website. Responds in 2-3 months ("sometimes longer if still considering manuscript for possible use in a forthcoming issue"). Pays 1 contributor's copy and a one-year subscription. Acquires first North American serial rights and reprint rights.

Tips "We tend to favor the narrative poem, the concrete crafted lyric, the persona poem, and the meditative place poem. Yet we try to leave some room for poems outside those parameters to keep some fresh air in our selection process."

◻ THE SOUTHEAST REVIEW

Dept. of English, Florida State University, Tallahassee FL 32306. (850)644-2773. E-mail: southeastreview@gmail.com; serpoetry@gmail.com. Website: www.southeastreview.org. Established 1979. **Contact:** Rebecca Hazelton, poetry editor.

Magazines Needs *The Southeast Review*, published biannually, looks for "the very best poetry by new and established poets." *The Southeast Review* is 160 pages, digest-sized. Receives about 5,000 poems/year, accepts less than 4%. Press run is 1,000 (500 subscribers, 100 libraries, 200 shelf sales); 100 distributed free. Single copy: $8; subscription: $15/year. Sample: $6. Make checks payable to *The Southeast Review*.

How to Contact Submit 3-5 poems at a time. Considers simultaneous submissions; no previously published poems. Accepts submissions by postal mail only; SASE required. Cover letter is preferred ("very brief"). Reads submissions year round. Time between acceptance and publication is up to 1 year. Seldom comments on rejected poems. Guidelines available for SASE, by e-mail, or on website. Responds in up to 3 months. Pays 2 contributor's copies. Acquires first North American serial rights. Reviews books and chapbooks of poetry. "Please query the Book Review Editor (serbookreview@gmail.com) concerning reviews."

Contest/Award Offerings Sponsors an annual poetry contest. Winner receives $500 and publication; 9 finalists will also be published. **Entry fee:** $15 for 3 poems. **Deadline:** March. Guidelines available on website.

☑ SOUTHERN CALIFORNIA REVIEW

3501 Trousdale Pkwy, Mark Taper Hall, THH 355J, University of Southern California, Los Angeles CA 90089-0355. E-mail: mpw@college.usc.edu. Website: college.usc.edu/mpw/experience/scr.cfm. **Contact:** Poetry Editor.

Magazines Needs *Southern California Review (SCR)*, published semiannually in the fall and spring, "is the literary journal of the Master of Professional Writing program at the University of Southern California. It has been publishing fiction and poetry since 1982 and now also accepts submissions of creative nonfiction, plays, and screenplays." Accepts poetry in experimental and traditional styles. Features new, emerging, and established authors. Has published poetry by Yevgeny Yevtushenko, Philip Appleman, Tomaz Salamun, Joyce Carol Oates, Bei Ling, and Denise Levertov. *Southern California Review* is about 140 pages, digest-sized, perfect-bound, with a semi-glossy color cover with original artwork. Press run is 1,000. Sample: $10.

How to Contact Submit up to 3 poems at a time. Considers simultaneous submissions, "but please note this in the cover letter and notify us immediately if your submission is accepted for publication elsewhere." No previously published poems. Reads submissions year round. Guidelines available for SASE or on website. Responds in 3-6 months. Pays 2 contributor's copies. Rights revert to poets upon publication; "author is asked to cite appearance in *Southern California Review* when the work is published elsewhere."

Contest/Award Offerings The Ann Stanford Poetry Prize.

☑ SOUTHERN HUMANITIES REVIEW

9088 Haley Center, Auburn University, Auburn AL 36849-5202. Website: www.auburn.edu/english/shr/home.htm. **Contact:** Dan Latimer and Chantel Acevedo, co-editors.

Magazines Needs *Southern Humanities Review*, published quarterly, is "interested in poems of any length, subject, genre. Space is limited, and brief poems are more likely to be accepted. Translations welcome, but also send written permission from the copyright holder." Has published poetry by Donald Hall, Andrew Hudgins, Margaret Gibson, Stephen Dunn, Walt McDonald, and R.T. Smith. *Southern Humanities Review* is 100 pages, digest-sized. Press run is 800. Subscription: $15/year. Sample: $5.

How to Contact Submit 3-5 poems at a time. No previously published poems or simultaneous submissions. No e-mail submissions. "Send poems in a business-sized envelope. Include SASE. Avoid sending faint computer printout." Responds in 2 months, "possibly longer in summer." Always sends prepublication galleys. Pays 2 contributor's copies. Copyright reverts to author upon publication. Reviews books of poetry in approximately 750-1,000 words. Send materials for review consideration.

Contest/Award Offerings Sponsors the Theodore Christian Hoepfner Award, a $50 prize for the best poem published in a given volume of *Southern Humanities Review*.

Tips "For beginners, we recommend study and wide reading in English and classical literature, and, of course, American literature—the old works, not just the new. We also recommend study of or exposure to a foreign language and a foreign culture. Poets need the reactions of others to their work: criticism, suggestions, discussion. A good creative writing teacher would be desirable here, and perhaps some course work, too; and then submission of work, attendance at workshops. And again, the reading: history, biography, verse, essays—all of it. We want to see poems that have gone beyond the language of slippage and easy attitudes."

☑ **SOUTHERN POETRY REVIEW**

Armstrong Atlantic State University, 11935 Abercorn St., Savannah GA 31419. (912)344-3196. E-mail: rrparham@aug.edu. Website: www.spr.armstrong.edu. **Contact:** Robert Parham, editor. Member: CLMP.

• Work appearing in *Southern Poetry Review* received a 2005 Pushcart Prize.

Magazines Needs *Southern Poetry Review*, published semiannually, is the second oldest poetry journal in the region. Wants "poetry eclectically representative of the genre; no restrictions on form, style, or content." Does not want fiction, essays, or reviews. Has published poetry by Cathy Smith Bowers, Albert Goldbarth, Robert Morgan, Linda Pastan, Margaret Gibson, and R. T. Smith. *Southern Poetry Review* is 70-80 pages, digest-sized, perfect-bound, with 80 lb. matte cardstock cover with b&w photography, includes ads. Receives about 8,000 poems/year, accepts about 2%. Press run is 1,200. Single copy: $6; subscription: $12 individuals, $15 institutions. Make checks payable to *Southern Poetry Review*.

How to Contact Submit 5-7 poems at a time (10 pages maximum). Lines/poem: subject to limitations of space. Considers simultaneous submissions (with notification in cover letter); no previously published poems ("previously published" includes poems published or posted online). No e-mail or disk submissions. Cover letter is preferred. "Include SASE for reply; manuscript returned only if sufficient postage is included." Reads submissions year round. Time between acceptance and publication is 6 months. Poems are circulated to an editorial board ("multiple readers, lively discussion and decision-making"). Sometimes comments on rejected poems. Guidelines available in magazine, for SASE, by e-mail, or on website. Responds in 3 months. Always sends prepublication galleys. Pays 2 contributor's copies. Acquires one-time rights.

Tips "We suggest that before submitting, writers read a current issue to get a feel for our journal."

$ ☑ **THE SOUTHERN REVIEW**

43 Allen Hall, Louisiana State University, Baton Rouge LA 70803-5005. (225)578-5108. Fax: (225)578-5098. E-mail: southernreview@lsu.edu. Website: www.lsu.edu/thesouthernreview. **Contact:** The Editors.

• Work published in *The Southern Review* has been included frequently in *The Best American Poetry* and *The Pushcart Prize* as well as *The Beacon's Best of 1999*.

Magazines Needs *The Southern Review*, published quarterly, "has been committed to finding the next new voices in literature. In our pages were published the early works of Eudora Welty, John Berryman, Delmore Schwartz, Peter Taylor, Randall Jarrell, Mary McCarthy, and Nelson Algren, to name only a few. More recently, we can claim Robert Pinsky, Michael S. Harper, and David Kirby as being among those whom we helped "discover." Has published poetry by Aimee Baker, Wendy Barker, David Bottoms, Nick Courtright, Robert Dana, Oliver de la Paz, Ed Falco, Piotr Florczyk, Rigoberto Gonzalez, Ava Leavell Haymon, and Philip Schultz. *The Southern Review* is 200 pages, digest-sized, flat-spined, with full color cover. Receives about 10,000 poetry submissions/year. Press run is 3,200 (2,100 subscribers, 70% libraries). Subscription: $40. Sample: $12.

How to Contact Submit up to 1-5 pages of poetry at a time. No previously published poems. No fax or e-mail submissions. "We do not require a cover letter, but we prefer one giving information about the author and previous publications." Reads submissions September-May. Guidelines available for SASE or on website. Responds in 1-2 months. Pays $25/printed page plus 2 contributor's copies. Acquires first North American serial rights. Staff reviews books of poetry in 3,000 words, multi-book format. Send materials for review consideration.

🌐 ☑ ◎ SOUTH POETRY MAGAZINE

PO BOX 3744, Cookham Maidenhead SL6 9UY, England. E-mail: south@southpoetry. org. Website: www.southmagazine.org. *SOUTH Poetry Magazine*, published biannually in Spring and Autumn, is "for the southern counties of England. Poets from or poems about the South region are particularly welcome, but poets from all over the world are free to submit work on all subjects." Has published poetry by Ian Caws, Stella Davis, Lyn Moir, Elsa Corbluth, Paul Hyland, and Sean Street. *SOUTH* is 68 pages, digest-sized, litho-printed, saddle-stapled, with gloss-laminated duotone cover. Receives about 1,500 poems/year, accepts about 120. Press run is 350 (250 subscribers). Single copy: £5.60; subscription: £10/year, £18/2 years. Make checks (in sterling) payable to *SOUTH Poetry Magazine*.

How to Contact No email submissions. Submit up to 3 poems at a time. No previously published poems or simultaneous submissions. Accepts disk submissions (if accompanied by hard copy). "Do not put name or address on manuscript. List poem titles on submission form (downloadable from website) or in cover letter with name and address." Selection does not begin prior to the deadline and may take up to eight weeks or more from that date." Time between acceptance and publication is up to 5 months. Guidelines available on website.

Tips "Buy the magazine. Then it will still be there to consider and publish your work, and you'll get the idea of the sort of work we publish. These are basic steps, and both are essential."

$ ☑ SOUTHWEST REVIEW

Southern Methodist University, P.O. Box 750374, Dallas TX 75275-0374. (214)768-1037. Fax: (214)768-1408. E-mail: swr@mail.smu.edu. Website: www.smu.edu/southwestreview. **Contact:** Willard Spiegleman, editor in chielf. Poetry published in Southwest Review has been included in The Best American Poetry and The Pushcart Prize .

Magazines Needs *Southwest Review*, published quarterly, prints fiction, essays, poetry, and occasional interviews. "We always suggest that potential contributors read several issues of the magazine to see for themselves what we like. We demand very high quality in our poems; we accept both traditional and experimental writing, but avoid unnecessary obscurity and private symbolism. We place no arbitrary limits on length but find shorter poems easier to fit into our format than longer ones. We have no specific limitations as to theme. Poems tend to be lyric and narrative free verse combining a strong voice with powerful topics or situations. Diction is accessible and content often conveys a strong sense of place." Has published poetry by Albert Goldbarth, John Hollander, Mary Jo Salter, James Hoggard, Dorothea Tanning, and Michael Rosen. *Southwest Review* is 144 pages, digest-sized, professionally printed, perfect-bound, with matte text stock cover. Receives about 1,000 poetry submissions/year, accepts about 32. Press run is 1,500. Subscription: $24. Sample: $6.

How to Contact No previously published poems or simultaneous submissions. Submit by mail or on website. Please note there is a $2 administrative fee for online submissions. Mailed manuscripts must be typed and should include SASE for a response. Guidelines available for SASE or on website. Responds within 1 month. Always sends prepublication galleys. Pays cash plus contributor's copies.

Contest/Award Offerings The Elizabeth Matchett Stover Memorial Award presents $250 to the author of the best poem or groups of poems (chosen by editors) published in the preceding year. Also offers The Morton Marr Poetry Prize.

⊘ THE SOW'S EAR POETRY REVIEW

217 Brookneil Dr., Winchester VA 22602. (864)379-8061. E-mail: sowsearpoetry@yahoo.com. Website: www.sows-ear.kitenet.net. **Contact:** Kristin Zimet, Submissions Editor. *The Sow's Ear Poetry Review*, published quarterly, wants fine poetry of all styles and lengths. "Excellent art in black and white complements the poems. We often take more than 1 poem by an author we like. The 'Community of Poets' feature presents group submissions; define 'community' as broadly as you like. The 'Crossover' feature showcases works that marry the written word with another art form (for example, lyrics with music, word collages, or special calligraphy)." Has published poetry by Robert Morgan, Elizabeth Spires, Virgil Suaárez, Susan Terris, and Franz Wright. *The Sow's Ear Poetry Review* is 32 pages, magazine-sized, professionally printed, saddle-stapled, with matte card cover. Receives about 3,000 poems/year, accepts about 75. Press run is 700 (600 subscribers, 15 libraries). Subscription: $27. Sample: $8. For subscriptions, contact Robert G Lesman, Managing Editor, P.O. Box 127 Millwood VA 22646.

How to Contact Submit up to 5 poems at a time. Considers simultaneous submissions "if you tell us promptly when work is accepted elsewhere"; no previously published poems, although will consider poems from chapbooks if they were never published in a magazine. Previously published poems may be included in 'Crossover' if rights are cleared. No e-mail submissions; postal submissions only. Include brief bio and SASE. Guidelines available for SASE, by e-mail, or on website. Responds in 3 months. Pays 2 contributor's copies. Acquires first publication rights. Inquire about reviews, interviews, and essays. Contest/Award offerings: *The Sow's Ear* Poetry Competition and *The Sow's Ear* Chapbook Contest (separate listings in Contests & Awards).

Tips "Four criteria help us judge the quality of submissions: 1) Does the poem make the strange familiar or the familiar strange, or both? 2) Is the form of the poem vital to its meaning? 3) Do the sounds of the poem make sense in relation to the theme? 4) Does the little story of the poem open a window on the Big Story of the human situation?"

⊕ ☐ SPEEDPOETS ZINE

86 Hawkwood St., Brisbane QL 4122, Australia. (61)(7)3420-6092. E-mail: geenunn@yahoo.com.au. Website: www.speedpoets.org. **Contact:** Graham Nunn, editor.

Magazines Needs *SpeedPoets Zine*, published monthly, showcases "the community of poets that perform at the monthly SpeedPoets readings in Brisbane, as well as showcasing poets from all around the world." Wants "shorter, experimental pieces." Does not want long submissions. Has published poetry by Robert Smith, Steve Kilbey, Brentley Frazer, Jayne Fenton Keane, Graham Nunn, and Marie Kazalia. *SpeedPoets Zine* is 28 pages, digest-sized, photocopied, folded and stapled, with color cover. Press run is 100. Single copy: $5 for overseas/interstate contributors. Payable to Graham Nunn via PayPal (in AUD only, or send well-concealed cash).

How to Contact Submit 2 poems at a time. Lines/poem: 25 maximum. Considers previously published poems. Accepts e-mail submissions (pasted into body of message—no attachments); no disk submissions. Cover letter is preferred. Reads submissions year round. Time between acceptance and publication is 2 weeks. Sometimes comments on rejected poems. Guidelines available by e-mail. Responds in 2 weeks. Rights revert to poet upon publication.

☑ SPILLWAY

P.O. Box 7887, Huntington Beach CA 92615-7887. (714)968-0905. Website: www.tebotbach. org. **Contact:** Mifanwy Kaiswer, publisher or Susan Terris, editor. Published annually in August, *Spillway* celebrates "writing's diversity and power to affect our lives." Open to all voices, schools, and tendencies. "We publish poetry, translations, reviews, essays, black-and-white photography, and color artwork and photography for the cover."

Magazines Needs *Spillway*, published semi-annually in June and December, celebrates "writing's diversity and power to affect our lives." Open to all voices, schools, and tendencies. "We publish poetry, translations, reviews, essays, black-and-white photography, and color artwork and photography for the cover." *Spillway* is about 100 pages, digest-sized, attractively printed, perfect-bound, with 2-color or 4-color card cover. Press run is 2,000. Single copy: $9; subscription plus $3 shipping and handling; one-year subscription $16 includes shipping and handling; two-year subscription $28. Make checks payable to Tebot Bach with *Spillway* in the notation line. "We recommend ordering a sample copy before you submit, though acceptance does not depend upon purchasing a sample copy."

How to Contact Submit 3-5 poems at a time (6 pages maximum total). Theme for December 2010 issue: 'All in the Family.' Theme for June 2011: 'First Time.' For more complete information about upcoming themes and submission periods, check out our website.Considers previously published poems ("only in rare instances") and simultaneous submissions ("say where also submitted"). E-mail submissions only to spillway2@tebotbach.org (Microsoft Word attachment); no disk or fax submissions. Cover letter is required. Include brief bio. Responds in up to 6 months. Pays 1 contributor's copy. Acquires one-time rights. Reviews books of poetry in 500-2,500 words. Send materials for review consideration.

☑ SPINNING JENNY

c/o Black Dress Press, P.O. Box 1067, New York NY 10014. E-mail: info@spinning-jenny. com. Website: www.spinning-jenny.com. **Contact:** C.E. Harrison, Editor.

Magazines Needs *Spinning Jenny*, published once/year in the fall (usually September), has published poetry by Abraham Smith, Cynthia Cruz, Michael Morse, and Joyelle McSweeney. *Spinning Jenny* is 96 pages, digest-sized, perfect-bound, with heavy card cover. "We accept less than 5% of unsolicited submissions." Press run is 1,000. Single copy: $8; subscription: $15 for 2 issues.

How to Contact Submit up to 6 poems at a time. No previously published poems or simultaneous submissions. Accepts submissions online only (see website for guidelines). Reads submissions September 15-May 15 only. Seldom comments on rejected poems.

Guidelines available on website. Responds within 4 months. Pays 3 contributor's copies. Authors retain rights.

☑ ◎ SPITBALL: THE LITERARY BASEBALL MAGAZINE

5560 Fox Rd., Cincinnati OH 45239. Website: www.spitballmag.com. **Contact:** Mike Shannon, Editor-in-Chief. *Spitball: The Literary Baseball Magazine*, published semiannually, is "a unique magazine devoted to poetry, fiction, and book reviews exclusively about baseball. Newcomers are very welcome, but remember that you have to know the subject; we do, and our readers do. Perhaps a good place to start for beginners is one's personal reactions to the game, a game, a player, etc., and take it from there." Writers submitting to *Spitball for the first time must buy a sample copy (waived for subscribers). "This is a one-time-only fee, which we regret, but economic reality dictates that we insist those who wish to be published in Spitball* help support it, at least at this minimum level." *Spitball* is 96 pages, digest-sized, computer-typeset, perfect-bound. Receives about 1,000 submissions/year, accepts about 40. Press run is 1,000. Subscription: $12. Sample: $6.

How to Contact Submit a "batch" of poems at a time ("we prefer to use several of same poet in an issue rather than a single poem"). Lines/poem: open. No previously published poems or simultaneous submissions. Cover letter is required. Include brif bio and SASE. "Many times we are able to publish accepted work almost immediately." Pays 2 contributor's copies."All material published in *Spitball* will be automatically considered for inclusion in the next *Best of Spitball* anthology."1) Poems submitted to *Spitball* will be considered automatically for Poem of the Month, to appear on the website. 2) "We sponsor the Casey Award (for best baseball book of the year) and hold the Casey Awards Banquet in late February or early March. Any chapbook of baseball poetry should be sent to us for consideration for the 'Casey' plaque that we award to the winner each year."

Tips "Take the subject seriously. We do. In other words, get a clue (if you don't already have one) about the subject and about the poetry that has already been done and published about baseball. Learn from it—think about what you can add to the canon that is original and fresh—and don't assume that just anybody with the feeblest of efforts can write a baseball poem worthy of publication. And most importantly, stick with it. Genius seldom happens on the first try."

⊕ ▢ SPLIZZ

4 St. Marys Rise, Burry Port, Carms SA16 0SH, Wales. E-mail: splizzmag@yahoo.co.uk. **Contact:** Amanda Morgan, editor.

Magazines Needs *Splizz*, published quarterly, features poetry, prose, reviews of contemporary music, and background to poets. Wants "any kind of poetry. We have no restrictions regarding style, length, subjects." Does not want "anything racist or homophobic." Has published Colin Cross (UK), Anders Carson (Canada), Paul Truttman (U.S.), Jan Hansen (Portugal), and Gregory Arena (Italy). *Splizz* is 60-64 pages, A5, saddle-stapled, includes ads. Receives about 200-300 poems/year, accepts about 90%. Press run is 150 (35 subscribers). Single copy: £2 UK; subscription: £8 UK. E-mail for current rates. Payments accepted in cash or paypal to splizz@tiscali.co.uk. No checks please.

How to Contact Submit 5 poems at a time. No previously published poems or simultaneous submissions. Accepts e-mail submissions (as attachment). Cover letter is required. Include short bio. Typed submissions preferred. Name and address must be included on each page of submitted work. Include SAE with IRCs. Time between acceptance and publication is 4 months. Often comments on rejected poems. **Charges criticism fee.** "Just enclose SAE/IRC for response, and allow 1-2 months for delivery. For those sending IRCs, please ensure that they have been correctly stamped by your post office." Guidelines available in magazine, for SASE (or SAE and IRC), or by e-mail. Responds in 2 months. Sometimes sends prepublication galleys. Reviews books/chapbooks of poetry or other magazines in 50-300 words. Send materials for review consideration. E-mail for further enquiries.

Tips "Beginners seeking to have their work published, send your work to *Splizz*, as we specialize in giving new poets a chance to see their work published alongside more established writers."

THE SPOON RIVER POETRY REVIEW

4241/Publications Dept., Illinois State University, Normal IL 61790-4241. E-mail: krhotel@ ilstu.edu. Website: www.litline.org/spoon. **Contact:** Kirstin Hotelling Zona, editor.

Magazines Needs *The Spoon River Poetry Review*, published biannually, is "one of the nation's oldest continuously published poetry journals. We seek to publish the best of all poetic genres, experimental as well as mainstream, and are proud of our commitment to regional as well as international poets and readers. *Spoon River* includes, alongside poems from emerging and established poets, original artwork and reviews solicited from poet-critics and translators. These essays situate selected books with regard to current poetic trends and conversations. In addition to poems across the United States and the world (in English translation), each issue publishes a *SRPR* Illinois poet feature (12-18 pages of unpublished poetry, an interview, and bio).The Summer/Fall issue also spotlights the winner and runners-up of our highly competitive editor's prize contest." *The Spoon River Poetry Review* is 128 pages, digest-sized, laser-set, with card cover. Receives about 3,000 poems/month, accepts 1%. Press run is 1,500. Subscription: $16. Sample: $10 (includes guidelines).

How to Contact Submit 3-5 poems at a time. Accepts simultaneous submissions "as long as you notify us immediately if a poem has been accepted elsewhere." Include name, e-mail, and address on every poem. Accepts submissions September 15-April 15. Comments on rejected poems "many times, if a poet is promising." Guidelines available in magazine or on website. Responds in 3 months. Pays a year's subscription. Acquires first North American serial rights. Reviews books of poetry. Send materials for review consideration.

Contest/Award Offerings Sponsors *The Spoon River Poetry Review* Editor's Prize Contest.

Tips "Read widely, across styles and time periods. We are looking for poems that are as intellectually and emotionally ambitious as they are attentive to technique. We seek your very best work in any form, and are especially interested in publishing a dynamic variety of poems in every issue."

SPOUT MAGAZINE

E-mail: editors@spoutpress.org. Website: www.spoutpress.com. **Contact:** Michelle Filkins, Poetry Editor.

Magazines Needs *Spout*, published approximately 3 times/year, aims to provide "a paper community of unique expression." Wants "poetry of the imagination; poetry that surprises.

We enjoy the surreal, the forceful, the political, the expression of confusion." No light verse, archaic forms or language. Has published poetry by Gillian McCain, Larissa Szporluk, Matt Hart, Joanna Fuhrman, Josie Rawson, and Richard Siken. *Spout* is 40-60 pages, saddle-stapled, with cardstock or glossy cover (different color each issue). Receives about 400-450 poems/year, accepts about 10%. Press run is 200-250 (35-40 subscribers, 100-150 shelf sales). Single copy: $5; subscription: $15.

How to Contact Submit up to 5 poems at a time. Considers previously published poems and simultaneous submissions. Cover letter is preferred. Time between acceptance and publication is 2-3 months. "Poems are reviewed by 2 of 3 editors; those selected for final review are read again by all three." Seldom comments on rejected poems. Guidelines available for SASE or on website. Responds in 4 months. Pays 1 contributor's copy.

Tips "Read a copy of the magazine to understand our editorial biases."

SPRING: THE JOURNAL OF THE E.E. CUMMINGS SOCIETY

129 Lake Huron Hall, Grand Valley State University, Allendale MI 49401-9403. E-mail: websterm@gvsu.edu. Website: www.gvsu.edu/english/cummings/Index.html. **Contact:** Michael Webster, editor.

Magazines Needs *Spring: The Journal of the E.E. Cummings Society*, published annually (usually in the fall), is designed "to broaden the audience for E.E. Cummings, and to explore various facets of his life and art." **Contributors are required to subscribe.** Wants poems in the spirit of Cummings, primarily poems of one page or less. Does not want "amateurish" work. Has published poetry by John Tagliabue, Jacqueline Vaught Brogan, and Gerald Locklin. *Spring* is about 180 pages, digest-sized, offset-printed, perfect-bound, with light cardstock cover. Press run is 400 (200 subscribers, 25 libraries, 200 shelf sales). Subscription or sample: $17.50.

How to Contact No previously published poems or simultaneous submissions. Accepts fax and e-mail (as attachment) submissions. Cover letter is required. Reads submissions May-August only. Seldom comments on rejected poems. Guidelines available for SASE. Responds in 6 months.

$ ST. ANTHONY MESSENGER

(Specialized: Catholic; spirituality/inspirational), 28 W. Liberty St., Cincinnati OH 45202-6498. Fax: (513)241-0399. Website: www.americancatholic.org. **Contact:** Christopher Heffron, poetry editor.

- *St. Anthony Messenger* poetry occasionally receives awards from the Catholic Press Association Annual Competition.

Magazines Needs *St. Anthony Messenger*, published monthly, is a mgazine for Catholic families, mostly with children in grade school, high school, or college. Some issues feature a poetry page that uses poems appropriate for their readership. Poetry submissions are always welcome despite limited need. "We seek to publish accessible poetry of high quality. Spiritual/inspirational in nature a plus, but not required." Considers poetry by young writers, ages 14 and older. *St. Anthony Messenger* is 60 pages. Press run 280,000. Sample: free for 9x12 SASE.

How to Contact Submit "a few" poems at a time. Lines/poem: under 25. No previously published poems. Accepts fax and e-mail submissions. "Please include your phone number and a SASE with your submission. Do not send us your entire collection of poetry. Poems must be original." Submit seasonal poems several months in advance. Guidelines available for SASE, by fax, or on website. Pays $2/line on acceptance plus 2 contributor's copies. Acquires first worldwide serial rights.

⊕ $ ☑ STAPLE MAGAZINE

114-116 St. Stephen's Rd., Sneinton, Nottingham NG2 4FJ, England. **Contact:** Wayne Burrows, Editor.

Magazines Needs *Staple*, published 3 times/year, accepts "poetry, short fiction, and articles about the writing process and general culture in relation to writing, plus some artwork and photography." *Staple* is about 150 pages, perfect-bound. Press run is 500 (350 subscribers). Single copy: £10; subscription: £25/year, £35/year overseas. Sample: £5.00 (back issue).

How to Contact Submit 6 poems or 1-2 stories/essays at a time. No previously published poems or simultaneous submissions. Cover letter with author bio note is preferred. Include SAE and 2 IRCs. Issues are themed, contact for details. Reads submissions by the following deadlines: end of March, July, and November. Sometimes comments on rejected poems. Responds in up to 3 months. Pays £10/single poem, £25/group of poems; £25/story or essay.

☐ STEPPING STONES MAGAZINE: A LITERARY MAGAZINE FOR INNOVATIVE ART

First Step Press, P.O. Box 902, Norristown PA 19404-0902. E-mail: info@fspressonline. org; editor@fspressonline.org. Website: www.fspressonline.org. **Contact:** Trinae A. Ross, publisher.

Magazines Needs *Stepping Stones Magazine: A Literary Magazine for Innovative Art*, published 4 times/year online, delivered as a PDF document, seeks "poetry as diverse as are the authors themselves. Poems should have something to say other than, 'Hi, I'm a poem please publish me.'" Does not want "poems that promote intolerance for race, religion, gender, or sexual preference." Has published poetry by Clayton Vetter, Michael Hathaway, and Ivan Silverberg. Receives about 300 poems/year, accepts about 10-15%. Reviews chapbooks, Websites, and other publications of interest to poets.

How to Contact Submit no more than 5 poems at a time. Considers previously published poems and simultaneous submissions. Prefers e-mail submissions; should include cover letter and formatted with a simple font and saved as .doc, .rtf, or .odf. Attach submissions and cover letter to e-mail and send to poetry@fspressonline.org. Read submissions year round. Guidelines available for SASE, by sending an e-mail to guidelines @fspressonline. org, or on website. Responds within 2 months. Pays one contributor's copy and free advertising space, though will implement a pay schedule when funding permits. Acquires one-time print and electronic rights.

Also Offers "Free advertising space is available for those wishing to promote their website, book, or other literary venture. The continuing goal of First Step Press is to provide sanctuary for new and established writers, to hone their skills and commune with one another within the comfort of our electronic pages."

Tips "The continued goal of *Stepping Stones Magazine: ALMIA* is to establish new poets with help from those more established in the poetry community. Your best chance of being published is to 1) read the guidelines, 2) follow the guidelines, and 3) be yourself. We are not looking for the next anyone..we are looking for the first you."

◐ ◎ THE WALLACE STEVENS JOURNAL

Clarkson University, Box 5750, 8 Clarkson Avenue, Potsdam NY 13699. (315)268-3987. Fax: (315)268-3983. E-mail: serio@clarkson.edu. Website: www.wallacestevens.com. **Contact:** Professor Josepeh Duemer, poetry editor (jduemer@clarkson.edu).

Magazines Needs *The Wallace Stevens Journal,* published semiannually by the Wallace Stevens Society, uses "poems about or in the spirit of Wallace Stevens or having some relation to his work. No bad parodies of Stevens's anthology pieces." Has published poetry by David Athey, Jacqueline Marcus, Charles Wright, X.J. Kennedy, A.M. Juster, and Robert Creeley. *The Wallace Stevens Journal* is 96-120 pages, digest-sized, typeset, flat-spined, with glossy cover with art. Receives 200-300 poems/year, accepts 15-20. Press run is 700. Subscription: $30 (includes membership in the Wallace Stevens Society). Sample: $10.

How to Contact Submit 1-4 poems at a time. No previously published poems, "though we have made a few exceptions to this rule.".No fax or e-mail submissions, "though requests for information are fine." Cover letter is encouraged, but keep brief. Send clean, readable copy. Responds in up to 10 weeks. Always sends prepublication galleys. Pays 2 contributor's copies. Acquires all rights. Returns rights with permission and acknowledgment. Staff reviews books of poetry. Send materials for review consideration "only if there is some clear connection to Stevens."

Tips "Please don't submit to *The Wallace Stevens Journal* if you have not read Stevens. We like parodies, but they must add a new angle of perception. Most of the poems we publish are not parodies but meditations on themes related to Wallace Stevens and those poets he has influenced. Those wishing to contribute might want to examine a previous issue."

▣ $ ◯ STICKMAN REVIEW

721 Oakwater Lane, Port Orange FL 32128. E-mail: poetry@stickmanreview.com. Website: www.stickmanreview.com.

Magazines Needs *Stickman Review,* published semiannually online, is dedicated to printing great poetry, fiction, nonfiction, and artwork. Wants poetry "that is literary in intent; no restrictions on form, subject matter, or style." Does not typically want "rhyming poetry."

How to Contact Submit no more than 5 poems at a time. Please wait until receiving a response before submitting again. Considers simultaneous submissions; no previously published poems. Accepts e-mail submissions only (as attachment in Word, .rtf or .txt, or pasted into body of message); no postal submissions. Cover letter is preferred. Reads submissions year round. Time between acceptance and publication is 4-6 months. "Currently, the editors-in-chief review all submissions." Rarely comments on rejected poems. Guidelines available on website. Responds in up to 6 months. Pays $10/poem, up to $20/author. Acquires first rights.

Tips "Keep writing and submitting. A rejection is not necessarily a reflection upon the quality of your work. Be persistent, trust your instincts, and sooner or later, good things will come."

☐ ◎ STILL CRAZY

E-mail: bkussow@hotmail.com. Website: www.crazylitmag.com. blog.crazylitmag.com. **Contact:** Barbara Kussow, editor.

Magazines Needs *Still Crazy*, published biannually in January and July, publishes "poetry, short stories, and some short nonfiction pieces by and about people over fifty years of age." Wants "poems that tell a story." Does not want "rhyming poetry, or poetry that is too sentimental." *Still Crazy* is magazine-sized. Single copy, paper: $9; download: $3; subscription: $16/year. Use PayPal or contact editor if you wish to pay by check.

How to Contact Submit 3-5 poems at a time. Lines/poem: 30 maximum. Occasionally considers previously published poems. Simultaneous submissions okay, but notify editor as soon as possible if work is accepted elsewhere. Submit by uploading via submission manager on website. Include short bio; tell editor you are over fifty or writing about someone over fifty. Reads submissions year round. Time between acceptance and publication is up to one year. Sometimes comments on rejected poems. Sometimes publishes theme issues. Guidelines available on website. Responds in 6 months. Sometimes sends prepublication galleys. Pays one contributor's copy. Acquires one-time rights. Rights revert to poet upon publication.

☒ ◐ STIRRING: A LITERARY COLLECTION

323 Oglewood Ave, Knoxville TN 37917. (607)765-6751. E-mail: eesmith81@gmail.com. Website: www.sundress.net/stirring/. **Contact:** Erin Elizabeth Smith, managing editor.

- "*Stirring*, published monthly online, is one of the oldest continually-published literary journals on the web and features poetry, short fiction, creative nonfiction, and photography by established and emerging writers."

Magazines Needs Wants free verse, formal poetry, etc. Doesn't want religious verse or children's verse. Has published poetry by Dorianne Laux, Sharon Olds, Patricia Smith, Chad Davidson. Receives about 1,500 poems/year, accepts 60.

How to Contact Submit 1-7 poems at a time by e-mail. Considers previously published poems and simultaneous submissions. Past submissions into body of e-mail message. Reads submissions year round. Time between acceptance and publication is 1-2 weeks. Poems are circulated to an editorial board. Sometimes comments on rejected poems. Guidelines available on website. Responds in 2-5 months. Acquires first North American serial rights.

$ ☐ ◎ ST. JOSEPH MESSENGER & ADVOCATE OF THE BLIND

537 Pavonia, Jersey City NJ 07306. (201)798-4141. Website: http://csjp.org. **Contact:** Editor. *St. Joseph Messenger & Advocate of the Blind*, published 3 times a year, prints "brief but thought-filled poetry." Does not want "lengthy and issue-filled poems." Receives 400-500 submissions/year, accepts about 50. *St. Joseph Messenger* is 12 pages, magazine-sized. Press run is 12,000. Subscription: $5. Sample: with guidelines and list of upcoming themes, available for 612 × 912 SASE and 2 first-class stamps.

How to Contact Sometimes comments on rejected poems. Publishes theme issues. Guidelines available for SASE. Responds within one month. Pays $5-15/poem plus 2 contributor's copies.

Tips "Most of the poets published in *St. Joseph Messenger* are previously unpublished."

$ ▢ ◎ STONE SOUP, THE MAGAZINE BY YOUNG WRITERS AND ARTISTS

P.O. Box 83, Santa Cruz CA 95063. (831)426-5557. Fax: (831)426-1161. E-mail: editor@ stonesoup.com. Website: www.stonesoup.com. **Contact:** Ms. Gery Mandel, editor.

• *Stone Soup* has received Parents' Choice and Edpress Golden Lamp Honor Awards.

Magazines Needs *Stone Soup*, published 6 times/year, showcases writing and art by children ages 13 and under. Wants free verse poetry. Does not want rhyming poetry, haiku, or cinquain. *Stone Soup* is 48 pages, 7x10, professionally printed in color on heavy stock, saddle-stapled, with coated cover with full-color illustration. Receives 5,000 poetry submissions/year, accepts about 12. Press run is 15,000 (14,000 subscribers, 3,000 shelf sales, 500 other). Subscription: membership in the Children's Art Foundation includes a subscription, $37/year. Sample: $5.

How to Contact No simultaneous submissions. No e-mail submissions. "Submissions can be any number of pages, any format. Include name, age, home address, and phone number. Don't include SASE; we respond only to those submissions under consideration and cannot return manuscripts." Guidelines available on website. Responds in up to 6 weeks. Pays $40, a certificate, and 2 contributor's copies plus discounts. Acquires all rights. Returns rights upon request. Open to reviews by children.

▢ THE STORYTELLER

2441 Washington Rd., Maynard AR 72444. (870)647-2137. E-mail: storyteller1@ hightowercom.com. Website: www.freewebs.com/fossilcreek. **Contact:** Regina Williams, Editor.

Magazines Needs *The Storyteller*, published quarterly, "is geared to, but not limited to, new writers and poets." Wants "any form, any subject, any style, but must have a meaning. Do not throw words together and call it a poem." Does not want "explicit sex, violence, horror, or explicit language. I would like it to be understood that I have young readers, ages 9-18." Considers poetry by children and teens. Has published poetry by Patrick Lobrutto, Bryan Byrd, and Gerald Zipper. *The Storyteller* is 72 pages, magazine-sized, desktop-published, with slick cover black and white photography, includes ads. Receives about 300 poems/ year, accepts about 40%. Press run is 700 (more than 600 subscribers). Single copy: $6 U.S., $8 Canada and foreign; subscription: $20 U.S., $24 Canada & foreign.

How to Contact Submit 3 poems at a time, 1 poem per page. Lines/poem: up to 40. Considers previously published poems and simultaneous submissions, "but must state where and when poetry first appeared." No e-mail submissions; postal submissions only. "However, if accepted, you will be asked to send material by e-mail, if possible." Cover letter is preferred. Manuscripts must be typed and double-spaced. "Make sure name and address are on each page submitted. We are getting many submissions without names." Time between acceptance and publication is 9 months. "Poems are read and discussed by staff." Sometimes comments on rejected poems. Guidelines available for SASE or on website. Responds in 1-2 weeks. Pays $1 per poem; does not provide contributor's copies. Acquires first or one-time rights. Reviews books/chapbooks of poetry by subscribers only. Send materials for review consideration to Jamie Johnson, assistant editor.

Contest/Award Offerings Sponsors a quarterly contest. "Readers vote on their favorite poems. Winners receive a copy of the magazine and a certificate. We also nominate for the Pushcart Prize." See website for yearly contest announcements and winners.

Tips "Be professional. Do not send 4 or 5 poems on 1 page. Send us poetry written from the heart."

▣ ◿ THE STRAY BRANCH

E-mail: thestraybranchlitmag@yahoo.com. Website: www.thestraybranch.org. **Contact:** Debbie Berk, editor/publisher.

Magazines Needs *The Stray Branch*, published twice per year, is a journal "looking to publish well-crafted material from experienced writers who are serious about their craft. Looking for honest, personal, edgy, raw, real life material that is relatable to the human condition known as existence in all its dark, flawed, secret self..exposed in the wounds that bleed upon the page and leave a scar within the skull of the reader. Open to subject matter but prefers edgy, raw material written from the gut that reflects the heart and human experience. Wants poetry by real people that can be understood by all readers. *The Stray Branch* prefers works of a darker nature." Does not want "over-schooled, arrogant, self-righteous, religious, political, erotic poetry, or happy and light, pretty poetry. Not interested in rants, tantrums, and the use of profanity that is not fitting to the piece. Please, be tactful and respectful of the language." Has published poetry by Andy Robertson, Keith Estes, Kate Sjostrand, Lena Vanelslander, Michael Grover, and Justin Blackburn.

How to Contact Submit 6 poems at a time. "Maximum length for poems is no longer than 1 page, shorter poems are preferred and stand a better chance." Considers previously published poems; no simultaneous submissions. (Considers poetry posted on a public website/blog/forum and poetry posted on a private, password-protected forum as published.) Accepts e-mail submissions (pasted into body of message); no fax or disk submissions. Cover letter is unnecessary. Reads submissions October-April. Sometimes comments on rejected poems. Guidelines available on website. Responds in 3 weeks. Acquires one-time rights ("includes material published on the web"). Rights revert to poets upon publication.

◻ STRAYLIGHT

University of Wisconsin-Parkside, English Dept., 900 Wood Rd., P.O. Box 2000, Kenosha WI 53141. (262)595-2139. Fax: (262)595-2271. E-mail: straylight@litspot.net. Website: www.straylightmag.com. **Contact:** Poetry Editor.

Magazines Needs *Straylight*, published biannually, seeks "poetry of almost any style as long as it's inventive." *Straylight* is digest-sized. Single copy: $10; subscription: $19. Make checks payable to *Straylight*.

How to Contact Submit 3-6 poems at a time. No previously published poems or simultaneous submissions. Accepts e-mail submissions (preferred, as .rtf or .doc attachment); no fax or disk submissions. Cover letter is required. "Include contact information on all pages of submission." Reads submissions August 15-April 15. Submit seasonal poems 3 months in advance. Time between acceptance and publication is 6 months. Never comments on rejected poems. Sometimes publishes theme issues. Upcoming themes available on website. Guidelines available for SASE or on website. Responds in 2 months. Pays 2 contributor's copies. Additional payment when funding permits. Acquires first North American serial rights. Rights revert to poet upon publication.

Tips "We suggest you buy a sample copy to get a feel for what we publish."

🌐 🖾 ☑ STRIDE MAGAZINE

E-mail: editor@stridemagazine.co.uk, submissions@stridemagazine.co.uk. Website: www. stridemagazine.co.uk. **Contact:** Rupert Loydell, editor.

Magazines Needs *Stride Magazine*, published online, is "a gathering of new poetry, short prose, articles, news, reviews, and whatever takes our fancy. *Stride* is regularly updated with new contributions."

How to Contact Submit 4-5 poems at a time. Accepts e-mail submissions (pasted into body of message; no attachments). "Attachments or snail mail without SAEs will not be considered or replied to."

☐ ◎ STRUGGLE: A MAGAZINE OF PROLETARIAN REVOLUTIONARY LITERATURE

P.O. Box 28536, Detroit MI 48228. (313)273-9039. E-mail: timhall11@yahoo.com. Website: www.strugglemagazine.net. **Contact:** Tim Hall, editor.

Magazines Needs *Struggle: A Magazine of Proletarian Revolutionary Literature*, published quarterly, focuses "on the struggle of the working people and all oppressed against the rich, dealing with such issues as racism, poverty, women's rights, aggressive wars, workers' struggle for jobs and job security, the overall struggle for a non-exploitative society, a genuine socialism." The poetry and songs printed are "generally short, any style; subject matter must criticize or fight—explicitly or implicitly—against the rule of the billionaires. We welcome experimentation devoted to furthering such content. We are open to both subtlety and direct statement." Has published poetry by Joseph Lampert, Shawn Crawford, ysabel Y. Gonzalez, Lisa Dawn Hilliker, Bob Vance, Louise Hammonds, Steve Moore, Traci Luker and Francee Bouvenire. *Struggle* is 36 pages, digest-sized, photocopied. Subscription: $10/year (4 issues); $12 for institutions, $15 for foreign, $5 for prisoners. Sample: $5 (for the now-customary double-sized issue of 72 pages). Make checks payable to "Tim Hall— Special Account (not to *Struggle*)."

How to Contact Submit up to 8 poems at a time. Accepts e-mail submissions (pasted into body of message, no attachments), but prefers postal mail. "Writers must include SASE. Name and address must appear on the opening page of each poem." Accepted work usually appears in the next or following issue. Comments on rejected poems "with every submission." Responds in 4 months, if possible, but often becomes backlogged. Pays one contributor's copy. "If you are unwilling to have your poetry published on our website, please inform us."

Tips "Show passion and fire. Humor also welcome. Prefer powerful, colloquial language over academic timidity. Look to Neruda, Lorca, Bly, Whitman, Braithwaite, Tupac Shakur, Muriel Rukeyser. Experimental, traditional forms both welcome. Especially favor: works reflecting rebellion by the working people against the rich; works against racism, sexism, militarism, imperialism; works critical of our exploitative culture; works showing a desire for—or fantasy of—a non-exploitative society; works attacking the Republican 'anti-terrorism' war frenzy and the Democrats' surrender to it."

⊛ ☑ ◎ STUDIO, A JOURNAL OF CHRISTIANS WRITING

727 Peel St., Albury NS 2640, Australia. (61)(2)6021-1135. Fax: (61)(2)6021-1135. E-mail: studio00@bigpond.net.au. **Contact:** Paul Grover, Publisher.

Magazines Needs *Studio, A Journal of Christians Writing*, published quarterly, prints "poetry and prose of literary merit, offering a venue for previously published, new, and aspiring writers, and seeking to create a sense of community among Christians writing." Also publishes occasional articles as well as news and reviews of writing, writers, and events of interest to members. Wants "shorter pieces [[of poetry]] but with no specification as to form or length (necessarily less than 200 lines), subject matter, style, or purpose. People who send material should be comfortable being published under this banner: *Studio, A Journal of Christians Writing*." Has published poetry by John Foulcher, Les Murray, and other Australian poets. *Studio* is 36 pages, digest-sized, professionally printed on high-quality recycled paper, saddle-stapled, with matte card cover. Press run is 300 (all subscriptions). Subscription: $60 AUD for overseas members. Sample: $10 AUD (airmail to U.S.).

How to Contact Lines/poem: less than 200. Considers simultaneous submissions. Cover letter is required. Include brief details of previous publishing history, if any. SAE with IRC required. "Submissions must be typed and double-spaced on one side of A4 white paper. Name and address must appear on the reverse side of each page submitted." Response time is 2 months. Time between acceptance and publication is 9 months. Pays 1 contributor's copy. Acquires first Australian rights. Reviews books of poetry in 250 words, single-book format. Send materials for review consideration.

Contest/Award Offerings Conducts a biannual poetry and short story contest.

Tips "The trend in Australia is for imagist poetry and poetry exploring the land and the self. Reading the magazine gives the best indication of style and standard, so send for a sample copy before sending your poetry. Keep writing, and we look forward to hearing from you."

☑ STUDIO ONE

Mary Commons, College of St. Benedict, 37 S. College Ave., St. Joseph MN 56374. E-mail: studio1@csbsju.edu. Website: http://clubs.csbsju.edu/studio1. **Contact:** Poetry Editor.

Studio One, published annually in May, is a "literary and visual arts magazine designed as a forum for local, regional, and national poets/writers. No specifications regarding form, subject matter, or style of poetry submitted." Considers poetry by children and teens. Has published poetry by Bill Meissner, Eva Hooker, and Larry Schug. *Studio One* is 50-80 pages, typeset, with soft cover. Receives 600-800 submissions/year. No subscriptions, but a sample copy can be obtained by sending a self-addressed, stamped manila envelope and $6 for p&h. Make checks payable to *Studio One*. Submissions are accepted August-December. The deadline is January 1 for spring publication. The reading/judging period between late November and February. Results will be sent by May. Submissions sent after the judging period concludes will be retained for consideration in the following year's publication.

How to Contact Submit no more than 5 poems at a time. Lines/poem: "poetry no more than 2 pages stands a better chance of publication." Considers simultaneous submissions;

no previously published poems. Accepts e-mail submissions (pasted into body of message); "clearly show page breaks and indentations." Seldom comments on rejected poems.

SUBTROPICS

University of Florida, P.O. Box 112075, 4008 Turlington Hall, Gainesville FL 32611-2075. E-mail: dleavitt@ufl.edu. Website: www.english.ufl.edu/subtropics. **Contact:** David Leavitt. "Magazine published 3 times/year through the University of Florida's English department. *Subtropics* seeks to publish the best literary fiction, essays, and poetry being written today, both by established and emerging authors. We will consider works of fiction of any length, from short shorts to novellas and self-contained novel excerpts. We give the same latitude to essays. We appreciate work in translation and, from time to time, republish important and compelling stories, essays, and poems that have lapsed out of print by writers no longer living."

How to Contact Submit in hard copy by mail. Please include cover letter with contact information included both on letter and on submission. Responds by e-mail. period from September 1-May 1. Does not return ms. Reading "We do not accept simultaneous submissions in poetry." Poets are paid $100 per poem.

Tips "Please read an issue of the magazine before you send us your work in order to get a feel for the kind of writing we publish. You'll see that we don't publish science fiction, fantasy, genre fiction, or anything with talking animals."

$ ☑ THE SUN

The Editorial Department, 107 N. Roberson St., Chapel Hill NC 27516. E-mail: tim@ thesunmagazine.org. Tim McKee, Managing Editor. **Contact:** Sy Safransky, Editor. *The Sun*, published monthly, is "noted for honest, personal work that's not too obscure or academic. "We favor poetry that is accessible and emotionally evocative." We avoid traditional, rhyming poetry, as well as limericks and haiku. We're open to almost anything else: free verse, prose poems, short and long poems." Has published poetry by Ellen Bass, Christopher Bursk, Steve Kowit, Alison Luterman, Naomi Shihab Nye, Ellery Akers, and Tess Gallagher. *The Sun* is 48 pages, magazine-sized, offset-printed on 50 lb. paper, saddle-stapled. Press run is 80,000 (70,000 subscribers, 500 libraries). Receives 3,000 submissions of poetry/ year, accepts about 30. Subscription: $36. Sample: $5.

How to Contact Submit up to 6 poems at a time. Considers previously published poems but strongly prefers unpublished work; no simultaneous submissions. "Poems should be typed and accompanied by a cover letter and SASE." Guidelines available for SASE or on website. Responds within 3-6 months. Pays $100-500 on publication plus contributor's copies and subscription. Acquires first serial or one-time rights.

▣ ◻ SUNKEN LINES

E-mail: dogger@sunkenlines.com. Website: www.sunkenlines.com. **Contact:** Dogger Banks, Poetry Editor.

Magazines Needs *Sunken Lines*, published biannually online, is a magazine of poetry, fiction, essays, and artwork "intended as a forum for talented writers looking for more exposure." Wants "poems that evoke a strong response in the reader, whether it be laughter, empathy, the conjuring of a strong image, or admiration of a witty line. Formal or (accessible) free verse." Does not want "poems that are excessively religious, offensive, or miserable." Has published poetry by Larry Rapant, Tony Gruenewald, Suzanne Harvey, Anna Evans, Paul Lench, and Bruce Niedt. Receives about 500 poems/year, accepts about 10%.

How to Contact Submit up to 5 poems at a time. Lines/poem: 40 maximum. Considers simultaneous submissions; no previously published poems. Accepts e-mail submissions (preferably pasted into body of message, or as attachment in MS Word or RTF format); no disk submissions. Cover letter is required. "Please be prepared to supply a short biography and optional photo upon notification of acceptance." Reads submissions year round. Time between acceptance and publication is up to 3 months. Poems are circulated to an editorial board. Sometimes comments on rejected poems. Guidelines available on website. Responds in 3 months. Acquires one-time rights. Rights revert to poet upon publication.

Tips "Check out current and back issues on website."

☑ SUNSPINNER

E-mail: sunspinnermagazine@yahoo.com. Website: www.sunspinner.org. **Contact:** Ellen Lewis and Lisa Swanstrom, editors. *Sunspinner*, published biannually online, is based in southern California and features "fiction and poetry from writers everywhere. There are no restrictions on style or subject matter, and submissions are always welcome." Has published poetry by Ryan G. Van Cleave, Lyn Lifshin, Linda Mastrangelo, and Gary Lehman.

How to Contact Submit 3-5 poems at a time. Considers previously published poems ("provided the author retains all rights") and simultaneous submissions. Accepts e-mail (pasted into body of message or as attachment in Microsoft Word) and disk submissions. Cover letter is preferred. "Please include a brief bio with each submission." Reads submissions year round. Time between acceptance and publication is 6 months to a year. Never comments on rejected poems. Guidelines available on website. Responds in 4-6 months. No payment. "Works accepted by *Sunspinner* will be archived for an indefinite period of time and removed at the author's request. Authors retain all rights to work featured in *Sunspinner*."

☑ SWEET ANNIE & SWEET PEA REVIEW

Sweet Annie Press, 7750 Highway F-24 W, Baxter IA 50028. (641)417-0020. E-mail: sweetann@pcpartner.net. *Sweet Annie & Sweet Pea Review*, published quarterly, features poetry and short stories. Wants "poems of outdoors, plants, land, heritage, women, relationships, olden times—simpler times." Does not want "obscene, violent, explicit sexual material, obscure, long-winded materials, overly religious materials." Does not accept unsolicited ms. Has published poetry by Patricia Rourke, Mary Ann Wehler, Ellaraine Lockie, Patricia Wellingham-Jones, Dick Reynolds, and Susanne Olson. *Sweet Annie & Sweet Pea Review* is 30 pages, digest-sized, offset-printed on bond paper with onion skin page before title page, saddle-stapled, with medium card cover with art. Receives about 200 poems/year, accepts 25-33%. Press run is 40. Subscription: $24. Sample: $7. Make checks payable to Sweet Annie Press.

How to Contact Submit 6-12 poems at a time. Considers simultaneous submissions; no previously published poems. No e-mail submissions. Cover letter is preferred. "Include phone number and personal comments about yourself." Strongly recommends ordering a sample issue prior to submitting; "preference is given to poets and writers following this procedure and submitting in accordance with the layout used consistently by this press." **Reading fee:** $5/author submitting. Time between acceptance and publication is 9 months. Often comments on rejected poems. Occasionally publishes theme issues. "We select for theme first, content second; narrow selections through editors." Pays one contributor's copy. Acquires all rights. Returns rights with acknowledgment in future publications. Will review chapbooks of poetry or other magazines of short length. Send materials for review consideration.

▣ ◎ SWELL

E-mail: swelleditor@yahoo.com. Website: www.swellzine.com. **Contact:** Jill Craig, Editor. "SWELL aims to reflect a spectrum of perspectives as diverse as the community from which it was born. Ideal publication candidates approach GLBT (gay/lesbian/bisexual/transgender) issues in a fresh way or present universal topics from a unique point of view. Pieces which avoid well-trodden areas of the GLBT canon are of particular interest. Fiction and nonfiction of all styles, as well as poetry and drama, are all acceptable forms for SWELL; aspiring contributors are also encouraged to experiment with the possibilities inherent in internet publication, such as multimedia compositions, creative hyperlinking, and works not easily categorized."

How to Contact Lines/poem: no works over 3,000 words total. Welcomes multiple submissions as long as the total submitted is under the maximum word count. Accepts e-mail submissions only. Responds in 1-2 months. Rights revert to poet upon publication.

Contest/Award Offerings "SWELL is pleased to sponsor a fiction contest. Prizes Awarded: First Prize: $250; Second Prize: $100; Third Prize: $50. See our website for details."

▨ SYCAMORE REVIEW

Dept. of English, Purdue University, 500 Oval Dr., West Lafayette IN 47907-2038. (765)494-3783. Fax: (765)494-3780. E-mail: sycamore@purdue.edu. Website: www.sycamorereview.com. **Contact:** Poetry Editor.

- Poetry published by *Sycamore Review* has appeared in *The Best American Poetry* and *The Pushcart Prize*.

Magazines Needs *Sycamore Review*, published semiannually in January and June, uses "personal essays, short fiction, short shorts, drama, translations, and quality poetry in any form. We aim to publish many diverse styles of poetry from formalist to prose poems, narrative, and lyric." Has published poetry by Denise Duhamel, Jonah Winter, Amy Gerstler, Mark Halliday, Dean Young, and Ed Hirsch. *Sycamore Review* is about 120 pages, 8x8, professionally printed, flat-spined, with matte color cover. Press run is 1,000 (200 subscribers, 50 libraries). Subscription: $12 ($14 outside U.S.). Sample: $7. Indiana residents add 5% sales tax. Make checks payable to Purdue University.

How to Contact Submit 3-6 poems at a time. with name and address on each page. Include SASE. Considers simultaneous submissions, if notified immediately of acceptance elsewhere; no previously published poems except translations. No fax or e-mail submissions. Cover letter is required. "Include phone number, short bio, and previous publications, if any, in cover letter." Put name and address on each page of ms, include SASE. Reads submissions August 1-March 1 only. Guidelines available for SASE or on website. Responds in 4-5 months. Pays 2 contributor's copies. Acquires first North American rights. After publication, all rights revert to author. Staff reviews books of poetry. Send materials for review consideration to editor-in-chief.

Tips "Poets who do not include a SASE do not receive a response."

🌐 $ ☑ TAKAHE

P.O. Box 13-335, Christchurch 8141, New Zealand. Website: http://www.takahe.org. nz. **Contact:** Poetry Editor. *Takahe* is published by Takahe Collective Trust, a nonprofit organization formed to help new writers and get them into print alongside established poets. A poem can range from about 10 lines to two pages, but we have published longer ones. All submissions should be in hard copy and accompanied by a cover letter and bio of 40/max words. Simultaneous submissions are acceptable, if advised on submission. Please notify editor immediately if work is accepted elsewhere. Contributors should not submit further material before previously submitted material has had a response. **Submissions:** No e-mail submissions, please. Mail poetry submissions. Use IRCs, not U.S. stamps for overseas submissions. Advise if you have e-mail." Time between acceptance and publication is 4 months. Often comments on rejected poems. Guidelines available for SASE. Responds in 3 months. "Payment varies, but currently $30 NZD total for any and all inclusions in an issue, plus 2 contributor's copies. Overseas contributors receive a year's subscription in lieu of cash." Acquires first or one-time rights.

How to Contact No simultaneous submissions. No e-mail submissions. "Please note: U.S. stamps should not be used on SAEs. They do not work in New Zealand. Please enclose IRCs or supply e-mail address." Cover letter is required.

Contest/Award Offerings The Takahe 2010 Poetry Competition awards 1st Prize: $250 NZD; 2nd Prize: $100 NZD; plus one-year subscriptions to *Takahe* to 2 runners-up. Submit as many poems as you wish, but each much be named separately on the entry form. Submissions must be unpublished and may not be entered in other contests. Poems must be in English and typed on A4 paper, with no identifying information on the ms. Include SASE with entry for results and/or return of entries (or SAE with IRCs for overseas entrants; may also add $2 NZD to entry fee for handling and postage). All entries considered for publication in *Takahe*. Guidelines and entry form available on website. Entry fee: $5 NZD/ poem. Deadline: September 30, 2010.

Ⓝ ☐ TALENT DRIPS EROTIC PUBLISHINGS

(216)799-9775. E-mail: talent_drips_eroticpublishing@lycos.com. Website: http:// ashygirlforgirls.tripod.com/talentdripseroticpublishings. **Contact:** Kimberly Steele, founder. *Talent Drips*, published bimonthly online, focuses solely on showcasing new erotic fiction.

Magazines Needs Wants erotic poetry and short stories.

How to Contact Submit 2-3 poems at a time, maximum 30 lines each by e-mail to talent_ drips_eroticapublishing@lycos.com. Considers previously published and simultaneous submissions. Accepts e-mail pasted into body of message. Reads submissions during publication months only. Time between acceptance and publication is 2 months. Guidelines available on website. Responds in 3 weeks. Pays $10 for each accepted poem. Acquires first rights, electronic rights. Work to be archived on the site for a year.

Contest/Award Offerings Talent Drips Erotic Publishings Poet of the Year Contest is held annually. Prizes: $75, $50, and certificate. Deadline: December 15. Guidelines on website.

Tips "Does not want sci-fi or fantasy submissions; mythical creatures having pointless sex is not a turn-on. Vampires are not a turn-on. I'm looking for more romantic—but still erotic—original plots than 'the beast takes the submissive maiden' stuff."

$ ◯ ◎ TALES OF THE TALISMAN

P.O. Box 2194, Mesilla Park NM 88047-2194. E-mail: hadrosaur@zianet.com. Website: www.talesofthetalisman.com.

Magazines Needs *Tales of the Talisman*, published quarterly, prints "well-written, thought-provoking science fiction and fantasy." Wants "strong visual imagery. Strong emotion from a sense of fun to more melancholy is good." Does not want "graphic/gory violence or poetry that strays too far from the science fiction/fantasy genre." Has published poetry by Mike Allen, Ian Watson, David Kopaska-Merkel, Terrie Leigh Relf, and Deborah P. Kolodji. *Tales of the Talisman* is 86 pages, 8¼ × 10½, printed on 60 lb. white paper, perfect-bound, with full-color cardstock cover. Receives about 500 poems/year, accepts up to 5%. Press run is 200 (100 subscribers). Single copy: $8; subscription: $20/year. Make checks payable to Hadrosaur Productions.

How to Contact Submit 1-5 poems at a time. Considers previously published poems; no simultaneous submissions. Accepts e-mail submissions (pasted into body of message); no disk submissions. "For e-mail submissions, place the word 'Hadrosaur' in the subject line. Submissions that do not include this will be destroyed unread. Postal submissions will not be returned unless sufficient postage is provided." Accepts submissions from January 1-February 15 and July 1-August 15. Cover letter is preferred. Time between acceptance and publication is one year. Occasionally comments on rejected poems. Guidelines available for SASE or on website. Responds in 1 month. Sends prepublication galleys on request. Pays $4/poem plus 1 contributor's copy. Acquires one-time rights.

Tips "Read absolutely everything you can get your hands on, especially poetry outside your genre of choice, and ask 'What if?' This is a great source for original speculative poems."

◲ TAPROOT LITERARY REVIEW

P.O. Box 204, Ambridge PA 15003. (724)266-8476. E-mail: taproot10@aol.com. **Contact:** Tikvah Feinstein, editor.

Magazines Needs *Taproot Literary Review*, published annually, is "a very respected anthology with increasing distribution. We publish some of the best poets in the U.S. We enjoy all types and styles of poetry from emerging writers to established writers to those who have become valuable and old friends who share their new works with us." Has published poetry by Shirley Barasch, Holly Day, Alena Horowitz, Chris Waters, Ellaraine Lockie, Craig Sipe, Greg Moglia, Elizabeth Swados, B.Z. Niditch and Robert Penick. *Taproot Literary Review* is about 95 pages, offset-printed on white stock, with one-color glossy cover. Circulation is 500. Single copy: $8.95; subscription: $7.50. Sample: $5.

How to Contact Submit up to 5 poems at a time. Lines/poem: 35 maximum. No previously published poems or simultaneous submissions. Accepts submissions by e-mail (pasted into body of message), but "we would rather have a hard copy. Also, we cannot answer without a SASE." Cover letter is required (with general information). Reads submissions September

1-December 31 only. Guidelines available for SASE. Sometimes sends prepublication galleys. Pays 1 contributor's copy; additional copies are $6.50 each. Open to receiving books for review consideration. Send query first.

Contest/Award Offerings Sponsors the annual Taproot Writer's Workshop Annual Writing Contest. 1st Prize: $25 and publication in *Taproot Literary Review*; 2nd and 3rd Prizes: publication. Submit 5 poems of literary quality, in any form, on any subject except porn, religion, and politics. **Entry fee:** $12/5 poems (no longer than 35 lines each); fee includes copy of *Taproot*. **Deadline:** December 31. Winners announced the following March.

Tips "We strive toward compiling the finest collection of poetry available and publish the best poetry we receive in a variety of styles and subjects, so long as it's literary quality, memorable, and speaks to us deeply. We love poetry that stuns, surprises, amuses, and disarms."

▣ ☑ TARPAULIN SKY

E-mail: editors@tarpaulinsky.com (inquiries) or submissions@tarpaulinsky.com (submissions). Website: www.tarpaulinsky.com. **Contact:** Poetry Editors. Established 2002. *Tarpaulin Sky*, published biannually in print and online, features "highest-quality poetry, prose, cross-genre work, art, photography, interviews, and reviews. We are open to all styles and forms, providing the forms appear inevitable and/or inextricable from the poems. We are especially fond of inventive/experimental and cross-/trans-genre work. The best indication of our aesthetic is found in the journal we produce: Please read it before submitting your work. Also, hardcopy submissions may be received by different editors at different times; check guidelines before submitting." Has published poetry by Jenny Boully, Matthea Harvey, Bin Ramke, Eleni Sikelianos, Juliana Spahr, and Joshua Marie Wilkinson. Receives about 3,000 poems/year.

How to Contact Submit 4-6 poems at a time. Considers simultaneous submissions; no previously published poems. Accepts e-mail submissions ("best received as attachments in .rtf or .pdf formats"); no disk submissions. Cover letter is preferred. Reads submissions year round. Time between acceptance and publication is 2-6 months. "Poems are read by all editors. We aim for consensus." Rarely comments on rejected poems. Guidelines available for SASE, by e-mail, or on website. Responds in 1-4 months. Pays in contributor's copies and "by waiving readings fees for Tarpaulin Sky Press Open Reading Periods." Always sends prepublication galleys (electronic). Acquires first rights. Reviews books/chapbooks of poetry.

☑ TAR RIVER POETRY

Erwin Building Mailroom, East Carolina University, Greenville NC 27858-4353. E-mail: TarRiverPoetry@gmail.com. Website: www.tarriverpoetry.com. **Contact:** Luke Whisnant, Editor. *Tar River Poetry*, published twice/year, is an "'all-poetry' magazine that publishes 40-50 poems per issue, providing the talented beginner and experienced writer with a forum that features all styles and forms of verse." Wants "skillful use of figurative language; poems that appeal to the senses." Does not want "sentimental, flat-statement poetry." Has published poetry by William Stafford, Sharon Olds, Carolyn Kizer, A.R. Ammons, and Claudia Emerson. Has also published "many other well-known poets, as well as numerous new and emerging poets." *Tar River Poetry* is 64 pages, digest-sized, professionally printed on salmon stock, with matte card cover with photo. Receives 6,000-8,000 submissions/year, accepts 80-100. Press run is 900 (500 subscribers, 125 libraries). Subscription: $12/year; $20/two years. Sample: $6.50.

How to Contact Submit no more than 5 poems at a time. No previously published poems or simultaneous submissions. Accepts e-mail submissions only; no print submissions. "Detailed submission instructions appear on the website, along with writer's guidelines." Check website for reading periods: "we do not read manuscripts from May through August—submissions will be returned unread." Rarely comments on rejections "due to volume of submissions." Guidelines available for SASE or on website. Responds in 6 weeks. Pays 2 contributor's copies. Acquires first rights. Reviews books of poetry in 4,000 words maximum, single- or multi-book format. Query for reviews.

Tips "Writers of poetry should first be readers of poetry. Read and study traditional and contemporary poetry."

▣ ☑ TATTOO HIGHWAY

E-mail: submissions@tattoohighway.org. Website: www.tattoohighway.org. **Contact:** Poetry Editor: Rochelle Nameroff. *On Hiatus until 9/15/2010. Do not send mss until then. Tattoo Highway*, published biannually online, is a journal of poetry, literary prose, new media, and art. "We're open to most styles; only criterion is quality." Wants "language that is fresh, vivid, and original; writing that is smart and a little edgy, that engages with the world beyond the writer's own psyche. We like formal poetry if well handled." Does not want "self-pity, navel-contemplation, clichés, workshop hackery." Has published poetry by Oliver Rice, Carol Frith, Paul Hostovsky, Lyn Lifshin, Doug Ramspeck, Judith Skillman. Receives about 800 poems/year, accepts about 50.

How to Contact Submit up to 5 poems at a time. Considers previously published poems (if they've appeared in small-circulation print journals; unpublished work preferred) and simultaneous submissions ("but please let us know promptly if you place your piece elsewhere"). Accepts e-mail submissions (pasted into body of message) only. "For hypertext or New Media (Flash, etc.) submissions, please provide a URL where we may view the work." Reading periods vary; "typically last about three months. Blind readings by editorial board. Several rounds of 'triage' during the reading period, usually handled by e-mail. Face-to-face editorial meeting shortly after submission deadline, where final selections are made. Editor and poetry editor have final say." Sometimes comments on rejected poems. "If a poem has its moments, though it doesn't quite work, we try to acknowledge that. We encourage near-misses to try us again." Regularly publishes theme issues. Guidelines available on website. Responds in up to 3 months ("usually within 1 week of deadline"). Always sends prepublication galleys. No payment. Acquires first electronic rights; rights revert to author 90 days after online publication date.

Contest/Award Offerings "Picture Worth 500 Words" contest for poetry/prose. No entry fee; small prizes. See guidelines on website.

Tips "Read some past issues before submitting." Upcoming Themes: Winter/Spring 2011: TH/21: Gambler's Choice, Summer/Fall 2011: TH/22: Gone to the Dogs (the Critters Issue).

⊞ ☑ THE TAYLOR TRUST: POETRY AND PROSE

P.O. Box 903456, Palmdale CA 93590-3456. E-mail: lavonne.taylor@sbcglobal.net. Website: thetaylortrust.wordpress.com. **Contact:** LaVonne Taylor, editor and publisher.

Magazines Needs *The Taylor Trust*, published quarterly, "considers ourselves egalitarian in that we accept most poetry forms. We also accept flash fiction, short stories, nonfiction. We publish more than one poem per author in each issue." Wants "all styles and forms. Prefers uplifting subject matter. Humorous poetry also accepted." Does not want "profanity or sexually explicit material. No age restrictions. Child must state age and give a short bio. Parental permission also required." Has published poetry by Mary L. Ports, Trisha Nelson, J.F. Connolly, Fredrick Zydek, John Fitzpatrick, Michael Lee Johnson. *The Taylor Trust* is 60-100 pages, digest-sized, press run, perfect bound with a heavy, clay-coated embossed stock full-bleed color photo background cover. Receives 800 poems/year; accepts 90%. Single copy: $10; subscription $40.

How to Contact Submit 6 poems at a time, between 4-100 lines. Considers previously published poems ("as long as the author owns the publication rights") and simultaneous submissions ("with the understanding that it is the author's duty to inform all concerned when a poem is accepted"). Accepts e-mail submissions pasted into body of e-mail message; disk submissions. Cover letter is required. "We require a bio of about 150-200 words with publication history adn any other information the author cares to provide. We prefer not to return declined hard copies, but if the author requests it, an SASE is required with postal submittals. SASEs are needed with requests for guidelines." Reads submissions year round. Submit seasonal poems 3 months in advance. Time between acceptance and publication is 3 months. Poems are circulated to an editorial board. Sometimes comments on rejected poems. Regularly published theme issues loosely based on the seasons. Upcoming themes available in magazine, by e-mail, and on website. Guidelines available for SASE, by e-mail, and on website. Responds in 1 week. Pays 1 contributor's copy. Acquires one-time rights, electronic rights, "selected poems from each print publication will be posted on the site." Rights revert to poet upon publication. Reviews poetry books, chapbooks, and other magazines and journals in 500-1,000 words.

Additional Information "Fee-based publishing on demand is available on a limited basis."

Tips "Follow the advice in *Poet's Market*. Behave professionally at all times. If your poetry is declined, try again with different subject matter or a different form."

☑ ◎ THE TEACHER'S VOICE

P.O. Box 150384, Kew Gardens NY 11415. E-mail: editor@the-teachers-voice.org. Website: www.the-teachers-voice.org. **Contact:** Andres Castro, founding/managing editor. (Specialized: the American teacher experience, from pre-K to university professor)

Magazines Needs *The Teacher's Voice*, was founded as an experimental hardcopy literary magazine and is now free and online. "We publish poetry, short stories, creative nonfiction, and essays that reflect the many different American teacher experiences." Wants "all styles and forms. We ask to see critical creative writing that takes risks without being overly self-indulgent or inaccessible. We welcome work that ranges from 'art for art's sake' to radically social/political. Writing that illuminates the most pressing/urgent issues in American education and the lives of teachers gets special attention." Has published poetry by Edward

Francisco, Sapphire, Hal Sirowitz, and Antler. Receives about 1,000 poems/year, accepts about 10%.

How to Contact Submit 3-5 poems at a time. Lines/poem: no limits. Considers previously published poems (if rights are held by the author) and simultaneous submissions (contact if submission has been accepted elsewhere). No e-mail or disk submissions. Send prose pieces under 2,000 words. Cover letter is preferred. "Are you a teacher, administrator, parent, student, librarian, custodian, coach, security officer, etc? We do not accept responsibility for submissions or queries not accompanied by a SASE with adequate postage." Reads submissions year round. Time between acceptance and publication is 4 months to 1 year. Poems are circulated to an editorial board. Guidelines available on website. Sometimes sends prepublication galleys "if requested." Acquires first rights and electronic reprint rights. Rights revert to poet "after work is first electronically published and archived on this site; no material on this site may be reproduced in any form without permission from their individual authors." No longer accepts online submissions.

Additional Information "Since we publish open as well as theme issues (that require enough thematic pieces to be compiled) and do rely on readership financial support, our publishing schedule and format may vary from year to year. We publish hardcopy limited press collections when funds allow. Our production goal is to showcase strong cohesive collections that support our mission and satisfy the needs of particular issues. For the moment, our new focus on electronic publishing is a matter of survival that offers many new possibilities and opportunities in keeping with the changing times."

Contest/Award Offerings Sponsors *The Teacher's Voice* Annual Chapbook Contest and *The Teacher's Voice* Annual Poetry Contest for Unpublished Poets. Guidelines for both contests available for SASE, by e-mail, or on website.

Tips "(1) Please, be daring. Take some personal risks in a few pieces. If you find it comfortable to write about your teaching experiences and students without ever making even subtle connections to history, current events, political and social institutions, and public policies, we may not be for you as we move ahead. (2) If you must, feel free to include a pseudonym in your cover letter. (3) If you are a teacher, become a poet. If you are a poet, become a teacher."

☑ ◎ TEXAS POETRY CALENDAR

Dos Gatos Press, 1310 Crestwood Rd., Austin TX 78722. (512)467-0678. E-mail: editors@ dosgatospress.org. Website: www.dosgatospress.org. **Contact:** Scott Wiggerman or Cindy Huyser, Co-Editors; David Meischen, Managing Editor.

Magazines Needs *Texas Poetry Calendar*, published annually in August, features a "week-by-week calendar side-by-side with poems with a Texas connection." Wants "a wide variety of styles, voices, and forms, including rhyme—though a Texas connection is preferred. Humor is welcome! Poetry *only*!" Does not want "children's poetry, erotic poetry, profanity, obscure poems, previously published work, or poems over 35 lines." *Texas Poetry Calendar* is about 144 pages, digest-sized, offset-printed, spiral-bound, with full-color cardstock cover. Receives about 600 poems/year, accepts about 70-75. Press run is 1,500; 70 distributed free to contributors. Single copy: $13.95 plus $3 shipping. Make checks payable to Dos Gatos Press.

How to Contact Submit 3 poems at a time. Lines/poem: 35 maximum, "including spaces and title." Considers simultaneous submissions; no previously published poems. No fax, e-mail, or disk submissions. Cover letter is required. "Include a short bio (100-200 words) and poem titles in cover letter. Also include e-mail address and phone number. Do not include poet's name on the poems themselves!" Reads submissions year round. Time between acceptance and publication is 3-4 months. Poems are circulated to an editorial board. Never comments on rejected poems. **"Entry fee for the *Texas Poetry Calendar* Awards ($5 for 3 poems) is required for all submissions—all poems submitted are eligible for cash awards."** (See Contest/Award Offerings below.) Guidelines available in magazine, by e-mail, or on website. Responds "only once a year, in spring." Sometimes sends prepublication galleys. Pays 1 contributor's copy. Acquires first, electronic, and reprint rights.

Contest/Award Offerings Sponsors the annual Texas Poetry Calendar Awards, offering 1st Prize: $250; 2nd Prize: $150; 3rd Prize: $75. "Award-winning poems receive special recognition in the calendar in which they are printed." Submit 3 poems. Guidelines available in magazine, by e-mail, or on website. **Entry fee:** $5 for 3 poems. **Deadline:** March 20 (postmark). "Judged by a nationally known poet—Robert McDowell, Naomi Shihab Nye, Kathleen Pierce, and Mark Doty."

$ ☑ ◎ THEMA

Thema Literary Society, P.O. Box 8747, Metairie LA 70011-8747. E-mail: thema@cox.net. Website: http://members.cox.net/thema. **Contact:** Gail Howard, Poetry Editor.

Magazines Needs *THEMA*, published triannually, uses poetry related to specific themes. "Each issue is based on an unusual premise. Please, please send SASE for guidelines before submitting poetry to find out the upcoming themes." Does not want "scatologic language, alternate lifestyle, explicit love poetry." Has published poetry by Rosalie Calabrese, Sharon Lask Munson, Robert Manaster, and Lori Williams. *THEMA* is 120 pages, digest-sized professionally printed, with glossy card cover. Receives about 400 poems/year, accepts about 8%. Press run is 400 (230 subscribers, 30 libraries). Subscription: $20 U.S./$30 foreign. Sample $10 U.S./$15 foreign.

How to Contact Submit up to 3 poems at a time. Include SASE. "All submissions should be typewritten on standard 8½ × 11 paper. Submissions are accepted all year, but evaluated after specified deadlines." Specify target theme. Editor comments on submissions. Upcoming themes and guidelines available in magazine, for SASE, by e-mail, or on website. Pays $10/poem and 1 contributor's copy. Acquires one-time rights.

Tips "Do not submit to *THEMA* unless you have one of *THEMA*'s upcoming themes in mind. And be sure to specify which one!"

ℕ THE VILLA

University of Wisconsin-Parkside, English Dept., Univ. of Wisconsin-Parkside, 900 Wood Rd., Box 2000, Kenosha WI 53414-2000. (262) 595-2139. Fax: (262) 595-2271. E-mail: villa@straylightmag.com. Website: http://straylightmag.com. Editor: Dean Karpowicz. **Contact:** Appropriate genre editor (revolving editors). The Villa is the web counterpart to Straylight Literary Arts Journal. We publish some crossover print material, but the Villa is centered on publishing work suited to a biannual magazine.

▣ ◯ THICK WITH CONVICTION

E-mail: twczine@yahoo.com. Website: www.angelfire.com/poetry/thickwithconviction. **Contact:** Arielle Lancaster-LaBrea and Kayla Middlebrook, editors. *Thick With Conviction*, published quarterly online, is "run by a couple of twenty-something women who are looking for fresh and exciting voices in poetry. We don't want to take a nap while we're reading, so grab our attention, make us sit up and catch our breath." Wants all genres of poetry, "poems that make us exhale a deep sigh after reading them. Basically, if we can't feel the words in front of us, we're not going to be happy. We'd like to see new and cutting edge poets who think outside the box, but still know how to keep things from getting too strange and inaccessible." Does not want "teen angst poems, religious poems, or greeting card tripe." Considers poetry by teens. Has published poetry by Kendall A. Bell, April Michelle Bratten, Rachel Bunting, Kristina Marie Darling, James H. Duncan, and Kelsey Upward. Receives about 300 poems/year, accepts about 15%.

How to Contact Submit 3-5 poems at a time. Lines/poem: no limit. Considers previously published poems; no simultaneous submissions. Accepts e-mail submissions (pasted into body of message; "any attachments will be deleted"); no disk submissions. Cover letter and bio is required. Reads submissions year-round. Submit seasonal poems 3 months in advance. Time between acceptance and publication is 3 months. Never comments on rejected poems. Guidelines available on website. Responds in "roughly 3-4 weeks." Acquires one-time rights. Rights revert to poet upon publication.

Tips "Please read the poems on our website to see what we're interested in. Read some up and coming poets on the web and don't fall into the traps of what one group of people tell you poetry is. Tell us something we've never heard or make us feel like we've been blindsided. We like that."

◯ THINK JOURNAL

P.O. Box 454, Downingtown PA 19335. (484)883-5806. E-mail: thinkjournal@yahoo.com. **Contact:** Christine Yurick, Editor.

Magazines Needs *Think Journal*, published quarterly, "focuses on words that have meaning, that are presented in a clear way, and that exhibit the skills demanded by craft. The journal prints work that achieves a balance between form and content. The most important traits that will be considered are form, structure, clarity, content, imagination, and style. *Think Journal* is 55 pages, digest-sized, desktop-printed, staple-bound with a cardstock cover containing original artwork. Single copy: $7; subscription: $20/year. Sample $6. Make checks payable to Christine Yurick.

How to Contact Submit 3-6 poems at a time, no restrictions in length. Accepts submissions by e-mail, mail. "Always include a SASE with submissions. Cover letter and brief biography preferred. Please include your e-mail address on the cover page for further communications. Include your name and address on each page of your submission." Reads submissions year round. Does not accept previously published or simultaneous submissions. Time between acceptance and publication is 6-12 months. Sometimes comments on rejected poems. Guidelines in magazine, for SASE, or on website. Responds in 2-3 months. Pays 1 contributor's copy. Acquires one-time rights. Rights revert to poet upon publication.

☑ THIRD COAST

Dept. of English, Western Michigan University, Kalamazoo MI 49008-5331. (269)387-2675. E-mail: editors@thirdcoastmagazine.com. Website: www.thirdcoastmagazine.com. **Contact:** Poetry Editors.

Magazines Needs *Third Coast*, published semiannually in March and September, is a national literary magazine of poetry, prose, creative nonfiction, translations, and drama. Wants "excellence of craft and originality of thought. Nothing trite." Has published poetry by Marianne Boruch, Terence Hayes, Alex Lemon, Philip Levine, David Shumate, Tomz Salamun, and Jean Valentine. *Third Coast* is 176 pages, digest-sized, professionally printed, perfect-bound, with 4-color cover with art. Receives about 2,000 poems/year, accepts about 1%. Press run is 1,000 (850 subscribers, 50 libraries, 100 shelf sales). Single copy: $9; subscription: $16/year, $28 for 2 years, $42 for 3 years. Sample: $6 (back issue).

How to Contact Submit up to 5 poems at a time via the Third Coast Submission Manager, found on website. Considers simultaneous submissions with notification; no previously published poems. Submissions by post will not be considered. Cover letter is preferred. "Poems should be typed single-spaced, with the author's name on each page. Stanza breaks should be double-spaced." Poems are circulated to assistant poetry editors and poetry editors; poetry editors make final decisions. Seldom comments on rejected poems. Guidelines available on website. Responds in 4 months. Pays 2 contributor's copies plus one-year subscription. Acquires first rights.

Contest/Award Offerings Sponsors an annual poetry contest. 1st Prize: $1,000 and publication; 4 finalists receive notification in prize-winning issue, possible publication, and a 3-year subscription. Guidelines available on website. **Entry fee:** $15, includes one-year subscription to *Third Coast*.

☑ THIRD WEDNESDAY: A LITERARY ARTS MAGAZINE

174 Greenside Up, Ypsilanti MI 48197. (734) 434-2409. E-mail: submissions@thirdwednesday. org; LaurenceWT@aol.com.

Magazines Needs Wants "all styles and forms of poetry are welcome, from formal to experimental. Emphasis is placed on the ideas conveyed, craft and language, beauty of expression, and the picture that extends beyond the frame of the poem." Does not want "hate-filled diatribes, pornography (though eroticism is acceptable), prose masquerading as poetry, first drafts of anything." Has published poetry by Wanda Coleman, Philip Dacey, Richard Luftig, Simon Perchik, Marge Piercy, Charles Harper Webb. Receives 800 poems/year. Press run is 125. Single copy: $8; subscription: $30. Make checks payable to Third Wednesday.

How to Contact Submit 1-5 poems at a time. Considers simultaneous submissions. Accepts submissions through e-mail, which is preferred to mail. Include SASE if submitting via postal mail. Reads submissions year round. Submit seasonal poems 3 months in advance. Time between acceptance and publication is 3 months. Poems are circulated to an editorial board. "Submissions are coded by executive editor and sent blind to members of editorial board; said members send up or down votes to executive editor who accepts pieces according to rule of majority." Sometimes comments on rejected poems. Guidelines available in magazine, by e-mail, and on website. Responds in 6-8 weeks. Pays $3-5 honorarium and 2 contributor's copies. Acquires first North American serial rights, electronic rights. "TW retains the right to reproduce accepted work as samples on our website." Rights revert to poet upon publication.

Tips "First and foremost, be a reader of contemporary poetry. Support the little magazines you wish to not disappear. Be professional in your correspondence; take risks with your poetry. If your poem does not surprise you during composition, it will fail to surprise the reader as well. A poem succeeds when its sounds and sense resonate both together and apart. Read samples of work from magazines to which you submit; blind submissions waste everyone's time. Proofread! Realize that rejection is nothing personal—aim high, but do so with a thick skin. Lastly, keep submitting—every market has its own flavor, and each editor has individual biases."

$ ☑ THE THREEPENNY REVIEW

E-mail: wlesser@threepennyreview.com. Website: www.threepennyreview.com. **Contact:** Wendy Lesser, Editor. *The Threepenny Review*, published quarterly, is "a national review of literature, performing and visual arts, and social articles aimed at the intelligent, well-read (but not necessarily academic) reader." Wants "formal, narrative, short poems (and others). No bias against formal poetry; in fact, a slight bias in favor of it." Has published poetry by Anne Carson, Frank Bidart, Seamus Heaney, Robert Pinsky, and Louise Gluück. *The Threepenny Review* is a 36-page tabloid. Receives about 4,500 submissions of poetry/year, accepts about 40 poems. Press run is 10,000 (8,000 subscribers, 150 libraries). Subscription: $25. Sample: $12.

Poetry Submit up to 5 poems at a time. Lines/poem: 100 maximum ("exceptions are possible"). No previously published poems or simultaneous submissions. No e-mail submissions accepted. Do not submit mss September-December. Guidelines available for SASE or on website. Responds in up to 2 months. Pays $200/poem plus one-year subscription. Acquires first serial rights. Guidelines available for SASE.

☑ TIGER'S EYE

Tiger's Eye Press, P.O. Box 2935, Eugene OR 97402. E-mail: tigerseyepoet@yahoo.com. Website: www.tigerseyejournal.com. **Contact:** Colette Jonopulos and JoAn Osborne, editors.

Magazines Needs *Tiger's Eye: A Journal of Poetry*, published semiannually, features both established and undiscovered poets. "Besides publishing the work of several exceptional poets in each issue, we feature two poets in interviews, giving the reader insight into their lives and writing habits." Wants "both free verse and traditional forms; no restrictions on subject or length. We welcome sonnets, haibun, haiku, ghazals, villenelles, etc. We pay special attention to unusual forms and longer poems that may have difficulty being placed elsewhere. Poems with distinct imagery and viewpoint are read and re-read by the editors and considered for publication." Has published poetry by Willis Barnstone, Kathy Kieth, Joyce Odam, Fiona Sze-Lorrain, and David Morse. *Tiger's Eye* is 64 pages, saddle-stitched. Receives 1,000 poems/year, accepts 100. Press run is 300. Single copy: $6; subscription: $11 for 2 issues. Make checks payable to Tiger's Eye Press.

How to Contact Submit 3-5 poems at a time, no multiple submissions. Considers simultaneous submissions with notification if a poem is accepted elsewhere; no previously published poems. No e-mail submissions. Cover letter is required. Include brief bio. SASE for notification only; no submissions are returned. Reads submissions year-round; deadlines are February 28 and August 31. Time between acceptance and publication is 3 months. "All poems are read by the editors, then filed as poems we definitely want to publish, those we are still considering, and those we aren't publishing. Our two featured poets are chosen, then letters and e-mails are sent out." Seldom comments on rejected poems. Guidelines available in magazine or on website. Responds in 6 months. Always sends prepublication galleys. Pays one contributor's copy to each poet, 2 to featured poets. Acquires one-time rights.

Additional Information *Tiger's Eye* nominates for *The Pushcart Prize*.

Contest/Award Offerings Tiger's Eye Annual Poetry Contest (see separate listing in Contests & Awards) and Editor's Choice Chapbook Contest. "Our annual poetry contest awards $500, $100, $50. Send 3 pages of poetry, cover letter with poet's name and contact information (no identifying information on mss pages) SASE, and $10 entry fee. **Deadline: February 28.** Our chapbook contest awards $100 and 25 copies of the winning chapbook. Do not send entire mss, but 5 pages of poetry, cover letter with poet's name and contact information (no identifying contact information on mss pages), SASE, and $10 entry fee. **Deadline: August 31.**

Tips "Poems with clean images, unique subjects, and strong voices have a good chance of being published in *Tiger's Eye*."

☑ TIMBER CREEK REVIEW

8969 UNCG Sta, Greensboro NC 27413. E-mail: timber_creek_review@hoopsmail.com. Willa Schmidt, assoc. editor. **Contact:** John M. Freiermuth, editor. Newsletter: 5½ × 8½; 76-84 pages; computer generated on copy paper; saddle-stapled with colored paper cover; some illustrations. "Fiction, humor/satire, poetry and travel for a general audience."

Magazines Needs *Timber Creek Review*, published quarterly, prints short stories, literary nonfiction, and poetry. Accepts all forms of poetry but does not want religious or pornographic. Has published poetry by Rod Farmer, Jan Ball, Robin Schectman, Joanna Solfrian, Barb Cranford, Richard Luftig, Robert Cooperman, Howard Winn, Edward M. O. Supranowicz, Maria Bennett, Carol Frith and Robert H. Deluty. *Timber Creek Review* is 80-84 pages, digest-sized, laser-printed, stapled, with colored paper cover. Receives about 1,000 poems/year, accepts about 8.5%. Press run is 150 (120 subscribers, 2 libraries, 30 shelf sales). Single copy: $5; subscription: $18; overseas mail add $8. Make checks payable to J.M. Freiermuth.

How to Contact Submit 3-6 poems at a time by U.S. mail. Lines/poem: 3 minimum, "rarely over 30." Considers simultaneous submissions; no previously published poems. No e-mail or disk submissions. Cover letter is expected. Reads submissions year round. Submit seasonal poems 10 months in advance. Time between acceptance and publication is 3-6 months. Never comments on rejected poems. Occasionally publishes theme issues. Guidelines available for SASE or by e-mail. Responds in up to 6 months. Pays one contributor's copy. Acquires first North American serial rights.

Tips "Turn off your TV and read that poety magazine that published your last poem, and maybe someone else will read your poem, too!"

☑ ◎ TIME OF SINGING, A MAGAZINE OF CHRISTIAN POETRY

P.O. Box 149, Conneaut Lake PA 16316. E-mail: timesing@zoominternet.net. Website: www.timeofsinging.com. **Contact:** Lora H. Zill, Editor.

Magazines Needs *Time of Singing, A Magazine of Christian Poetry*, published 4 times/year, seeks "poems that 'show' rather than 'tell.' The viewpoint is unblushingly Christian—but in its widest and most inclusive meaning." Wants free verse and well-crafted rhyme; would like to see more forms. Does not want "collections of uneven lines, sermons that rhyme, unstructured 'prayers,' and trite sing-song rhymes." Has published poetry by John Grey, Luci Shaw, Bob Hostetler, Tony Cosier, Barbara Crooker, and Charles Waugaman. *Time of Singing* is 44 pages, digest-sized, offset from typescript. Receives more than 800 submissions/year, accepts about 175. Press run is 250 (150 subscribers). Subscription: $17 USD, $21 USD Canada, $30 USD overseas. Sample: $4, or 2 for $7 (postage paid).

How to Contact Submit up to 5 poems at a time. Lines/poem: prefers less than 40, "but will publish up to 60 lines if exceptional." Considers previously published poems (indicate when/where appeared) and simultaneous submissions. Accepts e-mail submissions (pasted into body of message or as attachment). Poems should be single-spaced. Time between acceptance and publication is up to one year. Comments "with suggestions for improvement if close to publication." Guidelines available for SASE, by e-mail, or on website. Responds in 4 months. Pays 1 contributor's copy.

Contest/Award Offerings Sponsors theme contests for specific issues. Guidelines available for SASE, by e-mail, or on website.

Tips "Study the craft. Be open to critique. A poet is often too close to his/her work and needs a critical, honest eye. *Time of Singing* publishes more literary-style verse, not greeting card style. Cover letters aren't needed, but if you do send one, it's unprofessional to use it to explain what your poem means. It shows me you don't have the confidence in your work, and you don't trust me, your first reader, to 'get it.' Poems that have to be explained in a cover letter are almost always rejected."

▣ ☑ ◎ TORCH: POETRY, PROSE AND SHORT STORIES BY AFRICAN AMERICAN WOMEN

E-mail: poetry@torchpoetry.org. Website: www.torchpoetry.org. **Contact:** Amanda Johnston, editor.

Magazines Needs *TORCH: Poetry, Prose, and Short Stories by African American Women*, published semiannually online, provides "a place to celebrate contemporary poetry, prose, and short stories by experienced and emerging writers alike. We prefer our contributors to take risks, and offer a diverse body of work that examines and challenges preconceived notions regarding race, ethnicity, gender roles, and identity." Has published poetry by Sharon Bridgforth, Patricia Smith, Shia Shabazz, Ana-Maurine Lara, and Remica L. Bingham. Receives about 250+ submissions/year, accepts about 20. Number of unique visitors: 300+/month.

How to Contact Submit 3 poems at a time. No previously published poems or simultaneous submissions. Accepts e-mail submissions only (as one attachment). Send to poetry@torchpoetry.org with "Poetry Submission" in subject line. Cover letter is preferred (in the body of the e-mail). Reads submissions April 1-August 31 only. Time between acceptance and publication is 2-7 months. Sometimes comments on rejected poems. Sometimes publishes theme issues. Guidelines available on website. Always sends prepublication galleys. No payment. Acquires rights to publish accepted work in online issue and in archives. Rights revert to poets upon publication.

Also Offers "Within *TORCH*, we offer a special section called Flame that features an interview, biography, and work sample by an established writer as well as an introduction to their Spark—an emerging writer who inspires them and adds to the boundless voice of creative writing by Black women." A free online newsletter is available; see website.

Tips "Black women, write freely. Know that your words are wanted, needed, and safe here. Read the previous issues online for examples of the type of writing *Torch* publishes."

☐ ◎ TRANSCENDENT VISIONS

251 S. Olds Blvd., 84-E, Fairless Hills PA 19030-3426. *Transcendent Visions* is published once a year at the beginning of the year. It provides "a creative outlet for psychiatric survivors/ex-mental patients." Wants "experimental, confessional poems; strong poems dealing with issues we face. Any length or subject matter is OK, but shorter poems are more likely to be published." Does not want "rhyming poetry." Recently published work by White Elephant, Gabe Kaufman, Jamey Damert, Marc Pernaino, Teacup Mary, K.J. Kabza, and Arthur Longworth. *Transcendent Visions* is 50-60 pages, magazine-sized, photocopied, corner-stapled, with paper cover. Receives about 100 poems/year, accepts 20%. Press run is 250 (50 subscribers). Subscription: $6. Sample: $3. Make checks payable to David Kime. (Specialized: psychiatric survivors & ex-mental patients)

How to Contact We start reading submissions in May. Submit 5 poems at a time. Considers previously published poems and simultaneous submissions. Cover letter is preferred. "Please tell me something unique about you, but I do not care about all the places you have been published." Time between acceptance and publication is 3 to 9 months. Guidelines available for SASE. Responds in 4 months. Pays one contributor's copy. Acquires first or one-time rights. Staff reviews books/chapbooks of poetry and other magazines in 20 words. Send materials for review consideration. Recently published work by Gloria del Vecchio, Carolina Morales, George Held, Less Cammer, Leonard Cirino, and Kelley Jean White.

Tips "Find your own voice. Please send camera-ready poems, single-spaced. I don't like poems that go all over the page."

Ⓝ ◪ TRIBECA POETRY REVIEW

25 Leonard Street, New York NY 10013. E-mail: editor@tribecareview.org. Website: www. tribecareview.org. **Contact:** Kenlynne Rini, editor.

Magazines Needs *Tribeca Poetry Review*, published annually in October, is "a publication emerging out of the thick poetic history that is downtown New York. It seeks to expose its readers to the best smattering of poetry we can get our hands on. TPR will showcase new pieces by seasoned poets as well as illuminate the work of fresh voices." Wants "the kind of poetry that squirms in your head for days, hopefully longer, after reading it. Send us your best work. Will publish all forms (including traditional poesy, spoken word, or your experimental pieces) providing they translate well on the page, are intelligent, and well-crafted. New York City poets are always encouraged to submit their work, but this is NOT strictly a regional publication." Does not want "overly self-absorbed poems; pieces so abstract that all meaning and pleasure is lost on anyone but the poet; first drafts, goofy word play, trite nostalgia." Considers poetry by teens. "It's the poem itself that needs to resonate with readers, so the age of the poet means little. Occasionally, poetry by a 14 year old is more profound than the drivel generated by those adults who hang out unnecessarily in coffee shops and believe themselves 'poets.'" *Tribeca Poetry Review* is approximately 100 pages, digest-sized, professionally printed, flat-spine bound, with artwork cover. Press run is 500.

How to Contact Submit no more than 5 poems at a time up to 10 pages in total. No previously published poems or simultaneous submissions. Cover letter is required. "Please do not use your cover letter as a place to explain your poems. The letter is a place to introduce yourself and your work but not sell or explain either. Your name, address, contact phone and e-mail should be on each page submitted." Reads submissions year round. Time between acceptance and publication is up to 1 year. Sometimes comments on rejected poems. Guidelines on website. Responds in 2 months. Pays 2 contributor's copies. Acquires first North American serial rights.

☑ TULANE REVIEW

122 Norman Mayer, New Orleans LA 70118. E-mail: litsoc@tulane.edu. Website: www.tulane.edu/~litsoc. **Contact:** Kathleen Weaver, Poetry Editor. *Tulane Review*, published biannually, is a national literary journal seeking quality submissions of prose, poetry, and art. "We consider all types of poetry." Wants "imaginative poems with bold, inventive images." Has published poetry by Virgil Suaárez, Tom Chandler, Gaylord Brewer, and Ryan Van Cleave. *Tulane Review* is 60 pages, 7 × 9, perfect-bound, with 100# cover with full-color artwork. Receives about 1,200 poems/year, accepts about 30. Single copy: $5; subscription: $10. Make checks payable to *Tulane Review*.

How to Contact Submit up to 2 poems at a time. Lines/poem: 1-2 pages. Prose should be 5,000/max. Considers simultaneous submissions; previously published pieces will be considered. Accepts e-mail submissions; no fax or disk submissions. Cover letter is required. Include 1-3 sentence biography. Reads submissions year-round. Time between acceptance and publication is 3 months. "Poems are reviewed anonymously by a review board under a poetry editor's supervision. Recommendations are given to the editor, who makes final publication decisions." Often comments on rejected poems. Guidelines available in magazine, for SASE, by e-mail, or on website. Responds in 2 months. Pays 2 contributor's copies. Acquires first North American serial rights.

☑ ◎ THE TULE REVIEW

Sacramento Poetry Center, 1719 25th St., Sacramento CA 95816. (916)451-5569. E-mail: tulereview@sacramentopoetrycenter.org. Website: www.sacramentopoetrycenter.org. **Contact:** Theresa McCourt or Linda Collins.

Magazines Needs *The Tule Review*, published 1-2 times/year, uses "poetry, book reviews, and essays concerning contemporary poetry" Wants "all styles and forms of poetry." Primarily publishes poets living in the greater Sacramento area, but accepts work from anywhere. Has published poetry by Gary Snyder, Diane DiPrima, Jack Hirschman, Julia Connor, Joyce Odam, and Douglas Blazek. *The Tule Review* is 40-60 pages, digest-sized, perfect-bound, with cover artwork. Receives about 500 poems/year, accepts about 10-20%. Press run is 500; 50 distributed free to contributors and for review. Single copy: $10 ppd;

subscription: $30/year (includes *Poetry Now*, a monthly publication). Make checks payable to Sacramento Poetry Center.

How to Contact Submit up to 6 poems at a time. Lines/poem: 96 maximum. Considers previously published poems; no simultaneous submissions. Prefers e-mail (include poems in a single attachment). Include name, street, and e-mail address on each page of submission. Provide short, 5 line bio. Reads submissions year round. Submit seasonal poems 6 months in advance. Time between acceptance and publication is 1-6 months. Poems are circulated to an editorial board. Sometimes comments on rejected poems. Sometimes publishes theme issues. Guidelines and upcoming themes available by e-mail, or on website. Responds in 3-4 months. Pays 1 contributor's copy. Acquires first North American serial rights. Rights revert to poet upon publication. See website for other publications and contests.

Tips "Send us your best work!"

◧ ◎ TUNDRA: THE JOURNAL OF THE SHORT POEM

22230 NE 28th Place, Sammamish WA 98074-6408. E-mail: WelchM@aol.com. Website: http://sites.google.com/site/tundrashortpoem/. **Contact:** Michael Dylan Welch, Editor. *Tundra: The Journal of the Short Poem* showcases all short poetry, including haiku, tanka, and other genres. Wants "short poems of 13 or fewer lines rooted in immediate and objective imagery, including haiku and tanka." Does not want religious, topical, or confessional poetry. Has published poetry by Dana Gioia, X.J. Kennedy, Jane Hirshfield, Peter Pereira, Robert Bly, and Madeleine DeFrees. *Tundra* is 128 pages, digest-sized, offset-printed, perfect-bound, with glossy cover. Receives about 14,000 poems/year, accepts less than 1%. Press run is 1,200 (700 subscribers, 10 libraries, 50 shelf sales); 10 distributed free to such places as poetry centers. Single copy: $9; subscription: $21 for 3 issues. Make checks payable to Michael Dylan Welch.

How to Contact *NOTE: Due to a backlog of submissions, we advise you not to submit at this time. A notice welcoming submissions will appear on this site when the backlog clears. Thank you for your patience.* Submit 3-5 poems at a time ("up to 10 is okay if as short as haiku"). No previously published poems or simultaneous submissions. Accepts e-mail submissions (pasted into body of message; no attachments); no disk submissions. "Always include your full postal address with each e-mail submission." Cover letter is optional; "okay the first time you submit, but unnecessary thereafter unless you write something you are sure the editor needs to know. *Tundra* does not publish bios, so there's no need to include them except for the editor's information. Please include a #10 SASE with sufficient postage for return of the manuscript or for a response." Reads submissions year round. Time between acceptance and publication "varies, but is sometimes up to a year. The editor makes the sole decision, and may occasionally offer suggestions on poems whether accepted or returned. The editor will clearly indicate if he wants to see a revision." Recommends reading an issue before submitting, "but no purchase or subscription is required." Guidelines available for SASE, by e-mail, or on website. Responds in 3-4 months. Sometimes sends prepublication galleys. Pays 1 contributor's copy. Acquires first rights. "Rights revert to author after publication, but we may want to include selected poems on website in the future." Reviews books/chapbooks of poetry in 500-2,000 words, single- and multi-book format. Send materials for review consideration to Michael Dylan Welch.

Tips "If your work centers on immediate and objective imagery, *Tundra* is interested. All poems must be 13 or fewer lines, with only very rare exceptions (where each line is very short). If you think that a haiku is merely 5-7-5 syllables, then I do not want to see your work (see 'Becoming a Haiku Poet' online at www.haikuworld.org/begin/mdwelch. apr2003.html for reasons why). Due to the excessive volume of inappropriate submissions for *Tundra* in the past, I now encourage only well-established poets to submit."

◯ UP AND UNDER: THE QND REVIEW

P.O. Box 115, Hainesport NJ 08036. E-mail: qndpoets@yahoo.com. Website: www. quickanddirtypoets.com. **Contact:** Kendall Bell, editor.

Magazines Needs *Up and Under: The QND Review*, published annually in March, is "a journal with an eclectic mix of poetry: sex, death, politics, IKEA, Mars, food, and jug handles alongside a smorgasbord of other topics covered in such diverse forms as the sonnet, villanelle, haiku, and free verse. We are interested in excellent poetry with no bias between free verse or traditional forms." Does not want "greeting card verse, graphic pornography." Has published poetry by Dan Maguire, Gina Larkin, Leonard Gontarek, Autumn Konopka, John Grey and Taylor Graham. *Up and Under* is 50-60 pages, digest-sized, laser-printed, saddle-stapled, with card cover with photograph, includes ads. Receives about 300 poems/ year, accepts about 30 (or 10%). Press run is 100. Single copy: $7. Chapbooks are available online or through U.S. Mail. Make checks payable to Kendall Bell.

How to Contact Submit up to 5 poems at a time. Lines/poem: no limit. Considers simultaneous submissions (with notification); no previously published poems. Accepts e-mail submissions (pasted into body of message). Reads submissions September 1-December 30. Time between acceptance and publication is 3-6 months. Poems are circulated to an editorial board. Sometimes comments on rejected poems. Guidelines available in magazine, for SASE, or on website. Responds in 2-3 months. Pays 1 contributor's copy. Acquires one-time rights.

Tips "Take a moment to read the poems featured on our website before submitting. We prefer poetry that uses concrete imagery to engage all 5 senses."

⊕ ◑ ◎ URTHONA MAGAZINE

Abbey House, Abbey Road, Cambridge CB5 8HQ, England. E-mail: urthonamag@onetel. com. Website: www.urthona.com. **Contact:** Poetry Editor.

Magazines Needs *Urthona*, published biannually, explores the arts and Western culture from a Buddhist perspective. Wants "poetry rousing the imagination." Does not want "undigested autobiography, political, or New Age-y poems." Has published poetry by Peter Abbs, Robert Bly, and Peter Redgrove. *Urthona* is 60 pages, A4, offset-printed, saddle-stapled, with 4-color glossy cover, includes ads. Receives about 300 poems/year, accepts about 40. Press run is 1,200 (200 subscribers, plus shelf sales in Australia and America). "See website for current subscription rates." Sample (including guidelines): $7.99 USD, $8.99 CAD.

How to Contact Submit 6 poems at a time. No previously published poems or simultaneous submissions. Accepts e-mail submissions (as attachment). Cover letter is preferred. Time between acceptance and publication is up to 8 months. Poems are circulated to an editorial board and are read and selected by poetry editor. Other editors have right of veto.

Responds within 6 months. Pays 1 contributor's copy. Acquires one-time rights. Reviews books/chapbooks of poetry and other magazines in 600 words. Send materials for review consideration.

☑ U.S. 1 WORKSHEETS

P.O. Box 127, Kingston NJ 08528. E-mail: nscott29@aol.com.

Magazines Needs *U.S. 1 Worksheets*, published annually, uses high-quality poetry and, on occasion, short fiction. "We prefer complex, well-written work." Has published poetry by Alicia Ostriker, BJ Ward, James Richardson, Lois Marie Harrod, and Baron Wormser. *U.S. 1 Worksheets* is 112 pages, perfect-bound, with b&w cover art. Press run is 500. Subscription: 2 years for $15; sample copy $8. Back issues $5.

How to Contact Submit up to 5 poems at a time. Considers simultaneous submissions if indicated; no previously published poems. "We use a rotating board of editors. We read April 15-June 30, and can no longer return manuscripts. Enclose SASE for reply." Pays 1 contributor's copy.

Also Offers The U.S. 1 Poets' Cooperative co-sponsors (with the Princeton Public Library) a series of monthly poetry readings (U.S. 1 Poets Invite) at the Princeton Public Library. "There is no formal membership, only the willingness of participants to share their work."

Tips "Send us your best. Please note submission dates. We receive many good poems we cannot consider because they arrive far outside our reading period."

$ ☑ U.S. CATHOLIC

Claretian Publications, U.S. Catholic, 205 W. Monroe St., Chicago IL 60606. E-mail: literaryeditor@uscatholic.org. Website: www.uscatholic.org. **Contact:** Editor: Rev. John Molyneux, C.M.F. *U.S. Catholic*, published monthly, "engages a broad range of issues as they affect the everyday lives of Catholics." No restrictions regarding subject matter or form, although "we are not necessarily looking for religious themes." Wants "high quality poetry." Does not want light verse. Has published poetry by Naomi Shihab Nye. *U.S. Catholic* is 51 pages, magazine-sized, printed in 4-color, stapled. Receives about 1,000 poems/year, accepts about 12. Circulation is 33,000. Subscription: $22.

How to Contact Submit 3-5 poems at a time. Lines/poem: 50 maximum. Considers simultaneous submissions; no previously published poems. Accepts e-mail submissions (pasted into body of message; no attachments). Cover letter is preferred. "Always include SASE." Time between acceptance and publication is 3 months. Poems are circulated to an editorial board. Seldom comments on rejected poems. Guidelines available for SASE or on website. Responds in 3 months. Pays $75/poem and 5 contributor's copies. Acquires first North American serial rights.

⚑ $ ☑ ◎ VALLUM

P.O. Box 598, Victoria Station, Montreal QC H3Z 2Y6, Canada. E-mail: info@vallummag. com. Website: www.vallummag.com. **Contact:** Joshua Auerbach and Helen Zisimatos, editors.

Magazines Needs *Vallum: Contemporary Poetry*, published annually, is "an international journal featuring high-quality, well-crafted contemporary poetry; open to most styles, and to new and established poets." Considers poetry by children and teens. Has published poetry by Franz Wright, A.F. Moritz, George Elliott Clarke, John Kinsella, and Medbh McGuckian. *Vallum* is 100 pages, 7x812, digitally printed, perfect-bound, with color images on coated stock cover. Press run is 2,500. Single copy: $8.95; subscription: $17/year. Make checks payable to *Vallum*.

How to Contact Submit 4-7 poems at a time. No previously published poems or simultaneous submissions. No e-mail submissions. Cover letter is preferred. Include SASE (or SAE and IRC). Check website for submission deadlines. Sometimes comments on rejected poems. Always publishes theme issues. Guidelines available on website. Responds in 9-12 months. Pays honorarium and one contributor's copy. Acquires first North American serial rights. Reviews books/chapbooks of poetry in 500-700 words. Send materials for review consideration. Essays on poetics also considered. Query essays, interviews, and reviews by e-mail.

Tips "Hone your craft; read widely; be original."

▣ ☑ VALPARAISO POETRY REVIEW

Dept. of English, Valparaiso University, Valparaiso IN 46383-6493. (219)464-5278. Fax: (219)464-5511. E-mail: vpr@valpo.edu. Website: www.valpo.edu/vpr/. **Contact:** Edward Byrne, editor.

Magazines Needs *Valparaiso Poetry Review: Contemporary Poetry and Poetics*, published semiannually online, accepts "submissions of unpublished poetry, book reviews, author interviews, and essays on poetry or poetics that have not yet appeared online and for which the rights belong to the author. Query for anything else." Wants poetry of any length or style, free verse or traditional forms. Has published poetry by Charles Wright, Cornelius Eady, Dorianne Laux, Dave Smith, Claudia Emerson, Billy Collins, Brian Turner, Daisy Fried, Stanley Plumly, and Annie Finch. Receives about 9,000 poems/year, accepts about 1%.

How to Contact Submit 3-5 poems at a time (no more than 5). Considers previously published poems ("original publication must be identified to ensure proper credit") and simultaneous submissions. Accepts e-mail submissions (pasted into body of message, no attachments); no fax or disk submissions. **Postal submissions preferred.** Cover letter is preferred. Include SASE. Reads submissions year round. Time between acceptance and publication is 6-12 months. Seldom comments on rejected poems. Guidelines available on website. Responds in up to 6 weeks. Acquires one-time rights. "All rights remain with author." Reviews books of poetry in single- and multi-book format. Send materials for review consideration.

▦ ☑ VAN GOGH'S EAR: BEST WORLD POETRY & PROSE

French Connection Press, 12 rue Lamartine, Paris 75009 France. (33)(1)4016-0535. Fax: (33)(1)4016-0701. E-mail: frenchcx@club-internet.fr. Website: www.frenchcx.com. Established 2002. **Contact:** Ian Ayres, founder/editor.

• Poetry published in *Van Gogh's Ear* has appeared in *The Best American Poetry*.

Magazines Needs *Van Gogh's Ear*, published annually in April, is an anthology series "devoted to publishing powerful poetry and prose in English and English translations by major voices and innovative new talents from around the globe." Has published poetry by Marilyn Monroe, Tony Curtis, Yoko Ono, James Dean, Xaviera Hollander, and Charles

Manson. *Van Gogh's Ear* is 280 pages, digest-sized, offset-printed, perfect-bound, with 4-color matte cover with commissioned artwork. Receives about 1,000 poems/year, accepts about 30%. Press run is 2,000 (105 subscribers, 25 libraries, 1,750 shelf/online sales); 120 distributed free to contributors and reviewers. Single copy: $19; subscription: $36 for 2 years. "As a 501(c)(3) nonprofit enterprise, *Van Gogh's Ear* needs the support of individual poets, writers, and readers to survive. Any donation, large or small, will help *Van Gogh's Ear* continue to publish the best cross-section of contemporary poetry and prose. Because of being an anglophone publication based in France, *Van Gogh's Ear* is unable to get any grants or funding. Your contribution will be tax-deductible. Make donation checks payable to Committee on Poetry-*VGE*, and mail them (donations **only**) to the Allen Ginsberg Trust, P.O. Box 582, Stuyvesant Station, New York NY 10009. All U.S. checks/money orders for reading fees, subscriptions, and purchases must be made out to French Connection Press and sent to Michael Hathaway, 522 E. South Ave., St. John KS 67576-2212."

How to Contact Submit 6 poems or 2 prose pieces at a time. Lines/poem: 165 maximum (1,500 words maximum for prose). No previously published poems or simultaneous submissions. No fax, e-mail, or disk submissions. Cover letter is preferred. "**Send to the French Connection Press address only!** Please include SASE (or SAE with IRCs) or e-mail address along with a brief bio of up to 120 words." Reads submissions May 1-October 31. **Charges $10 (USD) reading fee for non-subscribers.** Time between acceptance and publication is one year. "Every submission is closely read by all members of the editorial board and voted upon." Seldom comments on rejections. "Our continued existence, and continued ability to read your work, depends mainly on subscriptions/donations. Therefore, we must ask that you at least purchase a sample copy before submitting work." Guidelines available in anthology or on website. Responds in 9 months. Always sends prepublication galleys. Pays 1 contributor's copy. Acquires one-time rights.

Tips "The goal of *Van Gogh's Ear* is for each volume to transport all who experience it into multifaceted realities that transcend color and culture through the uncensored pens of legendary and new talents from all walks of life. 'Intensity' is the key. And we are more than open to poets/writers who haven't been published before. Being published isn't as important as the work itself. Please note: Volume 7 will be the final volume of *Van Gogh's Ear*. We are currently accepting submissions for that volume."

⊕ ◯ VERANDAH

c/o Faculty of Arts, Deakin University, 221 Burwood Hwy., Burwood, Victoria 3125, Australia. (61)(3)9251-7134. E-mail: verandah@deakin.edu.au. Website: www.deakin.edu.au/verandah. **Contact:** Poetry Editor.

Magazines Needs *Verandah*, published annually in September, is "a high-quality literary journal edited by professional writing students. It aims to give voice to new and innovative writers and artists." Has published poetry by Christos Tsiolka, Dorothy Porter, Seamus Heaney, Les Murray, Ed Burger, and Joh Muk Muk Burke. *Verandah* is 120 pages, professionally printed on glossy stock, flat-spined, with full-color glossy card cover. Sample: $20 AUD.

How to Contact Submit bt mail or e-mail. However, electronic version of work must be available if accepted by *Verandah*. **Do not submit work without the required submission form (available for download on website).** Reads submissions by June 1 deadline (postmark). Guidelines available on website. Some prizes awarded. Pays one contributor's copy, "with prizes awarded accordingly." Acquires first Australian publishing rights.

Contest/Award Offerings Prizes awarded in each issue. Prize entry is automatic for Deakin students, no entry fee (student number is required). **Entry fee:** $10 AUD for first entry, $15 AUD for 3. Work submitted by non-Deakin students without an entry fee will not be considered for publication. **Deadline:** June 1. Guidelines available on website.

🌐 ☑ VERSAL

Amsterdam, Netherlands. E-mail: versaljournal@wordsinhere.com. Website: www. wordsinhere.com. **Contact:** Megan M. Garr, editor.

Magazines Needs *Versal*, published annually by wordsinhere, is the only English-language literary magazine in the Netherlands and publishes new poetry, prose, and art from around the world. "We publish writers with an instinct for language and line break, content and form that is urgent, involved, and unexpected." Has published poetry by Naomi Shihab Nye, Ben Doller, Marilyn Hacker, Emily Carr, Peter Shippy, William Doresky, Mary Miller, and Sawako Nakayasu. Receives about 1,000+ poems/year, accepts about 4%. Single copy: $15 USD. Ordering information available on website.

How to Contact Submit 3-5 poems at a time. Considers simultaneous submissions; no previously published poems. Accepts submissions online only (online submission system can be found on website. Reads submissions September 15-January 15. Time between acceptance and publication is 4-7 months. Poems are circulated to an editorial board. Sometimes comments on rejected poems. Guidelines available on website. Responds in 2 months. Sends prepublication PDF galleys. Pays 1 contributor's copy. Acquires one-time rights. Rights revert to poet upon publication.

Tips "Write as much as you can. Follow the guidelines. Resist the urge to send us poems about tulips, windmills, or sex and drug adventures. Support independent literary publishing: buy copies of *Versal* and any other lit mag you find."

☑ VERSE

Dept. of English, University of Richmond, Richmond VA 23173. Andrew Zawacki, Co-Editor. **Contact:** Brian Henry. *Verse*, published 3 times/year, is "an international poetry journal which also publishes interviews with poets, essays on poetry, and book reviews." Wants "no specific kind; we look for high-quality, innovative poetry. Our focus is not only on American poetry, but on all poetry written in English, as well as translations." Has published poetry by James Tate, John Ashbery, Barbara Guest, Gustaf Sobin, and Rae Armantrout. *Verse* is 128-416 pages, digest-sized, professionally printed, perfect-bound, with card cover. Receives about 5,000 poems/year, accepts 1%. Press run is 1,000. Single copy: $10; subscription: $18 for individuals, $39 for institutions. Sample: $6. Everyone submitting work to the print magazine will receive a free copy of Verse (cover price $12-15). All contributors to the print magazine will receive at least $200 (possibly more) plus two copies and a one-year subscription.There is no reading fee for submissions to the Verse site and no payment for contributors to the Verse site. All submissions to the print magazine will also be considered for the VERSE site, so if a portfolio isn't selected for the print magazine, individual pieces still might be accepted for the VERSE site.

⊕ THE VIEW FROM HERE MAGAZINE

E-mail: editor@viewfromheremagazine.com; rear.view.poetry@gmail.com. Website: www.viewfromheremagazine.com. **Contact:** Sydney Nash, poetry editor; Michael Kannengieser, fiction editor. "We are a print and online literary magazine designed and edited by an international team. We bring an entertaining mix of wit and insight all packaged in beautifully designed pages."

Magazines Needs *The View From Here*, published monthly, "showcases new, emerging talent as well as the seasoned voice. Our poets are word wizards, prophets, mystics, and lyricists who are unafraid to demand attention by painting the world with their vision. Our poets will leave you yearning for more of the way they see the universe." Wants avant garde, free verse, haiku, light verse, traditional poetry. Has published Cyndi Dawson, Todd Heldt.

How to Contact Submit up to 3 poems by e-mail, either as attachments or in the body of the message, plus a short bio and 3 most recent publishing credits with online links, if applicable. Does not accept previously published or simultaneous submissions. Please combine all poems into a single document.

$ ☑ THE VIRGINIA QUARTERLY REVIEW

P.O. Box 400223, Charlottesville VA 22904-4223. (434)924-3124. Fax: (434)924-1397. Website: www.vqronline.org. Established 1925.

Magazines Needs *The Virginia Quarterly Review* uses about 45-50 pages of poetry in each issue. No length or subject restrictions. Issues have largely included lyric and narrative free verse, most of which features a strong message or powerful voice. *The Virginia Quarterly Review* is 256 pages, digest-sized, flat-spined. Press run is 7,000.

How to Contact Submit up to 5 poems at a time. No simultaneous submissions. Accepts online submissions only at http://vqronline.org/submission/. Responds in 1-3 months. Guidelines available on website; do not request by fax. Pays $5/line.

Contest/Award Offerings Sponsors the Emily Clark Balch Prize for Poetry, an annual award of $1,000 given to the best poem or group of poems published in the *Review* during the year.

☑ ◎ THE WELL TEMPERED SONNET

87 Petoskey St., Suite 120, New Hudson MI 48165. E-mail: thewelltemperedsonnet@yahoo.com. **Contact:** James D. Taylor, II, editor/publisher.

Magazines Needs *The Well Tempered Sonnet*, published annually, features compositions in sonnet form only and "caters to those who love and appreciate the form Shakespeare made famous." Does not want "erotica, blasphemy, vulgarity, or racism." Considers poetry by children and teens. *The Well Tempered Sonnet* is magazine-sized, desktop-published, spiral-bound, with attractive heavy stock cover. Subscription: $25/year. Make checks payable to James Taylor. "We encourage submissions requesting subscriptions, details included in guidelines."

How to Contact Submit up to 5 poems at a time. Considers previously published poems; no simultaneous submissions. Accepts submissions by mail or e-mail. Seldom comments on rejected poems. Occasionally publishes theme issues. Guidelines available for SASE or on website. Responds ASAP. Always sends prepublication galleys.

Also Offers "We encourage and try to provide the means for interaction between other sonneteers."

Tips "A well composed sonnet is a piece of art. Understanding word usage is important in the development of the sonnet, as important as colors to a painter."

$ ◨ WESTERN HUMANITIES REVIEW

University of Utah, 255 S. Central Campus Dr., LNCO 3500, Salt Lake City UT 84112-0494. (801)581-6070. Fax: (801)585-5167. E-mail: whr@mail.hum.utah.edu. Website: www. hum.utah.edu/whr. **Contact:** Dawn Lonsinger, Managing Editor.

- Poetry published in *Western Humanities Review* has been selected for *The Best American Poetry* as well as the *Pushcart Prize* anthologies.

Magazines Needs *Western Humanities Review*, published semiannually in April and October, prints poetry, fiction, and a small selection of nonfiction. Wants "quality poetry of any form, including translations." Has published poetry by Charles Simic, Olena Kalytiak Davis, Ravi Shankar, Karen Volkman, Dan Beachy-Quick, Lucie Brock-Broido, Christine Hume, and Dan Chiasson. Innovative prose poems may be submitted as fiction or nonfiction to the appropriate editor. *Western Humanities Review* is 120-160 pages, digest-sized, professionally printed on quality stock, perfect-bound, with coated card cover. Receives about 1,500 submissions/year, accepts less than 5%. Press run is 1,000. Subscription: $16 to individuals in the U.S. Sample: $10.

How to Contact Considers simultaneous submissions but no more than 5 poems or 25 pages per reading period. No fax or e-mail submissions. Reads submissions October 1-April 1 only. Time between acceptance and publication is 1-3 issues. Managing editor and assistant editors makes an initial cut, then the poetry editor makes the final selections. Seldom comments on rejected poems. "We do not publish writer's guidelines because we think the magazine itself conveys an accurate picture of our requirements." Responds in up to 6 months. Pays 2 contributor's copies. Acquires first serial rights then rights revert to author.

Contest/Award Offerings Sponsors an annual contest for Utah writers.

◨ ◎ WESTVIEW: A JOURNAL OF WESTERN OKLAHOMA

Southwestern Oklahoma State University, 100 Campus Dr., Weatherford OK 73096. E-mail: james.silver@swosu.edu; westview@swosu.edu. *Westview: A Journal of Western Oklahoma*, published semiannually, is "particularly interested in writers from the Southwest; however, we are open to quality work by poets from elsewhere. We publish free verse, prose poems, and formal poetry." Has published poetry by Carolynne Wright, Miller Williams, Walter McDonald, Robert Cooperman, Alicia Ostriker, and James Whitehead. *Westview* is 64 pages, magazine-sized, perfect-bound, with full-color glossy card cover. Receives about 500 poems/year, accepts 7%. Press run is 700 (300 subscribers, about 25 libraries). Subscription: $15/2 years. Sample: $6.

How to Contact Submit 5 poems at a time. Cover letter is required, including biographical data for contributor's note. Comments on submissions "when close." Manuscripts are circulated to an editorial board. Responds within 4-6 months. Pays 1 contributor's copy.

◻ WESTWARD QUARTERLY: THE MAGAZINE OF FAMILY READING

Laudemont Press, P.O. Box 369, Hamilton IL 62341. (800)440-4043. E-mail: wwquarterly@ aol.com. Website: www.wwquarterly.com. **Contact:** Shirley Anne Leonard, editor.

Magazines/Journals

Magazines Needs *WestWard Quarterly: The Magazine of Family Reading* prints poetry. Wants "all forms, including rhyme—we welcome inspirational, positive, reflective, humorous material promoting nobility, compassion, and courage." Does not want "experimental or avant-garde forms, offensive language, depressing or negative poetry." Considers poetry by children and teens. Has published poetry by Jane Stuart, Brian Felder, Leland Jamieson, Joyce I. Johnson, Michael Keshigian, Arlene Mandell, J. Alvein Speers, Charles Waugaman. *WestWard Quarterly* is 32 pages, digest-sized, laser-printed, saddle-stapled, with inkjet color cover with scenic photos, includes ads. Receives about 1,500 poems/year, accepts about 10%. Press run is 150 (60 subscribers). Single copy: $4 ($6 foreign); subscription: $15/year ($18 foreign). Contributors to an issue may order extra copies at a discounted price. Make checks payable to Laudemont Press.

How to Contact Submit up to 5 poems at a time. Lines/poem: 40 maximum. Considers previously published poems and simultaneous submissions. Prefers e-mail submissions (pasted into body of message); no disk submissions. Reads submissions year round. Submit seasonal poems 3 months in advance. Time between acceptance and publication is "months." Often comments on rejected poems. Guidelines available for SASE, by e-mail, or on website. Responds in "weeks." Pays 1 contributor's copy. Acquires one-time rights.

Also Offers "Every issue includes a 'Featured Writer,' an article about 'Poets from the Past,' and a piece on improving writing skills or writing different forms of poetry."

☑ WHISKEY ISLAND MAGAZINE

English Dept., Cleveland State University, Cleveland OH 44115. **Contact:** Poetry Editor. *Whiskey Island Magazine*, published semiannually, prints poetry, fiction, creative nonfiction, and art. Wants "writing that engages the reader immediately. It's always good to be interesting early." Has published poetry by Denise Duhamel, H.L. Hix, James Allen Hall, Jay Hopler, and Wayne Miller. *Whiskey Island Magazine* is about 100 pages, digest-sized, professionally printed, perfect-bound, with glossy stock cover. Receives 1,000-1,500 poetry mss/year, accepts 6%. Press run is 1,000. Subscription: $12 domestic, $20 overseas. Sample: $6. Make checks payable to *Whiskey Island Magazine*.

☐ WHISPERS OF POETRY

E-mail: whispersofpoetry@aol.com. Website: http://whispers.forumotion.com/. *Whispers of Poetry* is "a poetry website devoted to publishing beginning and experienced poets. We accept all types and styles of poetry (with the exception of questionable material such as profanity or pornographic material, due to possible younger members). There are no fees involved for members. We created this site out of love for the art of poetry!" Considers poetry by children and teens. Has published poetry by Scarlett Wheeler, Tim Bullerwell, Melinda Blount, jacob erin-cilberto (fog), Che Sarto Francisco, and Larry Powers. Receives about 520 poems/year, accepts about 80%.

How to Contact Submit 3-5 poems at a time. Lines/poem: no limit. Considers previously published poems and simultaneous submissions. Accepts e-mail submissions (pasted into body of message; or use online form through the "Contact Us" link on website); no disk submissions. "Single-space poems. Include full name, e-mail address, pen name (if other than full name), and brief bio to be published on the website." Reads submissions year round. Submit seasonal poems one month in advance. Time between acceptance and publication is one day to one week. Always comments on rejected poems. "There are no requirements to submit; but if accepted, you would become a member; no charges for membership." Regularly publishes theme issues. Guidelines available by e-mail. Responds in one week. Acquires one-time rights.

Contest/Award Offerings Offers monthly contest. Features winner on "Star Poem" page on website (possibly other prizes to be announced). Deadline: 20th of each month. Guidelines available by e-mail or on website. "Each member receives a monthly newsletter describing the guidelines and theme for that month's contest. Members will have the ability to comment on posted material, but there will be no scoring system, for we believe in encouraging, not discouraging, poets in their endeavors. We also believe poetry is a work of art, and that art is created by feelings from the heart, not to be judged for style or content by others."

Tips "Never give up your dreams! If you are not accepted by one place, submit again, and again! Read the work on the site or in the magazine for which you are submitting to assure that your submission is suitable. Write from your heart!"

◔ WHITE PELICAN REVIEW

P.O. Box 7833, Lakeland FL 33813. **Contact:** Nancy Wiegel, editor.

Magazines Needs *White Pelican Review*, published semiannually in April and October, is dedicated to printing poetry of the highest quality. Wants "writing that goes beyond competency to exceptional acts of imagination and language." Has published poetry by Paul Hostovsky, Michael Hettich, Becky Sakellariou, Lyn Lifshin, and John Grey. *White Pelican Review* is about 48 pages, digest-sized, photocopied from typescript, saddle-stapled, with matte cardstock cover. Receives about 5,000 poems/year, accepts 3%. Circulation is 500. Single copy: $4; subscription: $8/year for individuals, $10/year for institutions. Make checks payable to *White Pelican Review*.

How to Contact Submit 3-5 poems at a time. Lines/poem: "optimal length is 32 lines plus title, although longer poems are given full consideration." No previously published poems or simultaneous submissions. Cover letter is required. SASE is a must. "Please include name, address, telephone number, and (if available) e-mail address on each page. No handwritten poems." Reads submissions year round. Time between acceptance and publication is 1-6 months. Poems are circulated to an editorial board. Seldom comments on rejected poems. Guidelines available for SASE. Responds in 6 months. Pays 1 contributor's copy. Acquires one-time rights.

Contest/Award Offerings The Hollingsworth Prize of $100 is offered to one distinguished poem published in each issue. No contest or fee is involved.

◪ ◲ WHITE WALL REVIEW

Dept. of English, Ryerson University, Jorgenson Hall, 5th Floor, 350 Victoria St., Toronto ON M5B 2K3, Canada. E-mail: wwr@ryerson.ca. Website: http://www.ryerson.ca/wwr/. **Contact:** The Editors. *White Wall Review*, published annually in August, focuses on printing "clearly expressed, innovative poetry and prose. No style is unacceptable." Has published poetry by Vernon Mooers and David Sidjak. *White Wall Review* is 90-144 pages, digest-sized, professionally printed, perfect-bound, with glossy card cover. Press run is 500. Subscription: $10 plus GST.

How to Contact Submit up to 5 poems at a time by mail only. Length: 5 pages/piece maximum. Cover letter is required. Include short bio. Guidelines available in magazine, for SASE. Responds "as soon as possible." Pays one contributor's copy.

Tips "Innovative work is especially appreciated."

▣ ◻ WILD GOOSE POETRY REVIEW

Central Piedmont Community College, Levine Campus, P.O. Box 35009, Charlotte NC 28235-5009. (704)330-4397. E-mail: Patricia.Bostian@cpcc.edu. Website: www. wildgoosepoetryreview.com.

Magazines Needs *Wild Goose Poetry Review*, published quarterly online, is a poetry journal with essays, reviews, and interviews. Wants "poetry that exudes a sense of place, that is well-crafted, with an eye to imagery and an ear to music." Does not want "erotica, abstract stream-of-consciousness, or gratuitous obscenities." Has published poetry by Anthony Abbott. Receives about 1,000 poems/year, accepts about 12%.

How to Contact Submit 3-5 poems at a time. Lines/poem: "no poems longer than two pages accepted." Considers simultaneous submissions; no previously published poems. Accepts e-mail submissions only as attachment; no disk submissions. Cover letter is preferred; include bio. Reads submissions year round. Time between acceptance and publication is up to 6 months. Poems are circulated to an editorial board. Guidelines available on website. Responds in 4-6 weeks. Rights revert to poet upon publication. Reviews books/chapbooks of poetry in 500 words. Send materials for review consideration to Patricia Bostian.

Tips "Read, read, read. Inspiration does not a poem make. Revise, revise, revise."

▣ ◿ WILD VIOLET

P.O. Box 39706, Philadelphia PA 19106-9706. E-mail: wildvioletmagazine@yahoo.com. Website: www.wildviolet.net. **Contact:** Alyce Wilson, editor. Established 2001.

Magazines Needs *Wild Violet*, published quarterly online, aims "to make the arts more accessible, to make a place for the arts in modern life." Wants "poetry that is well crafted, that engages thought, that challenges or uplifts the reader. We have published free verse, haiku, blank verse, and other forms. If the form suits the poem, we will consider any form." Does not want "abstract, self-involved poetry; poorly managed form; excessive rhyming; self-referential poems that do not show why the speaker is sad, happy, or in love." Has published poetry by Lyn Lifshin, Andrew H. Oerke, Erik Kestler, Anselm Brocki, Carol Frith, Richard Fammerée, Joanna Weston and Graham Burchell. Accepts about 15% of work submitted.

How to Contact Submit 3-5 poems at a time. Considers simultaneous submissions (with notification); no previously published poems. Accepts e-mail submissions (pasted into body of message, or as text or Word attachment); no disk submissions. Cover letter is preferred. Reads submissions year round. Submit seasonal poems 3 months in advance. Time between acceptance and publication is 3 months. "Decisions on acceptance or rejection are made by the editor." Seldom comments on rejected poems, unless requested. Occasionally publishes theme issues. Guidelines available by e-mail or on website. Responds in up to 3 months. Pays by providing a bio and link on contributor's page. Requests electronic rights to publish and archive accepted works. Reviews books/chapbooks of poetry in 250 words, single-book format. Query for review consideration.

Contest/Award Offerings Sponsors an annual poetry contest, offering 1st Prize: $100 and publication in *Wild Violet*; 2 Honorable Mentions will also be published. Guidelines available by e-mail or on website. **Entry fee:** $5/poem. Judged by independent judges.

Tips "Read voraciously; experience life and share what you've learned. Write what is hardest to say; don't take any easy outs."

◢ WILLARD & MAPLE

163 S. Willard St., Box 34, Burlington VT 05401. E-mail: willardandmaple@champlain.edu.
Magazines Needs *Willard & Maple*, published annually in spring, is "a student-run literary magazine from Champlain College's Professional Writing Program that publishes a wide array of poems, short stories, creative essays, short plays, pen & ink drawings, photographs, and computer graphics." Wants "creative work of the highest quality." Does not want any submissions over 10 typed pages in length; all submissions must be in English. Considers poetry by children and teens. Has published poetry by Frederick Zydek, Robert Cooperman, Meghan Schardt, Patrick Willwerth, and N.B.Smith. Willard & Maple is 200 pages, digest-sized, digitally printed, perfect-bound. Receives about 500 poems/year, accepts about 20%. Press run is 600 (80 subscribers, 4 libraries); 200 are distributed free to the Champlain College writing community. Single copy: $12. Contact Lulu Press for Contributor's Copy.
How to Contact Submit up to 5 poems at a time. Lines/poem: 100 maximum. Considers simultaneous submissions; no previously published poems. Accepts e-mail and disk submissions. Cover letter is required. "Please provide current contact information including an e-mail address. Single-space submissions, one poem/page." Reads submissions September 1 -March 31. Time between acceptance and publication is less than 1 year. "All editors receive a blind copy to review. They meet weekly throughout the academic year. These meetings consist of the submissions being read aloud, discussed, and voted upon." Seldom comments on rejected poems. Occasionally publishes theme issues. Upcoming themes available by e-mail. Responds in less than 6 months. Pays 2 contributor's copies. Acquires one-time rights. Reviews books/chapbooks of poetry and other magazines/journals in 1,200 words. Send materials for review consideration to the poetry editor.
Tips "The power of imagination makes us infinite."

▣ ◯ THE WILLOW

The Smithtown Poetry Society, P.O. Box 793, Nesconset NY 11767. (631)656-6690. Fax: (631)656-6690. E-mail: sherylmint@cs.com; editor@thesmithtownpoetrysociety.com. **Contact:** Sheryl Minter, Editor. *The Willow*, published quarterly online, features "new and upcoming poets alongside known poets. We also feature art, short stories, and poetry, regardless of length, that inspire intelligent thought and originality." Wants all forms of poetry. Does not want "poetry written without thought or in sing-song rhyme." Considers poetry by children and teens. Has published poetry by Marian Ford and Najwa Brax. Receives about 1,000 poems/year, accepts about 15%. Press run is 600; 300 distributed free to coffee shops. Single copy: $7; subscription: $20. Make checks payable to S. Minter.
How to Contact Submit up to 3 poems at a time. Lines/poem: 30 maximum (longer poems are considered but may take longer to publish, depending on magazine space; query before submitting). Considers previously published poems; no simultaneous submissions. Accepts disk submissions; no fax or e-mail submissions. Cover letter is preferred. "All submissions

must be typed, double-spaced, with submitter's name and address clearly printed. Please include a SASE for all submissions if you would like your original work returned." Reads submissions year round. Submit seasonal poems 6 months in advance. **Charges $1 reading fee.** Time between acceptance and publication is up to one year. Poems are circulated to an editorial board. Sometimes comments on rejected poems. Guidelines available in magazine, for SASE, by e-mail, or on website. Responds in 1 month.

Contest/Award Offerings The Smithtown Poetry Society Yearly Contest is open to all poets and offers 50% of the contest proceeds as first prize; "the other half goes to the distribution of *The Willow.*" Submit up to 3 poems, 20 lines maximum each. **Entry fee:** $5. **Deadline:** June 1. Guidelines available in magazine, for SASE, or on website. "All submissions may be edited for grammar and punctuation."

☑ WILLOW REVIEW

College of Lake County, 19351 W. Washington St., Grayslake IL 60030-1198. (847)543-2956. E-mail: com426@clcillinois.edu. Website: www.clcillinois.edu/community/willowreview. asp. Established 1969. **Contact:** Michael F. Latza, editor.

• *Willow Review* is partially supported by a grant from the Illinois Arts Council, a state agency.

Magazines Needs *Willow Review*, published annually, is interested in poetry, creative nonfiction, and fiction of high quality. "We have no preferences as to form, style, or subject, as long as each poem stands on its own as art and communicates ideas." Has published poetry by Lisel Mueller, Lucien Stryk, David Ray, Louis Rodriguez, John Dickson, and Patricia Smith. *Willow Review* is 88-96 pages, digest-sized, professionally printed, flat-spined, with a 4-color cover featuring work by an Illinois artist. Press run is 1,000. Subscription: $18 for 3 issues, $30 for 6 issues. Sample: $5 (back issue).

How to Contact Submit up to 5 poems at a time. Considers simultaneous submissions "if indicated in the cover letter"; no previously published poems. No e-mail submissions; postal submissions only. Include SASE; "manuscripts will not be returned unless requested." Reads submissions September-May. Guidelines available on website. Pays 2 contributor's copies. All rights remain with the author.

Contest/Award Offerings Prizes totaling $400 are awarded to the best poetry and short fiction/creative nonfiction in each issue.

Also Offers The College of Lake County Reading Series (4-7 readings/academic year) has included Thomas Lux, Isabel Allende, Donald Justice, Galway Kinnell, Lisel Mueller, Amiri Baraka, and others. One reading is for contributors to *Willow Review*. Readings, usually held on Thursday evenings and widely publicized in Chicago and suburban newspapers, are presented to audiences of about 150 students and faculty of the College of Lake County and other area colleges, as well as residents of local communities.

☑ WISCONSIN REVIEW

800 Algoma Blvd., University of Wisconsin-Oshkosh, Oshkosh WI 54902. E-mail: wisconsinreview@uwosh.edu. *Wisconsin Review*, published annually, is a "contemporary poetry, prose, and art magazine run by students at the University of Wisconsin Oshkosh." Wants all forms and styles of poetry. Does not want "poetry that is racist, sexist, or unnecessarily vulgar." Considers poetry by children and teens. "Minors may submit

material by including a written letter of permission from a parent or guardian." *Wisconsin Review* is 250 pages, digest-sized, perfect-bound, with 4-color glossy coverstock. Receives about 400 poetry submissions/year, accepts about 50; Press run is 2,000. Single copy: $10; subscription: $10 plus $3 extra per issue for shipments outside the U.S.

How to Contact Submit up to 5 poems at a time. Does not consider previously published poems or simultaneous submissions. Accepts e-mail submissions. "Online submissions are accepted only through manuscripthub.com." Type one poem/page, single-spaced, with name and address of writer on each page. Cover letter is required. Include 3-5 sentence bio and SASE if submitting by mail. Reads submissions September through May. Submit seasonal poems 6 months in advance. Time between acceptance and publication is 6-9 months. Sometimes comments on rejected poems. Guidelines available in magazine, for SASE, by e-mail, and on website. Responds in 4-6 months. Pays 2 contributor's copies. Reviews books and chapbooks of poetry, other magazines and journals. Send materials for review consideration to the editors.

Tips "We are open to any poetic form and style, and look for outstanding imagery, new themes, and fresh voices — poetry that induces emotions."

N ⊕ THE WOLF

E-mail: submissions@wolfmagazine.co.uk. Website: www.wolfmagazine.co.uk. Established 2002. **Contact:** James Byrne, editor.

Magazines Needs *The Wolf*, published 3 times per year, publishes "international translations, critical prose, and interviews with leading contemporary poets, which are frequently mentioned as distinguishing characteristics of the magazine. The poetry, however, comes purely through work submitted. There is no special treatment with regard to the consideration of any poet or poem. Since January 2008, *The Wolf* has benefited from Arts Council funding. Since receiving its grant the magazine has increased its content by a third and is perfect bound." $12 single issue, including postage and packing; $35 subscription. Accepts PayPal.

How to Contact Submit up to 5 poems by e-mail. Reads submissions year round. Guidelines available on website. Responds in 6 months. Pays 1 contributor's copy. Accepts reviews of poetry books between 800-1,500 words.

Additional Information Also accepts critical essays on any poetry subject between 2,000-3,000 words. Welcomes artwork or photographs.

⊘ THE WORCESTER REVIEW

Worcester County Poetry Association, Inc., 1 Ekman St, Worcester MA 01607. (508)797-4770. E-mail: rodgerwriter@myfairpoint.net. Website: theworcesterreview.org. **Contact:** Rodger Martin, managing editor.

Magazines Needs *The Worcester Review*, published annually by the Worcester County Poetry Association, encourages "critical work with a New England connection; no geographic limitation on poetry and fiction." Wants "work that is crafted, intuitively honest and empathetic." Has published poetry by Kurt Brown, Cleopatra Mathis, and Theodore Deppe. *The Worcester Review* is 160 pages, digest-sized, professionally printed in dark type on quality stock, perfect-bound, with matte card cover. Press run is 750. Subscription: $30 (includes membership in WCPA). Sample: $8.

How to Contact Submit up to 5 poems at a time (recommend 3 or less receive the most favorable readings). Considers previously published poems "if they do not conflict with our readership" and simultaneous submissions "if notified." Cover letter is required. Include brief bio. Poems should be typed on 8½ × 11 paper, with poet's name in upper left corner of each page. Include SASE for return of ms. Sometimes comments on rejected poems. Guidelines available for SASE or on website. Responds in up to 9 months. Pays 2 contributor's copies plus small honorarium. Acquires first rights.

Tips "Read some. Listen a lot."

☑ WRITE ON!! POETRY MAGAZETTE

P.O. Box 901, Richfield UT 84701-0901. E-mail: jimnipoetry@yahoo.com. **Contact:** Jim Garman, Editor.

Magazines Needs *Write On!! Poetry Magazette*, published monthly, features "poetry from poets around the world." Wants poetry of "any style; all submissions must be suitable for all ages to read." Does not want "adult themes or vulgar material." Considers poetry by children and teens. Has published poetry by Cathy Porter, B.Z. Niditch, Ron Koppelberger, and Betty Shelley. *Write On!!* is 24 pages, digest-sized, photostat-copied, saddle-stapled. Receives about 500 poems/year, accepts about 50%. Press run is 50. Single copy: $4. Sample: $3. Make checks payable to Jim Garman.

How to Contact Submit 1-6 poems at a time. Lines/poem: 6 minimum, 28 maximum. Considers previously published poems and simultaneous submissions. Accepts e-mail submissions (pasted into body of message, no attachments). Reads submissions year round. Submit seasonal poems 2 months in advance. Time between acceptance and publication is one month. Never comments on rejected poems. Occasionally publishes theme issues. Guidelines available by e-mail. Responds in "approximately" 3 weeks. No payment or free copies provided. "*WRITE ON!!* contains no ads, no sponsors, all costs are covered out of pocket or by those desiring a copy." Acquires one-time rights, "which return to author upon publication."

Tips "Send only your best material after it has been refined."

☑ WRITER'S BLOC

Dept. of Language & Literature, Texas A&M University-Kingsville, MSC 162, Kingsville TX 78363-8202. E-mail: c-downs@tamuk.edu. Website: www.tamuk.edu/langlit/writer's. htm. **Contact:** C. Downs, Faculty Sponsor.

Magazines Needs *Writer's Bloc*, published annually in October, prints poetry, fiction, creative nonfiction, and graphic art. "About half of our pages are devoted to the works of Texas A&M University-Kingsville students and half to the works of writers and artists from all over the world." Wants quality poetry; no restrictions on content or form. *Writer's Bloc* is 96 pages, digest-sized. Press run is 300. Subscription: $7. Sample: $7.

How to Contact Submit no more than 3 pages of poetry at a time ("prose poems okay"). Lines/poem: 50 maximum. No previously published poems or simultaneous submissions. No e-mail submissions; postal submissions only. "Submissions should be typed, double-spaced; SASE required for reply." Reads submissions September-January only. "Manuscripts are published upon recommendation by a staff of students and faculty." Seldom comments on rejected poems. Guidelines available in magazine or for SASE. "Acceptance letters are sent out in October." Pays 1 contributor's copy.

$ ⬚ ◎ WRITERS' JOURNAL

P.O. Box 394, Perham MN 56573. (218)346-7921. Fax: (218)346-7924. E-mail: writersjournal@ writersjournal.com. Website: www.writersjournal.com. **Contact:** Esther M. Leiper-Estabrooks, Poetry Editor.

Magazines Needs WRITERS" Journal, published bimonthly, offers "advice and guidance, motivation, and inspiration to the more serious and published writers and poets." Features 2 columns for poets: "Esther Comments" offers critiques of poems sent in by readers, and "Every Day with Poetry" discusses a wide range of poetry topics, often—but not always—including readers' work. Wants "a variety of poetry: free verse, strict forms, concrete, Oriental. Since we appeal to those of different skill levels, some poems are more sophisticated than others, but those accepted must move, intrigue, or otherwise positively capture me. 'Esther Comments' is never used as a negative force to put a poem or a poet down. Indeed, I focus on the best part of a given work and seek to suggest means of improvement on weaker aspects." Does not want anything "vulgar, preachy, or sloppily written." Considers poetry by children (school-age). Has published poetry by Lawrence Schug, Diana Sutliff, and Eugene E. Grollmes. WRITERS' Journal is 64 pages, magazine-sized, professionally printed, with paper cover. Receives fewer than 900 submissions/year, accepts about 25 (including those used in columns). Press run is 20,000. Single copy: $5.99; subscription: $19.97/year U.S., add $15 for Canada/Mexico, $30 for Europe, all others add $35. Sample: $6.

How to Contact Submit 3-4 poems at a time. Lines/poem: 25 maximum. No e-mail submissions; postal submissions only. Responds in up to 5 months. Pays $5/poem plus 1 contributor's copy.

Contest/Award Offerings Sponsors poetry contests for previously unpublished poetry. Submit serious verse only, on any subject or in any form, 25 lines maximum. "Submit in duplicate: one with name and address, one without." Receives fewer than 300 entries/ contest. Winners announced in The WRITERS' Journal, for SASE, and on website. **Entry fee:** $3/poem for each contest. **Deadline:** April 30, August 30, and December 30. Guidelines available for SASE or on website.

⬚ ◎ XAVIER REVIEW

(Specialized: focus on African American, Caribbean, Southern literature), Xavier University, 1 Drexel Dr., New Orleans LA 70125-1098. (504)520-7805. Fax: (504)520-7917. Website: www.xula.edu/review. Established 1980 (review), 1988 (press). **Contact:** Dr. Nicole P. Greene, Editor (review) or Robert Skinner, Managing Editor.

Magazines Needs Xavier Review, published semiannually, is a journal of poetry, fiction, translations, essays, and reviews (contemporary literature) for professional writers, libraries, colleges, and universities. "Our content includes a focus on African American, Caribbean, and Southern literature, as well as works that touch on issues of religion and spirituality. We do, however, consider quality works on all themes." Has published poetry by Chris Waters, Lisa Sisk, Mark Taksa, Glenn Sheldon, Christine DeSimone, and Holly Pettit. Press run is 300. Subscription: $10/year for individuals, $15/year for institutions. Sample: $5.

How to Contact Submit 3-5 poems at a time. Include SASE. "Overseas authors only may submit by e-mail attachment." Pays 2 contributor's copies; offers 40% discount on additional copies.

Additional Information *Xavier Review* Press publishes book-length works of poetry and prose. Recent publications include *Turning Up the Volume* by Patrice Melnick and *Vespers at Mount Angel* by Stella Nesanovich. Books are available through website or by e-mailing rskinner@xula.edu. Query via e-mail: rskinner@xula.edu. **"Manuscripts should not be sent without permission of the editor."**

Book/Chapbook Publishers

E very poet dreams of publishing a collection of his or her work. However, it's surprising how many poets still envision putting out a thick, hardbound volume containing hundreds of poems. In reality, poetry books are usually slim, often paperback, with varying levels of production quality, depending on the publisher.

More common than full-length poetry books (i.e., 50-150 pages by modern standards) are poetry *chapbooks*, small editions of approximately 24-32 pages. They may be printed on quality paper with beautiful cover art on heavy stock; or they may be photocopied sheets of plain printer paper, folded and stapled or hand-sewn along the spine.

In this section you'll find a variety of presses and publishers of poetry books and chapbooks. However, it's a reflection of how poetry publishing works in the early 21st century that many book/chapbook publishing opportunities appear in the Contest & Awards section instead. To thoroughly search for a publisher/press, consult the Chapbook Publishers index (starting on page 502) and the Book Publishers index (starting on page 505) for a complete roundup of publishers that are listed in this edition of *Poet's Market*.

HOW LISTINGS ARE FORMATTED

Content of each listing was provided or verified by a representative of the press or publisher (poetry editor, managing editor, owner, etc.). Here is how that content is arranged in each listing: **Symbols.** Icons at the beginning of each listing offer visual signposts to specific information about the book/chapbook publisher: (🆕) this market is recently established and new to *Poet's Market*; (✪) this market did not appear in the 2010 edition; (🖥) this market publishes primarily online (some books and chapbooks are indeed published online, sometimes as a PDF that can be printed out); (🍁) this market is located in Canada or (🌐) outside the U.S. and Canada; ($) this market pays a monetary amount (as opposed to a given number of author's copies); (❑) this market welcomes submissions from beginning poets; (◪) this market prefers submissions from skilled, experienced poets, will consider work from beginning poets; (◑) this market prefers submissions from poets with a high degree of skill and experience; (◎) this market has a specialized focus (listed in parentheses after publisher/press name); (⊘) this market does not consider unsolicited submissions; and (⊘) this market is closed to *all* submissions. (Keys to these symbols are listed on the inside covers of this book and on page 3.)

Contact information. Next you'll find the information you need to contact the press or publisher, according to what was provided for each listing: name (in bold) of the publisher/press (with areas of specialization noted in parentheses where appropriate); regular mail address; telephone number; fax number; e-mail address; website address; year the publisher/press was established; the name of the person to contact (or an editorial title); and membership in small press/publishing organization(s). (**Note:** If a publisher or press wants electronic submissions exclusively, no street address may be given.)

Book/Chapbook Needs. This section provides an overview of the publisher/press, including such helpful information as editorial preferences; how manuscripts are considered; the number and kinds of books and/or chapbooks produced; a list of recently published titles; and production information about the titles (number of pages, printing/binding details, type of cover, press run).

How to Submit. This section states whether a poet should query with samples or send the complete manuscript; possible reading periods; reading fees, if applicable; response time; payment amount/terms; and how to order sample copies.

Additional Information. Editors/publishers may use this section to explain other types of publishing activities (such as broadsides, postcards or anthologies), elaborate on some aspect of production—anything beyond the basic details of the submission process that readers may find of interest.

Contest/Award Offerings. This section discusses prizes and competitions associated with the publisher, with either brief guidelines or a cross-reference to a separate listing in the Contests & Awards section.

Also Offers. Describes other offerings associated with this publisher (i.e., sponsored readings, website activities such as blogs and forums, related poetry groups, etc.).

Advice. Provides direct quotes from the editor/publisher about everything from pet peeves to tips on writing to views on the state of poetry today.

GETTING STARTED, FINDING A PUBLISHER

If you don't have a publisher in mind, read randomly through the listings, making notes as you go. (Don't hesitate to write in the margins, underline, use highlighters; it also helps to flag markets that interest you with Post-It Notes). Browsing the listings is an effective way to familiarize yourself with the kind of information presented and the publishing opportunities that are available at various skill levels. If you're thinking of a specific publisher by name, however, begin with the General Index. Here all *Poet's Market* listings are alphabetized.

REFINE YOUR SEARCH

To supplement the General Index, we provide several more specific indexes to help you refine your marketing plan for your manuscript. Not every listing appears in one of these indexes, so use them only to reinforce your other research efforts. As mentioned earlier, the Chapbook Publishers Index and Book Publishers Index are good places to start when you have a poetry collection to submit. In addition, the following indexes may be helpful:

Openness to Submissions Index breaks out markets according to the symbols (□ ◨ ◙ ▦) that appear at the beginning of each listing—signposts that indicate the level of writing an editor/publisher prefers to see. (For an explanation of these symbols, see page 3, the inside covers of this book, or the handy tear-out bookmark just inside the front cover.)

Geographical Index sorts publishers/presses by state and by countries outside the U.S. Some publishers are more open to poets from their region, so use this index when you're pinpointing local opportunities.

Subject Index groups all markets into categories according to areas of special focus. These include all specialized markets (appearing with the ◎ symbol) as well as broader categories such as online markets, poetry for children, markets that consider translations, and others. Save time when looking for a specific type of publisher/press by checking this index first.

THE NEXT STEP

Once you know how to interpret the listings in this section and identify markets for your work, the next step is to start submitting your poetry collection. See "Getting Started (and Using This Book)" on page 2 and "Frequently Asked Questions" on page 7 for advice, guidelines for preparing your manuscript and proper submissions procedures.

Book/Chapbook Publishers

☑ AHSAHTA PRESS

1910 University Dr., Boise ID 83275. (208)426-3134. Fax: (208)426-4373. E-mail: ahsahta@ boisestate.edu. Website: http://ahsahtapress.boisestate.edu. **Contact:** Janet Holmes, editor.

Needs Ahsahta Press, which originally published contemporary poets of the American West, has since expanded its scope "to publish poets nationwide, seeking out and publishing the best new poetry from a wide range of aesthetics—poetry that is technically accomplished, distinctive in style, and thematically fresh." Has published *The True Keeps Calm Biding Its Story* by Rusty Morrison (James Laughlin Award, 2008), *Bone Pagoda* by Susan Tichy, *Case Sensitive* by Kate Greenstreet, *Quarantine* by Brian Henry, *Spell* by Dan Beachy-Quick, and *Saving the Appearances* by Liz Waldner.

How to Contact Considers multiple and simultaneous submissions. Reading period is temporarily suspended due to backlog, but the press publishes runners-up as well as winners of the Sawtooth Poetry Prize. Forthcoming, new, and backlist titles available on website. Most backlist titles: $9.95; most current titles: $17.50.

Contest/Award Offerings The Sawtooth Poetry Prize.

Tips "Ahsahta seeks distinctive, non-imitative, unpredictable, and innovatively crafted work. Please check our website for examples of what we publish."

$ ◯ AMSTERDAM PRESS

6199 State Hwy 43, Amsterdam OH 43903. (740)543-4333. E-mail: plainspoke@gmail. com. Website: www.amsterdampress.net. **Contact:** Cindy Kelly, editor.

Needs Amsterdam Press, publishes chapbooks and broadsides, wants "poetry of place, poetry grounded in sense images, poetry that leaps, and has a clear voice." Does not want "esoteric poetry that focuses on the universal." Manuscripts are selected through open submission. Chapbooks are 36 pages, laser-printed, saddle-stitched, with card cover and black and white art/graphics.

How to Contact Query first, with a few sample poems and a cover letter with brief bio and publication credits. Chapbook mss may include previously published poems. "Previously published poetry must be recognized on a separate page of mss." Responds to queries in 1-3 months; to mss in 1-3 months. Pays honorarium of $25-100 and 10 author's copies out of a press run of 100-300. Order sample books/chapbooks by sending $8 to Amsterdam Press, 6199 Steubenville Road SE, Amsterdam, OH 43903.

ANHINGA PRESS

P.O. Box 10595, Tallahassee FL 32302. (850)422-1408. Fax: (850)442-6323. E-mail: info@ anhinga.org. **Contact:** Rick Campbell, editor. "Publishes only full-length collections of poetry (60-80 pages). No individual poems or chapbooks."

- Publishes only full-length collections of poetry (60-80 pages). No individual poems or chapbooks.

How to Contact *"Anhinga Press is currently not accepting unsolicited manuscripts.* (By "unsolicited" we mean manuscripts we haven't already accepted or requested.) Our publication calendar is filled through March, 2010." Please check website for further updates. Submit query letter and 10-page sample by mail with SASE.

◩ ANVIL PRESS

P.O. Box 3008 MPO, Vancouver BC V6B 3X5, Canada. (604)876-8710. Fax: (604)879-2667. E-mail: info@anvilpress.com. **Contact:** Brian Kaufman. "Anvil Press publishes contemporary adult fiction, poetry, and drama, giving voice to up-and-coming Canadian writers, exploring all literary genres, discovering, nurturing, and promoting new Canadian literary talent. Currently emphasizing urban/suburban themed fiction and poetry; de-emphasizing historical novels."

How to Contact Submit 8-12 poems with SASE.

Tips "Get our catalog, look at our poetry. We do very little poetry-maybe 1-2 titles per year."

⊕ ARC PUBLICATIONS

Nanholme Mill, Shaw Wood Rd., Todmorden, Lancashire OL14 6DA, England. E-mail: arc.publications@btconnect.com. Website: www.arcpublications.co.uk. **Contact:** Tony Ward, managing editor, or Angele Jarman, marketing and music editor.

Needs Publishes "contemporary poetry from new and established writers from the UK and abroad, specializing in the work of world poets writing in English, and the work of overseas poets in translation."

How to Contact *"At present we are not accepting submissions but keep updated by visiting the website."*

ARCTOS PRESS

P.O. Box 401, Sausalito CA 94966-0401. (415)331-2503. E-mail: runes@aol.com. Website: www.arctospress.com.

Needs Arctos Press, under the imprint HoBear Publications, publishes 1-2 paperbacks/year. "We publish quality, perfect-bound books and anthologies of poetry, usually theme-oriented, in runs of 1,500. as well as individual poetry collections such as *Prism*, poems by David St. John; *Fire Is Favorable to the Dreamer*, poems by Susan Terris; J.D. Whitney, Lowell Jaeger, and others.

How to Contact "We do not accept unsolicited manuscripts. Accepts queries by e-mail."

◪ THE BACKWATERS PRESS

3502 N. 52nd St., Omaha NE 68104-3506. (402)451-4052. E-mail: thebackwaterspress@gmail.com. Website: http://www.thebackwaterspress.com. **Contact:** Greg Kosmicki, editor.

Needs "The Backwaters Press continues to accept manuscripts for consideration for publication through the Open Submissions category. We're looking for manuscripts between 65 and 80 pages in length. **There is a $25 reading fee.**"

How to Contact "Please see the website for complete details, or send a self-addressed, stamped envelope to 'Guidelines' at the above address, or e-mail with a subject line of 'Open Submission Guidelines.'" Books available through The Backwaters Press or Amazon.com.

Tips "The Backwaters Press is dedicated to publishing the best new literature we can find. Send your best work."

Book/Chapbook Publishers

☑ BARNWOOD PRESS

4604 47th Ave. S, Seattle WA 98118-1824. (206)225-6887. E-mail: barnwoodpress@ earthlink.net. Website: www.barnwoodpress.org. **Contact:** Tom Koontz, editor.

Needs Barnwood Press publishes 1 paperback and 1 chapbook of poetry/year. Has recently published *New and Selected Poems* by Robert Ronnow, *Hitler's Mustache* by Peter Davis, *Sheer* by Martha Collins, and *Whatever You Can Carry: Poems of the Holocaust* by Stephen Herz. Chapbooks are usually 12-32 pages, offset-printed, saddle-stapled, with paper covers with art; size varies.

How to Contact Query first with a few sample poems and cover letter with brief bio and publication credits. Responds to queries and mss in 1 month. Order sample books/chapbooks through website.

BEAR STAR PRESS

185 Hollow Oak Dr, Cohasset CA 95973. Website: www.bearstarpress.com. **Contact:** Beth Spencer, editor/publisher.

How to Contact The Dorothy Brunsman Poetry Prize awards $1,000 and publication by Bear Star Press to the best book-length ms by a poet who resides in the Western states (within Mountain or Pacific time zones, plus Alaska and Hawaii) and serves as their primary pool for finding new manuscripts. "You need not enter the contest to submit to us, but our first allegiance is to manuscripts that come with a reading fee since they help to keep the press going."

$ ☑ BIRCH BOOK PRESS

P.O. Box 81, Delhi NY 13753. Birch Brook Press "is a letterpress book printer/typesetter/designer that uses monies from these activities to publish several titles of its own each year with cultural and literary interest." Specializes in literary work, flyfishing, baseball, outdoors, theme anthologies, translations of classics, and books about books. Has published *Woodstoves & Ravens*, by Robert Farmer, *Shadwell Hills*, by Rebecca Lilly, *Seasons of Defiance*, by Lance Lee, *And This is What Happens Next*, by Marcus Rome, *Jack's Beans* by Tom Smith, and *Tony's World*, by Barry Wallenstein. Publishes 4 paperbacks and/or hardbacks/year. Specializes "mostly in anthologies with specific themes." Books are "handset letterpress editions printed in our own shop." **Offers occasional co-op contract.**P.O. Box 81, Delhi NY 13753. Fax: (607)746-7453. E-mail: birchbrook@copper. net (inquiries only). Website: www.birchbrookpress.info. Established 1982. **Contact:** Barbara de la Cuesta, poetry editor. Member: American Academy of Poets, Small Press Center, Independent Book Publishers Association, American Typefounders Fellowship.

Tips "Send your best work, and see other Birch Brook Press books."

$ ☑ BLACK LAWRENCE PRESS

115 Center Ave., Aspinwall PA 15215. E-mail: editors@blacklawrencepress.com. Website: www.blacklawrencepress.com. **Contact:** Diane Goettel, Executive Editor.

Needs Black Lawrence Press seeks "to publish intriguing books of literature: novels, short story collections, poetry. Will also publish the occasional translation (from the German and French)." Has published poetry by D.C. Berry, James Reidel, and Stefi Weisburd. Publishes 10-12 books/year, mostly poetry and fiction. Manuscripts are selected through open submission and competition (see below). Books are 48-400 pages, offset-printed or high-quality POD, perfect-bound, with matte 4-color cover.

How to Contact "Regular submissions are considered on a year-round basis. Please check the general submissions page on our website for the most up-to-date guidelines information before submitting." Responds in up to 4 months for mss, "sometimes longer depending on backlog." Pays royalties. Sample books available through website.

Contest/Award Offerings The St. Lawrence Book Award, The Hudson Prize, and The Black River Chapbook Competition (see separate listings in Contests & Awards).

ℕ ◐ BLACK OCEAN

(617)304-9011. Fax: (617)849-5678. E-mail: carrie@blackocean.org. Website: www. blackocean.org. **Contact:** Carrie Olivia Adams, poetry editor.

◐ BLUE LIGHT PRESS

1563-45th Ave., San Francisco CA 94122. E-mail: bluelightpress@aol.com.

Needs Blue Light Press publishes 3 paperbacks, 2 chapbooks/year. "We like poems that are imagistic, emotionally honest, and push the edge—where the writer pushes through the imagery to a deeper level of insight and understanding. No rhymed poetry." Has published poetry by Alice Rogoff, Tom Centolella, Rustin Larson, Tony Krunk, Lisha Adela Garcia, Becky Sakellariou, and Christopher Buckley. "Books are elegantly designed and artistic." Chapbooks are 30 pages, digest-sized, professionally printed, with original cover art. Chapbooks available for $10 plus $2 p books for $15.95 plus $3 p&h.

How to Contact Submission guidelines available for SASE or by e-mail. Does not accept e-mail submissions. **Deadlines:** January 30 full-sized ms) and June 15 for chapbooks. "Read our guidelines before sending your ms."

Contest/Award Offerings The Blue Light Poetry Prize and Chapbook Contest and Blue Light Book Award for Full-Length Ms.

Also Offers "We have an online poetry workshop with a wonderful group of American and international poets—open to new members 3 times per year. Send an e-mail for info. We work in person with local poets, and will edit/critique poems by mail; $40 for four poems."

Tips "Read some of the books we publish, including our new anthology. We like to publish poets with a unique vision and gorgeous or unusual language; poems that push the edge. Stay in the poem longer and see what emerges in your vision and language."

$ ◐ BOA EDITIONS, LTD.

250 N. Goodman Street, Ste 306, Rochester NY 14607. (585)546-3410. E-mail: ward@boaeditions.org. Website: www.boaeditions.org. Established 1976. **Contact:** Thom Ward, poetry editor and Peter Conners, fiction editor.

Needs BOA Editions, a Pulitzer Prize-winning, not-for-profit publishing house acclaimed for its work, reads poetry mss for the American Poets Continuum Series (new poetry by distinguished poets in mid- and late career), the Lannan Translations Selection Series (publication of 2 new collections of contemporary international poetry annually, supported by The Lannan Foundation of Santa Fe, NM), and The A. Poulin, Jr. Poetry Prize (to honor a poet's first book; mss considered through competition—see separate listing in Contests & Awards). Has published poetry by W.D. Snodgrass, John Logan, Isabella Gardner, Richard Wilbur, and Lucille Clifton. Also publishes introductions by major poets of those less well-known (Gerald Stern wrote the foreword for Li-Young Lee's *Rose*, for example). BOA now also publishes fiction manuscripts for its American Reader Series. Check BOA's website for when the house is accepting fiction manuscripts.

How to Contact Check website for reading periods for the American Poets Continuum Series and The Lannan Translation Selection Series. "Please adhere to the general submission guidelines for each series." Guidelines available for SASE or on website. Pays advance plus 10 author's copies.

Contest/Award Offerings The A. Poulin, Jr. Poetry Prize.

Also Offers Available for download from website are reading and teaching guides for selected titles; and Season Sampler chapbooks, which provide introductions to BOA poets and their work.

☑ BOTTOM DOG PRESS, INC.

P.O. Box 425, Huron OH 44839. E-mail: LsmithDog@smithdocs.net. Website: http://smithdocs.net. Allen Frost and Laura Smith, Associate Editors. **Contact:** Larry Smith, Director.

• Imprint: Bird Dog Publishing

Needs Bottom Dog Press, Inc., "is a nonprofit literary and educational organization dedicated to publishing the best writing and art from the Midwest." Has published poetry by Jeff Gundy, Jim Daniels, Maj Ragain, Diane di Prima, and Sue Doro. Publishes the Midwest Series, Working Lives Series, and Harmony Series (105 books to date).

How to Contact Guidelines available on website.

Tips "Please read some of our books and send us a query before submitting anything."

☑ CAROLINA WREN PRESS

120 Morris St., Durham NC 27701. (919)560-2738. Fax: (919)560-2759. E-mail: carolinawrenpress@earthlink.net. Website: www.carolinawrenpress.org. **Contact:** Andrea Selch, President.

Needs Publishes 1 poetry book/year, "usually through our poetry series. Otherwise we primarily publish women, minorities, and North Carolina authors." Has published *a half-red sea* by Evie Shockley, as well as poetry by William Pitt Root, Karen Leona Anderson, Jaki Shelton Green, and Erica Hunt.

How to Contact Query first to see if submissions are open. If so, send 10 pages of sample poems and cover letter with brief bio and publication credits. Include SASE for reply only. Accepts e-mail queries, but send only letter and description of work; no large files. Reads unsolicited poetry submissions during the month of February. "Your best bet is to submit as part of our biennial poetry contest held in autumn of even-numbered years (e.g., 2010)." Guidelines available for SASE, by e-mail, or on website. Responds to queries in 3 months; to mss in 6 months. Payment varies.

Contest/Award Offerings Carolina Wren Press Poetry Contest for a First of Second Book.

◙ CLEVELAND STATE UNIVERSITY POETRY CENTER

2121 Euclid Ave., RT 1841, Cleveland OH 44115-2214. (216)687-3986 or (888)278-6473. Fax: (216)687-6943. E-mail: poetrycenter@csuohio.edu. Website: www.csuohio.edu/ poetrycenter. **Contact:** Michael Dumanis or Rita Grabowski, Managers.

Needs The Cleveland State University Poetry Center publishes "full-length collections by established and emerging poets, through competition and solicitation, as well as occasional poetry anthologies, texts on poetics, and novellas. Eclectic in its taste and inclusive in its aesthetic, with particular interest in lyric poetry and innovative approaches to craft. Not interested in light verse, devotional verse, doggerel, or poems by poets who have not read much contemporary poetry." Recent CSU Poetry Center publications include *You Don't know What you Don't Know*, by John Bradley, *Clamor*, by Elyse Fenton, *Horse Dance Underwater*, by Helena Mesa, *Destruction Myth*, by Mathias Svalina, *Sum of Every Lost Ship*, by Allison Titus, *Trust*, by Liz Waldnere, and *Self-Portrait With Crayon*, by Allison Benis White.

Contest/Award Offerings The Cleveland State University Poetry Center First Book Award and Open Competition (see separate listings in Contests & Awards).

Additional Information "Most manuscripts we publish are accepted through the competitions. All manuscripts sent for competitions are considered for publication. Outside of competitions, manuscripts are accepted by solicitation only."

◘ COACH HOUSE BOOKS

(416)979-2217. Fax: (416)977-1158. **Contact:** Alana Wilcox, editor.

◙ COFFEE HOUSE PRESS

79 Thirteenth Avenue, Suite 110, Minneapolis MN 55413. (612)338-0125. Fax: (612)338-4004. E-mail: fish@coffeehousepress.org. Website: www.coffeehousepress.org. **Contact:** Christopher Fischbach, senior editor.

- Books published by Coffee House Press have won numerous honors and awards. Example: *The Book of Medicines* by Linda Hogan won the Colorado Book Award for Poetry and the Lannan Foundation Literary Fellowship.

Needs Publishes 4-5 poetry books/year. Wants poetry that is "challenging and lively; influenced by the Beats, the NY School, LANGUAGE and post-LANGUAGE, or Black Mountain." Has published poetry collections by Victor Hernandez Cruz, Anne Waldman, Eleni Sikelianos, and Paul Metcalf.

How to Contact As of press-time, Coffee House Press was not accepting unsolicited mss for at least six months. Check website for updates. Query first, with 8-12 sample poems and cover letter with brief bio and publication credits. "Please include a SASE for our reply and/or the return of your manuscript. Absolutely no phone, fax, or e-mail queries." Seldom comments on rejected poems. Responds to queries in 1 month; to mss in up to 8 months. Always sends prepublication galleys. Catalog available for SASE.

Also Offers Online sign-up for free e-newsletter.

✠ $ ☑ COTEAU BOOKS

Thunder Creek Publishing Co-op, 2517 Victoria Ave., Regina SK S4P 0T2, Canada. (306)777-0170. Fax: (306)522-5152. E-mail: coteau@coteaubooks.com. Website: www. coteaubooks.com. **Contact:** Acquisitions Editor.

Needs Coteau Books is a "small literary press that publishes poetry, fiction, drama, anthologies, criticism, young adult novels—**by Canadian writers only**." Has published *The Crooked Good* by Louise Bernice Halfe, *Wolf Tree* by Alison Calder, and *Love of Mirrors* by Gary Hyland.

How to Contact Submit mss (80-100 poems only) typed with at least 12-point font. No simultaneous or non-Canadian submissions. No e-mail or fax submissions. Cover letter is required. Include publishing credits and bio, and SASE for return of ms. Accepts poetry mss from September 1-December 31 only. Responds to queries and mss in 4 months. Always sends prepublication galleys. Author receives 10% royalties and 10 author's copies. Order samples by sending 9x12 SASE for catalog.

Additional Information website includes title and ordering information, author interviews, awards, news and events, submission guidelines, and links.

Tips "Generally, poets should have, at minimum, a number of publishing credits (single poems or series) in literary magazines and anthologies before submitting a manuscript."

☑ CROSS-CULTURAL COMMUNICATIONS

239 Wynsum Ave., Merrick NY 11566-4725. (516)868-5635. Fax: (516)379-1901. E-mail: cccpoetry@aol.com. Website: www.cross-culturalcommunications.com. **Contact:** Stanley H. or Bebe Barkan, or Mia Barkan Clarke. (Specialized: bilingual, translations, multicultural)

• See www.thedrunkenboat.com (Summer 2002 issue) for a profile and www. Poetryvlog.com for a video.\lang3082

Needs "Cross-Cultural Review began as a series of chapbooks (6-12 per year) of collections of poetry translated from various languages, and continues as the Holocaust, Women Writers, Latin American Writers, African Heritage, Italian Heritage, International Artists, Art & Poetry, Jewish, Israeli, Yiddish, Hebrew, Arabic, Armenian, American, Bengali, Brazilian (Portuguese), Bulgarian, Cajun, Catalan, Chicano, Chinese, Dutch & Flemish, Estonian, Finnish, Gypsy (Roma), Korean, Macedonian, Native American, Persian, Polish, Romanian, Russian, Serbian, Sicilian, Swedish, Scandinavian, Turkish, Ukrainian, Welsh, and Long Island and Brooklyn Writers Chapbook Series (with a number of other permutations in the offing)—issued simultaneously in palm-sized and regular paperback and cloth-binding editions, and boxed and canned editions, as well as audiocassette, CD, DVD, and videocassette. The Cross-Cultural International Writers Series, focusing on leading poets from various countries, includes titles by Leo Vroman (Holland) and Pablo Neruda (Chile). The Holocaust Series is for survivors. In addition to publications in these series, Cross-Cultural Communications has published anthologies and postcard and broadside portfolio collections by dozens of poets from many countries, a number in special bilingual limited editions, including such poets and translators as Laura Boss, August bover, Mia Barkan Clarke, Sultan Catto, Aleksey Dayen, Arthur Dobrin,

Kristine Doll, John Dotson, Robert Dunn, Sung-Il Lee, and more ." Sample chapbook: $10 postpaid.

How to Contact Guidelines available for SASE. Pays 10% of print run.

Additional Information New: *Cross-Cultural Review Chapbook* (CCRCB), an occasional series of 16-48 page limited edition chapbooks (print runs of 100-150 copies) focusing on poetry (bilingual preferred). Sample: $15 postpaid. Pays 5-10 copies. The Seventh Quarry/CCC chapbook series, co-edited with Peter Thabit Jones, features a pairing of a British poet with a non-British poet. 64 pages (print run of 250-500 copies). $15 (Int'l Money Order for direct shipment from Swansea, Wales). Pays 10 copies.

Also Offers "Cross-Cultural Communications continues, on an occasional basis, to organize events for international poets and writers."

$ ⊘ JOHN DANIEL & COMPANY

P.O. Box 2790, McKinleyville CA 95519. (707)839-3495. Fax: (707)839-3242. E-mail: dandd@danielpublishing.com. Website: www.danielpublishing.com. **Contact:** John Daniel, editor.

Needs John Daniel & Company, an imprint of Daniel & Daniel Publishers, Inc., is a general small press publisher, specializing in literature, both prose and poetry. "Book-length manuscripts of any form or subject matter will be considered, but we do not want to see pornographic, libelous, illegal, or sloppily written poetry." Has published *A Tiara For The Twentieth Century,* by Suzanne Richardson Harvey; *Shaking the Tree,* by Jeanne Lohmann; and *Sailing On Dry Land,* by Burton D. Wasserman. Publishes about 6 flat-spined poetry paperbacks/year. Books average 80 pages. Press runs average between 500-1,000. No longer issues a print catalog, but all books are shown and described on website.

How to Contact Query first, with 12 sample poems and cover letter with brief bio and publication credits. Considers simultaneous submissions. No fax or e-mail submissions. Responds to queries in 2 weeks; to mss in 2 months. Always sends prepublication galleys. Pays 10% royalties of net receipts. Acquires English-language book rights. Returns rights upon termination of contract.

Tips "Because we are downsizing our company, and therefore have less cash flow to work with, I'm sorry to say we are now publishing very little poetry. This doesn't mean we won't take a look at any manuscript we receive, but you should know that of late almost all poetry books we have published come out under our Fithian Press imprint, the imprint we use for copublishing."

⇄ ⊘ DESCRIBE ADONIS PRESS

297 Blake Blvd., #4, Ottawa ON K1L 6L6, Canada. Website: canadianzenhaikuhome. homestead.com/index.html.

Needs Describe Adonis Press publishes Japanese form poetry only, "especially haiku, but also senryu, renga, tanka, etc." Does not want any other form or genre of poetry. Publishes one poetry book/year, 5 chapbooks/year on average.

How to Contact Contact with up to 12 haikus via e-mail attachment in rtf form only. E-mail is through website form only. Format should be single-spaced with three blank lines between each haiku; subject line should read: "Submission of hiaku (or haikus) by [your name]." Must use Georgia Font 11 points, or, if absolutely unable to use that, in Times New Roman 11 point font. See website for complete guidelines and contact.

⚃ $ ☑ ÉCRITS DES FORGES

992-A, rue Royale, Trois-Rivières QC G9A 4H9, Canada. (819)840-8492. Website: www.ecritsdesforges.com. **Contact:** Stéphane Despatie, director.

Needs Écrits des Forges publishes poetry only that is "authentic and original as a signature. We have published poetry from more than 1,000 poets coming from most of the francophone countries: Andreé Romus (Belgium), Amadou Lamine Sall (Seéneégal), Nicole Brossard, Claude Beausoleil, Jean-Marc Desgent, and Jean-Paul Daoust (Queébec)." Publishes 45-50 paperback books of poetry/year. Books are usually 80-88 pages, digest-sized, perfect-bound, with 2-color covers with art.

How to Contact Query first with a few sample poems and a cover letter with brief bio and publication credits. Responds to queries in up to 6 months. Pays royalties of 10-20%, advance of 50% maximum, and 25 author's copies. Order sample books by writing or faxing.

◻ ETCHED PRESS

P.O. Box 3063, Wilmington NC 28406, (919)536-8258. E-mail: submit@etchedpress.com. Website: www.etchedpress.com. **Contact:** Kevin Dublin, editor.

Needs *Etched Press* publishes poetry chapbooks and anthologies. "We're interested mostly in well-written collections of poetry that aren't pretentious and have universal themes." Does not want "poetry that will be forgotten." Has published Melanie Faith's *Bright Burning Fuse*. Publishes 3 chapbooks/year. Manuscripts are selected through open submission. Chapbooks are 12-40 pages, sheet-fed press printed, saddle-stitched, with cover stock designed in collaboration wtih the author.

How to Contact "May submit via e-mail with the manuscript attached as a .doc or .pdf file complete with cover page that contains name, address, and e-mail. Any questions should be directed to inquiry@etchedpress.com." Responds to queries in 2 weeks; to mss in 3 months. Pays royalties of 25% and 25 author's copies (out of a press run of 150). Order sample books/chapbooks by sending $5 to Etched Press Sample Chapbook, P.O. Box 3063, Wilmington NC 28406.

Tips "Please, please, please don't send submissions in the body of an e-mail. Even though copying and pasting it into a word document isn't that difficult, it's a little bothersome, affects presentation, and the editor dislikes it just a little from the start. Selling poetry today is difficult in book form for anyone whose name isn't recognized. I think chapbooks are perfect for the world of poetry. They're cheaper, meaning a person may be more inclined to buy one. They're also intimate, meaning a person may feel closer to the author."

$ ▨ FARRAR, STRAUS & GIROUX/BOOKS FOR YOUNG READERS

Children's Editorial Dept., 175 Fifth Ave., New York NY 10010. (646)307-5151. Website: www.fsgkidsbooks.com. **Contact:** Children's Editorial Department.

Needs Publishes one book of children's poetry "every once in a while," in trade hardcover only. Open to book-length submissions of children's poetry only. Has published Valerie

Worth's *Peacock and Other Poems*, Tony Johnston's *An Old Shell*, and Helen Frost's *Keesha's House* (a novel in poems).

How to Contact Query first with sample poems and cover letter with brief bio and publication credits. Considers simultaneous submissions. Seldom comments on rejected poems. Send SASE for reply. Responds to queries in up to 2 months, to mss in up to 4 months. "We pay an advance against royalties; the amount depends on whether or not the poems are illustrated, etc." Also pays 10 author's copies.

☑ FINISHING LINE PRESS

P.O. Box 1626, Georgetown KY 40324. (859)514-8966. E-mail: FinishingBooks@aol.com. Website: www.finishinglinepress.com. **Contact:** Leah Maines, Poetry Editor.
• Member of CLMP

Needs Finishing Line Press seeks to "discover new talent" and hopes to publish chapbooks by both men and women poets who have not previously published a book or chapbook of poetry. Has published *Parables and Revelations* by T. Crunk, *Family Business* by Paula Sergi, *Putting in a Window* by John Brantingham, and *Dusting the Piano* by Abigail Gramig. Publishes 50-60 poetry chapbooks/year. Chapbooks are usually 25-30 pages, digest-sized, laser-printed, saddle-stapled, with card covers with textured matte wrappers.

How to Contact Submit up to 26 pages of poetry with cover letter, bio, acknowledgments, and **$12 reading fee**. Responds to queries and mss in up to 1 month. Pay varies; pays in author's copies. "Sales profits, if any, go to publish the next new poet." Sample chapbooks available by sending $6 to Finishing Line Press or through website.

Contest/Award Offerings The Finishing Line Press Open Chapbook Competition and the New Women's Voices Chapbook Competition (see separate listings in Contests & Awards).

Tips "We are very open to new talent. If the poetry is great, we will consider it for a chapbook."

⊕ $ ☑ FLARESTACK POETS

P.O. Box 14779, Birmingham, West Midlands B13 3GU, United Kingdom. E-mail: meria@ btinternet.com; jacquierowe@hotmail.co.uk. Website: www.flarestackpoets.co.uk. **Contact:** Meredith Andrea and Jacqui Rowe. Estab. 2008.

Needs Flarestack Poets wants "poems that dare outside current trends, even against the grain." Does not want "poems that fail to engage with either language or feeling." First chapbooks appearing in Autumn 2009. Publishes 8 chapbooks/year and 1 anthology. Manuscripts are selected through open submission and competition. "Our first chapbooks are winners of the 2009 Flarestack Poets Pamphlet competition. Thereafter we will consider open submissions." Chapbooks are 20-30 pages, professional photocopy, saddle-stitched, card cover.

How to Contact Quert first with a few sample poems and a cover letter with brief bio and publication credits. Manuscript may include previously published poems. Responds in 6 weeks. Pays royalties of 25% and 6 author's copies (out of a press run of 200). See website to order sample copies.

☑ FLOATING BRIDGE PRESS

PO Box 18814, Seattle WA 98118. E-mail: floatingbridgepress@yahoo.com. Website: www.floatingbridgepress.org.

Needs Floating Bridge Press publishes chapbooks and anthologies by Washington State poets, selected through an annual competition (see below). Has published *After* by Nancy Pagh, *In the Convent We Become Clouds* by Annette Spaulding-Convy, *Toccata & Fugue* by Timothy Kelly, and *The Former St. Christopher* by Michael Bonacci, among others. The press also publishes *Floating Bridge Review*, an annual anthology featuring the work of Washington State poets. *Floating Bridge Review* is 86-144 pages, digest-sized, offset-printed, perfect-bound, with glossy cardstock cover. For a sample chapbook or anthology, send $13 postpaid.

Contest/Award Offerings For consideration, **Washington State poets only** should submit a chapbook ms of 20-24 pages of poetry. In addition to publication, the winner receives $500, 15 author's copies, and a reading in the Seattle area. All entrants receive a copy of the winning chapbook and will be considered for inclusion in *Floating Bridge Review*. Poet's name must not appear on the ms. Include a separate page with ms title, poet's name, address, phone number, and acknowledgments of any previous publications. Include SASE for results only; mss will not be returned. **Entry fee:** $12. **Deadline:** usual reading period is November 1-February 15 (postmark). Considers previously published individual poems and simultaneous submissions. Manuscripts are judged anonymously.

Ⓝ ☑ FUTURECYCLE PRESS

P.O. Box 680695, Marietta GA 30068. (404)805-6039. Fax: (800)755-7332. E-mail: submissions@futurecycle.org. Website: www.futurecycle.org. **Contact:** Robert S. King, director & editor-in-chief.

- "FutureCycle Press publishes chapbooks and full-length collections of poetry. We consider unsolicited submissions throughout the year as well as those submitted to our annual book competition."

Needs Wants "poetry from highly skilled poets, whether well known or emerging. With a few exceptions, we are eclectic in our editorial tastes." Does not want concrete or visual poetry. Has published David Chorlton, John Laue, Temple Cone, Neil Carpathios. Publishes 4 poetry books/year and 2 chapbooks/year. Ms. selected through open submission and competition. "We read unsolicited mss. but also conduct a yearly poetry book competition." Books are 60-90 pages; offset print, perfect-bound, with glossy, full color cover stock, b&w inside. Chapbooks are 20-40 pages, offset print, saddle-stitched.

How to Contact Submit completes ms; no need to query. Read guidelines posted on website. May include previously published poems. Responds in 1 week. Pays royalties of 10% and 25 copies out of press run of 200.

☑ GERTRUDE PRESS

P.O. Box 83948, Portland OR 97283. E-mail: editor@gertrudepress.org. Website: www.gertrudepress.org. **Contact:** Eric Delehoy, founding editor. (Specialized: gay, lesbian, bisexual, transgendered, queer-identified & allied)

Needs Gertrude Press, a nonprofit 501(c)(3) organization, showcases and develops "the creative talents of lesbian, gay, bisexual, trans, queer-identified, and allied individuals."

Has published *Bone Knowing* by Kate Grant. Gertrude Press publishes 2 chapbooks/ year (1 fiction, 1 poetry) as well as *Gertrude*, a semiannual literary journal (see separate listing in Magazines/Journals). Manuscripts are chosen through competition only (see below). Chapbooks are 20-24 pages, offset-printed, saddle-stapled, with cardstock cover with art.

How to Contact Refer to guidelines for Gertrude Press Poetry Chapbook Contest. Order sample chapbooks for $10.

Contest/Award Offerings The Gertrude Press Poetry Chapbook Contest.

Ⓝ GHOST ROAD PRESS

(303)758-7623. E-mail: matt@ghostroadpress.com; evan@ghostroadpress.com. Website: ghostroadpress.com.

How to Contact *Not currently accepting submissions.* Query via e-mail. "Send an attachment (word or.rtf only) that includes a complete synopsis, a description of your marketing plan and platform and samples. To view a complete list of our titles and changing submission guidelines, please visit website." Responds in 2-3 months. Accepts simultaneous submissions.

⊕ ⊘ GINNINDERRA PRESS

P.O. Box 3461, Port Adelaide SA 5015, Australia. (61)(2)6258-9060. Fax: (61)(2)6258-9069. E-mail: stephen@ginninderrapress.com.au. Website: www.ginninderrapress.com. au. Established 1996.

• Please note: No longer accepting mss from writers residing outside of Australia.

Needs Ginninderra Press works "to give publishing opportunities to new writers." Has published poetry by Alan Gould and Geoff Page. Books are usually up to 72 pages, A5, laser-printed, saddle-stapled or thermal-bound, with board covers.

How to Contact Query first, with a few sample poems and a cover letter with brief bio and publication credits. Considers previously published poems; no simultaneous submissions. No fax or e-mail submisions. Time between acceptance and publication is 6 months. Seldom comments on rejected poems. Responds to queries within 1 week; to mss in 2 months.

⊠ $ ⊘ GOOSE LANE EDITIONS

469 King St., Ste 330, Fredericton NB E3B 1E5, Canada. (506)450-4251. Fax: (506)459-4991. Website: www.gooselane.com. **Contact:** Ross Leckie, Poetry Editor.

Needs Goose Lane is a small literary press publishing Canadian fiction, poetry, and nonfiction. **Considers mss by Canadian poets only.** Receives about 400 mss/year, publishes 15-20 books/year, 4 of which are poetry collections. Has published *Beatitudes* by Herménégilde Chiasson and *I & I* by George Elliott Clarke.

How to Contact "Call to inquire whether we are reading submissions." Accepts submissions by postal mail only. Guidelines available on website. Always sends prepublication galleys. Authors may receive royalties of up to 10% of retail price on all copies sold. Copies available to author at 40% discount.

Tips "Many of the poems in a manuscript accepted for publication will have been previously published in literary journals such as *The Fiddlehead*, *The Dalhousie Review*, or *The Malahat Review*."

GOTHIC PRESS

2272 Quail Oak, Baton Rouge LA 70808. 225-766-2906. E-mail: gothicpt12@aol.com. Website: www.gothicpress.com.

Needs Gothic Press publishes gothic, horror, and dark fantasy poetry in their Gothic Chapbook series. Wants poetry in "any form or style as long as gothic or horror elements are present." Does not want science fiction. Has published Bruce Boston, Joey Froehlich, Scott C. Hocstad. Manuscripts are selected through open submission. Chapbooks are 10-80 pages, offset, saddle-stapled, with cardstock cover or interior illustration by commission. Send samples of art.

How to Contact *Gothic Press no longer accepts unsolicited submissions, and seeks chapbooks by invitation only.*

Tips "Know Gothic literature well."

⊘ GRAYWOLF PRESS

250 Third Avenue North, Suite 600, Minneapolis MN 55401. Website: www.graywolfpress. org. **Contact:** Jeff Shotts, Poetry Editor.

- Poetry published in Graywolf Press collections has been included in *The Pushcart Prize*, and many books have won major awards.

Needs Graywolf Press is considered one of the nation's leading nonprofit literary publishers. "Graywolf introduces and promotes some of the most exciting and creative writers of our times." Considers only mss by poets widely published in magazines and journals of merit; **does not generally consider unsolicited mss but considers queries**. Has published poetry by Elizabeth Alexander, Vijay Seshadri, Tess Gallagher, Tony Hoagland, Matthea Harvey, D.A. Powell, and many more. Publishes around 9 collections of poetry, 1-2 collections of poetry in translation, and 1-2 collections of essays on poetry/year.

How to Contact *No unsolicited mss.* Query first, with 10 pages of poetry (as a sample from the ms) and cover letter with brief bio and publication credits through online submission form. See website for guidelines. SASE required for reply. No e-mail queries. Reads queries in January, May, and September. Responds to queries in 3-6 months. Order sample books through website, or request catalog through online submission form.

⟨⟩ ⊘ GUERNICA EDITIONS INC.

489 Strathmore Blvd., Toronto ON M4C 1N8, Canada. Website: www.guernicaeditions. com.

Needs "We wish to bring together the different and often divergent voices that exist in Canada and the U.S. We are interested in translations. We are mostly interested in poetry and essays on pluriculturalism." Has published poetry by Pier Paolo Pasolini, Pasquale Verdichio, Carole David, Jean-Marc Desgent, Gilles Cyr, Claudine Bertrand, Paul Beélanger, Denise Desaulets.

How to Contact Query with 1-2 pages of sample poems. Send SASE (Canadian stamps only) or SAE and IRCs for catalog.

Tips "We are interested in promoting a pluricultural view of literature by bridging languages and cultures. We specialize in international translation."

HIGH LYRICAL EXPERIMENTS

P.O. Box 141, Rehoboth NM 87322. E-mail: M_L_Perez@yahoo.com. Website: www. gallup.unm.edu/ ~ smarandache/ebooksliterature.htm.

Needs *High Lyrical Experiments* publishes 2-3 poetry paperbacks/year. Wants experimental poetry dealing with paradoxism. No classical poetry. See website for poetry samples. Has published poetry by Anatol Ciocanu, Nina Josu, and Al Bantos.

How to Contact Submit 3-4 poems at a time. No previously published poems or simultaneous submissions. Cover letter is preferred. Submit seasonal poems 1 month in advance. Time between acceptance and publication is 1 year. Seldom comments on rejected poems. Responds to queries in 1 month. Pays 100 author's copies. Order sample books by sending SASE.

Also Offers Free e-books available on website.

⊞ $ ⊘ HIPPOPOTAMUS PRESS

22 Whitewell Rd., Frome, Somerset BA11 4EL, England. (44)(1373)466653. Fax: (44) (1373)466653. E-mail: rjhippopress@aol.com. **Contact:** Roland John, Poetry Editor. (Specialized: Modernism)

Needs Hippopotamus Press publishes 6 books/year. "The Hippopotamus Press is specialized, with an affinity with Modernism. No Typewriter Poetry, Concrete Poetry, or Surrealism."

How to Contact Query first, with a few sample poems and cover letter with brief bio and publication credits. Considers simultaneous submissions and previously published poems. Responds in 6 weeks. Pays 7½-10% royalties plus author's copies. Request book catalog to purchase sample books.

⊘ HOLIDAY HOUSE, INC.

Editorial Dept., 425 Madison Ave., New York NY 10017. Fax: (212)421-6134. E-mail: info@ holidayhouse.com. Website: www.holidayhouse.com. **Contact:** Editor. (Specialized: poetry for children/teens)

Needs A trade children's book house. Has published hardcover books for children by John Updike and Walter Dean Myers. Publishes one poetry book/year, averaging 32 pages.

How to Contact *"The acceptance of complete book manuscripts of high-quality children's poetry is limited."* Please send the entire manuscript, whether submitting a picture book or novel by mail. Does not accept submissions by e-mail or fax.

⊠ $ ⊘ HOUSE OF ANANSI PRESS

110 Spadina Ave., Suite 801, Toronto ON M5V 2K4, Canada. (416)363-4343. Fax: (416)363-1017. Website: www.anansi.ca. **Contact:** Editors. (Specialized: work by Canadian

authors)110 Spadina Ave., Suite 801, Toronto ON M5V 2K4 Canada. (416)363-4343. Fax: (416)363-1017. Website: www.anansi.ca. Established 1967.

Needs House of Anansi publishes literary fiction and poetry by Canadian and international writers. "We seek to balance the list between well-known and emerging writers, with an interest in writing by Canadians of all backgrounds. We publish Canadian poetry only, and poets must have a substantial publication record—if not in books, then definitely in journals and magazines of repute." Does not want "children's poetry or poetry by previously unpublished poets." Has published *Power Politics* by Margaret Atwood and *Ruin & Beauty* by Patricia Young. Books are generally 96-144 pages, trade paperbacks with French sleeves, with matte covers.

How to Contact Canadian poets should query first with 10 sample poems (typed double-spaced) and a cover letter with brief bio and publication credits. Considers simultaneous submissions. Poems are circulated to an editorial board. Often comments on rejected poems. Responds to queries within 1 year, to mss (if invited) within 4 months. Pays 8-10% royalties, a $750 advance, and 10 author's copies (out of a press run of 1,000).

Tips "To learn more about our titles, check our website or write to us directly for a catalog. We strongly advise poets to build up a publishing reésumeé by submitting poems to reputable magazines and journals. This indicates 3 important things to us: 1, that he or she is becoming a part of the Canadian poetry community; 2, that he or she is building up a readership through magazine subscribers; and 3, it establishes credibility in his or her work. There is a great deal of competition for only 3 or 4 spots on our list each year—which always includes works by poets we have previously published."

☑ ALICE JAMES BOOKS

University of Maine at Farmington, 238 Main St., Farmington ME 04938. (207)778-7071. Fax: (207)778-7071. E-mail: ajb@umf.maine.edu. Website: www.alicejamesbooks.org.

Needs "The mission of Alice James Books, a cooperative poetry press, is to seek out and publish the best contemporary poetry by both established and beginning poets, with particular emphasis on involving poets in the publishing process." Has published poetry by Jane Kenyon, Jean Valentine, B.H. Fairchild, and Matthea Harvey. Publishes flat-spined paperbacks of high quality, both in production and contents. Does not want children's poetry or light verse. Publishes 6 paperback books/year, 80 pages each, in editions of 1,500.

How to Contact Manuscripts are selected through competitions (see below).

Contest/Award Offerings The Kinereth Gensler Awards and The Beatrice Hawley Award.

⊘ THE JOHNS HOPKINS UNIVERSITY PRESS

2715 N. Charles St., Baltimore MD 21218. Website: www.press.jhu.edu. Trevor Lipscombe, editor-in-chief (physics and mathematics; tcl@press.jhu.edu); Jacqueline C. Wehmueller, executive editor (consumer health and history of medicine; jwehmueller@press.jhu.edu); Henry Y.K. Tom, executive editor (social sciences; htom@press.jhu.edu); Wendy Harris, senior acquisitions editor (clinical medicine, public health, health policy; wharris@press.jhu.edu); Robert J. Brugger, senior acquisitions editor (American history, history of science and technology, regional books; rbrugger@press.jhu.edu); Vincent J. Burke, senior acquisitions editor (biology; vjb@press.jhu.edu); Matt McAdam, acquisitions editor (humanities, classics, and ancient studies; mlonegro@press.jhu.edu); Ashleigh McKown, assistant acquisitions editor (higher education; amckown@press.jhu.edu). 2715 N. Charles St., Baltimore MD 21218. Fax: (410) 516-6968. Website: www.press.jhu. edu. Established 1878.

Needs "One of the largest American university presses, Johns Hopkins publishes primarily scholarly books and journals. We do, however, publish short fiction and poetry in the series Johns Hopkins: Poetry and Fiction, edited by John Irwin."

How to Contact *"Unsolicited submissions are not considered."*

KATYDID BOOKS

1 Balsa Rd., Santa Fe NM 87508. Website: http://katydidbooks.com. **Contact:** Karen Hargreaves-Fitzsimmons and Thomas Fitzsimmons, editors/publishers.

Needs "We publish a series of poetry: Asian Poetry in Translation (distributed by University of Hawaii Press)."

How to Contact *Currently not accepting submissions.*

⊘ KITCHEN PRESS

E-mail: JustinAMarks@gmail.com. Website: http://www.kitchenpresschapbooks. blogspot.com/. Kitchen Press is not currently accepting unsolicited submissions.

⊘ KNOPF

1745 Broadway, New York NY 10019.

Needs Over the years Knopf has been one of the most important and distinguished publishers of poetry in the United States. Has published poetry by Cynthia Zarin, John Hollander, Kevin Young, Marge Piercy, and Edward Hirsch.

How to Contact *Does not consider unsolicited mss.*

▦ ⊘ LAPWING PUBLICATIONS

1 Ballysillan Dr., Belfast BT14 8HQ, Northern Ireland. +44 2890 500 796. Fax: +44 2890 295 800. E-mail: lapwing.poetry@ntlworld.com. Website: www.lapwingpoetry.com. **Contact:** Dennis Greig, Editor.

• Lapwing will produce work only if and when resources to do so are available.

Needs Lapwing publishes "emerging Irish poets and poets domiciled in Ireland, plus the new work of a suitable size by established Irish writers. Non-Irish poets are also published. Poets based in continental Europe have become a major feature. Emphasis on first collections preferrably not larger than 80 pages. Logistically, publishing beyond the British Isles is always difficult for 'hard copy' editions. PDF copies via e-mail are £3 or 3 per copy. No fixed upperl limit to number of titles per year. Hard copy prices are £8 to £10 per copy. No e-reader required." Wants poetry of all kinds, but, "no crass political, racist, sexist propaganda, even of a positive or 'pc' tenor." Has published Alastair Thomson, Clifford Ireson, Colette Wittorski, Gilberte de Leger, Aubrey Malone, and Jane Shaw Holiday. Pamphlets up to 32 pages, chapbooks up to 44 pages, books 48-112 pages; New Belfast binding, simulated perfect binding for books, otherwise saddle stitching.

How to Contact "Submit 6 poems in the first instance; depending on these, an invitation to submit more may follow." Considers simultaneous submissions. Accepts e-mail submissions in body of message or in DOC format. Cover letter is required. "All submissions receive a first reading. If these poems have minor errors or faults, the writer is advised. If poor quality, the poems are returned. Those 'passing' first reading are retained, and a letter of conditional offer is sent." Often comments on rejected poems. Responds to queries in 1 month; to mss in 2 months. Pays 20 author's copies; no royalties. "After initial publication, irrespective of the quantity, the work will be permanently available using 'print-on-demand' production; such publications will not always be printed exactly as the original, although the content will remain the same."

Tips "Clean; check spelling, grammar, punctuation, layout (i.e., will it fit a book page?); clear text. Due to limited resources, material will be processed well in advance of any estimated publishing date. The conventional publishing date system is abandoned. Work will be published when it is ready. We produce what is needed."

⊠ LETHE PRESS

(609)410-7391. E-mail: editor@lethepressbooks.com. Website: www.lethepressbooks. com. **Contact:** Steve Berman, publisher. "Lethe Press is a small press seeking gay and lesbian themed poetry collections." Distributes/promotes titles Lethe Books are distributed by Ingram Publications and Bookazine, and are available at all major bookstores, as well as the major online retailers.

How to Contact Send query letter. Accepts queries by e-mail.

⊘ LOONFEATHER PRESS

P.O. Box 1212, Bemidji MN 56619-1212. E-mail: books@loonfeatherpress.com. Website: loonfeatherpress.com.

Needs Loonfeather Press publishes a limited number of quality poetry books. Has published *Imaginarium* by Lynn Levin (a 2005 ForeWord Finalist); *The Rhubarb King* by Sharon Chmielarz; and *Traces in Blood, Bone, & Stone: Contemporary Ojibwe Poetry*, edited by Kimberly Blaeser.

How to Contact *Does not accept unsolicited mss. Does accept query letters/e-mails. Check website for updates.*

◔ LOUISIANA STATE UNIVERSITY PRESS

3990 West Lakeshore Dr., Baton Rouge LA 70808. (225) 578-6434. Fax: (225) 578-6461. E-mail: jeaster@lsu.edu. Website: www.lsu.edu/lsupress. **Contact:** John Easterly, Executive Editor.

Needs A highly respected publisher of collections by poets such as Claudia Emerson, David Kirby, Brendan Galvin, Fred Chappell, Marilyn Nelson, and Henry Taylor. Publisher of the Southern Messenger Poets series edited by Dave Smith.

How to Contact *"Currently not accepting poetry submissions, since the lists are full through 2014."*

⊘ LUNA BISONTE PRODS

E-mail: bennett.23@osu.edu. Website: www.johnmbennett.net. **Contact:** John M. Bennett, editor/publisher.

Needs Luna Bisonte Prods considers book submissions. "Interested in avant-garde and highly experimental work only." Has published poetry by Jim Leftwich, Sheila E. Murphy, Al Ackerman, Richard Kostelanetz, Carla Bertola, Olchar Lindsann, and many others.

How to Contact Query first, with a few sample poems and cover letter with brief bio and publication credits. "Keep it brief. Chapbook publishing usually depends on grants or other subsidies, and is usually by solicitation. **Will also consider subsidy arrangements on negotiable terms.**" A sampling of various Luna Bisonte Prods products is available for $20.

Tips "Be blank."

⊘ MAVERICK DUCK PRESS

E-mail: maverickduckpress@yahoo.com. Website: www.maverickduckpress.com. **Contact:** Kendall A. Bell, editor.

Needs Maverick Duck Press is a "publisher of chapbooks from undiscovered talent. We are looking for fresh and powerful work that shows a sense of innovation or a new take on passion or emotion. Previous publication in print or online journals will increase your chances of us accepting your manuscript." Does not want "unedited work." Recently published *Devil's road Down*, by Adrienne Odasso; *Hemispheres*, by Jeanpaul Ferro; *Inside Bone There's Always Marrow*, by Rachel Mallino and *Big Time*, by Don Kloss. Publishes 4-6 chapbooks/year. Manuscripts are selected through open submission. Chapbooks are 18-24 pages, photocopied, saddle-stapled, with cardstock covers (poet must provide desired cover art).

How to Contact Send manuscript in Microsoft Word format with a cover letter with brief bio and publication credits. Chapbook mss may include previously published poems. "Previous publication is always a plus, as we may be more familiar with your work. Chapbook manuscripts should have at least 20 poems." Pays 20 author's copies (out of a press run of 50).

Tips "Write and revise often. Read a lot of other poets. Your manuscript should be the strongest of your work."

$ ⊘ MEADOWBROOK PRESS

5451 Smetana Dr., Minnetonka MN 55343. (800)338-2232. Fax: (952-930-1940). E-mail: info@meadowbrookpress.com. Website: www.meadowbrookpress.com. (Specialized: anthologies; children's humor)

Needs Meadowbrook Press is "currently seeking poems to be considered for future funny poetry book anthologies for children." Wants humorous poems aimed at children ages 6-12. "Poems should be fun, punchy, and refreshing. We're looking for new, hilarious, contemporary voices in children's poetry that kids can relate to." Has published poetry by Shel Silverstein, Jack Prelutsky, Jeff Moss, Kenn Nesbitt, and Bruce Lansky. Published anthologies include *Kids Pick the Funniest Poems*, *A Bad Case of the Giggles*, and *Miles of Smiles*.

How to Contact "Please take time to read our guidelines, and send your best work." Submit up to 10 poems at a time; 1 poem to a page with name and address on each; include SASE. Lines/poem: 25 maximum. Considers simultaneous submissions. Time between acceptance and publication is 1-2 years. Poems are tested in front of grade school students before being published. Guidelines available for SASE or on website. Responds only if interested. Pays $50-100/poem plus 1 contributor's copy.

MELLEN POETRY PRESS

P.O. Box 450, Lewiston NY 14092-0450. **Contact:** Kelly Lang, Acquisitions Editor.

✷ MIDMARCH ARTS PRESS

300 Riverside Dr., New York NY 10025. E-mail: info@midmarchartspress.org. Website: www.midmarchartspress.org.

Needs Midmarch Arts Press publishes 4 paperbacks/year on the visual arts and one book of poetry. Has recently published *Rock Vein Sky*, by Charlotte Mandel; *Luminations*, art by Oriole F. feshbach for Wallace Stevens' poem "The Auroras of Autumn."

How to Contact Query by letter or e-mail prior to submitting anything.

✷ MILKWEED EDITIONS

1011 Washington Ave. S., Suite 300, Minneapolis MN 55415-1246. (612)332-3192. Fax: (612)215-2550. E-mail: editor@milkweed.org. Website: www.milkweed.org.

Needs Milkweed Editions is "looking for poetry manuscripts of high quality that embody humane values and contribute to cultural understanding." Not limited in subject matter. Open to writers with previously published books of poetry or a minimum of 6 poems published in nationally distributed commercial or literary journals. Considers translations and bilingual mss. Has published *Fancy Beasts*, by Alex Lemon, *Reading Novalis in Montana*, by Melissa Kwasny, and *The Book of Props*, by Wayne Miller.

How to Contact Submit through website. No fax or e-mail submissions. Do not send originals. Accepts and reads unsolicited mss all year. Guidelines available on website. Responds in up to 6 months. Order sample books through website.

✷ MOVING PARTS PRESS

10699 Empire Grade, Santa Cruz CA 95060-9474. (831)427-2271. E-mail: frice@movingpartspress.com. Website: www.movingpartspress.com. **Contact:** Felicia Rice, poetry editor.

Needs Moving Part Press publishes handsome, innovative books, broadsides, and prints that "explore the relationship of word and image, typography and the visual arts, the fine arts and popular culture." Published *Codex Espangliensis: from Columbus to the Border Patrol* (1998) with performance texts by Guillermo Goómez-Penña and collage imagery by Enrique Chagoya; *Cosmogonie Intime/An Intimate Cosmogony* (2005), a limited edition artists' book with poems by Yves Peyreé, translated by Elizabeth R. Jackson, and drawings by Ray Rice.

How to Contact *Does not accept unsolicited mss.*

⬚ ⊘ MULTICULTURAL BOOKS

Suite 307, 6311 Gilbert Rd., Richmond BC BC V7C 3V7, Canada. (604)277-3864. E-mail: jrmbooks@hotmail.com. Website: www.thehypertexts.com. www.mbooksofbc.com. **Contact:** Joe M. Ruggier, publisher.

Needs "MBooks of BC is a small press. We publish poetry, prose and poetry leaflets, prose, translations, children's writing, sound recordings, fiction, and literary nonfiction. We also have a publishing services division. We belong to an international circle of poets and editors committed to reforming the prevailing order by bringing about a traditionalist revival in writing." Publishes 1-6 books/year "depending on availability and quality." Manuscripts are selected through open submission. Books are 120+ pages, digitally photocopied, perfect-bound, with heavy color cardstock cover.

How to Contact Query first, with a few sample poems and a cover letter with brief bio and publication credits. Book mss may include previously published poems. "The only criteria is quality of work and excellence." Responds to queries in 2 months; to mss in 2 months. **Offers author-subsidy as well as publisher-subsidy options**; the selection process for the latter is extremely competitive and quality-conscious. "Authors who feel their work may be up to standard are welcome to query us with a sample or else submit an entire manuscript. All interested parties may consult our guidelines as well as our sample publication contract on website." Order sample books/chapbooks by contacting Joe M. Ruggier.

⬚ NEW ISSUES POETRY & PROSE

1903 W. Michigan Ave., Kalamazoo MI 49008-5463. (269)387-8185. Fax: (269)387-2562. E-mail: new-issues@wmich.edu. Website: wmich.edu/newissues. **Contact:** Managing Editor.

How to Contact Query first. All unsolicited mss returned unopened. "The press considers for publication only manuscripts submitted during its competition reading periods and often accepts two or more manuscripts for publication in addition to the winner. New Issues also sponsors the Green Rose Prize in Poetry, an award given to a collection of poems by a poet who has previously published one or more volumes of poetry. Submissions for the Green Rose Prize are accepted from May to the end of September, with winning manuscripts selected by the editors of New Issues."

⊘ NEW NATIVE PRESS

P.O. Box 661, Cullowhee NC 28723. (828)293-9237. E-mail: newnativepress@hotmail. com. Website: www.newnativepress.com. **Contact:** Thomas Rain Crowe, publisher.

Needs New Native Press has "selectively narrowed its range of contemporary 20th- and 21st-century literature to become an exclusive publisher of writers in marginalized and endangered languages. All books published are bilingual translations from original languages into English." Publishes about 2 paperbacks/year. Has published *Kenneth Patchen: Rebel Poet in America* by Larry Smith; Gaelic, Welsh, Breton, Cornish, and Manx poets in an all-Celtic-language anthology of contemporary poets from Scotland, Ireland, Wales, Brittany, Cornwall, and Isle of Man, entitled *Writing The Wind: A Celtic Resurgence* (The New Celtic Poetry); and *Selected Poems* by Kusumagraj (poet from Bombay, India) in the Marathi language. Books are sold by distributors in 4 foreign countries, and in the U.S. by Baker & Taylor, Amazon.com, library vendors, and Small Press Distribution. Books are typically 80 pages, offset-printed on glossy 120 lb. stock, perfect-bound, with professionally designed color cover.

How to Contact Query first, with 10 sample poems and cover letter with brief bio and publication credits. Considers previously published poems and simultaneous submissions. Time between acceptance and publication is up to 1 year. Always comments on rejected poems. Responds in 2 weeks. Pays in author's copies ("amount varies with author and title").

Tips "We are looking for work indicative of rare and unique talent—and original voices—using language experimentally and symbolically, if not subversively."

☐ NEW RIVERS PRESS

MSU Moorhead, 1104 Seventh Ave. S., Moorhead MN 56563. E-mail: kelleysu@mnstate. edu. Website: www.newriverspress.com. **Contact:** Suzanne Kelley, managing editor.

Needs New Rivers Press publishes collections of poetry, novels or novellas, translations of contemporary literature, and collections of short fiction and nonfiction. "We will continue to publish books regularly by new and emerging writers, especially those with a connection to Minnesota or to New York City, but we also welcome the opportunity to read work of every character and to publish the best literature available by new and emerging authors nationwide. Each October and November, through the MVP competition (see below), we choose 3 books, 1 of them national (genre will vary by year) and 2 regional." Has published *The Pact* by Walter Roers, *Nice Girls* by Cezarija Abartis, *Mozart's Carriage* by Dan Bachhuber, *The Volunteer* by Candace Black, *The Hunger Bone* by Deb Marquart, and *Real Karaoke People* by Ed Bok-Lee, and *Terrain Tracks* by Purvi Shah.

How to Contact Book-length mss of poetry, short fiction, novellas, or creative nonfiction are all considered. No fax or e-mail submissions. Guidelines and catalog available on website.

Contest/Award Offerings The Minnesota Voices Project (MVP) awards $1,000, a standard book contract, and publication of a book-length ms by New Rivers Press. Every third year, the poetry competition is national, open to anyone residing in the U.S.; 2 additional annual prizes (1 prose, 1 in any genre) are open only to residents of Minnesota or New York City. All previously published poems must be acknowledged. Considers simultaneous submissions "if noted as such. If your manuscript is accepted elsewhere during the judging, you must notify New Rivers Press immediately. If you do not give such notification and your manuscript is selected, your signature on the entry form gives New Rivers Press permission to go ahead with publication." Submit 50-80 pages of poetry. Entry form (required) and guidelines available on website. **Entry fee:** $20. **Deadline:** submit September 15-November 1 (postmark). 2008 poetry winners were Elizabeth Oness (*Fallibility*) and Maya Pindyck (*Friend Among Stones*). 2008 judge: Michael Hettich.

☑ ORCHISES PRESS

P.O. Box 320533, Alexandria VA 22320-4533. E-mail: lathbury@gmu.edu. Website: http:// mason.gmu.edu/ ~ lathbury. **Contact:** Roger Lathbury, poetry editor.

• Orchises Press prefers not to receive unsolicited mss.

⬛ PALETTES & QUILLS

330 Knickerbocker Ave., Rochester NY 14615. (585)456-0217. E-mail: palettesnquills@gmail.com. Website: www.palettesnquills.com. **Contact:** Donna M. Marbach, publisher/owner.

Needs Palettes & Quills "is at this point, a poetry press only, and produces only a handful of publications each year, specializing in anthologies, individual chapbooks, and broadsides." Wants "work that should appeal to a wide audience." Does not want "poems that are sold blocks of text, long-lined and without stanza breaks. Wildly elaborate free-verse would be difficult and in all likelihood fight with art background, amateurish rhyming poem, overly sentimental poems, poems that use excessive profanity, or which denigrate other people, or political and religious diatribes." Has published Cornelius Eady (reprints with permission), M.J. Iuppa, Katharyn Howd Machan, Tom Holmes, Liz Rosenberg, and Linda Allardt, among others. Published 1-2 chapbooks/year, occasional anthologies, and 3-5 broadsides.

How to Contact Query first with 3-5 poems and a cover letter with brief bio and publication credits for individual unsolicited chapbooks. May include previously published poems. Chapbook poets would get 20 copies of a run; broadside poets and artists get 5-10 copies and occasionally paid $10 for reproduction rights. Anthology poets get 1 copy of the anthology. All poets and artists get a discount on purchases that include their work.

Contest/Award Offerings Palettes & Quills Biennial Chapbook Contest, held biennially. Prize: $200 plus 50 copies of chapbook and discount on purchase of others. Guidelines available for SASE or on website. Entry fee: $20. Deadline: September 1. 2010 judge: Dorianne Laux.

Also Offers "From time to time, Palettes & Quills will put out a special call for poems for themed anthologies (e.g. Women Celebrating Women). Specific directions for such calls are posted on the website when they are announced and our available for SASE."

Tips "Please read the guidelines carefully and follow directions. Send individual poems for broadsides electronically in one file. Send chapbook mss. via snail mail. If you do not follow directions, your poetry may be dismissed unread."

⊘ PATH PRESS, INC.

1229 Emerson Street, Evanston IL 60201. (847)492-0177. Fax: (773)651-0210. E-mail: pathpressinc@aol.com. **Contact:** Bennett J. Johnson, president.

Needs Path Press is a small publisher of books and poetry primarily "by, for, and about African American and Third World people." Open to all types of poetic forms; emphasis is on high quality. Books are "hardback and quality paperbacks."

How to Contact Query first, with a few sample poems and cover letter with brief bio and publication credits. Submissions should be typewritten in ms format. Accepts submissions by e-mail (as attachment).

⬛ ◻ Pecan Grove Press

Box AL, 1 Camino Santa Maria, San Antonio TX 78228. (210)436-3442. Fax: (210)436-3782. E-mail: phall@stmarytx.edu. Website: http://library.stmarytx.edu/pgpress. **Contact:** H. Palmer Hall, editor/director. Member, CLMP. Pecan Grove Press is a poetry-only press and conducts one national chapbook competition each year. Aside from that, the press publishes approximately 7-8 books and chapbooks each year outside of the competition.

- Member, CLMP. "Pecan Grove Press is a poetry-only press and conducts one national chapbook competition each year. Aside from that, the press publishes approximately 7-8 books and chapbooks each year outside of the competition."

Needs "PGP publishes a variety of 'types' of poetry (narrative, lyrical, formal, free, hetero, gay, male, female, etc." Has published *Small Songs of Pain*, by Patricia Fargnoli; *Like Li-Po Laughing at the Lonely Moon,* by Chuck Taylor; *Oh Forbidden!,* by Jill Alexander Essbaum; *The Heat of What Comes*, by Joel Peckham; *Visiting Home*, by Paul Willis; *Rio Vertabral/ Vertabral River*, by Juan Arando Rojas. Publishes 5 poetry books/year, 3 chapbooks/year, and 1-2 anthologies/year. Manuscripts are selected through open submission. Books are 52-100 pages, off-set or laser print, perfect-bound with color index stock cover and full color art. Chapbooks are 32-45 pages, laser printed, perfect-bound, index stock cover with color in-house graphics.

How to Contact Submit complete ms with SASE for reply only. Mss. are recycled and will not be returned. Book/chapbook may include previously published poems. Prefers some record of publication in literary reviews prior to submission. Responds in 4 months. Pays poet 50% of proceeds after printing/binding costs are covered. Press run of 250 chapbooks and 500-1,000 for books. Pays 5 author's copies.

Contest/Award Offerings Annual chapbook contest with prize of $250 and 25 copies of chapbook. Submit 32-42 pages. Guidelines are on website. Entry fee: $15; deadline: January 15.

Additional Information "We are a non-profit, independent poetry press working under the umbrella of St. Mary's University in San Antonio, Texas."

Tips "We think chapbooks should cohere.poems should relate to each other like paintings in a one-person exhibition. Books should also work together instead of simply being a hodgepodge of poems."

$ ⊘ PELICAN PUBLISHING COMPANY

1000 Burmaster St., Gretna LA 70053. E-mail: editorial@pelicanpub.com. Website: www. pelicanpub.com. **Contact:** Nina Kooij, Editor-in-Chief.

Needs Pelican Publishing Company is a medium-sized publisher of popular histories, cookbooks, regional books, children's books, and inspirational/motivational books. Considers poetry for "hardcover children's books only (1,100 words maximum), preferably with a regional focus. However, our needs for this are very limited; we publish 20 juvenile titles per year, and most of these are prose, not poetry." Has published *Alaskan Night Before Christmas* by Tricia Brown and *Hawaiian Night Before Christmas* by Carolyn Macy. Two of Pelican's popular series are prose books about Gaston the Green-Nosed Alligator by James Rice, and Clovis Crawfish by Mary Alice Fontenot. Books are 32 pages, magazine-sized, include illustrations.

How to Contact Printout of ms with a cover letter including "work and writing backgrounds and promotional connections." No previously published poems or simultaneous submissions. Guidelines available for SASE or on website. Responds to mss in 3 months. Always sends prepublication galleys. Pays royalties. Acquires all rights. Returns rights upon termination of contract. Typically, Pelican books sell for $16.99. Write for catalog or visit website to view catalog and/or buy samples.

Tips "Except for the rhyme in our *Night Before Christmas* series, we try to avoid rhyme altogether, especially predictable rhyme. Monotonous rhythm can also be a problem."

⌀ PERUGIA PRESS

P.O. Box 60364, Florence MA 01062. E-mail: info@perugiapress.com. Website: www. perugiapress.com. **Contact:** Susan Kan, director.

Needs Perugia Press publishes 1 collection of poetry each year, by a woman at the beginning of her publishing career (first or second books only). "Our books appeal to people who have been reading poetry for decades, as well as those who might be picking up a book of poetry for the first time. Slight preference for narrative poetry." Has published *How to Live on Bread and Music*, by Jennifer K. Sweeney, *Two Minutes of Light,* by Nancy K. Pearson, *Beg No Pardon,* by Lynne Thompson, *Kettle Bottom,* by Diane Gilliam Fisher, *Lamb*, by Frannie Lindsay. Books are an average of 88 pages, perfect-bound. First print run is 800-1,200. Order sample books through website.

How to Contact *Manuscripts are selected through competition only.*

Contest/Award Offerings The Perugia Press Prize.

⌀ PLAN B PRESS

P.O. Box 4067, Alexandria VA 22303. (215)732-2663. E-mail: planbpress@gmail.com. Website: www.planbpress.com. **Contact:** Steven Allen May, president. (Specialized: experimental, concrete, visual poetry)

Needs Plan B Press is a "small publishing company with an international feel. Our intention is to have Plan B Press be part of the conversation about the direction and depth of literary movements and genres. Plan B Press's new direction is to seek out authors rarely-to-never published, sharing new voices that might not otherwise be heard. Plan B Press is determined to merge text with image, writing with art." Publishes poetry and short fiction. Wants "experimental poetry, concrete/visual work." Does not want "sonnets, political or religious poems, work in the style of Ogden Nash." Has published poetry by Lamont B Steptoe, Michele Belluomini, Jim Mancinelli, Lyn Lifshin, Robert Miltner, and stevenallenmay. Publishes 1 poetry book/year and 5-10 chapbooks/year. Manuscripts are selected through open submission and through competition (see below). Books/chapbooks are 24-48 pages, with covers with art/graphics.

How to Contact Query first, with a few sample poems and a cover letter with brief bio and publication credits. Book/chapbook mss may include previously published poems. Guidelines available on website. Responds to queries in 1 month; to mss in 3 months. Author keeps royalties. Pays varying number of author's copies; press run varies per book. Order sample books/chapbooks by writing to Plan B Press or through website.

Contest/Award Offerings The annual Plan B Press Poetry Chapbook Contest.

Tips "Writing reveals the mirror to your soul. Don't think about words until you are in the editing phase, and then only look for errors. Whatever sense your work makes is for the reader to ascertain, not you. You are a beacon, a transmitter."

⊞ ⊘ POETRY SALZBURG

University of Salzburg, Dept. of English, Akademiestrasse 24, Salzburg A-5020, Austria. (43) (662)8044-4422. Fax: (43)(662)8044-167. E-mail: editor@poetrysalzburg.com. Website: www.poetrysalzburg.com. **Contact:** Wolfgang Goertschacher, Andreas Schachermayr.

Needs Poetry Salzburg publishes "collections of at least 100 pages by mainly poets not taken up by big publishers." Publishes 6-8 paperbacks/year. Books are usually 100-350 pages, A5, professionally printed, perfect-bound, with card covers.

How to Contact Query first, with a cover letter with brief bio and publication credits. Suggests authors publish in *Poetry Salzburg Review* (see separate listing in Magazines/Journals) first. Responds to queries in 4 weeks; to mss in about 3 months. Payment varies.

⊌ PRESA :S: PRESS

P.O. Box 792, 8590 Belding Rd NE, Rockford MI 49341. **Contact:** Roseanne Ritzema, assistant editor. Presa :S: Press publishes "perfect-bound paperbacks and saddle-stitched chapbooks of poetry." Wants " imagistic poetry where form is an extension of content, surreal, experimental, and personal poetry." Does not want "overtly political or didactic material." Has published poetry books by Kirby Congdon, John Amen, Hugh Fox, Eric Greinke, Donald Lev, Lyn Lifshin, Stanley Nelson, and A.D. Winans. Publishes 2-3 poetry books/year, 1-2 chapbooks/year, and an occasional anthology. Manuscripts are selected through open submission. Books are 64-144 pages, laser-printed on 24 lb. paper, perfect-bound paperback with a laminated, color art cover. Chapbooks are 28-48 pages, laser-printed on 20-24 lb. paper, saddle-stitched with a color art cover. Anthologies are 250-325 pages, laser-printed, perfect-bound paperback with a laminated color art cover. Press runs 500-1,000 copies.

PRINCETON UNIVERSITY PRESS

41 William St., Princeton NJ 08540. (609)258-4900. Fax: (609)258-6305. Website: www.pupress.princeton.edu. **Contact:** Hanne Winarsky, Editor. "The Lockert Library of Poetry in Translation embraces a wide geographic and temporal range, from Scandinavia to Latin America to the subcontinent of India, from the Tang Dynasty to Europe of the modern day. It especially emphasizes poets who are established in their native lands and who are being introduced to an English-speaking audience. The series, many of whose titles are bilingual editions, calls attention to some of the most widely-praised poetry available today. In the Lockert Library series, each book is given individual design treatment rather than stamped into a series mold. We have published a wide range of poets from other cultures, including well-known writers such as Hoölderlin and Cavafy, and those who have not yet had their due in English translation, such as Goöran Sonnevi. Manuscripts are judged with several criteria in mind: the ability of the translation to stand on its own as poetry in English; fidelity to the tone and spirit of the original, rather than literal accuracy; and the importance of the translated poet to the literature of his or her time and country."

⊘ PUDDING HOUSE PUBLICATIONS

81 Shadymere Lane, Columbus OH 43213. (614)986-1881. E-mail: jen@puddinghouse.com. Website: www.puddinghouse.com. **Contact:** Jennifer Bosveld, publisher. (Specialized: social issues; popular culture reflected in poetry arts) S

Needs Pudding House Publications prints chapbooks, anthologies, and broadsides. Has over 1,200 titles in print. Provides "a sociological looking glass through poems that speak to the pop culture, struggle in a consumer and guardian society, and more—through 'felt experience.' Speaks for the difficulties and the solutions." Pudding House is also the publisher of the respected national archive, POETS' GREATEST HITS—an invitational. Has recently published *The Allegories* by Dan Sicoli, *Barb Quill Down* by Bill Griffin, *Sonnets to Hamlet* by David Rigsbee, *Mischief* by Charlene Fix, and over 700 others.

How to Contact Chapbooks considered outside of competitions, no query. Send complete ms and a cover letter with publication credits and bio. Now accepts manuscripts by e-mail. **Reading fee:** $15. Sometimes comments; "no more critiquing, too busy now." See main page at puddinghouse.com for chapbook guidelines.

Contest/Award Offerings Pudding House offers an annual chapbook competition. **Entry fee:** $15. **Deadline:** September 30. Guidelines available on website.

Also Offers "Our website is one of the greatest poetry websites in the country—calls, workshops, publication list/history, online essays, games, guest pages, calendars, poem of the month, poet of the week, much more." The website also links to the site for The Unitarian Universalist Poets Cooperative and American Poets Opposed to Executions, both national organizations.

Tips "Editors have pet peeves. I won't respond to or on postcards. I require SASEs. Love cover letters that are genuine, friendly, and don't state the obvious. Don't like poems with trite concepts or meaning dictated by rhyme. Thoroughly review our website; it will give you a good idea about our publication history and editorial tastes."

⊘ THE PUDDIN'HEAD PRESS

P.O. Box 477889, Chicago IL 60647. (708)656-4900. E-mail: phbooks@att.net. Website: www.puddinheadpress.com.

Needs The Puddin'head Press is interested in "well-rounded poets who can support their work with readings and appearances." Wants "quality poetry by active poets who read and lead interesting lives. We occasionally publish chapbook-style anthologies and let poets on our mailing lists know what type of work we're interested in for a particular project." Does not want experimental, overly political poetry, or poetry with overt sexual content; no shock or novelty poems. Has published poetry by Jared Smith, Carol Anderson, Larry Janowski, Sandy Goldsmith, and Norman Porter. Puddin'head Press publishes 2-3 books and 2-3 chapbooks per year. Books/chapbooks are 30-100 pages, perfect-bound or side-stapled ("we use various formats").

How to Contact "Please visit our website for submission guidelines." Poets must include SASE with submission. Responds to queries in 2 months. Pays various royalty rates "depending on the publication. We usually have a press run of 500 books." **About 10% of books are author subsidy-published.** Terms vary. Order sample books/chapbooks by sending $10 (price plus postage) to The Puddin'head Press (also available through Amazon). "Please visit our website and see what we publish."

Additional Information "In the last several years we have been increasingly active across the country. There are numerous readings and events that we sponsor. We do our own distribution, primarily in the Midwest, and also do distribution for other small presses. Please send a SASE for a list of our current publications and publication/distribution guidelines. We sell poetry books, not just print them. Submitted poetry is evaluated for its marketability and quality."

Also Offers "Extensive website with rare and used books, extensive links to who's who in poetry and online marketing."

Tips "It is difficult to find a quality publisher. Poets must have patience and find a press that will work with them. A good relationship between poet and publisher is important. Many good books will never be seen because the poet/publisher relationship is not healthy. If a poet is involved in the literary world, he will find a publisher, or a publisher will find him."

$ ☑ QED PRESS/CYPRESS HOUSE

Cypress House, 155 Cypress St., Fort Bragg CA 95437. (800)773-7782. Fax: (707)964-7531. E-mail: joeshaw@cypresshouse.com. Website: www.cypresshouse.com. **Contact:** Joe Shaw, Editor.

Needs QED Press publishes "clear, clean, intelligent, and moving work." Wants "concrete, personal, and spare writing. No florid rhymed verse." Has published poetry by Victoria Greenleaf, Luke Breit, Paula Tennant (Adams), and Cynthia Frank. Publishes 1 poetry book/year. Books are usually about 100 pages (75-80 poems), digest-sized, offset-printed, perfect-bound, with full-color cover.

How to Contact "We prefer to see 6 representative poems." Considers simultaneous submissions. Cover letter and SASE for return of materials are required. Time between acceptance and publication is up to 1 year. Poems are circulated to an editorial board. Responds to queries and mss in 1 month. Pays royalties of 7-12% and 25 author's copies (out of a press run of 500-1,000). Order sample books through website.

Also Offers Book packaging, and promotion and marketing services to start-up publishers.

$ ☑ RATTAPALLAX PRESS

(Specialized: the diversity of world cultures), 217 Thomas St., Suite 353, New York NY 10012. E-mail: info@rattapallax.com. Website: www.rattapallax.com. Established 1998. **Contact:** Poetry Editor.

Needs Rattapallax Press publishes "contemporary poets and writers with unique, powerful voices." Publishes 5 paperbacks and 3 chapbooks/year. Books are usually 64 pages, digest-sized, offset-printed, perfect-bound, with 12-pt. CS1 covers.

How to Contact Query first, with a few sample poems and cover letter with brief bio and publication credits. Include SASE. Requires authors to first be published in *Rattapallax* (see separate listing in Magazines/Journals). Responds to queries in 1 month; to mss in 2 months. Pays royalties of 10-25%. Order sample books from website.

☑ RED DRAGON PRESS

P.O. Box 320301, Alexandria VA 22320-4301. Website: www.reddragonpress.com.

Needs Red Dragon Press is a proponent "of works that represent the nature of man as androgynous, as in the fusing of male and female symbolism, and we support works that deal with psychological and parapsychological topics." Wants "innovative and experimental poetry and prose using literary symbolism and aspiring to the creation of meaningful new ideas, forms, and methods." Has published *The Distance of Ducks* by Louis Bourgeois, *Spectator Turns Witness* by George Karos, and *The Crown of Affinity* by Laura Qa. Publishes 3-4 chapbooks/year. Chapbooks are usually 64 pages, offset-printed on trade paper, perfect-bound.

How to Contact Submit up to 5 poems at a time with SASE. Considers previously published poems and simultaneous submissions. Cover letter with brief bio is preferred. **Reading fee: $5 for poetry and short fiction, $10 for novels.** Make checks or money orders payable to Red Dragon Press. Time between acceptance and publication is 8 months. "Poems are selected for consideration by the publisher, then circulated to senior editor and/or poets previously published for comment. Poems are returned to the publisher for further action, i.e., rejection or acceptance for publication in an anthology or book by a single author. Frequently, submission of additional works is required before final offer is made, especially in the process for a book by a single author." Often comments on rejected poems. Responds to queries in 10 weeks, to mss in one year. Purchase sample books at bookstores, or mail-order direct from Red Dragon Press at the above address.

RED MOON PRESS

P.O. Box 2461, Winchester VA 22604-1661. (540)722-2156. E-mail: jim.kacian@redmoonpress.com. **Contact:** Jim Kacian, Editor/Publisher.

Needs Red Moon Press "is the largest and most prestigious publisher of English-language haiku and related work in the world." Publishes 6-8 volumes/year, usually 3-5 anthologies and individual collections of English-language haiku, as well as 1-3 books of essays, translations, or criticism of haiku. Under other imprints, the press also publishes chapbooks of various sizes and formats.

How to Contact Query with book theme and information, and 30-40 poems or draft of first chapter. Responds to queries in 2 weeks, to mss (if invited) in 3 months. "Each contract separately negotiated."

Tips "Haiku is a burgeoning and truly international form. It is nothing like what your fourth-grade teacher taught you years ago, and so it is best if you familiarize yourself with what is happening in the genre (and its close relatives) today before submitting. We strive to give all the work we publish plenty of space in which to resonate, and to provide a forum where the best of today's practitioners can be published with dignity and prestige. All our books have either won awards or are awaiting notification. We intend to work hard to keep it that way."

$ RONSDALE PRESS

3350 W. 21st Ave., Vancouver BC V6S 1G7, Canada. (604)738-4688. Fax: (604)731-4548. E-mail: ronsdale@shaw.ca. Website: www.ronsdalepress.com. **Contact:** Ronald B. Hatch, Director.

Needs Publishes 3 flat-spined paperbacks of poetry per year—**by Canadian poets only**—classical to experimental. "Ronsdale looks for poetry manuscripts that show the writer reads and is familiar with the work of some of the major contemporary poets. It's also essential that you have published some poems in literary magazines. We have never published a book of poetry when the author has not already published a goodly number in magazines." Has published *Return to Open Water* by Harold Rhenisch, *Mother Time* by Joanne Arnott, *Cobalt 3* by Kevin Roberts, *Poems for a New World* by Connie Fife, *Steveston* by Daphne Marlatt, and *After Ted & Sylvia* by Crystal Hurdle.

How to Contact Query first, with a few sample poems and cover letter with brief bio and publication credits. Considers previously published poems and simultaneous submissions. Often comments on rejected poems. Responds to queries in 2 weeks, to mss in 2 months. Pays 10% royalties and 10 author's copies. Write for catalog to purchase sample books.

Tips "Ronsdale looks for Canadian poetry with echoes from previous poets. To our mind, the contemporary poet must be well-read."

ROSE ALLEY PRESS

4203 Brooklyn Ave. NE, #103A, Seattle WA 98105-5911. (206)633-2725. E-mail: rosealleypress@juno.com. Website: www.rosealleypress.com. **Contact:** David Horowitz.

• "Rose Alley Press does not consider unsolicited manuscripts."

$ ☒ SAM'S DOT PUBLISHING

E-mail: samsdot@samsdotpublishing.com. Website: www.samsdotpublishing.com. **Contact:** Tyree Campbell, managing editor. (Specialized: scifaiku, horror-ku, other minimalist poetry forms) Member: The Speculative Literature Foundation.

Needs Sam's Dot Publishing prints collections of scifaiku, horror-ku, and minimalist poetry. Publishes 2-3 chapbooks/year and one anthology/year. Manuscripts are selected through open submission. Chapbooks are 32 pages, offset-printed, saddle-stapled, with cardstock covers.

How to Contact Query first, with a few sample poems and a cover letter with brief bio and publication credits, up to 500 words. Chapbook mss may include previously published poems. Responds to queries in 2 weeks; to mss in 4-6 weeks. Pays royalties of 12.5% minimum and 1-2 author's copies (out of a press run of 50-100). Order sample chapbooks by sending $8 to Tyree Campbell/Sam's Dot Publishing.

Tips "It's up to the writer to take the first step and submit work. Some of our best poems have come from poets who weren't sure if they were good enough. A basic knowledge of writing traditional haiku is helpful."

☒ SARABANDE BOOKS, INC.

2234 Dundee Rd., Suite 200, Louisville KY 40205. (502)458-4028. E-mail: info@sarabandebooks.org. Website: www.SarabandeBooks.org. **Contact:** Sarah Gorham, editor-in-chief. Member: CLMP.

Needs Sarabande Books publishes books of poetry of 48 pages minimum. Wants "poetry that offers originality of voice and subject matter, uniqueness of vision, and a language that startles because of the careful attention paid to it—language that goes beyond the merely competent or functional. Has published poetry by Mark Jarman, Gerald Stern, Jean Valentine, Cate Marvin, Ralph Angel, Gabriel Fried, and Eleanor Lerman. Manuscripts are selected through our literary contests, invitation, and recommendation by a well-established writer. At least half of our list is drawn from contest submissions to the Kathryn A. Morton Prize in Poetry."

How to Contact Charges $10 handling fee with alternative option of purchase of book from website (e-mail confirmation of sale must be included with submission). See website for submission details. Open reading period in September only.

Contest/Award Offerings The Kathryn A. Morton Prize in Poetry (see separate listing).

Tips "We recommend that you request our catalog and familiarize yourself with our books. Our complete list shows a variety of style and subject matter."

⊘ SEAWEED SIDESHOW CIRCUS

P.O. Box 234, Jackson WI 53037. (414)791-1109. Fax: (262)644-0249. E-mail: sscircus@aol.com. Website: www.facebook.com/seaweedsideshowcircus. **Contact:** Andrew Wright Milam, Editor. Established 1994.

Needs Seaweed Sideshow Circus is "a place for young or new poets to publish a chapbook." Has published *Main Street* by Steven Paul Lansky and *The Moon Incident* by Amy McDonald. Publishes one chapbook/year. Chapbooks are usually 30 pages, digest-sized, photocopied, saddle-stapled, with cardstock covers.

How to Contact Query first, with 5-10 sample poems and cover letter with brief bio and publications credits. Responds to queries in 6-9 weeks; to mss in 6-9 months. Pays 10 author's copies (out of a press run of 100). Order sample chapbooks by sending $6.

⊕ ⊘ SECOND AEON PUBLICATIONS

19 Southminster Rd., Roath, Cardiff CF23 5AT, Wales. +44(29)2049-3093. Fax: +44(29)2049-3093. E-mail: peter@peterfinch.co.uk. Website: www.peterfinch.co.uk. **Contact:** Peter Finch, Poetry Editor.

• *Does not accept unsolicited mss.*

⊘ STEEL TOE BOOKS

Western Kentucky University, 1906 College Heights Blvd. #11086, Bowling Green KY 42101-1086. (270)745-5769. E-mail: tom.hunley@wku.edu. Website: www.steeltoebooks.com. **Contact:** Dr. Tom C. Hunley, Director. Established 2003.

Needs Steel Toe Books publishes "full-length, single-author poetry collections. Our books are professionally designed and printed. We look for workmanship (economical use of language, high-energy verbs, precise literal descriptions, original figurative language, poems carefully arranged as a book); a unique style and/or a distinctive voice; clarity; emotional impact; humor (word plays, hyperbole, comic timing); performability (a Steel Toe poet is at home on the stage as well as on the page)." Does not want "dry verse, purposely obscure language, poetry by people who are so wary of being called 'sentimental' they steer away from any recognizable human emotions, poetry that takes itself so seriously that it's unintentionally funny." Has published poetry by Allison Joseph, Susan Browne, James Doyle, Martha Silano, Mary Biddinger, John Guzlowski, Jeannine Hall Gailey, and others. Publishes 1-3 poetry books/year. Manuscripts are normally selected through open submission.

How to Contact "Check the website for news about our next open reading period." Book mss may include previously published poems. Responds to mss in 3 months. Pays

$500 advance on 10% royalties and 10 author's copies. Order sample books by sending $12 to Steel Toe Books. *Must purchase a manuscript in order to submit.* See website for submission guidelines.

SWAN SCYTHE PRESS

515 P Street, #804, Sacramento CA 95814. E-mail: jimzbookz@yahoo.com. Website: www.swanscythe.com. **Contact:** James DenBoer, editor.

- Swan Scythe Press has been awarded a California Arts Council Multicultural Entry Grant and a Fideicomiso para la Cultura Mexico-EUA/US-Mexico Fund for Culture Grant.

Needs "After publishing 25 chapbooks, a few full-sized poetry collections,and 1 anthology, then taking a short break from publishing, Swan Scythe Press is now re-launching its efforts with some new books, under a new editorship, in 2010. Our annual contest winner will be named in late June 2010. We have also begun a new series of books, called Poetas/ Puentes, from emerging poets writing in Spanish, translated into English. We will also consider manuscripts in indigenous languages from North, Central and South America, translated into English. Has published poetry by Emmy Peérez, Maria Melendez, John Olivares Espinoza, Karen An-hwei Lee, Pos Moua, and Walter Pavlich. Order sample books/chapbooks by sending $11 to Swan Scythe Press or order through website.

How to Contact Query first before submitting a manuscript via e-mail or through website.

$ ☑ SYNERGEBOOKS

205 S. Dixie Dr., Haines City FL 33844. (863)956-3015. E-mail: synergebooks@aol.com. Website: www.synergebooks.com. **Contact:** Deb Staples, acquisitions editor. Member: EPIC, PMA

Needs SynergEbooks specializes in "quality works by talented new writers in every available digital format, including CD-ROMs and paperback. Poetry must have a very unique twist or theme and must be edited." Does not accept unedited work. Has published poetry by Russell J. Fee, Brenda Roberts, Joel L. Young, and Pamela Jaskot. SynergEbooks publishes up to 50 titles/year, less than 1% of them poetry. Books are usually 45-150 pages, print-on-demand, with paperback binding. "All of our titles are digital. There is no guarantee that a book will be put into print."

How to Contact Query by e-mail preferred, with a few sample poems and a cover letter with brief bio and publication credits. "We prefer no simultaneous submissions, but inform us if this is the case." Accepts e-mail submissions (as attachment) only. "Please do not send poetry via postal mail. Valid, working e-mail address is required." Guidelines available on website. Responds to queries in 1 month; to mss in up to 5 months. Pays royalties of 15-40% for electronic formats; up to 15% for paperbacks.

Tips "We are inundated with more poetry than prose every month; but we will accept the occasional anthology with a unique twist that is original and high quality. New poets welcome."

⊡ TARPAULIN SKY PRESS

P.O. Box 189, Grafton VT 05146. E-mail: editors@tarpaulinsky.com. Website: www. tarpaulinsky.com. **Contact:** Christina Peet, co-editor. (Specialized: cross- & trans-genre work)

Needs Tarpaulin Sky Press publishes cross- and trans-genre works as well as innovative poetry and prose. Produces full-length books and chapbooks, hand-bound books and trade paperbacks, and offers both hand-bound and perfect-bound paperback editions of full-length books. "We're a small, author-centered press endeavoring to create books that, as objects, please our authors as much their texts please us." Has published books and chapbooks by Jenny Boully, Danielle Dutton, Joyelle McSweeney, Chad Sweeney, Andrew Michael Roberts, and Max Winter, as well as a collaborative book by Noah Eli Gordon as Joshua Marie Wilkinson.

How to Contact Writers whose work has appeared in or been accepted for publication in *Tarpaulin Sky* (see separate listing in Magazines/Journals) may submit chapbook or full-length manuscripts at any time, with no reading fee. Tarpaulin Sky Press also considers chapbook and full-length manuscripts from writers whose work has not appeared in the journal, but **asks for a $20 reading fee**. Make checks/money orders to Tarpaulin Sky Press. Cover letter is preferred. Reads periods may be found on the website.

⊘ TEBOT BACH

P.O. Box 7887, Huntington Beach CA 92615-7887. (714)968-0905. E-mail: info@tebotbach. org. **Contact:** Mifanwy Kaiser, editor/publisher.

Needs Tebot Bach (Welsh for "little teapot") publishes books of poetry. Has published *One Breath*, by Catharine Clark-Sayles, *Monkey Journal*, by Holly Prado; *Swagger and Remorse* by Richard Fox, *Dragon Ship* by Daniel F. Polikoff, and *A Cafeé in Boca* by Sam Pereira.

How to Contact Query first, with a few sample poems and cover letter with brief bio and publication credits. Include SASE. Responds to queries and mss, if invited, in 3 months. Time between acceptance and publication is up to 2 years. Write to order sample books.

Contest/Award Offerings The Patricia Bibby First Book Award.

Also Offers An anthology of California poets. Must be current or former resident of California in order to submit, but no focus or theme required for poetry. Submit up to 6 poems with "California Anthology" written on lower left corner of envelope. Accepts submissions by e-mail (pasted into body of message or as attachment in Word). Deadline for submission is in August of the year call for submissions in announced. Please check the website for calls for submissions. Also publishes *Spillway: A Literary Journal* (see separate listing in Magazines/Journals).

Ⓝ ⊡ TIGHTROPE BOOKS

602 Markham St., Toronto ON M6G 2L8, Canada. (647) 348-4460. Website: tightropebooks. com. **Contact:** Shirarose Wilensky, editor (fiction, poetry, nonfiction).

$ ☑ TOKYO ROSE RECORDS/CHAPULTEPEC PRESS

4222 Chambers, Cincinnati OH 45223. E-mail: chapultepecpress@hotmail.com. Website: www.TokyoRoseRecords.com. Established 2001. **Contact:** David Garza.

Needs Chapultepec Press publishes books of poetry/literature, essays, social/political issues, art, music, film, history, popular science; library/archive issues, and bilingual works. Wants "poetry that works as a unit, that is caustic, fun, open-ended, worldly, mature, relevant, stirring, evocative. Bilingual. Looking for authors who have a publishing history. No poetry collections without a purpose, that are mere collections. Also looking for broadsides/posters/illuminations." Publishes 1-2 books/year. Books are usually 1-100 pages.

How to Contact Query first with a few sample poems, or a complete ms, and a cover letter with brief bio and publication credits. Pays 50% of profits and author's copies. Order sample books by sending $5 payable to David Garza.

☒ TUPELO PRESS

P.O. Box 1767, North Adams MA 01247. (802)366-8185. Fax: (802)362-1882. E-mail: publisher@tupelopress.org. "We're an independent nonprofit literary press. Also sponsor these upcoming competitions: Dorset Prize: $10,000. Entries must be postmarked between Sept. 1 and Dec. 15, 2008. Guidelines are online; Snowbound Series chapbook Award: $1,000 and 50 copies of chapbook. Closed for 2008.Every July we have Open Submissions. We accept book-length poetry, poetry collections (48 + pages), short story collections, novellas, literary nonfiction/memoirs and up to 80 pages of a novel."

How to Contact Submit complete ms of 48-90 pages through online submission or via mail. during open submissions period of July. Please include the reading fee $25 and SASE for response.

TURKEY PRESS

6746 Sueño Rd., Isla Vista CA 93117-4904. Website: www.turkeypress.net. **Contact:** Harry Reese and Sandra Reese, poetry editors.

- "We do not encourage solicitations of any kind to the press. We seek out and develop projects on our own."

☒ THE UNIVERSITY OF AKRON PRESS

(330)972-5342. Fax: (330)972-8364. E-mail: uapress@uakron.edu. **Contact:** Thomas Bacher, Director and Acquisitions. "The University of Akron Press is the publishing arm of The University of Akron and is dedicated to the dissemination of scholarly, professional, and regional books and other content."

Needs "We publish two books of poetry annually, one of which is the winner of The Akron Poetry prize. We also are interested in literary collections based around one theme, especially collections of translated works."

How to Contact If you are interested in publishing with The University of Akron Press, please fill out form online.

⊘ THE UNIVERSITY OF CHICAGO PRESS

1427 E. 60th St., Chicago IL 60637. (773)702-7700. Fax: (773)702-2705 or (773)702-9756. Website: www.press.uchicago.edu. **Contact:** Randolph Petilos, Poetry Editor.

• Submissions by invitation only!

Needs "The University of Chicago Press has been publishing scholarly books and journals since 1891. Annually, we publish an average of four books in our Phoenix Poets series and four books of poetry in translation. Occasionally, we may publish a book of poetry outside Phoenix Poets, or as a paperback reprint from another publisher." Has published poetry by Peter Balakian, Don Bogen, Peter Campion, Gendun Chopel, David Gewanter, Reginald Gibbons, Fulke Greville, Randall Mann, Lucrezia Marinella, Greg Miller, Gabriela Mistral, Marguerite de Navarre, Robert Polito, Francisco de Quevedo, Atsuro Riley, Pedro Salinas, Gaspara Stampa, Sarra Copia Sulam, Garcilaso de la Vega, and Tom Yuill.

How to Contact *By invitation only.* No unsolicited mss.

ℕ VANHOOK HOUSE

925 Orchard St., Charleston WV 25302. E-mail: editor@vanhookhouse.com. Website: www.vanhookhouse.com. **Contact:** Jim Whyte, acquisitions, all fiction/true crime/military/war. "VanHook House is a small press focused on the talents of new, unpublished authors. We are looking for works of fiction and nonfiction to add to our catalog. No erotica or sci-fi, please. Query via e-mail. Queries accepted ONLY during submissions periods."

Needs "VanHook House is a small press focused on the talents of new, unpublished authors. We are looking for works of fiction and nonfiction to add to our catalog. No erotica or sci-fi, please. Query via e-mail. Queries accepted ONLY during submissions periods."

How to Contact "A collection MUST contain 200 individual poems to be considered." Query; submit 3 sample poems. Receives 20 mss/year. Pays authors 8-10% royalty on wholesale price. Advance negotiable. Time between acceptance and publication is 6 months. Responds in 1 month to queries; 2 months toproposals; 3 months to mss. Book catalog and guidelines free on request and available online at website.

⤢ ⊘ VEHICULE PRESS

P.O. Box 125 Station Place du Parc, Montreal QC H2X 4A3, Canada. (514)844-6073. Fax: (514)844-7543. E-mail: vp@vehiculepress.com. Website: www.vehiculepress.com. (Specialized: work by Canadian poets only)

Needs Vehicule Press is a "literary press with a poetry series, Signal Editions, publishing the work of Canadian poets only." Publishes flat-spined paperbacks. Has published *The Empire's Missing Links* by Walid Bitar, *36 Cornelian Avenue* by Christopher Wiseman, and *Morning Gothic* by George Ellenbogen. Publishes Canadian poetry that is "first-rate, original, content-conscious."

How to Contact Query before submitting.

$ ☑ WASHINGTON WRITERS' PUBLISHING HOUSE

C/O Brandel France de Bravo, 3541 S. Street, NW, Washington DC 20007. E-mail: wwphpress@gmail.com. Website: www.washingtonwriters.org. **Contact:** Patrick Pepper, president.

- Individual books by WWPH authors have been nominated for and/or won many awards, e.g. the Towson University Prize.

Needs Washington Writers' Publishing House publishes books by Washington, D.C.- and Baltimore-area poets through its annual book competition. "No specific criteria, except literary excellence." Has published books by Brandel France de Bravo, Carly Sachs, Bruce MacKinnon, Piotr Gwiazda, Moira Egan, Jane Satterfield, Jean Nordhaus, and Gray Jacobik. Publishes 1-2 poetry books/year.

How to Contact Washington Writers' Publishing House considers book-length mss for publication by poets living within 60 driving miles of the U.S. Capitol (Baltimore area included) through competition only (see below).

Contest/Award Offerings Offers $500 and 50 copies of published book plus additional copies for publicity use. Manuscripts may include previously published poems. Submit 2 copies of a poetry ms of 50-60 pages, single-spaced (poet's name should not appear on ms pages). Include separate page of publication acknowledgments plus 2 cover sheets: one with ms title, poet's name, address, telephone number, and e-mail address, the other with ms title only. Include SASE for results only; mss will not be returned (will be recycled). Guidelines available for SASE or on website. "Author should indicate where they heard about WWPH." **Entry fee:** $20. **Deadline:** July 1-November 1 (postmark). Order sample books on website or by sending $12 plus $3 s&h to Washington Writers' Publishing House, P.O. Box 15271, Washington DC 20003.

Tips "Visit website. Washington Writers' Publishing House is a nonprofit cooperative poetry press reflecting the cultural and racial diversity of the Greater Washington-Baltimore area. The winning poet becomes a member of the organization and should be prepared to participate actively in the work of the press, including such areas as publicity, distribution, production, and fundraising. Our tradition of poets actively working on behalf of other poets is essential to the continued vitality and success of WWPH. Contest entrants should be willing to make this commitment should their work be selected for publication. Membership in WWPH is an opportunity to work together with many of the best writers in the region."

☑ WHITE EAGLE COFFEE STORE PRESS

P.O. Box 383, Fox River Grove IL 60021-0383. E-mail: WECSPress@aol.com. Website: whiteeaglecoffeestorepress.com. White Eagle is a small press publishing 2-3 chapbooks/year. "Alternate chapbooks are published by invitation and by competition. Author published by invitation becomes judge for next competition." Wants "any kind of poetry. No censorship at this press. Literary values are the only standard." Does not want "sentimental or didactic writing." Has published poetry by Timothy Russell, Connie Donovan, Scott Lumbard, Linda Lee Harper, Scott Beal, Katie Kingston, and Brian Brodeur. Sample: $6.95. *Regular submissions by invitation only.*

⊘ WOODLEY MEMORIAL PRESS

English Dept., Washburn University, 1700 SW College Ave., Topeka KS 66621. **Contact:** Kevin Rabas, Acquisitions Editor.

Needs Woodley Memorial Press publishes 1-4 perfect-bound paperbacks/year, "most being collections from Kansas or with Kansas connections. Terms are individually arranged with author on acceptance of manuscript." Has published *Sunflower Sinner* by Cynthia Dennis, *Thailand Journal* by Denise Low, and *Kansas Poems of William Stafford.* Sample books may be ordered from Woodley Memorial Press.

How to Contact Guidelines available on website. Responds to queries in 2 weeks; to mss in 6 months. Time between acceptance and publication is 1 year.

Tips "We look for experienced writers who are part of their writing and reading communities."

Contests & Awards

This section contains a wide array of poetry competitions and literary awards. These range from state poetry society contests (with a number of modest monetary prizes) to prestigious honors bestowed by private foundations, elite publishers and renowned university programs. Because these listings reflect such a variety of skill levels and degrees of competitiveness, it's important to read each carefully and note its unique requirements. *Never* enter a contest without consulting the guidelines and following directions to the letter (including manuscript formatting, number of lines or pages of poetry accepted, amount of entry fee, entry forms needed and other details).

Important note: As we gathered information for this edition of *Poet's Market*, we found that some competitions hadn't yet established their 2010 fees and deadlines. In such cases, we list the most recent information available as a general guide. Always consult current guidelines for updates before entering any competition.

WHERE TO ENTER?

While it's perfectly okay to "think big," being realistic may improve your chances of winning a prize for your poetry. Many of the listings in the Contests & Awards section begin with symbols that reflect their level of difficulty:

Contests ideal for beginners and unpublished poets are coded with the (❑) symbol. That's not to say these contests won't be highly competitive—there may be a large number of entries. However, you may find these entries are more on a level with your own, increasing your chances of being "in the running" for a prize. Don't assume these contests reward low quality, though. If you submit less than your best work, you're wasting your time and money (in postage and entry fees).

Contests for poets with more experience are coded with the (◑) symbol. Beginner/unpublished poets are usually still welcome to enter, but the competition is keener here. Your work may be judged against that of widely published, prize-winning poets, so consider carefully whether you're ready for this level of competition. (Of course, nothing ventured, nothing gained—but those entry fees *do* add up.)

Contests for accomplished poets are coded with the (●) symbol. These may have stricter entry requirements, higher entry fees and other conditions that signal these programs are not intended to be "wide open" to all poets.

Specialized contests are coded with the (◎) symbol. These may include regional contests; awards for poetry written in a certain form or in the style of a certain poet; contests for women, gay/lesbian, ethnic, or age-specific poets (for instance, children or older adults); contests for translated poetry only; and many others.

There are also symbols that give additional information about contests. The ((◼) symbol indicates the contest is newly established and new to *Poet's Market*; the (◼) symbol indicates this contest did not appear in the 2010 edition; the (◼) symbol identifies a Canadian contest or award and the (◉) symbol an international listing. Sometimes Canadian and international contests require that entrants live in certain countries, so pay attention when you see these symbols.

ADDITIONAL CONTESTS & AWARDS

Contest information also appears in listings in other sections of the book (Magazines/Journals, Book/Chapbook Publishers, Conferences, Workshops & Festivals and Organizations). To make sure you don't overlook these opportunities, we've cross-referenced them under Additional Contests & Awards at the back of this section. For details about a contest associated with a market in this list, go to that market's page number.

WHAT ABOUT ENTRY FEES?

Most contests charge entry fees, and these are usually quite legitimate. The funds are used to cover expenses such as paying the judges, putting up prize monies, printing prize editions of magazines and journals, and promoting the contest through mailings and ads. If you're concerned about a poetry contest or other publishing opportunity, see "Is It a 'Con'?" on page 66 for advice on some of the more questionable practices in the poetry world.

OTHER RESOURCES

Widen your search for contests beyond those listed in *Poet's Market*. Many Internet writer's sites have late-breaking announcements about competitions old and new (see Additional Resources on page 461). Often these sites offer free electronic newsletter subscriptions, sending valuable information right to your e-mail inbox.

The writer's magazines at your local bookstore regularly include listings for upcoming contests, as well as deadlines for artist's grants at the state and national level. (See Additional Resources on page 461 for a few suggestions; also, Grants on page 456.) The Association of Writers & Writing Programs (AWP) is a valuable resource, including its publication, *Writer's Chronicle*. (See Organizations, page 475.) State poetry societies are listed throughout this book; they offer many contests, as well as helpful information for poets (and mutual support). To find a specific group, search the General Index for listings under your state's name or look under "poetry society" or "society."

Don't overlook your local connections. City and community newspapers, radio and TV announcements, bookstore newsletters and bulletin boards, and your public library can be terrific resources for competition news, especially regarding regional contests.

$ ☑ "DISCOVERY"/BOSTON REVIEW POETRY CONTEST

Unterberg Poetry Center, 92nd Street Y, 1395 Lexington Ave., New York NY 10128. (212)415-5759. E-mail: unterberg@92y.org. Website: www.92y.org/poetry. **Contact:** Contest Coordinator. The "Discovery" Poetry Contest is designed to attract large audiences to poets who have not yet published a book. Awards a cash prize to 4 winners, plus a reading at The Unterberg Poetry Center and publication in a literary journal of national distribution, to be announced. New guidelines available on website. Endowed by Joan L. and Dr. Julius H. Jacobson, II.

$ ☑ THE "STRONG RX MEDICINE" BEST POEM CONTEST

MARGIE, 1395 Lexington Ave., New York NY 10128. E-mail: margiereview@aol.com. Website: www.margiereview.com. **Contact:** Contest Coordinator. The "Discovery" Poetry Contest is designed to attract large audiences to poets who have not yet published a book. Awards a cash prize to 4 winners, plus a reading at The Unterberg Poetry Center and publication in a literary journal of national distribution, to be announced. New guidelines available on website. Endowed by Joan L. and Dr. Julius H. Jacobson, II. Offers $1000 prize and publication in MARGIE/The American Journal of Poetry (see separate listing in Magazines/Journals) for best poem. Twelve finalists are also published, and all entries will be considered for publication. Submissions must be unpublished. Considers simultaneous submissions. Submit 3 poems, 60 line limit/poem. Include cover sheet with poet's name, address, phone number, e-mail (if possible), and poem titles; no identifying information on poems. Include SASE for results only; mss will not be returned. Guidelines available by e-mail or on website. **Entry fee:** $15 for 3 poems; additional poems may be entered for $5 each. Make checks payable to MARGIE, Inc. **Deadline:** TBA

$ ☑ THE 46ER PRIZE FOR POETRY

8405 Bay Parkway, C8, Brooklyn NY 11214. E-mail: editors@theadirondackreview.com; angela@blacklawrencepress.com. Website: www.theadirondackreview.com/46erPrize. html. With Black Lawrence Press, *The Adirondack Review* (see separate listing in Magazines/Journals) offers the 46er Prize for Poetry, to be awarded once each year for a previously unpublished poem. Winner receives $400 and publication in *The Adirondack Review*. Honorable Mention poems will also be published and receive an honorarium of $30. Considers simultaneous submissions if notified immediately of acceptance elsewhere. Submit up to 3 original poems, unpublished in either print or on-line publications. Submissions should be sent to diane@blacklawrencepress.com with poet's name, address, phone number, and e-mail address included. E-mail should be titled 46er PRIZE SUBMISSION in subject line; poems must be pasted into body of message. Guidelines available by e-mail or on website. **Entry fee:** $5 for 1 poem, $8 for 2 poems, $10 for 3 poems. Make payment through website via PayPal. **Deadline:** December 31. Winners announced during the summer. Judges: The Adirondack Review editors.

$ ☑ THE 49TH PARALLEL POETRY AWARD

Western Washington University, Mail Stop 9053, Bellingham WA 98225. E-mail: bhreview@wwu.edu. Website: www.wwu.edu/~bhreview. The annual 49th Parallel Poetry Award offers 1st Prize of $1,000, plus publication in and a year's subscription to Bellingham Review (see separate listing in Magazines/Journals). Runners-up and finalists may be considered for publication. Submissions must be unpublished and not accepted for publication elsewhere. Considers simultaneous submissions, but work must be withdrawn from the competition if accepted for publication elsewhere. Submit up to 3 poems. "Poems within a series will each be treated as a separate entry." For each entry, include a 3x5 index card stating the title of the work, the category (poetry), the poet's name, phone number, address, and e-mail. "Make sure writing is legible on this card. Author's name must not appear anywhere on the manuscript." Include SASE for results only; mss will not be returned. Guidelines available for SASE or on website. **Entry fee:** $18 for first entry (up to 3 poems); $10 each additional poem. Make checks payable to Bellingham Review. "Everyone entering the competition will receive a complimentary two-issue subscription to Bellingham Review ." **Deadline:** entries must be postmarked December 1-March 15. 2009 winner was Elizabeth McLagan. 2009 judge: Paulann Peterson. Winners will be announced by July 2009.

ABZ PRESS FIRST BOOK POETRY PRIZE

P.O. Box 2746, Huntingon WV 25727-2746. E-mail: editorial@abzpress.com. Website: abzpress.com. Wants poetry manuscripts between 48-80 pages. "Each manuscript must be bound only with a binder clip. Include a table of contents, acknowledgements, and two title pages. One title page should have only the title. The second title page should have the author' s name, address, phone number with area code, and e-mail address. Please indicate any poetry books or chapbooks (with fewer than 48 pages) you may have published. Simultaneous submissions are OK with us. Include SASE to receive notice of contest winner. Let us know if you win another prize." Winner will receive $1000 and 50 free copies of the winning book. Guidelines available on website. Entry fee: $28; includes one copy of winning book. Deadline: "We read entries submitted between May 1-June 30."

$ ☑ AKRON POETRY PRIZE

The University of Akron Press, Akron OH 44325-1703. (330)972-5342. Fax: (330)972-8364. E-mail: marybid@uakron.edu. Website: www.uakron.edu/uapress/poetryprize. **Contact:** Mary Biddinger, Editor. Offers annual award of $1,000 plus publication of a book-length ms. Submissions must be unpublished. Considers simultaneous submissions (with notification of acceptance elsewhere). Submit 48 or more pages, typed, single-spaced; optional self-addressed postcard for confirmation. Mss will not be returned. Do not send mss bound or enclosed in covers. See website for complete guidelines. **Entry fee:** $25. **Deadline:** entries accepted May 1-June 15 only. Competition receives 500 + entries. 2009 winner was Oliver de la Paz for *Requiem For The Orchard*. 2010 judge: G.C. Waldrep. Winner posted on website by September 30. Intimate friends, relatives, current and former students of the final judge (students in an academic, degree-conferring program or its equivalent) were not eligible to enter the 2009 Akron Poetry Prize competition.

$ ☑ AGHA SHAHID ALI PRIZE IN POETRY

University of Utah Press, J. Willard Marriott Lib., Ste 5400, 295 S. 1500 East, Salt Lake City UT 84112. (801)581-6771. Fax: (801)581-3365. Website: www.uofupress.com/Agha-

Shahid-Ali. The University of Utah Press and the University of Utah Department of English offer an annual award of $1,000, publication of a book-length poetry ms, and a reading in the Guest Writers Series. Poems must be unpublished as a collection, but individual poems may have been previously published elsewhere. Considers simultaneous submissions; "however, entrants must notify the Press immediately if the collection submitted is accepted for publication elsewhere during the competition." Submit 48-64 typed pages of poetry, with no names or other identifying information appearing on title page or within ms. Include cover sheet with complete contact information (name, address, telephone, e-mail address). Submissions must be in English. Mss will not be returned. Guidelines available on website. **Entry fee:** $25/book submission. **Deadline:** 2011: February 1-April 15. Competition receives over 300 mss/year. 2009 winner was Jon Wilkins. 2009 judge: Ander Monson. Winner announced on press website in October; series editor contacts winning poet. Copies of winning books are available for $14.95 from University of Utah Press ((800)621-2736 for order fulfillment) or through website.

$ ☑ THE AMERICAN POETRY REVIEW/HONICKMAN FIRST BOOK PRIZE

1700 Sansom St. Suite 800, Philadelphia PA 19103. E-mail: sberg@aprweb.org; escanlon@aprweb.org. Website: www.aprweb.org. **Contact:** Stephen Berg and Elizabeth Scanlon, editors. Annual award to encourage excellence in poetry, and to provide a wide readership for a deserving first book of poems. Offers $3,000, publication of a book-length ms, and distribution by Copper Canyon Press through Consortium. Open to U.S. citizens writing in English and who have not yet published a book-length collection of poems which was assigned an ISBN. Send a poetry ms. of 48 pages or more, single-spaced, paginated, with a table of contents and acknowledgements. Include SASE for notification only and two title pages; one containing name, address, e-mail, phone number, and book title; second title page should contain the title only. Guidelines available on website. **Entry fee:** $25/book ms. **Deadline:** August 1-October 31, 2010 for 2011. 2010 winner was Melissa Stein (*Rough Honey*). 2010 judge was Mark Doty.

$ ◻ THE AMY AWARD FOR POETRY

Poets & Writers, 90 Broad St., Suite 2100, New York NY 10004. E-mail: admin@pw.org. Website: www.pw.org/about-us/amy_award. **Contact:** Elliot Figman, executive director. (Specialized: women age 30 & under living in NYC metropolitan area & Long Island; lyric poems) The Amy Award, sponsored by Poets & Writers, Inc. (see separate listing in Organizations), offers honorarium, books, plus a reading in NYC. **Entrants must be women 30 years of age or under who reside on Long Island or in the New York metropolitan region.** Submit 3 lyric poems of no more than 50 lines each, with SASE and brief biography. Guidelines available on website (posted in February). **Entry fee:** none. **Deadline:** to be announced (check website). Past winners include Genevieve Burger-Weiser, Lisabeth Burton, K.D. Henley, and Alexandra Wilder. "The Amy Award was established by Edward Butscher and Paula Trachtman of East Hampton in memory of Mrs. Trachtman's daughter, Amy Rothholz, an actor and poet who died at age 25."

$ ☑ ANABIOSIS PRESS CHAPBOOK CONTEST

(978)469-7085. E-mail: rsmyth@anabiosispress.org. Website: www.anabiosispress.org. **Contact:** Richard Smyth, editor. The Anabiosis Press Chapbook Contest offers $100 plus publication of the winning chapbook and 75 copies of the first run. Submit 16-20 pages of poetry on any subject. Include separate pages with a biography, table of contents, and acknowledgments for any previous publications. Include SASE with correct postage for return of ms. **Entry fee:** $12 (all entrants receive a copy of the winning chapbook). Make checks payable to The Anabiosis Press. **Deadline:** June 30 (postmark). Winners announced by September 30. 2009 winner was Meghan Brinson (*Fragrant Inferno*).

$ ☑ THE ANHINGA PRIZE FOR POETRY

Anhinga Press, Tallahassee FL 32302. (850)442-1408. Fax: (850)442-6323. E-mail: info@ anhinga.org. Website: www.anhinga.org. **Contact:** Rick Campbell, poetry editor. The annual Anhinga Prize awards $2,000, a reading tour of Florida, and publication of a book-length poetry ms. Guidelines available for SASE or on website. **Entry fee:** $25. **Deadline:** submit February 15-May 1. Past judges include Donald Hall, Joy Harjo, Robert Dana, Mark Jarman, and Tony Hoagland. Past winners include Frank X. Gaspar, Julia Levine, Keith Ratzlaff, and Lynn Aarti Chandhok, and Rhett Iseman Trull.

$ ARIZONA LITERARY CONTEST & BOOK AWARDS

Arizona Authors Association, 6145 W. Echo Lane, Glendale, AZ 85302. (623)847-9343. E-mail: info@azauthors.com. Website: www.azauthors.com. **Contact:** Toby Heathcotte, president. Arizona Authors Association sponsors annual literary contest in poetry, short story, essay, unpublished novels, and published books (fiction, nonfiction, and children's literature). Awards publication in *Arizona Literary Magazine*, prizes by Five Star Publications, Inc. and $100 1st Prize, $50 2nd Prize, and $25 3rd Prize in each category. Poetry submissions must be unpublished. Considers simultaneous submissions. Submit any number of poems on any subject up to 42 lines. Entry form and guidelines available on website or for SASE. **Entry fee:** $10/poem. **Deadline:** reads submissions January 1-July 1. Competition receives 1,000 entries/year. Recent poetry winners include Cappy Love Hanson and Margaret C Weber. Judges: Arizona authors, editors, and reviewers. Winners announced at an award banquet by November 8.

$ ☐ ARIZONA STATE POETRY SOCIETY ANNUAL CONTEST

37427 N. Ootam Rd., #104, Cave Creek AZ 85331. (480)575-1222. Website: www.azpoetry. org. Offers a variety of cash prizes in several categories ranging from $10-125; 1st, 2nd, and 3rd Prize winners are published in Sandcutters, ASPS's quarterly publication, which also lists names of Honorable Mention winners. See guidelines for detailed submission information (available for SASE or on website). **Entry fee:** varies according to category; see guidelines. **Deadline:** approximately September 15 (postmark). Competition receives over 1,000 entries/year. "ASPS sponsors a variety of monthly contests for members. Membership is available to anyone anywhere."

$ ◻ ART AFFAIR POETRY CONTEST

P.O. Box 54302, Oklahoma City OK 73154. Website: www.shadetreecreations.com. **Contact:** Barbara Shepherd. The annual Art Affair Poetry Contest offers 1st Prize: $40 and certificate; 2nd Prize: $25 and certificate; and 3rd Prize: $15 and certificate. Honorable Mention certificates will be awarded at the discretion of the judges. Open to any poet. Poems must be unpublished. Multiple entries accepted with entry fee for each and may be mailed in the same packet. Submit original poems on any subject, in any style, no more than 60 lines (put line count in the upper right-hand corner of first page). Include cover page with poet's name, address, phone number, and title of poem. Do not include SASE; poems will not be returned. Guidelines available on website. **Deadline:** October 1, 2009 (postmark). **Entry Fee:** $3/poem. Make check payable to Art Affair. Winners' list will be published on the Art Affair website in December. 2009 winners were Patti Landi-Zippilli, Maria Rachel Hooley, and David Dillon.

$ ◻ ARTIST TRUST FELLOWSHIPS

(Specialized: WA resident artists), 1835 12th Ave., Seattle WA 98122. (206)467-8734. Fax: (206)467-9633. E-mail: info@artisttrust.org. Website: www.artisttrust.org. **Contact:** Heather Helbach-Olds, Director of Programs. Artist Trust is a nonprofit arts organization that provides grants to artists (including poets) who are residents of the state. Applications for Grants for Artist Projects (GAP) are accepted each year in February; awards grants of up to $1,500. Applications for Fellowship Program are accepted in June of odd-numbered years; awards $7,500 merit-based awards. **Deadline:** GAP, February; Fellowship, second Friday of June in odd-numbered years. Each competition receives 200-300 literary entries/year. Most recent winners include Stacey Levine, Ann Pancake, and Brenda Miller. Also publishes a newsletter (4 times/year) full of information on arts-related topics and cultural issues; and Artists' Assets (published annually) full of resources for artists of all disciplines.

$ ☑ AUTUMN HOUSE POETRY PRIZE

P.O. Box 60100, Pittsburgh PA 15211. (412)381-4261. E-mail: msimms@autumnhouse.org. Website: http://autumnhouse.org. **Contact:** Michael Simms, editor. Offers annual prize of $2,500 and publication of book-length ms with national promotion. Submission must be unpublished as a collection, but individual poems may have been previously published elsewhere. Considers simultaneous submissions. Submit 50-80 pages of poetry ("blind judging—2 cover sheets requested"). Guidelines available for SASE, by e-mail, or on website. **Entry fee:** $25/ms. **Deadline:** June 30 annually. Competition receives 700 entries/year. 2009 winner was Jacqueline Berger. 2010 judge: Claudia Emerson. Winners announced through mailings and through ads in Poets & Writers , American Poetry Review , and Writer's Chronicle (extensive publicity for winner). Copies of winning books available from Amazon.com, Barnes & Noble, Borders, and other retailers. "Autumn House is a nonprofit corporation with the mission of publishing and promoting poetry. We have published books by Gerald Stern, Ruth L. Schwartz, Ed Ochester, Andrea Hollander Budy, George Bloch, Jo McDougall, and others." Advice: "Include only your best poems."

$ ☑ THE MURIEL CRAFT BAILEY MEMORIAL AWARD

4956 St. John Dr., Syracuse NY 13215. (315)488-8077. E-mail: poetry@comstockreview. org. Website: www.comstockreview.org. The annual Muriel Craft Bailey Memorial Award offers 1st Prize: $1,000; 2nd Prize: $250; 3rd Prize: $100; Honorable Mentions; plus publication of winners and selected finalists in The Comstock Review (see separate listing in Magazines/Journals). Submissions must be unpublished in any media, print or electronic. No simultaneous submissions. Submit poems of 40 lines each, beginning wtih the first line of text below the title (do not count blank lines). Put poet's name, address, phone number, and e-mail address on reverse side of each page. "We read each poem 'blind,' so we do not want to see your name on the front of the poem." Poems with identification visible to judges on the front side of page will be disqualified. Include SASE for results only; no poems will be returned. See our website for full guidelines. **Entry fee:** $5/poem. Make checks payable to The Comstock Review (combine fees on a single check for multiple entries). **Deadline:** reads May 1-July 1 (postmark). 2009 Judge: Maxine Kumin. 2010 judge: Charles Martin.

◗ THE BAILEY PRIZE

The Chrysalis Reader, 1745 Gravel Hill Rd., Dillwyn VA 23936. (434)983-3021. Fax: (434)983-1074. E-mail: chrysalis@hovac.com. Website: www.swedenborg.com/chrysalis. **Contact:** The Editor. (Specialized: open to upper-level undergraduate & graduate-level writing students) Celebrating more than 25 years of publishing established and emerging writers, *The Chrysalis Reader* offers The Bailey Prize, an annual publishing prize for undergraduate and graduate-level students. *The Chrysalis Reader,* published yearly in the fall, is an anthology of poetry, fiction, and nonfiction. Winners will be published in CR (see separate listing in Magazines/Journals), receive 3 copies of the issue, and have their work available online after print publication. The Bailey Prize is open to nominations by instructors of undergraduate and graduate-level courses. Instructors may submit a maximum of 3 nominations from their students' output within one academic year. Nominations may be any combination of previously unpublished poetry (100 lines maximum) or fiction or nonfiction (3,100 words maximum). "We welcome both traditional and experimental writing with an emphasis on insightful writing related to the *Chrysalis Reader's* annual theme. The 2011 theme is "The Marketplace." Submit one copy of each entry with writer's contact information. Include a cover letter and SASE. No e-mail or disk submissions. No nominated entries will be returned. Guidelines available on website. **Entry fee:** none. **Deadline:** All entries must be dated on or before May 31 to be considered for that year's publishing cycle.

$ ☑ THE WILLIS BARNSTONE TRANSLATION PRIZE

1800 Lincoln Ave., Evansville IN 47722. (812)488-1042. E-mail: evansvillereview@ evansville.edu. Website: english.evansville.edu/EvansvilleReview.htm. **Contact:** Kasey Bunner, editor. (Specialized: translations from any language) The annual Willis Barnstone Translation Prize offers an annual award of $1,000 and publication in The Evansville Review for translated poems from any language and any time period, ancient to contemporary. Submissions must be unpublished. Each translated poem must not exceed 200 lines. "Please staple the translation to a copy of the original (which identifies the original poet) and put the name, address, and phone number of the translator(s) on the back of the translation page." Accepts multiple entries (up to 10/translator). Include SASE for results; mss will not be returned. Guidelines available for SASE or on website. **Entry fee:** $5 for the first poem, $3 for each subsequent poem. Make checks payable to The University of Evansville. **Deadline:** December 1. Competition receives 400 entries/year. Winner will be announced in April in The Evansville Review and to entrants who provided SASEs.

$ ✪ BARROW STREET PRESS BOOK CONTEST

P.O. Box 1558, Kingston RI 02881. Website: www.barrowstreet.org. Barrow Street Press publishes one poetry book/year through the annual Barrow Street Press Book Contest. Winner receives $1,000 and publication. Submit a 50- to 70-page ms of original, previously unpublished poetry in English. Manuscript should be typed, single-spaced on white 8½ × 11 paper. Clear photocopies acceptable. Include 2 title pages and an acknowledgments page listing any poems previously published in journals or anthologies. Author's name, address, and daytime phone number should appear on first title page only, and nowhere else in ms. Include SASE for results only; no mss will be returned. Guidelines available on website. **Entry fee:** $25; include mailer with $2.13 postage for copy of winning book. Make checks payable to Barrow Street. **Deadline:** June 30. 2011 judge: TBA.

$ ✪ GEORGE BENNETT FELLOWSHIP

Phillips Exeter Academy, 20 Main St., Exeter NH 03833-2460. E-mail: teaching_opportunities@exeter.edu. Website: www.exeter.edu/english/bennett.html. Provides an annual $12,600 fellowship plus residency (room and board) to a writer with a ms in progress. The Fellow's only official duties are to be in residence while the academy is in session and to be available to students interested in writing. The committee favors writers who have not yet published a book-length work with a major publisher. Application materials and guidelines available for SASE or on website. **Entry fee:** $5. **Deadline:** December 1. Competition receives 190 entries.

$ ✪ THE PATRICIA BIBBY FIRST BOOK AWARD

Tebot Bach, P.O. Box 7887, Huntington Beach CA 92615-7887. E-mail: info@tebotbach.org. Website: www.tebotbach.org. **Contact:** Mifanwy Kaiser. The Patricia Bibby First Book Award offers $1,000 and publication of a book-length poetry manuscript by Tebot Bach (see separate listing in Book/Chapbook Publishers). Open to "all poets writing in English who have not committed to publishing collections of poetry of 36 poems or more in editions of over 400 copies." Submissions must be unpublished as a collection, but individual poems may have been previously published elsewhere. Considers simultaneous submissions, but Tebot Bach must be notified immediately by e-mail if the collection is accepted for publication. Partial guidelines: Submit 60-84 pages of poetry, letter-quality, single-spaced; clear photocopies acceptable. Use binder clip; no staples, folders, or printer-bound copies. Include 2 title pages: 1 (not fastened to ms) with ms title, poet's name, address, phone number, and e-mail address; the second (fastened to ms) with ms title only. Also include table of contents. Include SASP for notification of receipt of entry and SASE for results only; mss will not be returned. Complete guidelines available by e-mail or on website. **Reading fee:** $25. Make checks/money orders payable to Tebot Bach with reading fee and title of ms. on the notation line. **Deadline:** October 31 (postmark) annually. Winner announced each year in April. Judges are selected annually.

$ ☑ BINGHAMTON UNIVERSITY MILT KESSLER POETRY BOOK AWARD

Binghamton University Creative Writing Program, P.O. Box 6000, Binghamton NY 13902. (607)777-2713. Fax: (607)777-2408. E-mail: cwpro@binghamton.edu. Website: english. binghamton.edu/cwpro. **Contact:** Maria Mazziotti Gillan, award director. (Specialized: poets over 40) Offers annual award of $1,000 for a book of poetry judged best of those published that year by a poet over the age of 40. "Submit books published that year; do not submit manuscripts." Entry form and guidelines available for SASE, by e-mail, or on website. **Entry fee:** none; "just submit 3 copies of book." **Deadline:** March 1. Competition receives 500 books/year. 2008 winner was Ruth Stone. Winner will be announced in June in Poets & Writers and on website, or by SASE if provided. (**NOTE:** Not to be confused with the Milton Kessler Memorial Prize for Poetry sponsored by Harpur Palate).

$ ☑ BLUE LIGHT POETRY PRIZE AND CHAPBOOK CONTEST

3600 Lyon St., San Francisco CA 94122. E-mail: bluelightpress@aol.com. The Blue Light Poetry Prize and Chapbook Contest offers a cash prize and publication by Blue Light Press (see separate listing in Book/Chapbook Publishers). "The winner will receive a $100 honorarium and 50 copies of his or her book, which can be sold for $10 each, for a total of $600." Submit ms of 10-24 pages, typed or printed with a laser or inkjet printer. No e-mail submissions. Include SASE and postcard for notification of receipt of ms. Guidelines available with SASE or by e-mail. **Entry fee:** $10. Make checks payable to Blue Light Press. **Deadline:** June 15 for chapbook contest. Winner announced in November. Deadline is January 31 for full-length ms contest, 50-80 pages. Send e-mail for guidelines. Winner announced in June.

$ ☑ THE BOSTON REVIEW ANNUAL POETRY CONTEST

Boston Review, 35 Medford St., Suite 302, Somerville MA 02143. (617)591-0505. Fax: (617)591-0440. E-mail: review@bostonreview.net. Website: www.bostonreview.net. Offers $1,500 and publication in *Boston Review* (see separate listing in Magazines/ Journals). "Any poet writing in English is eligible, unless he or she is a current student, former student, or close personal friend of the judge." Submissions must be unpublished. Submit up to 5 poems, no more than 10 pages total, in duplicate. Include cover sheet with poet's name, address, and phone number; no identifying information on the poems themselves. No mss will be returned. Guidelines available for SASE or on website. **Entry fee:** $20 ($30 for international submissions); all entrants receive a one-year subscription to Boston Review. Make checks payable to Boston Review. **Deadline:** June 1 (postmark). Winner announced in early November on website. 2009 Winner: John Gallagher. 2010 judge: Peter Gizzi.

$ ☑ BOULEVARD EMERGING POETS CONTEST

PMB 325, 6614 Clayton Rd., Richmond Heights MO 63117. E-mail: kellyleavitt@ boulevardmagazine.org. Website: www.boulevardmagazine.org. **Contact:** Kelly Leavitt, managing editor. Annual Emerging Poets Contest offers $1,000 and publication in Boulevard (see separate listing in Magazines/Journals) for the best group of 3 poems by a poet who has not yet published a book of poetry with a nationally distributed press. "All entries will be considered for publication and payment at our regular rates." Submissions must be unpublished. Considers simultaneous submissions. Submit 3 poems, typed; may be a sequence or unrelated. On page one of first poem type poet's name, address, phone number, and titles of the 3 poems. Include 3x5 index card with poet's name, address, phone number, and titles of poems. Include SASP for notification of receipt of ms; mss will not be returned. Guidelines available on website. **Entry fee:** $15/group of 3 poems, $15 for each additional group of 3 poems; includes one-year subscription to Boulevard. Make checks payable to Boulevard. **Deadline:** June 1 (postmark). Judge: editors of Boulevard magazine. "No one editorially or financially affiliated with Boulevard may enter the contest."

$ ☑ THE BRIAR CLIFF REVIEW FICTION, POETRY AND CREATIVE NONFICTION CONTEST

3303 Rebecca St., Sioux City IA 51104-2100. Website: www.briarcliff.edu/bcreview. **Contact:** Jeanne Emmons, poetry editor. The Briar Cliff Review (see separate listing in Magazines/Journals) sponsors an annual contest offering $1,000 and publication to each First Prize winner in fiction, poetry, and creative nonfiction. Previous year's winner and former students of editors ineligible. Winning pieces accepted for publication on the basis of First-Time Rights. Considers simultaneous submissions, "but notify us immediately upon acceptance elsewhere." Submit 3 poems, single-spaced on 8½ × 11 paper, no more than 1 poem/page. Include separate cover sheet with author's name, address, e-mail, and poem title(s); no name on ms. Include SASE for results only; mss will not be returned. Guidelines available on website. **Entry fee:** $20 for 3 poems. "All entrants receive a copy of the magazine (a $15 value) containing the winning entries." **Deadline:** November 1. Judge: the editors of The Briar Cliff Review.

$ ☑ BRITTINGHAM PRIZE IN POETRY

University of Wisconsin Press, Dept. of English, 600 N. Park St., Madison WI 53706. E-mail: rwallace@wisc.edu. Website: www.wisc.edu/wisconsinpress/index.html. **Contact:** Ronald Wallace, Poetry Editor. The annual Brittingham Prize in Poetry is one of 2 prizes awarded by The University of Wisconsin Press (see separate listing for the Felix Pollak Prize in Poetry in this section). Offers $1,000 plus publication, with an additional $1,500 honorarium to cover expenses of a reading in Madison. Submissions must be unpublished as a collection, but individual poems may have been published elsewhere (publication must be acknowledged). Considers simultaneous submissions if notified of selection elsewhere. Submit 50-80 unbound ms pages, typed single-spaced (with double spaces between stanzas). Clean photocopies are acceptable. Include one title page with poet's name, address, and telephone number and one with title only. No translations. SASE required. Will return results only; mss will not be returned. Guidelines available for SASE or on website. **Entry fee:** $25. **NOTE:** $25 fee applies to consideration of same entry for the Felix Pollak Prize in Poetry—1 fee for 2 contest entries. Make checks/ money orders payable to University of Wisconsin Press. **Deadline:** submit September 1-27 (postmark). 2010 Brittingham Prize winner was Jennifer Boyden, *The Mouths of Grazing Things*. Qualified readers will screen all mss. Judge: "a distinguished poet who will remain anonymous until the winners are announced in mid-February."

$ ☑ BROKEN BRIDGE POETRY PRIZE

E-mail: lsspress@lintelsashandsill.org. Website: www.lintelsashandsill.org/press-guidelines/#highschool. The annual Broken Bridge Poetry Prize awards $150 plus publication in a special folio from LS&S Press with an introduction by the contest's judge, and publication of the winning poem in our online literary journal *Suss* following the folio's publication. **"Open only to students enrolled in independent secondary schools, grades 9-12."** Submit up to 1-3 poems. Guidelines available by e-mail or on website. **Entry fee:** none. **Deadline:** February 1.

$ ☑ DOROTHY BRUNSMAN POETRY PRIZE

Bear Star Press, 185 Hollow Oak Dr., Cohasset CA 95973. (530)891-0360. Website: www.bearstarpress.com. **Contact:** Beth Spencer, editor/publisher. The annual Dorothy Brunsman Poetry Prize awards $1,000 and publication by Bear Star Press to the best book-length ms by a poet who resides in the Western states (within Mountain or Pacific time zones, plus Alaska and Hawaii). "The contest also serves as our best pool for finding new voices." Submission must be unpublished as a collection, but individual poems may have been previously published elsewhere (as long as poet retains copyright). Considers simultaneous submissions (contact immediately if ms status changes). Submit ms of 50-65 pages of original poetry, in any form, on any subject. Use a plain 10-12 point font. Include separate cover sheet with poet's name, address, and phone number; no identifying information on mss pages. Include SASP for notification of receipt (do not send by Registered Mail); mss will not be returned. Guidelines available for SASE or on website. **Entry fee:** $20. **Deadline:** November 30 (postmark); reads mss in September, October, and November. Most recent winner was Robert Hill Long (*The Kilim of Dreaming*). Judge: mss judged in house. Winner notified on or before February 1; winner information posted on website. Copies of winning books available through website. "Send your best work; consider its arrangement. A 'wow' poem early on keeps me reading."

$ ☑ BURNSIDE REVIEW CHAPBOOK COMPETITION

P.O. Box 1782, Portland OR 97207. E-mail: sid@burnsidereview.org. Website: www. burnsidereview.org. **Contact:** Sid Miller, editor. The annual Burnside Review Chapbook Competition awards $200, publication, and 25 author's copies to winning poet. Guidelines available for SASE or on website. **Entry fee:** $15. **Deadline:** March 15-June 30. 2009 winner was Louise Mathias (*Above All Else the Trembling Resembles a Forest*). (See separate listing for Burnside Review in Magazines/Journals.)

⬚ $ CAA POETRY AWARD

Canadian Authors Association, Box 419, Campbellford ON K0L 1L0, Canada. Website: www.CanAuthors.org. (Specialized: Canadian poets) The CAA Poetry Award offers $1,000 CAD and a silver medal to Canadian writers for a poetry collection (by a single poet) published during the year. Guidelines available on website. **Entry fee:** $35 CAD/ title. **Deadline:** December 15; except for works published after December 1, in which case the postmark deadline is January 15. Competition receives 100 entries/year. 2009 winner was Elise Partridge (*Chameleon Hours*). All awards are given at the CAA Awards Banquet at the annual conference.

$ ⬚ GERALD CABLE BOOK AWARD

Silverfish Review Press, P.O. Box 3541, Eugene OR 97403. (541)344-5060. E-mail: sfrpress@earthlink.net. Website: www.silverfishreviewpress.com. **Contact:** Rodger Moody, Editor. Offers annual award of $1,000, publication by Silverfish Review Press, and 25 author copies to a book-length ms of original poetry by an author who has not yet published a full-length collection. No restrictions on the kind of poetry or subject matter; no translations. Individual poems may have been previously published elsewhere, but must be acknowledged. Considers simultaneous submissions (notify immediately of acceptance elsewhere). Submit at least 48 pages of poetry, no names or identification on ms pages. Include separate title sheet with poet's name, address, and phone number. Include SASP for notification of receipt and SASE for results; no mss will be returned. Accepts e-mail submissions in Word, plain text, or rich text; send entry fee and SASE by regular mail. Guidelines available for SASE, by e-mail, or on website. **Entry fee:** $20. Make checks payable to Silverfish Review Press. **Deadline:** October 15 (postmark). 2008 Winner was Eric Gudas (*Best Western and Other Poems*). Winner announced in March. Copies of winning books available through website. "All entrants who enclose a booksize envelope and $2.23 in postage will receive a free copy of a recent winner of the book award."

CAKETRAIN CHAPBOOK COMPETITION

P.O. Box 82588, Pittsburgh PA 15218. E-mail: caketrainjournal@hotmail.com. Website: www.caketrain.org/competitions. Annual chapbook contest sponsored by Caketrain literary journal. Can submit by mail with SASE or by e-mail.See website for guidelines. Winner receives a $250 cash prize and 25 copies of their chapbook. **Entry fee:** $15 for reading fee only or $20 for entry fee and copy of winning chapbook. **Deadline:** October 1. Past winners include Elizabeth Skurnick's *Check-In* (2005); Tom Whalen's *Dolls* (2007); Claire Hero's *afterpastures* (2008); Tina May Hall's *All the Day's Sad Stories* (2009); and Ben Mirov's *Ghost Machine* (2010).

$ ⬚ CAROLINA WREN PRESS POETRY CONTEST FOR A FIRST OR SECOND BOOK

120 Morris St., Durham NC 27701. (919)560-2738. Fax: (919)560-2759. E-mail: carolinawrenpress@earthlink.net. Website: www.carolinawrenpress.org. **Contact:** Contest Director. The biennial Carolina Wren Press Poetry Contest for a First or Second Book offers $1,000 and publication by Carolina Wren Press (see separate listing in Book/

Chapbook Publishers). Open only to poets who have published no more than 1 full-length collection (48 pages or more). Submissions must be unpublished as a collection, but individual poems may have been previously published elsewhere. Manuscripts that have been previously self-published or that are available online in their entirety are not eligible. Considers simultaneous submissions (notify immediately of acceptance elsewhere). Submit 2 copies of a poetry ms of 48-60 pages. Page count should include title page, table of contents, and optional dedication page. See guidelines for complete formatting and submission details. Include SASE for results only; mss will not be returned. Guidelines available for SASE, by e-mail, or on website (in September). **Entry fee:** $20. **Deadline:** December 1, 2010, 2012, 2014, etc. (postmark). 2010 judge: TBA. Past judges: William Pitt Root, Evie Shockley, Minnie Bruce Pratt. Copies of winning books available through website, Amazon, or local bookstore.

$ ☑ CAVE CANEM POETRY PRIZE

Cave Canem Foundation, Inc., 20 Jay Street, Suite 310-A, Brooklyn NY 11201. Website: www.cavecanempoets.org. (Specialized: African American) Offers "annual first book award dedicated to presenting the work of African American poets who have not been published by a professional press. The winner will receive $500 cash, publication, and 50 copies of the book." **U.S. poets only.** Considers simultaneous submissions, but they should be noted. "If the manuscript is accepted for publication elsewhere during the judging, immediate notification is requested." Send 2 copies of manuscript of 50-75 pages. The author's name should not appear on the manuscript. 2 title pages should be attached to each copy. The first must include the poet's name, address, telephone number, and the title of the manuscript; the second should list the title only. Number the pages." Include SASE for notification of receipt of ms; mss will not be returned. Guidelines available for SASE or on website. **Entry fee:** $15. **Deadline:** April 30. 2010 final judge: Elizabeth Alexander.

$ ☑ CIDER PRESS REVIEW BOOK AWARD

777 Braddock Lane, Halifax PA 17032. E-mail: editor@ciderpressreview.com. Website: http://ciderpressreview.com. **Contact:** Contest Director. The annual Cider Press Review Book Award offers $1,000, publication, and 25 author's copies. CPR acquires first publication rights. Initial print run is not less than 1,000 copies. Submissions must be unpublished as a collection, but individual poems may have been previously published elsewhere. Submit book-length ms of 48-80 pages. "Submissions can be made online using the submission form on the website or by mail. If sending by mail, include 2 cover sheets—1 with title, author's name, and complete contact information; and 1 with title only, all bound with a spring clip. Include SASE for results; manuscripts cannot be returned. Online submissions must be in Word for PC or PDF format, and should not include title page with author's name. The editors strongly urge contestants to use online delivery if possible." **Entry fee:** $25. All entrants will receive a copy of the winning book and a one-issue subscription to *Cider Press Review*. **Deadline:** submit September 1-November 30. 2010 judge: Patricia Smith.

$ ☑ CLEVELAND STATE UNIVERSITY POETRY CENTER FIRST BOOK

Dept. of English, 2121 Euclid Ave., Cleveland OH 44115-2214. E-mail: poetrycenter@ csuohio.edu. Website: www.csuohio.edu/poetrycenter/contest1.html. **Contact:** Poetry Center Manager. Offers $1,000, publication in the CSU Poetry Series, and a paid reading at Cleveland State for the best full-length volume of original poetry by a poet who has not published or committed to publish a collection of poetry in a book of 48 or more pages with a press run of at least 500 copies. "The CSU Poetry Center reserves the right to consider all finalists for publication." Considers simultaneous submissions; "please inform us if the manuscript is accepted elsewhere." "Eclectic in taste and inclusive in its aesthetic, with particular interest in lyric poetry and innovative approaches to craft. Not interested in light verse, devotional verse, doggerel, or poems by poets who have not read my contemporary poetry." Submit a minimum of 48 pages of poetry, numbered. Include table of contents and acknowledgements page. Include 2 cover pages: one with ms title, poet's name, address, phone number, and e-mail; one with ms title only. No identifying information on ms pages; no cover letter or biographical information. Clearly mark outside of mailing envelope and each cover page "First Book." Accepts multiple submissions with separate entry fee for each; send in the same envelope marked " Multiple." Include SASP for notification of receipt of ms (optional) and SASE for notification of results; mss are not returned. Guidelines available on website. **Entry fee:** $25. Make checks payable to Cleveland State University. **Deadline:** submit November 1-February 15 (postmark). Entrants notified by mail in summer. 2011 judge: Matthea Harvey (intimate friends, relatives, current and former students of the First Book judge, students in an academic degree-conferring program or its equivalent are not eligible to enter)."

$ ☑ CLEVELAND STATE UNIVERSITY POETRY CENTER OPEN COMPETITION

Dept. of English, 2121 Euclid Ave., Clevleand OH 44115-2214. E-mail: poetrycenter@ csuohio.edu. Website: www.csuohio.edu/poetrycenter/contest1.html. **Contact:** Center Manager. Offers $1,000 and publication in the CSU Poetry Series for the best full-length volume of original poetry by a poet who has published at least one full-length collection of poetry in a book of 48 pages or more with a press run of 500. The CSU Poetry Center reserves the right to consider all finalists for publication. No submissions previously published in their entirety (including self-published) or translations. Considers simultaneous submissions; "please inform us if the manuscript is accepted elsewhere. Eclectic in its taste and inclusive in its aesthetic, with particular interest in lyric poetry and innovative approaches to craft. Not interested in light verse, devotional versr, doggerel, or poems by poets who have not read much contemporary poetry." Submit a minimum of 48 pages of poetry, numbered. Include table of contents and acknowledgements page. Include 2 cover pages: one with ms title, poet's name, address, phone number, and e-mail; one with ms title only. No identifying information on ms pages; no cover letter or biographical information. Clearly mark outside of mailing envelope and each cover page "Open Competition." Include SASP for notification of receipt of ms (optional) and SASE for notification of results; mss are not returned. Guidelines available on website. **Entry fee:** $25. Make checks payable to Cleveland State University. **Deadline:** submit

November 1-February 15 (postmark). Entrants notified by mail in summer. 2011 juried by a committee headed by Michael Dumanis.

$ ☑ COLORADO PRIZE FOR POETRY

Center for Literary Publishing, Dept. of English, 9105 Campus Delivery, Colorado State University, Fort Collins CO 80523. (970)491-5449. E-mail: creview@colostate.edu. Website: http://coloradoreview.colostate.edu. **Contact:** Stephanie G'Schwind, Editor. The annual Colorado Prize for Poetry awards an honorarium of $1,500 and publication of a book-length ms. Submission must be unpublished as a collection, but individual poems may have been published elsewhere. Submit mss of 48-100 pages of poetry (no set minimum or maximum) on any subject, in any form, double- or single-spaced. Include 2 titles pages: one with ms title only, the other with ms title and poet's name, address, and phone number. Enclosed SASP for notification of receipt and SASE for results; mss will not be returned. Guidelines available for SASE or by e-mail. **Entry fee:** $25; includes one-year subscription to *Colorado Review* (see separate listing in Magazines/Journals). **Deadline:** submission period was October 1-January 14 for 2010. Winner announced in May. 2009 winner was Rob Schlegel (The Lesser Fields), selected by James Longenbach. 2010 judge was Donald Revell.

$ ☐ CONCRETE WOLF POETRY CHAPBOOK CONTEST

P.O. Box 1808, Kingston WA 98346. E-mail: concretewolf@yahoo.com. Website: http://concretewolf.com. **Contact:** Contest Coordinator. (Specialized: theme-centric chapbooks) Member: CLMP. The Concrete Wolf Poetry Chapbook Contest offers publication and 100 author copies of a perfectly bound chapbook. Considers simultaneous submissions if notified of acceptance elsewhere. "We prefer chapbooks that have a theme, either obvious (i.e., chapbook about a divorce) or understated (i.e., all the poems mention the color blue). We like a collection that feels more like a whole than a sampling of work. We have no preference as to formal or free verse. We probably slightly favor lyric and narrative poetry to language and concrete, but excellent examples of any style get our attention." Submit up to 26 pages of poetry, paginated. Include table of contents and acknowledgments page. Include 2 cover sheets: one with ms title, poet's name, address, phone number, and e-mail; one without poet's identification. Include SASE for results; mss will not be returned. Guidelines available on website. **Entry fee:** $20; include 6.5x9.5 envelope with $1.82 postage for a copy of the winning chapbook. Make checks payable to Concrete Wolf. **Deadline:** December 3 for 2011. Competition receives about 250 entries. Winner announced in February. Judge: editors and an anonymous guest judge, announced after the contest. Copies of winning chapbooks available through website.

THE CONNECTICUT RIVER REVIEW POETRY CONTEST

P.O. Box 270554, West Hartford CT 06127. E-mail: connpoetry@comcast.net. Website: ct-poetry-society.org/publications.htm. Prizes of $400, $200, and $100 will be awarded and winning poems will be published in *Connecticut River Review*. Send up to 3 unpublished poems, any form, 80 line limit. Include two copies of each poem: one with complete contact information in the upper right hand corner and one with NO contact information. Include SASE for results only (no poems will be returned). Winning poems must be submitted electronically following notification. Deadline: February 28. **Entry fee:** Entry fee: $15 for up to 3 poems. Simultaneous submissions acceptable if we are notified immediately when a poem is accepted elsewhere. Please make out check to Connecticut Poetry Society. See separate entries in Magazines and Organizations sections of this book.

$ ☑ CRAB ORCHARD SERIES IN POETRY FIRST BOOK AWARD

Dept. of English, Mail Code 4503, Faner Hall 2380, Southern Illinois Univ Carbondale, Carbondale IL 62901. Website: www.craborchardreview.siuc.edu. **Contact:** Jon Tribble, series editor. Dept. of English, Mail Code 4503, Faner Hall 2380, Southern Illinois University Carbondale, 1000 Faner Dr., Carbondale IL 62901. Website: www.siu.edu/ ~ crborchd. Established 1995. **Contact:** John Tribble, series editor. The Crab Orchard Series in Poetry First Book Award offers $2,500 ($1,000 prize plus $1,500 honorarium for a reading at Southern Illinois University Carbondale) and publication. "Manuscripts should be 50-75 pages of original poetry, in English, by a U.S. citizen or permanent resident who has neither published, nor committed to publish, a volume of poetry 40 pages or more in length (individual poems may have been previously published). Current students and employees of Southern Illinois University and authors published by Southern Illinois University Press are not eligible." See guidelines for complete formatting instructions. Guidelines available for SASE or on website. **Entry fee:** $25/submission; includes a copy of the summer/fall Crab Orchard Review (see separate listing in Magazines/Journals). Make checks payable to Crab Orchard Series in Poetry. **Deadline:** see guidelines or check website. 2009 winner was Traci Brimhall (*Rookery*).

$ ☑ CRAB ORCHARD SERIES IN POETRY OPEN COMPETITION AWARDS

Dept. of English, Mail Code 4503, Faner Hall 2380, Southern Illinois Univ Carbondale, Carbondale IL 62901. Website: www.craborchardreview.siuc.edu. **Contact:** Jon Tribble, series editor. The Crab Orchard Series in Poetry Open Competition Awards offer two winners $3,500 and publication of a book-length ms. "Cash prize totals reflect a $1,500 honorarium for each winner for a reading at Southern Illinois University Carbondale. Publication contract is with Southern Illinois University Press. Entrants must be U.S. citizens or permanent residents." Submissions must be unpublished as a collection, but individual poems may have been previously published elsewhere. Considers simultaneous submissions, but series editor must be informed immediately upon acceptance. Manuscripts should be typewritten or computer-generated (letter quality only, no dot matrix), single-spaced; clean photocopy is recommended as mss are not returned. See guidelines for complete formatting instructions. Guidelines available for SASE or on website. **Entry fee:** $25/submission; includes a copy of the winning Crab Orchard Review (see separate listing in Magazines/Journals). Make checks payable to Crab Orchard Series in Poetry. **Deadline:** see guidelines or check website. 2009 winners were Todd Hearon (*Strange Land*) and Jennifer Richter (*Threshold*).

$ ☑ LOIS CRANSTON MEMORIAL POETRY PRIZE

CALYX, Inc., P.O. Box B, Corvallis OR 97339. E-mail: calyx@proaxis.com. Website: www. calyxpress.org. CALYX (see separate listing in Magazines/Journals) offers the annual Lois Cranston Memorial Poetry Prize of $300, publication in CALYX , and a one-volume subscription. Finalists will be published on the CALYX website and receive a one-volume subscription. No previously published poems or simultaneous submissions. Submit up to 3 poems/entry (6 pages total maximum). Include separate cover letter with poet's name, address, phone number, e-mail address, and title(s) of poem(s). No names on poems. No mss will be returned. Guidelines available for SASE, by e-mail, or on website. **Entry fee:** $15 for up to 3 poems. Make checks payable to CALYX. **Deadline:** submit March 1-May 31 (inclusive postmark dates). Winners notified by October 30 and announced on Calyx's website. 2008 winner was Hilde Weisert ("Finding Wilfred Owen Again"). 2009 judge Marilyn Chin.

$ ☑ DANA AWARD IN POETRY

200 Fosseway Dr., Greensboro NC 27455. (336)644-8028 (for emergency questions only). E-mail: danaawards@pipeline.com. Website: www.danaawards.com. **Contact:** Mary Elizabeth Parker, Award Chair. Offers annual award of $1,000 for the best group of 5 poems. Submissions must be unpublished and not under promise of publication when submitted. Considers simultaneous submissions. Submit 5 poems on any subject, in any form; no light verse. Include separate cover sheet with name, address, phone, e-mail address, and titles of poems. Entries by regular mail only. Include SASE for winners list only; no mss will be returned. Guidelines available for SASE, by e-mail, or on website. **Entry fee:** $15 for 5 poems. **Deadline:** October 31 (postmark). Winner will be announced in early spring by phone, letter, and e-mail.

$ ◯ DANCING POETRY CONTEST

704 Brigham Ave., Santa Rosa CA 95404-5245. (707)528-0912. E-mail: jhcheung@comcast. net. Website: www.DANCINGPOETRY.com. **Contact:** Judy Cheung, contest chair. Annual contest offers 3 Grand Prizes of $100, five 1st Prizes of $50, ten 2nd Prizes of $25, and twenty 3rd Prizes of $10. The 3 Grand Prize-winning poems will be choreographed, costumed, premiered, and videotaped at the annual Dancing Poetry Festival at Palace of the Legion of Honor, San Francisco; Natica Angilly's Poetic Dance Theater Company will perform the 3 Grand Prize-winning poems. In addition, "all prizes include an invitation to read your prize poem at the festival, and a certificate suitable for framing." Submissions must be unpublished or poet must own rights. Submit 2 copies of any number of poems, 40 lines maximum (each), with name, address, phone number on 1 copy only. Foreign language poems must include English translations. Include SASE for winners list. No inquiries or entries by fax or e-mail. Entry form available for SASE. **Entry fee:** $5/poem or $10 for 3 poems. **Deadline:** May 15 annually. Competition receives about 500-800 entries. Winners will be announced by mail; Grand Prize winners will be contacted by phone. Ticket to festival will be given to all winners. Artist Embassy International has been a nonprofit educational arts organization since 1951, "Furthering intercultural understanding and peace through the universal language of the arts."

DELAWARE DIVISION OF THE ARTS

820 North French St., Wilmington DE 19801. (302)577-8278. Fax: (302)577-6561. E-mail: kristin.pleasanton@state.de.us. Website: www.artsdel.org. **Contact:** Kristin Pleasanton, art & artist services coordinator. Award "to help further careers of emerging and established professional artists." For Delaware residents only. Prize: $10,000 for masters; $6,000 for established professionals; $3,000 for emerging professionals. Judged by out-of-state, nationally recognized professionals in each artistic discipline. No entry fee. Guidelines available after May 1 on website. Accepts inquiries by e-mail, phone. Expects to receive 25 fiction entries. **Deadline: Beginning of August**. Open to any Delaware writer. Results announced in December. Winners notified by mail. Results available on website. "Follow all instructions and choose your best work sample."

$ ◧ DIAGRAM/NEW MICHIGAN PRESS CHAPBOOK CONTEST

Dept. of English, P.O. Box 210067, University of Arizona, Tucson AZ 85721. E-mail: nmp@ thediagram.com. Website: www.newmichiganpress.com/nmp. **Contact:** Ander Monson, Editor. The annual DIAGRAM /New Michigan Press Chapbook Contest offers $1,000 plus publication and author's copies, with discount on additional copies. Also publishes 2-4 finalist chapbooks each year. Submit 18-44 pages of poetry, fiction, mixed-genre, or genre-bending work (images okay if b/w and you have permissions). Include SASE. Guidelines available on website. **Entry fee:** $16. **Deadline:** April 1.

$ ▢ JAMES DICKEY PRIZE FOR POETRY

Georgia State University, P.O. Box 3999, Atlanta GA 30302-3999. Website: www. webdelsol.com/Five_Points. The annual James Dickey Prize for Poetry awards $1,000 and publication in Five Points. Submissions must be unpublished. Submit up to 3 typed poems, no more than 50 lines each. Include name and address on cover sheet. Enclose 2 SASEs: 1 to acknowledge receipt of ms, 1 for results. Guidelines available for SASE or on website. **Entry fee:** $20 domestic, $30 foreign (includes one-year subscription). Make checks payable to Georgia State University. **Deadline:** September1-December 1. Winner announced in spring.

$ ◪ DREAM HORSE PRESS NATIONAL POETRY CHAPBOOK PRIZE

P.O. Box 2080, Felton CA 95001-2080. E-mail: dreamhorsepress@yahoo.com. Website: www.dreamhorsepress.com. **Contact:** J.P. Dancing Bear, Editor/Publisher. "The Dream Horse Press National Poetry Chapbook Prize offers an $500, publication, and 25 copies of a handsomely printed chapbook." All entries will be considered for publication. Submissions may be previously published in magazines/journals but not in books or chapbooks. Considers simultaneous submissions with notification. "Submit 20-28 pages of poetry in a readable font with table of contents, acknowledgments, bio, e-mail address for results, and entry fee. Poet's name should not appear anywhere on the manuscript." Accepts multiple submissions (with separate fee for each entry). Manuscripts will be recycled after judging. Guidelines available on website. **Entry fee:** $15. Make checks/ money orders made payable to Dream Horse Press. **Deadline:** June 30. Recent previous winners include Amy Holman, Cyntha Arrieu-King, Charles Sweetman and Jason Bredle. 2010 judge: C.J. Sage.

$ ☑ T.S. ELIOT PRIZE FOR POETRY

Truman State University Press, 100 E. Normal, Kirksville MO 63501-4221. (660)785-7336. Fax: (660)785-4480. E-mail: tsup@truman.edu. Website: http://tsup.truman.edu. **Contact:** Nancy Rediger. Offers annual award of $2,000 and publication. "The manuscript may include individual poems previously published in journals or anthologies, but may not include a significant number of poems from a published chapbook or self-published book." Submit 60-100 pages. Include 2 title pages: 1 with poet's name, address, phone number, and ms title; the other with ms title only. Include SASE for acknowledgment of ms receipt only; mss will not be returned. Guidelines available for SASE or on website. **Entry fee:** $25. **Deadline:** October 31. Competition receives more than 500 entries/year. 2009 winner was David Moolten (*Primitive Mood*). 2009 judge: Virgil Suárez.

$ ☑ EMERGING VOICES

P.O. Box 6037, Beverly Hills CA 90212. (424)258-1180. Fax: (424)258-1184. E-mail: ev@penusa.org; pen@penusa.org. Website: www.penusa.org. Annual program offering $1,000 stipend and 8-month fellowship to writers in the early stages of their literary careers. Program includes one-on-one sessions with mentors, seminars on topics such as editing or working with agents, courses in the Writers' Program at UCLA Extension, and literary readings. Participants selected according to potential and lack of access to traditional publishing and/or educational opportunities. No age restrictions; selection is not based solely on economic need. Participants need not be published, but "the program is directed toward poets and writers of fiction and creative nonfiction with clear ideas of what they hope to accomplish through their writing. Mentors are chosen from PEN's comprehensive membership of professional writers and beyond. Participants are paired with established writers sharing similar writing interests and often with those of the same ethnic and cultural backgrounds." Program gets underway in January. See website for brochure and complete guidelines. **Deadline:** September 5. "Materials must arrive in the PEN offices by the submission deadline—no exceptions."

$ ☑ ERSKINE J. POETRY PRIZE

P.O. Box 22161, Baltimore MD 21203. E-mail: sreichert@smartishpace.com. Website: www.smartishpace.com. **Contact:** Stephen Reichert, editor. The annual Erskine J. Poetry Prize offers 1st Prize: $200 and publication of the winning poem in Smartish Pace (see separate listing in Magazines/Journals); 2nd and 3rd Prizes: winning poems will be published in Smartish Pace. Winners also receive additional Internet and advertising exposure. Honorable mention (usually 5 to 12) also published in Smartish Pace. All entries will be considered for publication in Smartish Pace. Submit 3 poems, with poet's name, address, e-mail, telephone number (preferred), and "Erskine J." at the top of each page of poetry submitted. Include bio. Entries may be submitted online or by e-mail (as attachment) or regular mail. Include SASE with postal entries. Guidelines available on website. **Entry fee:** $5/3 poems; additional poems may be submitted for $1/poem (limit of 12 poems). Make checks/money orders payable to Smartish Pace. **Deadline:** August 15. 2009 winners were Diane K. Martin (1st), Bethany Schultz Hurst (2nd), William Varner (3rd). There were seven finalists also published in Issue 17 of Smartish Pace. Judge: Stephen Reichert (editor).

⬚ $ ⬚ FAR HORIZONS AWARD FOR POETRY

The Malahat Review, University of Victoria, P.O. Box 1700, Stn CSC, Victoria BC V8W 2Y2, Canada. (250)721-8524. Fax: (250)472-5051. E-mail: malahat@uvic.ca. Website: www.malahatreview.ca. **Contact:** John Barton, editor. The biennial Far Horizons Award for Poetry offers $500 CAD, publication in The Malahat Review (see separate listing in Magazines/Journals), and payment at the rate of $40 CAD per printed page upon publication. Open to "emerging poets from Canada, the United States, and elsewhere" who have not yet published a full-length book (48 pages or more). Submissions must be unpublished. No simultaneous submissions. Submit up to 3 poems per entry, each poem not to exceed 60 lines; no restrictions on subject matter or aesthetic approach. Include separate page with poet's name, address, e-mail, and poem title(s); no identifying information on mss pages. No e-mail submissions. Do not include SASE for results; mss will not be returned. Guidelines available on website. **Entry fee:** $25 CAD for Canadian entries, $30 USD for US entries ($35 USD for entries from Mexico and outside North America); includes a one-year subscription to *The Malahat Review*. **Deadline:** May 1 (postmark) of alternate years (2010, 2012, etc.). 2008 winner: Tadzio Richards. Winner and finalists contacted by e-mail. Winner published in fall in *The Malahat Review* and announced on website, Facebook page, and in quarterly e-newsletter, *Malahat lite*.

$ ⬚ THE WILLIAM FAULKNER-WILLIAM WISDOM CREATIVE WRITING COMPETITION

The Pirate's Alley Faulkner Society, Inc., 624 Pirate's Alley, New Orleans LA 70116. (504)586-1609. Fax: (504)522-9725. E-mail: faulkhouse@aol.com. Website: www.wordsandmusic.org. **Contact:** Rosemary James, Award Director. Offers annual publication in *The Double Dealer*, cash prize of $750, gold medal, and travel and hotel expenses to attend the Society's writers conference and festival, Words & Music, a Literary Feast in New Orleans, with ms critiques and one-on-one consultations with well-known literary editors and agents. "Foreign nationals are eligible, but the society pays transportation to awards ceremony from U.S. cities only. Winners must be present at annual meeting to receive award." Submissions must be previously unpublished. Submit 1 poem of no more than 750 words on any subject in any English-language form. Multiple entries permitted. Entry form (required for each entry) and guidelines available for SASE or on website. **Entry fee:** $25/entry. **Deadline:** submit January 15-April 15 (postmark). "No entries before January 15, please." Competition receives 1,600 (for 7 categories) entries/year. 2009 winner was "Sacred Things," Rosemary Daniell. 2009 judged by poet and nonfiction writer Rodger Kamenetz. Winners are announced on the society's website between January 1 and January 15. "Competition is keen. Send your best work."

$ ⬚ THE FIELD POETRY PRIZE

Oberlin College Press, Oberlin College, 50 N. Professor St., Oberlin OH 44074. (440)775-8408. E-mail: oc.press@oberlin.edu. Website: www.oberlin.edu/ocpress. **Contact:** Linda Slocum, managing editor. The annual FIELD Poetry Prize for a book-length collection of poems offers $1,000 and publication in the FIELD Poetry Series. Submit non-returnable ms of 50-80 pages. Guidelines available for SASE or on website. **Entry fee:** $25; includes one-year subscription to FIELD (see separate listing in Magazines/Journals). Make checks payable to Oberlin College Press. **Deadline:** submit during May only (postmark). 2009 winner was Amy Newlove Schroeder (*The Sleep Hotel*).

$ ☑ THE ANNIE FINCH PRIZE FOR POETRY

The National Poetry Review, P.O. Box 2080, Aptos CA 95001-2080. E-mail: editor@ nationalpoetry review.com. Website: www.nationalpoetryreview.com. **Contact:** C.J. Sage, Editor. The Annie Finch Prize for Poetry offers $500 plus publication in The National Poetry Review (see separate listing in Magazines/Journals). All entries will be considered by the editor for publication. Submissions must be unpublished and uncommitted. Considers simultaneous submissions, "but if the work is selected by The National Poetry Review for the prize or for publication, it must be withdrawn from elsewhere unless you have withdrawn it from us two weeks before our acceptance." Submit up to 3 poems/entry (10 pages maximum per group of 3). Include cover letter with bio and contact information, including e-mail address for results. Complete guidelines available on website. **Entry fee:** $15/entry; accepts multiple submissions with separate entry fee for each 3-poem group. "If you include a small book-sized SASE with $1.30 postage with your entry, we will provide you a copy of the winner's issue." Make checks payable to The National Poetry Review. **Deadline:** April 30 (postmark).

$ ☑ THE FINISHING LINE PRESS OPEN CHAPBOOK COMPETITION

Finishing Line Press, P.O. Box 1626, Georgetown KY 40324. (859)514-8966. E-mail: FinishingBooks@aol.com. Website: www.finishinglinepress.com. **Contact:** Leah Maines, Poetry Editor. The Finishing Line Press Open Chapbook Competition offers a $1,000 cash award and publication. All entries will be considered for publication. Open to all poets regardless of past publications. Submit up to 26 pages of poetry. Include bio, acknowledgments, and cover letter. Guidelines available by e-mail or on website. **Entry fee:** $15. **Deadline:** July 15 (postmark) for 2010.

$ ☐ FLIP KELLY POETRY PRIZE, THE

6199 Steubenville Road SE, Amsterdam OH 43903. (740)543-4333. E-mail: editor@ amsterdampress.net. Website: www.amsterdampress.net. **Contact:** Cindy Kelly, editor. The Flip Kelly Poetry Prize offers a $150 honorarium for best chapbook and publication in Gob Pile Chapbook series. Two runners-up receive publication of chapbook in Gob Pile chapbook series. Chapbook submissions may include previously published works, with acknowledgment. Poems may be entered in other contests and/or under consideration elsewhere. Submit cover letter and copy of manuscript with poet's name, address, phone number. Guidelines and entry forms available for SASE, by e-mail, and on website. Entry fee: $15. **Deadline: December 31**. 2009 judge: TBA. Winners will be announced February 15 (or sooner). Copies of winning chapbooks will be available from amsterdampress. etsy.com for $8. " Amsterdam Press was founded in 2007." **Advice** " We favor the plain-spoken over the esoteric. We like specific, not universal."

$ ☑ THE ROBERT FROST FOUNDATION ANNUAL POETRY AWARD

(Specialized: poems written in the spirit of Robert Frost)The Robert Frost Foundation, Lawrence Library, 51 Lawrence St., Lawrence MA 01841. (978)725-8828. E-mail:

frostfoundation@comcast.net. Website: www.frostfoundation.org. Established 1997. Offers annual award of $1,000. Submissions may be entered in other contests. Submit up to 3 poems of not more than 3 pages each (2 copies of each poem, 1 with name, address, and phone number), written in the spirit of Robert Frost. Guidelines available for SASE and on website. **Entry fee:** $10/poem. **Deadline:** September 15. Competition receives over 600 entries/year. 2008 winner was Elizabeth Klise von Zerneck. Winning poem can be viewed on website.

$ ☑ KINERETH GENSLER AWARD

Alice James Books, University of Maine at Farmington, 238 Main St., Farmington ME 04938. (207)778-7071. Fax: (207)778-7071. E-mail: ajb@umf.maine.edu. Website: www. alicejamesbooks.org. **Contact:** Contest Coordinator. The Kinereth Gensler Award offers $2,000 and publication by Alice James Books (see separate listing in Book/Chapbook Publishers); winners become members of the Alice James Books cooperative, with a 3-year commitment to the editorial board. **Entrants must reside in New England, New York, or New Jersey.** Submissions must be unpublished as a collection, but individual poems may have been previously published elsewhere (in publications of less than 48 pages). Submit 2 copies of ms of 50-70 pages, typed single-spaced and paginated, with table of contents and acknowledgments page; bio is optional. Use binder clips; no staples, folders, or printer-bound copies. Title page of each ms copy must include poet's name, address, and phone number. Enclose SASP for acknowledgment of receipt of ms, #10 SASE for results; mss will not be returned. Guidelines available for SASE or on website. **Entry fee:** $25/ms. Make checks/money orders payable to Alice James Books. For a free book (does not apply to books not yet published), include an additional 6x9 envelope with $2.50 in postage attached; write title of selection on back of envelope. **Deadline:** October 2010. Judges: members of the Alice James Books Editorial Board. Winners announced in December. Copies of winning books available through website.

$ ☑ GERTRUDE PRESS POETRY CHAPBOOK CONTEST

P.O. Box 83948, Portland OR 97283. Website: www.gertrudepress.org. (Specialized: gay, lesbian, bisexual, transgendered, queer-identified & allied) Gertrude Press (see separate listing in Books/Chapbooks) sponsors an annual chapbook competition. Offers $50, publication, and 50 author copies (out of a press run of 200) to the winning poet. Individual poems may have been previously published; unpublished poems are welcome. Submit 16-20 pages of poetry (postal submissions only). "Poetry may be of any subject matter, and writers from all backgrounds are encouraged to submit." Include list of acknowledgments and cover letter indicating how poet learned of the contest. Guidelines available in Gertrude (see separate listing in Magazines/Journals), for SASE, by e-mail, or on website. **Entry fee:** $15; includes copy of the winning chapbook. **Deadline:** Submission period August 1, 2010-February 15, 2011.

$ ☑ ALLEN GINSBERG POETRY AWARDS

Poetry Center, Passaic Co. Community College, One College Blvd, Paterson NJ 07505-1179. (973)684-6555. E-mail: mgillan@pccc.edu. Website: www.pccc.edu/poetry. **Contact:** Maria Mazziotti Gillan, Editor/Executive Director. The Allen Ginsberg Poetry

Awards offer annual prizes of 1st Prize: $1,000, 2nd Prize: $200, and 3rd Prize: $100. All winning poems, honorable mentions, and editor's choice poems will be published in Paterson Literary Review (see separate listing in Magazines/Journals). Winners will be asked to participate in a reading that will be held in the Paterson Historic District. Submissions must be unpublished. Submit up to 5 poems (no poem more than 2 pages long). Send 4 copies of each poem entered. Include cover sheet with poet's name, address, phone number, and poem titles. Poet's name should not appear on poems. Include SASE for results only; poems will not be returned. Guidelines available for SASE or on website. **Entry fee:** $15 (includes subscription to Paterson Literary Review). Write "poetry contest" in memo section of check and make payable to PCCC. **Deadline:** April 1 (postmark). Winners will be announced the following summer by mail and in newspaper announcements. 2009 winners Eileen Moeller and Jose Antonio Rodriguez (1st), Josh Humphrey and Sarah Jefferis 92nd), and Kevin Carey (3rd).

▨ $ GOVERNOR GENERAL'S LITERARY AWARDS

The Canada Council for the Arts, P.O. Box 1047, 350 Albert St., Ottawa ON K1P 5V8, Canada. Website: www.canadacouncil.ca/prizes/GGLA. **Contact:** Diane Miljours, program officer. (Specialized: Canadian citizens/permanent residents; English- and French-language works) Established by Parliament, the Canada Council for the Arts "provides a wide range of grants and services to professional Canadian artists and art organizations in dance, media arts, music, theater, writing, publishing, and the visual arts." The Governor General's Literary Awards, valued at $25,000 CAD each, are given annually for the best English-language and best French-language work in each of 7 categories, including poetry. Non-winning finalists each receive $1,000 CAD. Books must be first edition trade books written, translated, or illustrated by Canadian citizens or permanent residents of Canada and published in Canada or abroad during the previous year (September 1 through the following September 30). Collections of poetry must be at least 48 pages long, and at least half the book must contain work not published previously in book form. In the case of translation, the original work must also be a Canadian-authored title. Books must be submitted by publishers with a Publisher's Submission Form, which is available on request from the Writing and Publishing Section of the Canada Council for the Arts. Guidelines and current deadlines on the website and available by mail, telephone, fax, or e-mail. 2009 winner for poetry in English was David Zieroth (*The Fly in Autumn*).

$ ◙ GRANDMOTHER EARTH NATIONAL AWARD

Grandmother Earth Creations, P.O. Box 2018, Cordova TN 38088. (901)309-3692. E-mail: Gmoearth@gmail.com. Website: www.grandmotherearth.org. **Contact:** Frances Cowden, Award Director. **Contact:** Frances Cowden, award director. Offers annual award of $1,250 with varying distributions each year; $1,250 minimum in awards for poetry and prose; $100 first, etc., plus publication in anthology; non-winning finalists considered for anthology if permission is given. Submissions may be published or unpublished. Considers simultaneous submissions. Submit at least 3 poems, any subject, in any form. Include SASE for winners list. Guidelines available for SASE or on website. **Entry fee:** $10 for 3 works, $2 each additional work. Entry fee includes a copy of the anthology.

Deadline: August 1. 2008 winners were Lynn Veach Sadler, Miriam Doege, Heather Halderman, Timothy Russell, and others. 2008 judge: Daniel Dalquist. Winners will be announced in October at the Mid-South Poetry Festival in Memphis. Copies of winning poems or books available from Grandmother Earth Creations.

$ ☑ GUGGENHEIM FELLOWSHIPS

90 Park Ave., New York NY 10016. (212)687-4470. E-mail: fellowships@gf.org. Website: www.gf.org. Guggenheim Fellowships are awarded each year to poets, as well as fiction and creative nonfiction writers, "on the basis of unusually distinguished achievement in the past and exceptional promise for future accomplishment." 2009 Fellowships were awarded to 34 writers; amounts averaged $36,672 each. Submit career summary, statement of intent, and no more than 3 published books. Guidelines, application form (required), and additional information available for SASE, by e-mail, or on website. **Deadline:** was September 15 for 2009 awards. **Entry fee:** none. 2009 Fellowship recipients in poetry were Saskia Hamilton, Joseph Harrison, Terrance Hayes, Lyn Hejinian, Laura Kasischke, Barbara Ras, Lisa Russ Spaar, Larissa Szporluk, and Daniel Tobin.

$ ☑ THE DONALD HALL PRIZE IN POETRY

AWP, Carty House, Mail Stop 1E3, George Mason University, Fairfax VA 22030-4444. E-mail: chronicle@awpwriter.org. Website: www.awpwriter.org. The Association of Writers & Writing Programs (AWP) sponsors an annual competition for the publication of excellent new book-length works, the AWP Award Series, which includes The Donald Hall Prize in Poetry. Offers annual award of $5,000 and publication for the best book-length ms of poetry (book-length defined for poetry as 48 pages minimum of text). Open to published and unpublished poets alike. "Poems previously published in periodicals are eligible for inclusion in submissions, but manuscripts previously published in their entirety, including self-published, are not eligible. As the series is judged anonymously, no list of acknowledgments should accompany your manuscript. You may submit your manuscript to other publishers while it is under consideration by the Award Series, but you must notify AWP immediately in writing if your manuscript is accepted elsewhere. Your manuscript must be submitted in accordance with the eligibility requirements, format guidelines, and entry requirements or it will be disqualified." Complete guidelines, including important formatting information, eligibility requirements, and required entry form available on website. **Entry fee:** $10 (AWP members) or $25 (nonmembers). Make checks/money orders payable in U.S. dollars only to AWP. **Deadline:** mss must be postmarked between January 1-February 28. 2009 winner was Bradley Paul (*The Animals All Are Gathering*). 2010 judge: Alberto Rios.

$ BEATRICE HAWLEY AWARD

Alice James Books, University of Maine at Farmington, 238 Main St., Farmington ME 04938. (207)778-7071. Fax: (207)778-7071. E-mail: ajb@umf.maine.edu. Website: www.alicejamesbooks.org. **Contact:** Contest Coordinator. The Beatrice Hawley Award offers $2,000 and publication by Alice James Books (see separate listing in Book/Chapbook Publishers). Winners have no cooperative membership commitment. "In addition to the winning manuscript, one or more additional manuscripts may be chosen for publication."

Entrants must reside in the U.S. Submissions must be unpublished as a collection, but individual poems may have been previously published elsewhere (in publications of less than 48 pages). Submit 2 copies of ms of 50-70 pages, typed single-spaced and paginated, with table of contents and acknowledgments page; bio is optional. Use binder clips; no staples, folders, or printer-bound copies. Title page of each ms copy must include poet's name, address, and phone number. Include SASP for acknowledgment of receipt of ms, #10 SASE for results only; mss will not be returned. Guidelines available for SASE or on website. **Entry fee:** $25/ms. Make checks/money orders payable to Alice James Books (write "Beatrice Hawley Award" on memo line). **Deadline:** December 1 (postmark) for 2010. Judges: members of the Alice James Books Editorial Board. Winners announced in April. Copies of winning books available through website.

$ ☑ JAMES HEARST POETRY PRIZE

North American Review, University of Northern Iowa, 1222 W. 27th St., Cedar Falls IA 50614-0516. (319)273-6455. Fax: (319)273-4326. E-mail: nar@uni.edu. Website: www. northamericanreview.org. The James Hearst Poetry Prize offers 1st Prize: $1,000; 2nd Prize: $100; and 3rd Prize: $50. All winners and finalists will be published in North American Review (see separate listing in Magazines/Journals). Submissions must be unpublished. No simultaneous submissions. Submit up to 5 poems, 2 copies each; **NO NAMES** on ms pages. Cover sheet is required (MS Word or PDF). Include SASP for acknowledgment of receipt of ms and #10 SASE for results (or provide e-mail address on cover sheet); mss will not be returned. Guidelines available for SASE, by fax, e-mail, or on website. **Entry fee:** $18 (includes one-year subscription). Make checks/money orders payable to North American Review. **Deadline:** October 31 (postmark).

$ ☑ TOM HOWARD/JOHN H. REID POETRY CONTEST

Tom Howard Books, c/o Winning Writers, 351 Pleasant St., PMB 222, Northampton MA 01060-3961. (866)946-9748. Fax: (413)280-0539. E-mail: johnreid@mail.qango. com. Website: www.winningwriters.com/poetry. **Contact:** John Reid, award director. Offers annual award of 1st Prize: $3,000; 2nd Prize: $1,000; 3rd Prize: $400; 4th Prize: $250; 5 High Distinction Awards of $200 each; and 6 Most Highly Commended Awards of $150 each. The top 10 entries will be published on the Winning Writers website. Submissions may be published or unpublished and may have won prizes elsewhere. Considers simultaneous submissions. Submit poems in any form, style, or genre. "There is no limit on the number of lines or poems you may submit." No name on ms pages; type or computer-print on letter-size white paper, single-sided. Submit online or by regular mail. Guidelines available for SASE or on website. **Entry fee:** $7 USD for every 25 lines (exclude poem titles and any blank lines from line count). **Deadline:** December 15-September 30. Competition receives about 1,000 entries/year. 2008 winner was Dawn Raymond ("Ghosts"). 2008 judges: John H. Reid and Dee C. Konrad. Winners announced in February at WinningWriters.com. Entrants who provide valid e-mail addresses will also receive notification.

$ ☑ HENRY HOYNS & POE/FAULKNER FELLOWSHIPS

Creative Writing Program, 219 Bryan Hall, P.O. Box 400121, University of Virginia, Charlottesville VA 22904-4121. (434)924-6675. Fax: (434)924-1478. E-mail: jsl9z@virginia.edu. Website: www.engl.virginia.edu/creativewriting/admissions.shtml. **Contact:** Jeb Livingood, Associate Director. (Specialized: MFA candidates in creative writing) Annual fellowships in poetry and fiction of varying amounts for candidates for the MFA in creative writing. Sample poems/prose required with application. **Deadline:** January 3, 2011. In 2010, 800 applicants for 10 fellowships.

$ ☑ THE LYNDA HULL MEMORIAL POETRY PRIZE

Crazyhorse, Dept. of English, College of Charleston, 66 George St., Charleston SC 29424. (843)953-7740. E-mail: crazyhorse@cofc.edu. Website: www.crazyhorsejournal.org. **Contact:** Prize Director. The annual Lynda Hull Memorial Poetry Prize offers $2,000 and publication in Crazyhorse (see separate listing in Contests & Awards). All entries will be considered for publication. Submissions must be unpublished. Submit online or by mail up to 3 original poems (no more than 10 pages). Include cover page (placed on top of ms) with poet's name, address, e-mail, and telephone number; no identifying information on mss (blind judging). Accepts multiple submissions with separate fee for each. Include SASP for notification of receipt of ms and SASE for results only; mss will not be returned. Guidelines available for SASE or on website. **Entry fee:** $16/ms for new entrants. Fee includes a one-year/2 issue subscription to Crazyhorse ; for each poetry ms entered and fee paid, subscription is extended by 1 year. Make checks payable to Crazyhorse ; credit card payments also accepted (see website for details). **Deadline:** September 1-December 15 (postmark). Winners announced by April. 2009 winnter: Kary Wayson. 2009 judge: James Tate.

$ ☐ INKWELL ANNUAL POETRY CONTEST

Manhattanville College, 2900 Purchase St., Purchase NY 10577. (914)323-7239. Fax: (914)323-3122. E-mail: inkwell@mville.edu. Website: www.inkwelljournal.org. **Contact:** Competition Poetry Editor. The Inkwell Annual Poetry Competition awards $1,000 grand prize and publication in *Inkwell* (see separate listing in Magazines/Journals) for best poem. Submissions must be unpublished. Submit up to 5 poems at a time, no more than 40 lines/poem, typed in 12 pt. font. Include cover sheet with poet's name, address, phone number, e-mail, and poems titles and line counts. No name or address should appear on mss. Also include Submission Checklist (download from website). Indicate "Poetry Competition" on envelope. Include SASE for results only; mss will not be returned. Guidelines available on website. **Entry fee:** $10 for first poem, $5 for each additional poem (USD only). Make checks payable to Manhattanville—Inkwell. **Deadline:** August 1-October 30 (postmark). 2011 judge: Mark Doty.

$ ☑ THE INTRO PRIZE IN POETRY

Four Way Books, P.O. Box 535, Village Station, New York NY 10014. (212)334-5430. E-mail: editors@fourwaybooks.com. Website: www.fourwaybooks.com. The Intro Prize in Poetry, offered biennially in even-numbered years, awards publication by Four Way Books (see separate listing in Book/Chapbook Publishers), honorarium ($1,000), and a reading at one or more participating series. Open to U.S. poets who have not yet published a book-length collection. "Submit one manuscript, 48-100 pages suggested. You may submit via e-mail or regular mail by the deadline. For complete information, you must refer to our guidelines on our website." **Entry fee:** $25. **Deadline:** March 31 (postmark). Winner announced by mail and on website. Copies of winning books available through Four Way Books online and at bookstores (to the trade through University Press of New England).

$ ☑ THE IOWA REVIEW AWARD IN POETRY

308 EPB, University of Iowa, Iowa City IA 52242. E-mail: iowa-review@uiowa.edu. **Contact:** Contest Coordinator. The Iowa Review Award in Poetry, Fiction, and Nonfiction presents $1,000 to each winner in each genre, $500 to runners-up. Winners published in The Iowa Review (see separate listing in Magazines/Journals). Submissions must be unpublished. Considers simultaneous submissions (with notification of acceptance elsewhere). Submit up to 10 pages of poetry, double- or single-spaced; one poem or several. Include cover page with poet's name, address, e-mail and/or phone number, and title of each work submitted. Personal identification must not appear on ms pages. Label mailing envelope "Contest: Poetry." Include SASP for confirmation of receipt of entry, SASE for results. Guidelines available on website. **Entry Fee:** $20 for entry and yearlong subscription. Make checks payable to The Iowa Review. **Deadline:** submit January 1-31 (postmark). 2009 winners were Anne Marie Rooney (1st prize) and Jennifer Militello (Runner-up). 2010 Judge: Brenda Hillman.

$ JOSEPH HENRY JACKSON AWARD

225 Bush Street, Suite 500, San Francisco CA 94104. (415)733.8500. Fax: (415)477.2783. E-mail: info@sff.org. Website: www.sff.org. (Specialized: northern CA or NV residents ages 20-35) The Joseph Henry Jackson Award offers $2,000 to the author of an unpublished work-in-progress of fiction (novel or short stories), nonfictional prose, or poetry. Applicants must be residents of northern California or Nevada for 3 consecutive years immediately prior to the March 31 deadline and must be between the ages of 20 and 35 as of the deadline. There are no applications for this award. Only applicant names submitted by a nominating jury will be considered. **Entry fee:** none. **Deadline:** March 31. Competition receives 150-180 entries.

$ ☐ JOHN WOOD COMMUNITY COLLEGE CREATIVE WRITING CONTEST

Business Office/Writing Contest, John Wood Community College, 1301 S. 48th St., Quincy IL 62305. Website: www.jwcc.edu. **Contact:** Kelli Langston. Offers annual award for original, unpublished poetry, fiction, and nonfiction. Categories include non-rhyming poetry, traditional rhyming poetry, plus a category for all other poetry forms (i.e., haiku, limerick, etc.). 1st, 2nd, and 3rd Prizes awarded in each category, plus Honorable Mention certificates. Cash prizes based on dollar total of entry fees. Guidelines available for SASE, by fax, e-mail, or on website. **Entry fee:** $5/poem; $7/nonfiction or fiction piece. **Deadline: April 1.** Competition receives 50-100 entries. "We are offering a new critiquing service of works submitted to the contest. **If you wish a written critique, you** must include an additional $5 per poem and/or $15 per story (include up to 3 pages). Critiques will be sent as soon as possible after judging."

$ ☑ JUNIPER PRIZE FOR POETRY

University of Massachusetts Press, Amherst MA 01003. (413)545-2217. Fax: (413)545-1226. E-mail: info@umpress.umass.edu. Website: www.umass.edu/umpress. **Contact:** Carla Potts. The University of Massachusetts Press offers the annual Juniper Prize for Poetry, awarded in alternate years for first and subsequent books. Prize includes publication and $1,500 in addition to royalties. In even-numbered years (2008, 2010, etc.), only "subsequent" books will be considered: mss whose authors have had at least 1 full-length book or chapbook (of at least 30 pages) of poetry published or accepted for publication. Self-published work is not considered to lie within this "books and chapbooks" category. In odd-numbered years (2009, 2011, etc.), only "first books" will beconsidered: mss by writers whose poems may have appeared in literary journals and/or anthologies but have not been published or accepted for publication in book form. Considers simultaneous submissions, "but if accepted for publication elsewhere, please notify us immediately. Manuscripts by more than 1 author, entries of more than 1 manuscript simultaneously or within the same year, and translations are not eligible." Submit paginated ms of 50-70 pages of poetry, with paginated contents page, credits page, and information about previously published books. Include 2 cover sheets: 1 with contact information, one without. Manuscripts will not be returned. Guidelines available for SASE or on website. **Entry fee:** $25. **Deadline:** submit August 1-September 29 (postmark). 2008 winner was L.S. Klatt (Interloper). Winners announced online in April on the press website.

$ ☐ BARBARA MANDIGO KELLY PEACE POETRY AWARDS

(805)965-3443. Fax: (805)568-0466. E-mail: wagingpeace@napf.org. Website: www. wagingpeace.org. **Contact:** Contest Director. Offers an annual series of awards "to encourage poets to explore and illuminate positive visions of peace and the human spirit." Awards $1,000 to adult contestants, $200 to youth in each 2 categories (13-18 and 12 and under), plus Honorable Mentions in each category. Submissions must be unpublished. Submit up to 3 poems in any form, unpublished and in English; maximum 30 lines/poem. Send 2 copies; put name, address, e-mail, phone number, and age (for youth) in upper right-hand corner of 1 copy of each poem. Title each poem; do not staple individual poems together. "Any entry that does not adhere to ALL of the contest rules will not be considered for a prize. Poets should keep copies of all entries as we will be unable to return them." Guidelines available for SASE or on website. **Entry fee:** Adult: $15 for up to 3 poems; 13-18: $5 for up to 3 poems; no fee for 12 and under. **Deadline:** July 1 (postmark). Judges: a committee of poets selected by the Nuclear Age Peace Foundation. Winners will be announced by October 1 by mail and on website. Winning poems from current and past contests are posted on the Foundation's website. "The Nuclear Age Peace Foundation reserves the right to publish and distribute the award-winning poems, including Honorable Mentions."

$ ☑ HAROLD MORTON LANDON TRANSLATION AWARD

The Academy of American Poets, 584 Broadway, Suite 604, New York NY 10012-3210. (212)274-0343 ext. 15. E-mail: awards@poets.org. Website: www.poets.org. **Contact:** Alex Dimitrov, awards coordinator. (Specialized: any language into English) Offers one $1,000 award each year to recognize a published translation of poetry from any language into English. Guidelines available for SASE or on website. **Deadline:** January 31, 2011 for a book published in 2010.

$ ☑ THE JAMES LAUGHLIN AWARD

The Academy of American Poets, 584 Broadway, Suite 604, New York NY 10012. Website: www.poets.org. The Academy of American Poets, 584 Broadway, Suite 604, New York NY 10012. (212)274-0343. Fax: (212)274-9427. E-mail: awards@poets.org. Website: www.poets.org. Offered since 1954. **Contact:** awards coordinator. Offers $5,000 prize to recognize and support a poet's second book (ms must be under contract to a publisher). Submissions must be made by a publisher in ms form. The Academy of American Poets purchases copies of the Laughlin Award-winning book for distribution to its members. Poets must be U.S. citizens. Entry form, signed by the publisher, required. Entry form and guidelines available for SASE (in January) or on website. **Deadline:** submissions accepted between January 1 and May 15. Winners announced in August.

$ ☑ THE LAUREATE PRIZE FOR POETRY

The National Poetry Review, P.O. Box 2080, Aptos CA 95001-2080. E-mail: editor@ nationalpoetryreview.com. Website: www.nationalpoetryreview.com. **Contact:** C.J. Sage, Editor. The Laureate Prize for Poetry, an annual award of $500 and publication in *The National Poetry Review* (see separate listing in Magazines Journals), "will honor 1 new poem that TNPR believes has the greatest chance of standing the test of time and becoming part of what we believe should be an ever-evolving literary canon. (We are talking about the future literary canon, not about trying to replicate the past.)" Submissions must be unpublished and uncommitted (not promised for first publication elsewhere). Considers simultaneous submissions, "but if the work is selected by TNPR for the prize or for publication, it must be withdrawn from elsewhere unless you have withdrawn it from us 2 weeks before our acceptance." Submit up to 3 poems (10 page maximum per group of 3). Include a brief bio, contact information, and poet's e-mail address for results. Guidelines available on website. **Entry fee:** $15/entry; accepts multiple submissions with separate entry fee for each 3-poem group. Make checks payable to The National Poetry Review. **Deadline:** August 31 (postmark).

☑ $ THE STEPHEN LEACOCK MEMORIAL MEDAL FOR HUMOUR

Stephen Leacock Associates, 4223, Line 12 North, R.R. #2, Coldwater ON L0K 1E0, Canada. (705)835-3218. Fax: (705)835-5171. E-mail: judith_rapson@gmail.com, don_ reid@sympatico.com. Website: www.leacock.ca. **Contact:** Ms. Judith Rapson, chair. (Specialized: humor by Canadian citizens) Award Chairman: Judith Rapson. Annual award of the Silver Leacock Medal for Humour and T.D. Canada Trust cash award of $10,000. "The winning author will also receive a cash price of $15,000, presented by the TD Financial Group. Each of four runners-up will be awarded cash prizes of $1,500."

Presented for a book of humor in prose, verse, drama, or any book form—by a Canadian citizen. "Book must have been published in the current year and no part of it may have been previously published in book form." Submit 10 copies of book, 8x10 b&w photo, bio, and entry fee. **Entry fee:** $100 CAD. **Deadline:** December 31. Competition receives 40-50 entries. 200

$ ▢ THE LEAGUE OF MINNESOTA POETS CONTEST

Website: www.mnpoets.org (see website for current contact information). **Contact:** Susan Stevens Chambers. Annual contest offers 18 different categories, with 3 prizes in each category ranging from $10-125. See guidelines for poem lengths, forms, and subjects. Guidelines available for #10 SASE, by e-mail, or on website. **Entry fee:** (nonmembers) $1/poem per category; $2/poem (limit 6) for Grand Prize category; (members) $5 for 17 categories; $1/poem (limit 6) for Grand Prize category. Make checks payable to LOMP Contest. **Deadline:** July 31. Nationally known, non-Minnesota judges. Winners will be announced at the October LOMP Conference and by mail. Additional information regarding LOMP membership available on website.

$ ☑ THE LEDGE POETRY AWARDS COMPETITION

40 Maple Ave., Bellport NY 11713. Website: www.theledgemagazine.com. **Contact:** Contest Director. Offers annual awards of 1st Prize: $1,000; 2nd Prize: $250; 3rd Prize: $100; and all 3 winners will be published in The Ledge (see separate listing in Magazines/Journals). All entries will be considered for publication. Submissions must be unpublished. Considers simultaneous submissions. "No restrictions on form or content. Excellence is the only criterion." Submit 3 poems. Include SASE for results or return of ms. Guidelines available on website. **Entry fee:** $10 for the first 3 poems, $3 for each additional poem; $20 subscription to The Ledge gains free entry for the first 3 poems. **Deadline:** April 30 (postmark). Winners announced in September.

$ ☑ THE LEDGE POETRY CHAPBOOK CONTEST

The Ledge Press, 40 Maple Ave., Bellport NY 11713. Website: www.theledgemagazine. com. **Contact:** Contest Director. The Ledge Poetry Chapbook Contest offers an annual prize of $1,000, publication by The Ledge Press, and 25 chapbook copies. Considers simultaneous submissions. Accepts multiple submissions with separate entry fee for each. " No restrictions on form or content. Excellence is the only criterion." Submit 16-28 pages of poetry with bio and acknowledgements, if any. Include title page with poet's name, address, phone number, and e-mail address (if applicable). Include SASE for results or return of ms. Guidelines available on website. **Entry fee:** $18; all entrants will receive a copy of the winning chapbook upon publication. **Deadline:** October 31. Sample chapbooks available for $8 postpaid. Winner announced in March.

$ ☑ THE LEVIS POETRY PRIZE

Four Way Books, Box 535, Village Station, New York NY 10014. (212)334-5430. Fax: (212)334-5435. E-mail: editors@fourwaybooks.com. Website: www.fourwaybooks.com. **Contact:** Martha Rhodes, director. The Levis Poetry Prize, offered biennially in odd-numbered years, offers publication by Four Way Books (see separate listing in Book/

Chapbook Publishers), honorarium ($1,000), and a reading at one or more participating series. Open to any poet writing in English. Entry form and guidelines available on website. **Entry fee:** $25. **Deadline:** March 31 (postmark). Winner announced by e-mail and on website. Copies of winning books available through Four Way Books online and at bookstores (to the trade through University Press of New England).

▣ $ ☑ LITERAL LATTE FOOD VERSE AWARDS

200 East 10th St., Suite 240, New York NY 10003. Website: www.literal-latte.com. **Contact:** Lisa Erdman. The annual Literary Latté Food for Verse Awards offers 1st Prize: $500 for best poem with food as an ingredient. All styles and subjects welcome. All entries considered for publication in Literal Latte (see separate listing in Magazines/Journals). Submissions must be unpublished. Include cover page with poet's name, address, phone number, e-mail, and poem titles/first lines; no identifying information on mss pages. Guidelines available by e-mail, or on website. **Entry fee:** $10 for up to 6 poems, $15 for 12 poems. Make checks/money orders payable to Literal Latté. **Deadline:** January 15 (postmark).

▣ $ ☑ LITERAL LATTE POETRY AWARDS

200 East 10th St., Suite 240, New York NY 10003. E-mail: litlatte@aol.com. Website: www.literal-latte.com. **Contact:** Lisa Erdman. The annual Literal Latté Poetry Awards offer 1st Prize: $1,000; 2nd Prize: $300; 3rd Prize: $200. All entries considered for publication in Literal Latté (see separate listing in Magazines/Journals). Submissions must be unpublished. All styles welcome, 2,000 words maximum/poem. Include cover page with poet's name, address, telephone number and e-mail; no identifying information on ms pages. Guidelines available by e-mail, or on website. Winners published in Literal Latté. **Entry fee:** $10 for up to 6 poems, $15 for 12 poems. Make checks/money orders payable to Literal Latté. **Deadline:** July 15 (postmark).

$ ☑ FRANCES LOCKE MEMORIAL POETRY AWARD

The Bitter Oldeander Press, 4983 Tall Oaks Dr., Fayetteville NY 13066-9776. (315)637-3047. Fax: (315)637-5056. E-mail: info@bitteroleander.com. Website: www.bitteroleander.com. **Contact:** Paul B. Roth. The Frances Locke Memorial Poetry Award offers $1,000, publication in *The Bitter Oleander* (see separate listing in Magazines/Journals), and 5 contributor's copies. Submit up to 5 poems, each no more than 2 pages in length, legibly typed or computer generated. Include poet's name, address, and phone number or e-mail on each poem. Include a short biography with submission. No e-mail submissions. Include SASE for results only; mss will not be returned. Guidelines available on website. **Entry fee:** $10 for up to 5 poems, $2 each additional poem. **Deadline:** June 15 (postmark). 2008 winner: Samantha Stiers.

⚡ $ ☑ LONG POEM PRIZE

The Malahat Review, University of Victoria, P.O. Box 1700, Stn CSC, Victoria BC V8W 2Y2, Canada. (250)721-8524. Fax: (250)472-5051. E-mail: malahat@uvic.ca. Website: www.malahatreview.ca. **Contact:** John Barton, editor. The biennial Long Poem Prize offers 2 awards of $500 CAD each for a long poem or cycle (10-20 printed pages). Includes publication in The Malahat Review (see separate listing in Magazines/Journals) and payment at $40 CAD per printed page upon publication. Open to "entries from Canadian, American, and overseas authors." Submissions must be unpublished. No simultaneous submissions. Submit a single poem or cycle of poems, 10-20 published pages (a published page equals 32 lines or less, including breaks between stanzas); no restrictions on subject matter or aesthetic approach. Include separate page with poet's name, address, e-mail, and title; no identifying information on mss pages. No e-mail submissions. Do not include SASE for results; mss will not be returned. Guidelines available on website. **Entry fee:** $35 CAD for Canadian entries, $40 USD for US entries ($45 USD for entries from Mexico and outside North America); includes one-year subscription to *The Malahat Review*. **Deadline:** February 1 (postmark) of alternate years (2011, 2013, etc.). 2009 winners: matt robinson, Marion Quednau. 2009 judges: Steve Noyes, Katia Grubisic, and Kathy Mac. Winners published in summer issue of *The Malahat Review*, announced in summer on website, Facebook page, and in quarterly e-newsletter *Malahat Lite*.

$ ☑ MAIN STREET RAG'S ANNUAL CHAPBOOK CONTEST

P.O. Box 690100, Charlotte NC 28227-7001. (704)573-2516. E-mail: editor@mainstreetrag. com. **Contact:** M. Scott Douglass, Editor/Publisher. Annual chapbook contest by Main Street Rag (see separate listing in Magazines/Journals) offers 1st Prize: $500 and 50 copies of chapbook. "As many as 19 runners-up have been published in previous contests, and every manuscript entered is considered for publication." All entrants receive a copy of the winning chapbook. Submit 24-32 pages of poetry, no more than 1 poem/page. Guidelines available for SASE, by e-mail, or on website. **Entry fee:** $17. **Deadline:** May 31st. 2008 winner was Kim Triedman (bathe in it or sleep).

$ ☑ MAIN STREET RAG'S ANNUAL POETRY BOOK AWARD

P.O. Box 690100, Charlotte NC 28227-7001. (704)573-2516. E-mail: editor@mainstreetrag. com. Website: www.MainStreetRag.com. **Contact:** M. Scott Douglass, Editor/Publisher. Main Street Rag' s Annual Poetry Book Award offers 1st Prize: $1,000 and 50 copies of book; runners-up may also be offered publication. Submit 48-84 pages of poetry, no more than 1 poem/page (individual poems may be longer than 1 page). Guidelines available for SASE, by e-mail, or on website. **Entry fee:** $20 (or $25 to include a copy of the winning book). **Deadline:** January 31. 2008 winner was Roy Seeger (The Boy Whose Hands Were Birds).

$ ☑ MANY MOUNTAINS MOVING POETRY BOOK CONTEST

Many Mountains Moving Press, 1705 Lombard St., Philadelphia PA 19146. E-mail: editors@ mmminc.org. Website: www.mmminc.org. **Contact:** Jeffrey Ethan Lee, senior poetry editor. The Many Mountains Moving Poetry Book Contest offers $1000 and publication of a book-length poetry ms by Many Mountains Moving Press. Open to all poets writing in English. More than half of ms may not have been published as a collection, but individual poems and chapbook-length sections may have been previously published if publisher gives permission to reprint. Accepts e-mail submissions (as an attachment, without any identification in the mss. itself). Considers simultaneous submissions "if the poet agrees to notify MMM Press of acceptance elsewhere." Submit 50-100 typed pages of poetry, single- or double-spaced. Include cover letter with ms title, brief bio, poet's name, address, phone number, and e-mail address(es). Poet's name must not appear anywhere on ms. Acknowledgments may be sent but are not required. Include SASE for results only; no mss will be returned. Guidelines available on website. **Entry fee:** $25; entitles entrant to discount on a subscription and discounts on any selected Many Mountains Moving Press books (use order form, available on website). Make checks/money orders payable to Many Mountains Moving Press. **Deadline:** August 14 (postmark). 2011 judge TBA.

$ ☑ THE MORTON MARR POETRY PRIZE

Southern Methodist University, P.O. Box 750374, Dallas TX 75275-0374. (214)768-1037. Fax: (214)768-1408. E-mail: swr@mail.smu.edu. Website: www.smu.edu/southwestreview. **Contact:** Prize coordinator. (Specialized: traditional poetry forms) The annual Morton Marr Poetry Prize awards 1st Prize: $1,000 and 2nd Prize: $500 to a poet who has not yet published a first book of poetry. Winners will be published in Southwest Review (see separate listing in Magazines/Journals). Submit 6 poems in a "traditional" form (e.g., sonnet, sestina, villanelle, rhymed stanzas, blank verse, et al). Include cover letter with poet's name, address, and other relevant information; no identifying information on entry pages. Manuscripts will not be returned. Guidelines available on website. **Entry fee:** $5/poem. **Deadline:** September 30 (postmark). 2007 winners: Gretchen Steele Pratt (1st Place), Bradford Gray Telford (2nd Place), Elizabeth Rosen (HM), and Chloë Joan Loópez (HM).

$ ☑ THE LENORE MARSHALL POETRY PRIZE

The Academy of American Poets, 584 Broadway, Suite 604, New York NY 10012. (212)274-0343. Fax: (212)274-9427. E-mail: awards@poets.org. Website: www.poets.org. **Contact:** Alex Dimitrov, awards coordinator. Offers $25,000 for the most outstanding book of poems published in the U.S. in the previous year. Contest is open to books by living American poets published in a standard edition (40 pages or more in length with 500 or more copies printed). Self-published books are not eligible. Publishers may enter as many books as they wish (books must be submitted in the year after their publication). Four copies of each book must be submitted and none will be returned. Guidelines, required entry form available for SASE or on website. **Entry fee:** $25/title. **Deadline:** entries must be submitted between April 1 and June 15.

$ ☑ MARSH HAWK PRESS POETRY PRIZE

P.O. Box 206, East Rockaway NY 11518-0206. E-mail: marshhawkpress1@aol.com. Website: www.MarshHawkPress.org. **Contact:** Prize Director. The Marsh Hawk Press Poetry Prize offers $1,000 plus publication of a book-length ms. Submissions must be unpublished as a collection, but individual poems may have been previously published elsewhere. Submit 48-70 pages of original poetry in any style in English, typed single-spaced, and paginated. Contest manuscripts may be submitted by electronic upload. See website for more information. If submitting via Post Office mail, the manuscript must be bound with a spring clip. Include 2 title pages: 1 with ms title, poet's name, and contact information only; 1 with ms title only (poet's name must not appear anywhere in the ms). Also include table of contents and acknowledgments page. Include SASE for results only; manuscript will not be returned. Guidelines available on website. **Entry fee:** $20. Make check/money order payable to Marsh Hawk Press. **Deadline:** April 30. 2009 winners was Neil de la Fleur for *Almost Dorothy*. 2010 Judge: Anne Waldman.

⊕ $ ◯ MELBOURNE POETS UNION NATIONAL POETRY COMPETITION

Melbourne Poets Union, P.O. Box 266, Flinders Lane VI 8009, Australia. Website: http://home.vicnet.net.au/~mpuinc. **Contact:** Leon Shann. Offers annual prizes of $1,500 AUD plus book vouchers, book prizes. Submissions must be unpublished. Submit unlimited number of poems on any subject, in any form, up to 50 lines. "Open to Australian residents living in Australia or overseas." Entry form and guidelines available for SASE (or SAE and IRC). **Entry fee:** $8 AUD; MPU members $7 AUD/poem; $14 AUD/2 poems; $18 AUD/3 poems. Under 18s (3) Aus 50c postage stamps or equivalent. **Deadline:** October 31. Competition receives over 500 entries/year. Winners announced on the last Friday of November by newsletter, mail, phone, and on website. "The $1,500 prize money comes directly from entry money, the rest going to paying the judge and costs of running the competition."

$ ◯ MILFORD FINE ARTS COUNCIL NATIONAL POETRY CONTEST

40 Railroad Ave., South, Milford CT 06460. E-mail: milfordfac@optonline.net. Website: www.milfordarts.org. **Contact:** Tom Bouton, Writer's Group Chairperson. Offers annual award of 1st Prize: $100; 2nd Prize: $50; 3rd Prize: $25; plus winners will be published in Milford Fine Arts Council's annual publication, *High Tide*. Submissions must be unpublished. No simultaneous submissions. Poems entered may not have won any other prizes or honorable mentions. Poets must be 18 years and older. "Poems must be typed single-spaced on white standard paper, 10-30 lines (including title), no more than 48 characters/line, on any subject, in any style, rhymed or unrhymed. Use standard font, clear and legible, 1 poem/page, no script or fax. NO foul language. No bio or date, only the words 'Unpublished Original' typed above the poem." Include poet's name, address, ZIP code, and phone number or e-mail address in the middle back of the submitted poem, no identifying information on the front of the page. Poems will be judged on form, clarity, originality, and universal appeal. "Entries may be considered for publication in *High Tide*. If you do not want your poems considered for publication, then you must print on the back of the poem (below your name, address, and ZIP code) 'For National Poetry Contest Only.'" Include SASE for results only, with NOTIFICATION printed on bottom left corner of envelope; no poems will be returned. Guidelines available for SASE or on website. **Entry fee:** $3 for one poem, $6 for 3 poems, $2 for each additional poem after 3. Contestants may enter an unlimited number of poems (will be judged individually, not as a group). Check or money order accepted, no cash. **Deadline:** March 31, 2010.

Ⓝ VASSAR MILLER PRIZE IN POETRY

1155 Union circle, #311336, Denton TX 76203-5017. (940)565-2142. Fax: (940)565-4590. Website: http://web3.unt.edu/untpress/. **Contact:** John Poch.

- "Annual prize awarded to a collection of poetry. Winner will receive $1000 and publication by University of North Texas Press." Judged by a "different eminent writer selected each year. Some prefer to remain anonymous until the end of the contest." Deadline: November 15. Fee: $25.

◘ MILLER WILLIAMS POETRY PRIZE

105 N. McIlroy Avenue, Fayetteville AR 72701. (479)575-4724. Fax: (479)575-6044. E-mail: lmalley@uark.edu; jewatki@uark.edu. Website: www.uapress.com. **Contact:** Julie Watkins, editor and Lawrence J. Malley, director and editor.
• Submit 60-90 pages of poetry. Submissions must be unpublished as a collection buy individual poems may have been published elsewhere. Copies of winning books available from University of Arkansas Press, $16, and through all bookstores and online sellers.

$ ◪ MISSISSIPPI REVIEW PRIZE

118 College Dr. #5144, Hattiesburg MS 39406-0001. (601)266-4321. E-mail: rief@ mississippireview.com. Website: www.mississippireview.com. *The Mississippi Review* Prize offers an annual award of $1,000 each in poetry and fiction. Winners and finalists comprise one issue of *Mississippi Review*. Submissions must be unpublished. Submit up to 3 poems/entry (totaling 10 pages or less). No limit on number of entries. Put "MR Prize" plus poet's name, address, phone number, e-mail address, and title(s) on page 1 of entry. Manuscripts will not be returned. **Entry fee:** $15/entry. Make checks payable to *Mississippi Review*. Each entrant receives a copy of the prize issue. **Deadline:** submit April 1-October 1 (postmark). Winners announced in January.

$ ◪ JENNY MCKEAN MOORE WRITER IN WASHINGTON

Dept. of English, George Washington University, Washington DC 20052. (202)994-6515. Fax: (202)994-7915. E-mail: dmca@gwu.edu. Website: www.gwu.edu/~english. Offers fellowship for a visiting lecturer in creative writing, currently about $55,000 for 2 semesters. Stipend varies slightly from year to year, depending on endowment payout. Teaching duties involve 2 workshops per semester—one for undergraduate students, the other free to the community. Apply with résumé and writing sample of 25 pages or less. Books may be submitted but will not be returned without SASE. Awarded to writers in different genres each year, typically alternating between poets and fiction writers. Check website for specific genre each year. **Deadline:** November 15.

$ ◪ THE KATHRYN A. MORTON PRIZE IN POETRY

Sarabande Books, Inc., P.O. Box 4456, Louisville KY 40204. (502)458-4028. E-mail: info@ sarabandebooks.org. Website: www.SarabandeBooks.org. **Contact:** Sarah Gorham, editor-in-chief. Member: CLMP. The Kathryn A. Morton Prize in Poetry is awarded annually to a book-length ms (at least 48 pages). Winner receives $2,000, publication, and a standard royalty contract. All finalists are considered for publication. Entry form and SASE are required. Accepts simultaneous submissions, but must be notified immediately if manuscript is accepted elsewhere. Guidelines available for SASE, by e-mail, or on website. **Entry fee:** $25. **Deadline:** submit January 1-February 15 (postmark) only. Competition receives approximately 1,400 entries. 2009 winner was Julia Story for her collection, *Post Moxie*. 2010 judge was Amy Gerstler. "To avoid conflict of interest, students in a degree-granting program or close friends of a judge are ineligible to enter the contest in the genre for which their friend or teacher is serving as judge. Sarabande, as a member of CLMP, complies with its Contest Code of Ethics."

$ ☑ NATIONAL BOOK AWARD

The National Book Foundation, 95 Madison Ave., Suite 709, New York NY 10016. E-mail: nationalbook@nationalbook.org. Website: www.nationalbook.org. Presents $10,000 in each of 4 categories (fiction, nonfiction, poetry, and young people's literature), plus 16 short-list prizes of $1,000 each to Finalists. Submissions must be previously published and **must be entered by the publisher**. General guidelines available on website; interested publishers should phone or e-mail the Foundation. **Entry fee:** $125/title. **Deadline:** see website for current year's deadline. 2010 poetry judges: Rae Armantrout, Cornelius Eady, Linda Gregerson, Jeffrey McDaniel, Brenda Shaughnessy. 2009 winner was Keith Waldrop, *Transcendental Studies: A Trilogy*.

$ ☑ THE NATIONAL POET HUNT CONTEST

(734)462-4400, ext. 5327. Fax: (734)462-4679. E-mail: macguffin@schoolcraft.edu. Website: www.macguffin.org. **Contact:** Carol Was, Poetry Editor. The National Poet Hunt Contest offers 1st Prize: $500 and publication in a future issue of *The MacGuffin*; may also award 2 Honorable Mentions and publication. Open to all writers. Submissions must be unpublished and may be entered in other contests. Submit 5 typed poems on any subject, in any form. One poem/page. Submissions are read blindly by the judge; contact information should not appear anywhere on the submission. Include name, address, phone number, e-mail address, and list of poem titles on 3x5 index card. Include SASE for winners' list only; entries will not be returned. Guidelines available for SASE, by e-mail, or on website. **Entry fee:** $15/entry (5 poems). Make checks payable to Schoolcraft College. **Deadline:** check website for current deadline. 2010 judge: Jim Daniels.

⊞ $ ☑ NATIONAL POETRY COMPETITION

Poetry Society, 22 Betterton Street, London WC2H 9BX, United Kingdom. E-mail: info@poetrysociety.org.uk. Website: www.poetrysociety.org.uk. **Contact:** Competition Organiser. The National Poetry Competition offers 1st Prize: £5,000; 2nd Prize: £2,000; 3rd Prize: £1,000; plus 7 commendations of £100 each. Winners will be published in Poetry Review (see separate listing in Magazines/Journals), and on the Poetry Society website and the top three winners will receive a year's free membership in the Poetry Society (see separate listing in Organizations). Open to anyone aged 17 or over. Entries "received from all around the world. All entries are judged anonymously and past winners include both published and previously unknown poets." Submissions must be unpublished (poems posted on Websites are considered published). Submit original poems in English, on any subject, no more than 40 lines/poem, typed on 1 side only of A4 paper, double- or single-spaced. Each poem must be titled. No identifying information on poems. Do not staple pages. Accepts online submissions; full details available on the National Poetry Competition pages on the Poetry Society website. Entry form (required) available for A5 SAE (1 entry form covers multiple entries, may be photocopied). Include SAE or SAP for notification of receipt of postal entries (confirmation of online entries will be e-mailed at time of submission); poems will not be returned. Guidelines available on website. **Entry fee:** £5 for first poem, £3 for each subsequent entry (Poetry Society members can enter a second poem free of charge). "Only sterling (checks, postal orders, money orders, or credit cards) will be accepted. All other payments will be returned. Checks must be drawn from UK banks." Make checks payable to the Poetry Society. **Deadline:** October 31.

$ ☑ THE NATIONAL POETRY REVIEW BOOK PRIZE

E-mail: nationalpoetryreview@yahoo.com. Website: www.nationalpoetryreview.com. **Contact:** C.J. Sage. The National Poetry Review Book Prize offers $1,000, publication of a book-length ms, and 15 author copies. All entries will be considered for publication. Submit 45-80 pages of poetry. Include cover letter with bio and acknowledgments page. **See website for entry address and details.** Include e-mail address (no SASEs; mss will not be returned). Guidelines available on website. **Fee:** $25. Make checks payable to The National Poetry Review. **Deadline:** September 30 (postmark).

$ HOWARD NEMEROV SONNET AWARD

The Formalist, 320 Hunter Dr., Evansville IN 47711. Website: theformalist.evansville. edu/contest.html. **Contact:** Mona Baer, contest coordinator. Although The Formalist has ceased publication, it continues to sponsor the annual Howard Nemerov Sonnet Award. Offers $1,000 prize; winner and 11 finalists will be published in Measure: A Review of Formal Poetry (see separate listing in Magazines/Journals). Submit original, unpublished sonnets, no translations; sonnet sequences acceptable, but each sonnet will be considered individually. Poets may enter as many sonnets as they wish. Poet's name, address, phone number, and e-mail address should be listed on the **back** of each entry. Enclose SASE for contest results; mss will not be returned. Guidelines available for SASE or on website. **Entry fee**: $3/sonnet. Make all checks payable to The Formalist. Entry fees from outside U.S. must be paid in U.S dollars via check drawn on a U.S. bank or by cash. **Deadline:** November 15 (postmark). 2009 winner Richard Wakefield. 2009 judge was David Middleton; 2010 judge was A. E. Stallings.

$ ☑ THE PABLO NERUDA PRIZE FOR POETRY

Nimrod, Literary Contest—Poetry, The University of Tula, 600 S. College, Tulsa OK 74104. Website: www.utulsa.edu/nimrod. **Contact:** Contest Coordinator. The annual Nimrod Literary Awards include The Pablo Neruda Prize for Poetry, which offers 1st Prize: $2,000 and publication in Nimrod: International Journal of Poetry and Prose (see separate listing in Magazines/Journals); and 2nd Prize: $1,000 and publication. Nimrod retains the right to publish any submission. Submissions must be unpublished. Work must be in English or translated by original author. Submit 3-10 pages of poetry (1 long poem or several short poems). Poet's name must not appear on ms. Include cover sheet with poem title(s), poet's name, address, phone and fax numbers, and e-mail address (poet must have a U.S. address by October of contest year to enter). Mark "Contest Entry" on submission envelope and cover sheet. Include SASE for results only; mss will not be returned. Guidelines available for #10 SASE or on website. **Entry fee:** $20; includes one-year subscription (2 issues) to *Nimrod*. Make checks payable to *Nimrod*. **Deadline:**

January 1-April 30 (postmark). 2009 winners were Mike Neslon ("Acacia") and Alicia Case ("Ascension" and Other Poems). Winners will be announced on Nimrod's website.

$ ☑ NERVE COWBOY CHAPBOOK CONTEST

P.O. Box 4973, Austin TX 78765. Website: www.jwhagins.com/ChapContest.html. The Nerve Cowboy Chapbook Contest offers 1st Prize: $200, publication, and 50 author's copies; 2nd Prize: $100, publication, and 30 author's copies. Submit 24-40 pages of poetry and/or short fiction. Include SASE for return of ms. Guidelines available on website. **Entry fee:** $10 (all entrants receive a copy of the winning chapbook and a discount on the 2nd Prize chapbook). Make checks payable to *Nerve Cowboy*. **Deadline:** January 31st of each year.

$ ☑ THE NEW ISSUES POETRY PRIZE

New issues Poetry & Prose, Dept. of English, Western Michigan University, 1903 W. Michigan Ave., Kalamazoo MI 49008-5331. (269)387-8185. Fax: (269)387-2562. E-mail: new-issues@wmich.edu. Website: www.wmich.edu/newissues. The New Issues Poetry Prize offers $2,000 plus publication of a book-length ms. Open to "poets writing in English who have not previously published a full-length collection of poems." Additional mss will be considered from those submitted to the competition for publication in the New Issues Press Poetry Series. Considers simultaneous submissions, but New Issues must be notified of acceptance elsewhere. Submit ms of at least 48 pages, typed, single-spaced preferred. Clean photocopies acceptable. Do not bind; use manila folder or metal clasp. Include cover page with poet's name, address, phone number, and title of the ms. Also include brief bio and acknowledgments page. No e-mail or fax submissions. Include SASP for notification of receipt of ms and SASE for results only; no mss will be returned. Guidelines available for SASE, by fax, by e-mail, or on website. **Entry fee:** $15. Make checks payable to New Issues Poetry & Prose. **Deadline:** November 30 (postmark). Winning manuscript will be named in May 2010 and published in Spring 2011. 2009 winner was SJudy Halebsky (*Sky = Empty*). "A national judge selects the prize winner and recommends other manuscripts. The editors decide on the other books considering the judge's recommendation, but are not bound by it." 2010 judge: Linda Gregerson.

$ ☑ NEW LETTERS PRIZE FOR POETRY

New Letters Awards for Writers, UMKC, University House, 5101 Rockhill Road, Kansas City MO 64110-2499. Website: www.newletters.org. The annual New Letters Poetry Prize awards $1,500 and publication in *New Letters* (see separate listing in Magazines/ Journals) to the best group of 3-6 poems. All entries will be considered for publication in *New Letters*. Submissions must be unpublished. Considers simultaneous submissions with notification upon acceptance elsewhere. Accepts multiple entries with separate fee for each. Submit up to 6 poems (need not be related). Include 2 cover sheets: 1 with poet's name, address, e-mail, phone number, prize category (poetry), and poem title(s); the second with category and poem title(s) only. No identifying information on ms pages. Accepts electronic submissions. Include SASE for notification of receipt of ms and entry number, and SASE for results only (send only 1 envelope if submitting multiple entries); mss will not be returned. Guidelines available for SASE or on website. **Entry fee:** $15 for first entry, $10 for each subsequent entry; includes cost of a one-year subscription, renewal, or gift subscription to *New Letters* (shipped to any address within the U.S.). Make checks payable to New Letters. **Deadline:** May 18 (postmark). 2009 winner was Heather Bell. 2009 judge was Kim Addonizio. "Current students and employees of the University of Missouri-Kansas City, and current volunteer members of the *New Letters* and BkMk Press staffs, are not eligible."

$ ◻ NEW MILLENNIUM AWARD FOR POETRY

New Millennium Writings, Room EM, P.O. Box 2463, Knoxville TN 37901. Website: www. newmillenniumwritings.com. Offers 2 annual awards of $1,000 each. Submissions must be unpublished and may be entered in other contests. Submit up to 3 poems, 5 pages maximum. No restrictions on style, form, or content. Include name, address, phone number, and a #10 SASE for notification. All contestants receive the next issue at no additional charge. Entry form available on website. Include SASE or e-mail address for results; mss will not be returned. Guidelines available for SASE or on website. **Entry fee:** $17. Make checks payable to *New Millennium Writings*. **Deadline:** June 17 and November 17 (each deadline may be extended once; check website for updates). Competition receives 2,000 entries/year. "2 winners and all finalists will be published." Most recent award winner was Patricia Jaggers. Enter online at www.WritingAwards.com.

$ ☑ NEW WOMEN'S VOICES CHAPBOOK COMPETITION

Finishing Line Press, P.O. Box 1626, Georgetown KY 40324. (859)514-8966. E-mail: FinishingBooks@aol.com. Website: www.finishinglinepress.com. **Contact:** Leah Maines, poetry editor.

$ ◻ NFSPS COMPETITIONS

90 High Farms Road, West Hartford CT 06107. Website: www.nfsps.org. **Contact:** Christine Beck. NFSPS sponsors a national contest with 50 different categories each year, including the NFSPS Founders Award of 1st Prize: $1,500; 2nd Prize: $500; 3rd Prize: $250. Rules for all contests are given in a brochure available from Caroline Walton, editor of Strophes newsletter, at 6176 West Pinedale Circle, Crystal River, FL 34429 (e-mail: carowaltonb@ embarqmail.com); or from Christine Beck at the address above; or on the NFSPS website. **Entry fee:** (for members) $1/poem or $8 total for 8 or more categories, plus $5/poem for NFSPS Founders Award (limit 4 entries in this category alone). Some categories are for members only. All poems winning over $15 are published in the ENCORE Prize Poem Anthology. NFSPS also sponsors the annual Stevens Poetry Manuscript Competition and the NFSPS College/University Level Poetry Awards (see separate listings this section).

$ ☑ THE NIGHTBOAT POETRY PRIZE

Nightboat Books, P.O. Box 10, Callicoon NY 12723. E-mail: info@nightboat.org. Website: www.nightboat.org. **Contact:** Stephen Motika. The Nightboat Poetry Prize offers an annual award of $1,000 plus book publication; finalists are announced. Submissions must be unpublished as a collection, but individual poems may have been previously published in journals; and collection may be entered simultaneously in other ms contests. Submit 48-100 pages of poetry (suggested length only), single-spaced, paginated, 1 poem/page, 1 side only. Manuscript must be typed, bound only by a clip. Include 2 title pages (1 with book title, name, address, telephone, and e-mail address; 1 with book title only), table of contents, and acknowledgments page. Poet's name should not appear anywhere in the ms, except on the first title page. Bio optional. Entry form and guidelines available for SASE, by e-mail, or on website. **Entry fee:** $25. **Deadline:** November 15 (postmark). 2008 winner was Paul Cisewski (*Ghost Fargo*). 2008 judge: Franz Wright. Winner announced by March on website, in Poets & Writers Magazine , and in a written letter to all entrants. "Nightboat Books has published books by Bruce Boone, Michael Burkard, Fanny Howe, Myung Mi Kim, Joshua Kryah, Douglas A. Martin, Juliet Patterson, and Natalie Stephens."

$ ☑ JESSE BRYCE NILES MEMORIAL CHAPBOOK AWARD

4956 St. John Dr., Syracuse NY 13215. (315)488-8077. E-mail: poetry@comstockreview. org. Website: www.comstockreview.org. The Jesse Bryce Niles Memorial Chapbook Award runs every other year, next in 2011, and offers $1,000 plus publication and 50 author's copies; each entrant also receives a copy. Submissions must be unpublished as a collection, but individual poems may have been previously published in journals. Considers simultaneous submissions "as long as the poet notifies us immediately upon acceptance elsewhere." Submit 25-34 pages of poetry, single-spaced (1 page = 38 lines maximum, including spacing between lines; poems may run longer than 1 page). **Manuscripts either too short or too long will be disqualified.** "Do not count title page, acknowledgments, dedication, or bio in the page length. Do not send illustrations, photos, or any other graphics attached to the poems. You may submit a table of contents, which may list the manuscript name only, not the poet's name (not counted in page total for manuscript)." Manuscripts should be paginated and secured with a binder clip; no staples or plastic covers. Include 2 cover pages: 1 with ms title, poet's name, address, phone number, and e-mail address; second with ms title only. List acknowledgments on a separate, removable page with same identifying information. Poet's name should not appear on poems. Include SASE for results only; mss will not be returned. Guidelines available for SASE or on website. **Entry fee:** $25/chapbook. **Deadline:** submit August 1-September 30 (postmark). **Offered every other year.** 2009 winner was Lynne Martin Bowman (*Water Never Sleeps*). 2009 judge: Kathleen Bryce Niles; all entries are screened by the editors of *The Comstock Review* (see separate listing in Magazines/Journals). Winner is notified in December. Copies of winning chapbooks are available for $12 saddle-stitched. E-mail for ordering details.

⊕ $ NSW PREMIER'S LITERARY AWARD "THE KENNETH SLESSOR PRIZE"

Website: www.arts.nsw.gov.au. (Specialized: Australian citizens only) Offers annual award of $30,000 for a book of poetry (collection or long poem) published in the previous year. **Open to Australian citizens only.** Books may be nominated by poets or by their agents or publishers. Write for entry form and guidelines or check website. **Deadline:** November (check guidelines). Winners will be announced in May. "Obtain copy of guidelines before entering."

$ OHIOANA POETRY AWARD

Ohioana Library Association, 274 E. First Ave., Suite 300, Columbus OH 43201. (614)466-3831. Fax: (614)728-6974. E-mail: ohioana@ohioana.org. Website: www.ohioana.org. (Helen and Laura Krout Memorial) (Specialized: native & resident OH authors) "Offers annual Ohioana Book Awards. Up to 6 awards may be given for books (including books of poetry) by authors born in Ohio or who have lived in Ohio for at least 5 years." The Ohioana Poetry Award of $1,000 (with the same residence requirements), made possible by a bequest of Helen Krout, is given yearly "to an individual whose body of published work has made, and continues to make, a significant contribution to poetry, and through whose work as a writer, teacher, administrator, or in community service, interest in poetry has been developed." **Deadline:** nominations to be received by December 31. Competition receives several hundred entries. 2009 Ohioana Poetry Award winner was William Greenway (*Everywhere at Once*). Ohioana Quarterly regularly reviews books by Ohio authors and is available through membership in Ohioana Library Association ($25/year).

$ ☐ OHIO POETRY DAY CONTESTS

Dept. of English, Heidelberg College, 310 East Market, Tiffin OH 44883. E-mail: wreyer@heidelberg.edu. Website: www.geocities.com/theohiopoetryassociation/. **Contact:** Bill Reyer, Contest Chair. Offers annual slate of 30-40 contest categories. Prizes range from $75 down; all money-winning award poems are published in an annual anthology (runs over 100 pages). Submissions must be unpublished. Submit 1 poem/category on topic and in form specified. Some contests open to everyone, but others open only to Ohio poets. "Each contest has its own specifications. Entry must be for a specified category, so entrants need rules." Entry form and guidelines available for SASE. **Entry fee:** $10 inclusive, unlimited number of categories. **Deadline:** usually end of May; see guidelines for each year's deadline. Competition receives over 4,000 entries/year. Winners and judges for most recent contest listed in winners' anthology. Judges are never announced in advance. Winners list available in August for SASE (enclose with poem entries); prizes given in October. Copies of annual prize anthologies available from Amy Jo Zook, contest treasurer (3520 State Route 56, Mechanicsburg OH 43044) for $9 plus postage (prices can differ from year to year). "Ohio Poetry Day is the umbrella. Individual contests are sponsored by poetry organizations and/or individuals across the state. OPD sponsors several and selects the Poet of the Year; have four memorial funds." Join mailing list at any time by sending contact information by postcard or letter. Advice: "Revise, follow rules, look at individual categories for a good match."

⊞ OPEN SEASON AWARDS

The Malahat Review, University of Victoria, P.O. Box 1700, Stn CSC, Victoria BC V8V 2Y2, Canada. Fax: (250)472-5051. E-mail: malahat@uvic.ca. Website: www.malahatreview.ca. **Contact:** John Barton, editor. The annual Open Season Awards offers $1000 CAD and publication in *The Malahat Review* (see separate listing in Magazines/Journals). The Open Season Awards accepts entries of poetry, fiction, and creative nonfiction. Submissions must be unpublished. No simultaneous submissions. Submit up to 3 poems per entry, each poem not to exceed 100 lines; one piece of fiction (2500 words max.), or one piece of creative nonfiction (2500 words max.), no restrictions on subject matter or aesthetic approach. Include separate page with writer's name, address, e-mail, and title(s); no identifying information on mss pages. No e-mail submissions. Do not include SASE for results; mss will not be returned. Guidelines available on Website. Entry fee: $35 CAD for Canadian entries, $40 USD for US entries, ($45 USD for entries from Mexico and outside North America); includes a one-year subscription to *The Malahat Review*. Deadline: November 1 (postmark) every year. 2010 winner in poetry category: Lorri Neilsen Glenn. Winner and finalists contacted by e-mail. Winners published in Spring issue of *Malahat Review* announced in winter on Website, facebook page, and in quarterly e-newsletter, *Malahat lite*.

$ ☑ THE ORPHIC PRIZE FOR POETRY

Dream Horse Press, P.O. Box 2080, Aptos CA 95001-2080. E-mail: dreamhorsepress@ yahoo.com. Website: www.dreamhorsepress.com. **Contact:** J.P. Dancing Bear, Editor/ Publisher. The Orphic Prize for Poetry offers an annual award of $1,000 and publication of a book-length ms by Dream Horse Press. All entries will be considered for publication. Both free and formal verse styles are welcome. Submissions may be entered in other contests, "but if your manuscript is accepted for publication elsewhere, you must notify Dream Horse Press immediately." Submit 48-80 pages of poetry, paginated, with table of contents, acknowledgments, and bio. Include separate cover letter with poet's name, biographical information, and e-mail address (when available). Poet's name should not appear anywhere on the ms. Manuscripts will be recycled after judging. Guidelines available on website. **Entry fee:** $25/ms entered. Entry fees are non-refundable. Make checks/money orders payable to Dream Horse Press. **Deadline:** August 31; check website for deadlines and details for subsequent years. Recent winners include: S.D. Lishan, Gaylord Brewer, Bruce Cohen, and Kyle McCord. Judging will be anonymous.

$ ☐ PACIFIC NORTHWEST WRITERS ASSOCIATION (PNWA) LITERARY CONTEST

PMB 2717-1420 NW Gilman Blvd., Suite 2, Issaquah WA 98027. (425)673-2665. Fax: (206)824-4559. E-mail: pnwa@pnwa.org. Website: www.pnwa.org. **Contact:** Kelli Liddane. "Calling all writers. Submit your writing to 12 categories for our annual literary contest." **Entry fee:** $35 for PNWA members, $50 for non-PNWA members per category. **Deadline:** February. Check website for specific date. Over $12,000 in prize monies. Winners will be announced at awards banquet at annual PWNA Summer Writers Conference in Seattle, WA. "The Pacific Northwest Writers Association, a nonprofit organization, is dedicated to Northwest writers and the development of writing talent from pen to publication through education, accessibility to the publishing industry, and participation in an interactive vital writer community. In addition to the annual literary contest, PNWA hosts an annual conference each summer in the Seattle area. See website for further membership and conference details."

$ ☑ THE PATERSON POETRY PRIZE

Poetry Center, Passaic Co. Community College, One College Blvd., Paterson NJ 07505-1179. (973)684-6555. E-mail: mgillan@pccc.edu. Website: www.pccc.edu/poetry.

Contact: Maria Mazziotti Gillan, editor/executive director. The Paterson Poetry Prize offers an annual award of $1,000 for the strongest book of poems (48 or more pages) published in the previous year. The winner will be asked to participate in an awards ceremony and to give a reading at The Poetry Center. Minimum press run: 500 copies. Publishers may submit more than 1 title for prize consideration; 3 copies of each book must be submitted. Include SASE for results; books will not be returned (all entries will be donated to the Poetry Center Library). Guidelines and application form (required) available for SASE or on website. **Entry fee:** none. **Deadline:** February 1 (postmark). Winners will be announced in Poets & Writers Magazine and on website. 2009 winner was Li-Young Lee for the book *Behind My Eyes*.

$ ☑ PAUMANOK POETRY AWARD

English Dept., Knapp Hall, Farmingdale State College, 2350 Broadhollow Rd., Farmingdale NY 11735. E-mail: brownml@farmingdale.edu. Website: www.farmingdale.edu. **Contact:** Dr. Margery L. Brown, director. Offers 1st Prize of $1,500 plus an all-expense-paid feature reading in their 2011-2012 visiting writers series. **(Please note: travel expenses within the continental U.S. only.)** Also awards two 2nd Prizes of $750 plus expenses for a reading in the series. Submit cover letter, 1 paragraph literary bio, and 3-5 poems (no more than 10 pages total), published or unpublished. Include cover page with name, address, and phone number. Guidelines available for SASE or on website. **Entry fee:** $25. Make checks payable to Farmingdale State University of New York, VWP. **Deadline:** by September 15 (postmark). Include SASE for results (to be mailed by late December); results also posted on website. Competition receives over 600 entries. 2009 winners were Annette Opalczynski (1st Prize) and Atar Hadari, Sharon Fain, and Holly Scalera (runners-up).

$ ☑ PAVEMENT SAW PRESS CHAPBOOK AWARD

321 Empire Street, Montpelier OH 43543-1301. E-mail: info@pavementsaw.org. Website: www.pavementsaw.org. **Contact:** David Baratier, editor. Pavement Saw Press Chapbook Award offers $500, publication, and 50 author copies. Open to all poets regardless of previous publication history. Submit up to 32 pages of poetry. Include signed cover letter with poet's name, address, phone number, e-mail, publication credits, a brief biography, and ms title. Also include 2 cover sheets: 1 with poet's contact information and ms title, 1 with the ms title only. Do not put poet's name on mss pages except for first title page. No mss will be returned. Guidelines available for SASE or on website. **Entry fee:** $15. "Every entrant will receive the equivalent cost of the entry fee in Pavement Saw Press titles." Make checks payable to Pavement Saw Press. **Deadline:** December 30 (entries must be postmarked by this date to be eligible). 2008 winner was Noah Eli Gordon (*Acoustic Experience*).

$ ☑ PEARL POETRY PRIZE

Pearl Editions, 3030 E. Second St., Long Beach CA 90803-5163. (562)434-4523. E-mail: pearlmag@aol.com. Website: www.pearlmag.com. **Contact:** Joan Jobe Smith, Marilyn Johnson, and Barbara Hauk, poetry editors. The annual Pearl Poetry Prize awards $1,000, publication, and 25 author's copies for a book-length ms. Guidelines available for SASE or on website. **Entry fee:** $20 (includes a copy of the winning book). **Deadline:** submit

May 1-June 30 only. 2008 winner was Alison Luterman (*See How We Almost Fly*). 2010 judge: Christopher Buckley.

$ ◻ JUDITH SIEGEL PEARSON AWARD

Wayne State University/Family of Judith Siegel Pea, 5057 Woodward Ave., Suite 9408, Detroit MI 48202. (313)577-2450. Fax: (313)577-8618. E-mail: rhonda@wayne.edu. **Contact:** Rhonda Agnew, Contest Coordinator. Offers an annual award of up to $500 for the best creative or scholarly work on a subject concerning women. The type of work accepted rotates each year: fiction in 2011, drama in 2012, poetry in 2013 (poetry, 20 pages maximum), essays in 2014. Open to all interested writers and scholars. Submissions must be unpublished. Submit 4-10 poems (20 pages maximum). Guidelines available for SASE or by fax or e-mail. **Deadline:** TBA.

$ PEN CENTER USA LITERARY AWARD IN POETRY

PEN Center USA, 269 South Beverly Dr. #1163 Beverly Hills, CA 90212. E-mail: awards@ penusa.org. Website: www.penusa.org. Contact: Literary Awards Coordinator: Hilary McCreery. Estab. 1982. Offered annually for fiction, creative nonfiction, research nonfiction, poetry, children's literature, translation, journalism, screenplay, teleplay and drama, published January 1-December 31 of the current year (2010). Open to authors west of the Mississippi River. Guidelines online. Deadline: December 31, 2010 (book categories); January 31, 2011 (non book categories). Charges: $35 fee. Prize: $1,000.

$ ☑ PERUGIA PRESS PRIZE

P.O. Box 60364, Florence MA 01062. E-mail: info@perugiapress.com. Website: www. perugiapress.com. **Contact:** Susan Kan, director. The Perugia Press Prize for a first or second poetry book by a woman offers $1,000 and publication. Poet must be a living U.S. resident with no more than 1 previously published book of poems (chapbooks don't count). Submissions must be unpublished as a collection, but individual poems may have been previously published in journals, chapbooks, and anthologies. Considers simultaneous submissions if notified of acceptance elsewhere. Submit 48-72 pages (white paper) "with legible typeface, pagination, and fastened with a removable clip. No more than 1 poem per page." Two cover pages required: 1 with ms title, poet's name, address, telephone number, and e-mail address; and 1 with ms title only. Include table of contents and acknowledgments page. No e-mail submissions. No translations or self-published books. Multiple submissions accepted if accompanied by separate entry fee for each. Include SASE for winner notification only; mss will be recycled. Guidelines available on website. **Entry fee:** $25. Make checks payable to Perugia Press. **Deadline:** submit August 1-November 15 (postmark). "Use USPS only, not FedEx or UPS." Winner announced by April 1 by e-mail or SASE (if included with entry). Judges: panel of Perugia authors, booksellers, scholars, etc.

$ ☑ THE RICHARD PETERSON POETRY PRIZE

Dept. of English, Mail Code 4503, Faner Hall 2380, Southern Illinois Univ Carbondale, Carbondale IL 62901. Website: www.craborchardreview.siuc.edu. **Contact:** Jon Tribble, managing editor. The Richard Peterson Poetry Prize offers $1,500 plus publication in the Winter/Spring issue of Crab Orchard Review (see separate listing in Magazines/Journals). "Submissions must be unpublished original work not under consideration elsewhere, written in English by a U.S. citizen or permanent resident. Name, address, telephone number, and/or e-mail address should appear only on the title page of manuscript; author's name should not appear on any subsequent pages. Mark 'poetry' on outside of envelope. Include #10 SASE for notification of winners." See guidelines for complete formatting instructions. Guidelines available for SASE or on website. **Entry fee:** $10/entry (3 poems, 100 line limit per poem, no more than 1 poem per page; poet may submit up to 3 separate entries if not entering the fiction or nonfiction categories of the contest). Each fee entitles entrant to a copy of the winter/spring Crab Orchard Review featuring the prize winner; include complete address. Make checks payable to Crab Orchard Review. **Deadline:** see guidelines or check website.

$ ☑ PLAN B PRESS POETRY CHAPBOOK CONTEST
P.O. Box 4067, Alexandria VA 22303. (215)732-2663. E-mail: planbpress@gmail.com. Website: www.planbpress.com. **Contact:** Contest Coordinator. The annual Plan B Press Poetry Chapbook Contest offers $225, publication by Plan B Press (see separate listing in Book/Chapbook Publishers), and 50 author's copies. Poems may be previously published individually. Accepts multiple submissions with separate fee for each. Submit up to 24 poems (48 pages total maximum) in English. Include table of contents and list of acknowledgments. Include e-mail address or SASE for notification of winner; mss will not be returned. Author retains copyright of poems, but Plan B reserves rights to layout and/or cover art and design. Guidelines available on website. **Entry fee:** $15. **Deadline:** March 1.

$ ☑ POETRY 2010 INTERNATIONAL POETRY COMPETITION
Atlanta Review, P.O. Box 8248, Atlanta GA 31106. E-mail: atlrev@yahoo.com. **Contact:** Dan Veach, Editor/Publisher. *Atlanta Review* (see separate listing in Magazines/Journals) sponsors an annual international poetry competition, offering $2,010 Grand Prize, 20 International Publication Awards (winners will be published in *Atlanta Review*), and 30 International Merit Awards (includes certificate, Honorable Mention in *Atlanta Review*, and free issue). Poems must not have been published in a nationally distributed print publication. Online entry available at journal website. For mail entry: put your name and address on each page (e-mail and phone optional). Include SASE for results only; no entries will be returned. Guidelines available on website. **Entry fee:** $5 for the first poem, $3 for each additional poem. Make checks payable to *Atlanta Review*. International entrants must use online entry. **Deadline:** March 1, 2010. Winners will be announced in August; Contest Issue published in October. Contest Issue available for $4, or free with $10 subscription to *Atlanta Review*.

$ ☑ THE POETRY COUNCIL OF NORTH CAROLINA ANNUAL POETRY CONTEST
E-mail: edcockrell@hotmail.com. Website: www.poetrycouncilofnc.wordpress.com. **Contact:** Ed Cockrell. The Poetry Council of North Carolina is "an organization whose sole purpose is to sponsor annual adult and student poetry contests and to publish the

winning poems in our book, Bay Leaves. There is no membership fee. All winners are invited to read their poems at Poetry Day in the fall of each year, either late September or early October." Open to residents and anyone with a "North Carolina connection" (persons born in NC, transients from other states who either attend school or work in NC, and NC residents temporarily out of state). Offers 4 adult and 2 student contests with prizes ranging from $10 to $35; all winning poems plus Honorable Mentions will be published in Bay Leaves (50+ pages, perfect-bound). Guidelines available for SASE or on website. **Entry fee:** $5/poem, 1 poem/contest. Students enter free. **Deadline:** see website. Competition receives 200+ entries/year. Winners list available for SASE, also appears in Bay Leaves and on website. Copies of Bay Leaves available from Poetry Council of North Carolina. "Please read the guidelines carefully. Send only your best work. You can enter only 1 poem in each contest."

$ ☑ POETRY SOCIETY OF AMERICA AWARDS

15 Gramercy Park, New York NY 10003. E-mail: psa@poetrysociety.org. Website: www. poetrysociety.org. Offers the following awards **open to PSA members only**: **The Writer Magazine/Emily Dickinson Award** ($250, for a poem inspired by Dickinson though not necessarily in her style); **Cecil Hemley Memorial Award** ($500, for a lyric poem that addresses a philosophical or epistemological concern); **Lyric Poetry Award** ($500, for a lyric poem on any subject); **Lucille Medwick Memorial Award** ($500, for an original poem in any form on a humanitarian theme); **Alice Fay Di Castagnola Award** ($1,000 for a manuscript-in-progress of poetry or verse-drama). The following awards are **open to both PSA members and nonmembers**: **Louise Louis/Emily F. Bourne Student Poetry Award** ($250, for the best unpublished poem by a student in grades 9-12 from the U.S.); **George Bogin Memorial Award** ($500, for a selection of 4-5 poems that use language in an original way to reflect the encounter of the ordinary and the extraordinary and to take a stand against oppression in any of its forms); **Robert H. Winner Memorial Award** ($2,500, to acknowledge original work being done in mid-career by a poet who has not had substantial recognition, open to poets over 40 who have published no more than one book). Entries for the **Norma Farber First Book Award** ($500) and the **William Carlos Williams Award** (purchase prize between $500 and $1,000, for a book of poetry published by a small press, nonprofit, or university press) **must be submitted directly by publishers**. Complete submission guidelines for all awards are available on website. **Entry fee:** all of the above contests are free to PSA members; nonmembers pay $15 to enter any or all of contests 6-8; $5 for high school students to enter single entries in the student poetry competition; high school teachers/administrators may submit unlimited number of students' poems (one entry/student) to student poetry award for $20. **Deadline:** submissions accepted October 1-December 22 (postmark). Additional information available on website.

$ ◻ THE POETRY SOCIETY OF VIRGINIA ADULT AND STUDENT CONTESTS

P.O. Box 341, Montpelier VA 23192-0341. E-mail: musicsavy45@yahoo.com. **Contact:** Judith K. Bragg. Adult contest offers many categories for original, unpublished poems—both specified and unspecified forms and topics. Student contest is school grade-specific.

Offers numerous cash prizes (varies by year). One poem per category may be submitted. Submit 2 copies of each poem. Both copies must have the category name and number on top left of page. One copy must contain poet's name, address, e-mail, and phone number on top right of page, as well as membership status. Guidelines available for SASE or on website (guidelines must be followed). **Entry fee:** $4/poem for adults; no fee for students and PSV members. ("Membership fee of $25 covers entries in all categories and can be sent with entry and membership form, available on website or for SASE.") Designate entries as "adult" or "student" and send to Contest Chair at the above address. **Deadline:** January 19 (postmark) annually (Edgar Allan Poe's birthday). Winning entries may be published in a booklet or on the PSV website unless author indicates otherwise on each poem entered. "Follow guidelines to ensure inclusion of poem in contest. Always include SASE for any return information."

$ ☑ FELIX POLLAK PRIZE IN POETRY

University of Wisconsin Press, Dept. of English, 600 N. Park St., Madison WI 53706. E-mail: rwallace@wisc.edu. Website: www.wisc.edu/wisconsinpress/index.html. **Contact:** Ronald Wallace, Poetry Series Editor. The annual Felix Pollak Prize in Poetry is one of 2 prizes awarded by the University of Wisconsin Press (see separate listing for the Brittingham Prize in Poetry). Offers $1,000 plus publication, with an additional $1,500 honorarium to cover expenses of a reading in Madison. Submissions must be unpublished as a collection, but individual poems may have been published elsewhere (publication must be acknowledged). Considers simultaneous submissions if notified of selection elsewhere. Submit 50-80 unbound ms pages, typed single-spaced (with double spaces between stanzas). Clean photocopies are acceptable. Include one title page with poet's name, address, and telephone number; one title page with title only. No translations. Include SASE for results only; mss will not be returned. Guidelines available for SASE or on website. **Entry fee:** $25. **NOTE:** $25 fee applies to consideration of same entry for the Brittingham Prize in Poetry—1 fee for 2 contest awards. Make checks/money orders payable to University of Wisconsin Press. **Deadline:** submit September 1-27 (postmark). 2010 Pollak Prize winner was Nick Lantz, *The Lightning That Strikes the Neighbors' House*. Qualified readers will screen all mss. Judge: "a distinguished poet who will remain anonymous until the winners are announced in mid-February."

$ ☑ THE JACKLYN POTTER YOUNG POETS COMPETITION

The Word Works, 1200 North Quaker Lane, Alexandria VA 22302. (703)931-5177. E-mail: wpe@episcopalhighschool.org. Website: www.worksdc.com. **Contact:** W. Perry Epes, director. (Specialized: Washington, DC-area high school students) The annual Jacklyn Potter Young Poets Competition is open to Washington, DC-are high school students. 2 winners receive an honorarium and read their original work at the Joaquin Miller Cabin in Rock Creek Park in an appearance with an established poet. The winners and other notable entrants will be recommended for a reading at the Nora School Poetry Series held in Silver Spring, MD. Submit 5-6 poems with poet's name, address, and phone number in the upper right corner of every ms page. Include a separate cover page with poet's name, address, phone number, e-mail address, name of school, grade, expected graduation date, and listed titles of poems submitted. Include SASE for results. **Deadline:** submit January 1-March 31.

$ ◙ A. POULIN, JR. POETRY PRIZE

BOA Editions, Ltd., 250 N. Goodman St., Suite 306, Rochester NY 14607. (585)546-3410. Website: www.boaeditions.org. Established 1976. **Contact:** Thom Ward, poetry editor. BOA Editions, Ltd. (see separate listing in Book/Chapbook Publishers) sponsors the annual A. Poulin, Jr. Poetry Prize for a poet's first book. Awards $1,500 and publication. Individual poems may have been previously published. Considers simultaneous submissions. Submit 48-100 pages of poetry, paginated consecutively, typed or computer-generated in 11 pt. font. Bind with spring clip (no paperclips). Include cover/title page with poet's name, address, and telephone number. Also include table of contents; list of acknowledgments; and entry form (available for download on website). Multiple entries accepted with separate entry fee for each. No e-mail submissions. Include SASP for notification of receipt and SASE for results. Mss will not be returned. Guidelines available on website in May. **Entry fee:** $25. **Deadline:** submit August 1-November 30 annually. 2010 judge: Thomas Lux. Winner announced in March 2011.

$ ◪ THE PRAIRIE SCHOONER BOOK PRIZE SERIES

201 Andrews Hall, P.O. Box 880334 University of Nebraska, Lincoln NE 68588-0334. (402)472-0911. Fax: (402)472-9771. E-mail: jengelhardt2@unl.edu. Website: http://prairieschooner.unl.edu. **Contact:** Contest Director. The annual Prairie Schooner Book Prize Series offers $3,000 and publication of a book-length collection of poetry by the University of Nebraska Press; one runner-up receives $1,000. Individual poems may have been previously published elsehwere. Considers simultaneous submissions if notified immediately of acceptance elsewhere. Submit at least 50 pages of poetry with acknowledgments page (if applicable). Poet's name should not appear on ms pages. Xeroxed copies are acceptable. Bind with rubber band or binder clip only. Include 2 cover pages: one with poet's name, address, phone number, and e-mail address; the other with ms title only. Include SASP for acknowledgment of receipt of ms and #10 SASE for results only; mss will not be returned. Guidelines available for SASE, by e-mail, or on website. **Entry fee:** $25. Make checks payable to Prairie Schooner. **Deadline:** January 15-March 15 annually. 2008 winner was Kara Candito (*Taste of Cherry*). Winners announced on website in early July, with results mailed shortly thereafter. (See separate listing for Prairie Schooner in Magazines/Journals.)

$ ◪ THE PSA NATIONAL CHAPBOOK FELLOWSHIPS

Poetry Society of America, 15 Gramercy Park, New York NY 10003. (212)254-9628. Fax: (212)673-2352. Website: www.poetrysociety.org. The PSA National Chapbook Fellowships offer 2 prizes of $1,000 and publication of winning chapbook mss, with distribution by the Poetry Society of America. Open to any U.S. resident who has not published a full-length poetry collection. **(Poets who apply to this contest may not apply to The PSA New York Chapbook Fellowships.)**Does not accept entries by fax or e-mail. Guidelines available for SASE or on website. **Entry fee:** $12 for both PSA members and nonmembers.

Make checks/money orders payable to Poetry Society of America. **Deadline:** submit October 1-December 22 (postmarked). 2010 judges: Kimiko Hahn and James Tate.

$ ☑ THE PSA NEW YORK CHAPBOOK FELLOWSHIPS

Poetry Society of America, 15 Gramercy Park, New York NY 10003. (212)254-9628. Fax: (212)673-2352. Website: www.poetrysociety.org. **Contact:** Contest Coordinator. (Specialized: open to NYC residents only) The PSA New York Chapbook Fellowships offer 2 prizes of $1,000 and publication of each of winning chapbook mss, with distribution by the Poetry Society of America. Open to any New York City resident (in the 5 boroughs) who is 30 or under and has not published a full-length poetry collection. **(Poets who apply to this contest may not apply to The PSA National Chapbook Fellowships.)** Does not accept entries by fax or e-mail. Guidelines available for SASE or on website. **Entry fee:** $12 for both PSA members and nonmembers. Make checks/money orders payble to Poetry Society of America. **Deadline:** submit October 1-December 22 (postmarked). 2010 judges: Cornelius Eady and Rosanna Warren. Additional information available on website.

$ ☑ THE PULITZER PRIZE IN LETTERS

709 Journalism, Columbia University, New York NY 10027. (212)854-3841. Fax: (212)854-3342. E-mail: pulitzer@pulitzer.org. Website: www.pulitzer.org. The Pulitzer Prize for Letters annually awards 2 prizes of $10,000 each and a certificate for the most distinguished books of poetry and fiction published during the preceding year (U.S. authors only). Anyone, including the author, may submit a book that's eligible. Submit 4 copies of published books (or galley proofs if book is being published after October 15), completed entry form, 1 photograph, and 1 biography. Entry form and guidelines available for SASE, by fax, or on website. **Entry fee:** $50. **Deadline:** October 15. Competition receives about 150 entries/year. 2007 poetry winner was Natasha Trethewey for Native Guard (Houghton Mifflin). 2007 judges: Cynthia Huntington, Rafael Campo, and Claudia Emerson.

PUSHCART PRIZE

P.O. Box 380, Wainscott NY 11975. (631)324-9300. Website: www.pushcartprize.com. **Contact:** Bill Henderson.

$ ☑ QUERCUS REVIEW PRESS POETRY SERIES BOOK AWARD

Quercus Review Press, Modesto Junior College, Div. of Lit & Language, 435 College Ave., Modesto CA 95350. Website: www.quercusreview.com. Quercus Review Press publishes 1 poetry book/year selected through the Poetry Series Book Award. Offers $1,000, publication, and 50 author's copies. Book mss may include previously published poems. Submit 46-96 pages in ms format. Include cover letter and SASE. Guidelines available on website. **Entry fee:** $20 ($25 to receive a copy of winning book). **Deadline:** June - October 15 (postmark). 2008 winner was Claire Zoghb (*Small House Breathing)*.

$ ☑ THE RAIZISS/DE PALCHI TRANSLATION AWARDS

The Academy of American Poets, 584 Broadway, Suite 604, New York NY 10012. (212)274-0343 ext 15. E-mail: awards@poets.org. Website: www.poets.org. **Contact:** Alex

Dimitrov, awards associate. (Specialized: Italian poetry translated into English) Awarded for outstanding translations of modern Italian poetry into English. A $5,000 book prize and a $25,000 fellowship are awarded in alternate years. Guidelines and entry form available for SASE or on website. **Deadline:** January 31.

$ ☑ RATTLE POETRY PRIZE

RATTLE, 12411 Ventura Blvd., Studio City CA 91604. (818) 505-6777. E-mail: timgreen@ rattle.com. Website: www.rattle.com. The RATTLE Poetry Prize awards 1st Prize of $5,000, plus ten $100 Honorable Mentions. Additional entries may be offered publication as well. Open to writers worldwide (see website for special international guidelines). Poems must be written in English (no translations). No previously published poems or works accepted for publication elsewhere. No simultaneous submissions. Submit no more than 4 poems/entry. Multiple entries by a single poet accepted; however, each 4-poem group must be treated as a separate entry with its own cover sheet and entry fee. Include cover sheet with poet's name, address, e-mail address, phone number, and poem titles. No contact information should appear on poems. Include SASE for results only; no poems will be returned. **Note:** Poems also may be entered through online submission on website. Guidelines available by e-mail or on website. **Entry fee:** $18; includes one-year subscription to RATTLE (see separate listing in Magazines/Journals). Make checks/ money orders payable to RATTLE (for credit card entries, see website). **Deadline:** August 1 (postmark). 2009 winner was Lynne Knight ("To the Young Man Who Cried Out.."). Judge: editors of RATTLE in blind review. Winners announced in September.

$ MARGARET REID POETRY CONTEST FOR TRADITIONAL VERSE

Tom Howard Books, c/o Winning Writers, 351 Pleasant St., PMB 222, Northampton MA 01060-3961. (866)946-9748. Fax: (413)280-0539. E-mail: johnreid@mail.qango. com. Website: www.winningwriters.com/margaret. **Contact:** John Reid, Award Director. Offers annual award of 1st Prize: $3,000; 2nd Prize: $1,000; 3rd Prize: $400; 4th Prize: $250; 5 High Distinction Awards of $200 each; and 6 Most Highly Commended Awards of $150 each. The top 10 entries will be published on the Winning Writers website. Submissions may be published or unpublished, may have won prizes elsewhere, and may be entered in other contests. Submit poems in traditional verse forms, such as sonnets, ballads, odes, blank verse, and haiku. No limit on number of lines or number of poems submitted. No name on ms pages; type or computer-print on letter-size white paper, single-sided. Guidelines available for SASE or on website. Submit online or by mail. **Entry fee:** $7 USD for every 25 lines (exclude poem title and any blank lines from count). **Deadline:** November 15-June 30. 2009 winner was Judith Goldhaber ("The Bewick's Wren"). 2009 judges: John H. Reid and Dee C. Konrad. Winners announced in December at WinningWriters.com; entrants who provide valid e-mail addresses also receive notification.

ROANOKE-CHOWAN POETRY AWARD

The North Carolina Literary & Historical Assoc., 4610 Mail Service Center, Raleigh NC 27699-4610. (919)807-7290. Fax: (919)733-8807. E-mail: michael.hill@ncdcr.gov. Website: ah.dcr.state.nc.us/affiliates/lit-hist/awards/awards.htm. **Contact:** Michael Hills, awards coordinator. (Specialized: NC resident authors) Offers annual award for "an original volume of poetry published during the 12 months ending June 30 of the year for which the award is given." Open to "authors who have maintained legal or physical residence, or a combination of both, in North Carolina for the 3 years preceding the close of the contest period." Submit 3 copies of each entry. Guidelines available for SASE or by fax or e-mail. **Deadline:** July 15. Competition receives about 15 entries. 2006 winner was James Applewhite (Selected Poems). Winner announced by mail October 15.

$ ☑ BEULLAH ROSE POETRY PRIZE

P.O. Box 22161, Baltimore MD 21203. E-mail: cbanks@smartishpace.com. Website: www.smartishpace.com. **Contact:** Clare Banks, associate editor. (Specialized: poetry by women) The annual Beullah Rose Poetry Prize for exceptional poetry by women offers 1st Prize: $200 and publication of the winning poem in *Smartish Pace* (see separate listing in Magazines/Journals); 2nd and 3rd Prizes: winning poems will be published in Smartish Pace. Winners also receive additional Internet and advertising exposure. Submit 3 poems, with poet's name, address, e-mail, telephone number (preferred), and "Beulah Rose Poetry Prize" at the top of each page of poetry submitted. Include bio. Entries may be submitted online or by e-mail (as attachment) or regular mail. Include SASE with postal entries. Guidelines available on website. **Entry fee:** $5 for 3 poems; additional poems may be submitted for $1/poem (12 poem maximum). Make checks/money orders payable to *Smartish Pace*. **Deadline:** November 1. Judges: Clare Banks and Traci O'Dea, associate editors.

☑ THE SACRAMENTIO POETRY CENTER BOOK PRIZE

PO Box 160406, Sacramento CA 95816. (916)451-5569. E-mail: buchanan@csus.edu. Website: www.sacramentopoetrycenter.org. **Contact:** Brad Buchanan. (Formerly the Cathy Washington Prize) The Sacramento Poetry Center Book Prize offers an annual prize of book publication, $1000, and 50 free copies of the winning book. Winning mss will be sold via Amazon.com and SPC website. Submissions must be unpublished as a collection, but individual poems may have been previously published elsewhere. Considers simultaneous submissions, with notification. Submit 48-70 pages of poetry. Include 2 title pages: name and contact information (including e-mail address, if possible) should appear on first title page only. Staff, volunteers, or board members of the Sacramento Poetry Center, or their relations, may not submit manuscripts for consideration in this contest. Guidelines available for SASE, on website, or by e-mail. **Entry fee**: $20. Check should be made out to The Sacramento Poetry Center. **Deadline**: April 1, 2011. Winner announced in June by e-mail. Copies of winning books available for $12 from The Sacramento Poetry Center. " The Sacramento Poetry Center is a non-profit organization dedicated to furthering the cause of poetry in the Sacramento area and nationwide. We welcome work from anyone, anywhere." **Advice**: "Never lose heart. SPC supports the CLMP Code of Ethics and will adhere to its precepts regarding contests, so we're as fair as it gets."

$ ☑ ERNEST SANDEEN PRIZE IN POETRY

Dept. of English, University of Notre Dame, Notre Dame IN 46556-5639. (574)631-7526. Fax: (574)631-4795. E-mail: creativewriting@nd.edu. Website: www.nd.edu/~ndr/

sandeen.html. **Contact:** Director of Creative Writing. The Sandeen Prize in Poetry offers $1,000 (a $500 award and a $500 advance against royalties from the Notre Dame Press) and publication of a book-length ms. Open to poets who have published at least 1 volume of poetry. "Please include a photocopy of the copyright and the title page of your previous volume. Vanity press publications do not fulfill this requirement. We will pay special attention to second volumes. Please include a vita and/or a biographical statement that includes your publishing history. We will be glad to see a selection of reviews of the earlier collection." Submit 2 copies of ms (inform if ms is available on computer disk). Include SASE for acknowledgment of receipt of ms and SASE for return of ms. **Entry fee:** $15; includes one-year subscription to Notre Dame Review (see separate listing in Magazines/Journals). Make checks payable to University of Notre Dame. **Deadline:** submit May 1- September 1, 2012. 2009 winner was Luisa Igloria (*Juan Luna's Revolver*). Winners announced by the end of January.

$ ☑ SAWTOOTH POETRY PRIZE

Website: ahsahtapress.boisestate.edu. The Sawtooth Poetry Prize, sponsored by Ahsahta Press (see separate listing in Books/Chapbooks), honors a book of original poetry in English by a single author. Offers a $1,500 for a book of poems. The winning volume will be published in January 2012 by Ahsahta Press. Translations are not eligible for this award. "Students and former students of Boise State University and of this year's judge may not enter; close friends of the judge are also not considered eligible." Considers simultaneous submissions, Submit 48-100 pages of poetry, single-spaced, printed on 1 side of 8½ × 11 or A4 page only. Include SASP for notification of receipt of ms and SASE (#10 business) for results; mss will not be returned. Guidelines available on website. **Entry fee:** $25/ms. Make checks payable to Ahsahta Press. (See website for payment options outside the U.S.) "Entrants will receive a copy of the winning book when it is printed if they include a 7x10 self-addressed mailer with $3.95 postage. Our books measure 6x8 and will not fit in smaller-sized mailers." **Deadline:** submit January 1-March 1 (postmark). "In addition to announcements in national publications, the winning book and author will be featured on the Ahsahta website, as will lists of finalists and semi-finalists." 2008 winner was Barbara Maloutas with The Whole Marie. 2011 judge: Paul Hoover. "Ahsahta Press, a member of the Council of Literary Magazines and Presses, conforms to the CLMP Code of Ethics and participated in its drafting." Winner will be announced in May

$ ☑ HELEN SCHAIBLE SHAKESPEAREAN/PETRARCHAN SONNET CONTEST

416 Gierz St., Downers Grove IL 60515. Website: www.poetsandpatrons.net. **Contact:** Barbara Eaton. The annual Helen Schaible Shakespearean/Petrarchan Sonnet Contest is open to anyone. **For sonnets only!** Offers 1st Prize: $50; 2nd Prize: $35; 3rd Prize: $15; plus 3 Honorable Mentions and 3 Special Recognitions (non-cash). **Submit only 1 entry** (2 copies) of either a Shakespearean or a Petrarchan sonnet, which must be original and unpublished. Entry must be typed on 8½ × 11 paper, double-spaced. Name and address in the upper right-hand corner on only 1 copy. All necessary guidelines appear in this listing. Include SASE with entry to receive winners' list. **Entry fee:** none. **Deadline:** September 1 annually (postmark). Competition receives 150 entries/year. Poets and

Patrons runs 4 workshops a year and Chicagoland Poety Contest. Open membership, $10. offer workshops in Chicago Public Library $10 each. "Read the guidelines—1 sonnet only!"

⚎ $ ◪ SHORT GRAIN CONTEST

Box 67, Saskatoon SK S7K 3K1, Canada. (306)244-2828. Fax: (306)244-0255. E-mail: grainmag@sasktel.net. Website: www.grainmagazine.ca. **Contact:** Mike Thompson, business administrator (inquiries only). The annual Short Grain Contest includes a category for poetry of any style up to 100 lines, offering 4 prizes with a first prize of $1,250 plus publication in Grain Magazine (see separate listing in Magazines/Journals). Each entry must be original, unpublished, not submitted elsewhere for publication or broadcast, nor accepted elsewhere for publication or broadcast, nor entered simultaneously in any other contest or competition for which it is also eligible to win a prize. Entries must be typed on 8½ × 11 paper. It must be legible. Faxed and/or electronic entries not accepted. No simultaneous submissions. A separate covering page must be attached to the text of your entry, and must provide the following information: poet's name, complete mailing address, telephone number, e-mail address, entry title, category name, and line count. An absolutely accurate word or line count is required. No identifying information on the text pages. Entries will not be returned. Include SASE for results only. Entry fee: $30 CAD; $36 US and international entrants; includes 1 year subscription to Grain Magazine. **Deadline:** April 1. Winning entries will be posted on the Grain Magazine website in August.

$ ◪ SLIPSTREAM POETRY CHAPBOOK CONTEST

Dept. W-1, P.O. Box 2071, Niagara Falls NY 14301-0071. (716)282-2616. E-mail: editors@ slipstreampress.org. Website: www.slipstreampress.org. **Contact:** Contest Director. The annual Slipstream Poetry Chapbook Contest awards $1,000, publication of a chapbook ms, and 50 author's copies. All entrants receive copy of winning chapbook and an issue of Slipstream (see separate listing in Magazines/Journals). Considers simultaneous submissions if informed of status. Accepts previously published work with acknowledgments. Submit up to 40 pages of poetry, any style, format, or theme. Manuscripts will not be returned. Guidelines available for SASE or on website. **Entry fee:** $20. **Deadline:** December 1. Latest winner is David Chorlton (*From the Age of Miracles*). Winner announced late spring/early summer.

$ ◪ SLOPE EDITIONS BOOK PRIZE

847 Bernardston Road, Greenfield MA 01301. E-mail: ethan@slope.org. Website: www. SlopeEditions.org. **Contact:** Christopher Janke, senior editor and Ethan Paquin, editor-in-chief. The Slope Editions Book Prize offers an annual award of $1,000 and publication of a book-length ms; author copies offered in lieu of royalties. Submissions must be unpublished as a collection. Submit 40-90 typed pages, bound only by a clip. Include 2 title pages: one with ms title, poet's name, address, phone number, and e-mail; and one with ms title only. Also include table of contents and acknowledgments page. Guidelines available by e-mail or on website. Do not include SASE or postcards for notification; they will not be returned. **Entry fee:** $20; entitles entrant to one Slope Editions book (see guidelines for details). Make checks/money orders payable to Slope Publishing Inc.

Deadline: March 15. 2010 judge was Franz Wright. 2009 winner was Crystal Curry (*Our Chrome Arms of Gymnasium*).

$ ▢ KAY SNOW WRITING AWARDS

9045 SW Barbur Blvd., Suite 5A, Portland OR 97219-4027. (503)452-1592. Fax: (503)452-0372. E-mail: wilwrite@willamettewriters.com. Website: www.willamettewriters.com. **Contact:** Elizabeth Shannon, award director. Offers annual awards of 1st Prize: $300; 2nd Prize: $150; 3rd Prize: $50 in several genres, including poetry. Submissions must be unpublished. Submit up to 2 poems (1 entry fee), maximum 5 pages total, on any subject, in any style or form, single-spaced, 1 side of paper only. Entry form and guidelines available for SASE or on website. **Entry fee:** $10 for members of Willamette Writers; $15 for nonmembers. **Deadline:** January 15-April 23 (postmarked) for 2011. Competition receives 150 entries. 2009 poetry winners were Daniel Sinderson, Caitlin Dwyer, and Diane Cammer. Winners will be announced July 20th. "Write and send in your very best poem. Read it aloud. If it still sounds like the best poem you've ever heard, send it in."

$ ◪ THE RICHARD SNYDER MEMORIAL PUBLICATION PRIZE

Ashland Poetry Press, 401 College Ave., Ashland University, Ashland OH 44805. **Contact:** Sarah Wells, managing editor. Offers annual award of $1,000 plus book publication in a paper-only edition of 1,000 copies. Submissions must be unpublished in book form. Considers simultaneous submissions. Submit 50-80 pages of poetry. **Entry fee:** $25. **Deadline:** April 30 annually. Competition receives 350 entries/year. 2009 Winner was Jason Schneiderman (*Striking Surface*). 2010 judge: David Wojahn. Winners will be announced in Writer's Chronicle and Poets & Writers. Copies of winning books available from Small Press Distribution, Baker & Taylor, and directly from the Ashland University Bookstore online. The Ashland Poetry Press publishes 2-4 books of poetry/year.

$ ◪ SOUL-MAKING LITERARY COMPETITION

Nob Hill, San Francisco Bay Area Branch, 1544 Sweetwood Dr., Broadmoor Vlg CA 94015-1717. (650)756-5279. Fax: (650)756-5279. E-mail: PenNobHill@aol.com. Website: www.soulmakingcontest.us. **Contact:** Eileen Malone, Award Director. Annual open contest offers cash prizes in each of 11 literary categories, including poetry and prose poem. 1st Prize: $100; 2nd Prize: $50; 3rd Prize: $25. Submissions in some categories may be previously published. Submit 3 one-page poems on soul-making theme; any form for open poetry category. No names or other identifying information on mss; include 3x5 card with poet's name, address, phone, fax, e-mail, title(s) of work, and category entered. Include SASE for results only; mss will not be returned. Guidelines available on website. **Entry fee:** $5/entry. **Deadline:** November 30. Competition receives 300 entries/year. Names of winners and judges are posted on website. Winners announced in January by SASE and on website. Winners are invited to read at the Koret Auditorium, San Francisco. Event is televised.

$ ◙ THE SPOON RIVER POETRY REVIEW EDITORS' PRIZE

4241 Dept. of English, Publications Unit, Illinois State University, Normal IL 61790-4241. Website: www.litline.org/spoon. **Contact:** Kirstin Hotelling Zona, editor. *The Spoon River*

Poetry Review Editors' Prize awards $1,000 to 1 winning poem; 2 runners-up will receive $100 each. Winning poem, runners-up, and honorable mentions will be published in the fall issue of *The Spoon River Poetry Review* (see separate listing in Magazines/Journals). Submissions must be unpublished. Submit 2 copies of 3 poems, maximum 10 pages total. On each page of 1 copy only include poet's name, address, and phone number. No fax or e-mail submissions. Include SASE for results only; mss will not be returned. Guidelines available for SASE or on website. **Entry fee:** $16; includes one-year subscription or gift subscription. (Indicate preference and include recipient's name and address.) **Deadline:** May 1 (postmark). 2009 winner was Rebecca Warren ("Doorway").

$ ☐ SPS STUDIOS BIANNUAL POETRY CARD CONTEST

Blue Mountain Arts, P.O. Box 1007, Dept. E, Boulder CO 80306. Website: www.sps.com. SPS Studios offers a biannual poetry contest with prizes of $300, $150, and $50 for each competition (winning poems are also published on the SPS website). "Poems can be rhyming or non-rhyming, although we find that non-rhyming poetry reads better. We suggest you write about real emotions and feelings and that you have some special person or occasion in mind as you write. Poems are judged on the basis of originality and uniqueness. English-language entries only, please. Enter as often as you like." All entries must be the original creation of the submitting poet, who must own all rights to the entries. Poet gives permission to SPS Studios, Inc. to publish and display the entry on the Web (in electronic form only) if the entry is selected as a winner or finalist. Contest is open to everyone except employees of SPS Studios and their families. Submit entries through online form or by postal mail. "If submitting by regular mail, please do not send us the only copy of your work. If you'd like your entry material returned, enclose a SASE. Label each submission with your name, snail mail address, phone number, and e-mail address (if you have 1)." Guidelines available on website. **Entry fee:** none. **Deadline:** June 30 and December 31. Winners will be contacted within 45 days of the deadline date.

⊞ ☑ THE ANN STANFORD POETRY PRIZE

3501 Trousdale Parkway, Mark Taper Hall, THH 355J, University of Southern California, Los Angeles CA 90089-0355. (213)740-3253. E-mail: scr@college.usc.edu. Website: www.usc.edu/dept/LAS/mpw/students/sca.php. **Contact:** Contest Coordinator. c/o Master of Professional Writing Program. The Ann Stanford Poetry Prize offers 1st Prize: $1,000; 2nd Prize: $200; 3rd Prize: $100. Winners will be published in the Fall edition of Southern California Review (see separate listing in Magazines/Journals). Submissions must be unpublished. Submit up to 5 poems. Include cover sheet with poem titles, poet's name, address, phone number, and e-mail. No identification on submission pages. Incomplete submissions will not be accepted. Include SASE for results. Guidelines available on website. **Entry fee:** $10 for up to 5 poems. All entrants receive a free issue of Southern California Review. **Deadline:** January 31.

$ ☑ WALLACE E. STEGNER FELLOWSHIPS

Creative Writing Program, Stanford University, Stanford CA 94305-2087. (650)725-1208. Fax: (650)723-3679. E-mail: mpopek@stanford.edu. Website: www.creativewriting.

standford.edu. **Contact:** Mary Popek, Program Administrator. Offers 5 fellowships in poetry of $26,000 plus tuition of over $7,000/year for promising writers who can benefit from 2 years of instruction and criticism at the Writing Center. "We do not require a degree for admission. No school of writing is favored over any other. Chronological age is not a consideration." **Deadline:** December 1 (postmark). Applicants may apply online. Competition receives about 600 entries/year for poetry. 2009/10 fellows in poetry were Joshua Edwards, Erica Ehrenberg, Keetje Kuipers, Brittany Perham, and Matthew Siegel.

$ THE WALLACE STEVENS AWARD

The Academy of American Poets, 584 Broadway, Suite 604, New York NY 10012-3210. Website: www.poets.org. Awards $100,000 annually to recognize outstanding and proven mastery in the art of poetry. **No applications are accepted**. 2009 winner was Jean Valentine. 2009 judges: Frank Bidart, Victor Hernández Cruz, Rita Dove, Marilyn Hacker, Lyn Hejinian, Edward Hirsch, Sharon Olds, Ron Padgett, Carl Phillips, Robert Pinsky, Kay Ryan, Gary Snyder, Susan Stewart, Gerald Stern, Ellen Bryant Voigt, and C. K. Williams.

$ ◻ STEVENS POETRY MANUSCRIPT CONTEST

22614 N. Santiam Hwy., Lyons OR 97358. E-mail: eberry@wvi.com. Website: www. nfsps.org. **Contact:** Eleanor Berry, contest chair. National Federation of State Poetry Societies (NFSPS) offers annual award of $1,000, publication of ms, and 50 author's copies. Individual poems may have been previously published in magazines, anthologies, or chapbooks, but not the entire ms as a collection. Simultaneous submissions allowed. Submit 48-70 pages of poetry by a single author, typewritten, or computer printed, beginning each poem on a new page. Pages numbered, with table of contents, but no author identification anywhere in ms. Include 2 title pages; 1 with no author identification, the other with name of poet, address, phone number, e-mail address and state poetry society member affiliation, if applicable. No staples or binders; plain manila folder and/or manuscript clip permitted. No illustrations. No disk submissions; no certified or registered mail. Optional: Include SASE for results only; mss will not be returned. Guidelines available for SASE or on website. **Entry fee:** $20 for NFSPS members; $25 for nonmembers. Make checks/money orders payable to NFSPS. **Deadline:** October 15 (postmark). Winners announced in January following deadline; entrants who include an e-mail address or SASE will be notified of winner. Book will be published by June and sold at annual NFSPS convention and winning poet (if present) will read from it. Copies of books available through NFSPS website.

$ ☑ THE RUTH STONE PRIZE IN POETRY

Vermont College, 36 College St., Montpelier VT 05602. (802)828-8517. E-mail: hungermtn@vermontcollege.edu. Website: www.hungermtn.org. **Contact:** Miciah Bay Gault, managing editor. The annual Ruth Stone Prize in Poetry offers $1,000 and publication in Hunger Mountain: The VCFA Journal of the Arts (see separate listing in Magazines/Journals); 2 Honorable Mentions receive $100 and are also published. Submit up to 3 poems, not to exceed 6 pages. **Entry fee:** $20. **Deadline:** December 10. Guidelines available for SASE or on website. "Include SASE and index card with poem titles and address; do not put name on poems."

$ ☑ MAY SWENSON POETRY AWARD

Utah State University Press, 7800 Old Main Hill, Logan UT 84322-7800. (435)797-1362. Fax: (435)797-0313. E-mail: michael.spooner@usu.edu. Website: www.usupress.org. **Contact:** Michael Spooner, director. The annual May Swenson Poetry Award offers $1,000 and publication by Utah State University Press for a full-length poetry collection. No restrictions on form or subject. Submit 50-100 pages of original poetry. Include cover sheet with poet's name and address. Include SASE for results; mss will not be returned. Guidelines available on website. **Entry fee:** $25; includes copy of winning book. **Deadline:** September 30 (postmark). 2009 winner was Jason Whitmarsh (*Tomorrow's Living Room*). 2010 judge: Grace Schulman. See website for latest winners and more information.

$ ☑ TANKA SOCIETY OF AMERICA INTERNATIONAL ENGLISH-LANGUAGE TANKA COMPETITION

1636 Edwards Drive, Point Roberts WA 98281-8511. E-mail: Jemrich@aol.com. Website: www.tankasocietyofamerica.com. Offers cash awards and publication of winning poems in *Ribbons* (see separate listing in Magazines/Journals), the journal of the Tanka Society of America (see separate listing in Organizations). All rights revert to poets after publication. Open to all except TSA officers and judges. Submissions must be unpublished. No simultaneous submissions. Submit any number of original tanka, in English. Guidelines and details available in March issue of Ribbons or on website. **Deadline**: May 10.

$ THE TEXAS INSTITUTE OF LETTERS POETRY AWARD

E-mail: Betwx@aol.com. Website: http://texasinstituteofletters.org. The Texas Institute of Letters gives annual awards for books by Texas authors, including including the Jesse Jones Award for Fiction, the Carr P. Collins Award for Nonfiction, and the Helen C. Smith Memorial Award for Best Book of Poetry. Books must have been first published in the year in question, and entries may be made by authors or by their publishers. Complete guidelines and award information available on website. **Deadline:** see website. Recent winners include: Lawrence Wright, *The Looming Tower*, Cormac McCarthy, *The Road*, Naomi Shibab Nye, *I'll Ask Three Times, Are You OK?*, Rick Bass, *"The Elephant."*

$ ☑ LENA-MILES WEVER TODD POETRY SERIES BOOK COMPETITION

Pleiades Press, Dept of English, University of Central Missouri, Warrensburg MO 64093. (660)543-8106. E-mail: pleiades@ucmo.edu. Website: ucmo.edu/englphil/pleiades. **Contact:** Wayne Miller, editor. The annual Lena-Miles Wever Todd Poetry Series Book Competition offers $1,000 and publication of a book-length ms. Open to all American writers, regardless of previous publication. Submission must be unpublished as a collection, but individual poems may have been previously published elsewhere. Submit at least 48 pages of poetry (one copy). Include 2 cover sheets: one with ms title, poet's name, address, and phone number; the second with ms title only. Also include acknowledgments page for previously published poems. Include SASE for results; for an additional large SASE with $1.24 postage affixed, entrant will receive a copy of the winning book. Guidelines available for SASE or on website. **Entry fee:** $15. Make checks/money orders payable to Pleiades Press. **Deadline:** September 30 (postmark). 2009 winner was Kevin Clark for *Self-Portrait with Expletives*. 2010 Final Judge: Alan Michael Parker.

$ ☑ TOWSON UNIVERSITY PRIZE FOR LITERATURE

(Specialized: book MD writer) Towson University, College of Liberal Arts, Towson MD 21252. (410)704-2128. Fax: (410)704-6392. E-mail: eduncan@towson.edu. Website: www.towson.edu. **Contact:** Chair of the English Dept. Offers annual prize of $1,000 "for a single book or book-length manuscript of fiction, poetry, drama, or imaginative nonfiction by a Maryland writer. The prize is granted on the basis of literary and aesthetic excellence as determined by a panel of distinguished judges appointed by the university. The first award, made in the fall of 1980, went to novelist Anne Tyler." Work must have been published within the 3 years prior to the year of nomination or must be scheduled for publication within the year in which nominated. Submit 5 copies of work in bound form or in typewritten, double-spaced ms form. Entry form and guidelines available on website (search "Towson Prize for Literature"). **Deadline:** June 15. Competition receives 8-10 entries. 2009 winner was Shelly Puhak (Stalin in Aruba, Black Lawrence Press, 2009).

$ ☑ TRANSCONTINENTAL POETRY AWARD

Pavement Saw Press, 321 Empire St., Montpelier OH 43543. E-mail: info@pavementsaw. org. Website: www.pavementsaw.org. **Contact:** David Baratier, editor. The Transcontinental Poetry Award offers $1,000, publication, and a percentage of the print run for a first book. "Each year, Pavement Saw Press will seek to publish at least 1 book of poetry and/or prose poems from manuscripts received during this competition, which is open to anyone who has not previously published a volume of poetry or prose. Writers who have had volumes of poetry and/or prose under 40 pages printed, or printed in limited editions of no more than 500 copies, are eligible." Submit 48-70 pages of poetry (1 poem/ page), paginated and bound with a single clip. Include 2 cover sheets: 1 with ms title, poet's name, address, phone number, and e-mail, if available, the second with ms title only (this sheet should be clipped to ms). Also include one-page cover letter (a brief biography, ms title, poet's name, address, and telephone number, e-mail, and poet's signature) and acknowledgments page (journal, anthology, chapbook, etc., and poem published). Include SASP for acknowledgment of receipt; SASE unnecessary as result will be sent with free book and no mss will be returned. Guidelines available for SASE or on website. **Entry fee:** $20; electronic submissions $27. "All U.S entrants will receive books, chapbooks, and journals equal to, or more than, the entry fee. Add $3 (USD) for other countries to cover the extra postal charge if sending by mail." Make checks payable to Pavement Saw Press. **Deadline:** reads submissions in June, July, and until August 15 (must have August 15 or earlier postmark).

$ ☑ TUFTS POETRY AWARDS

Center for Arts & Humanities at Claremont Graduate, University, 160 E. 10th St., Harper East B7, Claremont CA 91711-6165. (909)621-8974. Website: www.cgu.edu/tufts. The annual Kingsley Tufts Poetry Award offers $100,000 for a work by an emerging poet, "one who is past the very beginning but has not yet reached the acknowledged pinnacle of his/her career." 2010 winner is D.A. Powell (*Chronic*). The Kate Tufts Discovery Award ($10,000) is for a first book. To be considered for the 2011 awards, books must have been published between September 15, 2009 and September 15, 2010. Entry form and guidelines available for SASE or on website. 2010 winner is Beth Bachmann (*Temper*). Check website for updated deadlines and award information.

$ ☐ MARICA AND JAN VILCEK PRIZE FOR POETRY

New York University School of Medicine, OBV-A612, 550 First Ave., New York NY 10016. (212)263-3973. E-mail: info@BLReview.org. Website: www.BLReview.org. **Contact:** Stacy Bodziak. (Specialized: humanity, health, and healing.) The annual Marica and Jan Vilcek Prize for Poetry recognizes outstanding writing related to themes of health, healing, illness, the mind, and the body. Offers $1,000 for best poem and publication in Bellevue Literary Review (see separate listing in Magazines/Journals). All entries will be considered for publication. No previously published poems (including Internet publication). Submit up to 3 poems (5 pages maximum). Electronic (online) submissions only (as Word document with *.doc extension); combine all poems into one document and use first poem as document title. See guidelines for additional submission details. Guidelines available for SASE or on website. **Entry fee:** $15/submission, limit of 2 submissions per person (one-year subscription available for additional $5). **Deadline:** July 1. Winner announced in December. 2011 judge: Marie Ponsot. Previous judges include Naomi Shihab Nye (2009) and Tony Hoagland (2010).

$ ☑ WAR POETRY CONTEST

Winning Writers, 351 Pleasant St., PMB 222, Northampton MA 01060-3961. (866)946-9748. Fax: (413)280-0539. E-mail: adam@winningwriters.com. Website: www.winningwriters.com. **Contact:** Adam Cohen, Award Director. Offers annual award of 1st Prize: $2,000; 2nd Prize: $1,200; 3rd Prize: $600; 12 Honorable Mentions of $100 each. All prizewinners receive online publication at WinningWriters.com; selected finalists may also receive online publication. Submissions must be unpublished. Considers simultaneous submissions. Submit 1-3 poems of up to 500 lines total on the theme of war, any form, style, or genre. No name on ms pages, typed or computer-printed on letter-size white paper, single-sided. Submit online or by regular mail. Guidelines available for SASE or on website. **Entry fee:** $15 for group of 1-3 poems. **Deadline:** November 15-May 31. Competition receives about 650 entries/year. 2009 winner was Robert Hill Long for "Wolverine and White Crow", "Motivations", and "Insurrection and Resurrection." 2009 final judge: Jendi Reiter. Winners announced on November 15 at WinningWriters.com and in free e-mail newsletter. Entrants who provided valid e-mail addresses will also receive notification. (See separate listing for the Wergle Flomp Humor Poetry Contest in this section and for Winning Writers in the Additional Resources section.)

$ ☑ THE WASHINGTON PRIZE

Word Works Washington Prize, Dearlove Hall, Adirondack Community College, 640 Bay Road, Queensbury NY 12804. E-mail: editor@wordworksdc.com; nancellini@aol.com. Website: www.wordworksdc.com. **Contact:** Nancy White, prize administrator. The

Washington Prize offers $1,500 and publication of a book-length ms of original poetry in English by a living American poet (U.S. or Canadian citizen or resident). Submit a ms of 48-64 pages. Include two title pages, one with and one without author information, an acknowledgments page, a table of contents and a cover letter containing a brief bio. Attach acknowledgments and bio to title page with a staple. Use a binder clip to secure the ms. No scripts will be returned. Indicate the information source where you learned about The Washington Prize (for example, *AWP newsletter, Poets & Writers Magazine, the Word Work*s website). Send entries to this address only by First Class Mail: Nancy White, Word Works Washington Prize Administrator, Dearlove Hall, Adirondack Community College, 640 Bay Road, Queensbury NY 12804. **Entry fee:** $25 (includes copy of winning book). Make checks payable to The Word Works and should be drawn from a US Bank only. **Deadline:** submit January 15-March 1 (postmark). Winners announced in 2010. Book publication planned for January 2011.

$ ☑ ROBERT WATSON LITERARY PRIZES

The Greensboro Review, MFA Writing Program, 3302 HHRA Building, UNC Greensboro, Greensboro NC 27402-6170. Website: www.greensbororeview.org. **Contact:** Jim Clark, editor. The annual Robert Watson Literary Prizes include a $500 award for poetry. All entries meeting guidelines will be considered for publication in *The Greensboro Review* (see separate listing in Magazines/Journals). Submissions must be unpublished. No simultaneous submissions. Submit poems of any length, typed. No e-mail submissions. Include SASE for results or (with additional postage) for return of ms (mss will not be returned unless specifically requested by author). Guidelines available in magazine, for SASE, or on website. **Entry fee:** none. **Deadline:** December 31 (postmark) annually.

$ ☑ WERGLE FLOMP HUMOR POETRY CONTEST

Winning Writers, 351 Pleasant St., PMB 222, Northampton MA 01060-3961. (866)946-9748. Fax: (413)280-0539. E-mail: adam@winningwriters.com. Website: www.winningwriters.com. **Contact:** Adam Cohen, Award Director. Offers annual award of 1st Prize: $1,500; 2nd Prize: $800; 3rd Prize: $400; plus 12 Honorable Mentions of $75 each. All prizewinners receive online publication at WinningWriters.com. Submissions may be previously published. Considers simultaneous submissions. Submit 1 humorous poem of any length, in any form, but must be "a humor poem that has been submitted to a 'vanity poetry contest' as a joke. See website for examples." Entries accepted only through website; no entries by regular mail. Guidelines available on website. **Entry fee:** none. **Deadline:** August 15-April 1. Competition receives about 750 entries/year. 2009 winner was Randy Cousteau. 2009 judge: Jendi Reiter. Winners announced on August 15 at WinningWriters.com and in free e-mail newsletter. "Please read the past winning entries and the judge's comments published at WinningWriters.com. Guidelines are a little unusual—please follow them closely. See separate listing for the War Poetry Contest in this section and for Winning Writers in the Additional Resources section.

$ ☑ THE WHITE PINE PRESS POETRY PRIZE

White Pine Press, P.O. Box 236, Buffalo NY 14201. E-mail: wpine@whitepine.org. Website: www.whitepine.org. **Contact:** Dennis Maloney, Editor. The White Pine Press

Poetry Prize offers $1,000 plus publication for a book-length collection of poems by a U.S. author. Submissions must be unpublished as a collection, but individual poems may have been previously published elsewhere. Submit 60-80 pages of poetry, typed, with table of contents. Include cover sheet with poet's name, address, e-mail address, and phone number. No e-mail submissions. Include SASP for notification of receipt of ms and SASE for results only; mss will not be returned. Guidelines available for SASE or on website. **Entry fee:** $20. Make checks payable to White Pine Press. **Deadline:** submit July 1-November 30 (postmark). Winner of the 14th Annual Award was Ansie Baird for *In Advance of All Parting*. Judge: poet of national reputation. Winning books available from local booksellers and White Pine Press.

$ ☑ MARJORIE J. WILSON AWARD FOR BEST POEM CONTEST

P.O. Box 250, Chesterfield MO 63006-0250. E-mail: margiereview@aol.com. Website: www.margiereview.com. The Marjorie J. Wilson Award for Best Poem Contest offers $1,000 and publication in MARGIE (see separate listing in Magazines/Journals). All entries will be considered for publication. Submissions must be unpublished. Considers simultaneous submissions. Submit 3 poems, 60-line limit/poem. Include single cover sheet with poet's name, address, phone number, e-mail (if available), and poem titles. No names should appear on the poems themselves; do not send originals. Include SASE for results only; submissions will not be returned. Guidelines available for SASE or on website. **Entry fee:** $15 for 3 poems; $5 for each additional poem. Make checks payable to MARGIE, Inc. **Deadline:** To be announced.

WISCONSIN INSTITUTE FOR CREATIVE WRITING FELLOWSHIP

University of Wisconsin-Madison, Creative Writing, English Dept 6195B H.C. White Hall, 600 N. Park St, Madison WI 53706. (608)263-3374. E-mail: rfkuka@wisc.edu. Website: www.creativewriting.wisc.edu. **Contact:** Ron Kuka, program coordinator. Fellowship provides time, space and an intellectual community for writers working on first books. Receives approximately 300 applicants a year for each genre. Prize: $27,000 for a 9-month appointment. Judged by English Department faculty and current fellows. **Entry fee:** $40, payable to the Department of English. Applicants should submit up to 10 pages of poetry or one story of up to 30 pages and a résumé or vita directly to the program during the month of February. An applicant's name must not appear on the writing sample (which must be in ms form) but rather on a separate sheet along with address, social security number, phone number, e-mail address and title(s) of submission(s). Candidates should also supply the names and phone numbers of two references. Accepts inquiries by e-mail and phone. **Deadline: February**. "Candidates must not yet have published, or had accepted for publication, a book by application deadline." Open to any writer with either an M.F.A. or Ph.D. in creative writing. Please enclose a SASE for notification of results. Results announced by May 1. "Send your best work. Stories seem to have a small advantage over novel excerpts."

$ ☑ WORKING PEOPLE'S POETRY COMPETITION

Blue Collar Review, P.O. Box 11417, Norfolk VA 23517. E-mail: red-ink@earthlink.net. Website: www.partisanpress.org. The Working People's Poetry Competition offers $100 and a one-year subscription to Blue Collar Review (see separate listing in Magazines/ Journals) and "one year posting on of winning poem on our website. Poetry should be typed as you would like to see it published, with your name and address on each page. Include cover letter with entry." Guidelines available on website. **Entry fee:** $15 per poem. Make checks payable to Partisan Press. **Deadline: May 1**. Previous winner was Luke Salazar.

$ ☐ WRITERS-EDITORS NETWORK INTERNATIONAL WRITING COMPETITION

(formerly CNW/FFWA Florida State Writing Competition), Florida Freelance Writers Association, P.O. Box A, North Stratford NH 03590-0167. (603)922-8338. E-mail: contest@ writers-editors.com. Website: www.writers-editors.com. Established 1978. **Contact:** Dana K. Cassell, award director. Offers annual awards for nonfiction, fiction, children's literature, and poetry. Awards for each category are 1st Prize: $100 plus certificate; 2nd Prize: $75 plus certificate; 3rd Prize: $50 plus certificate; plus Honorable Mention certificates. Poetry submissions must be unpublished. Submit any number of poems on any subject in traditional forms, free verse, or children's. Entry form and guidelines available for SASE or on website. **Entry fee:** $3/poem (members), $5/poem (nonmembers). **Deadline:** March 15. Competition receives 350-400 entries/year. Competition is judged by writers, librarians, and teachers. Winners will be announced on May 31 by mail and on website.

ADDITIONAL CONTESTS & AWARDS

The following listings also contain information about contests and awards. Turn to the page numbers indicated for details about their offerings.

Grants

State & Provincial

Arts councils in the United States and Canada provide assistance to artists (including poets) in the form of fellowships or grants. These grants can be substantial and confer prestige upon recipients; however, **only state or province residents are eligible**. Because deadlines and available support vary annually, query first (with a SASE) or check Web sites for guidelines.

UNITED STATES ARTS AGENCIES

Alabama State Council on the Arts, 201 Monroe St., Montgomery AL 36130-1800. (334)242-4076. E-mail: staff@arts.alabama.gov. Website: www.arts.state.al.us.

Alaska State Council on the Arts, 411 W. Fourth Ave., Suite 1-E, Anchorage AK 99501-2343. (907)269-6610 or (888)278-7424. E-mail: aksca_info@eed.state.ak.us. Website: www.eed.state.ak.us/aksca.

Arizona Commission on the Arts, 417 W. Roosevelt St., Phoenix AZ 85003-1326. (602)771-6501. E-mail: info@azarts.gov. Website: www.azarts.gov.

Arkansas Arts Council, 1500 Tower Bldg., 323 Center St., Little Rock AR 72201. (501)324-9766. E-mail: info@arkansasarts.com. Website: www.arkansasarts.com.

California Arts Council, 1300 I St., Suite 930, Sacramento CA 95814. (916)322-6555. E-mail: info@caartscouncil.com. Website: www.cac.ca.gov.

Colorado Council on the Arts, 1625 Broadway, Suite 2700, Denver CO 80202. (303)892-3802. E-mail: online form. Website: www.coloarts.state.co.us.

Commonwealth Council for Arts and Culture (Northern Mariana Islands), P.O. Box 5553, CHRB, Saipan MP 96950. (670)322-9982 or (670)322-9983. E-mail: galaidi@vzpacifica. net. Website: www.geocities.com/ccacarts/ccacWebsite.html.

Connecticut Commission on Culture & Tourism, Arts Division, One Financial Plaza, 755 Main St., Hartford CT 06103. (860)256-2800. Website: www.cultureandtourism.org.

Delaware Division of the Arts, Carvel State Office Bldg., 4th Floor, 820 N. French St., Wilmington DE 19801. (302)577-8278 (New Castle Co.) or (302)739-5304 (Kent or Sussex Counties). E-mail: delarts@state.de.us. Website: www.artsdel.org.

District of Columbia Commission on the Arts & Humanities, 410 Eighth St. NW, 5th Floor, Washington DC 20004. (202)724-5613. E-mail: cah@dc.gov. Website: http://dcarts.dc.gov.

Florida Arts Council, Division of Cultural Affairs, R.A. Gray Building, Third Floor, 500 S. Bronough St., Tallahassee FL 32399-0250. (850)245-6470. E-mail: info@florida-arts.org. Website: http://dcarts.dc.gov.

Georgia Council for the Arts, 260 14th St., Suite 401, Atlanta GA 30318. (404)685-2787. E-mail: gaarts@gaarts.org. Website: www.gaarts.org.

Guam Council on the Arts & Humanities Agency, P.O. Box 2950, Hagatna GU 96932. (671)646-2781. Website: www.guam.net.

Hawaii State Foundation on Culture & the Arts, 2500 S. Hotel St., 2nd Floor, Honolulu HI 96813. (808)586-0300. E-mail: ken.hamilton@hawaii.gov. Website: http.state.hi.us/sfca.

Idaho Commission on the Arts, 2410 N. Old Penitentiary Rd., Boise ID 83712. (208)334-2119 or (800)278-3863. E-mail: info@arts.idaho.gov. Website: www.arts.idaho.gov.

Illinois Arts Council, James R. Thompson Center, 100 W. Randolph, Suite 10-500, Chicago IL 60601. (312)814-6750. E-mail: iac.info@illinois.gov. Website: www.state.il.us/agency/iac.

Indiana Arts Commission, 150 W. Market St., Suite 618, Indianapolis IN 46204. (317)232-1268. E-mail: IndianaArtsCommission@iac.in.gov. Website: www.in.gov/arts.

Institute of Puerto Rican Culture, P.O. Box 9024184, San Juan PR 00902-4184. (787)724-0700. E-mail: www@icp.gobierno.pr. Website: www.icp.gobierno.pr.

Iowa Arts Council, 600 E. Locust, Des Moines IA 50319-0290. (515)281-6412. Website: www.iowaartscouncil.org.

Kansas Arts Commission, 700 SW Jackson, Suite 1004, Topeka KS 66603-3761. (785)296-3335. E-mail: KAC@arts.state.ks.us. Website: http://arts.state.ks.us.

Kentucky Arts Council, 21st Floor, Capital Plaza Tower, 500 Mero St., Frankfort KY 40601-1987. (502)564-3757 or (888)833-2787. E-mail: kyarts@ky.gov. Website: http://artscouncil.ky.gov.

Louisiana Division of the Arts, Capitol Annex Bldg., 1051 N. 3rd St., 4th Floor, Room #420, Baton Rouge LA 70804. (225)342-8180. Website: www.crt.state.la.us/arts.

Maine Arts Commission, 193 State St., 25 State House Station, Augusta ME 04333-0025.

(207)287-2724. E-mail: MaineArts.info@maine.gov. Website: www.mainearts.com.

Maryland State Arts Council, 175 W. Ostend St., Suite E, Baltimore MD 21230. (410)767-6555. E-mail: msac@msac.org. Website: www.msac.org.

Massachusetts Cultural Council, 10 St. James Ave., 3rd Floor, Boston MA 02116-3803. (617)727-3668. E-mail: mcc@art.state.ma.us. Website: www.massculturalcouncil.org.

Michigan Council of History, Arts, and Libraries, 702 W. Kalamazoo St., P.O. Box 30705, Lansing MI 48909-8205. (517)241-4011. E-mail: artsinfo@michigan.gov. Website: www. michigan.gov/hal/0,1607,7-160-17445_19272—-,00.html.

Minnesota State Arts Board, Park Square Court, 400 Sibley St., Suite 200, St. Paul MN 55101-1928. (651)215-1600 or (800)866-2787. E-mail: msab@arts.state.mn.us. Website: www.arts.state.mn.us.

Mississippi Arts Commission, 501 N. West St., Suite 701B, Woolfolk Bldg., Jackson MS 39201. (601)359-6030. Website: www.arts.state.ms.us.

Missouri Arts Council, 815 Olive St., Suite 16, St. Louis MO 63101-1503. (314)340-6845 or (866)407-4752. E-mail: moarts@ded.mo.gov. Website: www.missouriartscouncil.org.

Montana Arts Council, 316 N. Park Ave., Suite 252, Helena MT 59620-2201. (406)444-6430. E-mail: mac@mt.gov. Website: www.art.state.mt.us.

National Assembly of State Arts Agencies, 1029 Vermont Ave. NW, 2nd Floor, Washington DC 20005. (202)347-6352. E-mail: nasaa@nasaa-arts.org. Website: www.nasaa-arts. org.

Nebraska Arts Council, 1004 Farnam St., Plaza Level, Omaha NE 68102. (402)595-2122 or (800)341-4067. Website: www.nebraskaartscouncil.org.

Nevada Arts Council, 716 N. Carson St., Suite A, Carson City NV 89701. (775)687-6680. E-mail: online form. Website: http://dmla.clan.lib.nv.us/docs/arts.

New Hampshire State Council on the Arts, 21/2 Beacon St., 2nd Floor, Concord NH 03301-4974. (603)271-2789. Website: www.nh.gov/nharts.

New Jersey State Council on the Arts, 225 W. State St., P.O. Box 306, Trenton NJ 08625. (609)292-6130. Website: www.njartscouncil.org.

New Mexico Arts, Dept. of Cultural Affairs, P.O. Box 1450, Santa Fe NM 87504-1450. (505)827-6490 or (800)879-4278. Website: www.nmarts.org.

New York State Council on the Arts, 175 Varick St., New York NY 10014. (212)627-4455. Website: www.nysca.org.

North Carolina Arts Council, 109 East Jones St., Cultural Resources Building, Raleigh NC 27601. (919)807-6500. E-mail: ncarts@ncmail.net. Website: www.ncarts.org.

North Dakota Council on the Arts, 1600 E. Century Ave., Suite 6, Bismarck ND 58503. (701)328-7590. E-mail: comserv@state.nd.us. Website: www.state.nd.us/arts.

Ohio Arts Council, 727 E. Main St., Columbus OH 43205-1796. (614)466-2613. Website: www.oac.state.oh.us.

Oklahoma Arts Council, Jim Thorpe Building, 2101 N. Lincoln Blvd., Suite 640, Oklahoma City OK 73105. (405)521-2931. E-mail: okarts@arts.ok.gov. Website: www.arts.state. ok.us.

Oregon Arts Commission, 775 Summer St. NE, Suite 200, Salem OR 97301-1280. (503)986-0082. E-mail: oregon.artscomm@state.or.us. Website: www.oregonartscommission. org.

Pennsylvania Council on the Arts, 216 Finance Bldg., Harrisburg PA 17120. (717)787-6883. Website: www.pacouncilonthearts.org.

Rhode Island State Council on the Arts, One Capitol Hill, Third Floor, Providence RI 02908. (401)222-3880. E-mail: info@arts.ri.gov. Website: www.arts.ri.gov.

South Carolina Arts Commission, 1800 Gervais St., Columbia SC 29201. (803)734-8696. E-mail: info@arts.state.sc.us. Website: www.southcarolinaarts.com.

South Dakota Arts Council, 711 E. Wells Ave., Pierre SD 57501-3369. (605)773-3301. E-mail: sdac@state.sd.us. Website: www.artscouncil.sd.gov.

Tennessee Arts Commission, 401 Charlotte Ave., Nashville TN 37243-0780. (615)741-1701. Website: www.arts.state.tn.us.

Texas Commission on the Arts, E.O. Thompson Office Building, 920 Colorado, Suite 501, Austin TX 78701. (512)463-5535. E-mail: front.desk@arts.state.tx.us. Website: www. arts.state.tx.us.

Utah Arts Council, 617 E. South Temple, Salt Lake City UT 84102-1177. (801)236-7555. Website: http://arts.utah.gov.

Vermont Arts Council, 136 State St., Drawer 33, Montpelier VT 05633-6001. (802)828-3291. E-mail: online form. Website: www.vermontartscouncil.org.

Virgin Islands Council on the Arts, 5070 Norre Gade, St. Thomas VI 00802-6872. (340)774-5984. Website: http://vicouncilonarts.org.

Virginia Commission for the Arts, Lewis House, 223 Governor St., 2nd Floor, Richmond VA 23219. (804)225-3132. E-mail: arts@arts.virginia.gov. Website: www.arts.state. va.us.

Washington State Arts Commission, 711 Capitol Way S., Suite 600, P.O. Box 42675, Olympia WA 98504-2675. (360)753-3860. E-mail: info@arts.wa.gov. Website: www. arts.wa.gov.

West Virginia Commission on the Arts, The Cultural Center, Capitol Complex, 1900 Kanawha Blvd. E., Charleston WV 25305-0300. (304)558-0220. Website: www. wvculture.org/arts.

Wisconsin Arts Board, 101 E. Wilson St., 1st Floor, Madison WI 53702. (608)266-0190. E-mail: artsboard@arts.state.wi.us. Website: www.arts.state.wi.us.

Wyoming Arts Council, 2320 Capitol Ave., Cheyenne WY 82002. (307)777-7742. E-mail: ebratt@state.wy.us. Website: http://wyoarts.state.wy.us.

CANADIAN PROVINCES ARTS AGENCIES

Alberta Foundation for the Arts, 10708-105 Ave., Edmonton AB T5H 0A1. (780)427-9968. Website: www.affta.ab.ca/index.shtml.

British Columbia Arts Council, P.O. Box 9819, Stn. Prov. Govt., Victoria BC V8W 9W3. (250)356-1718. E-mail: BCArtsCouncil@gov.bc.ca. Website: www.bcartscouncil.ca.

The Canada Council for the Arts, 350 Albert St., P.O. Box 1047, Ottawa ON K1P 5V8. (613)566-4414 or (800)263-5588 (within Canada). Website: www.canadacouncil.ca.

Manitoba Arts Council, 525-93 Lombard Ave., Winnipeg MB R3B 3B1. (204)945-2237 or (866)994-2787 (in Manitoba). E-mail: info@artscouncil.mb.ca. Website: www.artscouncil.mb.ca.

New Brunswick Arts Board (NBAB), 634 Queen St., Suite 300, Fredericton NB E3B 1C2. (506)444-4444 or (866)460-2787. Website: www.artsnb.ca.

Newfoundland & Labrador Arts Council, P.O. Box 98, St. John's NL A1C 5H5. (709)726-2212 or (866)726-2212. E-mail: nlacmail@nfld.net. Website: www.nlac.nf.ca.

Nova Scotia Department of Tourism, Culture, and Heritage, Culture Division, 1800 Argyle St., Suite 601, P.O. Box 456, Halifax NS B3J 2R5. (902)424-4510. E-mail: cultaffs@gov.ns.ca. Website: www.gov.ns.ca/dtc/culture.

Ontario Arts Council, 151 Bloor St. W., 5th Floor, Toronto ON M5S 1T6. (416)961-1660 or (800)387-0058 (in Ontario). E-mail: info@arts.on.ca. Website: www.arts.on.ca.

Prince Edward Island Council of the Arts, 115 Richmond St., Charlottetown PE C1A 1H7. (902)368-4410 or (888)734-2784. E-mail: info@peiartscouncil.com. Website: www.peiartscouncil.com.

Québec Council for Arts & Literature, 79 boul. René-Lévesque Est, 3e étage, Quebec QC G1R 5N5. (418)643-1707 or (800)897-1707. E-mail: info@calq.gouv.qc.ca. Website: www.calq.gouv.qc.ca.

The Saskatchewan Arts Board, 2135 Broad St., Regina SK S4P 1Y6. (306)787-4056 or (800)667-7526 (Saskatchewan only). E-mail: sab@artsboard.sk.ca. Website: www.artsboard.sk.ca.

Yukon Arts Funding Program, Cultural Services Branch, Dept. of Tourism & Culture, Government of Yukon, Box 2703 (L-3), Whitehorse YT Y1A 2C6. (867)667-8589 or (800)661-0408 (in Yukon). E-mail: arts@gov.yk.ca. Website: www.tc.gov.yk.ca/216.html.

Conferences, Workshops & Festivals

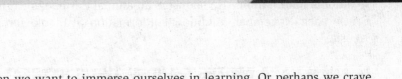

There are times when we want to immerse ourselves in learning. Or perhaps we crave a change of scenery, the creative stimulation of being around other artists, or the uninterrupted productivity of time alone to work.

That's what this section of Poet's Market is all about, providing a selection of writing conferences and workshops, artist colonies and retreats, poetry festivals, and even a few opportunities to go traveling with your muse. These listings give the basics: contact information, a brief description of the event, lists of past presenters, and offerings of special interest to poets. Contact an event that interests you for additional information, including up-to-date costs and housing details. **(Please note that most directors had not finalized their 2011 plans when we contacted them for this edition of *Poet's Market*. However, where possible, they provided us with their 2010 dates, costs, faculty names or themes to give you a better idea of what each event has to offer.)**

Before you seriously consider a conference, workshop or other event, determine what you hope to get out of the experience. Would a general conference with one or two poetry workshops among many other types of sessions be acceptable? Or are you looking for something exclusively focused on poetry? Do you want to hear poets speak about poetry writing, or are you looking for a more participatory experience, such as a one-on-one critiquing session or a group workshop? Do you mind being one of hundreds of attendees, or do you prefer a more intimate setting? Are you willing to invest in the expense of traveling to a conference, or would something local better suit your budget? Keep these questions and others in mind as you read these listings, view Web sites and study conference brochures.

Some listings are coded with symbols to provide certain "information at a glance." The (N) symbol indicates a recently established conference/workshop; the (✗) symbol indicates this conference/workshop did not appear in the 2010 edition; the (✿) symbol denotes a Canadian event and the (⊕) symbol one located outside the U.S. and Canada. The Additional Conferences & Workshops list at the end of this section cross-references conference, workshop and festival information in other sections of this book. To find out more, go to the page number indicated for each listing.

AMERICAN CHRISTIAN WRITERS CONFERENCES

P.O. Box 110390, Nashville TN 37222. (800)21-WRITE. E-mail: ACWriters@aol.com. Website: www.ACWriters.com. **Contact:** Reg Forder, director. Annual 2-day events. Holds 30 conferences/year in cities including Houston, Boston, Minneapolis, Chicago, St. Louis, Detroit, Atlanta, Miami, Phoenix, and Los Angeles. Location: usually a major hotel chain like Holiday Inn. Average attendance: 40-80.

Purpose/Features Open to anyone. Conferences cover fiction, poetry, writing for children. Offers poets ms critiques.

Costs/Accommodations Cost: $150-250. Participants responsible for all meals. Accommodations available on site.

Additional Information Also sponsors an annual Caribbean Christian Writers Conference Cruise each November. Additional information available for SASE, by e-mail, or on website.

⊞ ANAM CARA WRITER'S AND ARTIST'S RETREAT

Eyeries, Beara, Co. Cork , Ireland. (353)(027)74441. Fax: (353)(027)74448. E-mail: anamcararetreat@gmail.com. Website: www.anamcararetreat.com. **Contact:** Sue Booth-Forbes, director. Offers up to one-month individual retreats as well as workshops on a variety of creative subjects for writers and artists. Length of workshops varies with subject and leader/facilitator. Location: "Beara is a rural and hauntingly beautiful part of Ireland that is kept temperate by the Gulf Stream. The retreat sits on a hill overlooking Coulagh Bay, the mountains of the Ring of Kerry, and the Slieve Mishkish Mountains of Beara. The village of Eyeries is a short walk away." Average attendance: 5 residents at the retreat when working individually; 12-18 workshop participants.

Purpose/Features "Anam Cara is open to novice as well as professional writers and artists. Applicants are asked to provide a written description on the focus of their work while on retreat. Residencies are on a first-come, first-deposit-in basis." 2010 workshops included sessions on poetry, painting, haiku, creativity, creative nonfiction, fiction, screenwriting, and photography.

Costs/Accommodations 2010 cost: residency fee ranges from 600-700/week for individual retreats, depending on room, and includes full room and board; editorial consulting; laundry; sauna; hot tub overlooking Coulagh Bay; 5 acres of gardens, meadows, riverbank and cascades, river island, swimming hole, and several unique working spots, such as the ruin of a stone mill and a sod-roofed beehive hut. Workshop fees vary with subject and length; participants stay either at Anam Cara or at nearby B&Bs, a 10-minute scenic walk or 2-minute drive away. Transportation provided if needed. Details regarding transporation to Anam Cara available on website.

Additional Information Requests for specific information about rates and availability can be made through the website; also available by fax or e-mail.

⊞ ART WORKSHOPS IN GUATEMALA

4758 Lyndale Ave. S., Minneapolis MN 55419-5403. (612)825-0747. E-mail: info@artguat. org. Website: www.artguat.org. **Contact:** Liza Fourre, Director. Annual 10-day creative writing courses, held in February, March, July, and October. Location: workshops held in Antigua, the old colonial capital of Guatemala. Average attendance: limit 10 students.

Purpose/Features Art Workshops in Guatemala provides "the perfect getaway for creative writers of all skill levels looking for a memorable and inspiring writing/travel experience." Workshops include "Journey of the Soul" (with Sharon Doubiago) and "Snapshots in Words" (with Roseann Lloyd).

Costs/Accommodations 2009 cost: $1,845. Includes "tuition, lodging in a beautiful old colonial home, a hearty breakfast, ground transportation, and some pretty interesting cultural field trips."

Additional Information Individual poetry critiques included. Call, write, e-mail, or check website.

AUSTIN INTERNATIONAL POETRY FESTIVAL

(512)600-0837. E-mail: aipfdirector@gmail.com. Website: www.aipf.org. **Contact:** Ashley S. Kim, festival director. Annual 4-day, city-wide 19th annual festival including over 50 poetry events. 2011 dates: April 7-10. Location: Austin, TX. Average attendance: 300

Purpose/Features Open to the public. Poets register online at aipf.org. Over 25 International, National, Texas and Local Featured Poets in attendance, reading alongside over 250 registered poets at over 20 local Austin venues. 10 Adult Workshops. 10 Youth/teen events, 5 Music & poetry events, 2 Anthology competitions and 2 complete anthology readings (adult & youth), 2 Poetry slams, 1 All-Night Open Mic and a Saturday 7-Poet Symposium.

Costs/Accommodations Early poet registration is $35; Late poet registration fee (starting March 7th) is $50. Students and Senior Citizens $20. Includes anthology submission, festival program biography, one scheduled reading at one of AIPF's 15 venues, participation in all open mics, a catered meal, participation in all workshops (8+) and more.

Additional Information Anthology & Slam contests with Cash Prizes. Submission guidelines & Accommodations info available on website. Online registration process at www.aipf.org starts October 1st. Final Schedule and Festival Map available in March on the website. "Largest non-juried poetry festival in the U.S."

CAVE CANEM

20 Jay St., Suite 310-A, Brooklyn NY 11201. (718)858-0000. Fax: (718)858-0002. E-mail: alisonmeyers@ccpoets.org. Website: www.cavecanempoets.org. **Contact:** Alison Meyers, Executive Director. (Specialized: African American poets)584 Broadway, Suite 508, New York NY 10012. (212)941-5720. Fax: (212)941-5724. E-mail: alisonmeyers@ccpoets.org. Website: www.cavecanempoets.org. Established 1996. **Contact:** Alison Myers, executive director. Three-year fellowship, completed in five years. Successful candidates participate in an annual residency. Usually held last week in June. Location: University of Pittsburgh at Greensburg, PA. Average attendance: 54.

Purpose/Features Open to African American poets. Participants selected based on a sample of 6-8 poems. Offerings include workshops by fellows and faculty, evening readings. 2010 faculty included co-founders Toi Derricotte, Cornelius Eady, Colleen J. McElroy, Carl Phillips, Claudia Rankine, and Ed Roberson. Guest poet: Sapphire.

Costs/Accommodations 2010 cost: $500 for room and board. Tuition is free. For complete information, contact Cave Canem.

Additional Information Poets should submit 6-8 poems with cover letter. 2010 deadline:

January 31, 2010. Accepted poets notified by April 30. Cave Canem Foundation also sponsors the Cave Canem Poetry Prize and the Cave Canem Northwestern University Press Poetry Prize (see separate listing in Contests & Awards section).

THE COLRAIN POETRY MANUSCRIPT CONFERENCE

Concord Poetry Center, 40 Stow. St., Concord MA 01742. (978)897-0054. E-mail: conferences@colrainpoetry.com. Website: www.colrainpoetry.com. Established 2004. **Contact:** Joan Houlihan, founding director. Usually held 10 times/year in 3-day, weekend sessions. Location: Colrain, MA, Greenfield, MA, and others. Average attendance: 12 poets.

Purpose/Features "The first poetry conference realistically designed to set poets who have a completed manuscript or a manuscript-in-progress on a path toward book publication. Three-day intensive conference includes a manuscript preparation workshop and in-depth meetings with poetry press editors." Also offers evening poetry readings, an editorial panel Q& A, and an after-conference strategy session. 2009 faculty include Joan Houlihan (Concord Poetry Center), Frederick Marchant (Suffolk University), Jeffrey Levine (Tupelo Press), Martha Rhodes (Four Way Books), Jeffrey Shotts (Graywolf Press), Ellen Dore Watson (Smith College Poetry Center), and others.

Costs/Accommodations 2009 cost: $995-$1395, includes lodging, meals, and tuition.

Additional Information Details, application, and registration form available on website.

FINE ARTS WORK CENTER

24 Pearl St., Provincetown MA 02657. (508)487-9960. Fax: (508)487-8873. E-mail: workshops@fawc.org. Website: www.fawc.org. **Contact:** Dorothy Antczak, summer program director. Offers more than 70 weeklong and weekend workshops in poetry, fiction, and creative nonfiction. Location: The Fine Arts Work Center in Provincetown.

Purpose/Features The Fine Arts Work Center in Provincetown is "a nonprofit organization dedicated to providing emerging writers and visual artists with time and space in which to pursue independent work in a community of peers." Seven-month fellowships are awarded to poets and fiction writers in the emerging stages of their careers; professional juries make admissions decisions. The 2010 Summer Workshop program runs from June 13 through August 20, 2010.

Costs/Accommodations 2010 cost: Summer Workshop Program fees range $600-725. Accommodations available at the Work Center for $675 for 6 nights. Additional accommodations available locally.

Additional Information See website for details and an application form.

FISHTRAP

P.O. Box 38, Enterprise OR 97828. (541)426-3623. E-mail: director@fishtrap.org. **Contact:** Rick Bombaci, director. Holds annual summer workshops. 2010 dates: July 11-18. Location: "The old Methodist Camp at the edge of the Eagle Cap Wilderness." Average attendance: 12/workshop; 8 workshops offered, not all in poetry. Workshops followed by weekend "gathering" with readings, discussions, live music.

Purpose/Features Open to anyone. "Fishtrap's mission is to "promote good writing and clear thinking in and about the West; also to encourage and promote new writers." Offers poetry workshops, open mics, friendly and egalitarian atmosphere.

Costs/Accommodations 2010 cost: $450 for 5-day workshop; $75-250/person for cabin lodging; $50-200 for meals. Other accommodations available locally. Information on overnight accommodations available on website.

Additional Information Awards up to 5 fellowships. Covers room and board and workshop registration. Additional information available on website.

THE IWWG SUMMER CONFERENCE

The International Women's Writing Guild, P.O. Box 810, Gracie Station, New York NY 10028. (212)737-7536. Fax: (212)737-9469. E-mail: iwwg@iwwg.org. Website: www.iwwg.org. Established 1978. **Contact:** Hannelore Hahn, executive director. 2010 dates: July 30-August 6. Location: Brown University, Providence, RI. Average attendance: 450.

Purpose/Features Open to all women. Around 65 workshops offered each day. 2010 poetry staff included Marj Hahne, D.H. Melhem, Myra Shapiro, Susan Baugh, and Carol Peck.

Costs/Accommodations 2008 cost: $1,085 (single), $945 (double) for IWWG members; $1,130 (single), $990 (double) for nonmembers. Includes program and room and board for 7 nights, 21 meals at Skidmore College. Shorter conference stays available, such as 5 days or weekend. Commuters welcome.

Additional Information Post-conference retreat weekend also available. Additional information available for SASE, by e-mail, or on website.

JACKSON HOLE WRITERS CONFERENCE

P.O. Box 1974, Jackson WY 83001. (307)413-3331. E-mail: tim@jacksonholewriters conference.com. Website: www.jacksonholewritersconference.com. **Contact:** Tim Sandlin.

Purpose/Features Open to "all writers, fiction, poetry nonfiction, adventure/travel magazine, and young adult." Offers poets workshops, lectures, participant readings, and ms critiques. Poetry presenters for 2010 were: Laurie Kutchins, Jay Hopler, Kimberly Johnson, Kate Northrup, and H.L. Hix.

Costs/Accommodations 2010 cost was $355-385. Includes cocktail party, BBQ, and goodie bag with dining coupons. Accommodations available at area hotels.

Additional Information Brochure and registration form available by e-mail and on website.

JENTEL ARTIST RESIDENCY PROGRAM

Jentel Foundation, 130 Lower Piney Creek Rd., Banner WY 82832. (307)737-2311. Fax: (307)737-2305. E-mail: jentel@jentelarts.org. Website: www.jentelarts.org. One-month residencies throughout the year, scheduled the 15th of 1 month through the 13th of the following month. Application deadlines are September 15 and January 15 annually. Location: Banner, WY. Average attendance: 2 writers in any genre (also 4 visual artists in any media).

Purpose/Features Residency program for writers and visual artists who are U.S. citizens or from the international community currently residing in the U.S., are 25 years and older, and are not matriculated students. "Set in a rural ranch setting in the foothills of the Big Horn Mountains of North Central Wyoming, Jentel offers unfettered time and space to focus on the creative process, experience of Wyoming landscape, and interact as desired with a small community of writers and artists." Special features include Jentel Presents, a monthly evening of slide presentations and readings by residents in 1 of the surrounding communities.

Costs/Accommodations Residents are responsible for travel expenses and personal items. "Jentel provides a private accommodation in a shared living space, a comfortable private studio, and a stipend to help defray the cost of food and personal expenses. Staff takes residents grocery shopping weekly after the stipend is distributed. Staff will pick up and drop off residents at the airport and bus station in Sheridan, 20 miles from the ranch setting of Jentel." Accommodation provided in a large house with common living and dining areas; fully equipped kitchen; library with computer, printer, and Wireless Internet access; media room with television, DVD/video player, and CD player; spacious private bedroom; and separate private studio.

Additional Information Brochure and application form available for self-addressed mailing label and 58 cents postage, or on website.

THE KENYON REVIEW WRITERS WORKSHOP

Kenyon College, Gambier OH 43022. (740)427-5207. E-mail: writers@kenyonreview. org. Website: www.kenyonreview.org. **Contact:** Anna Duke Reach, Director of Summer Programs. Annual 8-day event. 2010 dates: June 19-26. Location: the Kenyon College campus. Average attendance: 10/class.

Purpose/Features Offers the time, setting, and community for writers to practice and develop their art. Focuses on the generation and revision of new work, although participants may bring works-in-progress. Offers poets one-on-one meetings with instructors, daily exercises and discussions, and public readings by distinguished visiting writers and workshop participants. 2010 poetry instructors were David Baker and Linda Gregerson.

Costs/Accommodations 2010 cost: $1,995 (includes tuition, room, and meals). A $200 discount is offered to returning participants. Participants are housed in modern campus apartments with computer access.

Additional Information College and non-degree graduate credit available. Online application form and writing sample submission available on website. Early application is encouraged as space is limited.

☐ KIMMEL HARDING NELSON CENTER FOR THE ARTS RESIDENCY PROGRAM

801 3rd Corso, Nebraska City NE 68410. 402-874-9600. Fax: 402-874-9600. E-mail: pfriedli@khncenterforthearts.org. Website: www.khncenterforthearts.org. **Contact:** Pat Friedli, Assistant Director. Residencies consisting of 2, 4, 6, or 8 week stays.

Purpose/Features See website for details. Application deadlines each year are March 1 and September 1.

Costs/Accommodations $25 application fee, participant responsible for all meals. $100/week stipend. Studios available on site.

KUNDIMAN POETRY RETREAT

245 Eighth Ave #151, New York NY 10011. E-mail: info@kundiman.org. Website: www.kundiman.org. **Contact:** Sarah Gambito, Executive Director.

Purpose/Features Open to Asian American poets. Offers poets workshops, lectures, faculty readings, fellow readings, and mentorship sessions with fellows. 2008 poetry presenters include Bei Dao, Tan Lin, and Aimee Nezhukumatathil.

Costs/Accommodations $350 - includes all housing and meal costs. Tuition is free to accepted fellows. Accommodations available on site.

Additional Information Guidelines available on website. Brochure and registration form available on website. "Open to Asian American poets. Renowned faculty will conduct workshops and provide one-on-one mentorship sessions with fellows. Readings and informal social gatherings will also be scheduled. Fellows selected based on sample of 6-8 poems and short essay answer. Applications should be received between February 1-March 1."

LIFE PRESS CHRISTIAN WRITERS' CONFERENCE

P.O. Box 2018, Cordova TN 38088. (901)309-3692. E-mail: gmoearth@gmail.com. Website: www.grandmotherearth.org. **Contact:** Frances Cowden, director. Annual one-day event. Location: Cordova, TN. Average attendance: 45.

Purpose/Features Open to all writers. Offers poets workshops, lectures, readings, and ms critiques. 2007 staff included Robert Hall, Florence Bruce, Cindy Beebe, and Sarah Hull Gurley.

Costs/Accommodations 2010 cost: $35 registration fee (includes one contest entry, critique of all entries, continental breakfast and lunch); $30 (includes registration with entries plus food, but no critique); or $25 (includes food, no entries); $20 fee for spouses. Information on overnight accommodations available in brochure.

Additional Information Individual poetry critiques available. Poets should submit a limit of 6 works/category and $10 fee. "One payment for all entries—send with entries." Sponsors contest for "poetry and prose in general, open to all writers. Other contests require attendance." National Awards for poetry (open to everyone, 50-line limit) are $50, $25, $15, and $10. Conference Awards for poetry (open to those who register for the conference, 30-line limit) are $50, $15, and $10. Entry fee: "$5 entitles you to one entry; $2 for each additional entry." Deadline: June 30. Critique from the judges is available for $10 for all entries. Guidelines available for SASE.

MONTEVALLO LITERARY FESTIVAL

Sta. 6420, University of Montevallo, Montevallo AL 35115. (205)665-6420. Fax: (205)665-6422. E-mail: murphyj@montevallo.edu. Website: www.montevallo.edu/english. **Contact:** Dr. Jim Murphy, Director. Annual day-long event. 2009 date: April 23. Location: several sites on the bucolic University of Montevallo campus. Average attendance: 60-100.

Purpose/Features Presents "a unique opportunity for participants to interact with some of the top writers in the country. Participants attend workshops in poetry, prose, or drama, working closely on their own writing with some of the country's most distinguished poets, fiction writers, playwrights, and writers of nonfiction." Offers poets readings, panels, workshops, and ms critiques. 2009 poetry workshop leader: Mitchell L.H. Douglas. Prior poetry workshop leaders have included Claudia Emerson, Angela Ball, Don Bogen, Andrew Hudgins, Rodney Jones, Jeff Thomson, Natasha Trethewey, Catherine Bowman, and Frank X Walker.

Costs/Accommodations 2009 cost: $45 for festival, including meals; $95 for festival, including meals and workshop. Offers overnight accommodations at Ramsay Conference Center on campus; rooms $40/night. Call (205)665-6280 for reservations. Free on-campus parking. Additional information available at www.montevallo.edu/cont_ed/ramsay.shtm.

Additional Information Poetry workshop participants submit up to 5 pages of poetry; e-mail as Word doc to Jim Murphy (murphyj@montevallo.edu) at least 2 weeks prior to festival. Brochure available on website. Information on upcoming festival available in February.

POETRY WEEKEND INTENSIVES

40 Post Ave., Hawthorne NJ 07506. (973)423-2921. Fax: (973)523-6085. E-mail: mariagillan@optonline.net. Website: www.pccc.edu/poetry. **Contact:** Maria Mazziotti Gillan, executive director. 40 Post Ave., Hawthorne NJ 07506. (973)423-2921. Fax: (973)523-6088. E-mail: mariagillan@msn.com. Website: www.pccc.cc.nj.us/poetry. Established 1997. **Contact:** Maria Mazziotti Gillan, executive director. Usually held 4 times/year in March, June, October, and December. Location: generally at St. Marguerite's Retreat House, an English manor house at the Convent of St. John the Baptist in Mendhan, NJ; also several other convents and monasteries. Average attendance: 26.

Purpose/Features Open to all writers. "The purpose of this retreat is to give writers the space and time to focus totally on their own work in a serene and beautiful setting away from the pressures and distractions of daily life." Sample theme: "Writing Your Way Home—Poetry of Memory and Place." "Writing weekend poets will find support and encouragement, stimulating activities leading to the creation of new work, workshop leaders who are actively engaged in the writing life, opportunities to read their work aloud to the group, a circle of writer friends, and networking opportunities." Poetry Weekend Intensives are led by Maria Mazziotti Gillan and Laura Boss. Other special features include one-on-one conferences with lead poet faculty.

Costs/Accommodations Cost $375, including meals. Offers a $25 early bird discount. Housing in on-site facilities included in the $375 price.

Additional Information Individual poetry critiques available. Poets should bring poems to weekend. Registration form available for SASE or by fax or e-mail. Maria Mazziotti Gillan is the director of the Creative Writing Program of Binghamton University—State University of New York, executive director of the Poetry Center at Passaic County Community College, and edits Paterson Literary Review. Laura Boss is the editor of Lips magazine. Fifteen professional development credits are available for each weekend.

⚌ SASKATCHEWAN FESTIVAL OF WORDS

Website: www.festivalofwords.com. Annual 4-day event. 2009 dates: July 16-19. Location: Moose Jaw Library/Art Museum complex in Crescent Park. Average attendance: about 4,000 admissions.

Purpose/Features "The Saskatchewan Festival of Words celebrates the imaginative uses of language, and features fiction and nonfiction writers, screenwriters, poets, children's authors, songwriters, dramatists, and film makers. Our festival is an ideal place for people who love words to mingle, promote their books, get acquainted, share ideas, conduct impromptu readings, and meet their fans." Offers poets workshops, readings, and open mics. 2009 program of 34 presenters included Jack Whyte, Marina Endicott, Joan Barfoot, Tom Wayman, Anna Porter, Bruce Dowbiggin, Sharon Pollock, and Mary Lou Finlay. 2010 dates were July 15-18.

Additional Information Complete information about festival presenters, events, costs, and schedule available on website. Festival presented by Saskatchewan Festival of Words Inc.

SOMOS, SOCIETY OF THE MUSE OF THE SOUTHWEST

P.O. Box 3225, Taos NM 87571. (575)758-0081. Fax: (575)758-4802. E-mail: somos@laplaza.com. Website: www.somostaos.org. P.O. Box 3225, 233B Paseo del Pueblo Sur, Taos NM 87571. (575)758-0081. Fax: (575)758-4802. E-mail: somos@laplaza.com. Website: www.somostaos.org. Established 1983. **Contact:** Dori Vinella, executive director. "We offer readings, special events, and workshops at different times during the year." Length of workshops varies. Location: various sites in Taos. Average attendance: 10-50.

Purpose/Features Open to anyone. "We offer workshops in various genres—fiction, poetry, nature writing, etc." Past workshop presenters have included Denise Chavez, Marjorie Agosin, Judyth Hill, Robin Becker, Sawnie Morris, and Lise Goett. Other special features include the 2-day Annual Taos Storytelling Festival in October, a Winter Writers Series (January-February), and Summer Writer's Series (July-August).

Costs/Accommodations See website for current information.

Additional Information Additional information available by fax, e-mail, or on website. "Taos has a wonderful community of dedicated and talented writers who make S.O.M.O.S. workshops rigorous, supportive, and exciting." Also publishes Chokecherries, an annual anthology.

SOUTHAMPTON WRITERS CONFERENCE

Stony Brook Southampton, 239 Montauk Hwy., Southampton NY 11968. (631)632-5030. E-mail: southamptonwriters@notes.cc.sunysb.edu. Website: www.stonybrook.edu/writers. **Contact:** Adrienne Unger, coordinator. Annual 11-day event. 2010 dates: July 14-25. Location: Stony Brook Southampton's seaside campus "in the heart of the Hamptons." Average attendance: 12/workshop.

Purpose/Features Open to new and established writers, graduate students, and upper-level undergraduate students. Offers poetry workshops and readings. 2010 poetry staff included Billy Collins and Thomas Lux.

Costs/Accommodations 2009 cost: $25 application fee; $2,175 for workshop, room and board; $1,575 workshop only (includes breakfast and lunch). Accommodations available on site.

Additional Information "Evening events will feature regular faculty and award-winning visiting authors. Participants will also enjoy a rich schedule of formal and informal social gatherings—author receptions, open mic nights, and special literary events. Early application is encouraged." Brochure and registration form available by e-mail or on website.

SPLIT ROCK ARTS PROGRAM SUMMER WORKSHOPS

University of Minnesota, 360 Coffey Hall, 1420 Eckles Ave., St. Paul MN 55108-6084. (612)625-1976. E-mail: srap@cce.umn.edu. Website: www.cce.umn.edu/splitrockarts. **Contact:** Anastasia Faunce, Program Director. Three day seasonal retreats and summer series of weeklong and 3-day workshops in creative writing, visual art, and design. 2010 dates: June 13-July 23. Locations: University's Twin Cities campus and Cloquet Forestry Center in Northern MN. Average attendance: 500.

Purpose/Features Open to anyone over 18 years old interested in writing and literature. Offers writers a variety of workshops in all genres and with renowned faculty. 2010 faculty included Nancy Carlson, Robin Hemley, Matthew Specktor, Michael Martone, Joyce Sutphen, Catherine Watson, Larry Watson, Carole Boston Weatherford, and more.

Costs/Accommodations 2010 cost: $555 tuition (noncredit); undergraduate/graduate credit available for additional fee. Scholarships available. Participants responsible for most meals. Accommodations available on site or at area hotels. Registration opens in late February. Additional information available on website.

SQUAW VALLEY COMMUNITY OF WRITERS POETRY WORKSHOP

P.O. Box 1416, Nevada City CA 95959. (530)470-8440. E-mail: info@squawvalleywriters. org. Website: www.squawvalleywriters.org. Established 1969. **Contact:** Brett Hall Jones, executive director. Annual 7-day event. 2010 dates: July 17-24. Location: The Squaw Valley USA's Lodge in the Sierras near Lake Tahoe. Average attendance: 60 for poetry.

Purpose/Features The Poetry Program is founded "on the belief that when poets gather in a community to write new poems, each poet may well break through old habits and write something stronger and truer than before. To help this happen we work together to create an atmosphere in which everyone might feel free to try anything. In the mornings we meet in workshops to read to each other the work of the previous 24 hours; each participant also has an opportunity to work with each staff poet. In the late afternoons we gather for a conversation about some aspect of craft. On several late afternoons staff poets hold brief individual conferences." 2010 poetry staff includes Kazim Ali, Forrest Gander, Brenda Hillman, Evie Shockley, Dean Young.

Costs/Accommodations 2010 cost: $760 for poetry tuition (includes 6 evening meals), $25 reading/application fee. Accommodations extra. "We arrange housing for participants in local houses and condominiums at a variety of rates." Information on overnight accommodations available on website.

Additional Information A limited amount of financial aid is available. Brochure available by e-mail (include mailing address for response) or on website. Also publishes the annual

Squaw Valley Community of Writers Omnium Gatherum and Newsletter containing "news and profiles on our past participants and staff, craft articles, and book advertising."

STEAMBOAT SPRINGS WRITERS CONFERENCE

P.O. Box 774284, Steamboat Springs CO 80477. (970)879-8138. E-mail: info@steamboatwriters.com. Website: www.steamboatwriters.com. **Contact:** Susan de Wardt, director. Annual one-day event usually held in mid-July. Location: a "renovated train station, the Depot is home of the Steamboat Springs Arts Council—friendly, relaxed atmosphere." Average attendance: 35-40 (registration limited).

Purpose/Features Open to anyone. Conference is "designed for writers who have limited time. Instructors vary from year to year, offering maximum instruction during a weekend at a nominal cost." Previous poetry instructors include Marilyn Krysl, Matthew Cooperman, David Mason, Renate Wood, Jim Tipton, and Donald Revell.

Costs/Accommodations 2010 cost: $60 before May 19; then $70. Includes pre-conference gathering, seminar and catered luncheon. "A variety of lodgings available."

Additional Information Brochure and registration form available for SASE, by e-mail, or on website. Optional: Friday evening readings by participants (no cost).

⊕ T NEWYDD WRITERS' CENTRE

Llanystumdwy, Criccieth, Gwynedd WA LL52 0LW, United Kingdom. (44) (1766) 522 811. Fax: (44) (1766) 523 095. E-mail: post@tynewydd.org. Website: www.tynewydd.org. **Contact:** Executive Director. Runs courses throughout the year, as well as writers' retreats. Location: Tŷ Newydd, The National Writers' Centre for Wales. Average attendance: maximum of 16 on any course.

Purpose/Features Open to anyone over 16 years of age. Courses are designed to "promote the writing and understanding of literature by providing creative writing courses at all levels for all ages. Courses at Ty Newydd provide the opportunity of working intimately and informally with two professional writers." Courses specifically for poets of all levels of experience and ability are offered throughout the year.

Costs/Accommodations 2010 cost: 5 nights' stay £525 (single room) and £450 (shared room). Please refer to website for costs in respect to shorter courses and further information about accommodation.

Additional Information Brochure and registration form available for SASE, or request by e-mail.

UNIVERSITY OF NORTH DAKOTA WRITERS CONFERENCE

Dept. of English, Box 7209, University of North Dakota, Grand Forks ND 58202. (701)777-3987. E-mail: writersconference@und.nodak.edu. Website: www.writersconference.und.edu. **Contact:** Kathy King, administrative director. Established 1970. Annual 4- to 5-day event. 2011 dates: March 29-April 2. Location: the University of North Dakota Memorial Union. Average attendance: 3,000-5,000. "Some individual events have as few as 20, some over 1,000."

Purpose/Features Offers poets panel discussions, readings, and book signings. 2010 poetry staff included Frank X. Walker and Saul Williams.

Costs/Accommodations All events are free and open to the public. Accommodations available at area hotels. Information on overnight accommodations available on website.

Additional Information Schedule and other information available on website.

VERMONT STUDIO CENTER

P.O. Box 613, Johnson VT 05656. (802)635-2727. Fax: (802)635-2730. E-mail: writing@ vermontstudiocenter.org. Website: www.vermontstudiocenter.org.. **Contact:** Gary Clark, Writing Program Director. From 2-12 weeks, year-round; most residents stay for 4 weeks. Community size: 50 + writers and visual artists/month.

Purpose/Features "The Vermont Studio Center is an international creative community located in Johnson, Vermont, and serving more than 600 American and international artists and writers each year (50 per month). A Studio Center Residency features secluded, uninterrupted writing time, the companionship of dedicated and talented peers, and access to a roster of two distinguished Visiting Writers each month. All VSC Residents receive three meals a day, private, comfortable housing and the company of an international community of painters, sculptors, poets, printmakers and writers. Writers attending residencies at the Studio Center may work on whatever they choose—no matter what month of the year they attend." Offers poets participant readings.

Costs/Accommodations "The cost of a 4-week residency is $3,750. Generous fellowship and grant assistance available. "Accommodations available on site. "Residents live in single rooms in ten modest, comfortable houses adjacent to the Red Mill Building. Rooms are simply furnished and have shared baths. Complete linen service is provided. The Studio Center is unable to accommodate guests at meals, overnight guests, spouses, children or pets."

Additional Information Fellowships application deadlines are February 15, June 15 and October 1. Writers encouraged to visit website for more information. May also e-mail, call, fax.

WESLEYAN WRITERS CONFERENCE

Wesleyan University, Middletown CT 06457. (860)685-3604. Fax: (860)685-2441. E-mail: agreene@wesleyan.edu. Website: www.wesleyan.edu/writers. Established 1956. **Contact:** Anne Greene, director. Annual 5-day event. 2010 dates: Thurs June 17-Mon, June 21. Location: the campus of Wesleyan University "in the hills overlooking the Connecticut River, a brief drive from the Connecticut shore. Wesleyan's outstanding library, poetry reading room, and other university facilities are open to participants." Average attendance: 100.

Purpose/Features "The conference welcomes everyone interested in the writer's craft, and participants are a diverse, international group. Both new and experienced writers are welcome. You may attend all of the seminars, including poetry, the novel, short story, fiction techniques, literary journalism, memoir, and multi-media work." Offers poets workshops, seminars, lectures, readings, ms critiques, meetings with editors and agents, and special panel presentations. Recent poetry presenters include Honor Moore, Mark Doty, Peter Gizzi, Elizabeth Willis, Sherwin Bitsui, Jeffrey Harrison, Laura Cronk, Ravi Shankar.

Costs/Accommodations See website for current rates. 2010 cost: $850 tuition only); $1,125 day student rate with meals; $1,298 boarding student rate (includes tuition, meals, room for 5 nights). Accommodations available on site or at area hotels. Information on overnight accommodations available on website.

Additional Information Scholarships/teaching fellowships offered. Additional information available by phone, fax, or on website.

WINTER POETRY & PROSE GETAWAY IN CAPE MAY

18 North Richards Ave., Ventnor NJ 08406. (888)887-2105. E-mail: info@wintergetaway. com. Website: www.wintergetaway.com. **Contact:** Peter E. Murphy, founder/director. Annual 4-day event. 2011 dates: January 14-17. Location: The Grand Hotel on the Oceanfront in Historic Cape May, NJ. Average attendance: 200 (10 or fewer participants in each poetry workshop).

Purpose/Features Open to all writers, beginners and experienced, over the age of 18. "This is not your typical writers' conference. Energize your writing with challenging and supportive workshops that focus on starting new material. Advance your craft with feedback from our award-winning faculty including Pulitzer Prize and National Book Award winners. The focus in on helping you improve and advance your skills and features a variety of poetry and prose workshops, each with 10 or fewer participants." Previous faculty has included Renee Ashley, Laure-Anne Bosselaar, Kurt Brown, Catherine Doty, Mark Doty, Stephen Dunn, Douglas Goetsch, Kathleen Graber, James Richardson, and many more. Workshops are available in poetry manuscript, poetry chapbook, memoir, creative nonfiction, novel, short story, children's market, songwriting, and more.

Costs/Accommodations Workshop held in historic Cape May, New Jersey. See website or call for current fee information.

Additional Information Brochure and registration form available on web site. "The Getaway is a conference where you will write! You will receive feedback but the workshops emphasize creating new material or revising works in progress. It is open to all writers, beginners and experienced, over the age of 18. Teachers can earn 17 hours of professional development credit as well as graduate credit from Rutgers University."

Resources

ADDITIONAL CONFERENCES/WORKSHOPS/FESTIVALS

The following cross-references listings in other sections of this book that include information about conferences, workshops, conventions and festivals. Among these are state and local poetry groups that may offer a variety of workshop opportunities for their members.

Resources

Organizations

There are many organizations of value to poets. These groups may sponsor workshops and contests, stage readings, publish anthologies and chapbooks or spread the word about publishing opportunities. A few provide economic assistance or legal advice. The best thing organizations offer, though, is a support system to which poets can turn for a pep talk, a hard-nosed (but sympathetic) critique of a manuscript or simply the comfort of talking and sharing with others who understand the challenges, and joys, of writing poetry.

Whether national, regional or as local as your library or community center, each organization has something special to offer. The listings in this section reflect the membership opportunities available to poets with a variety of organizations. Some groups provide certain services to both members and nonmembers.

These symbols may appear at the beginning of some listings: The (▧) symbol indicates a recently established organization new to *Poet's Market*; the (▨) symbol indicates this organization did not appear in the 2010 edition; the (▧) symbol denotes a Canadian organization and the (▦) symbol one headquartered outside the U.S. and Canada.

Since some organizations are included in listings in the other sections of this book, we've cross-referenced these listings under Additional Organizations at the end of this section. For further details about an organization associated with a market in this list, go to that market's page number.

To find out more about groups in your area (including those that may not be listed in *Poet's Market*), contact your YMCA, community center, local colleges and universities, public library and bookstores (and don't forget newspapers and the Internet). If you can't find a group that suits your needs, consider starting one yourself. You might be surprised to discover there are others in your locality who would welcome the encouragement, feedback and moral support of a writer's group.

92ND STREET Y UNTERBERG POETRY CENTER

1395 Lexington Ave., New York NY 10128. (212)415-5760. E-mail:unterberg@92y.org. Website: www.92y.org/Poetry. Established 1939. The Unterberg Poetry Center offers "students of all ages the opportunity to hone their skills as writers and deepen their appreciation as readers." Offers annual series of readings by major literary figures (weekly readings late September through May), writing workshops, master classes in fiction and poetry, and lectures and literary seminars. Also co-sponsors the "Discovery"/ Boston Review Poetry Contest (see separate listing in Contests & Awards). This year's deadline is January 14, 2011 by 5 pm.

⊕ ACADEMI—YR ACADEMI GYMREIG/THE WELSH ACADEMY

(44)(29)2047-2266. Fax: (44)(29)2049-2930. E-mail: post@academi.org. Website: www. academi.org. Academi is the Welsh National Literature Promotion Agency and Society of Writers and is open to "the population of Wales and those outside Wales with an interest in Welsh writing." Currently has 2,000 members. Levels of membership/dues: associate, full, and fellow; £15/year (waged) or £7.50/year (unwaged). Offerings include promotion of readings, events, conferences, exchanges, tours; employment of literature-development workers; publication of a quarterly events magazine; publication of a literary magazine in Welsh (*Taliesin*). Sponsors conferences/workshops and contests/awards. Publishes A470: What's On In Literary Wales , a magazine appearing quarterly containing information on literary events in Wales. Available to nonmembers for £15 (annual subscription). Academi is also a resident company of the Wales Millenium Centre, where it runs the Glyn Jones Centre, a resource centre for writers and the public. Additional information available for SASE (or SAE and IRC), by fax, e-mail, or on website.

AMERICAN BOOKSELLERS FOUNDATION FOR FREE EXPRESSION

275 7th Ave., Suite 1504, New York NY 10001. (212)587-4025 ext. 15. Fax: (212)587-2436. E-mail: chris@abffe.com. Website: www.abffe.com. "The American Booksellers Foundation for Free Expression is the bookseller's voice in the fight against censorship. Founded by the American Booksellers Association, ABFFE's mission is to promote and protect the free exchange of ideas, particularly those contained in books, by opposing restrictions on the freedom of speech; issuing statements on significant free expression controversies; participating in legal cases involving First Amendment rights; collaborating with other groups with an interest in free speech; and providing education about the importance of free expression to booksellers, other members of the book industry, politicians, the press and the public." Levels of membership/dues: $50. "ABFFE is the bookseller's voice in all free speech controversies involving books and other written material. We alerted booksellers to the dangers posed by the USA Patriot Act and helped them communicate their concerns to Congress. We are also active on the local level. ABFFE opposes efforts to ban books in public schools and libraries and files amicus briefs in cases challenging school censorship." Additional information available on website.

ARIZONA AUTHORS ASSOCIATION

6145 W Echo Lane, Glendale, AZ 85302. (623)847-9343. E-mail: info@azauthors.com. Website: www.azauthors.com. Established 1978. **Contact:** Toby Heathcotte, president.

Provides education and referral for writers and others in publishing. Statewide organization. Currently has 200 members. Levels of membership/dues: Published, Unpublished (seeking publication), Professional (printers, agents, and publishers), and Student; $45/year for authors, $30/year students, $60/year professionals. Sponsors conferences, workshops, contests, awards. Sponsors annual literary contest in poetry, short story, essay, unpublished novels, and published books (fiction, children's, and nonfiction). Publishes Arizona Literary Magazine and Arizona Authors Newsletter . Members meet monthly. Additional information available on website.

THE BEATLICKS

1300 El Paseo Road, Suite G #308, Las Cruces NM 88001. E-mail: beatlickjoe@yahoo.com. Website: www.beatlick.com. International organization open to "anyone interested in literature." Currently has 200 members. "There is no official distinction between members, but there is a core group that does the work, writes reviews, organizes readings, etc." Offerings include publication of work (have published poets from Australia, Egypt, India, and Holland) and reviews of books and venues. Publishes Beatlick News 4 times/year, a networking tool designed to inform poets of local events and to bring awareness of the national scene. "We include poems, short fiction, art, photos, and articles about poets and venues." Submit short pieces, no vulgar language. "We try to elevate the creative spirit. We publish new voices plus well-established talents." Subscription: $15/year. Additional information available for SASE or by e-mail. "We promote all the arts."

BRIGHT HILL LITERARY CENTER

P.O. Box 193, 94 Church St., Treadwell NY 13846-0193. (607)829-5055. Fax: (607)829-5054. E-mail: wordthur@stny.rr.com. Website: www.brighthillpress.org. Bright Hill Literary Center serves residents in the Catskill Mountain region, greater New York, and throughout the U.S. Includes the Bright Hill Library & Internet Center, with "thousands of volumes of literary journals, literary prose and poetry, literary criticism and biography, theater, reference, art, and children's books available for reading and research (noncirculating, for the time being). Wireless Internet access is available." Sponsors workshops for children and adults. Sponsors contests/awards (Bright Hill Press book and chapbook competitions; see separate listings in Contests & Awards). Publishes 5-7 books of poetry each year.

◘ BURNABY WRITERS' SOCIETY

E-mail: info@bws.bc.ca. Website: www.bws.bc.ca. Corresponding membership in the society, including a newsletter subscription, is open to anyone, anywhere. Currently has 100 members. Levels of membership/dues: regular ($30 CAD); students/seniors ($20 CAD/year). Sample newsletter in return for SASE with Canadian stamp. Holds monthly meetings at The Burnaby Arts Centre (located at 6450 Deer Lake Ave.), with a business meeting at 7:30 followed by a writing workshop or speaker. Members of the society stage regular public readings of their own work. Sponsors open mic readings for the public. Sponsors a poetry contest open to British Columbia residents. Competition receives about 100-200 entries/year. Past contest winners include Mildred Tremblay,

Irene Livingston, and Kate Braid. Additional information available on website or news blog at burnabywritersnews.blogspot.com.

CALIFORNIA STATE POETRY SOCIETY

CSPS/CQ, P.O. Box 7126, Orange CA 92863. E-mail: pearlk@covad.net. The California State Poetry Society "is dedicated to the adventure of poetry and its dissemination. Although located in California, its members are from all over the U.S. and abroad." Levels of membership/dues: $30/year. Benefits include membership in the National Federation of State Poetry Societies (NFSPS); 4 issues of California Quarterly (see separate listing in Magazines/Journals), *Newsbriefs*, and *The Poetry Letter*. Sponsors monthly and annual contests. Additional information available for SASE.

◪ CANADIAN POETRY ASSOCIATION

331 Elmwood Dr., Suite 4-212, Moncton NB E1A 1X6, Canada. (506)204-1732. Fax: (506)380-1222. E-mail: poemata@live.ca; poemata@live.com. Website: www. canadianpoetryassoc.com. "We promote all aspects of the reading, writing, publishing, purchasing, and preservation of poetry in Canada. The CPA promotes the creation of local chapters to organize readings, workshops, publishing projects, and other poetry-related events in their area." Membership is open to anyone with an interest in poetry, including publishers, schools, libraries, booksellers, and other literary organizations. Levels of membership/dues: $35 CAD/year; seniors, students, and fixed income, $25 CAD; International, $45 USD. Publishes a magazine, Poemata , featuring news articles, chapter reports, poetry by new members, book reviews, markets information, announcements, and more. Membership form available for SASE or on website. Also sponsors The CPA Annual Poetry Contest, with 3 cash prizes plus up to 10 Honorable Mentions. **Open to the public.** Winning poems published in Poemata and on CPA website. **Deadline:** June 30, 2010. Guidelines available for SASE or on website. "Send in your best verse!"

COLUMBINE POETS OF COLORADO

8989 Yukon St., Westminster CO 80021. (303)431-6774. E-mail: anitajg5@aol.com. Website: http://columbinepoets.pbworks.com. **Contact:** Anita Jepson-Gilbert, secretary/treasurer. Statewide organization open to anyone interested in poetry. Currently has around 100 members in 3 Chapters, now in Denver, Salida, and Loveland, CO. An affiliate of the National Federation of State Poetry Societies (NFSPS). Levels of membership/dues: $15 for Members-at-Large, (includes membership in the national and state societies), and $35 (includes membership in the national, state, and local Foothills Chapter in Denver). Offerings for the Denver Foothills Chapter include weekly workshops and monthly critiques. Sponsors contests, awards for students and adults, an Annual Poetry Fest and some publications. Additional information available with SASE, by phone or e-mail.

CONNECTICUT POETRY SOCIETY

P.O. Box 702, Manchester CT 06040. E-mail: connpoetry@comcast.net. Website: www. ct-poetry-society.org/. Established 1978. **Contact:** Christine Beck, president. The Connecticut Poetry Society is a nonprofit organization dedicated to the promotion and enjoyment of poetry through chapter meetings, contests, and poetry-related events.

Statewide organization open to non-Connecticut residents. Currently has about 175 members. Levels of membership/dues: full, $25/year; student, $10/year. Membership benefits include automatic membership in The National Federation of State Poetry Societies (NFSPS); a free copy of The Connecticut River Review , a national poetry journal published by CPS (see separate listing in Magazines/Journals); opportunity to publish in Long River Run II , a members-only poetry journal; quarterly CPS and NFSPS newsletters; annual April poetry celebration; and membership in any of 10 state chapters. Sponsors conferences and workshops. Sponsors The Connecticut River Review Annual Poetry Contest, The Brodinsky-Brodine Contest, The Winchell Contest, and The Lynn Decaro High School Competition. Members and nationally known writers give readings that are open to the public. Members meet monthly. Additional information available by SASE or on website.

GEORGIA POETRY SOCIETY

P.O. Box 2184, Columbia GA 31902. E-mail: gps@georgiapoetrysociety.org. Website: www. georgiapoetrysociety.org. Statewide organization open to any person who is in accord with the objectives to secure fuller public recognition of the art of poetry, stimulate an appreciation of poetry, and enhance the writing and reading of poetry. Currently has 200 members. Levels of membership/dues: Active, $30 ($40 family), fully eligible for all aspects of membership; Student, $15, does not vote or hold office, and must be full-time enrolled student through college level; Lifetime, same as Active but pays a one-time membership fee of $500, receives free anthologies each year, and pays no contest entry fees. Membership includes affiliation with NFSPS. Holds at least one workshop annually. Contests are sponsored throughout the year, some for members only. "Our contests have specific general rules, which should be followed to avoid the disappointment of disqualification. See the website for details." Publishes Georgia Poetry Society Newsletter , a quarterly, and The Reach of Song , an annual anthology devoted to contest-winning poems and member works. Each quarterly meeting (open to the public) features at least one poet of regional prominence. Also sponsors a monthly open mic at the Columbus Library (Macon Rd) in Columbus, GA (open to the public). Sponsors Poetry in the Schools project. Additional information available on website.

HAIKU SOCIETY OF AMERICA

P.O. Box 31, Nassau NY 12123. E-mail: hsa-9AT@comcast.net. Website: www.hsa-haiku. org. The Haiku Society of America is composed of haiku poets, editors, critics, publishers, and enthusiasts dedicated to "promoting the creation and appreciation of haiku and related forms (haibun, haiga, renku, senryu, sequences, and tanka) among its members and the public." Currently has over 800 members. Levels of membership/dues: $33 U.S.; $30 seniors or full-time students (in North America); $35 USD in Canada and Mexico; $45 USD for all other areas. Membership benefits include a year's subscription (3 issues in 2007) to the Society's journal, Frogpond (see separate listing in Magazines/Journals), and to the quarterly HSA Newsletter ; the annual information sheet; an annual address/e-mail list of HSA members; and eligibility to submit work to the members' anthology. Administers the following annual awards: The Harold G. Henderson Awards for haiku, The Gerald Brady Awards for senryu, The Bernard Lionel Einbond Awards for renku,

The Merit Book Awards, and The Nicholas Virgilio Haiku Awards for youth. Guidelines available in the newsletter or on website. Meets quarterly at various locations throughout the U.S. Additional information available for SASE or on website.

INTERNATIONAL WOMEN'S WRITING GUILD

P.O. Box 810, Gracie Station, New York NY 10028. (212)737-7536. Fax: (212)737-9469. E-mail: iwwg@iwwg.org. Website: www.iwwg.org. A network for the personal and professional empowerment of women through writing. Levels of membership/dues: $55/year (domestic and overseas). The Guild publishes a quarterly 32-page journal, Network, which includes members' achievements, contests, calendar, and extensive publishing opportunities. Other benefits include regional/local writing groups and kitchen tables, agent list, and dental and vision insurance, health insurance in New York City. "We offer approximately 8 writing workshops throughout the U.S., including the weeklong summer conference held at Brown University in Providence, Rhode Island. Poetry workshops are interspersed in the conference programs." Additional information available by fax, e-mail, or on website.

IOWA POETRY ASSOCIATION

2325 61st St., Des Moines IA 50322. (515)279-1106. Website: www.iowapoetry.com. Established 1945. **Contact:** Lucille Morgan Wilson, editor. Statewide organization open to "anyone interested in poetry, with a residence or valid address in the state of Iowa." Currently has about 425 members. Levels of membership/dues: Regular ($8/year) and Patron ($15 or more/year; "same services, but patron members contribute to cost of running the association"). Offerings include "semiannual workshops to which a poem may be sent in advance for critique; annual contest—also open to nonmembers—with no entry fee; IPA Newsletter , published 5 or 6 times/year, including a quarterly national publication listing of contest opportunities; and an annual poetry anthology, Lyrical Iowa , containing prize-winning and high-ranking poems from contest entries, available for $10 postpaid. No requirement for purchase to ensure publication." Semiannual workshops "are the only 'meetings' of the association." Additional information available for SASE or on website.

THE LOFT LITERARY CENTER

Suite 200, Open Book, 1011 Washington Ave. S, Minneapolis MN 55414. (612)215-2575. E-mail: loft@loft.org. Website: www.loft.org. "The Loft is the largest and most comprehensive literary center in the country, serving both writers and readers with a variety of readings, Spoken Word performances, educational programs, contests and grants, and writing facilities." Supporting members (starting at $60/year - $25 for students/low income) receive benefits including discounted tuition, admission charges, and contest fees; check-out privileges at The Loft's Rachel Anne Gaschott Resource Library; rental access to the Book Club Meeting Room and writers' studios and more. Information on additional benefit levels, classes/workshops, contests and grants, and readings by local and national writers available at the website.

MASSACHUSETTS STATE POETRY SOCIETY

64 Harrison Ave., Lynn MA 01905. E-mail: msps.jcmaes@comcast.net. Website: http://mastatepoetrysociety.tripod.com/. Dedicated to the writing and appreciation of poetry and promoting the art form. Statewide organization open to anyone with an interest in poetry. Currently has 200 members. Levels of membership/dues: $15/year. Member benefits include subscription to Bay State Echo , published 5 times/year with members' news and announcements; members-only contests; round-robin critique groups; members-only annual anthology; workshops at society meetings; and automatic membership in National Federation of State Poetry Societies (NFSPS). Sponsors contests open to all poets. Guidelines available for SASE or on website. Members or nationally known writers give readings that are open to the public. Sponsors open mic readings for members and the public for National Poetry Day. Members meet 5 times/year. Additional information available for SASE or on website.

MOUNTAIN WRITERS SERIES

Mountain Writers Center, 2804 S.E. 27th Ave., #2, Portland OR 97202. "Mountain Writers Series is an independent nonprofit organization dedicated to supporting writers, audiences, and other sponsors by promoting literature and literacy through artistic and educational literary arts events in the Pacific Northwest." Currently has about 150 members. Levels of membership/dues: Basic ($50); Student/Retired ($25); Family ($75); Contributing ($100); Supporting ($500); and Patron ($1,000). Mountain Writers Series offers intensive one-day and 2-day workshops, weekend master classes, 5-week, 8-week, and 10-week courses about writing." Authors who have participated recently include David James Duncan, Linda Gregg, C.K. Williams, Li-Young Lee, Kim Addonizio, and David St. John. Sponsors readings that are open to the public. Nationally and internationally known writers are sponsored by the Mountain Writers Series Northwest Regional Residencies Program (reading tours) and the campus readings program (Pulitzer Prize winners, Nobel Prize winners, MacArthur Fellows, etc.). Additional information available for SASE, by fax, e-mail, or on website.

NATIONAL WRITERS UNION

256 West 38th St., 7th Floor, New York NY 10018. (212)254-0279. E-mail: nwu@nwu.org. Website: www.nwu.org. Poets eligible for membership if they've published at least 5 poems, or if they've written 5 poems and are actively writing and trying to publish their work. Other standards apply for various forms of writing (see website). Offers members such services as a grievance committee, contract guidelines, health insurance, press credentials, and caucuses and trade groups for exchange of information about special markets. Levels of membership/dues: $120 for those earning less than $5,000/year; $195 for those earning $5,001-15,000; $265 for those earning $15,001-30,000; and $315 for those whose writing income is between $30,001 and $45,000; and $340 for those whose writing income is more than $45,000/year. Membership form available online. Members receive monthly NWUsletter, and e-newsletter. See website for complete information.

Resources

NEW HAMPSHIRE WRITERS' PROJECT

2500 North River Rd., Manchester NH 03106. (603)314-7980. Fax: (603)314-7981. E-mail: info@nhwritersproject.org. Website: www.nhwritersproject.org. Statewide organization open to writers at all levels in all genres. Currently has 700+ members. Levels of membership/dues: $55/year; $25/year for seniors and students. Offerings include workshops, seminars, an annual conference, and a literary calendar. Sponsors daylong workshops and 4- to 6-week intensive courses. Also sponsors the biennial New Hampshire Literary Awards for outstanding literary achievement (including The Jane Kenyon Award for Outstanding Book of Poetry). Publishes *NH Writer*, a quarterly newsletter for and about New Hampshire writers. Members and nationally known writers give readings that are open to the public. Additional information available by fax, e-mail, or on website.

NORTH CAROLINA WRITERS' NETWORK

P.O. Box 21591, Winston-Salem NC 27120. (336)293-8844. E-mail: mail@ncwriters. org. Website: www.ncwriters.org. Supports the work of writers, writers' organizations, independent bookstores, little magazines and small presses, and literary programming statewide. Currently has 1,100 members. Levels of membership/dues: $75/year; seniors/ students, $55/year. Membership benefits include The Writers' Network News , a 24-page quarterly newsletter containing organizational news, national market information, and other literary material of interest to writers; and access to the NCWN online resources, other writers, workshops, writer's residencies, conferences, readings and competitions, and NCWN's critiquing and editing service. Annual fall conference features nationally known writers, publishers, and editors, held in a different North Carolina location each November. Sponsors competitions in short fiction, nonfiction, and poetry for North Carolina residents and NCWN members. Guidelines available for SASE or on website.

THE POETRY FOUNDATION

444 N. Michigan Ave., Suite 1850, Chicago IL 60611-4034. (312)787-7070. Fax: (312)787-6650. E-mail: mail@poetryfoundation.org. Website: http://poetryfoundation.org. "The Poetry Foundation is an independent literary organization committed to a vigorous presence for poetry in our culture. It exists to discover and celebrate the best poetry and to place it before the largest possible audience. Initiatives include publishing Poetry magazine (see separate listing in Magazines/Journals); distributing Ted Kooser's *American Life in Poetry* newspaper project; funding and promotion of Poetry Out Loud: National Recitation Contest (in partnership with the National Endowment for the Arts and state arts associations); *Poetry Everywhere*, a series of short poetry films airing on public television and on transportation systems across the country; *The Essential American Poets* podcast series featuring seminal recordings of major American Poets reading from their work, as selected by former Poet Laureate Donald Hall; and www.poetryfoundation. org, an award-winning comprehensive online resource for poetry featuring an archive of more than 6,500 poems by more than 600 classic and contemporary poets. The site also includes the poetry blog "Harriet," poetry-related articles, a bestseller list, video programming, a series of poetry podcasts, and reading guides about poets and poetry. The Poetry Foundation annually awards the Ruth Lilly Poetry Prize, of $100,000, and the Ruth Lilly Poetry Fellowships, 5 annual awards of $15,000 to young poets to support their

further studies in poetry. In 2004 the Foundation established a family of prizes called the Pegasus Awards to honor under-recognized poets and types of poetry (The Neglected Masters Award, The Emily Dickinson First Book Award, The Mark Twain Poetry Award, The Randall Jarrell Award in Criticism, The Children's Poet Laureate, and The Verse Drama Award). Additional information available on website. "

🌐 POETRY LIBRARY

The Saison Poetry Library, Royal Festival Hall, London SE1 8XX, England. (44)(207)921-0943/0664. Fax: (44)(207)921-0607. E-mail: info@poetrylibrary.org.uk. Website: www.poetrylibrary.org.uk. **Contact:** Chris McCabe and Miriam Valencia, assistant librarians. A "free public library of modern poetry. It contains a comprehensive collection of all British poetry published since 1912 and an international collection of poetry from all over the world, either written in or translated into English. As the United Kingdom's national library for poetry, it offers loan and information services and a large collection of poetry magazines, cassettes, compact discs, videos, records, poem posters, and cards; also press cuttings and photographs of poets."

🌐 THE POETRY SOCIETY

22 Betterton St., London WC2H 9BX, England. (44)(207)420-9880. One of Britain's most dynamic arts organizations, with membership open to all. "The Poetry Society exists to help poets and poetry thrive in Britain today. Our members come from all over the world, and their support enables us to promote poetry on a global scale." Publishes Poetry Review (see separate listing in Magazines/Journals), Britain's most prominent poetry magazine, and Poetry News , the Society's newsletter, as well as books and posters to support poetry in the classroom. Runs the National Poetry Competition (see separate listing in Contests & Awards) and The Foyle Young Poets of the Year Award (for poets aged 11-17), as well as many other competitions, services, and education projects for readers and writers of poetry. "Visit the website for a full idea of the range of activities The Poetry Society is engaged with."

POETRY SOCIETY OF NEW HAMPSHIRE

31 Reservoir, Farmington NH 03835. (603)332-0732. E-mail: poetrysocietyofnh@gmail.com. A statewide organization for anyone interested in poetry. Currently has 200 members. Levels of membership/dues: Junior ($10); Regular ($20). Offerings include annual subscription to quarterly magazine, The Poet's Touchstone ; critiques, contests, and workshops; public readings; and quarterly meetings with featured poets. The Poet's Touchstone is available to nonmembers for $6 (single issue). Members and nationally known writers give readings that are open to the public. Sponsors open mic readings for members and the public. Additional information available for SASE or by e-mail. "We do sponsor a national contest four times a year with $100, $50, and $25 prizes paid out in each one. People from all over the country enter and win."

THE POETRY SOCIETY OF SOUTH CAROLINA

P.O. Box 1090, Charleston SC 29402. E-mail: flatbluesky@hotmail.com. Website: www.poetrysocietysc.org. The Poetry Society of South Carolina supports "the reading, writing, study, and enjoyment of poetry." Statewide organization open to anyone interested in poetry. Offers programs in Charleston that are free and open to the public September-May (except for members-only holiday party in December). Currently has 150 members. Levels of membership/dues: $15 student, $25 individual, $35 family, $50 patron, and $100 business or sponsor. Membership year runs July 1-June 30. Membership benefits include discounts to PSSC-sponsored seminars and workshops held in various SC locations; a copy of the annual Yearbook of contest-winning poems; eligibility to read at the open mic and to enter contests without a fee; and an invitation to the annual holiday party. Sponsors a monthly Writers' Group, a January open mic reading featuring PSSC members, a Charleston Poetry Walk during Piccolo Spoleto in June, and a May Forum leading to an audience-selected poetry prize. Sponsors two yearly contests, totaling 20-25 contest categories, some with themes; some are open to all poets, others open only to SC residents or PSSC members. Guidelines available on website. **Deadline:** November 15 (Fall round) and February 15 (Spring round). Also offers the Skylark Prize, a competition for SC high school students. Sometimes offers a chapbook competition. Members and nationally known writers give readings that are open to the public. Poets have included Billy Collins, Henry Taylor, Cathy Smith Bowers, and Richard Garcia, as well as emerging poets from the region. Additional information available by e-mail or on website.

POETRY SOCIETY OF TENNESSEE

18 S. Rembert, Memphis TN 38104. E-mail: RSTRpoet@cs.com. Website: www.tpstn.org. **Contact**: Russell H. Strauss. Purpose is "to promote writing, reading, and appreciation of poetry among members of the society and the community; to improve poetry writing skills of members and local students. State poetry society, with some out-of-state members. Affiliate of National Federation of State Poetry Societies (NFSPS). Current membership about 70. Dues $20 a year for adults, $25 to include the yearbook (Tennessee Voices); $8 for students, including yearbook. Yearbook contains names, addresses, e-mail addresses of officers and members; winning poems by members and student members; and more. Society activities include programs with speakers; poetry contests, readings, and workshops; one meeting a year dedicated to students; plus Mid-South Poetry Festival first Saturday in October with workshop and prizes. Poetry readings about four times a year in local restaurants and bookstores. Regular meetings at 2 p.m. on first Saturday of each month (September-May) in basement of Evergreen Presbyterian Church across from Rhodes College (Parkway at College St.). No meetings in summer months. Newsletter Tennessee Voices Bulletin) every 2 months to members or for SASE.

THE POETRY SOCIETY OF TEXAS

610 Circle View Dr., Dallas TX 75248. (817)477-1754. E-mail: jlstrother@sbcglobal.net. Website: www.poetrysocietyoftexas.org. "The purpose of the society shall be to secure fuller public recognition of the art of poetry, to encourage the writing of poetry by Texans, and to kindle a finer and more intelligent appreciation of poetry, especially the work of living poets who interpret the spirit and heritage of Texas." Poetry Society of Texas is a member of the National Federation of State Poetry Societies (NFSPS). Has 25 chapters in cities throughout the state. Currently has 300 members. Levels of membership/dues: Active ($25) for native Texans, Citizens of Texas, or former Citizens of Texas who were

active members; Associate ($25) for all who desire to affiliate; also Student ($12.50); Sustaining; Benefactors; and Patrons of the Poets. Offerings include annual contests with prizes in excess of $5,000 as well as monthly contests (general and humorous); 8 monthly meetings; annual awards banquet; annual summer conference in a different location each year; round-robin critiquing opportunities sponsored at the state level; and Poetry in Schools with contests at state and local chapter levels. "Our monthly state meetings are held at the Preston Royal Branch of the Dallas Public Library. Our annual awards banquet is held at the Crown Plaza Suites in Dallas. Our summer conference is held at a site chosen by the hosting chapter. Chapters determine their meeting sites." PST publishes A Book of the Year , which presents annual and monthly award-winning poems, coming contest descriptions, minutes of meetings, by-laws of the society, history, and information. Also publishes the Poetry Society of Texas Bulletin , a monthly newsletter that features statewide news documenting contest winners, state meeting information, chapter and individual infor! mation, news from the NFSPS, and announcements of coming activities and offerings for poets. "A Book of the Year is available to nonmembers for $8." Members and nationally known writers give readings. "All of our meetings are open to the public." Additional information available for SASE, by e-mail, or on website.

POETS HOUSE

10 River Terrace, New York NY 10282. (212)431-7920. Fax: (212)431-8131. E-mail: info@ poetshouse.org. Website: www.poetshouse.org. Poets House, a national poetry library and literary center, is a "home for all who read and write poetry." Levels of membership/ dues: begin at $50/year; along with other graduated benefits, each new or renewing member receives free admission to all regularly scheduled programs. Resources include the 50,000-volume poetry collection, conference room, exhibition space, a programming hall, and a Children's Room. Over 200 annual public programs include panel discussions and lectures, readings, seminars and workshops, and children's events. In addition, Poets House continues its collaboration with public library systems, Poetry in The Branches, a multi-faceted program model to help libraries nationwide create a complete environment for poetry locally (see website for information). Finally, each year Poets House hosts the Poets House Showcase, a comprehensive exhibit of the year's new poetry releases from commercial, university, and independent presses across the country. (**Note: Poets House is not a publisher.**) Copies of new titles become part of the library collection, and comprehensive listings for each of the books are added to Directory of American Poetry Books , a free, searchable online database featuring over 50,000 poetry titles published 1996-2007. "Poets House depends, in part, on tax-deductible contributions of its nationwide members." Additional information available by fax, e-mail, or on website.

QUINCY WRITERS GUILD

E-mail: chillebr@adams.net. **Contact:** Carol Hillebrenner, treasurer. Purpose is "to encourage writers to write and, if they wish, get published." Regional organization open to all those who love to write and want mutual support in their passion. Currently has 18 members. Levels of membership/dues: $15/year. Offers "support, encouragement, whatever information we can gather for each other, and special speakers on the writing

Resources

craft." Often meet at Bickford Cottage the first Monday of most months. Sponsors conferences/workshops. Publishes a newsletter about upcoming meetings and "anything the editor thinks might interest others." E-mail newsletter is free for one year. Additional information available by e-mail.

SCIENCE FICTION POETRY ASSOCIATION

PO Box 4846, Covina CA 91723. E-mail: SFPATreasurer@gmail.com. Website: www. sfpoetry.com. **Contact:** Samantha Henderson, treasurer. The Science Fiction Poetry Association was founded "to bring together poets and readers interested in science fiction poetry (poetry with some element of speculation, usually science fiction, fantasy, or horror)." Levels of membership/dues: $21 USD (U.S., Canada, Mexico) for one-year memberships/renewals; $25 USD for overseas. Membership benefits include 6 issues/year of Star*Line (see separate listing in Magazines/Journals), a journal filled with poetry, reviews, articles, and more; one issue of the annual Rhysling Anthology of the best science fiction poetry of the previous year; opportunity to nominate one short poem and one long poem to be printed in the anthology, and to vote for which poems should receive that year's Rhysling award; half-priced advertising on the SFPA website, with greater subject matter leeway than non-members; eligibility to vote for SFPA officers (or run for officer); mailings with the latest news. Additional information available on website.

⊞ SCOTTISH POETRY LIBRARY

5 Crichton's Close, Edinburgh EH8 8DT, Scotland. (44)(131)557-2876. Fax: (44)(131)557-8393. E-mail: reception@spl.org.uk. Website: www.spl.org.uk. A reference information source and free lending library; also lends by post. Arranges poetry-writing workshops throughout Scotland, mainly for young people. The library has a web-based catalog available at www.spl.org.uk, which allows searches of all the library's resources, including books, magazines, and audio material—over 30,000 items of Scottish and international poetry. Need not be a member to borrow material; memberships available strictly to support the library's work. Levels of membership/dues: £25 individual; £15 concessionary/low-waged;; £40 organizational. Benefits include semiannual newsletter, annual report, new publications listings, and book offers. The School of Poets is open to anyone; "at meetings, members divide into small groups in which each participatn reads a poem, which is then analyzed and discussed." Meetings normally take place at 7:30 p.m. on the second Tuesday of each month at the library. Also offers a Critical Service in which groups of up to 6 poems, not exceeding 200 lines in all, are given critical comment by members of the School: 15 for each critique (with SAE). Publishes the Scottish Poetry Index , a multi-volume indexing series, photocopied, spiral-bound, that indexes poetry and poetry-related material in selected Scottish literary magazines from 1952 to present; an audio CD of contemporary Scottish poems, The Jewel Box (January 2000); and various anthologies available from www.spl.org.uk. A wide range of poetry events takes place throughout the year. Additional information available by e-mail or on website.

WISCONSIN FELLOWSHIP OF POETS

2105 E. Lake Bluff Blvd., Shorewood WI 53211. E-mail: nevers@wisc.edu. Website: www. wfop.org. President: Lester Smith. Statewide organization open to residents and former residents of Wisconsin who are interested in the aims and endeavors of the organization. Currently has 485 members. Levels of membership/dues: Active ($25); Student ($12.50). Sponsors biannual conferences, workshops, contests and awards. Publishes Wisconsin Poets' Calendar , poems of Wisconsin (resident) poets. Also publishes Museletter , a quarterly newsletter. Members or nationally known writers give readings that are open to the public. Sponsors open mic readings. Additional information available for SASE to WFOP membership chair at the above address, by e-mail, or on website.

☑ THE WORD WORKS

P.O. Box 42164, Washington DC 20015. E-mail: editor@wordworksdc.com. Website: www.wordworksdc.com. Word Works is "a nonprofit literary organization publishing contemporary poetry in single-author editions." Levels of membership/dues: $35 (basic), $50 (sustaining). Membership benefits at the basic level include choice of 2 books from The Word Works book list, newsletter, and 20% discount on additional book orders; in addition to these benefits, sustaining members are eligible for on-line critique of several poems via email. Sponsors an ongoing poetry reading series, educational programs, and the Hilary Tham Capital Collection (2010 judge will be Denise Duhamel). Sponsors The Washington Prize, one of the older manuscript publishing prizes, and The Jacklyn Potter Young Poets Competition (see separate listings in Contests & Awards). Additional information available on website.

✪ WRITERS' FEDERATION OF NOVA SCOTIA

1113 Marginal Rd., Halifax NS B3H 4P7, Canada. (902)423-8116. Fax: (902)422-0881. E-mail: talk@writers.ns.ca. Website: www.writers.ns.ca. Purpose is "to foster creative writing and the profession of writing in Nova Scotia; to provide advice and assistance to writers at all stages of their careers; and to encourage greater public recognition of Nova Scotian writers and their achievements." Regional organization open to anybody who writes. Currently has 800+ members. Levels of membership/dues: $45 CAD annually ($20 CAD students). Offerings include resource library with over 2,500 titles, promotional services, workshop series, annual festivals, mentorship program. Sponsors the Atlantic Writing Competition for unpublished works by beginning writers, and the annual Atlantic Poetry Prize for the best book of poetry by an Atlantic Canadian. Publishes Eastword , a bimonthly newsletter containing "a plethora of information on who's doing what; markets and contests; and current writing events and issues." Members and nationally known writers give readings that are open to the public. Additional information available on website.

✪ WRITERS GUILD OF ALBERTA

11759 Groat Rd., Edmonton AB T5M 3K6, Canada. (780)422-8174. Fax: (780)422-2663. E-mail: mail@writersguild.ab.ca. Website: www.writersguild.ab.ca. Established 1980. Founded to "provide a community of writers which exists to support, encourage, and promote writers and writing; to safeguard the freedom to write and read; and to advocate for the well-being of writers." Provincial organization open to emerging and professional writers. Currently has over 1,000 members. Offerings include retreats/conferences; monthly events; bimonthly magazine that includes articles on writing and a market section; weekly electronic bulletin with markets and event listings; and the Stephan G. Stephansson Award for Poetry (Alberta residents only). Additional information available by phone, e-mail, or on website.

ADDITIONAL ORGANIZATIONS

The following listings also contain information about organizations. Turn to the page numbers indicated for details about their offerings.

Resources

Poets in Education

Whether known as PITS (Poets in the Schools), WITS (Writers in the Schools), or similar names, programs exist nationwide that coordinate residencies, classroom visits and other opportunities for experienced poets to share their craft with students. Many state arts agencies include such "arts in education" programs in their activities (see Grants on page 456 for contact information). Another good source is the National Assembly of State Arts Agencies (see below), which offers an online directory of contact names and addresses for arts education programs state-by-state. The following list is a mere sampling of programs and organizations that link poets with schools. Contact them for information about their requirements (some may insist poets have a strong publication history, others may prefer classroom experience) or check their websites where available.

The Academy of American Poets, 584 Broadway, Suite 604, New York NY 10012-5243. (212)274-0343. E-mail: academy@poets.org. Website: www.poets.org (includes links to state arts in education programs).

Arkansas Writers in the Schools, WITS Director, 333 Kimpel Hall, University of Arkansas, Fayetteville AR 72701. (479)575-5991. E-mail: wits@cavern.uark.edu. Website: www. uark.edu/ ~ wits.

California Poets in the Schools, 1333 Balboa St. #3, San Francisco CA 94118. (415)221-4201. E-mail: info@cpits.org. Website: www.cpits.org.

e-poets.network, a collective online cultural center that promotes education through videoconferencing (i.e., "distance learning"); also includes the *Voces y Lugares* project. Website: http://learning.e-poets.net (includes online contact form).

Idaho Writers in the Schools, Log Cabin Literary Center, 801 S. Capitol Blvd., Boise ID 83702. (208)331-8000. E-mail: info@thecabinidaho.org. Website: www.thecabinidaho. org.

Indiana Writers in the Schools, University of Evansville, Dept. of English, 1800 Lincoln Ave., Evansville IN 47722. (812)488-2962. E-mail: rg37@evansville.edu. Website: http://english.evansville.edu/WritersintheSchools.htm.

Michigan Creative Writers in the Schools, ArtServe Michigan, 17515 W. Nine Mile Rd., Suite 1025, Southfield MI 48075. (248)557-8288 **OR** 1310 Turner St., Suite B, Lansing MI 48906. (517)371-1720 (toll free at (800)203-9633). E-mail: online form. Website: www.artservemichigan.org.

National Assembly of State Arts Agencies, 1029 Vermont Ave. NW, 2nd Floor, Washington DC 20005. (202)347-6352. E-mail: nasaa@nasaa-arts.org. Website: www.nasaa-arts.org.

National Association of Writers in Education (NAWE), P.O. Box 1, Sheriff Hutton, York YO60 7YU England. (44)(1653)618429. Website: www.nawe.co.uk.

Oregon Writers in the Schools, Literary Arts, 224 NW 13th Ave., Suite 306, Portland OR 97209. (503)227-2583. E-mail: john@literary-arts.org. Website: www.literary-arts.org/wits.

PEN in the Classroom (PITC), Pen Center USA, Þco Antioch University, 400 Corporate Pointe, Culver City CA 90230. (310)862-1555. E-mail: pitc@penusa.org. Website: www.penusa.org/go/classroom.

"Pick-a-Poet," The Humanities Project, Arlington Public Schools, 1439 N. Quincy St., Arlington VA 22207. (703)228-6299. E-mail: online form. Website: www.humanitiesproject.org.

Potato Hill Poetry, 6 Pleasant St., Suite 2, South Natick MA 01760. (888)5-POETRY. E-mail: info@potatohill.com. Website: www.potatohill.com (includes online contact form).

Seattle Writers in the Schools (WITS), Seattle Arts & Lectures, 105 S. Main St., Suite 201, Seattle WA 98104. (206)621-2230. Website: www.lectures.org/wits.html.

Teachers & Writers Collaborative, 520 Eighth Ave., Suite 2020, New York NY 10018. (212)691-6590 or (888)BOOKS-TW (book orders). E-mail: info@twc.org. Website: www.twc.org. "A catalog of T&W books is available online, or call toll-free to request a print copy.

Texas Writers in the Schools, 1523 W. Main, Houston TX 77006. (713)523-3877. E-mail: mail@witshouston.org. Website: www.writersintheschools.org.

Writers & Artists in the Schools (WAITS), COMPAS, Landmark Center, Suite 304, 75 Fifth St. West, St. Paul MN 55102-1496. (651)292-3254. E-mail: daniel@compas.org. Website: www.compas.org.

Youth Voices in Ink, Badgerdog Literary Publishing, Inc., P.O. Box 301209, Austin TX 78703-0021. (512)538-1305. E-mail: info@badgerdog.org. Website: www.badgerdog.org.

Glossary of Listing Terms

A3, A4, A5. Metric equivalents of 11¾ × 16½, 8¼ × 11¾, and 5⅞ × 8¼ respectively.

Acknowledgments page. A page in a poetry book or chapbook that lists the publications where the poems in the collection were originally published; may be presented as part of the copyright page or as a separate page on its own.

Anthology. A collection of selected writings by various authors.

Attachment. A computer file electronically "attached" to an e-mail message.

AUD. Abbreviation for Australian Dollar.

b&w. Black & white (photo or illustration).

Bio. A short biographical statement often requested with a submission.

CAD. Abbreviation for Canadian Dollar.

Camera-ready. Poems ready for copy camera platemaking; camera-ready poems usually appear in print exactly as submitted.

Chapbook. A small book of about 24-50 pages.Circulation. The number of subscribers to a magazine/journal.

CLMP. Council of Literary Magazines and Presses; service organization for independent publishers of fiction, poetry, and prose.

Contributor's copy. Copy of book or magazine containing a poet's work, sometimes given as payment.

Cover letter. Brief introductory letter accompanying a poetry submission.

Coverstock. Heavier paper used as the cover for a publication.

Digest-sized. About 5½ × 8½, the size of a folded sheet of conventional printer paper.

Download. To "copy" a file, such as a registration form, from a website.

Electronic magazine. See *online magazine*.E-mail. Mail sent electronically using computer and modem or similar means.

Euro. Currency unit for the 27 member countries of the European Union; designated by EUR or the INSERT EURO symbol.

FAQ. Frequently Asked Questions.

Font. The style/design of type used in a publication; typeface.

Galleys. First typeset version of a poem, magazine, or book/chapbook.

GLBT. Gay/lesbian/bisexual/transgender (as in "GLBT themes").

Honorarium. A token payment for published work.Internet. A worldwide network of computers offering access to a variety of electronic resources.

IRC. International Reply Coupon; a publisher can exchange IRCs for postage to return a manuscript to another country.

JPEG. Short for *Joint Photographic Experts Group*; an image compression format that allows digital images to be stored in relatively small files for electronic mailing and viewing on the Internet.

Magazine-sized. About 8½ × 11, the size of an unfolded sheet of conventional printer paper.

ms. Manuscript.

mss. Manuscripts.

Multi-book review. Several books by the same author or by several authors reviewed in one piece.

Offset-printed. Printing method in which ink is transferred from an image-bearing plate to a "blanket" and then from blanket to paper.

Online magazine. Publication circulated through the Internet or e-mail.

p&h. Postage & handling.

p&p. Postage & packing.

"Pays in copies." See *contributor's copy*.

PDF. Short for *Portable Document Format*, developed by Adobe Systems, that captures all elements of a printed document as an electronic image, allowing it to be sent by e-mail, viewed online, and printed in its original format.

Perfect-bound. Publication with glued, flat spine; also called "flat-spined."

POD. See *print-on-demand*.

Press run. The total number of copies of a publication printed at one time.

Previously published. Work that has appeared before in print, in any form, for public consumption.

Print-on-demand. Publishing method that allows copies of books to be published as they're requested, rather than all at once in a single press run.

Publishing credits. A poet's magazine publications and book/chapbook titles.

Query letter. Letter written to an editor to raise interest in a proposed project.

Reading fee. A monetary amount charged by an editor or publisher to consider a poetry submission without any obligation to accept the work.

Rich Text Format. Carries the .rtf filename extension. A file format that allows an exchange of text files between different word processor operating systems with most of the formatting preserved.

Rights. A poet's legal property interest in his/her literary work; an editor or publisher may acquire certain rights from the poet to reproduce that work.

ROW. "Rest of world."

Royalties. A percentage of the retail price paid to the author for each copy of a book sold.

Saddle-stapled. A publication folded, then stapled along that fold; also called "saddle-stitched."

SAE. Self-addressed envelope.

SASE. Self-addressed, stamped envelope.

SASP. Self-addressed, stamped postcard.Simultaneous submission. Submission of the same manuscript to more than one publisher at the same time.

Subsidy press. Publisher who requires the poet to pay all costs, including typesetting, production, and printing; sometimes called a "vanity publisher."

Tabloid-sized. 11 × 15 or larger, the size of an ordinary newspaper folded and turned sideways.

Text file. A file containing only textual characters (i.e., no graphics or special formats).

Unsolicited manuscript. A manuscript an editor did not ask specifically to receive.

URL. Stands for "Uniform Resource Locator," the address of an Internet resource (i.e., file).

USD. Abbreviation for United States Dollar.website. A specific address on the Internet that provides access to a set of documents (or "pages").

Resources

Glossary of Poetry Terms

This glossary is provided as a quick-reference only, briefly covering poetic styles and terms that may turn up in articles and listings in *Poet's Market*. For a full understanding of the terms, forms, and styles listed here, as well as common literary terms not included, consult a solid textbook or handbook, such as John Drury's *The Poetry Dictionary* (Writer's Digest Books).

Abstract poem: conveys emotion through sound, textures, and rhythm and rhyme rather than through the meanings of words.

Acrostic: initial letters of each line, read downward, form a word, phrase, or sentence.

Alliteration: close repetition of consonant sounds, especially initial consonant sounds. (Also known as *consonance*.)

Alphabet poem: arranges lines alphabetically according to initial letter.

American cinquain: derived from Japanese haiku and tanka by Adelaide Crapsey; counted syllabic poem of 5 lines of 2-4-6-8-2 syllables, frequently in iambic feet.

Anapest: foot consisting of 2 unstressed syllables followed by a stress (- - ').

Assonance: close repetition of vowel sounds. Avant-garde: work at the forefront—cutting edge, unconventional, risk-taking.

Ballad: narrative poem often in ballad stanza (4-line stanza with 4 stresses in lines 1 and 3, 3 stresses in lines 2 and 4, which also rhyme).

Ballade: 3 stanzas rhymed *ababbcbC* (*C* indicates a refrain) with envoi rhymed *bcbC*.

Beat poetry: anti-academic school of poetry born in '50s San Francisco; fast-paced free verse resembling jazz.

Blank verse: unrhymed iambic pentameter.

Caesura: a deliberate rhetorical, grammatical, or rhythmic pause, break, cut, turn, division, or pivot in poetry.

Chant: poem in which one or more lines are repeated over and over.

Cinquain: any 5-line poem or stanza; also called "quintain" or "quintet." (See also *American cinquain*.)

Concrete poetry: see *emblematic poem*.

Confessional poetry: work that uses personal and private details from the poet's own life.

Consonance: see *alliteration*.

Couplet: stanza of 2 lines; pair of rhymed lines.

Dactyl: foot consisting of a stress followed by 2 unstressed syllables (' - -).

Didactic poetry: poetry written with the intention to instruct.

Eclectic: open to a variety of poetic styles (as in "eclectic taste").

Ekphrastic poem: verbally presents something originally represented in visual art, though more than mere description.

Elegy: lament in verse for someone who has died, or a reflection on the tragic nature of life.

Emblematic poem: words or letters arranged to imitate a shape, often the subject of the poem.

Enjambment: continuation of sense and rhythmic movement from one line to the next; also called a "run-on" line.

Envoi: a brief ending (usually to a ballade or sestina) no more than 4 lines long; summary.

Epic poetry: long narrative poem telling a story central to a society, culture, or nation.

Epigram: short, witty, satirical poem or saying written to be remembered easily, like a punchline.

Epigraph: a short verse, note, or quotation that appears at the beginning of a poem or section; usually presents an idea or theme on which the poem elaborates, or contributes background information not reflected in the poem itself.

Epitaph: brief verse commemorating a person/group of people who died.

Experimental poetry: work that challenges conventional ideas of poetry by exploring new techniques, form, language, and visual presentation.

Fibs: short form based on the mathematical progression known as the Fibonacci sequence; syllable counts for each line are 1/1/2/3/5/8/13 (count for each line is derived by adding the counts for the previous two lines).

Flarf: a malleable term that may refer to 1) poetic and creative text pieces by the Flarflist Collective; any poetry created from search engine (such as Google) results; any intentionally bad, zany, or trivial poetry.

Foot: unit of measure in a metrical line of poetry.Found poem: text lifted from a non-poetic source such as an ad and presented as a poem.

Free verse: unmetrical verse (lines not counted for accents, syllables, etc.).

Ghazal: Persian poetic form of 5-15 unconnected, independent couplets; associative jumps may be made from couplet to couplet.

Greeting card poetry: resembles verses in greeting cards; sing-song meter and rhyme.

Haibun: originally, a Japanese form in which elliptical, often autobiographical prose is interspersed with haiku.

Haikai no renga: see *renku*.

Hay(na)ky: a 3-line form, with 1 word in line 1, 2 words in line 2, and 3 words in line 3.

Haiku: originally, a Japanese form of a single vertical line with 17 sound symbols in a 5-7-5 pattern. In English, typically a 3-line poem with fewer than 17 syllables in no set pattern, but exhibiting a 2-part juxtapositional structure, seasonal reference, imagistic immediacy, and a moment of keen perception of nature or human nature. The term is both singular and plural.

Hokku: the starting verse of a renga or renku, in 5, 7, and then 5 sound symbols in Japanese; or in three lines, usually totaling fewer than 17 syllables, in English; the precursor for what is now called haiku. (See also *haiku*).

Iamb: foot consisting of an unstressed syllable followed by a stress (- ').Iambic pentameter: consists of 5 iambic feet per line.

Imagist poetry: short, free verse lines that present images without comment or explanation; strongly influenced by haiku and other Oriental forms.

Kyrielle: French form; 4-line stanza with 8-syllable lines, the final line a refrain.

Language poetry: attempts to detach words from traditional meanings to produce something new and unprecedented.Limerick: 5-line stanza rhyming *aabba*; pattern of stresses/line is traditionally 3-3-2-2-3; often bawdy or scatalogical.

Line: basic compositional unit of a poem; measured in feet if metrical.

Linked poetry: written through the collaboration of 2 or more poets creating a single poetic work.Long poem: exceeds length and scope of short lyric or narrative poem; defined arbitrarily, often as more than 2 pages or 100 lines.

Lyric poetry: expresses personal emotion; music predominates over narrative or drama.

Metaphor: 2 different things are likened by identifying one as the other (A = B).Meter: the rhythmic measure of a line.

Minute: a 12-line poem consisting of 60 syllables, with a syllabic line count of 8,4,4,4,8,4,4,4, 8,4,4,4; often consists of rhyming couplets.

Modernist poetry: work of the early 20th century literary movement that sought to break with the past, rejecting outmoded literary traditions, diction, and form while encouraging innovation and reinvention.

Narrative poetry: poem that tells a story.

New Formalism: contemporary literary movement to revive formal verse.

Nonsense verse: playful, with language and/or logic that defies ordinary understanding.

Octave: stanza of 8 lines.

Ode: a songlike, or lyric, poem; can be passionate, rhapsodic, and mystical, or a formal address to a person on a public or state occasion.

Pantoum: Malayan poetic form of any length; consists of 4-line stanzas, with lines 2 and 4 of one quatrain repeated as lines 1 and 3 of the next; final stanza reverses lines 1 and 3 of the previous quatrain and uses them as lines 2 and 4; traditionally each stanza rhymes *abab*.Petrarchan sonnet: octave rhymes *abbaabba*; sestet may rhyme *cdcdcd*, *cdedce*, *ccdccd*, *cddcdd*, *edecde*, or *cddcee*.

Prose poem: brief prose work with intensity, condensed language, poetic devices, and other poetic elements.

Quatrain: stanza of 4 lines.

Refrain: a repeated line within a poem, similar to the chorus of a song.

Regional poetry: work set in a particular locale, imbued with the look, feel, and culture of that place.

Renga: originally, a Japanese collaborative form in which 2 or more poets alternate writing 3 lines, then 2 lines for a set number of verses (such as 12, 18, 36, 100, and 1,000). There are specific rules for seasonal progression, placement of moon and flower verses, and other requirements. (See also *linked poetry*.)

Rengay: an American collaborative 6-verse, thematic linked poetry form, with 3-line and 2-line verses in the following set pattern for 2 or 3 writers (letters represent poets, numbers indicate the lines in each verse): A3-B2-A3-B3-A2-B3 or A3-B2-C3-A2-B3-C2. All verses, unlike renga or renku, must develop at least one common theme.

Renku: the modern term for renga, and a more popular version of the traditionally more aristocratic renga. (See also *linked poetry*.)

Rhyme: words that sound alike, especially words that end in the same sound.

Rhythm: the beat and movement of language (rise and fall, repetition and variation, change of pitch, mix of syllables, melody of words).

Rondeau: French form of usually 15 lines in 3 parts, rhyming *aabba aabR aabbaR* (R indicates a refrain repeating the first word or phrase of the opening line).

Senryu: originally, a Japanese form, like haiku in form, but chiefly humorous, satirical, or ironic, and typically aimed at human foibles. (See also *haiku* and *zappai*.)

Sequence: a group or progression of poems, often numbered as a series.

Sestet: stanza of 6 lines.

Sestina: fixed form of 39 lines (6 unrhymed stanzas of 6 lines each, then an ending 3-line stanza), each stanza repeating the same 6 non-rhyming end-words in a different order; all 6 end-words appear in the final 3-line stanza.

Shakespearean sonnet: rhymes *abab cdcd efef gg*.Sijo: originally a Korean narrative or thematic lyric form. The first line introduces a situation or problem that is countered or developed in line 2, and concluded with a twist in line 3. Lines average 14-16 syllables in length.

Simile: comparison that uses a linking word (*like, as, such as, how*) to clarify the similarities.

Sonnet: 14-line poem (traditionally an octave and sestet) rhymed in iambic pentameter; often presents an argument but may also present a description, story, or meditation. Spondee: foot consisting of 2 stressed syllables (' ').

Stanza: group of lines making up a single unit; like a paragraph in prose.

Strophe: often used to mean "stanza"; also a stanza of irregular line lengths.

Surrealistic poetry: of the artistic movement stressing the importance of dreams and the subconscious, nonrational thought, free associations, and startling imagery/ juxtapositions.

Tanka: originally, a Japanese form in one or 2 vertical lines with 31 sound symbols in a 5-7-5-7-7 pattern. In English, typically a 5-line lyrical poem with fewer than 31 syllables in no set syllable pattern, but exhibiting a caesura, turn, or pivot, and often more emotional and conversational than haiku.

Tercet: stanza or poem of 3 lines.

Terza rima: series of 3-line stanzas with interwoven rhyme scheme (*aba, bcb, cdc* . . .).

Trochee: foot consisting of a stress followed by an unstressed syllable (' -).

Villanelle: French form of 19 lines (5 tercets and a quatrain); line 1 serves as one refrain (repeated in lines 6, 12, 18), line 3 as a second refrain (repeated in lines 9, 15, 19); traditionally, refrains rhyme with each other and with the opening line of each stanza.

Visual poem: see *emblematic poem*.

Waka: literally, "Japanese poem," the precursor for what is now called tanka. (See also *tanka*.)

War poetry: poems written about warfare and military life; often written by past and current soldiers; may glorify war, recount exploits, or demonstrate the horrors of war.

Zappai: originally Japanese; an unliterary, often superficial witticism masquerading as haiku or senryu; formal term for joke haiku or other pseudo-haiko.

Zeugma: a figure of speech in which a single word (or, occasionally, a phrase) is related in one way to words that precede it, and in another way to words that follow it.

Chapbook Publishers Index

A poetry chapbook is a slim volume of 24-50 pages (although chapbook lengths can vary; some are even published as inserts in magazines). Many publishers and journals solicit chapbook manuscripts through competitions. Read listings carefully, check Web sites where available, and request guidelines before submitting. See Frequently Asked Questions on page 7 for further information about chapbooks and submission formats.

Special Indexes

Book Publishers Index

The following are magazines and publishers that consider full-length book manuscripts (over 50 pages, often much longer). See Frequently Asked Questions on page 7 for further information about book manuscript submission.

Special Indexes

Openness to Submissions Index

In this section, all magazines, publishers, and contests/awards with primary listings in *Poet's Market* are categorized according to their openness to submissions (as indicated by the symbols that appear at the beginning of each listing). Note that some markets are listed in more than one category.

☐ WELCOMES SUBMISSIONS FROM BEGINNING POETS

☑ OPEN TO BEGINNERS AND SKILLED POETS

Special Indexes

Special Indexes

☻ PREFERS SKILLED AND EXPERIENCED POETS

◎ SPECIALIZED FOCUS

Special Indexes

Geographical Index

This section offers a breakdown of U.S. publishers and conferences/workshops arranged alphabetically by state or territory, followed by listings for Canada, Australia, France, Ireland, Japan, the United Kingdom, and other countries–a real help when trying to locate publishers in your region as well as conferences and workshops convenient to your area.

Publishers of Poetry

COLORADO
Book/Chapbook Publishers

Publishers of Poetry

NORTH CAROLINA
Book/Chapbook Publishers

Publishers of Poetry

Special Indexes

Special Indexes

Special Indexes

Subject Index

This index focuses on markets indicating a specialized area of interest, whether regional, poetic style, or specific topic (these markets show a ◎ symbol at the beginning of their listings). It also includes markets we felt offered special opportunities in certain subject areas. Subject categories are listed alphabetically, with additional subcategories indicated under the "Specialized" heading (in parentheses behind the market's name). **Pease Note:** 1) This index only partially reflects the total markets in this book; many do not identify themselves as having specialized interests and so are not included here. 2) Many specialized markets have more than one area of interest and will be found under multiple categories. 3) When a market appears under a heading in this index, it does not necessarily mean it considers only poetry associated with that subject, poetry only from that region, etc. It's still best to read all listings carefully as part of a thorough marketing plan.

Automobiles

Bilingual/Foreign Language

Buddhism

Catholic

Christian

Special Indexes

Form/Style Asian

Gay/Lesbian/Bisexual/Transgendered

Poetry by Children

Special Indexes

Poetry for Children

Poetry for Teens

Religious Poetry

Science Fiction

Senior Citizen/Aging

Social Issues

Specialized various

Spirituality/Inspirational

Special Indexes

Women various

Working Class Issues

Writing

General Index

B

M